ARCHITECTURAL
WORKING DRAWINGS

ARCHITECTURAL WORKING DRAWINGS

FOURTH EDITION

RALPH W. LIEBING

JOHN WILEY & SONS, INC.
New York, Chichester, Weinheim, Brisbane, Singapore, Toronto

Copyright © 1999 by John Wiley & Sons. All rights reserved.

Published simultaneously in Canada.

No part of this publication may be reproduced, stored in a retrieval
system or transmitted in any form or by any means, electronic,
mechanical, photocopying, recording, scanning or otherwise,
except as permitted under Sections 107 or 108 of the 1976 United
States Copyright Act, without either the prior written permission of
the Publisher, or authorization through payment of the appropriate
per-copy fee to the Copyright Clearance Center, 222 Rosewood
Drive, Danvers, MA 01923, (978) 750-8400, fax (978) 750-4744.
Requests to the Publisher for permission should be addressed
to the Permissions Department, John Wiley & Sons, Inc., 605
Third Avenue, New York NY 10158-0012, (212) 850-6011, fax (212)
850-6008, E-Mail: PERMREQ @ WILEY.COM.

This publication is designed to provide accurate and authoritative
information in regard to the subject matter covered. Is is sold with
the understanding that the publisher is not engaged in rendering
professional services. If professional advice or other expert
assistance is required, the services of a competent professional
person should be sought.

Library of Congress Cataloging-in-Publication Data

Liebing, Ralph W., 1935-
    Architectural working drawings/Ralph W. Liebing.
        p.   cm.
    Includes bibliographical references and index.
    ISBN 0-471-34876-7 (alk. paper)
    1. Architecture—Working drawings.   I. Title.
NA2713.L54   1999
720'.28'4—dc21   98–51777

Printed in the United States of America
10 9 8 7 6 5 4 3 2 1

To my family, who stood by to help through each edition.

To all of my colleagues who encouraged and supported me.

To my readers—I hope I've helped!

Notice to the Reader

Contents

Preface to the Fourth Edition

It's a wonderful experience to be asked to produce the fourth edition of *Architectural Working Drawings*—a true privilege that we never envisioned.

In fact, no thought was ever given to where this book might go, or how many people it may serve. We (I and my co-author, the late Mimi Ford Paul) tried initially to fill the need we had, to have a text available that truly showed what working drawings were about and the type of effort that was required. We tried to instill the spirit of *Architectural Working Drawings* (AWD) in our students at that time, as it was evident that things were changing. In that change we felt the need to provide our students (and other readers) with a fundamental understanding of why working drawings exist, what they are destined to do on each project, their tremendous value, and the essential need for them.

This edition, beyond a milestone, is a transition. The book in its first three editions has covered a period of more than 20 years. These years fell roughly in the center of a 50-year period that has seen a rapid and almost unbelievable transformation in the architectural profession, its tasks, and its products. But there remains a need for basic and fundamental understanding and respect for the process and the product.

In 1950 architectural students were still being trained/taught in the use of the "ruling pen," a confounding device with two parallel nibs between which one inserted India ink. But this device came near the end of the "ink-on-linen" era,

when working drawings were produced totally with pen and ink on linen media. Good translucent tracing papers and vellum were in wide use.

By 1970 computers began to appear, but only in larger firms. They had not, as yet, caught on. Then their use was usually confined to repetitive work, where portions of drawings could be placed in the "library" and then reused in different locations and orientations—mind-boggling! Most of their use was in the design functions, and not so much in working drawings. Mylar film came along as a replacement for the "1000H" rag paper medium that was widely used (along with a good deal of vellum). At first, though, a special waxy "lead" had to be used on the mylar, which came with slick face surfaces only. Later, a grainy-textured drafting surface was added to one or both faces, on which regular drafting lead would not work.

By 1990, the computer-aided drafting (CAD) controversy was in full swing—many swore by it, others at it. Tradition hung on, primarily because of high computer costs, rapidly evolving (and fairly expensive) software, and the inability to decide what was right for a particular firm. Although some in the profession, for various reasons, moved easily and quickly, as in other professions and trades, the architectural profession, overall, lagged in moving to CAD. It moved slowly, in spurts, almost reluctantly and with no real drive. The prime function, architecturally, was the three-dimensional work that could be done in preliminary designing, for assessing a project electronically, and for presentation drawings. Working drawing work still lagged as software programs came on-line through material manufacturers, other disciplines, and, slowly but surely, in the architectural mode. Yet traditional values were revered and maintained as if the use of CAD was acquiescence to some evil that would mark one as "unprofessional." Oddly enough, that stigma was pronounced years before, when firms attempted to reduce the cost of repetitive work in other ways.

In looking now toward the twenty-first century, we can not deny that marvelous and more adventurous times lie ahead. It is difficult to envision what computer technology will be able to produce and offer to the profession. The human effort may be reduced by the added capabilities of CAD devices, but there will still be a need to have a person discern what should happen, how, and when. We simply offer the thought that what will have to be done, then, will be better done if the values and standards, adaptions of techniques, and the insight gained in the previous century are used as stepping stones. Rather than discarding the old (and obsolete, as some will hold), just perhaps we will see that the professional manipulations of the past are more than worthy of reuse and improvement and can be set forth as the true measure of good professionally produced architectural working drawings.

We sincerely hope this edition helps in this, as did its predecessors.

RALPH W. LIEBING

Cincinnati, Ohio
June 1999

Preface to the
First Edition

Why write a book about architectural working drawings? It had to be done; such a book has been sadly lacking. In our years of teaching we have reviewed many texts concerned with "architectural drafting." All, in our opinion, came up short. The authors flirted with the real problems while giving the impression that by reading their books the readers would automatically become good draftsmen or architects.

We do not pretend to be able to create draftsmen and practitioners. We have tried to analyze (or dissect, if you will) each drawing and to give some insight to its content, some approaches to its successful completion, and some applicable techniques.

Much has been written about specifications; the standard CSI format, Master Specification, and detailed papers on each finite section are available. No one, though, has approached the critical area of working drawings and the requisite care demanded. Some feel that standardization is the proper route to pursue. This may be the case, but the basic drawings and some of their inherent problems must be understood before a standard method of production can be accepted.

We feel that students deserve broad exposure; the same latitude is equally valuable to young graduate architects and practitioners. High school is not too soon to start the exposure. Today many junior high schools have excellent courses in construction methodology. These courses, accompanied by the substance of this book, can provide a fully rounded background for the high school student, who can then evaluate the contributions of allied professions and trades to better advantage.

College-level architecture students need a comprehensive frame of reference to make a better evaluation of their education and experience. To sell students a "pat" system of drawing production is really shortchanging them. Students must be free to progress, as they can, from a strong basic background. Again, understanding comes before manipulation of the "systems."

This book is our answer. We sincerely felt that a "gap" existed, and our intention was to narrow the gap, if not close it entirely.

Our sincere gratitude is extended to all those individuals, firms, and associations that so graciously (and patiently) helped with this effort:

Our draftsmen: Terry Ross, Mark Bidwell, David Wilson, Paul Volpe, and Gary Mitchell;

Glaser & Myers & Associates, Inc., for allowing us to use portions of their drawings as our illustrations;

Mr. Robert E. Stauder of Hellmuth, Obato, & Kassabaum for providing us with illustrations of freehand detailing;

The AIA *Journal* for use of "Task Force, Number One" data in connection with new symbols, designators, and schedules;

The Construction Specifications Institute for allowing us to quote from their pamphlet, *Relating*

PREFACE TO THE FIRST EDITION

Drawings and Specifications, and to reproduce the "Standard Specification Format";

The American Institute of Steel Construction for providing data on rolled steel sections and welding;

The Concrete Reinforcing Steel Institute for permitting us to use the "bar chart" and "cards";

The Victor O. Schinnerer Company for allowing us to quote statistics on professional liability and causes of lawsuits against design professionals;

Miss Kathy Cunningham for her excellent typing (and retyping) and the rapid production of the final manuscript;

The American National Metric Council and the Standards Association of Australia for providing current conversion data;

Mr. DeForrest R. Roggenbach, AIA, Corporate Director of Architecture for Smith, Hinchmann, & Grylls, Associates, Inc., for allowing us to use his illustrations and outline, "Detail Cycle," as the basis for our "Concept of Detailing";

Miss Betty J. Ritter for encouraging us initially; and last but not least,

Mr. William Dudley Hunt Jr., FAIA, for his help, advice, and extreme patience.

RALPH W. LIEBING
MIMI FORD PAUL

Cincinnati, Ohio
October 1976

xiv

Acknowledgments

No one ever successfully undertakes and completes an exercise like writing or revising a book such as this without infinite kindness, help, support, and encouragement from many people.

Many of those who have given such help since before the first edition have now passed on. Yet some remain, and some new people have come to the fore.

Of course, there are various parties, including Amanda Miller at John Wiley & Sons, who have seen fit to allow this fourth edition with, we hope, the same anticipation that we have—that we can truly aid and inform new young professionals and assist them in their budding careers. We hope the very kind attention that has brought *Architectural Working Drawings* a good reputation will be present again and, more important, that we can measure up to it.

Our sincere and heartfelt thanks to two very special people. First, Kevin Giglio, whose knowledge of computer operations is deep, true, and expert. Kevin assisted willingly on every occasion (and they were many) with good humor and good results; his support and help has been invaluable. And Christy Richardson-Burger, a very quiet, astute, and meticulous young architect, who did many of our CAD presentations. Her skill, understanding, drive, and good nature are deeply appreciated. So, too, in much the same measure we acknowledge several other great folks: Greg Rebennack, Sarah Davey-Kleiner, Steve Knipper, and Jamie Dobrozsi (the latter two being more experienced registered architects, as well as CAD-fluent, and also our bosses).

We are also grateful to a gentleman who came into our life and left again shortly, Kaye Stabler. Verbose and outspoken are quiet in comparison with Kaye—but the guy knows his stuff. Older, and with wide-ranging practical experience, Kaye knows the ins and outs of CAD, how it has impacted the production of working drawings and, more important, how it now can be made to aid, or confound, good document production.

This has really been a wonderful collaboration, involving all of these people, who with their wide range of skill and experience have offered advice, direction, criticism, and valued support. They have helped and supported; they have reviewed and suggested. They all have contributed more than they would admit.

We fear that it is totally inadequate, but we hope a simple but heartfelt "thanks" comes close to expressing our sincere gratitude.

RESPONSIBILITY—
A detachable burden easily shifted to the shoulders
of God, Fate, Fortune, Luck, or one's neighbors.

—AMBROSE GWINETT BIERCE

God is in the details.

—APHORISM OF LUDWIG MIES VAN DER ROHE

1

Introduction

The true essence of this book has always been, and remains, the fact that in the face of change and choice, not everything is "cut and dry," nor fully resolved. For this reason, this book is not solely about the machines, attributes, capacities, and nuances of computer-aided drafting (CAD). Rather, it is, in part, about how all these can, should, and must support CAD's correct place in the creation and execution of proper communications instruments (architectural working drawings) that support, enable, and facilitate project construction.

Simply, it is about the results that CAD, *if properly and well handled*, can produce.

Many of the examples and illustrations were manually produced, but they still present certain values, principles, and techniques that remain fully valid, if not eminently improved, when applied through CAD. That is the *informed application* of CAD*, utilizing those attributes that enhance the final drawing products—and in a far shorter period of time.

Even in its finest hour, CAD is benign and incapable of making determinations or decisions on its own. It is here that the "informed" element—

the human—is required. In simplest terms, we ask, "What, exactly, do we want CAD to do in this instance?" Therefore, any of the examples in this book could be products of CAD, and the mere fact that "the hand" produced them does not reduce their inherent value as lessons and examples that illustrate a particular point in the progression of working drawing production.

Because lines are the basis for all drawings, we must come to understand and appreciate what they are and what we want them to portray. In thinking of lines (for CAD or manual work), we must decide:

The beginning and the end

The location, angle, or rotation

The relative importance, the consistency

The value—how light or dark

The type—solid, dotted, dashed (and the variations in the latter two)

The configuration—straight, drafted, curved, angled

The added notation if required
(————SS————, for example)

Our theme is that the best professional effort, from this point on, combines the new and better attributes of CAD with the well-founded, tried,

---

* "Informed application" means adjusting CAD capabilities to use them in accord with, or to meet, a criterion other than that set into the CAD program normally or by default—for example, adjusting line weight to darker or lighter than that provided by the basic software program.

INTRODUCTION

and proven values of the past. Many of the standard notations, types of lines, values of lines, and so on, were established some time ago and prevail today as well-known, easily recognizable designations. There is no need (and indeed it is a danger) to use CAD to try to create a new set of such designations. And perhaps more important to the new professional, there is no stigma connected with use of prevailing (albeit "old") information and designations, so long as they remain pertinent.

This is no cry to stop, to tenuously retain the status quo, or to regress in favor of manual drawings and older elements. Rather, we hope to show that applying proven values and techniques of the past *in CAD operations* will result in documents that are better than ever. CAD will add a consistency (if we "will" it) that was not necessarily present in manual efforts. We now know more, have more information coming to us continually, and we have a system of display for our work that enhances the work and produces faster results. Intelligently utilizing the best of the past and the best of the present can do nothing but make our total effort better.

> It is highly preferable, if not ideal, in working drawing production today, to execute and enhance the work using CAD, but also by still utilizing traditional (manual drafting) guidelines, standards, values, and techniques.
>
> —Anonymous

Architects, by virtue of their contracts with their clients, are responsible for producing a great many different types of drawing. Each has a specific function and each is produced at a different time during the contract period.

Basically, the drawings consist of the preliminary, or schematic, design drawings, the design development drawings, and the construction documents. The schematic drawings, or preliminary designs, in which the scope of the contract and project is defined, represent the various working areas, and it is these areas that are interrelated to form a workable plan. Here the basic design concept, the building or the project, is shown on elevations and perspective drawings, which can be developed into finished sketches or renderings that will be given to the client for approval.

Most people outside the profession know these drawings only as they see them in published announcements of a project. Others may encounter renderings that are displayed from time to time in

various ways, but few are familiar with the totality of the preliminary phase.

During the design development phase the preliminary drawings are given more definition and meaning by the addition of technical information, such as that dealing with the structural, electrical, and mechanical systems. The design is indeed developed during this stage. The basic concept of the project, the sketches and renderings that are produced in the preliminary phase, is given over to the technical needs of the project so that the building can be built.

When we approach the production of the construction documents, we begin to convert the design concept into feet and inches, into door swings, window and door frames, types of equipment, and different construction materials. It is in this phase that the design concept begins to take physical shape and provides the technical information the contractor(s) will need to construct the building. It is also at this time when a commitment must be made to produce documents, drawings, specifications, details, and other construction information that will faithfully communicate the design concept; working drawings do not function to set out a new design!

In the practice of architecture,

Planning is the foundation;

Design is the solution;

Documentation is the method;

Construction Administration is the reality;

Successful Projects are the results!

Building construction is one of the most important industries in the United States today. Needs change, and the demand for more and varied designs is constant. Some structures become obsolete; others must be built to accommodate new ideas. New designs must be conceived and new approaches taken, and with this we must keep tabs on all the drawings to be produced. No contractor can take an original design concept and construct a building. These conceptual drawings are the ideas, the basics of the project, but they are not the sum of the information required by the contractor.

Architecture involves a great many things, primary of which are the artistic and aesthetic phases of building construction. Architecture is concerned with the principles of design betterment (balance, scale, massing, proportion, rhythm, and unity). From the first preliminary idea for a project, to the approved design concept, we keep in mind that the documentation of the project is necessary to bring it to completion. Thus, we must be able to express the intangible attributes of the design concept in a real, physical manner. That is, we must build the project with various materials and techniques of installation so they accurately bring forth the design concept. What originates as an idea must now become a full-size, real "thing"! The finished project can be a joy to the eye, but that wonderment of building is composed of a tremendous amount of detail, parts, systems, and subsystems, all linked together. Each must be thought through to maintain the design concept and in no way detract from it. The design concept is created, and indeed lives, as an abstract, an intangible, a delicate balance of taste and function. The parts of this living concept are real and tangible.

Each project progresses through the architect's office in a set manner, in a series of planned stages—some imposed by contract, some to ensure the best job possible.

But when we talk of what is entailed in producing working drawings, we are referring to work that requires roughly 50 percent of the architect's fee (the payment from the client to the architect). Obviously, if a professional devotes half of the fee to this one phase, it gives strong credence to the drawings' being most valuable in the construction of the facility. Simply, they are vital to producing the correct work in every aspect of the project.

Thousands of decisions are made during the working drawing phase, and hundreds of thousands of items may be involved. Many persons treat this phase of the work in an offhand manner; others try to ignore it completely—but it will not be denied. It must happen! There is no shortcut! There is no easy way to convert the project from the original concept into a structure without incorporating feet and inches and producing all the minute details of the working drawings.

Over the years systems have changed, new materials have been introduced, and method approaches to the working drawings have been updated. Quite often these changes are not cataloged but become matters of procedure tied to one office or another. Many new techniques are being introduced, and architectural offices are benefiting from workshop and seminar experiences.

An architect is no longer regarded as a mere dilettante; the word *profit* is an honorable addition to his or her vocabulary. Profit is not to be ignored, for the architect is in business and this business is to make money. One of the more profitable aspects of the practice rests with the construction document phase, not, however, with the cost of the project. Because so much of the fee is tied to this phase, the architect realizes the importance of procedures, of trying new methods to produce the most efficient, complete, and accurate set of drawings for each project. Not every procedure works for everyone; not every system is exactly right. To find the most economical and efficient procedure is not an easy task. Consider the many decisions and the many hands required.

Architects are no longer termed "guys who draw blueprints"; they are respected members of the construction industry. Architects produce the workability that must be introduced into every project, participate in every phase, and understand what is to be done to make the drawings as complete as possible.

Tremendous amounts of money are often spent, and only minimal errors can be tolerated. However, human beings are fallible and mistakes, though quickly rectifiable, will happen. It is most important that young architects, student architects, draftsmen, or drafting technicians anticipate the impact of every line, circle or semicircle, and note that they enter on a drawing. They must be totally aware while they are working on the various media that the end result, or print, must be clear and complete so that the information may be properly transmitted from the office to the workers on the site.

Everything must be in its place, everything must work together; no gaps are allowed, and no overlaps or duplications are permissible. This is a major aspect of the working drawing phase.

At the end of a project the building is opened. Certainly the architect will accept the credit due for the project that he or she has designed, for it is that architect's idea that has been realized in brick and mortar and all the other materials. It is his or her sense of design that has proportioned the building to make it pleasing to the eye; it is that architect's idea that stands constantly as a reminder of his or her efforts. A good architect knows that any project will have passed through a tough working phase, that the original concept will have been changed into feet and inches, arrowheads and notes, leader lines and dimensions.

> One of the nobler professional goals of every architect should be—That every project is completed, closed-out, and delivered with the same verve, intensity, anticipation, interest, effort, attention to detail, dedication, enthusiasm, skill, poise, and concern for the project, as were present and employed when the project first came into the office; all to the client's complete satisfaction and pleasure.

The contractors also take credit for the project when completed, but they too know that it could not exist even with their efforts if working drawings had not been available to them.

This book has been written to provide a basic understanding of contract documents (contract drawings and specifications), in particular, the working drawings. A great deal has been written about the format and procedures established for writing specifications; therefore, the subject is not included extensively in this book, although specifications are part of the construction documents. Updated techniques used in working drawings are equally important. There have been many advances that allow us to produce better drawings in less time. The need for a good guide to drafting that covers the entire construction industry, and not just residential work, is overwhelming. Heavy construction demands more and more highly detailed documents than single-family housing. We must have an honest approach to these drawings to show the range of work involved.

This book has no system to sell, because each office adopts its own procedures. It is not a self-teaching guide, because such devices do not succeed. This book is best used in a setting that involves an instructor to supplement the information it contains. It has not been regionalized, but it has been generalized to disseminate reasonable information to the widest audience. We present absolute realities with our working drawings; each type of drawing is broken down to demonstrate what must be included—the *how* and *why* of procedures changing from office to office or from region to region. Here, then, is an outline, a beginning, for students or young practitioners: approaches they may care to adopt or, at a minimum, approaches from which they may discover others of their own derivation. It is hoped that each person using this book may find valuable ideas to adapt, modified or not.

We are dealing with an area of construction drawing too long ignored. Many have considered the drawings to be necessary evils, but we all know that they are important enough to mean success or failure. To put this book in the context of office and contract language, the preliminaries have been approved and the renderings and models have been made and presented. The client is pleased with the design, design development is complete, and now the construction drawings begin. On their completion they will be "put out" for bids by various contractors.

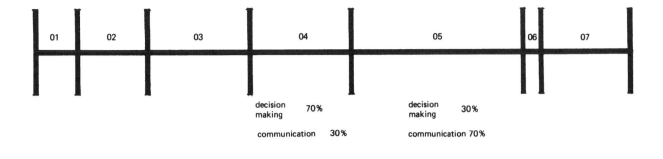

decision
making   70%

communication   30%

decision
making   30%

communication 70%

PROJECT PHASES

01 — Project Concept
02 — Programming
03 — Schematics
04 — Design Development
05 — Contract Documents
06 — Bidding
07 — Construction Services

Illustration shows the breakdown of the project into the several phases that are required to prepare the documents and move to completion. The AIA Basic Services are contained in Phases 03–07. Note the importance of communication in the contract document (working drawing) phase.

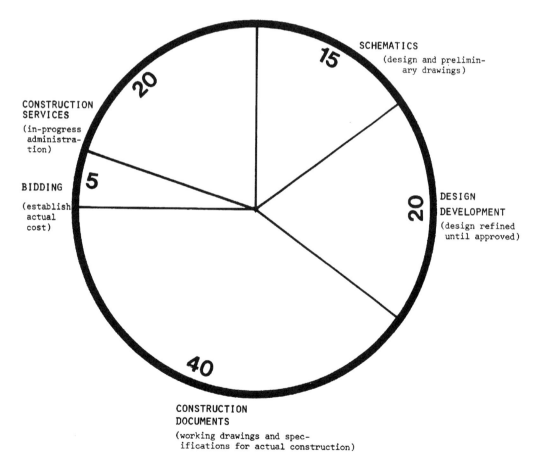

Chart depicts the traditional allocation of the available fee for production of the project. Note in particular that almost one-half of this fee is expended for working drawings and specifications! With modem methods, and systems drafting, the 40 percent for Construction Documents can be reduced to about 30 percent, with Schematics and Design Development each being increased 5 percent; in other words, with less time spent in production, more time can be allocated to design and design refinement.

2

The Role Of Working Drawings

The primary role, or function, of working drawings (sometimes called "contract" or "construction" drawings) is to convert design data into construction information and to clearly communicate that information to contractors. The drawings must provide and transmit a complete, faithful, and accurate *graphic* depiction of the project's design concept, to scale—a major portion of the construction information required to build the project. These are the vehicles by which the design professional applies technology to the project's design concept and communicates the same to construction personnel so they know what is to be done, how, and with what. The essence of the working drawings is that they are the design professional's interpretation of how the project should be built to satisfy the client's program for the project. That satisfaction relates directly to the very reason for the project, and the resolution of the client's problems, needs, and desires.

In this context, working drawings are not intended for, nor do they exist for, the enhancement or gratification of the design professional. The drawings (and the effort to produce them) should be geared to their utilization as the documents used most directly in the field; that is, they will be taken to the actual work area/location (on the site) and used by construction workers as they erect or install work. (The other contract documents—Agreement and Specifications—are used primarily as administrative, office, and legal instruments). Because of their function, the drawings have to provide the necessary construction information in a graphic form that the workers can use directly in their effort to construct the project as designed. This is not to say that the specifications are any less important, but they usually explain or expand on the graphic information used by the workers; they are more usable by project managers, expediters, and those interested in ordering, receiving, and moving material as necessary for the progress of the project.

The best architecture firms, with select client types, are paid for their knowledge, *not* their CADD systems.

—Raymond F. Kogan, AIA
Zweig White & Associates, Inc.
Washington, D. C.

The importance of working drawings is perhaps best reflected in the requirements of the Intern Development Program (IDP) of the American Institute of Architects (AIA) and the National Council of Architectural Registration Boards (NCARB). Here roughly 25 percent of the total postgraduate professional experience required must be gained through working drawing work. This is more than three times the experience required in any other aspect of practice. The requirement of 135 training units equates to 1,080 actual clock hours, or 27 full-time workweeks, devoted strictly to working drawings. Although this is a substantial amount of time, there should be no illusion that one can be fully oriented, trained, and knowledgeable about working drawings within this period.

This IDP requirement reflects the lack of time devoted to working drawings in the academic environment. Many may say that working drawings are better "taught" in the office, but we submit that understanding their intent and content, along with developing some minimal skills, is an academic effort. True, refinement and wider experience through IDP and practice is both preferable and more easily achieved, but the schools certainly can make a good effort at providing some fundamental training. Isn't it reasonable for good drafting techniques, habits, and skills to be required and developed in the production of school projects?

Ancillary activities of the profession associated with working drawings include code research, materials research, specification writing, and document coordination and checking. All of these are also required experience factors in the IDP program. This gives increased credence to their value, as well as the need for a good understanding of working drawings and practice in their production.

An individual professional may be much more interested and active in one aspect of practice than others (i.e., design, document production, contract administration, etc.) and may thus tend to pigeon-hole him- or herself. However, whether or not there is a concentration on a specialty (either personally or throughout a firm), there is a prevailing technological aspect to the architect's work. This technology encompasses one fundamental premise (an understanding of and respect for the design process and concept) and two basic forms (materials/systems and documentation).

According to George M. White, FAIA, former architect of the U.S. Capitol, "Without in any way diminishing the work of celebrated designers, why not recognize the architects who deliver a project—whose talents are as valuable and as difficult to come across as those of a first-rate designer? Thousands of architects are solving the myriad problems associated with the design and construction of society's shelter every day. Let's sing the praises of these as yet unsung heroes, as well as those at the forefront of design.

The executive architect, who is ultimately responsible for making a project happen, must be on top of every aspect of its design and construction. Consider the awesome responsibility of realizing Dulles Airport, for example. Then consider that designer [architect] Eero Saarinen's name is the only one linked to it in the public record."

> The profession itself has been slow to recognize that design expertise has its counterparts in other aspects of practice.
> —George M. White, FAIA
> Former architect of the Capitol

If the dictionary defines *architecture* as "the art and science of designing and erecting buildings and other structures," can we not restate it as

The application of technology (science) in a manner and combination so as to bring a concept (artistic idea) to functional realization.

In essence, without the application of technology, the concept will remain just that—an idea, a thought, an unrealized design. And where does that technology reside?

The two elements—design concept and technology—are not necessarily equals; rather, they are mutually supporting. Each needs the other to produce another example of architecture. Obviously, the design (concept) is the more visible and the element most celebrated (or maligned). Awards honor and celebrate good design, but very few, if any, recognize good construction, good detailing, or excellence in physically achieving a concept. There are even competitions and appropriate awards for specification writing. However, the overwhelming number of plaques and citations on office walls mark excellence or achievement in design, but very few in drawing production.

The minds and hearts of architects vary, finding expression and satisfaction in different aspects of the profession and professional work. Although repugnant to some, the fact remains that a massive array of architectural/construction technology *must* be present and properly applied, *in every project*. It is a major and dangerous breach of professional understanding and direction for one to embrace only the design, aesthetical, and overall concept of a project. No project proceeds successfully from concept to reality without the application of proper technology in minute detail.

> The architect should be equipped with the knowledge of many branches of study and varied kinds of reasoning, for it is by his judgement that all work done by others is put to the test . . . it follows, therefore, that architects who have aimed at acquiring manual skill without scholarship have never been able to reach a position of authority to correspond to their pains, while those who relied upon theories and scholarship were obviously hunting the shadow, not the substance.
> —Vitruvius *On Architecture*
> Book 1 [25 B.C.]

What is the technology of architecture? It is generally recognized that an architect is a combination of artist and engineer, with the "art" aspect emphasized. For the most part, this is true because most architects have an initial and abiding concern about a project's aesthetic appeal, impact, and propriety. But this, in the minds of most architects, is not the entire story of a project. Architecture is, of course, a visual art that presents projects that remain and endure. They are not momentary glimpses of near-perfection as in the dance. The basic charge to every architect, from the client, is to produce a pleasing and attractive structure—at least in the eyes of the client. Most often the client is not completely sure of what he or she wants or needs and is unwittingly asking to be led to good form and pleasant presentations.

Appeal, of course, is quite profound in that it is the attribute of a project that is seen and assessed by the casual viewer as well as the professional observer. It is the overall pleasing or striking impression of the project that is foremost, because this is the expression of the project most readily apparent. It expresses the image and "message"

of the client. The basic inner working and relationships of the project and the actual construction are present, of course, but the observation of these aspects is restricted to those who are looking into them. The clients, their staffs, tenants, and other users are usually more concerned with how the building functions for their operation(s) and their work environment. In addition, there is a measure of pride and prestige in working in a well-designed, beautiful, and impressive structure. The construction, however, is more than likely forgotten until something goes wrong or becomes a problem. Yet both function and construction of the project were integral parts of the program that produced the structure; they were designed just as much as the overall concept that produced the project's aesthetic virtues.

> The architect must approach design with a fundamental grasp of building materials and methodology . . . the architect must have an expertise in construction along with design ability.
> —AIA, papers submitted for
> 1993 Walter Wagner Education Forum

It is virtually indisputable that working drawings have been transformed, in complexion, over the last 10 to 15 years. Their intent has remained exactly as it has been for decades, but growing utilization of new and better production techniques has contributed to an overall change. There has also been a change in the concept somewhat, but little that touches on the reason for the existence of the drawings. Most all of this is tied directly to the increasing use of computer-aided drafting (CAD) for the production of the drawings.

Part of the uniqueness of the design/documentation/construction process is the fact that the project starts with an overall vision, plan, or concept. It is envisioned in its final state, as evidenced by the preliminary drawings and renderings, which appear quite often in announcements of new projects. The designer, with little regard for minute detail, fashions the idea into an overall scheme that encompasses, addresses, and resolves all factors involved in the project. These include the owner's needs and desires and the public voice—the codes and other regulations. The scheme addresses what must be done, or what is necessary to communicate the basic idea of the project. Through design development more and more details are added, but it is in document production that each small portion or piece is analyzed to see exactly how it may be constructed, related to other parts, and brought to reality in the project. This is a painstaking, careful, and vigorous effort, but time well spent when a project is successfully realized and the design concept is correctly and distinctly revealed.

So the project process is not strictly evolutionary, but one of taking an overall concept and dissecting, expanding, developing, and "constructing" it on paper in written and graphic terms, item by item, transforming a design concept into technical information that can be used by contractors. This application of technology to all work items, from the largest to the smallest, in turn facilitates construction, which brings the concept to reality as a finished project. Perhaps *facilitating* is a better term to apply to the process.

Technology, then, is not something to be feared or avoided, nor something that can be obviated or ignored; it is a given, a necessity—its application an unavoidable task, a foregone conclusion. Architects and architecture students have to fully understand, appreciate, and respect this necessity, even though they may choose to concentrate their individual efforts on more conceptual or aesthetic premises.

For the technological aspects of a project to perform as required, there must be a fundamental and in-depth understanding of the process of design preceding the creation and development of the approved design concept. Moreover, there must be full and abiding respect for that concept and a firm resolve to bring it to full reality, faithfully and completely. Both of these values, understanding and respect, are necessary for a successful project. They should be introduced to and instilled in the entire staff who will process the project in its various phases. Otherwise, detailing, specification writing, and field observation will be virtually rudderless, without guidance or goal. Although the design concept may exist only in schematic/presentation drawings, renderings, and/or a model, these provide guidance for the other work. At least, here, there is "something to shoot for," a distinct goal. A great deal of time, talent, imagination, skill, knowledge, and experience are required to bring presentation instruments to fruition. There usually need not be a formal education process to get design information to staff members, but some effort is required to convey the perspective of the project, the quality to be achieved, and the process that will produce the project documents.

Staffers who have pursued a professional education (toward registration) may have some degree of the requisite understanding and respect. Part of their education may entail "practice instruction," which covers the various work phases of the professional, for each project, and their interrelationships. Still, some may need to be reminded of these aspects, and even prompted to embrace these values more fully. Keep in mind that some persons may have already found or moved toward their own narrow professional niches which lie elsewhere, removed somewhat from the technological aspects of the project.

Other staffers, including architectural technicians, may have to be made more aware of the need for their understanding and respect. Their normal work position in the professional office is usually in the technology area (documentation, to be precise). Often their training has been so narrow as to exclude any instruction, reference, or allusion to the proper handling of a project, the work required in each phase, or the movement of the design concept to a finished project. However, this is so vital to the success of a project that time is well spent in giving the required training in the office.

In this instruction there should be no effort toward making design the "everything" of the project. Design will dominate, but it must be supported, enhanced, and facilitated by the applied technology—it cannot stand alone! Well-designed projects that are not properly conceived functionally and/or are improperly detailed, documented, or constructed will fail in a relatively short period of time, some of which come to ill-serve their occupants either because of failures in their systems or because of mere deterioration. For example, many of Frank Lloyd Wright's houses had confounding leaky roofs, difficult to resolve once discovered; Michael Graves came under severe criticism for his choice of materials on his Portland (Oregon) building. There is a need for the professional to be extremely prudent in the choices made and how these function and interrelate within the total project.

A new thought!

Good design is the result of good detailing; good detailing is complex and highly technical. Why not, then, award outstanding detailing, so the public comes to know the correct message, that good architecture requires both!

—Howard L/ Filiere Jr., NCARB
Cleveland, Ohio

In these and similar situations, it is quite evident that technology must be present in its best form, but must retain its proper relationship and not overcome or obviate the features necessary to convey the concept. This is not necessarily a ticklish process, but the staff must be together on the issue, moving in lockstep toward their common goal: a successful (and profitable) project. It should *not* be perceived that bad design can be "saved" by good technology. Bad technology, however, can ruin the best of designs!

To bring a design concept to reality, there must be a process of selecting the materials to be used for the project. These must be combined into systems, where possible, or distinct details that gather and utilize them to formulate "pieces" of construction. Professional offices and individual architects tend to reuse materials and systems that they have used previously. In many cases, this is acceptable practice. However, in almost every project there are nuances and requirements that necessitate new materials, details, systems, and applications/installations or new ways of utilizing "old" materials. There should never be any hesitation on the part of the designer to seek and investigate new materials. Most offices retain some sort of library, formal or otherwise, in which they store product information. This, along with the normal array of manufacturer sources, sales/technical representatives, and so on, provides a wide range of data that can be accessed. The specification writer in an organization is frequently the repository of product availability and technical information on the use of products. (Eero Saarinen, however, retained a full-time staffer to do nothing but research materials.) Where needed, additional information must be sought out, evaluated, discussed, and only then incorporated into the design scheme.

Being an integral part of the project's technology, searching for a material may fall to the architectural technician. The project architect could, for instance, ask the technician to find a number of possibilities for analysis and deeper consideration. Of course, the project architect, or other architect/staffers could perform this work as well. The main point is that incorporation of new materials and systems is not an off-hand process, done without regard to prudent assessment.

Fundamental to this entire process is a working knowledge of construction materials. This should include some information as to basic raw materials, production, fabrication, processing, testing,

> **The [professional's] duty to investigate products is limited to how to apply the product on the project.**
> **[Professionals] are not responsible for the design of the product itself.**
> —Kenneth M. Elovitz
> Attorney/Engineer
> Foxboro, Massachusetts

availability, costs, and so forth. No one person may have all of this data at hand for every product, but an office organization should use its entire technical staff as a resource. Experience on other projects or with other firms can prove to be a great value in the material selection process. Obviously, there will be times where some experimentation or risk taking is required. Every effort should be expended to find out everything possible about a material under consideration. At least there should be a comfortable level of confidence before use of the material is approved. Lenient selection, shoddy incorporation, and lack of professional attention can lead to drastic consequences: claims, disputes, recurring problems, failures, and the like, up to and including litigation. The John Hancock Tower built in Boston is an outstanding example of a project gone wrong because of many unfortunate factors that contributed to the overall concept.

The sequence, in the field at the job site, entails the crew leader ascertaining, from the working drawings, the work to be performed and the materials and equipment required for the work. By this time, most of the materials should be on-site, but the specifications must be checked to ensure that the correct material is placed as required. For example, there may be several types and thicknesses of plywood on-site. The crew leader must then determine the type and the specific thickness needed in the work the crew is to perform. Where there are two types and two thicknesses required, the drawings should distinguish the type, thickness, size, and shape of the sheets or pieces in their correct locations and relationships. From this example it can be seen that the specifications provide valuable information (regarding the types, sizes, thicknesses, and other features of the plywood), but it is the working drawings that provide the specific direction, sizes and shapes required to the workers.

THE ROLE OF WORKING DRAWINGS

As noted elsewhere, the professionals producing the working drawings and specifications must

---

Manufacturers: Subject to compliance with requirements, provide ties and anchors by one of the following:

AA Wire Products Co.
Dur-O-Wal, Inc.
Heckman Building Products Co.
Hohmann & Barnard Inc.
Masonry Reinforcing Corp. of America
National Wire Products Industries

For anchorage of brick veneer, through sheathing to framing behind, provide manufacturers standard 16-gauge, galvanized, 1–1/4" wide by 3–1/2" long corrugated bent plate with 1–1/2" bend and 5/16" dia. punched/drilled hole for No.12 dia. screw attachment to structural framing; same as Heckman No. 187.

A. Corrugated ties that are bent in an L-shape and nailed at the very top of the tie will have virtually no strength in tension. If the vertical leg is not tight against the sheathing, there may also be very little strength in transferring inward loads. The nails should always be placed as close to the bend in the tie as possible. As the wall moves out under suction wind loads, the tie will bend at the nail attachment. The greater the distance between the fastener and the horizontal portion within the wall, the greater will be this bending force on the tie. The Brick Industry Association recommends in BIA Technical Note 28 that corrugated wall ties for residential wood frame construction be 20-gauge or heavier and that they be attached with 8d nails at a distance no greater than 5/8 inch from the bend in the tie.

The nails should be attached to the wood studs. If the tie is nailed merely into plywood sheathing, it will have very little strength in resisting outward loads. The nails can pull out of the plywood, and the plywood can deflect between the studs.

An example of the type and amount of detail contained in specifications for a small item that is noted, and shown in its location on the drawings. Also, shown here is a brief explanation of the items [which information is not part of the specifications]

---

be very careful as to what information goes on which document. It is wholly inappropriate to list on a drawing too much information about a product that does not affect the work or installation, or to note how and what is to be accomplished. Likewise, it is improper to attempt to verbally depict the work or project in a lengthy written dissertation in the specifications. The professionals must learn, early on, that some things are better drawn and others are best described in words. In general, the specifications will elaborate on the attributes of the material or system (size, thickness, finish, type, etc.). The role of the drawings is to show the specific installation(s) as to exact size (shown to scale), configuration, attachment, relationship to other parts/pieces and material, and so forth. (see illustration) There is a pressing and prevailing need for clarity and directness in the drawings, to the point that they are self-evident or self-explanatory. Techniques and media may vary, but clarity, directness, and ease of readability are paramount. This is not the place for the design professional to be "cute," divisive, unique, or innovative; nothing should be used or incorporated that disrupts clear communication—nothing that gives pause or causes question.

Design professionals in today's construction climate can ill afford to create documents that confuse or confound the erectors. There have been several different formats or systems developed for the production of working drawings. Few have really caught on, because they served more to undo traditional communication lines and formats than to enhance or better them. Not only is there a need to separate information into written and graphic forms, but there is a need to understand how the information will be used—by whom, in what environment, and for what reason. All of this must be considered and thought through very carefully.

Naturally, there is some crossover, as absolute and strict lines between the forms of information cannot be drawn. However, experience and exposure to experienced people can help in sensing and understanding how the data can be separated and properly placed. Part of the role of the drawings is to cross-reference information between drawings and between drawings and specification. A lack of cross-referencing, or inadequate cross-referencing, in the working drawings can prove detrimental to on-site progress and proper construction.

Oddly enough, the role of the working drawings is to dissect the design concept for the project, then examine, determine, and portray every portion of the work required. The designer of the project creates an overall scheme, but does not deal with the details of how the scheme is to be achieved (constructed). In the main, projects require a "set" of drawings. In a few small projects the complete project work may be confined to one sheet. However, it is not at all unusual for a project to require upward of 50 sheets just for the architectural work, and projects requiring hundreds of sheets are not out of the ordinary. Beyond these drawings are those required for the other disciplines— HVAC (heating, ventilating, air-conditioning), plumbing, electrical, fire protection, site/civil engineering, utilities, landscaping, furnishings, and so on. Understanding the requisite interrelationships and coordination of all this information is crucial to successfully producing sets of project documents that result in successful projects.

All architects can think "big picture."
But if you can't execute the details, you've lost it!
—Reb Haizlip, AIA
Principal Architect
Williamson, Haizlip & Pounders, Inc.

All design and drafting personnel, including junior drafters and students, have to understand the *priority* of their work, as well as the "fit" or interrelationship with the work of others. Rarely is work on working drawings done in isolation. Obviously, there are a lot of drawings required in any set of architectural or construction drawings, and a lot of information. However, by setting and understanding the personal priorities based on those set by the project architect, one can approach the work of getting all of this done in proper sequence and in good, well-coordinated order.

For example, consider three primary aspects of a set of project documents: *configuration/size, height,* and *construction.* Immediately, these translate into *floor plan(s),* which deal with shape (configuration) and size, in the form of length and width, and the intricacies of the room layout. *Exterior elevations* add the element and relationship of

height, giving the third dimension to the project. *Wall sections,* which cut through the exterior walls (primarily) reveal the construction of the project, or just how the building/project is to be built, interrelated, and so forth.

What Percentage of the contractors' profit is contained in the Change Orders resulting from discrepancies in your documents?

Without all three of these aspects of the project, the documents are incomplete, inadequate, and unacceptable/useless! There is no sense issuing such documents to contractors, for bidding or construction, when they do not contain all of the information required. If some information is not available, the contractor(s) will either be forced to ask numerous questions (which is confusing and time-consuming) or will attempt to fill in the data on their own. That usually will prove to be a detriment to the project, inasmuch as the contractor(s) do not know the thinking, reasoning, and rationale behind the design and documentation of the project.

Further, these three categories of drawings form the base of information for the other drawings in the set and contribute heavily to the success of those other drawings. Everything after these basic drawings enhances, expands, or adds to these drawings; these other drawings clarify, amplify, detail, dissect, reveal, coordinate, enlarge, or complete the basic drawings. Like the smaller pieces in a jigsaw puzzle, they are needed to complete the entire picture, even though they are smaller (in size/scope) and perhaps in the amount of information they project (a single-colored border piece of a puzzle, for example).

It must also be said that these priorities *should not* be avoided or ignored in favor of other, less important drawings simply because the others can be more easily or more rapidly produced on CAD systems, nor should drawings be produced just for the sake of using the computer. A set of several tens of drawings may appear impressive. It may indicate a "tremendous work effort." However, such drawings can prove to be quite improper, inadequate, or even useless where they do not provide the required information. One cannot install a "beautifully depicted elevator shaft" in a building that has no walls (none shown on the drawings)!

The mere fact that one likes, is intrigued by, or is drawn to particular materials, systems, or areas of a project is irrelevant to this process. Projects are *not* produced to meet the whims of staff, but rather to carefully delineate the work required by the program to produce the client's project. Obviously, the major systems of the project will initially dominate the work; general schemes and concepts will be brought forward to transform client programming into working documents. Details will dominate the work in the finishing phases, as truly "the specific" rules. General ideas, concepts, terms, and so on, must be converted to usable construction information in a very specific manner. This directly follows the progression, but does so in a developmental setting, in sequence, and with priorities set, followed, and met.

Of course, it is possible to find minute detail of fairly obscure portions of the project immediately, but this does not mean that they are then immediately incorporated into the project documents. Too many things change, too often, in the course of production to install firm, final determinations, information, or details right away or early in the process. Proper priority must be given each piece of data. To do less than this is to often require that "finished work" be abandoned, deleted, worked over, or radically revised to meet new project requirements—this is professional disaster.

It is neither prudent nor wise to allow obscure, minor cosmetic or utilitarian details to drive the project. The process is to develop (evolve) the general schemes into the detailed explanations, not vice versa. Every project has a basic and fundamental set of pieces and systems that are vital to a successful, proper functioning and a safe project/structure. To these an endless variety of cosmetic finishes and utilitarian items are added. So to make decisions early on about remote or superficial aspects of the finished building(s) and have them drive or force decisions about structural, mechanical, and other general matters, including aesthetics and conceptual considerations, is fundamentally wrong and quite counterproductive.

No item of clothing is designed around a button selected first; no automobile is designed around a selected spark plug. Details and finishes should be conceived and considered as enhancements and explanations of the design concept and its overall scheme and systems—the execution of the concept. Finishing touches mean just

that: relatively minor additions and revisions and fine-tuning of the project's major considerations.

The production of a set of working drawings can be most intimidating. At some point, one realizes the terrifying reality that several, if not all, of the drawings are "in progress," none finished, and all requiring massive amounts of additional work. To this, in the office, one must add the inevitable time limit at which point the project must be finished and biddable.

Yet in spite of all this, the movement toward completion is accomplished in the same shuffling fashion as information is received, modified, and developed specifically for the project. It is good to perceive this process as an inverted pyramid. (See chart below) In this way, the work of documentation starts literally at a particular point— upon approval of the design concept (scheme) and completion of the design development phase of work. Progress is made from the initial point as information becomes available, each layer adding to the breadth of the project. Although completion of information gathering and incorporation can be seen as a "wide field," the time frame and percentage of "incompleteness" become increasingly narrow until they reach a point, the "out-the-door-for-bidding" point (let's get paid!).

In all of this, the documentation process has moved from the conceptual to the very general, to the controlled general, to the specific. This approach is taken in response to the importance of the information or the construction detail/system to the project. Of course, the complete package or "set" is the final product being pursued. Its completeness, appropriateness, and accuracy are derived directly from the process that produced the set of documents; that is, the end not only justifies the means, the end reflects the means.

The end, however, can be adversely affected by overdetailing. This means, simply, that showing too much is as great an error as showing too little. In addition, sacrificing initial research, study, review, design, and modification of systems in favor of detailing small, mundane, or relatively unimportant pieces of the project will usually result in faulty documentation. Emphasis will occur in the wrong places; more crucial items will be inadequately covered, or worse, not covered at all. Specific information will be in place, but will have no frame of reference, that is, will not be tied into a greater or more general scheme. The information, then, is useless!

Where these items are requirements, systems, or concepts of some significance, the project will suffer in numerous ways: cost elevation, safety compromise, disputes, complaints, claims, dissatisfied client(s), and the degrading of the professional's reputation.

Detail is important and necessary to the project overall (as it defines and refines the project's features), but it is not the driving force. It must be applied to the other major aspects of the project, in proper sequence and in proportion to the support it lends the project.

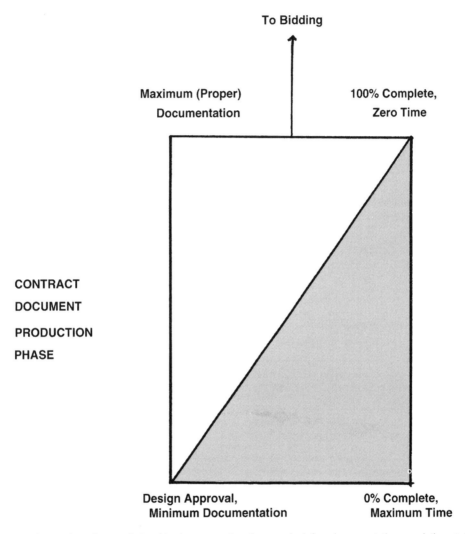

This chart shows the direct relationship between the time period for documentation, and the state of completeness of the documents.

3

A Perspective On Working Drawings

A new consumer protection group is being formed to find ways to reduce fire-related deaths . . . the first action of the new group will be the formulation of a handbook for the filing of lawsuits, against design professionals, for fire-related death.

Such news items as this should greatly elevate the awareness and concern of every design professional; they have not done so over the last 10 to 15 years. In addition, a series of disasters again have served to show the fragility and vulnerability of the various design and construction professions; none has gone unscathed. In some cases, professionals saw their careers completely destroyed because of the ways in which they chose to practice. Moreover, a crisis in the liability insurance industry added to the malaise and struck fear in the professionals. Premiums rose, inordinately, yet fees coming to the professionals remained unchanged, or in terms of buying power, actually declined.

Clearly, professionals were under siege on many fronts and were literally forced, in the main, to seek new configurations in which to carry on their affairs and practices. However, even then,

due to the strong mitigative trend, professionals were, and still are, finding themselves involved in more and more court cases, often on most tenuous grounds. One study forecasted on the average a suit every 3 years. The alarming reality of practice must and can be dealt with in every phase of the work.

It seems, then, more than appropriate, even in a book on working drawings, to set out this new perspective. Even within the relatively short life span of the previous editions of this book, conditions have changed dramatically. Practice is much different now than in the late 1970's, and this includes production of working drawings.

In the construction industry, there is a propensity to be myopic—to be almost mindless beyond one's current purview. Obviously, there is much beyond a design concept before it can become a "perfect," prize-winning project. The award plaque on the wall and the new copy in the company brochure are most prestigious, but the "wearing" of the project is also a worthwhile consideration, and perhaps a truer measure of the success of the building. Thus, the mere welding of two structural members, the installation of glass, the use of proper fire ratings for finish materials or assemblies, and such other intricate details should not be perceived, executed, or dismissed lightly.

The architect's purview, on every project, must be to realize that only faithful execution of the design concept, both in documentation and in the actual working, will result in the project's being satisfactory to the client and a contender for awards.

Every principal, associate, project architect, or job captain in charge of production must be constantly vigilant to ensure that the contract documents are not perceived or produced in an offhand, mindless, disjointed, or seemingly disparate fashion, without direct relevance to the project. Staff education, involvement, and motivation are necessary.

Should any of those negative characteristics be carried over into practice, they will eventually have a devastating effect. Therefore, the professional's staff should be made aware of and instructed about their status as "agents" of the professional. The legal concept of agency is crucial in that the professional is being contractually bound by virtue of the actions of others. Few professionals observe, monitor, oversee, perform, or review every line and sentence that staffers include in the contract documents. However, the work of the staffers becomes direct contract obligations of the professional (and others). Any failure, error, misrepresentation, illegality, or other malady in the documents becomes a potential problem for the professional. Some of these may be caught early and problems avoided. Some may be minor and easily remedied; others could become major impositions or threats. A few could be so serious as to result in litigation.

Confidence and trust in staff and loyalty to employer become hallmarks and key issues of successful practice. Both deserve full airing in the office and complete understanding by all. Even good-intentioned or unwitting gaffs can become problems. Assumptions are deadly. Questions by staff should be openly encouraged, with unqualified assurance of no stigma, and fully resolved. Indeed, it is essential to make every effort to create an open, communicative, harmonious, strongly directional production atmosphere.

Architectural practice, it must be remembered, is carried on within a vast and complex legal framework; from personal registration, to code compliance, to business affairs, the law requires distinct paths and hallmarks of legality and compliance. There is an impressive litany of case law that deals with professional practice, and much of it with architectural practice. Court cases are not new, although the incidence of cases has increased. In most of the cases reviewed for this effort, a common thread is found as the basis for suit. Wherever some uncommon, rather irrational, nonprudent, or "cloudy" procedure is used, suit will follow. The cases are rather telling in that straightforward, clearly defined, and well-executed contracts and projects will usually give little cause for litigation. Apparently, most practitioners recognize this fact and attempt, even through exaggerated means, to provide the correct scenario for the project. The professional should neither attempt to perform "above and beyond" (the contract) nor allow the owner to extract services or documents for which no provision(s) have been made. This is not to shirk the duty of the contract, but rather to perform in full accord with an appropriately drawn contract, fair to all, and apropos to the project. In reality, this is part of the "quality" built into each project.

The "Who cares?" attitude has led directly to massive expenditures for insurance and litigation. The professional seeking protection is caught in a vicious circle. To remain competitive, the fees charged must be low. To maintain low fees, there is a great tendency to shortcut work, including document production. Something has to give. Realizing this, the professional sees the need to protect the practice by purchasing "errors and omissions" (malpractice) insurance. This coverage, however, has become inordinately expensive, with some premiums being increased as much as 1,000% in just one year's time. This is due to excessive awards in some court cases and to the high frequency of claims and suits.

Yet almost every owner will seek to reduce professional fees to a minimum while retaining the requirement for a "perfect" (and profitable) project. The owner must realize that impossibly low fees will result, more frequently, in suspect projects. It is easier (all too easy) though, to squeeze fees and litigate any (and all) shortcomings. Not realizing or understanding that excellence in the production of working drawings lies in complete and coordinated documents, an owner may think that professional fees can (and should) be reduced. Too often the owner sees the professional as a "necessary evil." This misdirected and myopic view neglects the fact that the professional is the owner's agent, acts for and on behalf of the client/owner, and is the entity who translates the owner's project concepts into the hard reality called construction information. Obviously, the owner, in reducing the professional fee, is acting counter to his or her own best interest.

With reduced fees, time and money are not available to the professional for producing fully comprehensive documents, complete and coordinated in every way. Contractors (as seen in Chapter 4), finding less than adequate documents, have no choice but to seek changes or directions from the owner (with whom they have a contract) who usually will rely on the professional for that "gap-closing" information. If the professional has arranged protective cover by noting the inadequate time and money to produce correct documents, the cost is billed to the owner over and above the contractual price.

Therefore, in exercising their option in the areas of cost and scope (see the discussion in Chapter 14), owners always need to be reminded that quality, in both their project and the documentation required to produce it, is a factor of cost, whether in the initial professional fee or later in unforeseen added costs. The issue of fee versus quality of documentation is one that the professional should address when discussing the fee initially and throughout the project as other issues and changes occur. It is far better to address this matter than to allow slippage in quality and client confidence/relationships, which can cause damage to the professional that may take years, if not decades, to repair.

This situation, in part, is not without help in the industry. In early 1989 the provincial government of British Columbia (Canada) investigated the requirement that, by statute, 6% of a total project cost must be allocated to structural design. This occurred when a roof on a major business building collapsed and it was found that only 2% of the cost had been used for the structural design fee. While well intentioned to enhance public safety, this solution falls short of the best answer. Rather, only after there has been a satisfactory determination as to the qualifications and abilities of the professional should a fee be set; preferably a negotiated fee that assures the professional adequate time for exploration, design, production, checking, and a decent profit level, all in full accord with the requirements of the project.

Several other recent disasters have been caused by the failure of systems or combinations of materials that were mishandled or misdesigned. Given that some were due to faulty contractual arrangements, it is questionable whether more time would have prevented the problems. To some degree then, professionals have contributed directly to their own increased liability exposure by ignoring their legal responsibilities or by "adjusting" their methods of practice in regard to transferring responsibility and establishing accountability. Professionals must be ready to accept their multiple responsibilities. It is when one begins to "unload," or transfer one's responsibility to others, that crises occur. Clearly, it is important to understand what responsibility is transferred and what is retained. Often, it is impossible to completely divest oneself of responsibility without adjustments in the contract. These situations are taken up in the *Manual of Professional Practice: Quality in the Constructed Project,* published by the American Society of Civil Engineers (ASCE). Although not all professional groups have endorsed the draft of this book, it is, at a minimum, a good checklist for design professionals, be their projects large or small. Responsibility does not vary in direct proportion to the size of a project; it is foolhardy to think otherwise.

Lawsuits are filed over a broad range of issues, not least among them contract documents (including working drawings). Issues such as cost overruns, payment for extra work that is not properly documented, field instructions left unverified, delays resulting from slow approval, refusals to approve or issue change orders, and unclear plans and specifications are commonplace.

Although most lawsuits involve contractual and procedural matters, technical issues are involved in the vast majority of disputes and claims. Fortunately, not all claims result in suits, but, like disputes, they still require excessive amounts of time, money, and effort to resolve. However, some technical issues are litigated. Very little litigation is rooted in the design or design development phases of work. Rather, most technical suits (which begin as disputes and claims) are rooted in the contract documents and matters contained in the working drawings. In the main, these issues are money oriented, with lawsuits almost certain in cases that result in casualty: injury or death to a project worker or another person. So things that appear in the office to be mundane, routine, or inconsequential, really can impact a project (and a professional practice) quite adversely.

A PERSPECTIVE ON WORKING DRAWINGS

In a year's time, approximately 40 percent of insured design professional firms are sued. Although the majority of the suits are groundless, it is still costly to the professionals to address the action and defend themselves. Where situations can be resolved through issuance of a change, there is still a cost (perhaps in hundreds of dollars) to the firm for the processing of the order. Similarly, where major lapses, omissions, conflicts, or contradictions occur, the design firm's cost of resolution can rise to several thousands, or tens of thousands, of dollars.

This underscores the need for well conceived and executed drawings and faithful construction; moreover, as-built drawings are very valuable in establishing this scenario. Thus, if there are changes after the final construction and these lead to a disaster, the responsibility falls to someone other than the design professional. Of course, where failures can be traced to the contract documents, there will be direct and quick reflection on the professional.

Thus, working drawings and the drafting staff are directly involved in the avoidance of problems, disputes, and litigation. Every drafter should be fully aware of this on a fairly continuous basis, not as intimidation but as a factual aspect of his or her work. Literally every line drawn has an impact on the project; nothing is frivolous. All too often some drafting personnel are left without definitive direction or perspective of how their "grunt" work contributes to a project. This can lead to "mindlessness" in the very sequence where decisions for the project are made. Any part of this process can be the flaw that will unravel the project in the future. Oddly enough, it is this production phase of the work that is often compromised, financially, to reduce the disproportionate amount of the fee that must be allocated to it. And there is an added threat when the work engages the tremendous new technology, both in new construction materials and methods, and tools, such as computer-aided drafting and design (CADD), used in document production. Some recent reports show that computers in the hands of principals tend to move decisions from the documentation phase forward to earlier work phases. By "locking in" features very early in the process, later phases will be somewhat inhibited by the lack of flexibility. This could produce adverse results, in the long run, for the project. Although this may be a good device for acquiring more of the fee earlier, it may not be best for overall quality in the project. Simply, the practice must be fully attuned to its liability exposure in every phase of the work, or its chances for intrusive problems are greatly enhanced.

All of these indications show that the professional is more than well advised to practice in a straightforward and extremely careful manner. However, this all falls short of requiring a "perfect" performance by the professional. In the case of *Seiler v. Ostarly*, 525 SO.2D 1207 (La. App. 1988), the court held that the architect does not guarantee a perfect plan, nor even a satisfactory result, where the owner/architect contract does not state or require the same. From this we can conclude that if the professional acts with care and reason and adheres to a prevailing standard of care, fewer problems will be encountered.

Usually professional efforts are measured, by a court, against a standard of practice. This standard varies from locale to locale, but reflects the level and direction of "normal," prudent practice among like professionals under the same or similar circumstances (as those at issue). Although the standard is unwritten, professionals within a given region create the standard by the very methods they employ in their work. Every architect practices within the parameters of such a standard of "reasonable care" (also known as "practice standard"). It is difficult to define this standard, but a process of thought may help to do so. By asking the following questions, the professional (or staffer) can run a self-analysis of his or her performance/action against the standard;

- Is this the right thing to do?
- Is it the best for the circumstances, as I know them?
- Is my reasoning explainable to others?
- Can I defend this decision/position?
- Have I apportioned the risk properly?
- Have I taken, unnecessarily, too much risk for myself?
- Am I genuinely comfortable with this decision?
- Will the outcome be favorable?

This mental process should be engrained in the professional early on (in college, actually) so it is second nature and continuous, and although not pervasive, it becomes a strong guide in every aspect of the work.

To illustrate the risk of working outside the standard, one has only to look to two court cases. In *Huang v. Garner*, 157 Cal. App. 3D 404 (1984), and its quote from *Burran v. Dambold*, 422 F. 2D 133 (10th Cir. 1970), the professional is found guilty of "negligence per se," where the building was not designed in compliance with the building code. Further, this professional breech was so compelling that *no* evidence was required in regard to the standard of care. Simply, designs by professionals *must* be in compliance with the prevailing building code, *period.*

This very scenario is addressed by several states, which require design professionals to make several "visits" to the construction site to ensure that the work is proceeding in accord with the approved drawings and, hence, with the prevailing code(s). At least one other state requires via a "seal law" (where design by registered professionals is mandatory) that the professionals engage in ongoing code education, file standardized permit application forms (with code analysis), file statements of design responsibility, and, in addition, perform the verification "visits" required by the other states. Although some may see this as a nuisance to the practice, it does directly involve the design professionals with the code professionals in a cooperative effort to protect public health, safety, and welfare—a statutory charge to both.

Although construction has become more complex, and so necessarily the documents to produce it, fundamentally the basis of the drawings remains much the same. Without a good working knowledge of these fundamentals one can never hope to produce the very intricate details, complex drawings, and complete documentation so very necessary to a successful project. It is obvious that our buildings are no longer festooned with custom-made, individualized ornament and other such distinctive features produced only through pain-staking drawing of full-sized details. Much of today's work can be, and is, ordered by model number, but transpose two digits in that number and see the havoc. This is not to suggest that modern-day working drawings require less effort. In fact, they require more, mainly because of the overall complexity of projects and the hectic atmosphere in which we must practice. Yet with the current necessity for speed comes a commensurate increase in the risk of error, simply because speed requires faster processes, allowing less and less time for finite design and careful thought and

precious little time for coordination and objective checking of the documents.

Contending with the requisite speed can entice a professional into divesting him- or herself of as much responsibility (and work) as possible, mainly by delegating more aspects of the project to other professionals or to third parties. This practice carries high risk. Hence, it has been very easy for professionals to move to extensive use of exculpatory clauses in their contract documents. These clauses are basically "disclaimers," which are set forth to disavow, repudiate, or deny responsibility, guilt, blame, or even connection with certain conditions or situations. Here, in lieu of complete and in-depth staff review, the professional seeks to lay responsibility on others and attempts to invoke other codes, standards, regulations, and the like, hoping that where any of these are violated the exculpatory clause will be applicable and protective (to the professional). Often these clauses are too broad and intangible in trying to mitigate errors or omissions in the contract documents. They will almost always fail where they are unduly vague, uncertain, or risky,. Contractors are not to be made to "exercise clairvoyance" in noting and resolving ambiguities in the documents (*Blount v. United States* 346 F 2D 962). Yet even the 1987 edition of AIA Form A201 approaches this very scenario.

Contractors will usually assume that if their work is performed in accord with the plans and specifications, it will meet not only their contractual obligations, but also all codes, standards, and other regulatory requirements. No broadly worded clause will change this reaction. Although, the professional's concern is somewhat understandable, broadly based documents and exculpatory clauses may not be the best method for resolving ambiguities besetting the contractor. Courts usually will find for the contractor(s) where the contract or documents create conflicts or ambiguities (*Mac Knight Flintic Stone Co. v. The Mayor*, 160 N.Y. 72; *Green v. City of New York*, 283 App. Div. 485).

The concept and use of exculpatory clauses have a direct impact on working drawings. It has been shown that the professional need not produce a "perfect" plan but, at the same time, must produce a proper and adequate plan that will allow construction of the project. If errors are rampant in those plans, the cost of the project may escalate, putting the professional in danger of suit by the owner. Yet it is also shown that total reliance on the clauses may very well *not* provide the protection sought by the professional. The best direction then has to lie in producing the "best" documents possible, using a standard of care as the measure throughout, and incorporating the exculpatory clauses in a very judicious manner.

In addition, one must be aware that the courts have ruled that the professional cannot shift the basic responsibility for the proper preparation of the plans (contract documents) to the owner, a building inspector, or any other person to whom the professional has delegated all or a portion of the preparation (see, respectively, cases of *Simpson Bros. Corp. v. Merrimac Chem Co.*, 248 Mass. 346, 142 N.E. 922; *Johnson v. Salem Title Co.*, 246, 425 p.2D 519 (1967); *Johnson v. Salem Title* at 409, 425 P. 2D at 519). Neither can the professional evade the basic responsibility even where the contractor fails to check the plans, or discover the defects in them [(*Chiavernin v. Vail*, 61 R.I. 117, 200A.) 462 (1938); *Covil v. Robert & Co.*, 112 Ga. App. 163, 144 S.E. 2D 450 (1965)].

Nevertheless, several courts have taken a very enlightened view of the design professional. Those courts have noted that professionals are different from contractors by virtue of " . . . education, training, experience, licensing, and professional stature," to such a degree that " . . . limitation on their tort liability would not reduce the care with which they performed their tasks . . ." (*Zapata v. Burns*, 542 A. 2D 700 (Sup. Ct. Conn. 1988). In essence, the court is saying that the professional will act as a *professional,* and can be held under a shorter term of limitations.

Working drawings have been part of professionals' responsibilities, in some form, even from the most ancient of times. There has always been a need for communication on every construction project, in every era, no matter how primitive. From scratchings in the sand made with a stick, to the chalk drawings on the trestleboards of the Master Builders (architects) for King Solomon's temple, to the Greeks in the Golden Age, to Rome in its grandeur and demise, there were at least "temporary" instructions, drawings, or other visual communications. Consider, further, the cutting plans used long-term through the centuries required to build magnificent Gothic cathedrals. The forms and terms may have changed, but never the intent: clear, concise, complete, decisive, proper, *professional* instructions/communications.

Where time and speed (i.e., economic issues) begin to impinge on any of these attributes, the professional and his or her staff had better include yet another consideration—*care.* Thus, the documents become:

Clear: at the cost of almost anything (show and tell what you mean, and mean what you show and tell),

Concise: brief, but not to the point of ambiguity, evasiveness, or "gaposis" (all that needs to be there—nothing more),

Complete: a most worthy goal, but subject to normal human foibles (each item within itself *and* in relation to other things), and

Care: sensitivity to what is needed; a stride toward a "job well done" (realization that the final project is worth extra effort, early on).

Therefore, neither principal nor junior drafter should perceive working drawings (or specifications) to be "busy" or "throw-away," time-filling work, relegated to the most junior staff. They are *not* relegated, but rather should be delegated to staff who are the best available for that work. Only with a careful studied, enlightened, monitored, and fully coordinated staff effort, well motivated, will the risk of problems of all kinds be reduced and responsibilities met.

One-Liner Thoughts, Theories, and Concepts
(Worth review, pondering, discussion, and understanding)

- Simple buildings require only simple documents (not always so).
- CAD or hand-drawn drawings that look good are correct and well coordinated; sloppy drawings, produced either way cannot be complete and well coordinated (both statements are wrong).
- If every item and decision is thought out correctly, no errors will result (except that time and complexity do not allow such thought all the time; and who decides what is "correct"?).
- Errors and conflicts are unavoidable, but they can be minimized (true).
- Errors, even though undesirable, are not really important, because they will all be worked out in the field (bad concept; not good practice; if attempted, the professional loses control of the project).
- Drawings are really necessary only for getting a building permit (that is but one purpose; another, among many, is giving a firm and exact description of what the owner wants built).
- Errors on drawings are irrelevant inasmuch as the owner and the contractors will change everything anyway (and will all more than likely be dissatisfied, engaged in disputes, regulation violations, claims, and possibly litigation).
- Preplanning the documentation, using checklists throughout the process, using meaningful checks and back-checks, and coordinating between documents are continuous hard work, but usually produce better projects (true).
- The size of the documents (number of sheets) and amount of detail on the drawings are direct indications of the project cost; i.e., the bigger and more detailed, the greater the cost (not so!).
- Diligence, striving for excellence, and doing the right thing are major virtues of professionalism (absolutely).
- Makes no difference who makes the errors; it is the effort to find and correct them that is of utmost importance (true).
- Architects tend to have a more global or overall view and concept of a project; many consultants become totally engaged in their narrow realms of work, without thinking of others (unfortunately, true).
- The degree of project success is elevated, directly, by the number of errors found and resolved (true).
- There are errors of omission (forgetting/not doing things) and errors of miscoordination (things done, but isolated from one another and not properly interrelated).
- For architects committed to excellence, checking for and finding errors is an emotional, not an intellectual, experience (true).
- The best reviewer for the final check before issuing the documents is an experienced and knowledgeable (about construction) professional who has not been related to the project (new, fresh eyes find things more quickly and more reliably).
- Working drawings (and specifications) will never be perfect (but as in a game of horseshoes, the closer the better).

4

General Overview of Working Drawings

The work of the architect is not confined to the design of a project. Although it is important that the architect properly program the project (ascertaining the necessities and parameters) to develop an appropriate design concept, it is equally important that all of the relevant information regarding the subsequently approved concept be conveyed to the constructors in the field. Between the activities of designing the project and communicating complete and pertinent information, lies a vast amount and sequence of work, all of which is part of the architect's charge. This entails the conversion and documentation of the design concept into usable construction information. Here materials and systems must be selected, construction details developed to show exactly how various portions of the project are to be built, and specifications and drawings executed to convey the necessary information in a form that is readily usable in the field. Working drawings are a part of this entire work and communications sequence—and a very important part.

Computer-aided drafting (CAD) has revolu-

tionized the production of architectural working drawings.

> **The act of architecture is not finished when the design is done, but when the building is built. However, most students see and are taught that a design is the end product.**
> —Gerald G. Weisbach, FAIA
> Registered Architect/Attorney
> San Francisco, California

A good motivating thought to encourage all professionals to think ahead, and to think in complete and coordinated ways

Although late in coming to the profession, CAD has now evolved into the standard in most offices for at least most, if not all, functions in the production of working drawings. In its early stages, CAD was perceived by architects as a design tool that provided the electronic depiction of a concept—a new project that was not yet reality. Through electronic manipulations, the project could quickly be changed: expanded, rotated, reoriented, and so forth. Eventually, with the continual development of new software, you could walk through a project—electronically, that is—while the structure (in concept form) unfolded and changed around you as you progressed along a path. This was a tremendous process for designers, who no longer had to produce a series of study perspective sketches to present new or differing views of a project. Of course, this electronic process was readily embraced by the profession in this context.

Working drawing production, however, was slower to evolve. As late as the early 1980s, there was still college-level instruction in hardline (manual) drafting. This was the predominant method for producing the drawings used for the actual construction work. There were, only naturally, many professionals who took hold of the CAD concept early on, and through their fascination and growing expertise in computers, incorporated it into their entire professional operation—working drawings and all. This was the "cutting edge." Similarly, because word processing was one of the first, and most impressive, computer functions, architectural specification writing was also a very early use of the computer and its marvelous, rapid manipulative powers. In other fields closely related to architecture any requirement for calculation (such as structural analysis) was almost immediately computerized. This was done mainly because of the set routine or method for such calculation; it was an unchanging methodology whose results varied with varied input. Architectural working drawings, however, were not appropriate for this approach.

Overall, beyond the architectural profession, computerization was exploding in many directions and incorporating new software functions almost daily. What had been novel and intriguing in the 1970s was now commonplace, readily available, and continually changing, adding new features and functions, much of them very specific to products, processes, and operations. This, of course, occasioned a strong and instantaneous reaction in the education system. It was quite obvious that computers were, indeed, "the wave of the future." Schools of all types immediately began to buy the equipment and convert their curricula to offer more computer operations, which included drawing with the computer—that is, CAD.

Drawing, of course, is not confined to the architectural profession, and the schools sought to meet the demand for CAD operators, no matter what type of drawing they were to produce—tool design, machine design, civil engineering,

structural engineering, mechanical engineering, and many others, including architectural drawing. CAD training proliferated, particularly in the secondary and vocational schools. It was felt that if you could operate the computer, you could learn to be productive using any of the still expanding array of software and the mind-boggling myriad of new functions and capabilities.

In some technical and community college curricula (leading to two-year associate degrees) CAD instruction was structured in such a way that a new discipline was addressed in each term or semester. This instruction had to be skimpy and minimal if it addressed anything more than the particular functions required in that new discipline. In essence, CAD was being taught in the same context as typing. That is, once you learned the operation of the machine, you could adjust and work in any work environment. But things were not, and still are not, that simple.

Educational institutions that teach CAD as an entity unto itself leave the student without a framework in which to utilize that system. For example, one can manipulate the machine and software very well, but without a meaningful and in-depth knowledge of architecture and construction, the application of the manipulations can be of marginal value or useless. Secondary and vocational schools and technical/community colleges often provide this type of CAD training. It matches the level of instruction assigned to, or established in, such institutions. College-level professional programs that include CAD instruction, in the main, provide the fundamental background of construction methods and materials, their architectural applications, and so on, which then can be applied, developed, and displayed utilizing CAD. This major change in emphasis and context is of primary importance in any discussion of the use and/or success of a CAD program.

A good deal of postsecondary academic training tends to direct CAD efforts toward enhancement of the design process, rather than toward the development and processing of construction drawings. Some major schools of architecture even refuse to incorporate CAD instruction in their curricula, but even then, the students use the program in their work. Overall, however, the situation has been changing in some ways. One issue, though, should be specifically addressed in the use of the CAD process; that is refinement. With so many software programs, options, "bells and whistles," and the tremendous capabilities of any CAD system, it is a real shame that top-quality documents are not always produced. This is not a shortcoming of the CAD machinery, but rather of the users, the operators.

There is a tremendous level of fascination in computerdom. It revolves around what the latest software can do—how much faster, how much better. However, in the production of architectural working drawings, this enthusiasm must be tempered, if not tethered, to the end product, its content, format, clarity, and so on. Operators and users are developing more slowly than the software capabilities. Although these people have changed somewhat, they still are charged with meeting and serving the needs of very traditional tradesworkers.

The discussion in the article "Does CAD Boost Productivity?" (*Architecture,* June 1997, p.160) is still of interest and value today. There has been no major directional change or innovation that has definitively resolved the issues of productivity, cost of operation, training, and equipment mentioned there. The software and hardware have changed, become better and faster, with added capabilities, but the fundamental issues that an office is well-advised to seriously consider, in regard to computerization, remain. The article is also quick to note the breadth of computer use in offices and the type of operations that are used. Not every office uses the computer in the same manner, for the same operations, and to the same degree. Use will change (and increase) as staff turnover brings more and more CAD-literate personnel on board. This is nothing more than normal movement to a new technology, wherein some offices are more aggressive than others. But it is also noteworthy that the change in staff orientation elevates concern about issues of constructability, understanding of document content, intent, and use, along with the other issues addressed in this effort. Obviously, not many offices are in this position, but buying cutting-edge computer equipment and giving it over to an ill-trained staff that has little background or sense of values in the production of working drawings and construction, relegates the machinery to nothing more than an expensive gadget. Each of these issues has to be reviewed from a cost-impact perspective, as they are part of the overall ongoing price of computerization.

This was borne out sometime later in another article. In "Look for Higher Technology Benefits," [ARCHITECTURAL RECORD, December, 1998, p. 139], the results of a survey of offices shows that within offices there are quite different opinions about the value of CAD. It seems that those who use, or are closely allied with CAD operations, extol its virtues, and see great value and endless prospects for the system. Firm principals and other higher-level managers do not see this as having an impact or lasting cost effectiveness on their business goals and operations. Additionally, the principals saw no change in the number of errors, omissions, change orders, etc. because of the use of CAD.

This is a crucial observation or perception. It shows that the use of the CAD technology does not necessarily translate into better documents. This, of course, vividly shows that the use of CAD still needs the construction knowledge, and the understanding of document content and intent to be successful. This, in turn, is a direct reflection of the operator's background, education, perspective, and contribution; these all must have a strong construction orientation.

Many professionals still perceive CAD as something that their clients forced them into; an annoyance, really, rather than a new system for better practice. Hence, the operations have been given over to junior staff, who have little if any understanding of the business operations of practice and construction. In the main, though, they are well versed solely in CAD operations. Here lies the current gap in many offices. This is reflected, somewhat, in a letter from architect Charles Maggio [ARCHITECTURAL RECORD, December, 1998, p. 12]. Mr. Maggio notes that many projects do not have experienced [or registered] professionals in the actual documentation. This, having been given order to less experienced persons, is creating continuing problems on the projects. Some of this is seen in added professional liability, and in diminished reputations for the firms, as well as a continuation of the normal range of project problems.

Even now [at what some see as a "late date"] things regarding CAD in offices are not all that settled, much less resolved. With all of its innovation, speed, and capabilities, CAD is not being used to further the basic goals and intentions of the firms. This only proves that there is still a distance for many firms to go. There is a lingering need for understanding and adjustment to bring a firm's computer operations and business goals into alignment. Of course, this requires participation by both principals and those in the technology. It also shows that new professionals need to be well rounded in their education and training, so they can both appreciate and utilize the proper use of technology in the business of the firm. This is so very true because in the future the professionals who are now "those in technology," will be the principals, and will establish their own business concepts, and values. Hopefully, at that time they will better understand the needs and value of the documentation; and the truest measure of the system within a firm will still be the degree to which the principals see it as a direct contributor to the overall goals of the practice.

The ultimate purpose of CAD in an architectural office lies beyond the mere operation of a computer. It lies in crafting a skill in a way that allows one to facilitate that skill through use of a computer, and in achieving the goal-accurate, legible, well-executed, helpful, communicative working drawings. It may be helpful to look at a more generalized but studious and considered opinion/philosophy of computerization and CAD. This surely will put a different perspective on the discussion and may help to bring focus and greater understanding to our task.

Malcolm McCullough, associate professor of architecture at the Harvard Graduate School of Design, has written a book titled *Abstracting Craft*. This is not precisely a study of CAD, but rather of skill and craft within a computerized setting. He speaks to the application of mental capacity in conjunction with technical skills. For example, McCullough notes the following random thoughts:

> . . . view computer-mediated design like . . . traditional crafts like pottery making or weaving.

> Our use of computers ought not to be so much for automating tasks as for abstracting craft.

> . . . view a skilled CAD user as much more than a technically sophisticated mouse-clicker.

> . . . now look to the day when praise will go to those who control computers much like the architects of latter day "who could make a pencil sing!"

McCullough goes to some length to tie craft with artisanry, artistry, industry, and skill. He also notes specifically that

> ultimately the use of the computer is the combining of the skillful hand with the reasoning mind. To relate directly to CAD, isn't this indeed what our mind-set should be? To manipulate without

direction or regard for the final product is a hollow, nonproductive waste of time, in regard to working drawings.

Further, McCullough looks at the word *craft* as it is now used as a verb. We now craft memos, for example, meaning that we adjust, fine-tune, and hone the final product. To develop a skill into a craft, there is a need to couple physical activity with mental astuteness. Mindless machines can be highly productive in merely turning out the same object time and time again. But this generally is not an aspect of architecture and construction. Granted there are prototype buildings and standardized materials and systems, but in most every case there is a need to recombine these in different ways to produce yet another project; that is, every project is different, even if we start with the same resources.

Can we not agree that the skillful use of CAD is a wonderful accomplishment in and of itself? The real essence of CAD, however, is to allow the crafting of the display of information in an appropriate form. To manipulate the computer programming to find the best route or format for the display at hand is purely and solely an exercise of a developed computer skill. But it is when one is able to then add correct and pertinent architectural and construction information and knowledge that one utilizes the entire array of CAD-driven abilities. Remember, it is the person (operator, user, technician, architect, engineer, drafter, designer, etc.) who is the repository of the knowledge, know-how, and ability to craft information. The computer contains only that knowledge given it previously, and it cannot evaluate or retrieve it on its own or develop any new version or revision.

Comprehension Applied Definitively
—Another way of defining CAD, and of showing the intent of the method

This all may seem to be another version of "CAD is just another drafting tool." This, however, is a true middle-of-the-road comment, and certainly not derogatory. Without such "tools" much of the information and knowledge (not to speak of creative works, including architecture) may find an extremely difficult route to expression. For example, the quill pen in Jefferson's hand allowed him to craft the language of the

Declaration of Independence. Would the same wonderful document not have been produced if Jefferson had had access to a computer? The only difference would be the use of a different skill, medium, and equipment.

The same holds true for CAD. Knowledge and know-how, applied through the skilled use of the medium of computerized drafting, can be crafted, changed, expanded, reduced, rotated, and whatever else, until the proper end result-fully developed and fully usable—can be produced.

CAD, we must always remember, is "command-driven." It is incapable of producing anything on its own initiative. Moreover, it can produce anything, when directed, from the very good to the very bad, but that production is the outgrowth of what the operator tells the machine to do. Therefore, it is obvious that it is the operator's skills and knowledge we must be concerned with—not the machine, nor the software, nor the latest fad of cutting-edge developments of production systems.

> **You cannot endow the best of machines with initiative—the jolliest of steamrollers will not plant flowers!**
> —Walter Lippman
> American teacher, editor, and journalist

Both hardware and software are manipulated by the operator, who has total control over what is and what is not done. Any failing in the final product is the result, more than 95 percent of the time, of operator error; at other times it is caused by confusion in commands, whereby the computer produces what it "thinks" is correct, or purely mechanical failure.

We are now in a situation where new students and professionals coming into the architectural profession are lacking almost all knowledge of the values and techniques used in manual drafting. With this is coupled a lack of technical, field-oriented know-how and a fundamental understanding of what architectural working drawings are all about. Their expertise lies in CAD operations, many of which do not even address architecture-oriented software. This places the profession in a position of having to retrain or upgrade new personnel to ensure that their con-

tributions to project work are direct, usable, and valuable.

Granted that this situation is a function of the transition from full manual drafting to 100 percent CAD operations, but there is a need to understand what is happening and what is being lost in the process. It is not an attempt to stop time or to try to negate CAD and relegitimize manual work. In the very near future the older professionals who were schooled and experienced in manual drafting and basic working drawing rationale will be gone. Their replacements will be those who were educated in the CAD context only. This is a harbinger of deterioration in both the process of producing working drawings and in the final results. To establish context, let us look at the manual system.

Instructors teaching manual drafting used a grading system that covered not only the accuracy of the drawing, but the success with which the drafting work was executed. In other words, not only did the drawing have to be an accurate representation, but it also had to use expressive and appropriate lines, employed with varying techniques, weights, widths, and so forth. Overall, the accuracy of the work required it to be in a fully legible, readable style that easily and properly conveyed the message of the drawing.

With CAD, however, accuracy is almost automatic and lines can be produced "in a flash," based solely on the command of the operator. But herein lies the problem. If the operator is unaware of, among other things, the need and has no "feel" for line work variants, and does not understand what different line weights can represent, the drawing produced will be bland, perhaps illegible (if too many layers of information are overlaid), and not easily read by field personnel. In this situation, not only does the drawing become a problem to the instructor (what, now, is the basis for grading?—we hope not just how quickly it was done!), but the work is not of much value to the project, because it may confuse, confound, or cause too many questions.

There is no doubt that the development and use of computer-aided drafting (CAD) has had a major impact on the production of architectural working drawings. However, even with all of the successful uses of CAD, it appears that there should be a tempering of its use. There is need for consideration of a more mature, judicious, controlled, and refined use of CAD. This is particularly true for new and emerging professionals

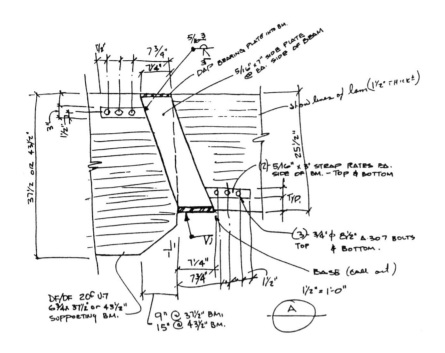

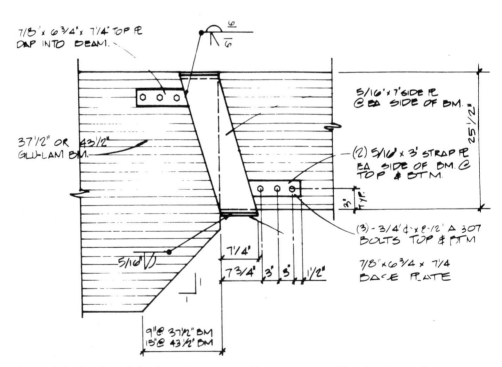

A typical office assignment; the hand sketch [top] must be converted into a proper working drawing detail, as done via manual drafting [bottom], but could be done via CAD just as well (students) who do not have knowledge of, or a grounding in, the traditional, manual methods of drawing. In addition, they lack the understanding of what those methods, techniques, and values established and imposed and, more specifically, what good they can contribute to the CAD process.

The controversy is long gone. CAD is not only here but is performing extremely well, and there is tremendous potential that the software of the future will continue to enhance the capabilities of the system. The use of the system is increasing and broadening into more offices and more functions. There can be no quarrel about this. There are, however, residual issues. These involve, for the most part, operator, use, and conceptual considerations. For example, the following are fairly typical issues:

• Emphasizing speed at the cost of readability
• Simply not taking time to refine and utilize features of CAD that will produce better drawing products
• Relying on color-coded displays to evaluate final (plotted) drawings, when this is patently misleading; the lack of "feel" for what the final product could and should be
• Misleading orientation and education on the use of CAD in its best format (usually a fault of secondary education)

CAD has had an influence on the concept and standards (values) associated with working drawings. Much of the movement to, and utilization of, CAD is attributed to the speed with which drawings can be produced. Perhaps more important, CAD drawings can be revised, relocated, expanded or reduced (in scope) in mere seconds. This lends an air of expedience to the process, which is certainly an attribute that cannot be denied. Every manager is seeking time-saving measures in order to meet tight (or unreasonable) budget and time restraints. But strictly relying on the expeditious use of CAD really shortchanges its capabilities and belies much of its good.

To take and use only what a CAD system can produce, and to limit our output of what the software offers, is to limit the quality of the products we produce. Although the computer programmer and software engineer can include marvelous abilities, they cannot include a decision-making device that replaces the human mind or the determination it can make. It is not Pollyanna-ish to state that the human capability is required to make a "good thing" (CAD) better.

In the evolution toward CAD, many have either overlooked or, for some reason, discarded the values, standards, and techniques of the traditional manual drafting system. But we suggest that there is no direct correlation between these and what CAD offers. The manual drafting attributes were developed, refined, and used for different reasons, but their basic concept is as sound today as it was in the past. Manual drafting was successful, in large measure, owing to the amount of graphite put on the paper; that is, sharp dark lines produced the same in the reproduction process; lighter lines reproduced their kind as well. In this process, it came to be known that drawings were enhanced, clarified, and made more readable by calling attention to some lines while allowing others to act as support or reference lines. This modulation of line weights introduced a sparkle into the final prints (reproductions of the original tracings), so that even the most untrained eye was drawn to important information, and guided away from other data, simply by the weight or intensity of the lines. They acted much like elements that guide a viewer to the center of focus in a painting or a photograph.

This technique was so widely and commonly used that it became a well-recognized standard within the construction industry. Some lines came to represent certain features, all the time. Particular line weights came to identify certain objects or materials, as opposed to others. Some types of drawings (sections, for example) used lines to define small, thin materials that were closely related but difficult to discern if not clearly shown. All this still survives and is needed today. However, CAD does not have the decision-making power of the human to use certain lines in certain places at certain times; it cannot evaluate the need for greater clarity, more separation, or more differentiation. This, then, falls to the CAD operator who *can* make these decisions and can then command the CAD system to produce the required result.

The most important idea here is that an "old" standard/technique is still valid and still able to make good better. A secondary aspect is that this is not an inherent function of CAD, but rather of a knowledgeable human who is in control of the CAD format and capabilities and who can best decide what is best used for the best result.

In manual drafting the "feel" for the drawing was always there. Because the drafter was producing the drawing directly (i.e., what was put on the tracing was the drawing), there was an immediate sense of whether or not the line was appropriate to its task. Of course, lines were scaled as accurately as could be done by eye, but the weight, width, and type of line were of equal importance. The ultimate criterion for a successful line was whether or not it would survive, as required for its task, when reproduced. Reproduction was accomplished by exposing the line to a strong light. The graphite that made up the line was intended to stop the light, to some degree, so that the sensitized paper below would not be fully exposed to the light. That paper was literally a negative. Where the full light struck it, the sensitive chemical was "burned off"; where the light was interrupted by the line, a line would appear on the paper. Where the drawn line was too timid or light, it would not create a line on the paper; it was simply not heavy enough to stop the penetration of light.

In CAD, the operator is not given this direct cause-and-effect feel in the production of a drawing. Unless there is a conscious understanding about each line, they could all be produced merely as the machine is programmed. If the operator gives no change of command, the line becomes a default function—whatever is set in the machine's formatting will be done automatically. Therein lies the problem. Moreover, the operator can be deluded into thinking that the lines are distinct and separated one from the other because they are colored differently on the monitor. Again, this is a faulty assumption, as the coloring on the monitor has no effect on the type or value (intensity) of the line produced.

At this point, several concepts must be addressed:

- The operator must understand what is to be produced,
- The operator must command the machine to produce what the operator deems to be correct and
- There must be flexibility in thinking to allow for changes in pen setting and other commands required to give the desired result

It is very important that these considerations be given attention and thought, that they be resolved as company policy and as individual concerns.

The end need for architectural working drawings has not changed. Despite the new information systems, production systems, software capabilities, and other sophistications, the workers in the field require all of the information necessary to construct the project—in a clear, complete, well-coordinated, and easily read and assimilated form. This constitutes a direct and formidable challenge, not to computerization or to CAD, but to those who utilize those means to communicate their desires and anticipate a final project as they envision it.

Architectural drawings have always been different from those in other engineering disciplines. This is true for design and presentation documents as well as for working drawings. So, too, are the techniques used to produce the drawings. This has all evolved into what are now called "traditional" standards, which were really developed by and through the process of manual drafting. One might ascribe this evolution to the art orientation of architecture. However, there is a good deal of sound rationale, including the standards that still survive. Most of this entails line work—the use of different types of lines, varied line weights (intensities and/or widths), their intersections, their meaning, that which they define and indicate, and so forth. It is self-defeating (disastrous) to perceive, think, or assert that architectural drafting—in whatever mode or form—and the production of working drawings are merely the recording of information, that is to say, "So long as it appears on the drawings, no matter the form, format, style, readability, or cross-reference." Rather, the working drawings have to be prepared in the same manner as the work is done on the job—closely fitted, scribe to fit, cleanly cut, neat, true, well crafted, and of highest quality workmanship in full accord with contract obligations.

The lines often speak for themselves merely by the type of line used and how pronounced or light it may be. This technique tends to add modulation, emphasis, expression, and readability to a drawing. The lines can sharply identify the work at a glance.

Because they are long-enduring standards, much of the construction industry is quite aware of and attuned to the line work of architectural working drawings. The general construction trades are trained in reading the prints (drawings) and understand any variations pointed out to them. Print reading, for the other trades, is directed toward the specific type of drawings they can expect to encounter for their work. In addition, there is at least minimal training in reading architectural drawings, inasmuch as the trade work must be fitted into the overall architectural project scheme.

None of this makes one type of drawing better than another; it is strictly a matter of the intended use and the tradition, repeated use, and established standards used for production. Only a few textbooks utilize actual working drawings (as does this book) that distinctly show the various techniques and how they aid reading and use. Most texts are published using printed lines for drawings, which tends to give student drafters a false impression—not every line is "perfect," of even width, and of constant value or intensity.

One of the functions of this book is to act as an instrument that interfaces with several concepts. Unlike training manuals for CAD or other texts addressing working drawings, this effort supports no fixed system or program. Rather, we are trying to provide a common ground between traditional manual drafting standards and the current CAD system. In making changes, CAD has also imparted, created, or fostered a new attitude and perspective among drafting personnel. Although, of course, not patently "bad" or misleading, this new outlook is somewhat amiss. We seek not to stop time or to impose outmoded standards. We seek only to add moderation, incorporation of helpful and appropriate standards (some that are of long-standing), and to inform readers as to what architectural working drawings are all about, why they exist, what they are intended to do, how their content influences project work, progress, and cost.

It is unfortunate that the simple attraction of manipulating a computer has come to overwhelm the reason a document is being made, what its content should be, and how best to portray the work. All this, in conjunction with the correct technology, has to be understood as the correct and valuable use of the CAD process. The full array of features and capabilities in computer software may come to naught, in many cases, when there is no implementation of correctness and/or properly conceived and depicted materials, systems, assemblies, and so forth. Only a drafter/operator trained in architecture, engineering, and construction methods, materials, and allied technology can achieve suitable documentation.

The simple fact that the outline of an area can be "clicked" and suddenly filled with a material symbol does not necessarily mean that the drawing is a success. In fact, this could make the drawing marginally effective, confusing, or misdirected. Although this type of task is easily done (and quickly), it may not have added information or clarity to the drawing; if not, it is ill advised. Think for a minute: Is a verbal message, quickly but indistinctly given, good in the final analysis? By the same token, is drawing done quickly, but in need of later explanation or clarification, a good product?

The true value of a drawing (even the smallest of details) lies not in the fact that it was quickly produced. Rather, it is in the quickness with which it contributes *directly* to a project—easily read, complete, easily understood, easily assimilated, easily utilized in the actual work.

Expedience puts a new twinkle in the eye of every person concerned with budgets, production hours, and the like. But expedience should not be in the driving force in the production of working drawings. Speed is admirable when combined with excellence in the communicative value of a drawing. Here is where traditional values come into play and where understanding of drawing intent and content must be present. Expedience should be the force to produce a "good, correct, readable, helpful, and complete" document in the shortest amount of time. Where that time can be shortened by utilizing CAD, all the better, but this does not mean minimizing or marginalizing time without regard for the product produced.

However, the "charm" of expedience has led to several rather negative nuances. First is a rigidity of mind that tends to force everything into one method of operation. Basically, what the CAD machine is set up to do is what gets done, without regard for other standards. From this the conclusion may be drawn that CAD can be "all things to all people," which simply is not true if one gives due consideration to the products developed by each of the professional disciplines. For instance, there may be a lack of varying pen sets in plotters that allow the use of different arrays of lines for the various disciplines. In addition, it is much easier to declare, rigidly, that all work can (and should?) be accomplished in the same manner, format, context, scheme, and/or technique. Finally, there is the matter that drawings—architectural drawings in particular—are being required in many cases, to be done in the same way as those in other professions. Here the intent and content of the drawings differs drastically, as do the direction they take and the standard (traditional?) manner in which the work is done.

There is no assertion that CAD is bad or improper (or unprofessional). Rather, the argument is that CAD is frequently viewed as the end result, the epitome of professional expertise and relevance. Some people speak of CAD in somewhat derogatory terms, noting it as "nothing more than another pencil." Certainly this ignores the tremendous value and capability that CAD brings to project documentation. But reality says that, indeed, CAD is the vehicle or method by which the required information is portrayed, just like the drafting pencil. (Perhaps we should consider CAD as today's tool of choice). The problem may be that we do not, as yet, consider CAD as commonplace as the pencil—something that is merely taken for granted. Nor do all professionals recognize and utilize the flexibility available in CAD, just as it exists in the pencil. For example, can one not produce a large array of different types, weights of lines from the same pencil?

The time is fast approaching when want ads will no longer address CAD in terms such as "CAD skills desirable (helpful)." Rather, there will be an assumption that anyone seeking a drafter's position in an architect's office will know CAD. Certainly, in the time of manual drafting no ads appeared that said, "drafting (drawing) skills desirable." The assumption was that if one wanted to be a drafter, one could draw.

Even now the ads are mainly used to identify the software being used in an office, so that those who do not know that program need not apply (the innuendo being that the office does not want to train new personnel on its software system). This, indeed, shows a very distressing situation. With the rapid and continuing proliferation of new software, one is very hard put to stay abreast of it and to be skilled in all such programs. Offices today change software when there is a new need or where the new attributes provide better and faster production methods, along with new capabilities. One would think it will all settle out eventually, but this is not likely as research and development in the computer industry thrives on and is aggressively producing a new and better hard- and software at an almost alarming rate. The professional offices that seek to adjust and accept new programs will eventually have to accept the fact that training goes hand in glove with the new programming.

The schools simply do not have the time or resources to teach every program available. This fact poses a tremendous challenge to educators who present CAD instruction. Although basic operations constitute one track, specific software is now becoming ever more imposing. The graduate must simply be aligned with a basic architectural software program or he or she will be relegated to entry-level employment at best. When a person is CAD trained, but only in basics, and has no orientation toward any specific software, that person, if hired, is a liability requiring training while not being productive for a period of time. Many offices do not or cannot accept this entire financial burden, particularly when they can hire other persons who have the necessary specific skills.

Perhaps this situation is best illustrated in a comment by the resources manager of a major engineering company:

> I would want to see a portfolio. I would expect to see, from a technical school, knowledge of detailing different types of buildings and materials, some knowledge of building codes, NFPA, NEC, etc. I would also expect them to have strong CADD skills in AutoCAD and MicroStation. Although I would not necessarily expect this from a technical school, a student who showed strong promise in use of Adobe Photo Shop, and knew all the right equipment to have for photographic quality "photomontages" would be a plus . . . a desire to either become the "best" architectural detailer in town, or to become a licensed architect.
>
> —Victoria Kahle, RA
> Resources Manager
> Fluor Daniel, Cincinnati

Working drawings simply must talk the talk of the construction project. Together with the specifications, the drawings should speak directly to the work required and how that work is to be accomplished. These two contract documents (the agreement between owner and contractor being the third contract document), combined with information from other sources, show and describe the exact requirements of the project as do no other instruments or documents. In this situation, there is a very distinct and demanding onus placed on the document production sequence,

Sources of Construction Project Requirements

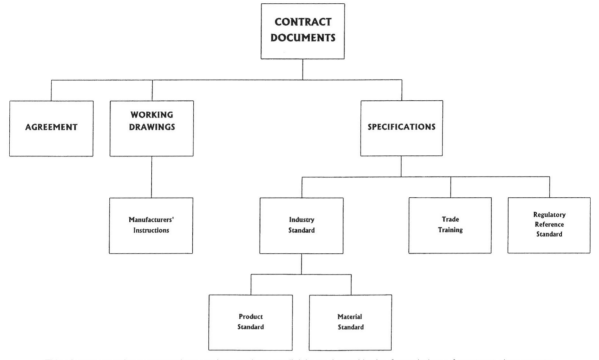

This chart notes the sources that can be, and are available and used in the formulation of contract documents. Note the number of sources from industry and not from professional sources

and that is to produce the very best documents possible. This obligation is tied to legal and administrative matters, as well as to the technical construction information.

Too often professionals forget that the technology of the construction project is really the work that makes the project "fly." No one disputes the fact that good architecture involves only pleasing and handsome buildings; ugliness is never rewarded. But to bring the well-conceived design concept to the point of being a usable structure, technology is the vehicle. This involves the conversion of many concepts (within the overall predominant *design* concept) into hard construction *facts*, which are interrelated, combined, and presented. Correctly done, this will enable the actual construction in the correct and proper manner. Without this effort, in the working drawings and specifications, the project will find a hard route to re-

ality; in fact, it more than likely will never be built.

Graphic delineation of architectural/construction projects is a legal as well as a functional necessity. By being part of the contract documents, the drawings are legal instruments. They show what must be done to fulfill the contract in place between owner and contractor. Their relationship, legally, starts with the work being accomplished "in accordance with the drawings and specifications." The owner is legally responsible to turn over fully adequate and complete drawings (and specifications) to the contractor for execution; the contractor is legally bound to produce the work displayed and described.

Doubtless, one could describe all of the necessary project requirements, and construction, in written form, but the resulting documents would be so voluminous, cumbersome, and complex that they would be virtually impossible to use. The proverbial "A picture is worth a thousand words" is never more apropos than in the instance of construction documents. Most legal concepts and aspects, however, defy "depiction." Drawings then become truly coequal with their associated specifications, as each relies on the other to complete the array of information (written and drawn) necessary to fully explain a portion of the work or the project itself. Either type of documentation is usable, but not in full without the other. The best criterion is that some things are best shown by graphic representation (drawings), others are best described in words.

In the creation of these documents, and the drawings in particular, some marvelous opportunities are now available to young and budding architectural professionals. What they do in contributing to the production of the drawings has a direct and important impact on the actual work and project. The increased use and development of computer-aided drafting (CAD) has opened many new directions and changed the face of project documentation.

A result has been a drastic change in over some 20 years. There is still some dispute as to working drawings whether the new drawings are better than those produced in the past. It is clear, however, that not all changes have added to the betterment of the drawings. Many professionals are of the opinion that something has been lost along the path of transition. There are some deep, disturbing, and quite troubling concerns, most of which are seated in but a few items:

- Lack of construction knowledge on the part of those now producing the drawings, as well as lack of field experience
- Lack of knowledge of and regard for traditional (past) standards, techniques, values, and criteria for drawing production and for drawing intent and content
- Education, starting in high school and voc-ed, that overemphasizes the use of computer-aided drafting by teaching only the manipulations of the machines
- Utter disregard, and almost disdain, on the part of students and far too many faculty, for producing quality documents with valid information correctly shown
- The lack of a will or impetus to correct these concerns by incorporating the capabilities of CAD with refined production methods and proper construction methods, materials, and details

This opinion, held by many practicing professionals, was echoed in a 1997 survey, noted in *Consulting-Specifying Engineer* magazine, in which the following comments (also applicable to architects) were included:

From my experience, most [engineering] professors do not have the clear knowledge or the know-how of dealing with actual conditions in practice. . . . Hence, engineers today have very little or no drafting knowledge. How can they design if they have no concept of details?

The growing utilization of CAD has contributed to this change, but also to major changes in the concept and perhaps even in the intent of the documents. Most of the change, however, is tied directly to the increasing use of CAD, the skill level of CAD operators, the differential in educational goals, and the proliferation of software programs for use in the production of the drawings. Additional factors are the acceptance of differing values, the available levels of skill and knowledge, and the transition from traditional to modern methods. Other aspects are related to the ease with which drawings can be produced. Time-consuming tasks of the past are now achieved in seconds—but are they equal in quality? It appears that the values applied today are too often directed more by how easily a task is done than by how properly it is done. Although this issue creates a division of opinion in the profession, it is a key to the success of every project.

In many professional offices the tremendous capability and speed of CAD has made expedience the primary, if not the sole, criterion in the production of drawings. With the inherent ease of performing CAD tasks, drawings can be created in mere seconds but, unfortunately, also in an almost mindless manner. Herein is great potential for creating construction problems. One can be fully satisfied with a drawing and the time it took in production, yet still have a substandard, inadequate, or wholly inappropriate piece of communication. The value of the drawing is not in the short time needed for production, or the utilization of several innovative features of CAD, but in the *content, instruction, and inherent value of the information* to the field personnel. For this reason, there is a greater onus on the drafters (which may

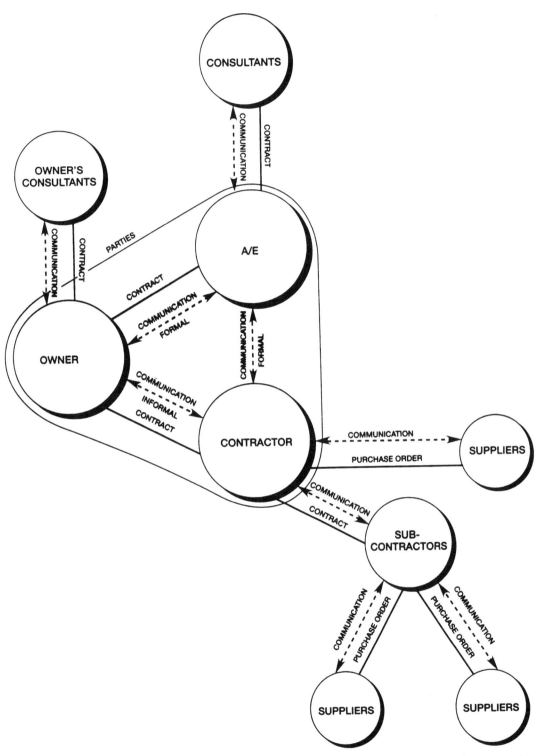

This figure shows the complete project configuration, as to contractual and communication obligations and responsibilities. It helps to explain the necessary inner workings of the project "behind the scenes" [i.e., activities supporting and facilitating the actual construction work]

be unknown to many) to understand and meet the responsibilities they have to both their clients and the contractors involved—production of readable and accurate drawings.

In his book, Construction Failures, second edition, civil engineer Jacob Feld points out, early on, that failure in construction is not confined to instances of collapse, be it partial or complete. Rather, Feld defines failure as . . . "behavior not in agreement with expected conditions of stability, or as lacking freedom from necessary repair, or as noncompliance with the desired use and occupancy of the completed structure."

This necessitates, Feld continues, "much more emphasisellipsisin technical education to teach what not to do, and when to say 'no,' rather than to give the impression to the untutored and inexperienced mind that blind compliance with minimal code provisions and reports of committees, signed by all members after several years of disagreement, but with ultimate consent to the strongest willed majority, is a guarantee of sufficiency.

Failures, as Feld defines them, "occur in all types of structures."

A fact not often reflected upon, much less mentioned or discussed, is that the true users of architectural working drawings and specifications are not the clients, but the contractors. This concept is vividly described in a very insightful article "Listening to Contractors" (*Architectural Record*, February 1998, p. 54). In a candid, surprisingly amicable panel discussion, there was agreement as to where architectural efforts are amiss and what the root causes are (improperly low fees, imposed by owners/clients, which provide inadequate budgets for coordinated, complete, and comprehensive professional services). The article also touches on the professionals' use of CAD and the results the contractors see.

Yet in the vast majority of cases, contractors had little input to the process of documentation and design. Documents in many cases tended to be incomplete (almost open-ended), uncoordinated, and contradictory. Contractors were made to guess and assume what was meant and required—a position they did not appreciate and

one that created all sorts of problems with both professionals and owners. All of the contractors' personnel had to be extremely flexible and quite aware of varying procedures, formats, methods, and designations so they could move to, easily assimilate, and use the variant and improper documents. Even within rather confined regions of the country, the variation between professional offices was most noticeable and often quite drastic. In addition, there was a good deal of contradiction and confusion in even the simplest of items, wherein a material symbol, for example, meant one thing on one set of drawings and something quite different on a set from another office.

Of course, the role of the construction manager (CM) comes immediately to mind. For in this arena, the CM does find voice, usually mandated by the owner through the contractual process. In like manner, the design/build firm is a more obvious user, having direct and usually high-profile input into the documentation as well as the overall design concept.

In all of this, the design professional (here let it be the architect) becomes a player with varying roles. In the traditional design/bid/build process (and the versions we now have) the professional is left, almost exclusively, to his or her own devices. Documents are formatted—for the most part, where owners make no demands—as the professional deems necessary, timely, and profitable. In this endeavor, engineers have outstripped architects in the ready use of CAD and other computerized programs. However, many aspects of engineering involve calculations with specific results, to a greater extent than the subjective and more conceptual work of the architect (taste has yet to be computerized!).

Too often, particularly in the past, architects have thought that part of their creativity lay in the unique and "clever" ways they used to produce sets of drawings. Often this involved new vocabularies and assignment of work spaces ("envelopes" in which only one trade was to work; others must ask permission to pass through or work therein). Although it has been used for some time, the 16-Division specifications format of the Construction Specifications Institute (CSI) evolved from the frustration of contractors and other users. The same work or materials had appeared in different locations in "the specs," depending on where the individual professional offices placed them. It was, for years, a scavenger hunt for contractors, subs, material suppliers, manufacturers' reps, much less the workers on the job site itself.

The previously noted article may not resolve the professionals' fee problems, but it certainly highlights the necessity to produce the best possible documents no matter what the restrictions of time and fee may be. Each office needs to address that issue, on each project!

Construction workers remain unmoved and unimpressed when given CAD drawings to work with. How the information was developed and placed on the drawings is completely irrelevant to these workers—unless there are problems in the drawings. What the workers are seeking is the information they need to erect the structure in the clearest, most complete terms and in a quickly read format. They have no time to differentiate between lines that appear the same but mean different things. They have no time to try to extract information from a maze of lines and symbols so overlaid, confusing, or unintelligible that the drawing is virtually unreadable. Few job superintendents will take the time that one did several years ago. This "super" actually took colored pencils and color-coded related/corresponding lines on a drawing so he could begin to read and understand all the drawing portrayed. The line work was marginal and similar in tone, weight, and type but attempted to show some seven different surfaces and profiles, each superimposed on the one below.

The drawing in this example was manually drafted, but the lesson it illustrates is most pertinent to CAD. First, the intent was ill conceived; it was trying to show too much. Second, the content was marginalized by the confusion created by all the similar lines. The simple use of different line weights, better understanding of what needed to be shown, and a critical review of this drawing would have resolved much of its difficulty. The same guidelines could have been applied had the drawing been done via CAD.

If, indeed, we expect workers to produce the project work properly, shouldn't we, as professionals, prepare the documents they use in like manner? If we are sloppy, disorganized, indistinct, ambiguous, inadequate in communication, and outside our contract, won't the same be excused or allowed on the job site?

The basic responsibility lies in the value of the drawing to the contractors; this, in turn affects the client. Where a drawing is murky, indistinct, incomplete, unreadable, or otherwise marginal, the contractors will be challenged to execute the work. This can directly influence the cost of the project (the impact on the owner). In the bid-ding process or other early project work, the contractors will easily see the problems inherent in the documents and will reflect those difficulties in their pricing. Moreover, inappropriate documents can lead to claims for added time of construction and/or additional compensation.

Thus, it is clear that the professional must be able not only to produce appropriate documents but also to recognize what is or is not appropriate, what should be included/excluded, and how best to display the information. However, it must be realized and understood that the training of new architects (like the training of engineers, as mentioned earlier) is not given in an even-handed manner. Although the project sequence breaks the work down into several phases, the greatest educational/training effort is not applied to the largest segment (in time, effort, and fee expenditure) of the sequence. Almost every school of architecture puts heavy emphasis on design and design theory. There is no denying that this is the fundamental direction of the profession, but the academic problem is that the other segments of practice are subjugated—some virtually ignored, some totally disregarded. This is most unfortunate, because the student is short-changed by being denied the opportunity to become familiar with the entire range of professional activities, their interrelationships, their impact on the project, and the client's perception. Similarly, students may not come to grasp the totality of a project and what must occur for the design concept to become reality. Understandability, time for professional training is extremely limited, such that the schools simply cannot teach "everything there is to know" about architecture. Because of the inordinate emphasis on design, in many cases there is no inclination to teach a fully rounded, generalist curriculum. It would be extremely helpful, though, if there could be some uniform accommodation for at least an orientation, minimal as it may be, to every phase of professional work. The student could then begin to appreciate all that is expected and involved in the profession and could better understand the process of bringing a design concept to fruition.

. . . [There is a prevailing] perception of technology as an annoying, minor boundary condition. . . . Technical subjects have always been the stepchild of architectural education and have been largely neglected . . . [creating] crisis in architectural education with the NAAB [National

Architectural Accrediting Board] and practitioners demanding quick changes and schools often slow to react.

—T. F. Peters in
Journal of Architectural Education, 1986

Many professionals still find working drawings tedious, a chore, "fee-eating," risky, and sometimes even unnecessary. It is not quite clear, though, how one portrays or communicates an entire construction project without the help (at least) of some drawings. There appears to be no flaw in the time-tested use of a combination of words (specifications) and pictures (drawings) to convey all of the required information to contractors, suppliers, workers, and even client(s). The methods may have changed, but certainly not the need for proper technical information; that need has increased tremendously.

The process of documentation is usually both intensive and extensive. It is imposing in that only the best of documents can clearly, adequately/fully and properly explain the concept of the project and the construction required to be performed. It is wide ranging in that even relatively small or restricted areas of the concept/project can entail numerous and complex details. Often what appears or seems simple is, in the end, difficult to convey in documentation. This is reflected in the complexity of the detail(s) and the need for careful and expert depiction/description. Then, too, the process is further complicated by the imposition of one system on another, or yet another. The interface and interplay of these systems must work in the final analysis (and project), but getting them built or installed is intricate and difficult even with decent documentation.

> **Design professionals should ensure all details are carefully and clearly documented in plans and specifications.**
>
> **Details and loose ends should not be left to contractors, nor essential performance and reliability features to code authorities to assure compliance.**
>
> —Consulting-Specifying Engineer, May 1997

The design professional is responsible for controlling the project, and its documentation. Literally, what is shown on the documents is what is required and expected from the construction.

Obviously, the better the documentation the better the chance for accurate, proper, and more than satisfactory construction in the finished project. This goes directly to the minimizing of potential problems—the first noted premise.

However, by combining and utilizing traditional values and techniques with CAD, documents can be refined, adding clarity, giving proper emphasis, increasing understanding, enhancing ease of reading assimilation and application, and increasing production in the actual work. This is a matter of using knowledge of what needs to be done and incorporated, why, and how that can best be accomplished. Then using CAD to execute this process, the best possible product (document) can result. Notice that this approach is not machine oriented, but rather a function of a knowledgeable, capable, and well-prepared human operators.

One thing, however, has not (and will not be) changed—that is the need, on every project, for clear, concise, accurate, and complete documentation of the project work for easy assimilation and use by the workers. Perhaps the charge now is to use this aspect as the lasting goal and to adapt the methods and techniques to this goal. We may also have to overcome our prejudices, our peeves, our quirks, our inflexibility, and ourselves.

With the increasing number of professional offices practicing architecture only to the extent of "plans and specs" (and no construction oversight services), it becomes more incumbent that the documents be closer to perfect—all-inclusive, errorless, well coordinated and referenced and giving a clear, exact, and thorough depiction of what is intended. Because the documents are the only (and limited) involvement of the professional, there is no opportunity to interpret, revise or correct them during construction. Even the best of these efforts will leave some matters unresolved or to be resolved by others (more than likely to the detriment of the project). In the event of unclear, ambiguous, confusing, contradictory, incomplete, or inaccurate documents, the professional can become the target of claims or litigation. So the mere fact that the professional chooses to reduce liability, by not providing construction services, does not excuse or eliminate liability for poor products. Although, the new professionals may not be fully attuned to this situation, their tasks remain to produce sets of coherent documents, well executed, well coordinated, accurate, and true to the design concept approved by the client. Two issues immediately arise: How does one best do this? And how does one know what to do? Perhaps one concise statement will suffice:

> **The understanding of the content (what to show and say) of the documents is the crux of the quandary; how (by what media, technique, format, etc.) you transmit this information contributes little to the information and, hence, is really almost irrelevant.**

To explain: It is necessary that only "correct information" be conveyed. Correct information is the technical data and the form in which it is shaped (words or various forms of drawings). That information can be successfully transmitted by any of several methods, but its fundamental relevance and accuracy are essential, its clarity, brevity, and completeness (words/drawings) quintessential.

We need to take a little time to ponder:

- What do I have to communicate?
- How can I best transmit it—words only?
    Drawings only?
    Drawing(s)/some words?
    Mostly words/some drawings?
  Of course, everything is a combination of words and pictures, as the normal technique is to show work and describe it (see illustration on page 42).
- What type of drawing will best convey the message(s)?
- What should I cover via drawing notes? What via specification?
- What production system is being used, manual drafting, composite drafting, CAD, etc.? Is it appropriate in this instance?

An old adage covers this situation: It is not so much the messenger, as the message that is important.

In architectural working drawings, this is exactly the case; nothing transcends the information that must be transmitted to enable the successful completion of the project. To provide such information it is necessary to understand *what* is required (content) and *how* best to present it (choice of media, view, projection, etc.).

For the technological aspects of a project to perform as required, there must be a fundamental and in-depth understanding of the process of design that has preceded the creation and development of the approved design concept. There must be full respect for that concept and a resolve to bring it to full reality, faithfully and completely. Both of these values, understanding and respect, are necessary for a successful project. They should be given to and instilled in the entire staff who will process the various phases of the project work. Otherwise, detailing, specification writing, and field observation will be virtually rudderless, without guidance or goal. Although the design concept may exist only in schematic/presentation drawings, renderings(s), and/or a model, these provide guidance to the other work. At least here there is "something to shoot for"—a goal. A great deal of time, talent, imagination, skill, knowledge, and experience are required to bring the presentation instruments to fruition. There usually is not, and need not be, a formal education process to get design information to the staff, but some effort is required to convey the perspective of the project, the quality to be achieved, and the process that will produce the project documents.

As part of the process of bringing a design concept to reality, there must be a method for selecting the materials to be used for the project. The design concept tells what is to be produced in the final project. Material and system selection tells what is to be used to produce the actual construction of the concept. Fundamental to this entire process is a working knowledge of construction materials. This should include some information on basic raw materials, production, fabrication, processing, testing, availability, costs and so forth. No one person may have all of this data at hand for every product, but an office organization should use its entire technical staff as a resource. Experiences on other projects or with other firms can prove to be of great value in the material selection process. These must be combined into systems, where possible, or into distinct details which gather and utilize them to formulate "pieces" of construction.

At this point attention must be centered on how the best result can be provided. Selection of materials may now be shown in the rough conceptual drawings in the manufacturer's literature, or perhaps it is still in the mind of the project architect or others. The focus must be on determining what to show (how materials and systems are

04151: Vertical Concrete Masonry Control Joint

The detail is one that is quite valid. Here it is shown with "keynoting" [see discussion in Chapter 35]. In addition the written material explains what is required to execute this detail, and the 5-digit number indicate the specifications Section in which this information will be placed.

Description

A vertical concrete masonry control joint is used to accommodate horizontal movement caused by shrinkage and thermal expansion and contraction.

This detail is used in commercial construction where steel or concrete columns support the floor and ceiling structure or where the masonry is used as a load-bearing wall. See Detail 04152 for vertical expansion joints in brick. See Detail 04153 for expansion joints in load-bearing composite walls.

Limitations of Use

- For concrete masonry exterior walls.
- Does not include horizontal control pints.
- Does not include reinforcing for seismic loads.

Detailing Considerations

- Through-wall building expansion joints must be provided to accommodate differential structural movement, settling, and movement caused by seismic activity.

- Shear lugs should be used to transfer lateral wind loads from one side of the joint to the other.
- Joint reinforcement must be discontinuous at control joints.
- Joint reinforcement is generally spaced at every other bed joint.

Coordination Required

- Locate control joints at points of least bending moment or at supports.
- Control joints should be located at changes in wall height or thickness; at pilasters, recesses, and chases; at one side of all wall openings; and at wall intersections.
- Control joints should be designed to provide masonry panels that are as square as possible. The ratio of length to height (aspect ratio) should be as close to one as practical, but not more than three.
- Joint reinforcement and bond beams must not be placed across a control joint.
- Mortar accelerators containing calcium chloride should not be used with reinforcing anchors and ties.
- Space control joints according to Table 2–1.

Table 2-1 Maximum horizontal spacing of vertical control joints in exterior concrete masonry walls, in feet

Maximum annual relative humidity	Vertical spacing of bed joint reinforcement, inches	Type of masonry	
		Type I	Type II
Greater than 75%	None	12	6
	16	18	10
	8	24	14
Between 50% and 75%	None	18	12
	16	24	16
	8	30	20
Less than 50%	None	24	18
	16	30	22
	8	36	26

Source: <u>Masonry Structural Design for Buildings,</u> TM 5-809-3, Department of the Army, Navy, and Air Force, August 1982.

Likely Failure Points

- Joint cracking if horizontal reinforcement is continued across joint or mortar used in joint.

Materials
04100 Grout
Fine or coarse grout, ASTM C 476.
Ultimate compressive strength (28 days) of at least 2500 psi.

04153 Flexible anchor
Vertically adjustable, type to suit support.
16 gauge, mill galvanized, ASTM A 527, G90.
Optional: Stainless steel, 18-8, Type 302/304, Cold rolled, annealed, ASTM A 240.
Spaced 16 inches on center

04155 Shear lug
Used to transfer lateral wind loads from one side of the joint to the other.
Made of polyvinyl chloride (PVC) or hard rubber.

04157 Joint reinforcement
Material:
Fabricated from hard-tempered, cold-drawn steel wire, ASTM A 82.
If reinforcement carries horizontal loads, reinforcement should be the deformed type.
Minimum No. 9 gauge, but not more than one-half the thickness of the bed joint. 2-wire, truss type.

Class 3, ASTM A 641 for partially embedded joint reinforcement (0.08 ounces of zinc per square foot of wire).
Use ties conforming to ASTM A 153, Class B-3, in very corrosive environments (1.50 ounces of zinc per square foot of wire) or use stainless steel ties conforming to ASTM A 167.
Size of horizontal reinforcement determined by structural requirements of the wall.

Execution:
Ends of joint reinforcement should be placed from 1/2 inch to 2 inches from expansion/control joint and not be continuous through control joints.
Lap joint reinforcement 6 inches elsewhere in wall.
Place 16 inches on center vertically and under the top course of masonry.
Place extra reinforcement in the first two bed joints above and below openings and extend 24 inches beyond the opening.
Center reinforcement with longitudinal wires centered over each face shell.
Lay reinforcement on bare masonry, then place mortar and slightly wiggle wire to get some mortar under the reinforcement.

04220 Concrete unit masonry
Materials:
ASTM C 90, Grade N.
Type 1, moisture controlled, and Type 2, nonmoisture controlled are available, but Type 1 is subject to less shrinkage and is best used in arid climates.
Sash block used to accept shear lug.

7910 Backer rod
Closed cell polyethylene foam, with the diameter at least 25 percent greater than the joint width.

07920 Sealant
Materials:
One-part polysulfide or polyurethane, ASTM C 920, Type S, Grade NS, Class 25.
Execution:
Sealant depth equal to the width of the joint up to 1/2 inch, with a minimum depth of 1/4 inch. Sealant depth 1/2 inch for joint widths from 1/2 inch to 1 inch.
For sealants with a +/-25 percent movement capability, the joint width should be four times the expected movement of the joint.
Proper priming and backer rods required.

located and combined for the construction) and how this information can be conveyed to workers in the most direct, clear, and complete manner. This sequence for CAD directly parallels the hand drafting process, and the criteria are the very same; only the process changes. With time and money such imposing factors in the production of any project, the tendency now is to use the CAD capabilities quickly and far to indiscriminately. The use of CAD must be controlled and directed. It is simply too easy to produce a drawing that adds nothing to the project knowledge (except, possibly, confusion). Needless line work, covering entire areas with nonproductive portrayals of material symbols, or drab, expressionless line work where no line weight variation is used can lead to "monotone" drawings in which readability may be impaired, impact is nondescript, and confusion or murkiness is pervasive. Simply said, the product will be better (and more rapidly done) only when the operator incorporates manual drafting concepts and techniques and when the needs, intent, and content of the final product are known to and met by the architect/technician/operator.

With the use of CAD, there is no need to concern oneself with dropping ink on a drawing, smearing graphite over a sheet (while working over other work),or otherwise marring a drawing/product. But there is still a possibility of producing an unclear confusing, unreadable drawing. In addition, the drawing can still be ill conceived, poorly delineated, and of quite limited value. An early axiom about computers still holds true: "Garbage in, garbage out." The benign computer produces only as it is *commanded*. It must be told what to do, and how.

Therefore, they who tell the machines what to do *must* know, well, what is to be produced or delineated. They must engage and utilize the best techniques available to produce a good result. As repugnant as this may be to some mavens of the computer, it is still absolutely true that old-fashioned, manual drafting standards and techniques are still perfectly valid and are used with this technology. CAD, in the final analysis, when used skillfully and judiciously, is really another, but marvelous, drafting tool, by far exceeding any pencil or pen. It is another way to produce drawings—the very same drawings required throughout the years, but produced by hand.

Using CAD is no stigma. Times change and technology evolves, mostly for the better. But we should not be so engrossed in the machine that we lose sight of the need to fully utilize its abilities within the context of existing and traditional standards and requirements.

Let us propose the following scenario:

- Learn the basics of construction materials.
- Learn the basics of construction systems.
- Learn what resources are available for added information.
- Understand the principles of "sectioning" and detailing."
- Learn from each project how materials can be combined, fitted, and made to work together.
- Learn CAD operations and the capabilities of the more widely used software programs.
- Seek out and learn old, traditional, but still valid, manual drafting standards and techniques; gain an understanding of the reasoning behind them.
- Learn and exercise a strict discipline over your use of CAD, consistent with the traditional standards/techniques; exercise control and restraint; produce the results you want (which differ from mere "wide-open" implementation of CAD features).
- Learn and understand the intent of each drawing type; understand the function of each drawing and what it should contain to perform its function.
- Combine all this into a personal scheme for knowing what should be done, why, and how you can best achieve the needed result; understand how that result will be used and what function it lends to the field personnel and to the actual construction.

> **Professionalism is a personal attribute that one acquires—It cannot be inherited; it cannot be bequeathed.**
>
> **Only they, having made the acquisition, who put to use that knowledge, that skill, and with all of their ability and complete dedication of purpose, can be truly called a "professional."**
>
> —R.E. Onstad

Professionalism (*as defined in the illustration*) is a most intangible virtue and a very personal one. One is *not* a professional by mere acclamation, nor according to what machines he or she uses. Professionalism in architecture is seated in an attitude—an uncompromising, disciplined approach to correctness—and excellence in work performed in every phase of a project. It is also related to dedication and sincere, innate caring about one's work.

Frank Bucaro, a teacher on moral theology and ethics, has said, "Values are what you believe; ethics is what you do." Architects need to be aware that there is a code of ethics available to help guide them through the often confusing world of professional conduct.

When the American Institute of Architects adopted a new Code of Ethics and Professional Conduct in 1987, it was framed around three sets of principles: the canons (the broad principles of conduct); ethical standards (goals that members should be reaching in their professional performance and behavior); and mandatory rules of conduct (whose violation is grounds for disciplinary action by the AIA).

There is often confusion about ethical matters, particularly at the level of standards of care, the rules of behavior that are derived from the entire set of ethics and that apply to the daily practice of architecture. Standards of care help determine questions of liability, particularly where reasonable care, skill, competence, and diligence fall below community standards.

Often there is no simple answer in determining a standard of care. In my work as a forensic architect and member of an ethics committee, I have seen architects judged responsible for falling below the standards of care for many reasons, including the following:

1. They did not properly coordinate drawings and specifications in the architectural and engineering disciplines.

2. They improperly designed roofs, balconies, window and door openings, and below-grade waterproofing.

3. They did not prepare specifications tailored for a particular project.

4. They prepared ambiguous documents that caused extra work and/or delays.

5. They accepted improper substitutions.

6. They performed improper contract administration observations.

7. They improperly certified payments for the contractor.

How do standards of care apply to the real world? The following overview of complaints received by the AIA/Los Angeles Ethics Committee relating to standards of care provides some examples:

The architect should have been at the job site more during construction. In agreements between architect and owner, the architect should specify the number of visits or number of hours set aside for periodic observations.

The architect didn't give us what we asked for. If an owner presents the architect with a program and specific requirements, the architect must incorporate them. The architect cannot ignore any portion of the program or the specifics.

The architect was found to be unlicensed. Any person discovered to be practicing architecture without a license must be reported to the state board of architectural examiners. That person is committing fraud by impersonating an architect.

A drafting service prepared plans that were stamped by the architect. Any architect who signs or seals construction documents that were prepared by others without his or her direct knowledge or supervision has violated the state's regulatory rules and an AIA rule of conduct.

An architect did not receive credit on a project. One of the most frequent complaints is failure to acknowledge contributions of colleagues such as designers on the team.

Employees and consulting engineers never received payment from the architect. Lack of compensation is a common problem leading to the filing of an ethics complaint.

An architect was not able to get copies of his or her work. Most architects allow their departing employees to obtain copies of their work, with the departing employee generally bearing the cost of the reproductions. Because of the confidential nature of certain projects, an employee may be asked to sign a confidentiality agreement.

Ethics committees of the AIA are available at all levels to assist architects in interpreting ethical matters. Yet, while colleagues can help architects to clarify the Code of Ethics, in many ways our choices remain personal. As folk singer David Wilcox says: "We answer for the consequences of our choices."

Edward K Takahashi AL4, CCS, is a forensic architect and partner-in-charge of the Forensic Section of the O'Leary Terasawa Partners in Los Angeles. He is also the Ethics Committee Chairman of AIA/Los Angeles.

Measured, legally, by a professional standard of care (see Chapter 3, "A Perspective on Working Drawings," it is eminently obvious that the true professional brings and interjects a new tone, vision, or element into every project. Part of that project is its documentation, and professionalism is manifest in the quality of the documentation. The professional will always seek to present the best design, the best information, the best detailing in the best format of fully coordinated, clear, and well-executed documents—including working drawings.

Part of the charge of this book is to relate and impart the concept of a *professional* approach to working drawings. It is hoped that we can aid each reader in establishing an understanding of this approach and at least respect for these documents, whether or not he or she works actively in document production. A true professional working in this context can achieve the proper and desired results through correct and astute manipulation of any medium—red pencil, yellow wood pencil, drafting lead holder, special lead, ink, composite (cut and paste) drafting, photographic drafting, and, yes, CAD. Combining wise, informed, professional manipulation with the marvelous capabilities of a CAD system should ensure that every set of project documents are presented at their very best. (Excellence in design concept certainly adds further enhancement and credence to the project scheme.) There is also a pervasive need for human sensitivity to refinement of the process. There is a need to recognize that the end result, a legible, complete, descriptive drawing, is the preeminent issue—not merely exercising the computer's capabilities nor the spectrum of its techniques.

Project documents can suffer in the selection of media where there is a lack of understanding, skill, restraint, sensitivity, and full operative flexibility. The traditional principles of architectural drawing remain: line weight variation, good lettering (adjusted to proper size to fit the associated drawing), clarity and readability via uncluttered drawings, scale adjusted to fit the work being depicted, and so on. It is no criticism of CAD to say that simply because the equipment is capable of performing a function does not mean you must use it, or use it to its fullest extent. Not every brick on an elevation need be shown simply because you can block out the area, click on the "brick symbol" icon, and have the area immediately filled with brick. What have you contributed to the project? Basically, nothing. You gain nothing by full rendering of working drawings in a manner similar to presentation drawings. No one (we hope) is going to count the bricks and estimate from that count. The process is simply unnecessary, even though the time expended would be minuscule. Moreover, the result can be a muddy, murky, or confused drawing—too many lines for no productive reason. Small areas of *proper* material symbology are helpful and recommended to aid readability and understanding. However, do not allow yourself to be taken in by CAD's abilities and library figures. You control the content, and *you* can manipulate what CAD does. There is absolutely no reason for not using the same "drafting refinements"

and techniques in CAD or composite drafting as are present in good manual drafting; the drawings and the project will be the better for their use. Yet some may quarrel with this statement. Their only concern is that the information be there—damn the style, technique, readability, clarity. Better, though, to approach any job in a fully professional manner, prepared to exercise the best of drafting skills and abilities, than to attempt quality work with less than quality techniques.

Before beginning the documentation of a project, the process and format of that work should be determined. Usually the project architect assembles his or her production team and goes over the standards involved and the type of documents to be produced. These can include everything from sheet media, to sheet size, title block layout and data, to use of office standards, to the particular standards that the client may request or demand. All this is preliminary to drawing the first line. However, such preplanning is necessary to form a context for the work. Obviously, not every drafter is free to "explore" or produce drawings as he or she sees fit, nor in the style or format that person may deem appropriate.

Each drafter, however, must take an active part in the preparation for the work. There is a need to resolve the sequence of the drawings (in the set), the content of the drawings, the scale(s) to be used, the layout of sheets (depending on the size of the project, use of match lines, etc.), the relationship of drawings one to the other and their cross-referencing, and the fundamental "how-to" of the drawings individually. Basically, this is setting a course for producing the *best* presentation of the information to all parties, particularly the contractors.

The process of producing working drawings requires some sophistication and some forethought. In fact, there are three distinct levels of involvement (knowledge/understanding, expertise, skill) required. Although they need not be outlined in a formal list, as this is generally a mental exercise, the following may be helpful:

Level 1—Knowledge/Understanding
- What needs to be shown?
- Why is this necessary?
- What problem(s) need to be resolved?
- What are the correct material selection(s)?
- What shapes, sizes, and interfaces have to be created?
- What fastening devices will be required?

- How many and what kind (legal, technical, etc.) of restrictions may apply?

Level 2—Expertise

- How large an area of work should be included? (Should more than one drawing be used?)
- What scale is appropriate for the amount of detail required?
- What type of drawing projection would be best?
- Can a standardized (previously used, banked) drawing be retrieved and reused and/or modified?
- Can it be anticipated that the new drawing will qualify as a standardized drawing for future use? (Change format, if yes.)
- What line weights should be used?
- Where are notes and dimensions best placed?
- How will this drawing fit on the sheet?
- Should it be located and/or combined with related drawings? If so, in what combination?
- What cross-referencing will be required (to and from the new drawing)?

Level 3—Skill, with Forethought and Planning

- Is CAD the best technique to use to make this drawing?
- What CAD operations/manipulations will be required?
- Can library figures be used or adapted?
- What size lettering is appropriate for the size of the drawing?
- Which of CAD's greatest assets can be utilized?
    Ability to copy
        Entire drawings
        Individual views
        Portions of larger work (for details, etc.)
    Ability to edit
        A piece of work or any portion thereof
        Add, subtract, or manipulation of entire layers
        Layers of information (even creating new or additional drawings by so doing)
        Combining disparate pieces of information, without regard to scale, into a drawing
        Retain and retrieve work (details, drawings)
        Quickly change line weights, other attributes

Move drawings/views from place to place in set
Automatically update related work when changes are made in one drawing

As noted earlier, the production staff should be made an integral part of the design/production team. Although this is more of a management function, it is also important that each drafter "pick up" the responsibilities delegated to him or her. Envision this as a relay race, if you will, with responsibility as the "baton." The aim is the same as in a foot race—finishing in a timely, winning manner. Sometimes you set records, sometimes you merely finish—best to do it in good style.

The following is a brief list and commentary regarding work on working drawings. This is a process that each drafter should review continually, certainly at the start of each project, and, indeed, for each new drawing for a project. This program encompasses nine basic thoughts or rules:

- Plan every step of each drawing, detail, and sheet.
- Develop a way of checking your work.
- Know/understand what decisions you will have to make.
- Find out the applicable standards for your work.
- Draft from the reader/users' point of view.
- Cooperate/communicate and work with others.
- Assume nothing; determine your main and secondary duties and responsibilities.
- Think for yourself; be resourceful; ask questions but try to have a possible solution at hand for verification; be helpful to the process and all involved.
- With each task, concentrate on improving one aspect of your skills.

The facts are undeniable—computerized production of contract documents, particularly working drawings, will continue to increase and will become ever more refined. This refinement will bring added sophistication to the process and will provide a growing number of options and capabilities to the operator/designer/drafter.

The case we intend to make is that all of the slogan-like nomenclature regarding the capabilities of a computer system are meaningless and

ASSUME NOTHING

Assumption leads to wrong conclusions, misjudgments, miscalculations, errors, misinformation, wrong guesses, procrastination, contract deviations, and numerous other assorted, but usually adverse, maladies regarding the work, progress, interrelationships, or the project as a whole.

productively useless where there is not an understanding, knowledgeable, construction-astute person at the keyboard. Rotation, electronic space walking, color graphics, and speed aside, if there is no understanding of what material/system to use, how to connect or interface it with others, and how and what to communicate in the construction of the system, the computer becomes superfluous. The wondrous machine must be directed toward its assigned task, as a laser scalpel is in brain surgery.

In addition to the professional nuances, the matter of personal caring about the work comes into play. Regardless of your current station in life (graduate, degreed—bachelor, associate, master—registered professional, co-op student, designer/operator), the success of the project you are working on depends directly on how much you care.

Caring also has a direct impact on the cost of the project. For example, if you show a detail requiring work that is not normally done or is not normally done as you show it, the cost of the project will increase. Simply because there is a question as to what will be required if you insist on having a detail done your way, the added cost is justified, to your client's detriment.

TO CRAFT IS TO CARE!

—Malcolm McCullough
Associate Professor of Architecture
Harvard Graduate School of Design

Any junior drafter, CAD operator, co-op student, or graduate architect can, and does, have a direct, imposing bearing on a project. This is achieved through the work of that single person — line work, notations, correctness, dimensioning, readability of drawing, proper and complete cross-referencing, and so on. Actually, the preparation of the documents requires as much control and supervision as the actual construction work. There is as much need to control and properly use CAD as there is to install the work in the field.

You have to care about each line—what it does and does not do and, more important, what it is supposed to do; so, too, with each note, word, dimension, indication, symbol. Be aware and sensitive to conditions. Does the door open into a brick wall? Why is a door opening cross-hatched? Be alert to misspellings. Do your dimensions add up to overalls? Do things look neat, controlled, and orderly?

Each drafter/operator needs a personal sense of dedication and drive to produce quality documents. This can be achieved through an understanding of the control he or she has over the CAD process and how this control can be used to produce proper, careful, thorough, and readable documents. In understanding content, intent, and methods to produce quality, professionals need only to care enough to exercise properly the equipment and processes at hand.

Indeed, do the drawings look as if a responsible, knowledgeable professional produced them? This is the clear challenge.

It is unfortunate that the attraction of working on a computer has come to overwhelm the reason a document is being made, what its content should be, and how best to portray the work. All of this, in conjunction with the correct technology, must be understood as the correct and valuable use of the CAD process. All "bells and whistles" of computer software are for naught, in many cases, when there is no implementation of correct procedure and/or properly conceived and depicted materials, systems, and assemblies. Only a technician trained in architecture, engineering and construction methods and materials and allied technology can achieve suitable documentation.

Education in CAD methodology includes the basic fundamentals of terminology, formatting procedure, and correct keying to perform the required task(s). From this base of information and skill, the budding CAD operator needs to proceed to more specific information (in some cases, course study terminates with merely achieving skill in basic operations). There is no "CAD industry," per se that is a direct counterpart to the tool design/making industry, or the architectural and engineering professions. Rather, like typing, the generic CAD function can be adapted and used in other work and functions. In some such instances, additional skills and knowledge must be developed to address the specific task or work to be done.

In the past, prior to computerization, most professional offices had staff members who were employed entirely in document production. These were young people who started perhaps as office runners and gradually sought, and were given, added instruction and an opportunity to become part of the drafting staff. Others were architectural and engineering graduates who, for one reason or another, never felt the need to become registered. All of these people became "professional drafters." However, by being trained on the job, they were able to add technical knowledge to their drafting skills, to the point that many such offices had senior chief drafters who were never registered, but who became major factors and influences in the production of documents. Their knowledge was office gained, based on problems and solutions resolved in various projects.

There is still a need for staffers who can function in much this way, not necessarily as chief drafters, but who can bring architectural and construction knowledge to a project, solve problems, and contribute to the production of quality and proper documentation. A budding professional or a technician who utilizes technology instruction and knowledge, presented through enlightened use of CAD, can become a valuable and integral part of any project team. A person with such combined skills should not confine his or her efforts to one aspect or the other. This may be something that should be talked through with an employer. Such an employee is more productive, per hour/dollar paid (and billed) and can rise to greater status and position than one who remains as a more passive CAD operator. The joy of this work is in actively contributing and being a valued part of the effort.

> The most precious asset any professional controls is knowledge of the discipline and the skill to apply it effectively. Over the long run it is more important to maintain the value of this asset than the office, the furniture, the computer hardware, or even the bank account.
>
> —Robert Gutman, PhD
> Author, *Architectural Practice: A Critical View*
> Lecturer, Social/Behavioral factors in design, Princeton University

5

The Production of Working Drawings

lthough the role of the entire set of drawings is to depict the project work in toto, each drawing sheet and/or each individual drawing has its own subrole, which entails showing various-sized portions of the project work. Subsequent chapters contain a general discussion of the various drawing/sheet types and their roles. In addition, a checklist is included, showing the information and drawings that usually appear on each type of sheet. Both for convenience and to save space, each single sheet in a set usually contains more than one type of drawing. Some drawings, such as floor plans, are so expansive as to take up all available drawing space on a single sheet. For very large projects, floor plans may require a series of sheets to depict just a single level.

The intent of this chapter is to provide a general outline and set of basic guidelines as working drawing standards. These are aimed at assisting the young professional and drafter in correctly arranging and depicting information pertaining to the drawing documents. (*Note:* This list is not all-inclusive; see Chapter 14 and subsequent chapters for more discussion and specific checklists of items to be included on drawings; also review office checklists and those published by other sources.)

General Concepts

1. The theory of working drawings. An art of communicating; the method used by design professionals* to convey graphic information to contractor(s) regarding a construction project; in particular, materials, methods of assembly, quantity, location, extent, configuration, and design intent (concept) information to construct the building project. The drawings are part of the contract documents;** hence, they are legal and binding documents.
2. A building project = building + structural system + all building services (mechanical) systems and utilities + site modifications.

---

* A design professional is a registered architect or engineer who is engaged in the design and construction of building projects.
** Contract documents are the contract agreement, the working drawings, and the specifications, in concert with one another.

51

3. Working drawings are a combination of words and pictures that convey different types of information to the contractor(s).

   These documents are drawn to scale (a small unit of measure is used to represent 1 ft (12 in.) and are usually two-dimensional, drawn to the correct size and in correct relationships (no distortion nor foreshortening as in perspective drawing).

   They do not, however, contain all of the information required to build the project; a set of written "specifications" is required. These add more, but new information and really *supplement* and *complement* the drawings.

   Only by using both of these documents can the contractor(s) truly review, see, and understand all the work they are to perform.

4. On the working drawings, there are several different types of notes:

   a. *Demolition Notes.* Used for removal of trees, vegetation, fences, existing structures, earth, etc. necessary to permit completion of the new project.

   b. *Construction, or Plan, Notes.* Used to "call out" (indicate, designate, show, name) materials, methods of assembly, quality, or design intent (concept) information needed to define a particular item or situation found on the sheet on which the note occurs. Be very specific with the information each of these notes gives to the contractor.

   c. *Landscape Notes.* Used only for extensive vegetation, plantings, and earth (contour) modifications. Call out both existing and new vegetation (size and quantity when applicable) and, as necessary, planting information or modifications to existing work.

   d. *General Notes.* Used to transfer information that is held common to either the sheet, discipline, or project on which it is found; usually refer, in general terms, to numerous items shown in other types of notes.

5. Sheet numbers. It is necessary that each sheet be given a distinctive number; this permits easy access, reference, and coordination of information between persons using the drawings. For example, persons talking on the telephone can easily refer to a specific sheet merely by citing its number.

   Numerous systems are in use, and each professional office has a standard of some sort that it uses. For example, on fairly large projects (more than 10 drawing sheets) sheets may be numbered as follows:

   "A" Series. Architectural Drawings: defining dimensional, aesthetics, materials, and methods used in the project.

   "S" Series. Structural Drawings: defining everything to do with the structural features of the project (footings, foundations, columns, beams, joists, etc.).

   "C" Series. Civil Drawings: showing and defining work of a civil engineering nature, such as grading (contour modifications), drainage, roads/drives/walks. Used only on extensive, more complicated projects or when breaking civil work out (defining it) on the site improvement plan to improve and simplify communication.

   "L" Series. Landscape Drawings: defining landscape work and vegetation modifications. Used only on more extensively landscape projects or where such work is to be specifically called out on the Site Improvement Plan to simplify communication.

   "P" Series. Plumbing Drawings: used to show and define the materials, methods, locations, equipment, fixtures, piping, and intent of the plumbing system (including storm drainage) for the project. May be combined with HVAC (heating, ventilating, and air-conditioning) information where work is limited in scope.

   "M" Series. Mechanical Drawings: used to show and define the materials, methods, locations, systems, equipment, and intent of the HVAC work on the project. On small projects the plumbing work may be included, provided that work is modest in extent.

   "E" Series. Electrical Drawings: used to show and define the materials, fixtures, methods, locations, equipment, and intent of the electrical system for the project.

6. More extensively detailed drawings and specifications = *more control* by the designer over the aesthetics, quality, and durability of a building project

   Less extensively detailed drawings and specifications = *less control* by the designer and owner over the aesthetics, quality, and durability of a building project (more control by contractor, whose main concern is money = less cost and more profit)

   This is a *very important* point, as the design

professional is an agent for the owner (acting in his or her behalf) and control is the key to a fully successful project (meeting all requirement of the owner). Control *cannot* and *should not* be released, given over to or abdicated to any one else, particularly the contractor(s).

It is also an important aspect in the work of any drafter working for a design professional in any capacity; the rule is fundamental and must be understood and followed.

7. A cover sheet is used on most projects and is quite helpful in many cases. This may be a separate sheet or simply a portion of a sheet that has some construction work shown on it. Basically, the cover sheet contains the following:

   a. Vicinity or location map clearly showing the project site; can be a state map (where necessary) and/or a portion of a local street map.

   b. Complete name of the project and any pertinent information such as project number, phase of work, etc.

   c. Full address (street and number, etc.) of the job site.

   d. Names of design professionals and consultants.

   e. Name of owner (board of directors, pastor, company president, mayor, city council, department members, as they apply to the project).

   f. Registration seal of the design professional; this is required, in several states by law, on *all* sheets of all projects except residences.

   g. Date project is issued and goes out for bidding; also occurs on *each* sheet.

   h. Index of *all* drawings contained within the set; shows sheet titles and sheet numbers.

   i. On some projects (as an option) a rendering of the project is included on the cover sheet.

8. Drawing sequence. Though not a sacred ordering, the listing given in the following section can be modified, added to, or deleted from, as deemed necessary (order may be varied from project to project). This is but one example of sheet numbering (use of a decimal system allows for inserting other sheets at a later date) and possible content (varied as the project requires). Working drawings numbering, as noted in the preceding item 5 is not magical; with fewer than approximately 10 sheets, numbering should be simply consecutive.

INDIVIDUAL DRAWING REQUIREMENTS

Site Improvement (Site, Plot) Plan

1. In a drawing containing actual survey information (by a registered land surveyor), show all property lines with a heavy line (long dash, two short dashes, long dash) and the bearing (meets and bounds) for each line (for example, N85°32'41"E, 158.94'); this denotes the direction of the property line and its length. At property corners (the point where property lines change direction), indicate the intersection of the property lines with a small dot or a hollow circle. Show benchmarks (points that show grade elevations as used by the surveyor) with a solid circle or target bullseye, and a note.

2. Show and call out all concrete paving, aprons, curbs, curb cuts, stoops, sidewalks, etc. Thoroughly dimension as appropriate (width, height, etc.). Indicate, as appropriate, by plan note all finishes, control and expansion joints, etc.

3. Show and call out all items, trees, structures (of all types), fences, etc. that exist; note specifically, or show in dotted line, those to be removed for the new construction.

4. Locate *new* building with dimension to two property lines (one to side or building, and one to front or rear). This should indicate the foundation wall locations.

   Indicate the building in one of two ways:

   a. As a "footprint," using a heavy, bold line around the perimeter, showing exterior columns (if any)

   b. As a roof plan (bird's-eye view), indicating slopes of roof, drains, parapet (top of wall) caps, etc. Also dash in the building footprint where it is set inside the roof line (this shows any roof overhang); dimension to footprint, not to roof line.

5. Show North arrow. If there is a wide difference, note with magnetic (true) North and building (or plan) North, which aligns with the walls of the building plan.

6. Show grade elevation of all contour lines (contour lines connect points of like elevation above a benchmark, or at sea level). Show existing contours in medium-weight dashed lines, new or modified contour routes and

locations in heavy, dark solid lines. Note the numerical value of each contour line in at least two places.

Indicate the grade elevation of the first floor (or grade level) of the building within the building footprint; crosshatch the entire footprint of the building in a medium tone.

7. Show the locations and sizes of *all* existing utility lines on the property and in the adjoining street; show new utility lines into building from existing sources; be sure to note the type of line (water, sanitary sewer, storm sewer, gas, etc.). Also show utility meter and shutoff valve locations if outside building.

Where appropriate, show the Siamese Y valve location for the fire sprinkler system. This must be accessible to all fire apparatus on a paved surface, with backup area, turnaround, or continued access around building. (For some projects it is advantageous to include a separate site plan devoted entirely to the utilities and the mechanical and electrical trade work.

In some jurisdictions, the fire service requires a fire protection plan. This is a modified site plan showing fire protection equipment, sprinkler connections, annunciators, fire pumps, utility shutoffs, building exits, driveways, radii, fire hydrants, fire mains; location of trees, high tension wires, and other items that may impede or affect fire fighting, access, or other emergency services.)

8. Indicate and call out the site drainage system: piping, area wells, dry wells, culverts (including diameters and materials), surface drainage swales, retention/detention basins, underwalk drains. Roof drains and collection drains should be taken to "daylight" or tied into a storm drainage system; call out and so indicate. Many residences use splash blocks beneath downspouts; call out where used.

9. Show, indicate, and call out in detail all new site improvements: drives, walks, parking areas, handicapped ramps, fences, decorative features (pillars, light posts, archways, entrance features, other structures, etc.), bridges, fountains, etc. Detail these features and locate properly.

In particular, dimension parking areas in relationship to the building proper. Call out and show wheel blocks, paving materials, striping, planting areas; dimension the parking bays and aisles in a string dimension and call out the total number of parking stalls in each bay. Note and locate parking area lighting standards and all signage, both painted and erected.

10. Call out and note all new landscaping materials by legend or plan note; indicate type, quantities, and spacing (if required) for each plant type. Note all sodded, seeded, or hydromulched areas; show extent.

Floor Plan(s)

1. If information is available, lay out the structural grid (column centerlines) for the building; then carefully, and as accurately as possible, scale out and draw in the walls and partitions for the building; establish and show/indicate door, window, and other wall openings.

Designate column grid centerlines with 1/2" or 3/8" diameter circles on the ends of the centerlines *outside* the building's dimensions (these can be widely spaced, away from interference with the drawing information). Assign numbers to one set of column lines and letters to those perpendicular to the first. Draw in all columns: proper material, cover, etc.

2. By single-string dimensions (as much as possible) locate and align all interior wall dimensions from face of studding to face of studding; call out wall finish materials and show thickness by Plan Note or by General Note, with Plan Notes as the exceptions (to the General).

3. Indicate fire walls, fire separation walls, and other special walls/partition types; change hatching for change in detail or construction; call out locations (dimension), methods, and materials.

All walls and partitions in the preceding items 2 and 3 should have a distinctive hatching applied, via hand drafting, CAD drafting, or application of reproducible adhering tapes, to distinguish one type from another and make plan reading easier.

4. Envision four distinct lines of dimensions around the exterior of the building:
   a. Out-to-out (overall) of the extremes of the building walls.
   b. The next line (moving in toward the building wall) dimensions between column cen-

terline (grid) lines, and the edges of wall corners (indicate to what location dimension is taken); this line may not be required on every project.

c. The next closest line to the building dimensions the "wings," offsets, jogs, angled walls, and major portions of the building.

d. Closest to the building is the dimension line that locates door, window, and other wall openings in relation to each other and to the corners of the building masses.

Indicate "rough opening" (RO) or "masonry opening" (MO). Use dimensions to the centerline of openings in *wood frame* walls only. Where bands of windows or glass are used, these should be dimensioned to the center of the mullions (vertical members between glass panels). Call out the type of system, glass type, thickness, etc. (note should be made of panels, etc. that are typical, that is, repeatedly used around the building).

5. Indicate *all* rooms and spaces with an area name and/or a room number. Most professional offices have a standard regarding room/area/space indications. In the main, however, assign room numbers in clockwise order, in adjacent fashion, beginning at the main entrance and working around the building perimeter, then toward the interior. In many instances it is helpful to use a number that indicates the floor or level on which the room is located (example: Room 112 = first floor, room 12). Ensure, in any event, that every space is numbered, without duplication. Rooms added after initial numbering can be designated as 112A, 112B in relation to the numbered room nearby.

6. Indicate and call out fire extinguisher cabinets, drinking fountains, counter and work tops, (including those in rest rooms), fixtures, built-in cabinetry, shelving, closet shelves and rods, electric panel locations, phone panels, utility entrances, telephone booths, and all other features to be built or supplied under the contract.

If these items occur in an area that is to be enlarged in plan (larger scale), show the feature on the larger plan *only*.

7. Call out and indicate (heavy dashed lines) portions of the floor plan that are to be enlarged, for detailing and clarification purposes, in another location within the working drawing set (for example, rest rooms, kitchens, specially equipped rooms).

8. Provide a distinctive door and window symbol/designator, for *each* opening. In residential work the window and door sizes and hardware information may be located at the opening.

In larger and commercial projects, a designator should be used and the complete associated information listed in a window or door schedule. Many different systems are in use, but *it is not wise to use any system that counts the number of units*—this should be left to the contractor(s).

9. Locate, indicate, and call out with heavy, distinctive designators, building sections (cross- and longitudinal) cut through the entire building. Use other distinctive designators for identifying details in the construction.

10. Ensure proper title and scale indication for *each* floor plan.

In some cases the complete plan of a building will not fit on a sheet. Here, *match lines* can be used to sever the building into several portions, each of which is shown on a sheet; a "key plan" at small scale, showing the entire building, is required, with an indication of what portion of the building is shown on the sheet. Match lines require heavy, distinctive designators.

11. Call out, if and where appropriate, radical changes in ceiling height(s), floor levels, critical beam locations (bulkhead) if no reflected ceiling plan is planned/used; exposed features, beams, etc., should be located and called out. All of this work should be shown with dashed lines and dimensioned as necessary.

12. In Chapter 18, on floor plans, there is a checklist of specific items relating to floor plans, indicating which should be depicted, where used, or required.

Exterior Elevations

1. Exterior elevations are orthographic views of the outside faces of a building (two-dimensional). They are *always* projected at 90 degrees to the surface being viewed. The required number of elevations varies with the layout (shape) of the building.

Where walls are angled, they should not be shown in an angled or foreshortened view; an additional elevation view is required at the 90-degree projection to the angled wall.

Curved walls should be drawn as if they were "pulled out flat," that is, showing the true (arched) length of the wall.

Elevations should be drawn at the proper scale, with vertical "verticals" and horizontal "horizontals" (nothing should be optically correct, as in perspective, and nothing should be distorted or foreshortened).

2. Call out critical vertical dimensions at *both* sides of *each* elevation as appropriate; ensure that dimensions extend to an actual point or establishable level: top of masonry, joist bearing, etc. Vertical items needing location including the following:
   a. Bottom and top of footing (indicate depth below grade)
   b. Top of foundation wall
   c. Top of sill plate; top of double top plate (wood)
   d. Top of wall, masonry, parapet
   e. Bearing level of roof joists
   Use a distinctive designator at each grade/elevation note (a "target," ⊕⊕, for example).

3. Indicate roof pitch (slope triangle or slope per foot) for sloping and pitched roofs; *do not* indicate top of ridge as an elevation on a pitched roof.

4. Properly locate and call out wall section designators where they apply; run designator down into the wall, but not through the entire wall height. Indicate detail cuts or other locations.

5. Show the configuration of the *new, finished* grade line as it is to appear at completion of the project (uneven, sloped, graded, raised, lowered, etc.); this is the heaviest line on the sheet (and is *not* a flat drafted line) and should extend well beyond the ends of the building in its proper location. Existing grade is often shown in a dashed line, somewhat lighter, but also in its proper configuration.

6. Indicate all spread footings, foundation walls, column pads, pilasters, stepped footings, and other features that would appear *on the outer face* of the building; do not show interior features. All work below the finished grade line should be dashed.

7. Show and call out special vertical locations as necessary for clarity: windowsill and head height (indicate RO or MO as appropriate),

centerlines of circular windows and arches, vents, louvers, and major items of mechanical equipment on the surface of the building.

8. Pochet (hatch; use standard symbols for materials in elevation, not in section) *only* on selected and confined portions of the elevations (not over the entire drawing, unless this is office standard). Help to define design intent, and call out location of all exposed materials, joints, etc. Be specific, but do not use specification language or extensive notes (the specifications writer usually assigns the proper terms to be used).

Building (Cross and Longitudinal) Sections

1. Building sections involve cutting the building across the short dimension (the cross section), or lengthwise (longitudinal section) to reveal both construction and relationships of construction systems and areas. "Sectioning" is much like slicing a sandwich, which reveals all the details of the "interior construction."

2. Show, usually at the scale of the exterior elevations, the overall mass sections(s) of the building at the point of the cut; the section (cut) line may be offset to go through a variety of spaces. Offsets *must* be taken *only* at right angles to the cutting plane.

3. Show and indicate major structural features, using minimal detail (slabs, walls, floors, trusses, roofs, beams, girders, foundation walls, footings, etc. (Think of the section as an index to the construction.)

4. Indicate each space cut by the section by its name and room number. In these spaces, show interior elevation(s) of walls beyond (those you would see looking in the direction of the cutting plane) *only if* there is new or critical information resulting and not revealed elsewhere in the working drawing set.

5. Indicate and call out, with a heavy, dashed line (or a solid line) those portions of the building section that are "blown up" (increased in scale) into details.

6. Indicate and call out with designators (targets, bullseyes) all critical vertical dimensions similar to elevations; extensive dimensioning *is not* required.

Wall Sections and Details

1. Wall sections are created by sectioning (cutting) the building vertically, from the bottom of the footing through the roof or parapet construction.

   To reduce the extent of the drawing, portions of the wall construction that are similar, redundant, repetitive, etc., can be deleted by inserting a *pair* of break lines (this usually occurs about mid-way between floor assemblies).

2. There is a relationship between the scale of wall sections and the use and scale of "blown-up" details. The smaller the scale of the wall section, the greater the need for associated blown-up details. Obviously, where work is shown at a small size, there is need for more, better, clearer, and larger-scaled information.

   This relationship, and the scales and drawings involved, are usually the subject of description in the office standards manual. Scales of 1-1/2", 1", 3/4", or even 1/2" = 1'-0" can be used, as deemed proper.

3. There is no fixed number of wall sections; this varies with the complexity of the construction and the number of different wall types and detailing involved. Wherever wall construction changes (even in fairly minor ways), another wall section is advisable, if not required. This does not mean that every note must be reproduced, but the *new* information must be shown; proper references to other information can be made.

4. Identify materials by both call-out note and material symbol; use proper line weight variations to distinguish between materials, especially thin materials; do this an adequate number of times to eliminate any doubt as to whether or where a material is used.

   A new method (if the office allows it) for call outs on a wall section is to use a numbered designator for each item, device, material, or situation, with one set of notes applied or typed on the sheet. This greatly reduces the amount of lettering required and offers a cleaner, more easily read sheet.

5. Provide, call out, and designate pertinent vertical dimensions as done for those on the exterior elevations.

6. Provide and call out all pertinent horizontal dimensions, aligning identical levels in the various sections, across the sheet.

7. There should be no reluctance to creating another detail; remember, we are trying to communicate a lot of information without speaking directly to the other person(s) involved. We must be clear, complete. We must define intent (what we want) so that we can maintain control of the project.

   Locations of details can be identified by heavy dashed or solid lines (around the area in question) or by note.

8. Some parts of details *direct* work ("provide masonry wall ties @ 24"o.c., each way") or *require* some work ("flashing") through their notes and by leader lines that literally point to, *and touch*, a particular item.

   In general, details show and indicate (1) items required, (2) work required, (3) methods of placement, (4) attachment required, (5) a better view of the work involved, and (6) other aspects of the design professional's *intent*.

Foundation Plan

(Can be combined with the basement plan in some projects.)

1. The foundation plan is really a form of floor plan, in that it is a horizontal section that looks *down* on the foundation and footing system. The scale is usually the same as that of other floor plans; in fact, there must be a direct relationship between floor plan and foundation plan (match lines similar, etc.).

   Again, instead of laying out the entire plan, one can often overlay the floor plan and use it as the base for the foundation plan; this ensures coordination and correlation between these plans.

2. In many instances the footing/foundation layout and information can be overlaid (superimposed) on the basement floor plan. Where this becomes too involved and complex, separate plans should be used.

3. Show foundation walls, with pilasters (where used) and other extraordinary features, in a solid line; indicate cut-outs, slots, beam pockets (wall recesses for steel beams), masonry and slab ledges, and other features that must be formed into the concrete foundation wall.

4. Indicate all bearing walls, column piers, columns, etc. that provide support for the floor above.

5. Show all spread, isolated, continuous, and other footings in their proper locations, sizes, and configurations, with a dashed line.

6. Indicate slabs on grade; note slab thickness, reinforcing, materials, penetrations, moisture protection, subsurface treatment, perimeter expansion joints, other concrete joints, etc.

7. Completely dimension the plan; interior string dimension to locate all walls, wall thickness, openings, etc.; exterior dimensions are the same as those of the floor plan. Locate and dimension steps in footings, joints, and openings.

8. Identify, detail, and dimension crawl space areas and unexcavated areas (for slab on grade).

9. Add the proper material symbols in several isolated areas: at sides of openings, changes in materials, corners, etc.

10. Show detail and section cuts; make associated drawings as necessary to define foundation systems. Show and call out location and types/number of reinforcing used.

   Call out and indicate beam and concrete masonry unit (CMU) lintel locations and similar related items and construction.

Framing Plan(s)—Floor(s) and Roof(s)

1. Show the footprint of the building, with all bearing walls and columns (that support the framing) in medium-weight, solid lines; call out all members with proper industry designators; provide overall dimensions as indicated on the plan. (If all interior walls and partitions, bearing and nonbearing are shown, *do not* show door openings, etc.)

2. Indicate with heavier lines the centerlines of beams (wood, steel, composite), with proper call-out notes.

   Over the beam system, draw, in heavy lines, the centerlines of a portion of the floor/roof joist layout (*not every* joist need be shown). Dimension as and where required; otherwise, indicate repetitive spacing of members. Call out manufacturer, specification number, industry designator, etc. (a proper note would be 2" × 10" joists @ 2'-0" o.c. = 88'-0"). Indicate by an arrow with two half-arrowheads the *span* of the

joists (need *not* touch each bearing) in each bay.

3. Define completely the system and all associated items in construction: bridging, decking, sheathing, accessories, anchors, trim (eave, ridge, edge closure boards) to provide a complete structural system.

4. Indicate applicable details, building and wall sections; show additional detail to clarify installation.

5. Framing systems, other than joists (glu-lam beams and arches, steel bar joists, light steel framing, composite beams, trusses for floors and roofs, etc.) are depicted in essentially the same manner.

Schedules (General)

There is a tremendous amount of information that must be incorporated, and shown on a set of working drawings. This is made more complex where the project in toto, or the construction itself, is very involved, complex, intricate, and/or crucial. Drawings often become overburdened with both written and graphic material, to the point that the documents become almost unreadable. Such excess can adversely affect the work, and perhaps the project as a whole.

The use of schedules allows for the display, in a very orderly fashion, of much of that information. In fact, one should always be looking for opportunities to combine data in a chart (schedule) form, always seeking to aid in clarifying the information and making it more readily readable and usable.

Examples of these forms include schedules for room finishes, doors, windows, openings, louvers, lintels, beams, columns, reinforcing, equipment, hardware, footings, piers, caissons, test borings, light fixtures, electric panels (several types), partitions, other fixtures, and symbols. Most professional offices have standard schedule formats.

Room Finish Schedule

1. Room finishes can be displayed in either legend or schedule form. In legend form, the information is placed within the space in question and appears as a note, perhaps using abbreviations to reduce the size of the note.

2. In some formats, the Room Finish Schedule is part of a sheet(s) devoted entirely to various

schedules. In this case, placing it at the extreme right side of the sheet aids the use of the schedule in relating it to the various spaces. Here the set pages can be folded back to reveal the schedule, and with only slight manipulation, the space being revised. In some projects the Room Finish Schedule is typed and bound into the Project Manual.

3. This schedule can be either a bar or matrix type (examples will be offered in the classroom). Selection of the form to be used is usually based on the available time for preparation and ease of use.

4. Lay out the schedule, from left to right, as follows:
   • Room Number (from the floor plan)
   • Room Name
   • Floor Covering (structure can be left exposed)
   • Base (board)
   • Wainscot (if applicable for partial wall coverage)
   • Walls; subdivide into four columns for N, S, W, and E walls
   • Ceiling; subdivide into "material" and "height" columns
   • Remarks—a sizable column for notes, details, specifics, modifiers, references

5. General Notes can be used that refer to the Room Finish Schedule, but they *must not* contain specification text or information (do not, for example, note the name and color of the carpeting). Usually these notes are few in number and address specific/unique conditions or apply general principles in the form of a reminder.

Door and Window Schedules

1. Show and call out doors and windows in *both* written and graphic form; that is, show elevations of *each* type of unit and use a written, column format for associated information (size, material, manufacturer, model number, etc.); cross-reference the two formats.

2. Choose a scale for the graphic portion of each schedule that adequately depicts the units in detail.

3. Show head, jamb, and sill details for both types of units; show vertical and horizontal dimensions and specific features (louvers, glass lights

in doors; special hardware or glazing in windows).

4. Examples will be presented in class; however, the Door Schedule is best formatted as follows (columnized left to right):
   • Door Number or Mark (designator used on plan)
   • Number of doors in opening—single, pair
   • Size: width, height, thickness (in this order) in feet/inches as applicable
   • Material: face material and core construction (solid, hollow, insulated, lead lined, or other special construction required)
   • Glazing: explain any glass panels in door
   • Finish: painted, aluminum, plastic laminate, prefinished
   • Type or style, taken from the elevations
   • Frame: material and type, special features
   • Details: list separately the title of the head, jamb, and sill detail for each door
   • Fire Rating (of opening): applies to *both* door and frame
   • Hardware Set: list set number as described in specifications for Finish Hardware
   • Remarks/Comments: list special conditions/exceptions/refurbishing/replacements, etc.

5. Include as well all special doors and frames (roll-up window closure over service counters, etc.); show elevation(s) and make proper entries in the Door Schedule itself. Call out thickness, width, height, material, and other pertinent dimensions.
   Note: Care should be taken to observe standard conditions; for example, in a CMU wall the frame height is best set at 7'-4" inasmuch as this corresponds with block coursing.

6. The Window Schedule is also set up in a grid pattern, with columns left to right, as follows:
   • Window Number (and mark or designator used on plans)
   • Manufacturer (coordinate with specifications)
   • Size: rough or masonry openings; usually width by height
   • Material: as specified
   • Glazing: type as specified
   • Details: usually in three columns—head, jamb, and sill
     Note: Where several detail conditions apply to the same window unit, use a different symbol on the plans.
   • Finish: as specified

- Remarks or comments: allow ample space to list unusual conditions, requirements
7. Window wall and storefront glazing systems are *not* included in the schedules. Use notes, elevations, and so forth, on the plans themselves.

Require field verification of opening sizes.
8. In simple (smaller) projects these schedules can be modified and reduced to simple elevations, with proper detail references at the head, jamb, and sill.

No drawing, whether produced by CAD or not, should—

- **Create more questions than it answers.**
- **Leave no hint of what it depicts, where it is applied, or what is to be done.**
- **Leave drafter or user scratching his or her head in confusion.**
- **Let the drafting style/technique get in the way of the message being sent.**
- **Mislead or give any wrong impression or direction.**
- **Try to do or show too much.**
- **Sacrifice readability for any other feature or attribute.**
- **Be so badly executed that it is an artistic masterpiece but a technical flop—the presentation must fully support the information.**

6

Coordination of Working Drawings and Specifications

Today *coordinate* has become a buzz-word, which is almost thrown away. Its real impact is too often lost, as many people merely nod toward that function without really addressing what is involved. In the production of architectural working drawings, however, coordination is an essential, major, and pervasive activity that cannot be sloughed off, ignored, or simply nodded to. Coordination, in fact, is an activity that ensures that the correct information is given in text and drawings, in the correct format, and in the correct location both on the documents and within the project work. It is part of a design professional's responsibility, just as applying and administering the correct medication is part of a physician's responsibility.

The proper coordination of working drawings and specifications is as simple as it is complex. In its simplest form, the overriding general principle is that the drawings and specifications are insep-arable companions—partners, if you like. They should not be separated or used in isolation, one from the other. Note that there is no claim of equality for this partnership; each of the docu-ments has its proper influence on the project, but only in the presence of the other. No project can be built using only the specifications or only the drawings.

Some legal aspects apply in this matter. First, a contract (and the drawings and specifications *are* legal contract documents) should be read as a whole. That is, no conclusion or determination should be based on a single, isolated portion of either drawings or specifications. Second, they are generally considered to be complementary and supplementary, meaning that they support each other and that one requires the input or informa-tion contained in the other. Third, it is generally held and accepted that "what is shown/described in one [of the documents] is as binding, contrac-tually, as if shown/described in both." This fur-ther reinforces the proposition of inseparability.

Judges and attorneys (in particular) love to try to separate out the specifications, as these people have a strong penchant to "work words." Sensing that few words have a strict, absolute single meaning, a good attorney can make any word mean something else, usually to his or her advantage, by changing the attitude, perspective, or approach to the word in question. Of course, there is no inclination on the part of architects and engineers to engage in such wordsmithing. Rather, they seek to be explicit, direct, accurate, and as clear as possible. Some owners, for varying reason, also seek to set a "pecking order" for the documents, but they should be dissuaded from trying to do this. Without question, setting one of the documents as superior to the other is a dangerous practice. By separating information that is fully intended to be read and used as a whole, an ambiguous scenario is created that is difficult to resolve and often the cause of disputes and even litigation.

Now comes the harder part. Ideally, the drawings and specifications are developed concurrently. As information is added to one, it should (*must*) be commensurately added to the other. Granted, there are many administrative items that are contained wholly within the specifications, but technical items tend to be contained in two parts—written and illustrated. When the information is incorporated into the project documents as they are produced, there is far less chance for errors or for leaving out vital items. Gaps are difficult to find later, often even more difficult to resolve without disrupting other work. Unresolved gaps lead to extra costs, disputes, and needless difficulties.

Information changes many times throughout the production of a project's documents and actual construction. All such changes must be reflected in the documents. Of course, it would be a needless effort, and quite costly, to continually issue full sets of new drawings and specifications. However, this can be done on a reduced scale. Bulletin drawings, addenda, change orders, and field instructions are issued, as required, at different stages of a project. All must be made part of the contract documentation, as these items augment, revise, or otherwise modify the originally distributed drawings and specifications.

To reflect such changes, some professionals add a provision in the Supplementary Conditions of the Contract (making changes to the General Conditions of the Contract, which are usually preprinted, standard forms). Special note should

Supplementary Conditions
The following provisions supplement and modify the General Conditions of the Contract for Construction, American Institute of Architects Document A- 201, 15th Edition, 1997. Portions of the General Conditions that are not modified by these Supplementary Conditions shall remain in effect as written.

ADD under Section 1.2, Correlation and Intent of the Contract Documents, the following provision:

1.2.4 In the event of conflicts or discrepancies among the Contract Documents, interpretations will be based on information taken from the documents in thefollowingorder:

1. Change Orders
2. Field Instructions (Both 1 and 2, in reverse chronological order, starting with last issued)
3. The Agreement
4. Addenda, in reverse chronological order, starting with last issued
5. The Supplementary Conditions
6. The General Conditions
7. Drawings and Specifications Full-size or large-scale details or drawings shall govern small-scale drawings, which they are intended to amplify. Details or conditions indicated for a portion of the Work but that are not repeated fully for other portions shall apply throughout to all similar portions except as otherwise specifically noted. In the case of an inconsistency between Drawings and Specifications or within either Document not clarified by addendum, the better quality or greater quantity of Work shall be provided in accordance with the Architect's interpretation.

Note: This list of documents has also been advocated by the Construction Specifications Institute (CSI).

Sample modification for use in the Supplementary General Conditions

be taken, however, that this type of modified provision is in no way intended nor does it attempt to create a new legal precedence or status for the various documents. It is, rather, merely a clarifying statement indicating how the professional will use the most current information in making any interpretations as the work progresses.

Here the professional, in consultation with the client, can list the order in which documents will be held. This does not, however, indicate precedence of one over the others, nor does it set a distinct pecking order for the documents. It merely reflects the status of a document by virtue of when it was issued, and how that issue influences the contract documents (which include the Agreement or contract, the drawings, and the specifications).

Completed drawings and specifications are first issued for bidding. They may be modified during the bidding process by issuance of addenda. These changes basically update the documents to new or correct information, revise project information, and answer questions from bidders. Addenda, however, are fully binding when the contract is signed. Usually the contract makes note and lists provisions that all drawings, specifications, *and* issued addenda are integral parts of the contract (Agreement), including them in the legal context of the project contract.

As work progresses (moving toward fulfilling the contract), other changes will be required. Some are items within the documents that are unclear, inadequate, or perhaps even incorrect. Other changes come from field conditions different from those expected, unavailability of material or systems, changes desired by the owner, and the like. These can be merely Field Instructions (formalized in writing, not by word of mouth) making changes that have no impact on either contract cost or contract time (period noted in the contract for construction to be completed). Where such changes involve either cost and/or time, a formal, fully executed Change Order is required. In either case, however, this is another form of updating the basic contract and is considered as "later information" that modifies the project contract.

To properly relate all of these updating documents, often a provision, such as seen in the illustration above, will be used. Note that the language alludes to how the documents will be considered, *not* to how they rank or take precedence one over the other(s). This distinction is preeminent and must be fully understood by all involved.

The first order of business here is to set out,

as best we can, what information goes where (see illustration). Although the actual information is not as cleanly segregated as shown on the chart, it closely follows this outline. There will be some overlap and redundancy—but it is better that there be no gaps. Some decisions about location of data may be required, but they should be coordinated with minimal redundancy.

Naturally, some information is better shown by drawing, other information requires and is better described in words. For example, it is difficult to describe relationships of materials to each other—angles, fasteners, varied thicknesses, and so on. Likewise, it is difficult (if not impossible) to depict an attribute, capability, or inherent ingredient of a material or system.

One learns early that voluminous notes on drawings can take up too much space, which could be used for other drawings, and are often not as accurate as specifications. Moreover, inaccuracies are too easily included and less likely to be discovered (as objective review of drawings is not a widely used practice these days). Specifications are usually proofread at least once before they are printed, bound, and issued. It cannot be overemphasized that many dollars can be involved where two numbers are merely transposed in a model number listed in a note. Such an error sounds simple and inconsequential, but it is not. First, the item matching the incorrect number may be totally wrong for the project, if it is not wrong in color, performance, or size. Either way, there is need for remedial action, both administratively and physically (both expensive) to change-out and make the correction(s).

It must be understood that every piece of project information has several relationships, all of which must be observed and resolved. Each has a relationship to

- The complete array of project documents (the "set" of contract documents)
- Other associated drawing sheets (to make references, to draw information from, or to expand/complete those items)
- The specifications (by providing the visual aspect of the information)
- Other ancillary drawings (which, when combined, provide complete information)

The following illustrations are examples of the coordination of project information. One example shows how various systems relate to the same

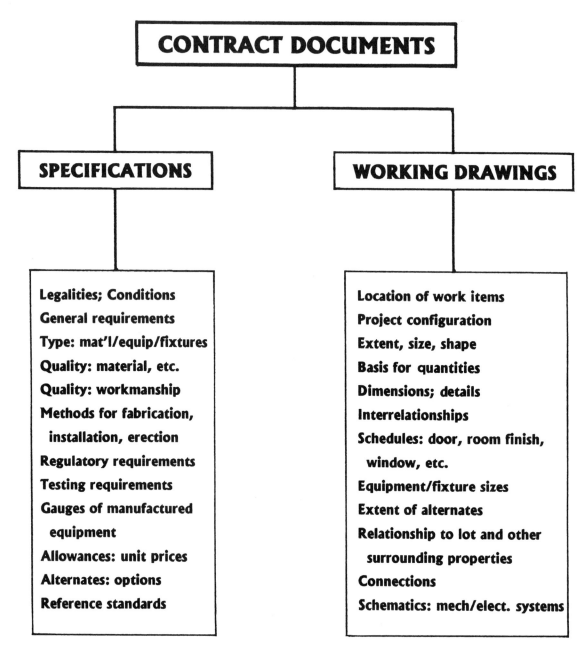

This chart depicts the breakdown of information, and where it should be located in the contract documents. Note that most of the items in the specification are more suitable for written explanation instead of some graphic display.

floor plan layout and area. The other notes how information is applied to the project, by reference, although the complete "package" of information is contained in various drawings located on different sheets.

The proper documentation of architectural projects involves not only the concept of "set," but also the requisite interrelationships and co-ordination. Understanding this is crucial to producing project documents that result in successful projects.

There are many things that we call, or use as, "sets"—dishes, golf clubs, tires, tennis games, and so forth. The word itself alludes to a group of

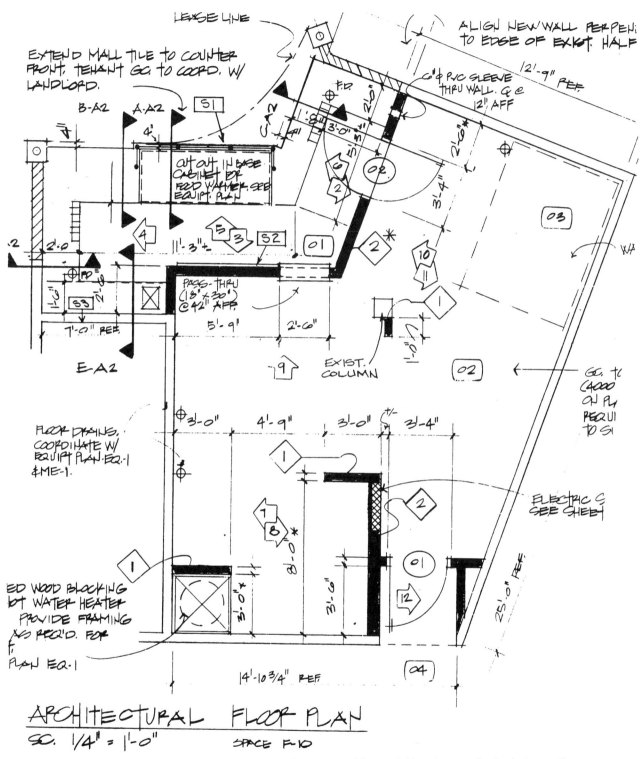

ARCHITECTURAL FLOOR PLAN
SC. 1/4" = 1'-0"   SPACE F-10

Following is a series of plans, each depicting another aspect of the work. Note the coordination between these plans and the ease of reading how the work fits together.

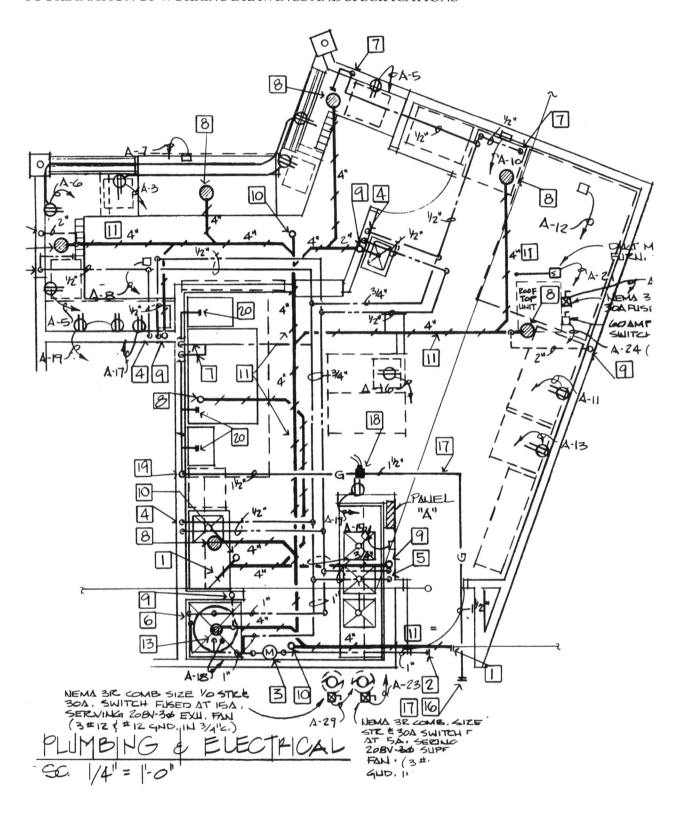

PLUMBING & ELECTRICAL

SC. 1/4" = 1'-0"

NEMA 3R COMB SIZE 1/0 STR &
30A. SWITCH FUSED AT 15A.
SERVING 208V-3Φ EXH. FAN
(3 #12 & #12 GND. IN 3/4"C.)

NEMA 3R COMB. SIZE
STR & 30A SWITCH F
AT 5A. SERING
208V-3Φ SUPF
FAN. (3 #.
GND. I

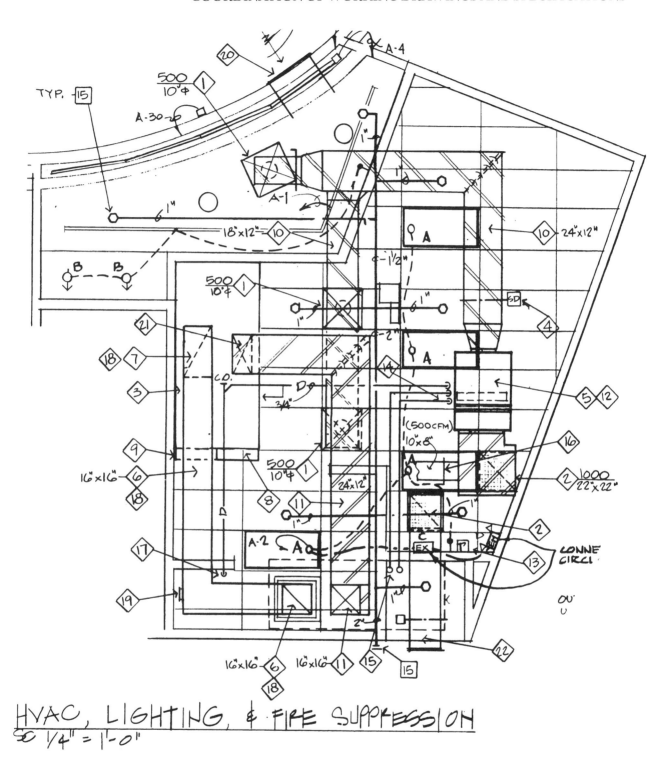

HVAC, LIGHTING, & FIRE SUPPRESSION
SC 1/4" = 1'-0"

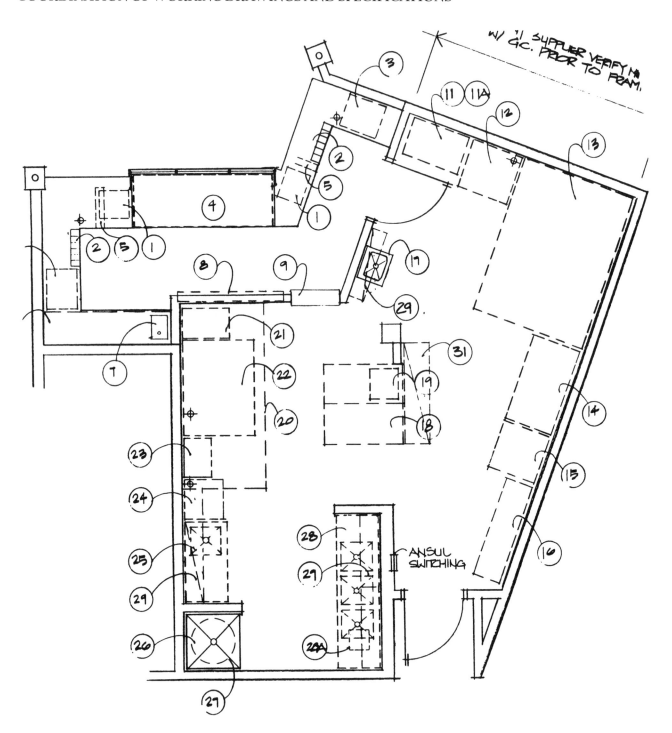

EQUIPMENT PLAN
SC. 1/4" = 1'-0"

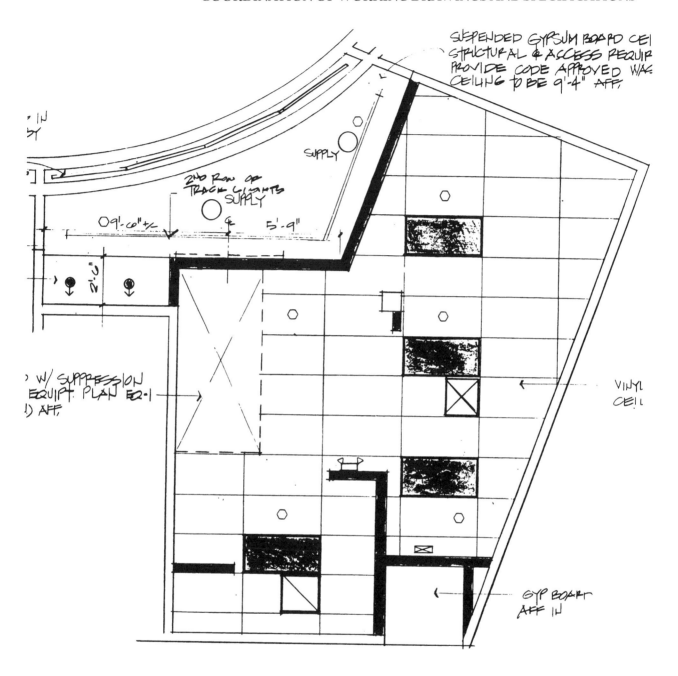

REFLECTED CEILING PLAN
SC. 1/4" = 1'-0"

closely related but different items, combined to form an entity, interrelated and interworking. So it is with architectural working (contract) drawings. An apt metaphor is a set of golf clubs. Each club in the set is unique in shape, angle, and use. Combined, the clubs provide the player with a full array of tools that allow for every condition or challenge the golf course presents. Misuse of a club can result in a bad result, which impairs a good hole, game, or completion. Some clubs may be used very little, but they are still available (in the bag) should a condition arise that requires their unique capacity (the sand wedge, for example). This is a direct parallel to the various drawings, types of views, and other presentations within a set of working drawings. One must have them at the ready, for use when appropriate and helpful, and certainly when they add, contribute, or clarify project information and where they facilitate a good and complete game (the project).

In some sets, the individual items can be used at random or for very specific circumstances. The interrelationship with other parts of the set is put aside. However, because of the necessarily tight interrelationship of information within architectural projects, things often change several times during project production. From early in the production of the documents, it is absolutely necessary to proceed in a very close, careful, thoughtful, prioritized, meticulous, and fully coordinated manner. This may seem like an extraordinary approach, but there is so much information, close coordination is essential to ensure that no other path works. Axioms that apply to other types of work also apply here: "The specific rules the general"; "Proceed at your own risk."

Hence, a set of working drawings is best produced through a series of small incremental steps, "shuffling," if you will. Progress is governed by the information available to be portrayed on an individual sheet. A lack of information indicates that the sheet cannot now be started, or that the sheet cannot be finished completely at this time. This situation directly shows the importance of gathering information and then developing it.

The following table is similar to those used by architectural firms in assessing the amount of time needed to produce sheets of drawings. Although this chart notes a period of hours, it is not required that these all be expended at one time; that is, the total hours shown will accumulate over several weeks or even months. Drawings cannot be started and finished, for the most part, in one sitting; they progress as information is made available over a period of time. For example, it is not possible to work on a floor plan from the beginning to the end, in one time period; usually the necessary information is developed through work on other drawings and from other sources.

A disgusted contractor was once heard to say, "They ought to box these drawings and sell them as jigsaw puzzles." His dilemma is not uncommon; some working drawings can be puzzling. Although many factors contribute to the confusion, a major cause is a lack of coordination. The metaphor can be applied if we see each item of construction information as a piece of a jigsaw puzzle, each of which is made to fit into one or more of the others. This is also the pattern of the working drawings. Few, if any, pieces of information can stand alone, totally isolated. Sometimes in a surge of inspiration we grit our teeth and resolve to finish a drawing once and for all. In a major portion of the working drawing phase such resolution simply does not work. Most drawings are tied to and influenced by so many particulars that appear on other drawings that they can never be entirely finished at any given stage. If we choose to follow inspiration, there is a high risk of having to revise a "finished" drawing, which is always messy, both literally and figuratively.

The distinctive shape or color of the pieces often makes the border of the puzzle the easiest part to solve. In like manner we can devise some parameters for the working drawings. General standards must be met—for example, items such as title blocks, borders, and schedules. Furthermore, large areas of the drawings can be finished separately, but must later be incorporated into the whole.

Generally speaking, when the architectural office is in full production, almost every drawing sheet of the project will be active, although one person (the project architect or job captain) will be in full charge. At this point it is vital that any new information be imposed wherever applicable. Coordination becomes a complex and difficult task. A busy office may have several projects in production at the same time, and the drafting force must be careful to enter all relevant data on the project sheets to which they pertain. If one piece is missing, the puzzle cannot be finished; if a piece is somehow misplaced and made to fit where it does not belong, the puzzle will be a mass of confusion.

Architecture Department
Execution Phase
Working Drawings: estimate of hours

Drawing/Sheet Type	Hours/Sheet (Average)	Modifier	Total Hours/Sheet	Comments
Cover Sheet/Title Block	30			
Composite Floor Plan	200			
Demolition Plan	20	Minor Project: 1	20	
		Complex Project: 3	60	
		Minor Project: .6	12	Warehouses, general storage, etc.
Floor Plans	100	Standard Project: 1	100	Manufacturing plants, offices
		Complex Project: 1.5–1.8	150–180	Pilots plants, laboratories, etc.
Furniture Plans	60			
Reflected Ceiling Plans	60			
Roof Plans	100			
Large-Scale Plans	100	Minor Project: .75	75	Simple surface features/materials
Exterior Elevations	50	Standard Project: 1	50	Multiple surface planes/materials
		Complex Project: 1.5	75	Multiple surface planes/materials penetrated by multiple types of windows/openings, ducts, etc. or complex pattern/siding designs built into facade
Interior Elevations	100			
Room Finish Schedule	100			
Door Schedule/Details	160			
Equipment/Furniture Schedule	80			
Building Sections	80			
Plan Details	100			
Section Details	100			
Wall Sections	120			
Stair/Elevator Sections	100			
Interior Partition Types	20			
Ceiling Details	20			
Roof Details	40			
Miscellaneous Interior Details	40			
Special Casework Details	60			

Notes:

1. Estimates to be reviewed with Architectural Lead or Department Head.

2. Lead to verify complexity of projects; hours shown are "go-by" and should be reviewed in relation to project complexity.

3. Leads to determine hours split between arhcitect and CAD, pending experience level of project staff.

Every drafter must be aware of the impact of his or her work on the reputation of the office and the quality of its products. This person must be made to see the principle of coordinating the drawings and should follow it to the best of his or her ability. It is far easier to do the work as it occurs than to try to insert information at the end of the project. Nearing completion, projects in any office are hurriedly coordinated; those working on various phases of the drawings will have information to be added, and in the confusion of getting the job out for reproduction and bidding, not every facet can be fully covered.

The plan of the main floor of a structure is the most vital drawing in the set and is derived from the preliminary program that reflects the owner's needs. It directly influences the layout of the entire building. Every other drawing in the set receives some information from it.

Once the layout is set by areas and sizes and locations are established, the floor plan from which the exterior elevations and preliminary sketches are developed is executed. The same principle is followed through the working drawings. The basement plan, for example, must reflect the shape of the main floor and other elements and systems proceeding downward to connections, such as basements and elevator shafts. Similarly, the upper floors either reflect or have some direct relation to the main floor. It helps if elevator shafts rise vertically without offsets or positional changes.

Other floors may be smaller, or larger, than the main floor, but each will still relate to it. There must be agreement between floors in every respect.

The chart illustrates the interrelationship of the drawings. The multifaceted influence of the floor plan is easy to see. It is interesting to note also that relatively minor drawings often have input for more than one major drawing. Example: the landscape plan. The minor drawing may greatly affect the work. Large-scale drawings, which usually show only a portion of the project, take precedence over small-scale drawings. The larger scale reduces scope but increases accuracy, which could drastically change that portion of the project. Similarly, a minor equipment plan could influence the basic plan by showing a need for more space to accommodate its function. This interplay among drawings is continuous.

Every office aims for zero defects in its documents; many come close, although this is not to say that the perfect set of drawings has never been produced. With so many materials, processes, and persons involved in the construction, some adjustments must be made.

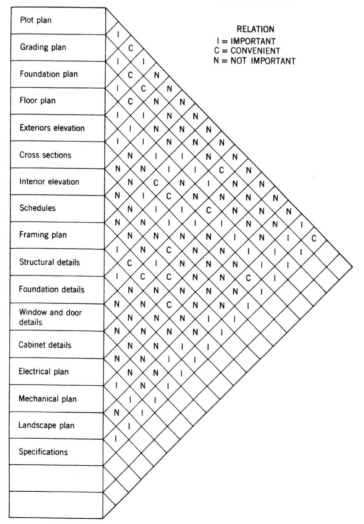

RELATIONSHIP OF CONSTRUCTION DOCUMENT DRAWINGS

This chart shows the relative interrelation of various drawings, one to another. I indicates an important relationship; C indicates a convenient relationship; N denotes a relative unimportant relationship.

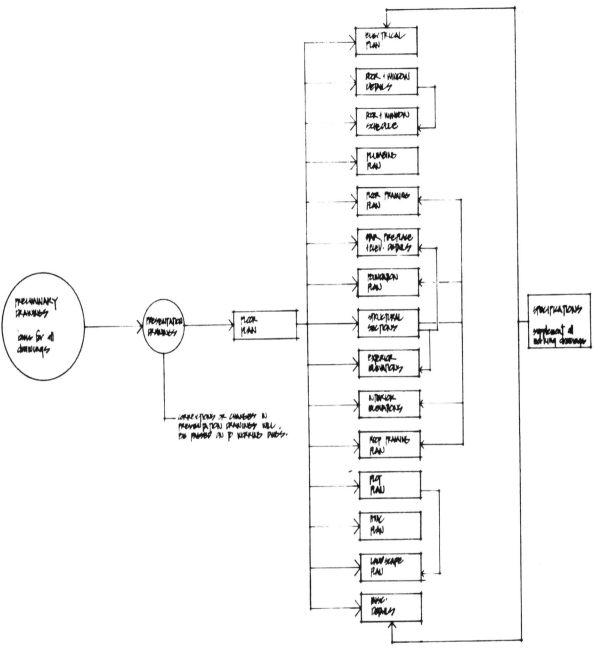

This chart shows the relationships within a set of working drawings. The owner's requirements are channeled into the floor plan. This drawing is usually the first produced, for all others develop from it. Note also the ties between drawings that indicate one-way or two-way exchanges of information.

COORDINATION OF WORKING DRAWINGS AND SPECIFICATIONS

If working drawings were compared to a jig-saw puzzle of many pieces, the relation between them and the specifications could be considered relatively simple. The simplicity, however, would be extended only to the number of pieces. Here there would be just two—the drawings and the specifications. The pieces would be constructed to show a mass of interconnections, all of which would fit together in only one way, thus presenting a problem difficult to solve.

In the *General Conditions of the Contract for Construction*, published by the American Institute of Architects, the contract documents are described as being complementary; the requirements are as binding for one element as for all. This means that all the information when tied together in one bundle cannot be contradictory but must provide the contractor with a complete package. In dealing with the working drawings and specifications, which constitute only a part of the contract documents, we must be extremely concerned with their display.

Perhaps the best guide, or reference, is a module published by the Construction Specifications Institute (CSI). In particular, we refer to Fundamentals and Formats Module FF/090, "Coordinating Drawings and Specifications" (part of the *CSI Manual of Practice*). It should, of course, be used only in the current edition. In this module one statement tells the whole story: "Ideally, the drawings show the form of construction, whereas the specifications establish its quality." As long

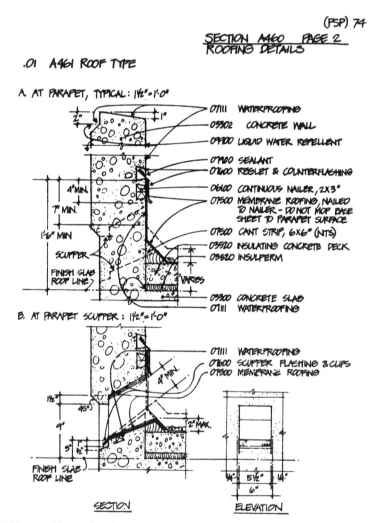

Mahlum and Mahlum, architects, Seattle, Washington
Although this detail may never appear on the drawings in this condition, it is an excellent in-house document to show how various materials in the work are accounted for in the specifications (numbers and notes on the right are specification references).

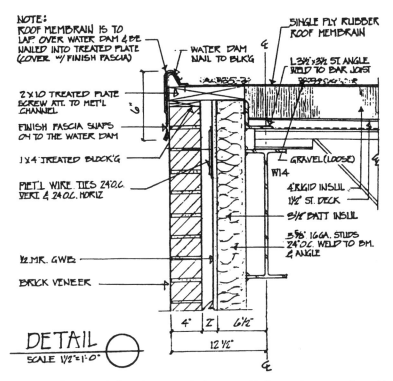

NOTE:
ROOF MEMBRAIN IS TO
LAP. OVER WATER DAM & BE
NAILED INTO TREATED PLATE
(COVER W/ FINISH FASCIA)

2 X 10 TREATED PLATE
SCREW ATT. TO MET'L
CHANNEL

FINISH FASCIA SNAPS
ON TO THE WATER DAM

1 X 4 TREATED BLOCK'G

MET'L WIRE TIES 24"O.C.
VERT & 24 O.C. HORIZ

½ M.R. GWB

BRICK VENEER

WATER DAM
NAIL TO BLK'G

SINGLE PLY RUBBER
ROOF MEMBRAIN

L 3½ x 3½ ST ANGLE
WELD TO BAR JOIST

GRAVEL (LOOSE)

W14

4" RIGID INSUL
1½ ST. DECK
3½ BATT INSUL

3⅝ 16 GA. STUDS
24"O.C. WELD TO BM.
& ANGLE

DETAIL
SCALE 1½"=1'-0"

4" | 2 | 6½"
12 ½"

Although the detail looks fairly good, there is a great deal wrong with it, namely, poor notes, which should not be placed on the drawings, misspellings, and poor coordination.

as this distinction is upheld, the drawings and the specifications will perform as required. Data that are too complicated to be shown on the drawings can be written into the specifications; at the same time, construction products listed in the specifications must be properly located on the drawings. Although this detail may never appear on the drawings in this condition, it is an excellent in-house document to show how various materials in the work are accounted for in the specifications (numbers and notes on the right are specification references).

The construction industry today contains such a complexity of operations and so wide a variety of trades, materials, components, equipment, sub-contractors, and sub-subcontractors that "errors and omissions" are inevitable. As long as these errors continue to appear in the contract documents, the bidding process will be undermined, the owner will pay higher prices, and poor or faulty construction will result. Errors are certain to lead to waste, confusion, and delay.

The beginning point in any sound relationship between the two elements rests in the establishment by the specifications writer of the nomenclature required for all parts of the building. This nomenclature should be consistent in order to avoid confusion among all concerned. Improper terminology and confusion results when old specifications are copied or terms that are not relevant to the current project are introduced. An example of proper nomenclature would be the term "vapor barrier," shown on the drawings and repeated in the specifications. Alternate terms such as roofing, roof membrane, or plastic membrane should not be substituted in one or the other.

To categorize the parts, the drawings should show the following information:

1. Location of each material assembly, component, or accessory
2. Sizes, including thicknesses and all other significant dimensions of all field-assembled components
3. Identification consistent with the established nomenclature of all preassembled or prefabricated components or equipment described in the specifications
4. Diagrams of specifically fabricated connections

Specifications should include the applicable parts of the following:

1. Quality control
2. Optional materials or methods
3. Required guarantees
4. Required products
5. Acceptable manufacturers
6. Required physical properties
7. Required performance
8. Type and grade of finish
9. Fabrication method
10. Installation methods

The CSI module is but one in a tremendous storehouse of information and techniques assembled by the Institute. This information is highly recommended for a good foundation in specifications writing. The *CSI Manual of Practice* is the basic reference unit.

The specifications should list the materials and equipment in terms of general requirements, specific products, and execution. Although the drawings and specifications contain a vast store of information, it differs greatly in kind. The module is comprehensive. It describes the relations between the parts and points out that the drawings are the means of showing shape, location, and dimensions. It explains the need for consistent nomenclature and urges that indiscriminate usage at the whim of members of the design team be avoided. It cautions against the use of exceedingly comprehensive notes that cover too much information, much of which truly belongs in the specifications. A vigorous system to achieve improved results is suggested:

1. Consistent labeling on all drawings
2. Notes on the drawings that do not conflict with specification requirements
3. A procedure for linking and cross-referencing drawings and specifications.

The Institute also suggests that only generic names be employed. If a material is to be identified, it should be given a generally accepted symbol, schedule of symbols, or name. No further descriptive information is necessary.

Too many notes have a tendency to obscure the drawing, increase research time and, as shown before, promote inconsistency and duplication. Notes that identify parts of the work to be done by specific contractors should not appear on the drawings; the scope items belong in the specifications. Trade names should be banned on all drawings. Even when the specifications refer to proprietary products, the designations on the drawings must remain generic. In some cases, however, acceptance of a substitute would necessitate revision; for example, a common notation calls for the use of Durowal rather than horizontal masonry reinforcement. Durowal is, of course, the name of a company, and the appearance of this note on the drawing would preclude the use of products manufactured by others.

Repetitive items, such as doors and windows, should be simplified. The drawings should include only the detail necessary to identify the materials and components. The specifications will complete the information necessary to define the quality. Location and contents of schedules vary greatly; schedules may be placed in the specifications rather than on the drawings, but no matter where they appear, the information should be complete.

Because the primary purpose of the drawings is to illustrate the construction, their order may vary but it should always facilitate the work of the contractor. The sequence of the work should be kept in mind as the drawings are collated; for example, it is a good idea to present preliminary site work and demolition drawings first, then the foundation drawings, followed by the superstructure drawings, and so on throughout the building.

Because this chapter concerns itself primarily with working drawings and only secondarily with specifications, we have devoted less discussion to specifications themselves. It is really the specifications, and no clever layout or composition by the draftsman, that allow the drawings to remain uncluttered.

The American Institute of Architects (AIA) now has a Professional Development Program which is aimed at the simplification and clarification of construction documents. Called "Con-Doc," the program proposes the reformatting of documents to integrate fully their information in a more easily accessed system. The program is linked directly to the CSI 16-Division format for construction specifications, which is a well-established system for the logical location of construction information. Further, by making this linkage, ConDoc moves the drawings into a direct and valuable relationship with the specifications; this has not been widely done previously. The use of a common format obviously reduces confusion in tracking information and greatly enhances coordination and use of the documents; in a sense it "intercombines" drawings and specs.

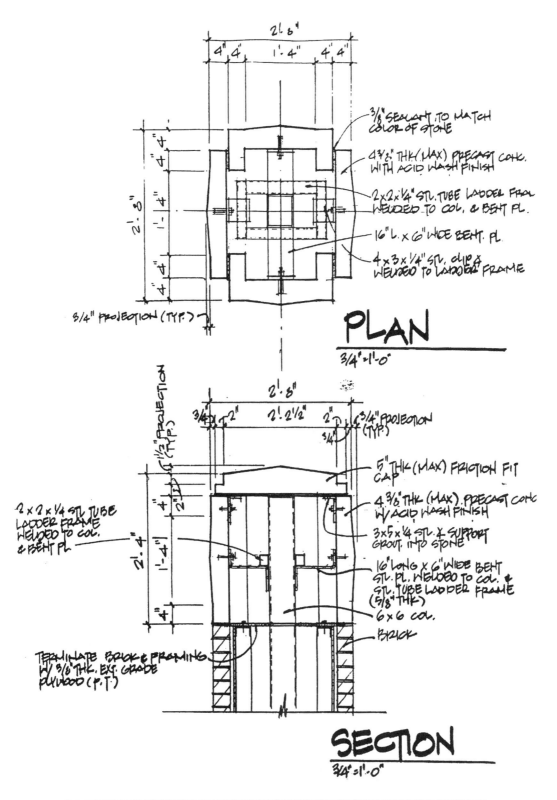

PLAN
3/4"=1'-0"

SECTION
3/4"=1'-0"

3/8" SEALANT TO MATCH COLOR OF STONE

4 3/8" THK (MAX) PRECAST CONC. WITH ACID WASH FINISH

2x2x1/4" STL. TUBE LADDER FRAME WELDED TO COL. & BENT PL.

16" L. x 6" WIDE BENT. PL.

4 x 3 x 1/4" STL. CLIP & WELDED TO LADDER FRAME

3/4" PROJECTION (TYP.)

2'.8"

4" 4" 1'.4" 4" 4"

4" 4" 4" 1'.4" 4" 4"

2'.8"

2'.8"

3/4" 2" 2'.2 1/2" 2" 3/4"

3/4" PROJECTION (TYP.)

1 1/2" PROJECTION (TYP.)

5" THK (MAX) FRICTION FIT CAP

4 3/8" THK (MAX) PRECAST CONC. W/ ACID WASH FINISH

3x5x1/4 STL. X SUPPORT GROUT INTO STONE

16" LONG x 6" WIDE BENT STL. PL. WELDED TO COL. & STL. TUBE LADDER FRAME (5/8" THK)

6 x 6 COL.

BRICK

2x2x1/4 STL. TUBE LADDER FRAME WELDED TO COL. & BENT PL

2'.4"

4" 1'.4" 4"

2" 2"

TERMINATE BRICK & FRAMING W/ 3/8" THK. EXT. GRADE PLYWOOD (P.T.)

ARCHITECTURAL CAST STONE

DRAWING NUMBER

PROJECT NAME INSTITUTE FOR ECONOMICS

The system almost exclusively uses the "keynoting" system of notations (see Chapter 34) of the drawings. In this, the keynotes are really expressions of CSI section numbers, combined with pertinent suffixes that distinguish one item from another. The designator replaces the note that would be used on the tradition drawing to identify or explain the particular item. Keynoting, of course, is intended by concept to remove extensive notes on the drawings and combine them in one area on the drawing sheet, or onto other sheet(s). Thus, one can see the inherent simplification, and the discipline, achieved immediately by ConDoc.

But the new system goes further, in that the keynote can be directly and easily traced to the pertinent specifications section, which further and completely explains the construction item in question.

Overall, ConDoc provides a method to improve both quality of work and the coordination of documents. These attributes, combined with simplification of production methods and production time savings, lead directly to increased profit. In addition, the system can be applied to either manual or computerized production techniques.

In 1997, CSI developed its Uniform Drawing System. The system consists of three modules: "Drawing Set Organization," "Sheet Organization," and "Schedules." Added to these will be modules on drafting conventions, symbols/terms and abbreviations, notation, layering, and plotting guidelines. The overall intent is to provide professionals with an organized system, for adoption, that interrelates various tools for the organization and presentation of working drawings.

The system is packaged in a three-ring binder and is also available with a CD-ROM. The latter contains electronic file formats in DGN (for MicroStation users), DWG (for AutoCAD users), and DXF (which can access either of the others and other less familiar systems). There are layout templates for some 16 different sheet sizes, as well as formats for some two dozen schedules in various software formats.

The drawing set module organizes, through use of standards relating to content of the set, the order of drawings, identification of each sheet and the file names for the same. It sets out specific designations for the various disciplines, to basically customize the drawing/file. Similar provisions are available for other special circumstances.

In the past there have been other such attempts at organization. Usually these were developed by individual offices, or to meet a need of a particular client or project. In the main, a set was divided by discipline: site development and improvements, architectural/structural, plumbing, fire protection, and so on. The set was bound, with the sheets located in a sequence that roughly followed that of the imminent construction. Individual sheets were indicated both by number and by a letter prefix indicating the discipline: A for architectural, S for structural, P for plumbing, and so on. To allow for the insertion of additional sheets (late in the process), many offices used a decimal system: A1, A1.1, A1.2, and so forth.

It is quite obvious, however, that in an electronic environment, it is wise to develop a system that is fully compatible with, and uses the same basic attributes as, other portions of the computerized programming.

Drawing sheets are organized in the second module. This notes the various and preferred sheet sizes and includes definition of the overall drawing area, title blocks, and production reference areas. Each is displayed with its content and configuration. The module also, sets out a location system, which is coordinate-based. This provides for far easier location of details and other items within the set and is the basis for all cross-referencing throughout the various drawings in the set. This module provides a consistent and reliable system.

The schedule module sets out standard formats for several different types of schedules. These include standardized format, content, and proper terminology. It also gives guidelines for producing other schedules that projects may demand. Overall, there is a suggested system that organizes the filing of schedules and their identification.

All of these modules, and one can suppose those in the future, provide a method for a correct and easily used system in each case. Through the implementation of this method (perhaps with some local adjustments or modifications) the process can be done once and established as an office standard. There is no doubt that with such an approach, the amount of time needed to set up project documentation will be reduced, which, of course, will free revenue for other activities. Even though many firms have used this method before (and may still be using similar systems), it appears that these systems will prove superior owing to their orientation toward computer operations, including retrieval and storage of data.

specs./drafting room coordination

Spec. Section No. _____

Project _XYZ Co, Bldg_____ Job No. _78-761_

Item: _Steel doors & frames_____

Source: ☐ Sweets ☒ Shelf ☐ Soft-file ☐ Other
M.W.Rasmussen (file no,) _____ (specify)

Manufacturer _Ceco_____ Model No._Dr = Regent_
_Fr = CF 34_

Designate below the features, finishes, options, modifications, etc.
required for this project.

Galv. Doors & Frames
Doors prefinished w/ Texture finish
Color as selected - Non-standard

Frames 14 ga.
Doors 16 ga. - Full flush type
Special Decorative Hardware

Grout Frames

Sample

Approved Equals: Manufacturers _____ Model No. _____
Steelcraft _Dr=L16 fr=STd_

Attachments: ☒ Spec. Data ☒ Catalog detail ☐ Catalog specification

☒ copy of det. as drawn for this proj. ☐ Other _____

Prepared by: _____ Date: _5/14/80_
(Draftsman)

Approved by: _____ Date: _5/16/80_
(Job Captain or Project Architect)

spec. coordination: Spec. Section No. is on drawings yes ___ no X

Item only in spec., not detailed yes ___ no X

This item also affects Section No. _Hdw._

Date copy rec'd in spec dept.: _____

Chapman, Cobeen, Desai, Sakata, Inc.
Architecture, Planning, Interior Design, Graphic Design
Example of a standard office sheet for enhancing the coordination between the drafting room and the specifications writer. Not only handy, but a very important instrument for overall project control.

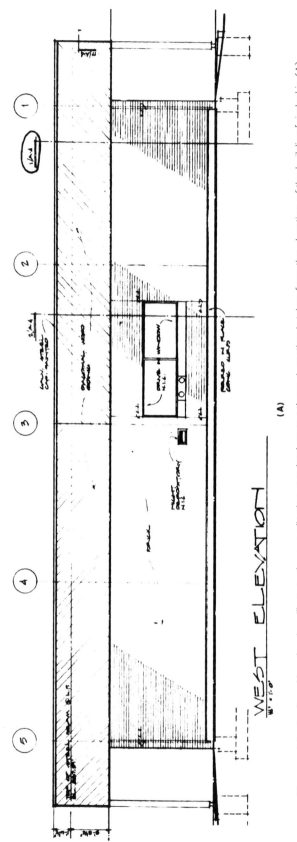

(A)

These architectural working drawings illustrate the coordination required among them. A section is taken from the elevation of the building [circled in (A) in the elevation drawing]; it is shown again, at increased scale and in greater detail, on the section detail sheet (B). Reference is also made to the roofing construction at the cant ship; this blown up detail appears in (C). The progression necessary for proper construction visualization is presented in these three drawings and correlated in the specifications.

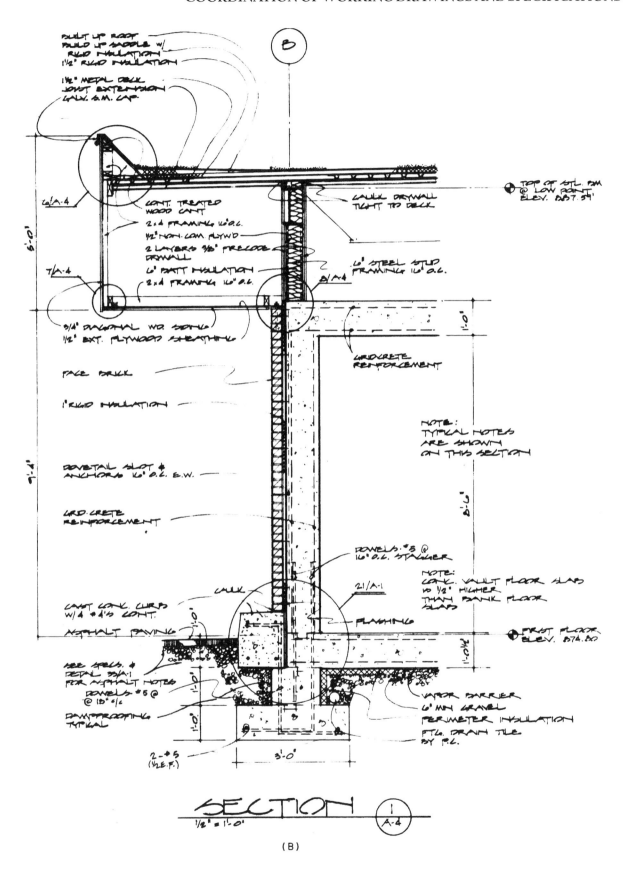

SECTION $\frac{1}{A-4}$

1/2" = 1'-0"

(B)

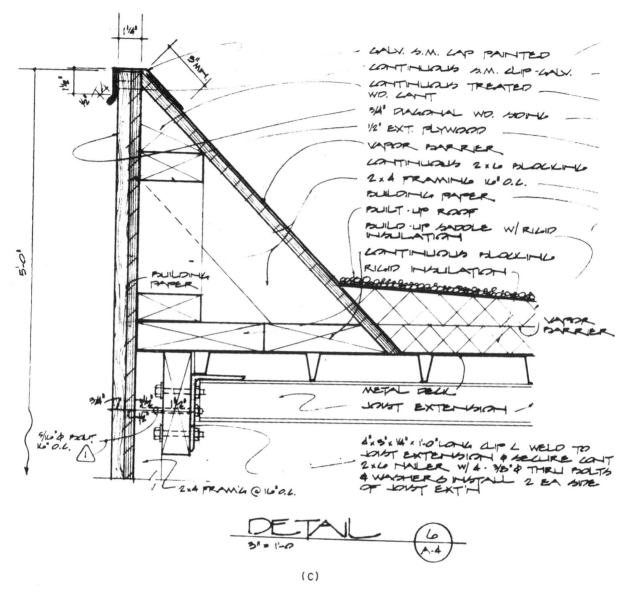

GALV. S.M. CAP PAINTED
CONTINUOUS S.M. CLIP-GALV.
CONTINUOUS TREATED WD. CANT
3/4" DIAGONAL WD. SDG.
1/2" EXT. PLYWOOD
VAPOR BARRIER
CONTINUOUS 2×6 BLOCKING
2×4 FRAMING 16" O.C.
BUILDING PAPER
BUILT-UP ROOF
BUILD-UP SADDLE W/ RIGID INSULATION
CONTINUOUS BLOCKING
RIGID INSULATION

BUILDING PAPER

VAPOR BARRIER

METAL DECK
JOIST EXTENSION

3/4"

5/16"∅ BOLT 16" O.C.

2×4 FRAM'G @ 16" O.C.

4"×3"×1/4"×1'-0" LONG CLIP ∠ WELD TO JOIST EXTENSION & SECURE CONT. 2×6 NAILER W/ 4- 3/8"∅ THRU BOLTS & WASHERS INSTALL 2 EA. SIDE OF JOIST EXT'N

DETAIL
3" = 1'-0

6 / A-4

(C)

This entire program has been coordinated with the revised edition of CAD Layer Guidelines, which has been published by the AIA.

Very few items of work on a construction project are depicted and installed alone. (See the discussion of sets earlier in this chapter.) Everything seems to be tied to other work, or at least to other drawings that expand on, or use the information to explain more fully, the work they show. Consider a flagpole, for example. Although standing alone, seemingly in the middle of nowhere, the flagpole needs a foundation detail (to illustrate its anchorage to the ground). In addition, it will appear on the site plan, which shows the correct location, associated walks, curbing, benches,

and so forth. It could possibly appear on the landscape plan if there is a complex of plantings near or around it. In some cases, the pole may also appear on the exterior elevations (where it has some impact on the building elevation).

Some items are repeated several times over in the same project but are drawn just once. Proper reference and coordination are required to place such an item in its several locations. Scale also plays a major role in the documentation, and coordination effort. As the need increases to be ever more specific in showing the work, the scale must increase; sometimes very small items are drawn at full size (their exact size). Not adjusting scale to the level of detail required can result in

1.05 PROTECTION

    A. Delivery and Storage: Keep materials dry during delivery and storage. Protect against exposure to weather and dampness.

        1. Stack lumber and plywood off ground and provide air circulation.

        2. Store millwork items and finish trim within the building in a dry and heated area.

PART 2 PRODUCTS

2.01 MATERIALS

    A. Framing and Blocking Lumber:

        1. ''Standard grade'' Douglas Fir or yellow pine: treated per ASTM E84, FR-S and UL 723 with flame spread of 25 or less. Each piece to bear UL FR-S label.

        2. Plywood Sheathing: Exterior grade DFPA C---D; treated per ASTM E84, FR-S and UL 723 with flame spread of 25 or less; thickness shown on drawings.

    B. Wood Facia, Soffits and Trim: Clear, all heart No. 1, V.G.

        1. Siding 3/4"$\times$ 6"''V'' edged, T & G, K.D.

        2. 3/4"S4S K.D. Redwood.

    C. Plastic Laminate: 1/16"Phenolformaldehyde plastic laminate---Formica, G. E. Tex-O-Lite or Nevamer. Plastic veneers shall be mounted on backings as detailed. Color and pattern as selected by Architect.

    D. Millwork as noted: Select Red Oak.

    E. Wood Shelves: Wood particle board with solid wood edge banding: Size and thickness, shown on drawings.

    F. Building Paper: Asphalt saturated ASTM 226.

    G. Miscellaneous: Provide the following miscellaneous Items:

        1. Where adjustable shelves are shown provide adjustable standards and brackets. Knapp & Vogt, series #255 Standards, #256 Supports. Furnish 4 standards per shelving unit with 4 supports per shelf.

3.03 EXTERIOR MILLWORK

    A. Install Facia, Soffits and finish trim as shown on drawing as specified herein.

        1. Install building paper horizontally over plywood sheathing, lap 2 inches at sides and 6 inches at ends.

        2. Install siding with tongue turned up and as detailed on drawings.

        a. Toe-nail siding through tongue with galvanized ring-shank 1½"nails.

        3. Install trim and moldings in single, unjointed lengths for runs less than 10'. For longer runs, use only one piece less than 10'in any straight run. Stagger joints in adjacent members.

3.04 INTERIOR MILLWORK AND CASEWORK

    A. The extent of Millwork and Casework is shown on the drawings which includes but is not limited to the following items: Tellers Counters,

Specifications relating to the work in the three preceding illustrations are reproduced in part to point out the correlation that is necessary between drawings and written instructions. It is not enough that the drawings tie together; the specifications must work with the drawings by supplementing the information, not repeating it.

either illegible drawings or work that is poorly or inadequately shown.

There is a direct correlation between a drawing, its scale, its contribution, and the type of information it provides. The following is a brief chart of explanation:

> **The more specific the drawing (a detail, for example),**
>> **the smaller the area of work shown,**
>>> **the larger the scale,**
>>>> **the more the drawing "informs"**
>>>>> **without reference to other drawings,**
>>>>>> **the more it depicts an end result,**
>>>>>>> **a final configuration.**

In the reverse, if the drawing is general or overall in scope (an exterior elevation of one entire side of a building), the area involved is larger and the scale must be smaller (to show the entire drawing on one sheet). The drawing will reference other, more specific drawings (details, sections, etc.), and it tends to depict a concept or overall view, but not the specifics of how the construction is created.

The start of the detailing process requires the drafter to assess the relative importance of the various items, the need for their appearance (if used at all), and, in turn, their proper line weights in the presentation. This review must be a very objective process, with the drafter remembering that showing "everything" is not necessarily the correct thing to do. In fact, it can be patently wrong, particularly if it in any way confuses reading and understanding the detail or contributes to making it "too liney" and needlessly complex.

The illustration is a good example of several previously noted maladies:

- Line weights poorly conceived
- Drawing too "liney"
- Information shown needlessly
- Detail unduly complex for no good reason

The assessment process starts with establishing what is to be shown, then adding the other items to be incorporated, that will further explain the construction of, or around, the primary item. For example, structural steel columns, in the project frame, are to be surrounded by concrete masonry unit (CMU) enclosures. These vary from column to column to meet differing conditions. Thus, the assessment is as follows: (1) We need to show the columns and (2) how each is enclosed with CMU. The priorities are obvious (the columns and the CMU surround are the primary features).

To this must be added dimensions, profiles (bullnose, etc.), proper relationships, anchors, and so on. However, there is no need to show the horizontal masonry wall reinforcing. This would add a number of lines and really add nothing that cannot be noted (on the drawing and/or in the specifications). Again, the illustration shows the latter, and it makes the drawing too liney, too complex, and places line weight emphasis in the wrong place. The detail has been degraded and readability compromised. In the normal sequence of a project, the production of contract (working) drawings or documents is not a process that must start from a dead stop. Rather, the schematic (preliminary) design documents will have been further developed and have had at least minimal detail begun: thus, the design development phase of the work.

The working drawings start with those documents, which are augmented and further detailed into the full, finished set of working drawings. In reality, three things must come together at this stage:

- The design development drawings and decisions
- The programming documents
- A checklist of project tasks that must be performed, including a list of materials, systems, drawings, details, and the like, which appear in some form in every project

The first two items refer to, discuss, and note the uniqueness of the project, and the third relates the common, mundane, and "usual" items that are necessary for a complete project. These may be upgraded or enhanced to be more in keeping with the uniqueness of the project, but they nonetheless need identification and a decision as to whether they are required, and if so, in what form.

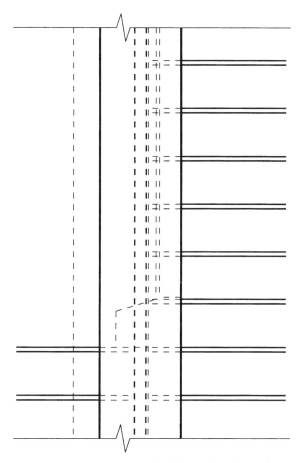

A detail that, more than likely, should never have been drawn. It shows only the elevation of an aluminum cover over a wall expansion joint; does that really need to be detailed? But it goes on to also show the wall, a window and sill, and a brick pilaster which occur well beyond the plane of the joint. Can you identify each "layer"?

7

Drafting Tools

Nothing is more frustrating than to tackle a job only to find that the knowledge is adequate but the tools are lacking. This is particularly true in drafting, architectural design, and the production of working drawings.

The ever increasing use of computer-aided drafting (CAD) has fostered a new and very different sequence for purchasing drafting tools and equipment. Although it does not address specific equipment purchases, Chapter 35 contains a wider discussion of CAD and its equipment requirements. However, to provide a full-breadth discussion, we have included this chapter, which is certainly still valid for many professionals and students in various portions of project work. Indeed, there are still many in professional offices who use manual techniques in some of their tasks.

A large array of drafting equipment is available from the artists and architects supply houses, reproduction firms, and discount stores located in any large city. Anyone who is interested in producing working drawings and fully intends to make them a life's work should be more than a bit concerned about the kind of equipment he or she buys. This is not to say that a person must purchase expensive equipment to cover the full range of possibilities in all drafting situations. Every manufacturer produces several lines of equipment, beginning with a scholastic line of good tools and

instruments that is usually of lower quality and price than the professional demands.

The purchasing sequence may take quite a number of years. In fact, as a piece of equipment is acquired or replaced, it should be in the back of a drafter's mind to improve his or her tools. A basic rule is to buy the best quality one can afford at any given time. It is always advisable to choose the better-known and reputable manufacturer's products; in this way good design and accuracy, when accuracy is essential, are ensured. Although the product may not be guaranteed, the larger firms are concerned with their reputations and will make adjustments when defects deem them necessary.

Fortunately, or unfortunately, new equipment is constantly appearing on the scene. These tools are improvements on older items or are new items for new situations. Again, a drafter does not need every piece of new equipment, but it is to his or her own benefit to watch for the latest improvement and to buy it if it will help that person in his or her work. It goes without saying that the drafter must be prepared to treat the equipment with respect and care for it properly. The tools are at the mercy of the user, and any abuses heaped on them will be reflected in their performance. It is foolhardy to spend money on good equipment only to abuse it, to break it, or to misuse it in any way.

Nearly everyone who reads this book will have some knowledge of mechanical or architectural drawing. For this reason minimum attention will be given to the basic instruments. Rather, we shall concentrate on suggestions for desirable acquisitions. Most architectural and engineering firms supply their staffs with the larger, more expensive, and little-used tools. This practice varies among firms, but in general, if a drafter provides his or her own for daily use, that person will be adequately equipped.

Ideally, the more sophisticated equipment includes some kind of drafting machine, either track or bar type, for keeping constant angles. The parallel bar can be moved about the board freely, and angles can be turned quickly and locked in place. Well-designed drafting room layouts permit drafting machines to cover large areas of the drafting boards without creating a space problem. These machines are expensive and are not widely used in architectural work, but they offer a fine degree of accuracy, so necessary in tool and die, machine, and other fine tolerance designs.

The T square has always been the mainstay as a parallel edge. The head of the T square must be kept firmly in touch with the edge of the board to ensure parallel lines. Inaccuracies occur when the entire head is not in contact with the edge, when it is jarred by some other force, or when the screws that hold the head and blade together are loosened. Many draftsmen prefer the parallel rule (Jacob's ladder), which is fastened to the board by cables locked in place to ensure parallel lines. These cables do limit, to some degree, the amount of equipment that can be kept on the board; the parallel edge is restricted by the cables and cannot be lifted more than an inch from the board's surface. The parallel rule, however, does allow the draftsman to forget about the "head

problem," for there is no head. When properly installed, it eases drafting chores by dependably producing parallel lines.

Drawing board designs vary considerably. Standard drafting tables are quite common and have worked well through the years. The standard board is mounted on an artist's stand or on four legs with a table frame. Many offices, and frequently individuals who work at home, use an inexpensive door that is easily converted into a fine drafting table. The door can be mounted on cleats on the wall or on sawhorse frames. Wooden drafting tables, or doors, do not offer the most desirable surface for drafting; the use of a drafting board pad is recommended. "Battleship" linoleum has always been popular because of its resilient surface, but a vinyl covering that can be laminated to the board is now available. This covering, obtainable in a light green shade that is easy on the draftsman's eyes, is washable. The uncovered wood surface of a drawing board lacks resiliency and quickly becomes scored and grooved, which, of course, adversely affects subsequent drawings. Hard surfaces, such as plastic laminates, again provide no resiliency. A hard lead on a hard surface will actually slit the paper. It is not necessary to cover the entire surface of the board. A storage area and a light on one edge, neither of which requires covering, are desirable.

Drafting tables are office equipment; the portable board is made of basswood or white pine and is either laminated or specially constructed to prevent warping and splitting. Portable boards are usually fabricated of horizontal strips of wood, with vertical strips at either side to provide a true edge for a T square. Some are laminated with a plywoodlike facing on the top, but this facing does not provide the best drafting surface.

The tendency of students entering architectural school is to buy a large number of drafting instruments. This can be expensive, and in many instances such students are "taken" because they have bought things about which they know little or nothing. A student really requires only a few pieces from an entire set, and it is wiser to be selective. The most commonly used instrument is a 6-inch bow compass with extension arms. It is preferable that it be equipped with a thumb wheel that allows accurate measurement of radii. Many friction-hinge compasses on the market have a tendency to collapse or expand as a circle is drawn. In some offices a large beam compass for extremely large circles may be provided.

(Top, opposite) Drafting equipment includes several types of scale: triangular, rounded, and flat beveled. All but the triangular come in 6- and 12-inch sizes. The standard size of a bow compass is 6 inches, although other sizes are available. Shown also is a set bow compass. Points that can be adjusted to various radii lie along the beam or bar. Standard T squares can be bought in various lengths.

(Bottom, opposite) The parallel rule, or bar, is attached directly to the board and requires no action to keep it square on the paper. The cables hold the bar in position. The only drawback in this unit is that equipment cannot be stored on the board.

A full-scale protractor and half-circle units are shown. Triangles can be obtained in various sizes; a good size is 8 or 10 inches. French curves are available in numerous sizes. Shown at right is a wooden drawing board with metal edges.

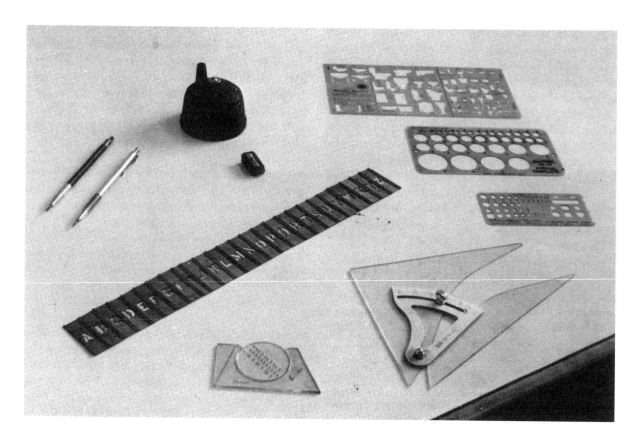

The beam compass can be a one-piece item, or it can be a metal or wood bar to which the pinpoint and drafting point are attached. Again, this is an instrument that the individual need not necessarily acquire, but it is available.

In addition to the board and parallel edge, there must be some accommodation for angular drawing. For this we use a triangle. A good-quality triangle is approximately 0.06 inch thick; thicker sections are more stable and are available in a wide range of prices and qualities. Thinner triangles, which are difficult to handle and are subject to warping and basic inaccuracies, are made for economy. Triangles should be tested for trueness; their edges should be straight and accurate, and bevels in the cut outs should be provided for ease of handling. Of course, it is important that the drafting edges of all triangles be undamaged and free of nicks.

It is the individual's choice, but a range of triangles is advisable. A 4-inch, 45-degree triangle is handy for toning (/poché) and applying symbols to drawings and for working in small areas. A 6- or 8-inch, 30–60-degree triangle and a 45-degree triangle of the same size will meet most needs. It is a good idea to add something in the range of a 14-inch, 30–60-degree triangle to the tool kit. This variety of sizes allows flexibility and a wide range of capabilities.

Also worthwhile is the adjustable triangle, which obviates the need for a chain of triangles to achieve an unusual angle. With this triangle the proper angle can be set and locked for use.

It is also possible to procure lettering triangles in which holes are punched to give evenly spaced guidelines. Some triangles are produced in colors that ease eyestrain to some extent, but again this is a matter of choice.

Another requirement is a good-quality protractor, either 180- or 360-degree. A 6- or 8-inch protractor will allow for accurate angular measurements. A basic French curve or an irregular

curve is an asset in the personal toolbox, but extensive ship's curves are expensive and have limited application. Also available are "snakes," or flexible curves, which usually have a lead core and an outer coating of plastic. These snakes can be formed to any particular curve required but are especially adaptable to the long curves encountered in road work. The French curve is applicable to curves of lesser extent.

Scales are produced in various shapes and materials: solid wood, solid plastic, and basswood with plastic edges. Almost all scales are machine-divided for accuracy and precision. The basswood with plastic edges is probably the highest quality and most expensive scale available. It is important for the drafter to obtain an architect's and a civil engineer's scale. Both should be 12 inches long. The architect's scale in the 6-inch length is convenient as a pocket aid. Most offices provide 18-inch scales with 1/8 and 1/4 inch divisions. The longer scale can be useful, though not mandatory.

All scales should be cared for to prevent chipping or splitting; they should be kept clean without rubbing off the markings, which should be scored into the face of the edge and filled with paint. The divisions should not be merely printed on the face. Cost will dictate quality and accuracy.

The biggest change in drafting equipment has occurred in the lead holder. For a great many years wooden pencils came in a full range of lead weights (hard to soft). There were special long-point sharpeners, and the point was finished on a sandpaper block or pad. Today this method has declined in use, and most draftsmen now use mechanical lead holders and stick lead.

Lead holders come in various styles and lengths and with many grips, body shapes, and weights. Some have indicators for the type of lead they contain. The individual choice is broad. The newest on the market is a 0.5 millimeter lead holder (also available in 0.3 and 0.7 millimeter). Sticks of lead can be loaded and stored in the holder, which provides automatic feeding. By virtue of the small size of the lead, no sharpening is required. These new holders are handy and efficient.

Sharpeners add more equipment to the toolbox. There is a rotary lead pointer that contains a sandpaper insert and another that consists of blades in a little cylinder. Automatic lead pointers are electrically operated. Caution is needed with all these devices to eliminate daggerlike points that will snap under the least pressure or pierce the paper. The degree of roundness for

(Opposite) Both lead holders take any lead, but the lower one has a clip for pocket use. Two lead pointers, the upper, a rotary type with sandpaper inserts, the lower, a twist type with inner knife blades. Only one style of rather sterile letters is possible with this template (center). Three common templates: the upper is for plumbing, the center for circles, and the lower is applicable to doors and other architectural features. The Ames lettering guide allows consistent spacing of guidelines for hand lettering. The adjustable curve ("snake") can be made to conform to any shape.

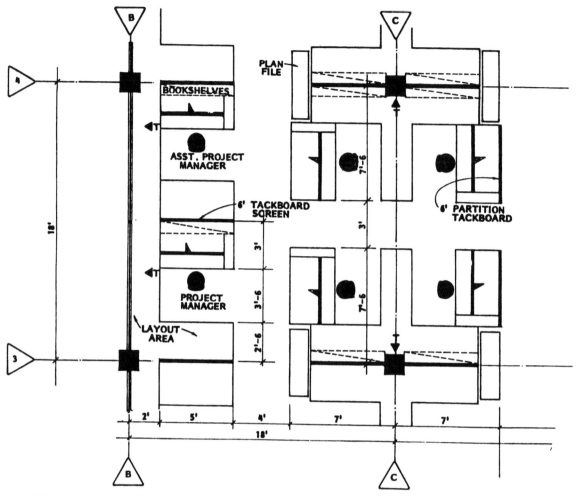

Hansen, Lind, Meyer, P.C.
It is impossible to depict the "ideal" workstation because of individual and firm requirements. Above is a good arrangement of separate stations and a grouping for a project team. Note ample drawing space, reference space, privacy, and yet openness for intercommunication.

the drafting point is a matter of choice, but some slight roundness is a must.

As we describe later, there is a technique of drafting that maintains the point for long periods of work. A well-chosen sharpener underlies this technique, however.

Some experimentation in the selection of lead is necessary. The drafter must determine the weight of lead that works best for him or her. In changing from one drafting medium to another (e.g., from paper to mylar film), the drafting technique, as well as the quality and type of lead, may have to change. Mylar film will take lead much more readily, give a blacker line with a harder

lead, and still produce excellent results. As a rule, two or three grades of lead should be all that any draftsman would use if working consistently on construction documents; 2-H lead is most common, although a heavier-handed drafter may have to resort to a 3-H lead, and someone who has superior control of his or her line work may get by with an H lead. The conventional stick lead has a clay content in which the drafter may often encounter dry spots or moments. These dry spots will not produce the desired line and may actually score the medium; therefore, the best procedure is to resharpen the lead or break the bad portion out of the stick. The new range of lead holders for the finer sticktype leads provides smoother and improved line work without the danger of scoring the sheet.

While they are on the drafting board, it is important that all sheets be kept clean to the best of the drafter's ability. Of course, a job may take a great deal of time, during which the sheets are constantly taken up and stored or worked on by many persons; the lead will smudge and the sheets will become dirty. For this reason the draftsman should be devoted to keeping the work as clean and neat as is humanly possible. Drafting powder or a dry-cleaning bag, known as a "bunny bag" because it is composed of ground eraser material, may be used. A drafting board brush, another essential part of the draftsman's kit, must be soft-bristled. This brush is for dusting the sheet, not for scrubbing across it, and should never be used for any other purpose.

Erasers must be kept at hand. It has been said that the eraser is society's greatest invention. The architectural draftsman should keep in mind that to make a mistake is no great sin if found in time, the right questions asked, and the situation remedied. The place to make mistakes is in the drafting room, on paper! In a comparatively short time, the change can be made. When making a change, however, it should be done completely and thoroughly, without any line work remaining and without any subsequent "ghosting" of the medium. Ghosting is caused by indentations or slits in the paper that will continue to reproduce on each print. Perhaps the most widely used eraser is the Pink Pearl, which is a rubber type; however, a newly developed vinyl eraser, usually white, is available in small blocks. It is advisable also to have a stick eraser, which, in conjunction with an eraser shield, permits the correction of small areas of a drawing. This combination makes meticulous eradication possible.

Mentioned with triangles was a useful instrument known as a lettering guide, perhaps the best of which is the Ames. This guide can be rotated to provide the spacing of guidelines as wanted, a capability that produces uniformity in lettering size and an overall neat appearance.

In speaking of lettering guides, we come to the matter of templates. Templates are produced in a vast number of configurations for a great many purposes in drafting. Templates are definitely a shortcut; their use should be mastered efficiently and properly by the new draftsman. Most common is the circle template, which hap-

pily reduces the use of the compass. The individual template usually has 40 to 60 holes of various sizes and is especially handy for such indications as door swings. From there, templates go hither and yon, taking in everything from furniture layouts to North arrows, arrowheads to bolt heads, and configurations of metal decks, toilet room equipment, and specialty items. In addition to the circle template, a template with variety of rectangles, squares, hexagons, triangles, and other shapes is recommended, for in many instances the symbols used for windows, doors, and room numbers are some sort of geometric figure.

An extensive range of templates is not a necessity, but the two mentioned will be helpful. Something in the furniture template area is also handy to have. Templates are widely available and, when a special need develops, easily acquired.

The architectural draftsman would be well-advised to buy a plumbing template in which the configurations of the various fixtures are cut for quick reproduction on plans or room elevations. Templates in various ellipses are myriad. Unless the desired ellipsis is known, these templates will prove valueless, for the axes change and the templates seldom fit the situation at hand.

From this point the tool kit can be expanded more or less as desired. It is always helpful, for instance, to have a small slide rule or calculator for quick calculations. Drafting tape is provided by the office, but little is done with thumbtacks, for they destroy a drafting surface. An electric eraser, usually supplied by the office, is especially suited to ink work and to the eradication of large areas. Great caution must be exercised; do not bear down on the sheet or remain in one area for longer than is needed to lift the lead. An electric eraser will penetrate the drafting medium quickly with disastrous results. A mat knife used for cutting paper belongs in every tool kit, and a special chisel blade will be needed for cutting board. The wise draftsman will have at hand a cardboard mailing tube in which to store drawings to prevent them from becoming mangled or crushed. A small case or tackle box is suitable for storing tools.

Colored pencils and dry markers or felt-tip pens are convenient additions to the kit. All are part of today's office supplies. Colored pencils are employed for marking prints in the working drawing phase and for corrections and notations on shop drawings.

DRAFTING TOOLS

Ink is used to a limited degree, although engineering offices in particular may still be quite active in ink work. Perhaps the greatest advancement in ink drafting has been the drawing instrument in fountain pen form. The old nib-type ruling pen is no longer used; it was a dangerous tool in that it constantly dropped ink and was difficult to control. The new fountain pens must be kept clean. These pens have a tubular point with a small needle that allows the proper flow of ink from the barrel reservoir. Well known is the Rapidograph by Kohinoor. Most offices have multipoint sets mounted in a humidor container in which the temperature can be monitored to keep the pens in good condition. With reasonable care and soap and water the pens can be kept clean and free-flowing. Points of various sizes are interchangeable in the standard barrel. Several systems are produced by different manufacturers, and the draftsman's choice remains an individual matter.

Each reader of this book will have developed some technique in a particular area of interest, and some may be more advanced than others by virtue of background or talent. Without offering a drafting course and teaching no system, certain observations regarding the drafter and his or her environment seem pertinent. These observations are predicated on the drafting station at which the drafter is situated, the conditions under which he or she works, and the drafter's basic approaches. It is essential that the drafting station have a firmly mounted board that will not wobble. The drafter may sit on a stool or a chair, or may stand, as he or she wishes. All boards are adjustable except those with four fixed legs. The drafter, or CAD operator should have some space available (table or counter) usually to the left side, on which to spread out reference drawings and other material which she or he is using in doing the work at hand. The best nightly storage is within fireproof files, which will safeguard these very valuable documents, be they finished or unfinished. Also, it must be remembered that paper is not dimensionally stable, and humidity adversely affects all types of paper (tracing and plotting papers included). If the sheets are to remain on the board, or simply out overnight, they should be covered with cover sheets, cloths, or other non-paper materials. Paper taped down should have the two upper, or lower corners freed, to reduce wrinkling and creases that occurs if they remain securely fastened.

In this book drafting techniques are pointed out with each drawing. Architectural drawing is different, in that good work to some is merely acceptable to others. Mechanical drawing and machine design drawing require extreme accuracy, which is not necessarily true of architectural drawing. The type of line work that architects use, the variation of lines, the crossed intersections, all are unique to architectural drafting.

The most important thing to remember is that all information must appear on the drawings in proper form and in good condition so that it can be reproduced easily. Many gadgets are available—for example, a typewriter that mounts directly on the drafting board to facilitate typing notes on the sheets, and stick-on decals by which we can place vital pieces of information. Most of the notes, however, are still lettered on by the drafter.

The drafter requires proper tools and a command of those tools to do the assigned work to the best of his or her ability.

The photo shows the rather typical CAD workstation. Here a PC is outfitted with a menu [or digitizer] board, which has the various commands and library figures incorporated in it.

This photo shows a two-monitor CAD system, more than likely used for MicroStation, Parch, and software programs with expanded capabilities, including 3-D depiction; the same display can be continued across the screens or 2 different displays can be used.

	REFERENCE NOTES-STRUCTURAL	SPECIFICATION SECTION NUMBERS	WALL CENTERLINES	NON-PRINT REFERENCE	ADDENDA AND BULLETIN "BUBBLES"	"CHANGE INDICATION" LEVEL		LEGEND + SCHEDULE GRAPHICS		LEGEND + SCHEDULE TEXT	REFERENCE NOTES-ELECTRICAL	REFERENCE NOTES-MECHANICAL
CTRL+ALT												
ALT	EQUIPMENT-OWNER PURCHASED	BEAM CENTERLINES	REFERENCE SYMBOLS, SYMBOL TEXT	MATCHLINES, BREAKLINES, TARGETS	DOOR SYMBOLS, HOLE ANNOTATION	WINDOW SYMBOLS	WALL FIRE RATINGS	DRAWING TITLES, SCALE		TEXT	REFERENCE NOTES-PLUMBING	GENERAL EQUIPMENT
CTRL	WINDOWS + WINDOW SILLS	ROOM NAMES WITH UNDERLINE	SHAFTS	ELEVATORS, ESCALATORS	DOOR FRAME	STAIR WALKLINES	PLUMBING FIXTURES	TOILET PARTITIONS, HANDICAP HANDRAILS		DEMO PLUMBING	EXISTING PLUMBING	
SHIFT	STAIRS, HANDRAILS, BREAKLINES	SLABS, AREA PAT., CONCRETE	NOTES, MISC. TEXT, LEADERS	ROOM NUMBERS	CASEWORK + MILLWORK	BEAM EDGES	SHEET BORDER	NORTH ARROW, GRAPHIC SCALE	DRAWING SHEET INFORMATION	ROOM PERIMETER SHAPE	CURTAIN WALL CENTERLINES	CURTAIN WALL MULLIONS + GLASS
KEY	WALL EDGES	DOORS, DOOR SWINGS, HOLES	COL. STL. JOIST	GYP. MTL. WALL, ROOF. DECKING	COLUMN GRIDLINES	COLUMN GRID TAGS	WALL PAT. BLOCKING	LOCK AXIS TOGGLE	EXISTING ELEMENTS	DEMOLITION	CEILING REFERENCES	DIMENSION TEXT

This is a prompting panel for use with MicroStation software. This replaces the digitizer board, and uses the function keys to enable various attributes, such as layer, line, colors, etc.

8

Lettering

Architectural working drawings are not just illustrations of buildings. They are collections of bits of information, each of which is vital to the building process. These drawings combine lines and words, for it is impossible to build a project with only the lines or only the words.

A simple notation consisting of one word or one short phrase may save the work of drawing several lines. When it is more efficient to draw an object than to describe it, we use the line technique, but it is often simpler to provide written instructions. It is always possible to gain time if we can somehow cut corners, for even today a great deal of precious time is spent on lettering.

An important requirement for each new draftsman or architect is the development of a good lettering technique and a good personal alphabet. The first requirement of good lettering is that it be legible. Most architects develop distinctive styles by adding some sort of artistic touch of their own. That is all right, for each of us values individuality, but at all times legibility is more important than any special effect. Some offices demand that all drawing sheets have a set look, as if they had been done by the same draftsman. The student must be able to produce several different types of lettering, and in learning the different styles, must master the basic letter forms. Individuality can be added later.

Lettering can enhance a drawing by making it simple to interpret and easy to understand, or the final effect can be ruined by sloppy, careless work. Carelessness and sloppiness have no place on a working drawing; neither is it a place to be "cute" by playing guessing games with the its users. Each letter character should be unique—never similar to any other letter or symbol.

The initial approach to lettering on architectural drawings is the selection of the correct lead or the right pencil for the particular need. Although one may have had a great deal of experience, it is essential to review the Gothic capital letter forms—a vertical, single-stroke, technical alphabet. It is nothing fancy, but this alphabet contains all the basics. Once the review has been made, the letter shapes must be retained in the personal alphabet. Good lettering is predicated on a knowledge of these letter forms and a practiced hand. There is no quick way and no shortcut to good lettering. A knowledgeable foundation and constant practice lead to proficiency.

For each word, phrase, line, or paragraph of lettering, guidelines must be drawn; use lines for the top and bottom of each line of characters. Some persons employ a third, intermediate line for a particular alphabet, but this is not a mandatory practice. Aim for accuracy and develop speed as accuracy is gained.

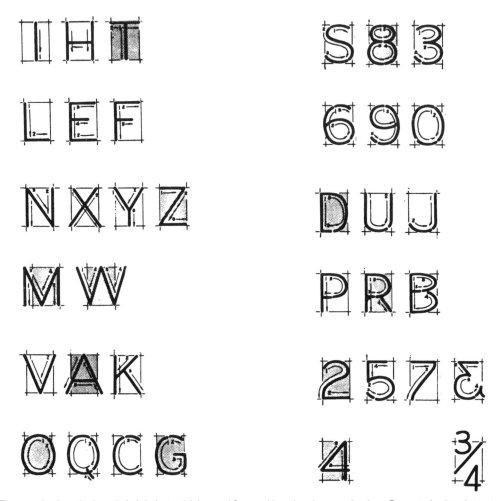

The standard vertical capital alphabet widely used for working drawing production. Groups depict characters of similar construction. Individual variation should start only after this basic alphabet is mastered.

Several types of lettering alphabet may be adopted; the choice depends on personal preference or on the preference of the office: vertical capital letters, vertical lowercase letters, and both capital and lowercase letters with slanted axes. One learns by experience when a particular type is advantageous or superfluous. Several personal alphabets shown in the examples typify both practice and students' work and may be copied or modified.

Another excellent source of good, uniform, legible lettering can be found in the comic sections and political cartoons of any newspaper. The cartoonist must get the point across and sometimes uses strictly line work. Most of the time, however, words must be added to make the characterization real and believable. The need for lettering is obvious. This is also true of working drawings.

Many systems are available to help with good lettering. In addition to the straight, freehand lettering system, with just the hand and pencil

---

(Top, opposite) Four excellent examples of hand lettering are illustrated. Although done by different people in individual styles, the characters are crisp and well formed. Both upper- and lowercase letters and Arabic numerals are shown. The lettering is strong and well spaced. Each example is representative of the fluent everyday work of the draftsman. Even with changes in style, the basic vertical axis is used. Note the slated examples.

(Bottom, opposite) Some of the more common lettering errors. The top line is self-explanatory and a defect that must be watched carefully (this error is eased to some degree by the new fine leads). The centerline is poor lettering. More care is needed on character strokes and forms. The rest is a good example of what not to do.

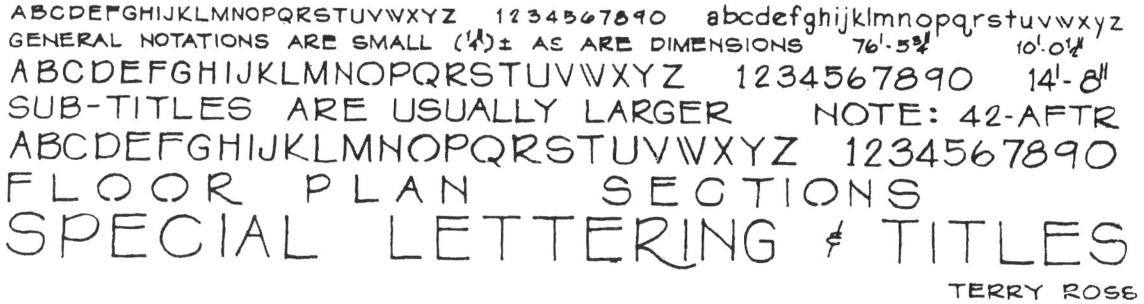

ABCDEFGHIJKLMNOPQRSTUVWXYZ 1234567890 abcdefghijklmnopqrstuvwxyz
GENERAL NOTATIONS ARE SMALL (1/4)± AS ARE DIMENSIONS 76'-5¾" 10'-0¼"
ABCDEFGHIJKLMNOPQRSTUVWXYZ 1234567890 14'-8"
SUB-TITLES ARE USUALLY LARGER NOTE: 42-AFTR
ABCDEFGHIJKLMNOPQRSTUVWXYZ 1234567890
FLOOR PLAN SECTIONS
SPECIAL LETTERING & TITLES

TERRY ROSS

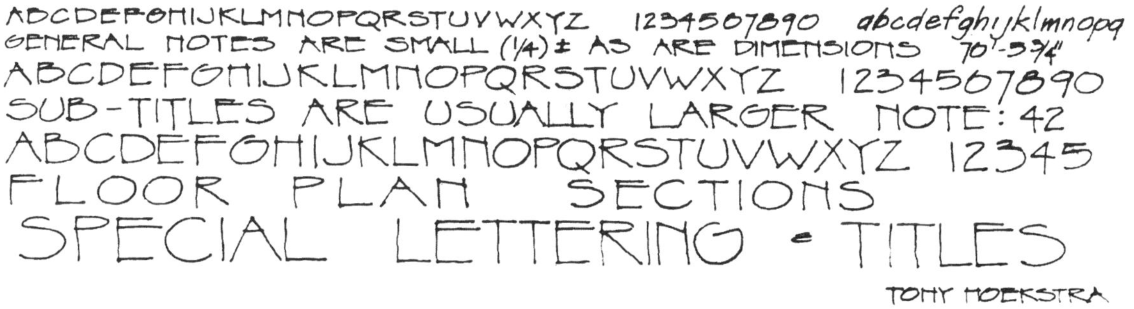

ABCDEFGHIJKLMNOPQRSTUVWXYZ 1234567890 abcdefghijklmnopq
GENERAL NOTES ARE SMALL (1/4)± AS ARE DIMENSIONS 70'-5¾"
ABCDEFGHIJKLMNOPQRSTUVWXYZ 1234567890
SUB-TITLES ARE USUALLY LARGER NOTE: 42
ABCDEFGHIJKLMNOPQRSTUVWXYZ 12345
FLOOR PLAN SECTIONS
SPECIAL LETTERING = TITLES

TONY HOEKSTRA

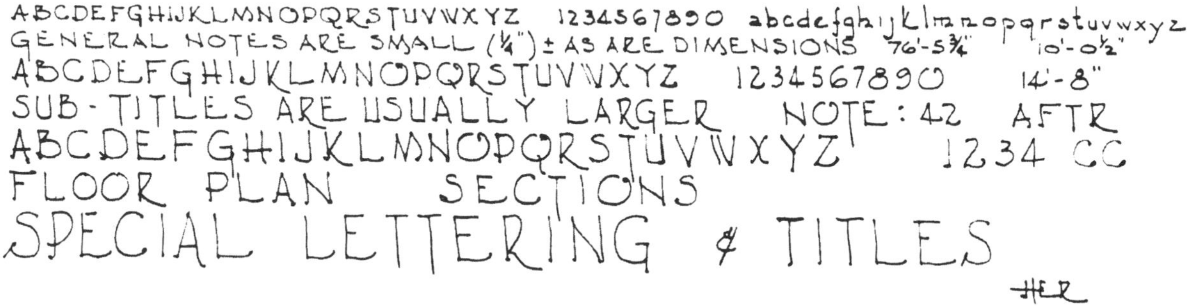

ABCDEFGHIJKLMNOPQRSTUVWXYZ 1234567890 abcdefghijklmnopqrstuvwxyz
GENERAL NOTES ARE SMALL (1/4")± AS ARE DIMENSIONS 76'-5¾" 10'-0½"
ABCDEFGHIJKLMNOPQRSTUVWXYZ 1234567890 14'-8"
SUB-TITLES ARE USUALLY LARGER NOTE: 42 AFTR
ABCDEFGHIJKLMNOPQRSTUVWXYZ 1234 CC
FLOOR PLAN SECTIONS
SPECIAL LETTERING & TITLES

HR

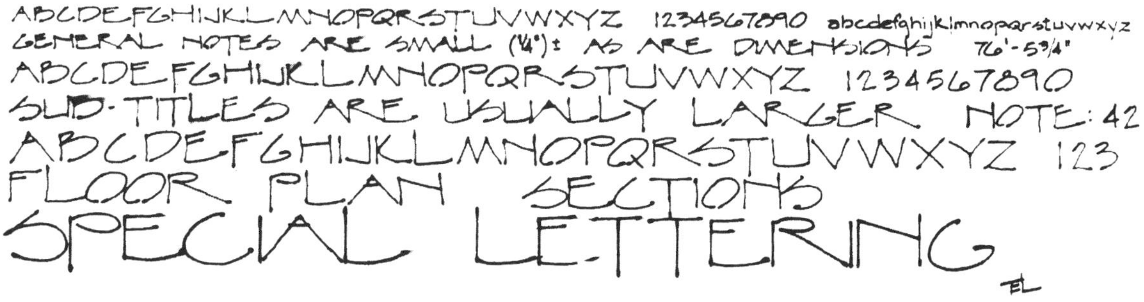

ABCDEFGHIJKLMNOPQRSTUVWXYZ 1234567890 abcdefghijklmnopqrstuvwxyz
GENERAL NOTES ARE SMALL (1/4")± AS ARE DIMENSIONS 76'-5¾"
ABCDEFGHIJKLMNOPQRSTUVWXYZ 1234567890
SUB-TITLES ARE USUALLY LARGER NOTE: 42
ABCDEFGHIJKLMNOPQRSTUVWXYZ 123
FLOOR PLAN SECTIONS
SPECIAL LETTERING

EL

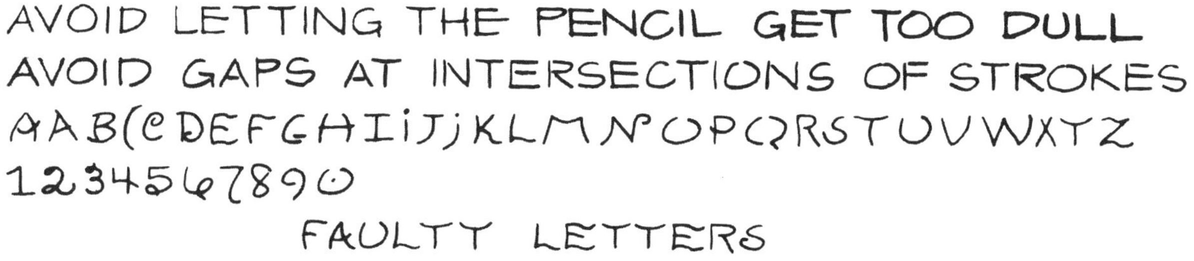

AVOID LETTING THE PENCIL GET TOO DULL
AVOID GAPS AT INTERSECTIONS OF STROKES
AAB(CDEFGHIJjKLMNOPQRSTUVWXYZ
1234567890

FAULTY LETTERS

AaBbCcDdEeFfGgHhIiJjKkLlMmNnOoPpQqRrSsTtUuVvWwXxYyZz1234567890

AaBbCcDdEeFfGgHhIiJjKkLlMmNnOoPpQqRrSsTtUuVvWwXxYyZz1234567890

AaBbCcDdEeFfGgHhIiJjKkLlMmNnOoPpQqRrSsTtUuVvWwXxYyZz1234567890

 AABBCCDDEEFFGGHHIIJJKKLLMMNNOOPPQQRRSSTTUUVVWWXXYYZZ1234567890

AaBbCcDdEeFfGgHhIiJjKkLlMmNnOoPpQqRrSsTtUuVvWwXxYyZz1234567890

AaBBCcDdEEFFGGHHIiJJKkLLMMNNOOPPQQRRSSTTUUVvWwXxYYZz1234567890

AaBbCcDdEeFfGgHhIiJjKkLlMmNnOoPpQqRrSsTtUuVvWwXxYyZz1234567890

AaBbCcDdEeFfGgHhIiJjKkLlMmNnOoPpQqRrSsTtUuVvWwXxYyZz1234567890

AaBbCcDdEeFfGgHhIiJjKkLlMmNnOoPpQqRrSsTtUuVvWwXxYyZz1234567890

AaBbCcDdEeFfGgHhIiJjKkLlMmNnOoPpQqRrSsTtUuVvWwXxYyZz1234567890

AaBbCcDdEeFfGgHhIiJjKkLlMmNnOoPpQqRrSsTtUuVvWwXxYyZz1234567890

AaBbCcDdEeFfGgHhIiJjKkLlMmNnOoPpQqRrSsTtUuVvWwXxYyZz1234567890

AaBbCcDdEeFfGgHhIiJjKkLlMmNnOoPpQqRrSsTtUuVvWwXxYyZz1234567890

AABBCCDDEEFFGGHHIIJJKKLLMMNNOOPPQQRRSSTTUUVVWWXXYYZZ1234567890

AaBbCcDdEeFfGgHhIiJjKkLlMmNnOoPpQqRrSsTtUuVvWwXxYyZz1234567890

AaBBCcDdEeFFGGHHIiJJKkLLMMNNOoPPQQRRSSTTUUVvWwXxYYZz1234567890

AaBbCcDdEeFfGgHhIiJjKkLlMmNnOoPpQqRrSsTtUuVvWwXxYyZz1234567890

AaBbCcDdEeFfGgHhIiJjKkLlMmNnOoPpQqRrSsTtUuVvWwXxYyZz1234567890

AaBbCcDdEeFfGgHhIiJjKkLlMmNnOoPpQqRrSsTtUuVvWwXxYyZz1234567890

AaBbCcDdEeFfGgHhIiJjKkLlMmNnOoPpQqRrSsTtUuVvWwXxYyZz1234567890

Numerous fonts are available on computers, including one [at the asterisk] that closely resembles hand-drafted architectural lettering.

MONOTXT
AaBbCcDdEeFfGgHhIiJjKkLlMmNnOoPpQqRrSsTtUuVvWwXxYyZz
1234567890

ROMANS
AaBbCcDdEeFfGgHhIiJjKkLlMmNnOoPpQqRrSsTtUuVvWwXxYyZz
1234567890

ROMAND
AaBbCcDdEeFfGgHhIiJjKkLlMmNnOoPpQqRrSsTtUuVvWwXxYyZz
1234567890

ROMANT
AaBbCcDdEeFfGgHhIiJjKkLlMmNnOoPpQqRrSsTtUuVvWwXxYyZz
1234567890

Examples of other commonly used fonts available for use on CAD drawings.

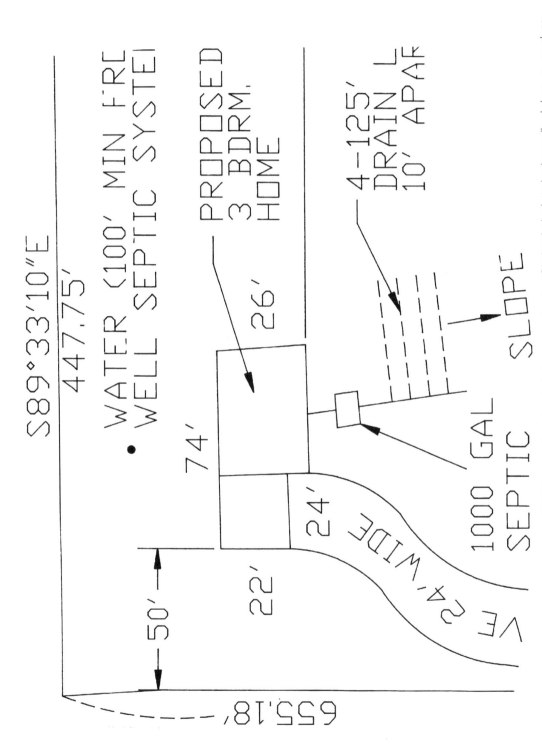

S89°33'10"E
447.75'
WATER (100' MIN F'RL
WELL SEPTIC SYSTE
PROPOSED
3 BDRM.
HOME
4-125'
DRAIN L
10' APAF
74'
26'
50'
22'
24'
1000 GAL
SEPTIC SLOPE
E 24' WIDE
655.18'

This is an example where the indiscriminate use of CAD has produced a wholly improper drawing. Obviously the lettering is needlessly large; so much so that it dwarfs and obscures the drawing itself. Lettering can be emphasized, if necessary, in several other ways that will better serve the drawing overall.

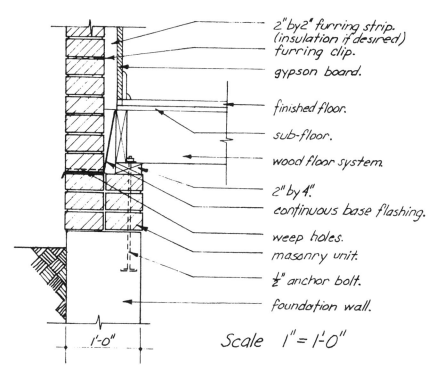

2" by 2" furring strip.
(insulation if desired)
furring clip.
gypson board.

finished floor.
sub-floor.
wood floor system.

2" by 4".
continuous base flashing.
weep holes.
masonry unit.
½" anchor bolt.
foundation wall.

1'-0"

Scale 1" = 1'-0"

The use of lowercase lettering is encouraged by some offices. The same approach to uniformity should be taken as with any lettering system. Do not intermix lower- and uppercase alphabets, in any event.

at work, we can employ templates, cut-out shapes that act as mechanical aids. Templates standardize our lettering, but most of them are decidedly lacking in artistic effect.

We can also adopt the Leroy system, which is a template with a scriber holding an ink or lead point that produces good-quality lettering. With slight adjustments, the lettering is made on a slant axis from the vertical. The variety of templates available with this system permits the choice of upper- and lowercase letters as well as letters of various sizes.

For smaller drawings we can use the typewriter, which, of course, is neat and fast but limited in size of the characters obtainable. In addition, the spacing is fixed between both letters and lines. Some are equipped with interchangeable sets of letters, but even with an extended carriage, drawings cannot always be fitted into the roller for the required notation.

Another system has been developed in which we can type on a decal material that can be fixed to the drawing. This method is discussed in Chapter 32, on composite drafting. Again, multiple notes that must be fitted close to the points to which they refer impose a limit on our choice.

A machine known as the Vari-typer is fast and neat and unlimited in the size of sheet it can accept. The Vari-typer provides type that is easily erased when changes are required. Many different type styles and sizes are available. In the last few years rub-on, or transfer, lettering has become popular, again in a wide variety of sizes and typefaces. This lettering is easy to apply to a drawing but not so easily corrected as the product of the Vari-typer. The rub-on and transfer process is slow for mass lettering; therefore, it is used for titles and important pieces of information that we wish to emphasize.

No matter what system is selected, hand lettering, template, or transfer, the lettering is only as good as the spacing allowed. Only the Vari-typer and typewriter give us automatic spacing, but with the distinct disadvantage that it is fixed. In the other systems the spacing is variable, an advantage when deftly used. In hand lettering we must be adaptable to the allotted space and to the impact of our lettering. Most frequently the more important pieces of information require a change of size, perhaps even style, in order to make an instantaneous impression on the viewer.

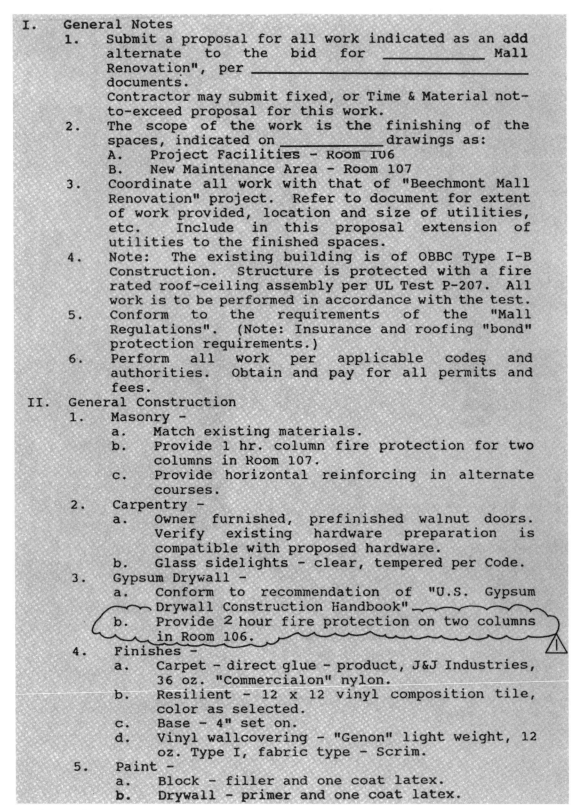

I. General Notes
  1. Submit a proposal for all work indicated as an add
     alternate to the bid for _____ Mall
     Renovation", per _____
     documents.
     Contractor may submit fixed, or Time & Material not-
     to-exceed proposal for this work.
  2. The scope of the work is the finishing of the
     spaces, indicated on _____ drawings as:
     A.   Project Facilities - Room 106
     B.   New Maintenance Area - Room 107
  3. Coordinate all work with that of "Beechmont Mall
     Renovation" project. Refer to document for extent
     of work provided, location and size of utilities,
     etc. Include in this proposal extension of
     utilities to the finished spaces.
  4. Note: The existing building is of OBBC Type I-B
     Construction. Structure is protected with a fire
     rated roof-ceiling assembly per UL Test P-207. All
     work is to be performed in accordance with the test.
  5. Conform to the requirements of the "Mall
     Regulations". (Note: Insurance and roofing "bond"
     protection requirements.)
  6. Perform all work per applicable codes and
     authorities. Obtain and pay for all permits and
     fees.
II. General Construction
  1. Masonry -
     a.   Match existing materials.
     b.   Provide 1 hr. column fire protection for two
          columns in Room 107.
     c.   Provide horizontal reinforcing in alternate
          courses.
  2. Carpentry -
     a.   Owner furnished, prefinished walnut doors.
          Verify existing hardware preparation is
          compatible with proposed hardware.
     b.   Glass sidelights - clear, tempered per Code.
  3. Gypsum Drywall -
     a.   Conform to recommendation of "U.S. Gypsum
          Drywall Construction Handbook".
     b.   Provide 2 hour fire protection on two columns
          in Room 106.
  4. Finishes -
     a.   Carpet - direct glue - product, J&J Industries,
          36 oz. "Commercialon" nylon.
     b.   Resilient - 12 x 12 vinyl composition tile,
          color as selected.
     c.   Base - 4" set on.
     d.   Vinyl wallcovering - "Genon" light weight, 12
          oz. Type I, fabric type - Scrim.
  5. Paint -
     a.   Block - filler and one coat latex.
     b.   Drywall - primer and one coat latex.

"Lettering" produced by a typewriter and then applied to the drawing master of reproducible.

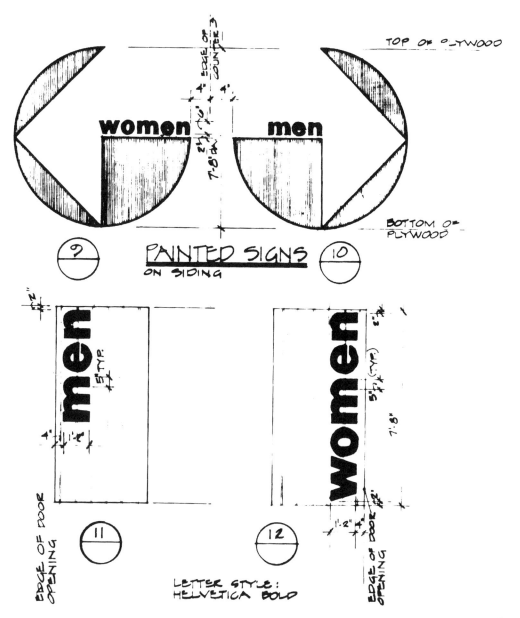

women   men

PAINTED SIGNS
ON SIDING

⑨   ⑩

⑪   ⑫

LETTER STYLE:
HELVETICA BOLD

Standard rub-on or transfer lettering is bold and black and calls instant attention to title, caption, or note. The hand lettering is scaled to the importance of its information.

LETTERING

A title should carry more weight than one small note that defines one small detail of construction. Sheet titles, which cover a large variety of drawings, need a different type of lettering, perhaps smaller in size but with a bolder stroke. Many systems are available to us to support our work, not detract from it. To confine all lettering to one size and one style merely defeats the purpose.

This precaution is also appropriate when one is using computer-aided drafting (CAD) equipment in the production of drawings. Often, in trying to maximize the speed of such systems, the operator does not vary the size of the lettering or adjust it to the drawing involved. This can lead to "oversized" lettering, which tends to distract from the drawing itself. This, of course, can occur in any system of lettering, but it seems that there is a particular problem with the use of CAD. One should always keep in mind that there is a need to make a complementary relationship between drawing and lettering, so they properly reflect the information without one distracting from, or dominating, the other. (See examples throughout text.)

Many key words are applied to lettering: *clear, concise, legible,* and *distinctive.* Lettering should combine legible and decorative characters with rapid production. In the everyday production of drawings another word should come to the mind: *fluency.* Just as we are able to speak at a rapid rate if the need arises, we must also be able to letter quickly. No one can put in a full day's work bent over a drafting board doing nothing but lettering. It is tiresome but important; so important, in fact, that the success of the drawing often relies on it. Good lettering comes only with practice, and with practice we learn spacing and fluency.

A number of symbols widely known and accepted in the industry often help to reduce the amount of lettering needed. Symbols and abbreviations used on drawings must be commonly known, defined in a legend attached to them, or explained by note.

A few key pointers may be helpful:

1. Find the proper pencil or lead weight for the style selected.
2. Use top and bottom guidelines at all times.
3. Proportion the characters to the style.
4. Ensure the integrity of the letter form to avoid confusion; "A" is "A," not delta.

There should be no hesitation in reading the drawing because a "4" resembles a "9," but each alphabetic and numeric character should stand on its own. Make sure that all intersections are sharp points on the guidelines and that the letters touch or possibly cover them. All horizontals are to be drawn from left to right, including the start of curves. Avoid fuzzy line work that allows an uppercase "B" to be mistaken for "13." Try to individualize the lettering alphabet with a weighted accent of stroke at the top and bottom of each character. Each line should have a definite starting and end point, without fadeout or whipped ends. Use a firm, deliberate stroke and learn to space lettering, whether in the context of a paragraph or standing alone as a title. Often a little extra care in spacing will be needed if a title must be fitted into an established space. We must provide an adequate but not excessive area between lines of lettering sufficient to make them readable. For the highest production we should standardize our proportions by working toward uniform size. A letter improperly formed should be erased and done again. Do not attempt to work over or modify a poorly done letter; begin again.

To learn spacing and formation of letters, the following words provide good practice: piling,

Each of these hand-lettered notes, carefully aligned and spaced, contains more than one line. Distinct paragraphing is required.

106

DWG: A 2.01

DOOR SCHEDULE

RM NAME	NO.	DOOR FRAME LABEL	SIDELIGHT	SIZE	HDWR SET	REMARKS
RECEPTION	106A	HM HM 1 HR		3'0"X 7-2"	1	
CLOSET	106B	HM WCS		2'4"X 8'6"	2	MODIFY LNDLRD FRNSHD DOOR
CLOSET	106D	HM WCS		3'0"X 8'6"	2	LANDLORD FURNISHED DOOR
MKT DIR	106E	HM WCS	YES	3'0"X 8'6"	3	LANDLORD FURNISHED DOOR
MANAGER	106F	HM WCS	YES	3'0"X 8'6"	3	LANDLORD FURNISHED DOOR
OPERATIONS	106G	HM WCS	YES	3'0"X 8'6"	3	LANDLORD FURNISHED DOOR
TOILET RM	106H	HM WCS		3'0"X 8'6"	4	LANDLORD FURNISHED DOOR
LEASING RECP	106J	HM HM 1 HR		3'0"X 7-2"	1	
PROJECT DIR	106K	HM WCS	YES	3'0"X 8'6"	3	LANDLORD FURNISHED DOOR
LEASING	106L	HM WCS	YES	3'0"X 8'6"	3	LANDLORD FURNISHED DOOR
CONFERENCE	106M	HM WCS	YES	3'0"X 8'6"	3	LANDLORD FURNISHED DOOR
WORK ROOM	106N	HM WCS		3'0"X 8'6"	3	LANDLORD FURNISHED DOOR
STORAGE	107A	HM HM 1 HR		6'0"X 7'2"	6	
HOUSEKPNG	107B	HM HM 1 HR		3'0"X 7-2"	7	
SECURITY	107C	HM HM		3'0"X 7-2"	8	HALF-GLASS DOOR
MAINT DIR	107D	HM HM		3'0"X 7-2"	8	HALF-GLASS DOOR
RECEPTION	107E	HM HM 1 HR		3'0"X 7-2"	1	
TOILET RM	107F	HM HM		2'8"X 7-2"	9	
LOCKERS	107G	HM HM		3'0"X 7-2"	10	
WORK AREA	107H	HM HM 3 HR		3'0"X 7-2"	11	
WORK AREA	107J	HM HM		3'0"X 7-2"	12	
MAINTENANCE	107K	HM HM		6'0"X 7'2"	13	GALV DOOR AND FRAME
SHOWER	107L	HM HM		3'0"X7'-2"	9	

SET 1
HINGES, 1 1/2PR, BB
LOCKSET, CLASSROOM
CLOSER

SET 2
HINGES, 2 PR
LOCKSET, CLO

SET 3
HINGES, 2 PR
LOCKSET, OFFICE

⚠

SET 4
HINGES, 2 PR
LOCKSET, TOILET RM

SET 6
HINGES, 3 PR
LOCKSET, STORERM
CLOSERS/ COORDINATOR
AUTO FLUSH BLTS
INTEG ASTRAGAL

SET 7
HINGES, 1 1/2PR
LOCKSET-STORERM
CLOSER

SET 8
HINGES, 1 1/2PR
LOCKSET, OFFICE

SET 9
HINGES, 1 1/2PR
LOCKSET, TOILET RM

SET 10
HINGES 1 1/2 PR
CLOSER
PASSAGE SET

SET 11
HINGES 1 1/2 PR
CLOSER
LOCKSET, OFFICE

SET 12
HINGES 1 1/2 PR
LOCKSET, OFFICE

SET 13
HINGES, 3 PR
PR FLUSH BOLTS
LOCKSET, CLASSRM
THRESHOLD
RAIN DRIP AT HEAD
WEATHERSTRIPPING
GJ-4 DOOR STOP

HARDWARE NOTES
PROVIDE SLIENCERS
LOCKSETS, HD CYLINDRICAL
BASIS - RUSWIN "STYLEMAKER"
KEY AS DIRECTED
NOTE LABEL **REQM'TS**
WALL BUMPERS-GJ-WB50

A door schedule with CAD-produced lettering. (Note revision added with manual lettering.)

SOUTH AVONDALE FIREHOUSE
FOR THE
CITY OF CINCINNATI   DIVISION OF FIRE
FOREST AVENUE   CINCINNATI, OHIO

(A)

NEW BRANCH OFFICE BUILDING
FOR THE
CINCINNATUS SAVINGS & LOAN CO
SPRINGDALE RD.   CINCINNATI, OHIO

(B)

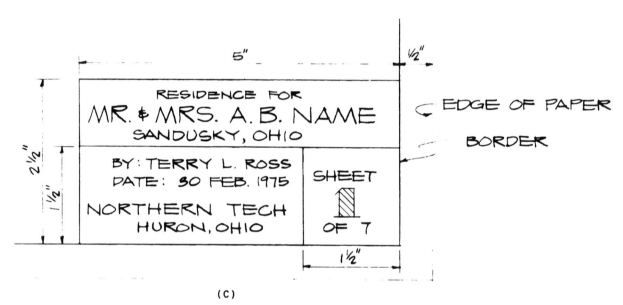

(C)

(A) A title block done with a mechanical lettering device is executed in ink with a Leroy stylus and several different sizes of lettering template. (B) This hand-lettered title block shows the distinctive styling achieved with a carefully controlled individual alphabet. The title has been spaced according to the importance of the words it contains. (C) In this typical title block no preprinted sheet material has been used. Attention has been given in this well-designed title block to the overall balance of the separate parts as well as to the size of the lettering.

occurs, foundation, soil, barrier, barricade, high, motor, nail, opening, overhang, plinth, blocking, millwork, lookout, kickplate, joint, door, caisson, acoustical, airspace, whaler, void, sash, plot plan, bolt, anchor, joist, batter board, building, column, duct, conditioning, floor, grout, jamb, louver, rawl plug, scaffolding, toggle, grommets, gravel, gym, waterproof, addition, base, estimate, lowest, progress, sealant, topographical, matte, concrete, vitrified, clay, sanitary, roofing, shelving, façade, exitway, lag-screw, vapor, frame, sidelight, walks, ocular, truss, gusset, vaulted, cathedral, scissors, vinyl, acrylic, latex, wall covering, surveyor, asphalt, macadam, fascia, valley, box, isocyanurate, composite, foam, transom, slate, adhesive, spacer, Glasweld, cast stone, plywood, envelope, waterstops, window, glass, glazing, subsurface, matting, drainage, architectural, and geotextile.

FRANKLIN GOTHIC

MICROGRAMMA BOLD EXTENDED

MICROGRAMMA LIGHT EXTENDED

MISTRAL

PEIGNOT MEDIUM

PEKIN

PLACARD BOLD CONDENSED

STENCIL

Sunset Script

WATUSI

A

A1

A1

A1

a

A1
a

Aa1
Aa1
Aa1
Aa1
Aa1

This chart shows the variation available in "rub-on" lettering. Many of the typefaces are decorative and not readily adaptable to working drawings in architecture. One popular face is Microgramma, which is used for titles and even for title sheets. Again, it is most important that a good clear typeface be selected for architectural work.

This chart shows the variation in size that the "rub-on" lettering provides. Although not all sizes are made in all typefaces, the selection is large. It is also a good example of the lettering that cannot be produced by hand or template. This form is a great time saver and has been used to advantage in many attractive presentations.

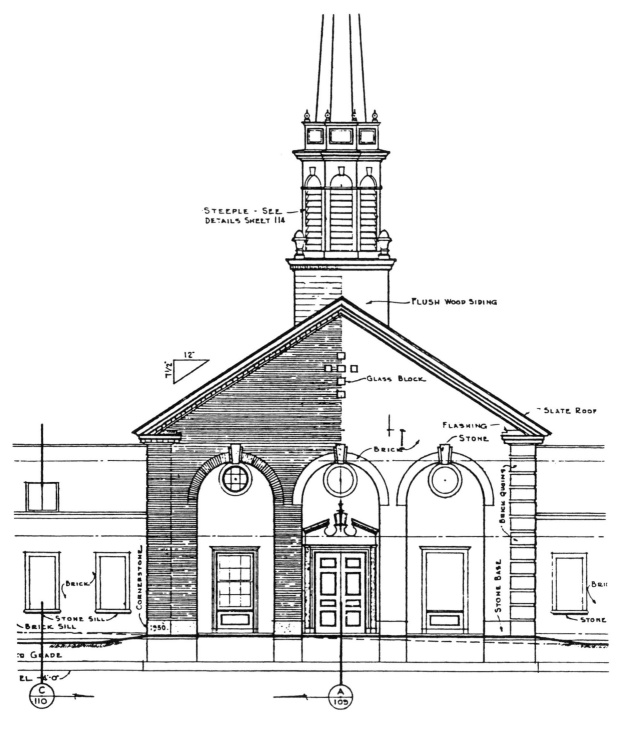

STEEPLE - SEE —
DETAILS SHEET 114

FLUSH WOOD SIDING

12"

7½"

GLASS BLOCK

SLATE ROOF

FLASHING
STONE

BRICK

BRICK QUOINS

CORNERSTONE

STONE BASE

BRICK

BRICK

STONE SILL
BRICK SILL

1950.

STONE

C
110

A
109

TO GRADE

EL - 4'-0"

ELEVATION - A

A well-executed drawing from days past. Note the "old-style" Roman lettering used in the title. This drawing was produced with pencil on linen.

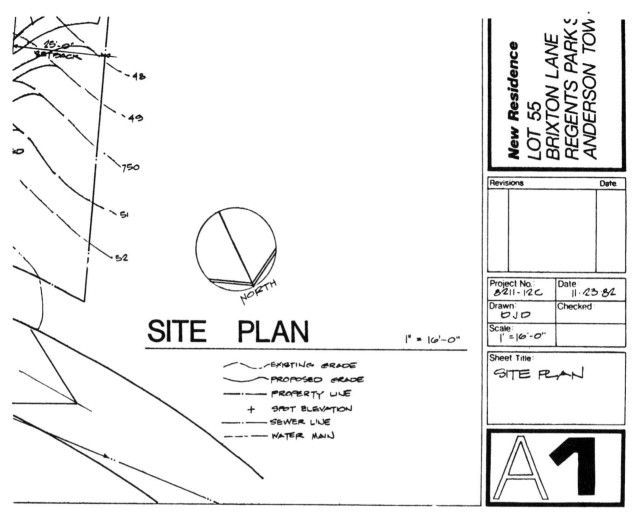

A portion of an actual working drawing sheet, which has utilized freehand, printed, and stick-on lettering (title block titles are printed; sheet number is stick-on).

9

Geometry and Scaling

That much of the work on working drawings is concerned with points, lines, and straight dimensions seems obvious. We find that a basic knowledge of geometry is necessary. In reality, basic training for working drawings requires the application of geometry and its various constructions and the adaptation of orthographic projection, in addition to sectioning and other auxiliary projections. Each of these fundamentals is equally important. In this chapter we show how we adapt them to our architectural working drawings. Each fundamental must be mastered so that when it becomes necessary to make a selection, the preferred method, as well as the dexterity, will be at hand.

The geometry of the work is nothing more than basic common sense. Geometry provides us with the ability to lay out general graphic shapes and helps us to deal with straight-line objects. Geometry is also the method by which we can produce various curves, from the simple circle to the multicentered curve with several radii. Of course, all geometry begins with a point, a specific location with no particular dimension, except that we find a simple pencil dot is a gross exaggeration of the true point.

A string of dots provides us with a line. Here, again, no width is intended; rather we rely on a representation. However, when we draw geometric curves and straight lines, we have specified directions and we can refer to a limited portion of the line. A straight line can continue to infinity in both directions if we do not give it some specific dimension.

A circle is the simplest of curved lines; in truth, it is a string of points all of which emanate as ends of radii starting at a single point in the center. The diameter is twice the length of the radius; it completes a cross-sectional dimension of the circle.

The circle is an example of the simple geometry that must be used on architectural working drawings. Following are some simple constructions that may be helpful from time to time. They are repeated here for convenience and are not meant to be basic construction information; the illustrations simply review the instructions.

Scaling in architectural work is vital. It is assumed that some knowledge of this subject has been acquired and that the reader knows the architectural scales. All drawings, with few exceptions (vicinity plans, isometric details, plumbing riser diagrams), should be drawn to scale. The scale should be maintained throughout the drawing. Of course, scale within the drawing does not change. At times, circumstances force the draftsman to show a feature not to scale (NTS). This may happen when a dimension changes radically and redrawing would be a burden, in which case all such dimensions must be identified as NTS.

The scaling should be done carefully and thoroughly. As many dimensions as possible should be given with one "set" of the scale; that is, do not scale one dimension and move the scale. Each move will produce errors that will accumulate, and at the end of the scaling a large, compounded error will have been built into the run. This error occurs most frequently when scaling between two fixed lines or points. It is handy to find scales that can be substituted to prevent scale movement; for example, a drawing at 1" = 1'-0" has a line of 9-inch dimension. Instead of scaling each one, use the 3/4-inch scale (a foot on this scale will equal 9 inches on the 1-inch scale) to measure these dimensions. No scale movement is required.

It is important to be accurate, but in architectural work the tolerances do not approach the ten-thousandths mandatory with machine design drawings. This does not suggest, however, that sloppy scaling can be tolerated.

It is also important that the correct, or proper, scale be selected for the drawings. Obviously, the more work that is to be shown on a drawing, the smaller the scale to be used; for example, a building plan that depicts a building several hundred feet long, is done at 1/8-inch, or 1/16-inch scale, never at 1½ inches. At the same time, details showing very confined areas of the work are useless if they are drawn too small (1/8-inch in lieu of 1½ inches, for example). It is good to keep some general principles in mind, and of course, one's experience will bring almost an automatic selection of scale. The principles, however, are

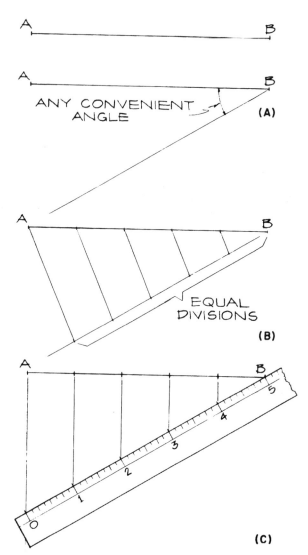

(A) ANY CONVENIENT ANGLE

(B) EQUAL DIVISIONS

(C)

The line AB is to be divided into a number of equal parts by the method shown in (B) and (C). First, draw any convenient angle from one end of the line. Connect the other with a point on the angled line. Divide the angled line into the number of parts desired for the other line. By using parallel lines, the first line will be equally subdivided; (C) shows the division of the angled line.

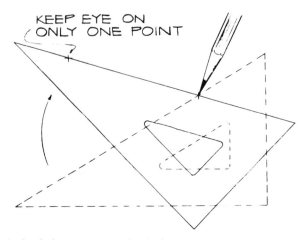

KEEP EYE ON ONLY ONE POINT

A simple but correct method of aligning points and using the triangle as a straightedge to produce a line. It can also be used to draw two lines from the same point (the pencil point).

(1) the more work to be shown, the smaller the scale and (2) the more detailed the work to be shown, or the smaller the area to be shown, the larger the scale.

This selection also is a factor in the readability of the drawing. Although the drafter may think that all the data can be shown at a selected scale, it may be that it *should not* be shown at that scale, because the data will be crowded (not crammed, it is hoped) together. It is good to remember that drawings, just like books, rely on the "white space" between the information for both separation of the data and to aid in reading the material. This small consideration can have a very drastic effect on how easily the project documents can be used in constructing the work; it is very important to everyone concerned.

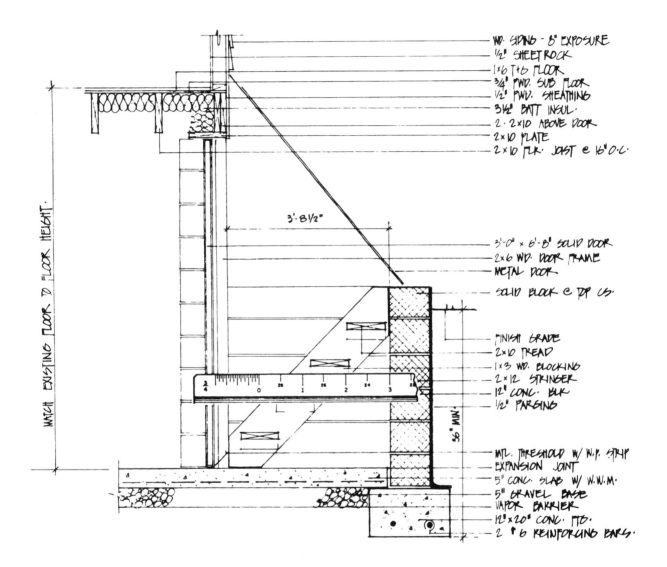

SECTION @ BASEMENT DOOR
SCALE ¾" - 1'-0"

A scale is superimposed on this detail to illustrate its proper use. To maintain the various parts in proper relation, accuracy is most important.

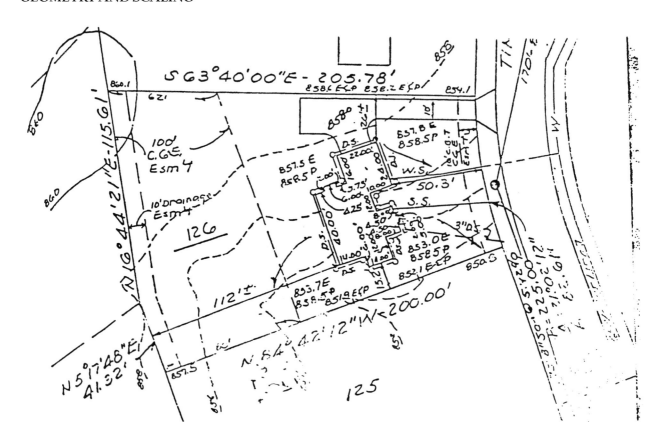

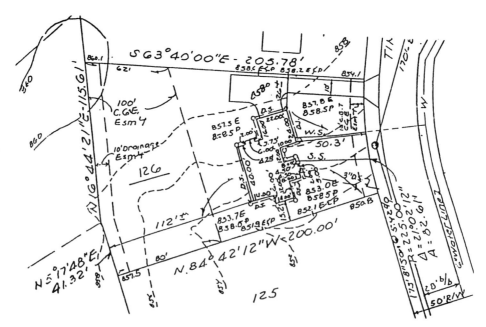

The examples show portions of the same plot plan, but at different scales. Note the difference in readability when the information is larger and more openly spaced.

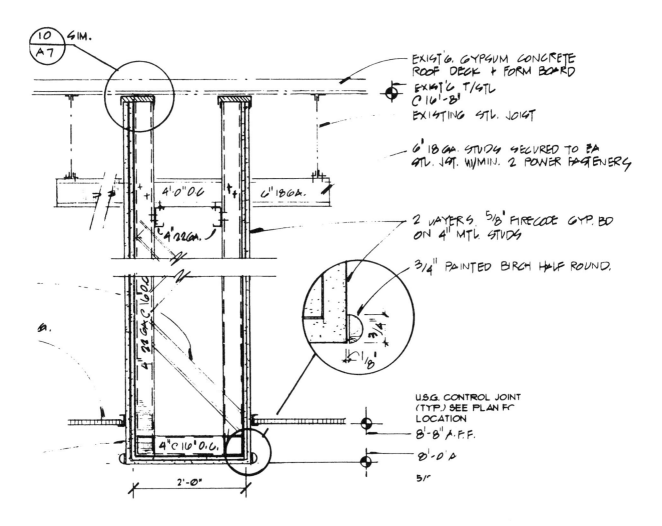

EXIST'G. GYPSUM CONCRETE ROOF DECK + FORM BOARD

EXIST'G T/STL
C 16'-8"

EXISTING STL. JOIST

6" 18 GA. STUDS SECURED TO EA STL. JST. W/MIN. 2 POWER FASTENERS

2 LAYERS. 5/8" FIRECODE GYP. BD ON 4" MTL. STUDS

3/4" PAINTED BIRCH HALF ROUND.

3/4"

1/8"

U.S.G. CONTROL JOINT (TYP.) SEE PLAN FC LOCATION

8'-8" A.F.F.

8'-0" ±

5/±

4'-0" O.C.   6" 18 GA.

4" 22 GA.

4" 22 GA. C 16' O.C.

4" C 16" O.C.

2'-0"

10
A7   SIM.

CEILING DROP

SCALE: 3/4"=1'-0"

An example of a deliberate decision to make an additional drawing at a larger scale to ensure that the work is shown in a clear and fully detailed manner.

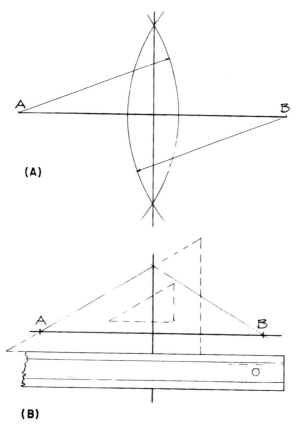

(A)

(B)

Two methods of constructing a perpendicular bisector of a line. Arcs are drawn in (A) by using radii greater than one-half the line length (the same radius is used for both arcs). When they intersect, above and below the line, they form points. A line drawn through these points is the perpendicular bisector of the given line. The same division is produced in (B) by using the 30-degree triangle. A line drawn through both ends of the given line will intersect, and a vertical triangle line through this intersection will again be the perpendicular bisector.

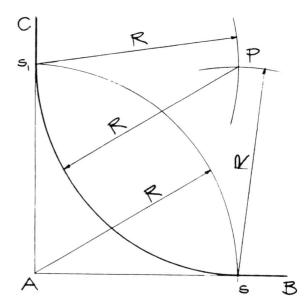

This example describes a method of inscribing a curve between the two lines. Using the radius (which must be known) and point A as the center, swing the arc that crosses both lines (at s and s₁). From these two points, using the same radius, swing two short intersecting arcs (point P). Again with the given radius, construct the curve desired from this point (P), taking care that the curve is tangent to the lines at points s and s₁.

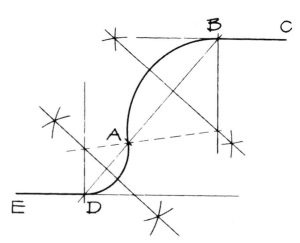

The first section of a continuous curve between two fixed points (or lines) starts at D; the compound curve terminates at B. The radii for the two curves should be laid off (these are the solid lines perpendicular to points B and D). The centers are connected by the dotted line; the points, by the solid line DB. Point A, the intersection of the two segments of the curve, is established.

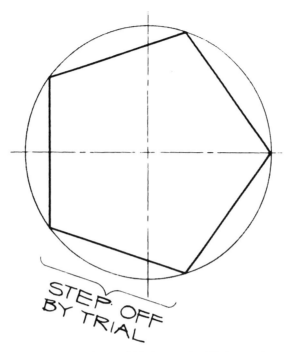

STEP OFF
BY TRIAL

This pentagon, whose five angles must add up to 360 degrees (or 72 degrees in each), is formed by trial and error. It is impossible for the eye to discern these angles, but an adjustable triangle can be used. Otherwise, step off straight lengths around the circle until five equal sides are achieved.

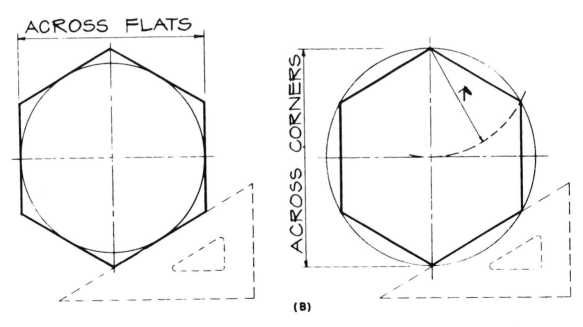

ACROSS FLATS

ACROSS CORNERS

(A)

(B)

A hexagon can be formed in two ways: (A) shows the hexagon circumscribed on a given circle by using the 30-degree angle of the triangle. As shown, the given distance would be "across the flats." (B) fits the hexagon into a circle. The known distance is across the corners. The 30-degree angle and the radius are used to form the "hex."

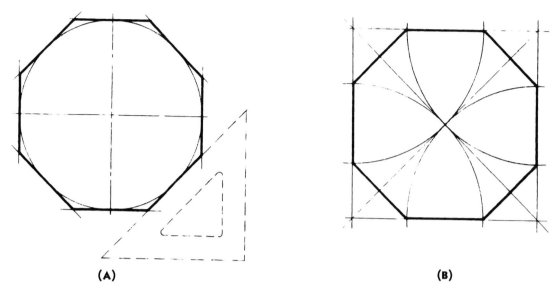

(A) **(B)**

(A) shows the formation of an octagon. To circumscribe the figure around a given circle, use 45-degree lines as a tangent and connect with horizontal and vertical lines. (B) describes the method of producing this figure within a given square. Draw the diagonals of the square and, using the corners as centers, draw part circles from one side to the other. Their radii should be equal to the length of one-half the diagonal. The points projected onto the perimeter of the drawing are then connected to produce the octagon.

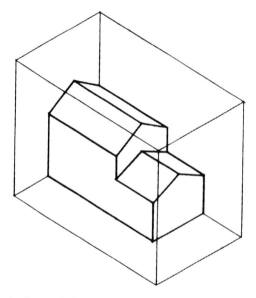

Orthographic projection is the basis of all working drawings. Imagine that the building is in a glass box. By viewing one side at a time and drawing on the glass side, the observer can produce five views of the building (it is possible to produce a sixth (bottom) view, but it is not used in architectural work). These drawings show the four building elevations and roof plan.

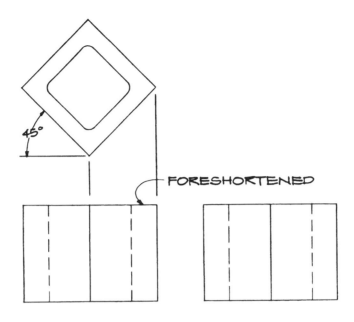

FORESHORTENED

45°

TILTED

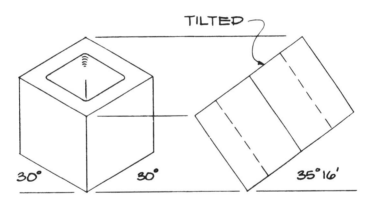

30°   30°   35° 16'

ISOMETRIC PROJECTION

Illustration of the basic principle for isometric drawing. Note subject is rotated and tilted, so that three surfaces are visible in one drawing. This is a very handy technique for complicated details that are not easily depicted otherwise.

GEOMETRY AND SCALING

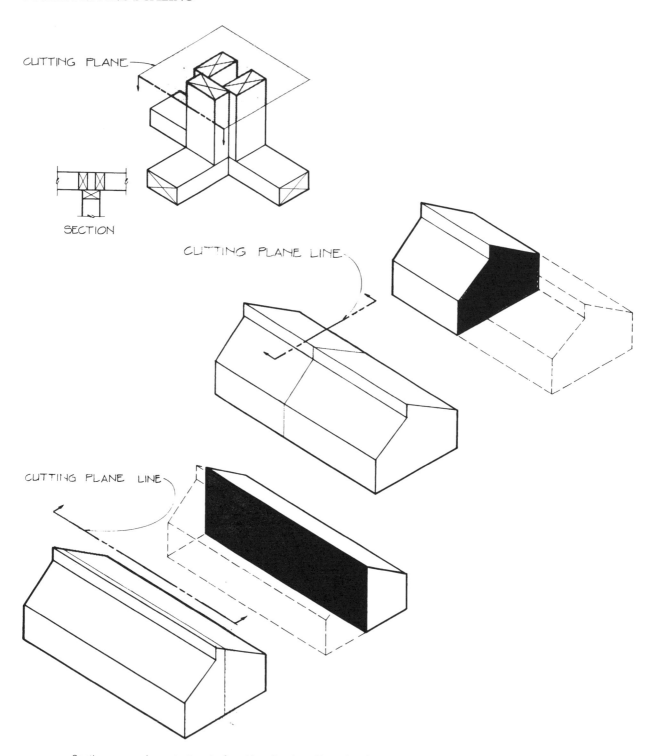

CUTTING PLANE

SECTION

CUTTING PLANE LINE

CUTTING PLANE LINE

Sections are an important part of working drawings. Examples show the basic principles of sections: the plan (horizontal section), the cross section, and the longitudinal section.

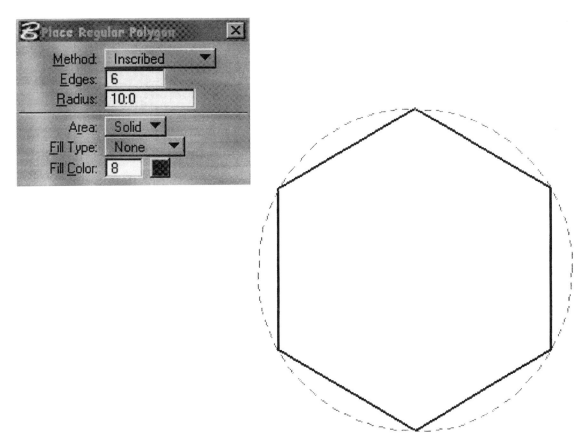

CAD obviously simplifies the creation of a polygon. By merely entering "Method, Edges, and Radius" in the palette, the polygon is quickly and automatically produced. Easy modification of the three palette requirements will produce any of a massive range of polygons, as may be required—even those with a very unusual number of sides [try figuring out an eleven-sided figure by manual means]

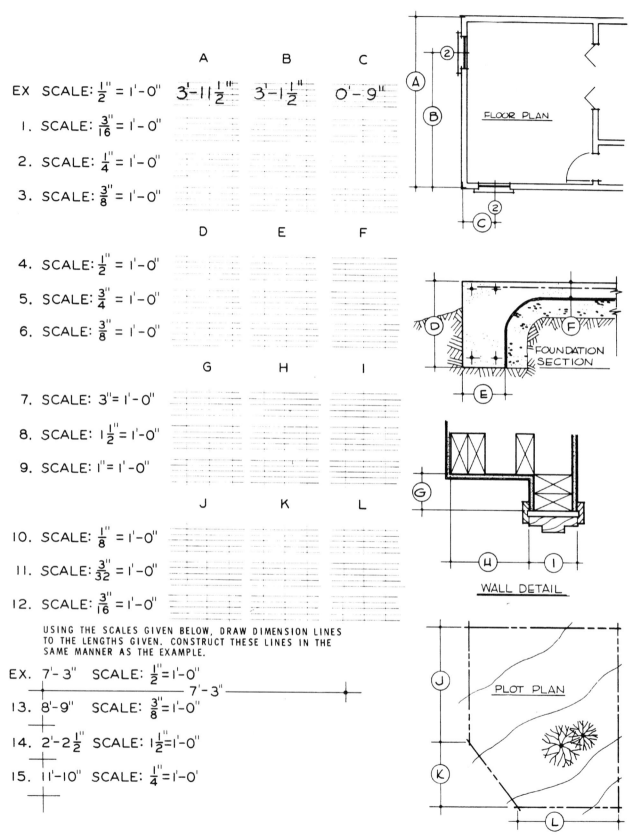

	A	B	C
EX SCALE: $\frac{1}{2}'' = 1'-0''$	$3'-11\frac{1}{2}''$	$3'-1\frac{1}{2}''$	$0'-9''$
1. SCALE: $\frac{3}{16}'' = 1'-0''$			
2. SCALE: $\frac{1}{4}'' = 1'-0''$			
3. SCALE: $\frac{3}{8}'' = 1'-0''$			

	D	E	F
4. SCALE: $\frac{1}{2}'' = 1'-0''$			
5. SCALE: $\frac{3}{4}'' = 1'-0''$			
6. SCALE: $\frac{3}{8}'' = 1'-0''$			

	G	H	I
7. SCALE: $3'' = 1'-0''$			
8. SCALE: $1\frac{1}{2}'' = 1'-0''$			
9. SCALE: $1'' = 1'-0''$			

	J	K	L
10. SCALE: $\frac{1}{8}'' = 1'-0''$			
11. SCALE: $\frac{3}{32}'' = 1'-0''$			
12. SCALE: $\frac{3}{16}'' = 1'-0''$			

USING THE SCALES GIVEN BELOW, DRAW DIMENSION LINES
TO THE LENGTHS GIVEN. CONSTRUCT THESE LINES IN THE
SAME MANNER AS THE EXAMPLE.

EX. $7'-3''$ SCALE: $\frac{1}{2}'' = 1'-0''$

$\longmapsto$ ———— $7'-3''$ ————— +

13. $8'-9''$ SCALE: $\frac{3}{8}'' = 1'-0''$

14. $2'-2\frac{1}{2}''$ SCALE: $1\frac{1}{2}'' = 1'-0''$

15. $11'-10''$ SCALE: $\frac{1}{4}'' = 1'-0'$

Using an architect's scale, measure the lines as indicated [use the scale noted] and list your answers

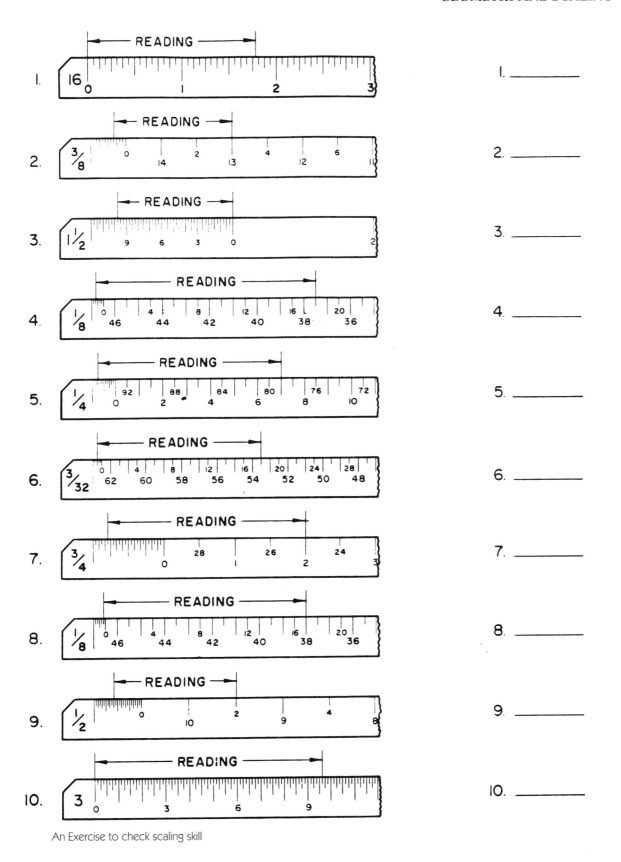

An Exercise to check scaling skill

1. _____

2. _____

3. _____

4. _____

5. _____

6. _____

7. _____

8. _____

9. _____

10. _____

10

Lines and Drafting Expression

I t is most important in drafting architectural working drawings that the information be conveyed correctly, simply, and clearly. Expression in the drawing is mainly concerned with the technique employed. Working drawings are an important part of the total architectural service in that we must first communicate with tradespeople, estimators, and contractors—indeed, everyone concerned with the construction of the project. These people rely totally on the architectural working drawings for the technical information they need to build the building. A definite effort should be made to make the drawings expressive and at the same time give way to local convention. In the final analysis we must produce accurately scaled drawings that properly illustrate all the parts.

It can be a great help to the final product if the drafter has enough knowledge to put him- or herself in the place of the tradesman, the carpenter, or the contractor. In this way the drafter can determine how easily the drawings can be read or whether the information required is readily available without searching through the entire set. When the information is found, it should transmit the drafter's ideas with a minimum of effort, a minimum consistent with a minimum of misinterpretation.

Lines are one of the most expressive aspects of working drawings. Every line drawn should have some significance or there really is no reason for its existence. This significance, of course, can vary quite a bit and can be directly conveyed to the user by virtue of the weight or width of the line. Example: If a line has little importance, it should be light; on the other hand, if a line makes an important contribution to the drawing, it should be heavy and perhaps broad. Each line must be evaluated before it is drawn, and this comes only with practice. If we become too shy and produce a very light tracing, much of the line work will be lost in the reproduction process. Here we must consider the lecturer and the monotone delivery that puts an audience to sleep. Just as in lettering, "monotone" drafting has no place in the architectural working drawing. Line variation, or contrast of lines, contributes directly to the success of the drawings.

This principle should also be exercised in using computer-aided drafting (CAD) equipment for the production of the drawings. Too often operators either use one line weight for all of

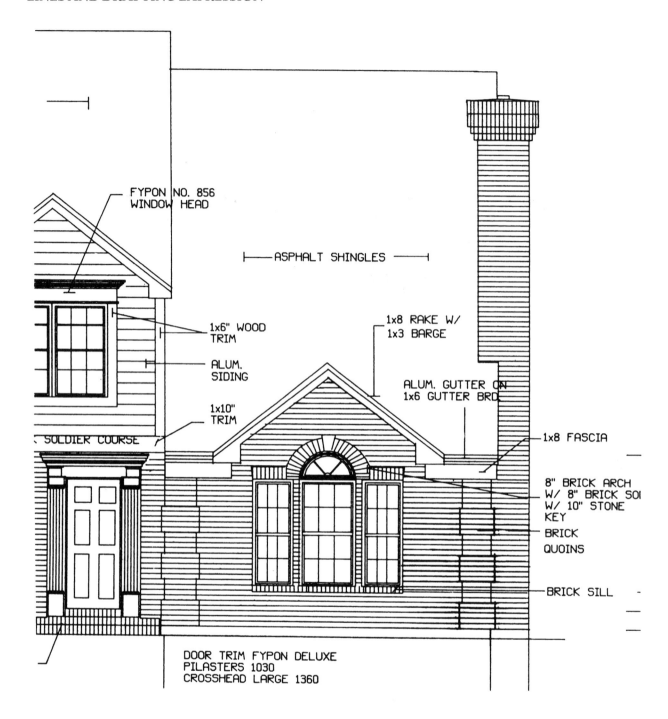

FYPON NO. 856
WINDOW HEAD

ASPHALT SHINGLES

1x6" WOOD
TRIM

ALUM.
SIDING

1x10"
TRIM

1x8 RAKE W/
1x3 BARGE

ALUM. GUTTER ON
1x6 GUTTER BRD.

SOLDIER COURSE

1x8 FASCIA

8" BRICK ARCH
W/ 8" BRICK SOI
W/ 10" STONE
KEY

BRICK
QUOINS

BRICK SILL

DOOR TRIM FYPON DELUXE
PILASTERS 1030
CROSSHEAD LARGE 1360

the lines in the drawing or rely on the preset "default" settings of the software program. Both of these practices basically give up control of the process to the computer, allowing it to do what someone else has programmed into the system without any knowledge of the circumstances of the project at hand. Although neither of these is a problem with the technical aspect of the project, it is a tremendous aid to user readability when line weights are *properly* varied, using several different line weights. This aids, significantly, the ease of reading the drawings by more distinctly differentiating between various materials and elements of the construction.

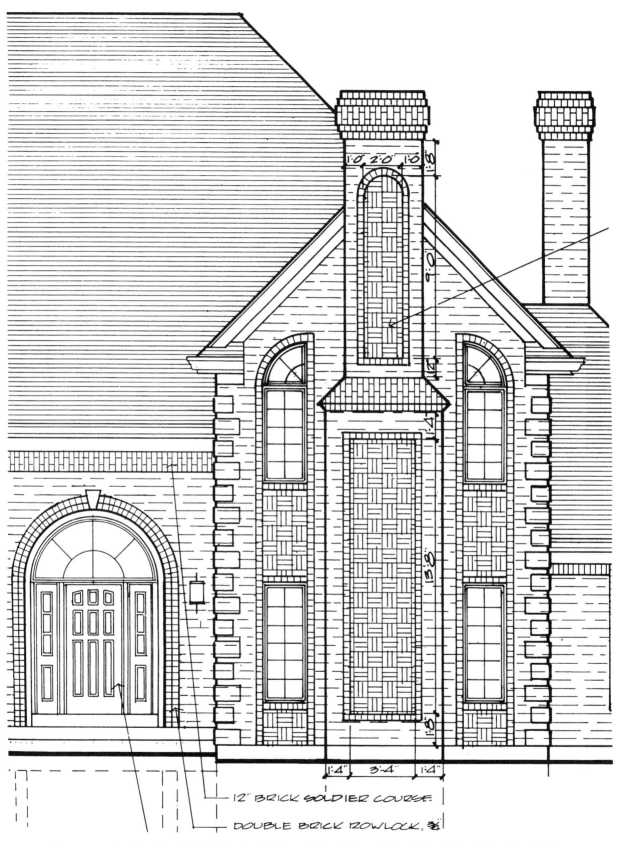

12" BRICK SOLDIER COURSE

DOUBLE BRICK ROWLOCK, ⅜

These examples show the distinct advantage to line weight variation, which adds both "sparkle" and readability to the drawing. Note drawing produced with CAD.

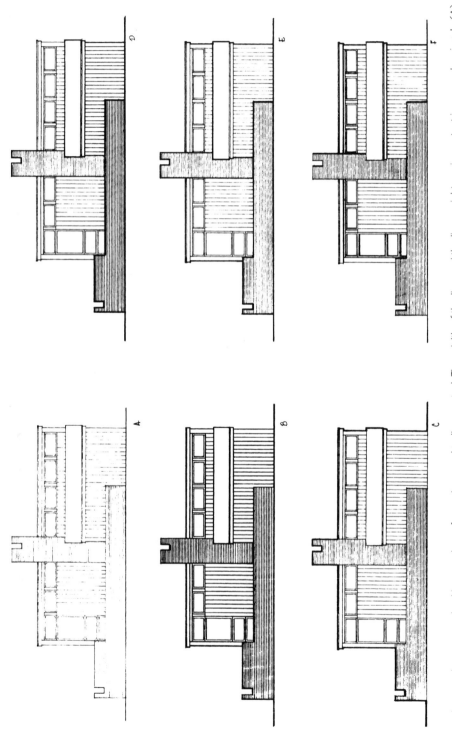

Drawings can be approached in a number of ways in regard to line control. The width of the line and the line weight are important in every drawing. In (A) all lines are the same tone, and the drawing looks washed out. In (B) too much compensation has been made; the lines lack variation and are too heavy. The profile method is shown in (C); a dark line defines the profile of the building. This is a better drawing because of its variation. In (D) the lines are toned to show depth; the closer the object to the viewer, the darker the lines. (E) is perhaps the best drawing; the profile lines and planes of the building are dark. Lighter lines characterize the work appearing "on" the planes. The shadow principle is applied in (F). A direction of light is established, and the lines are varied to show shadows on the faces of the buildings.

All CAD programs have the capacity for changing line weights as the operator desires. Some forethought is required on the part of the operator. In older systems there may be a need to change plotter pens, and in newer systems alternative commands may have to be injected into the program to ensure that line weight variation is produced. The extra effort is clearly worthwhile.

Care must also be taken that there is no undue reliance on, or misconception about, the various colors used for lines on the CAD visual display. The colors are used solely to differentiate between various surfaces or materials, but they do *not* indicate the density, width, or intensity of the line work. Colors are used to separate information on the operator's screen, but do not translate to the finished product. Often the eye will register the colored lines as a valid and satisfactory presentation, but the plotted result will be imperfect, if not wholly improper. This is one of the major differences between CAD and manual operations. With CAD a line can appear to be one thing, when in fact it is something quite different as to value and weight (in manual work, the drafter sees, immediately, what the line is and whether its weight is correct). If this CAD "hazard" is not kept firmly in mind constantly, the best of drawings, technically, may prove to be most inadequate when plotted. This is a major checkpoint for the validity of the CAD work and is an integral part of the operator's level of care in the production of the drawing(s). CAD can and should be manipulated/modified in this instance—always—to ensure the most readable document possible.

In addition, at a minimum the concept of three line weights (one for total object outline, one for planes within the object, and one for circumstances/conditions occurring on the planes) must be followed as in other architectural presentations. The configuration of the entire construction depicted in the detail is the "object." The architectural material symbols are the various "planes." The other circumstances are such things as the reinforcing, ties, strap, leader lines, and so forth, which are vital but need not be depicted meticulously (inasmuch as they are, mainly, described in the specifications and are of such small size that trying to show them to scale is doomed to failure).

It would be well to study examples of good line work to learn where to place emphasis and, of course, where to restrain it. In reality, the heavy line is used more and is more effective in most situations. Examples in this chapter show how a plan or elevation can be improved with a heavy outline that actually silhouettes the object. This silhouetting also applies, for example, to the cut portions of materials in a section. It is also generally accepted that the grade line or roof overhang will be shown in a heavy line to make an immediate impression on the user. A number of techniques are illustrated here for the use of lines, but it can easily be seen from the examples that line variation must be a part of our drafting technique.

While we are varying the lines, we must be concerned with consistency in the line work. Lead pencils, for instance, must be kept sharp, although various pressures can be used. It should also be understood that lines can be gone over, if done carefully, to increase the emphasis. In some instances ink will give a heavy black massing to important lines. One good habit for a draftsman to acquire is the application of extra pressure to the beginning and ending of all pencil lines; these lines will then show a definite starting and stopping point without fading off. It is not good practice to show "fizzled out" or ragged endings. Architectural drawing differs from other types of drafting in that the line work is more distinctive and pleasing if there are slight extensions, or crosses, at intersections, rather than a sharp point. This technique is actually simpler, because in laying out the drawing we are extending its lines beyond their permanent dimensions and are reducing our effort by allowing this slight deviation. This is not done in a haphazard way with giant intersections, but by recognizing the crossing point with only slight emphasis.

Every kind of line should be taken into account in drafting expression. Many types of broken or dashed lines are used on a drawing and, again, should be done carefully and with added expression. If a dashed line appears in the drawing, it has importance and should be treated in direct proportion to its value. Hidden objects, hidden surfaces, or alternate positions of various features are often shown by dashed lines and should be given emphasis by adding slight pressure at their ends. The dashes should not be too widely spaced; at the same time, variety can be added to the intervals—for example, a line of long dashes and rather short intervals. It is most important, however, when showing a broken line, that the same motif be retained for its entire length; that is to say, the intervals and the dashes should be uniform. This uniformity should be carried out

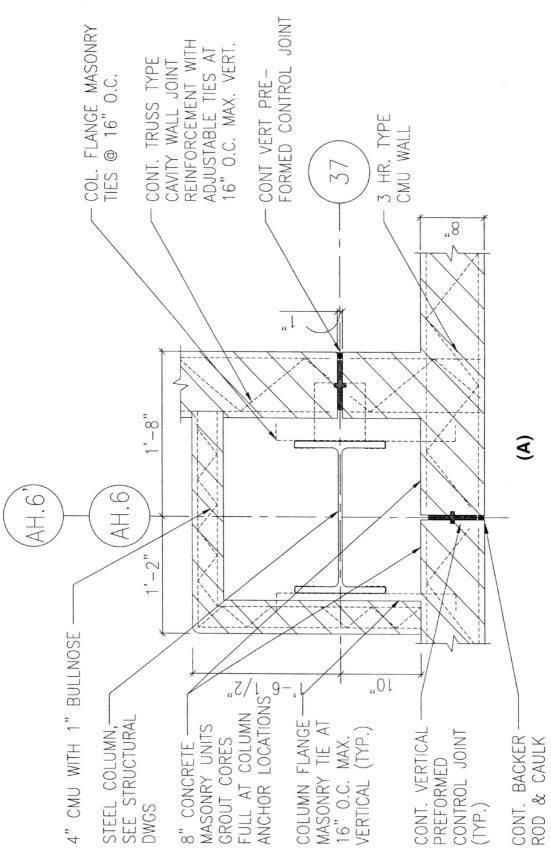

(A)

The series of four drawings [of the same detail], which follows is included to show the variation that CAD operations can produce, and how the use of varying line weights can aid the overall readability and use of the drawing. Drawing A depicts the detail, with all lightweight lines; Drawing B uses all dark line weights. In Drawing C, a middle-ground medium line weight was used for all lines. The final drawing, D, uses a combination of line weights; this is the method highly recommended for use. Of course, the operator needs to be alert, and the system modified to allow such variation. Also, there is a need to follow established office standards, which may vary from this recommendation. [See Case Studies in CAD Detailing in Chapter 35]

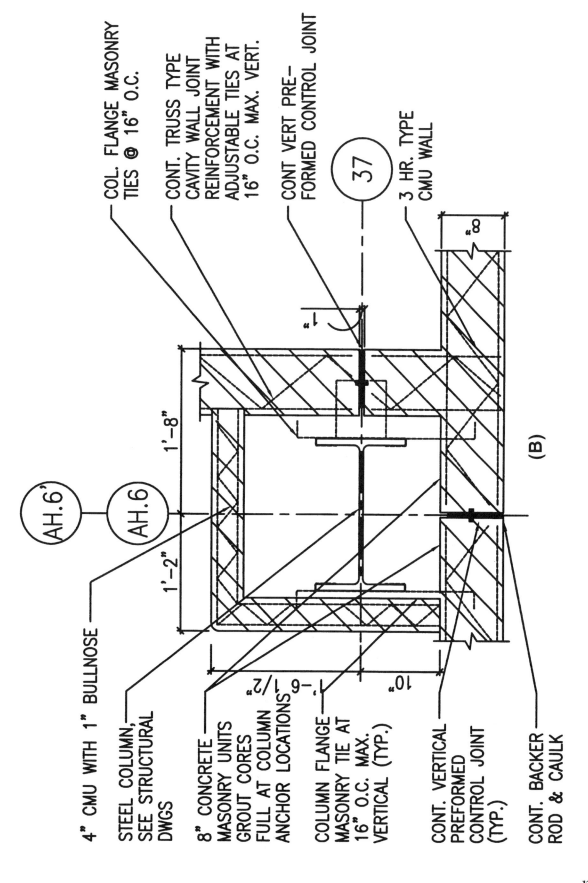

(B)

4" CMU WITH 1" BULLNOSE

STEEL COLUMN, SEE STRUCTURAL DWGS

8" CONCRETE MASONRY UNITS GROUT CORES FULL AT COLUMN ANCHOR LOCATIONS

COLUMN FLANGE MASONRY TIE AT 16" O.C. MAX. VERTICAL (TYP.)

CONT. VERTICAL PREFORMED CONTROL JOINT (TYP.)

CONT. BACKER ROD & CAULK

COL. FLANGE MASONRY TIES @ 16" O.C.

CONT. TRUSS TYPE CAVITY WALL JOINT REINFORCEMENT WITH ADJUSTABLE TIES AT 16" O.C. MAX. VERT.

CONT VERT PRE– FORMED CONTROL JOINT

3 HR. TYPE CMU WALL

133

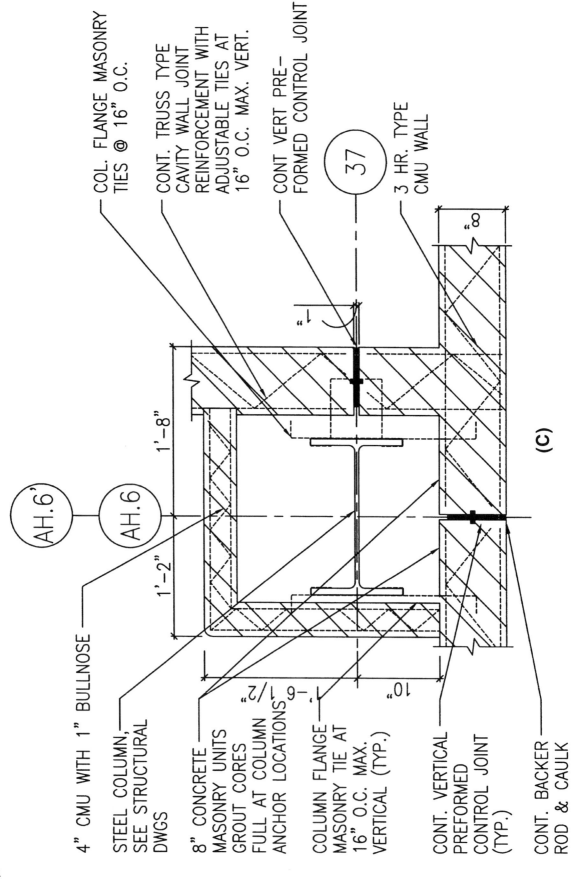

COL. FLANGE MASONRY TIES @ 16" O.C.

CONT. TRUSS TYPE CAVITY WALL JOINT REINFORCEMENT WITH ADJUSTABLE TIES AT 16" O.C. MAX. VERT.

CONT VERT PRE-FORMED CONTROL JOINT

37

3 HR. TYPE CMU WALL

AH.6

AH.6

4" CMU WITH 1" BULLNOSE

STEEL COLUMN, SEE STRUCTURAL DWGS

8" CONCRETE MASONRY UNITS GROUT CORES FULL AT COLUMN ANCHOR LOCATIONS

COLUMN FLANGE MASONRY TIE AT 16" O.C. MAX. VERTICAL (TYP.)

CONT. VERTICAL PREFORMED CONTROL JOINT (TYP.)

CONT. BACKER ROD & CAULK

(C)

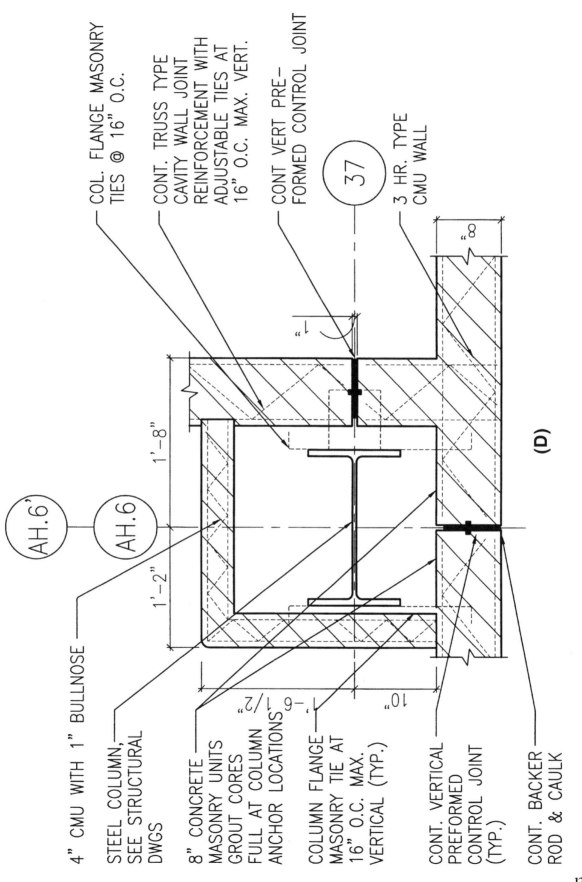

COL. FLANGE MASONRY TIES @ 16" O.C.

CONT. TRUSS TYPE CAVITY WALL JOINT REINFORCEMENT WITH ADJUSTABLE TIES AT 16" O.C. MAX. VERT.

CONT VERT PRE-FORMED CONTROL JOINT

37

3 HR. TYPE CMU WALL

4" CMU WITH 1" BULLNOSE

STEEL COLUMN, SEE STRUCTURAL DWGS

8" CONCRETE MASONRY UNITS GROUT CORES FULL AT COLUMN ANCHOR LOCATIONS

COLUMN FLANGE MASONRY TIE AT 16" O.C. MAX. VERTICAL (TYP.)

CONT. VERTICAL PREFORMED CONTROL JOINT (TYP.)

CONT. BACKER ROD & CAULK

AH.6'

AH.6

(D)

135

throughout the drawing in that the same character of line work should describe like objects. A drawing can become excessively complicated when one object overrides another, and extreme care must be taken in the execution of broken lines.

Object lines, of course, should carry the most impact, because here we are describing the parameters of the object—the outline. The range of line weights varies between this object line and the extension lines (for the dimensions), which are drawn in a much lighter line weight.

So far we have talked of the drafted line on working drawings, but another set of lines, the leaders, or leader lines, which are drawn from a note or a dimension to the point of application on the drawing, must be included. These leaders can be straight, drafted, curved, or freehand. It is good practice to include an arrowhead or dot on the object end of the leader. Although various techniques have been devised, the most effective leaders are those that can be immediately identified and are in no way confused with the object lines or other parts of the drawing. They should appear as connectors between the notes and objects and should never be open to misinterpretation. This is the purpose of the more angular leader or some type of offset curve. Usually, the leaders are added after the notation has been entered. It is important that these connectors be prevented from forming a "spaghetti overlay." Instead, they should be drawn neatly, without crossing one another, in a direct route to the points to which they apply. A leader should start at the beginning or end of a note, but never at some midpoint. There are times when a circle or balloon may be employed for more effective identification of parts; for example, in structural drawings to call out reinforcing bars.

Leaders are often used to show angles in geometric shapes; circles may be shown, perhaps, by radii or diameter, and other dimensioning is not necessary.

BREAK LINES: Fine lines with offsets to show a break in or the termination of a partial view.

Used to eliminate unimportant portions of detail. Break lines may be done freehand.

CENTER LINES: Fine lines made with alternate dots and long dashes to indicate symmetry about an axis and to locate centers of window and door symbols. Lines should be extended beyond the outline of the object or view.

CUT LINES: Prominent broken lines consisting commonly of two dots and a dash motif to indicate the plane of a section. Arrowheads on either end show direction of view. A circular detail designator may be incorporated at either end as well.

DIMENSION LINES: Fine lines with arrowheads at either end to show length, width, thickness, and depth of a given dimension. Numerical dimensions are placed above and centered along the line.

EXTENSION LINES: Fine lines relating dimension lines to that item being dimensioned (sized). Should not touch object or feature; extend beyond dimension line.

HIDDEN LINES: Medium-weight broken lines composed of uniform dashes indicate hidden surfaces or intersections; in sections they show features occurring beyond our view. Also used to show old construction.

LEADERS: Fine lines with an arrow or dot at the point to which they apply. Drawn at an angle from note to point of application; leader lines never cross other leader lines! They may be drawn freehand.

OUTLINES: Prominent lines representing surface edges or the intersection of two surfaces. As the heaviest lines in a drawing, they separate the object, or material, from the surrounding space.

POCHÉ: Fine line work, usually vertical, horizontal, or angular; gives the surface the appearance of a halftone. Line work made with conventional symbols of the materials, used in elevations and sections.

(text continues on p. 152)

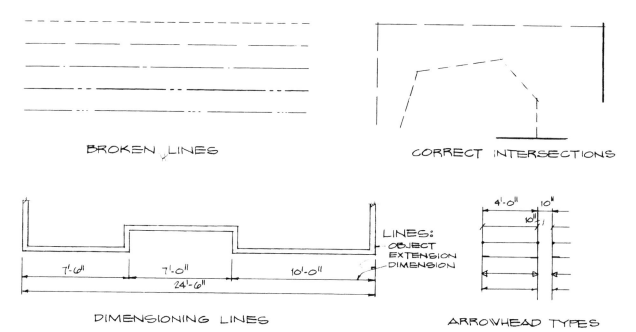

BROKEN LINES

CORRECT INTERSECTIONS

DIMENSIONING LINES

LINES:
OBJECT
EXTENSION
DIMENSION

ARROWHEAD TYPES

Many factors must be recognized in the production of working drawings. A variety of broken (or dotted) lines allows the draftsman to show detail in a distinctive manner. Lines slightly crossed are good practice. Note the distinction between lines in the dimensioning procedure. Here, variation in line weight is essential. Dimensions can be defined by a number of terminations. They must be used consistently (but not all in one set of drawings) and should be crisp and clear. Also make sure that they are exactly placed to direct the dimension to the point required.

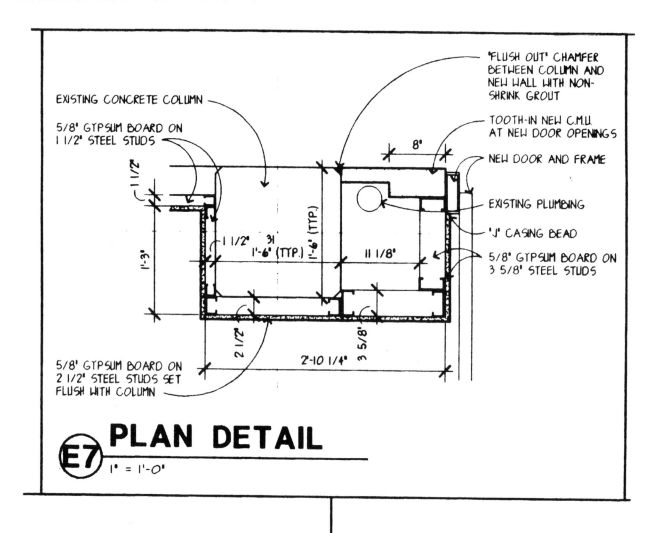

EXISTING CONCRETE COLUMN

5/8" GYPSUM BOARD ON
1 1/2" STEEL STUDS

'FLUSH OUT' CHAMFER
BETWEEN COLUMN AND
NEW WALL WITH NON-
SHRINK GROUT

TOOTH-IN NEW C.M.U.
AT NEW DOOR OPENINGS

NEW DOOR AND FRAME

EXISTING PLUMBING

'J' CASING BEAD

5/8" GYPSUM BOARD ON
3 5/8" STEEL STUDS

5/8" GYPSUM BOARD ON
2 1/2" STEEL STUDS SET
FLUSH WITH COLUMN

1 1/2"
3"
1'-6" (TYP.)
1'-6" (TYP.)
11 1/8"
8"
1'-3"
2 1/2"
3 5/8"
2'-10 1/4"

Ⓔ7 PLAN DETAIL

1" = 1'-0"

Existing work should always be shown in lighter weight lines; new work in dark lines. Check this drawing for inconsistent use of lines.

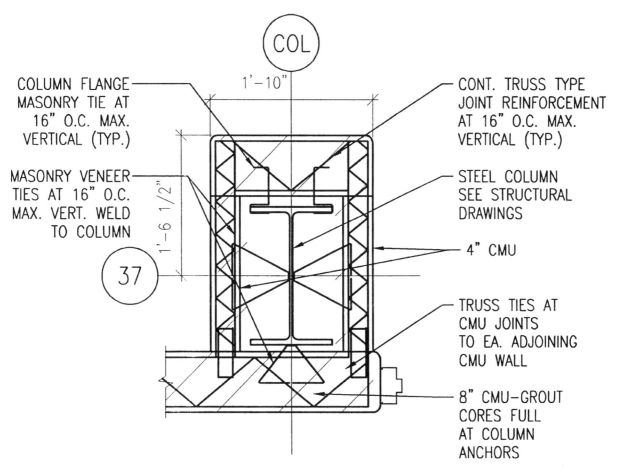

COL

1'-10"

COLUMN FLANGE
MASONRY TIE AT
16" O.C. MAX.
VERTICAL (TYP.)

MASONRY VENEER
TIES AT 16" O.C.
MAX. VERT. WELD
TO COLUMN

1'-6 1/2"

37

CONT. TRUSS TYPE
JOINT REINFORCEMENT
AT 16" O.C. MAX.
VERTICAL (TYP.)

STEEL COLUMN
SEE STRUCTURAL
DRAWINGS

4" CMU

TRUSS TIES AT
CMU JOINTS
TO EA. ADJOINING
CMU WALL

8" CMU-GROUT
CORES FULL
AT COLUMN
ANCHORS

This detail does not follow the "3 line" theory. Note that the darker lines show items that are stock items and of lesser importance, relatively, than the lines of the walls themselves, for example. Good information is here, but the line work could be of greater assistance in readability of the drawing.

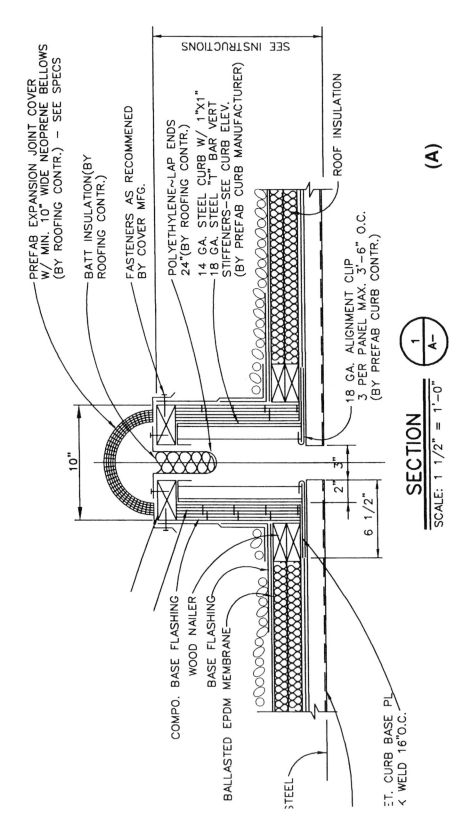

SECTION

SCALE: 1 1/2" = 1'-0"

(A)

These two details show distinctly the need for variation in line weight. Note, in B that the use of dark lines help distinguish the various materials; in A everything appears the same, and is difficult to distinguish one from the other.

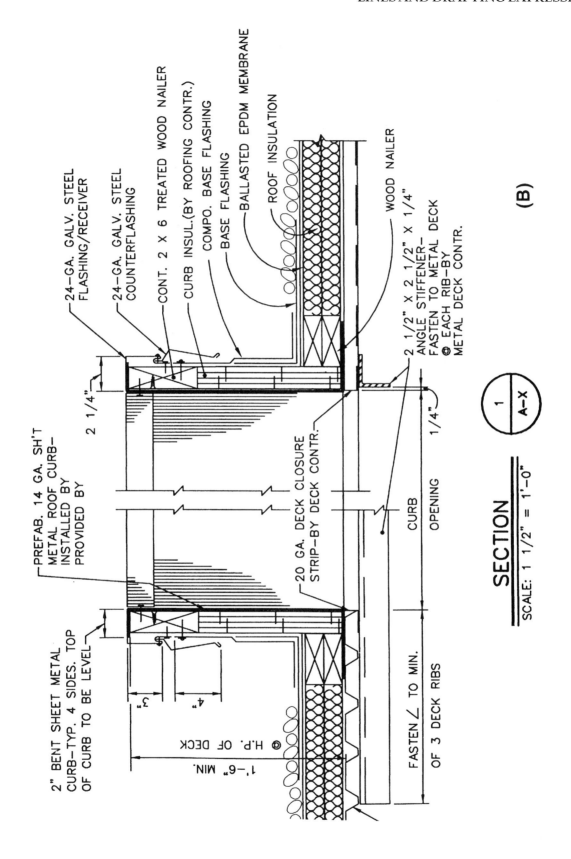

SECTION

SCALE: 1 1/2" = 1'-0"

(B)

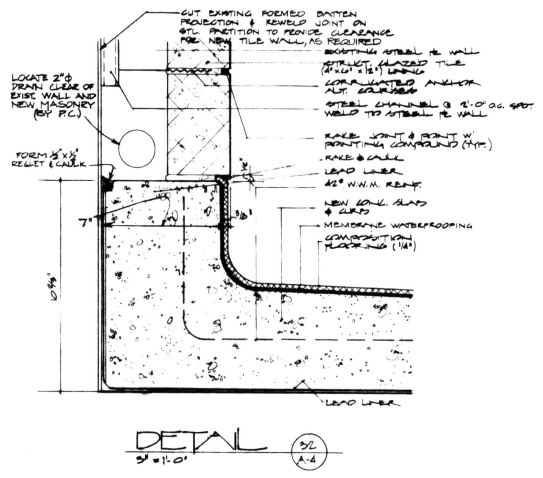

CUT EXISTING FORMED BATTEN PROJECTION & REWELD JOINT ON STL. PARTITION TO PROVIDE CLEARANCE FOR NEW TILE WALL, AS REQUIRED

EXISTING STEEL PL WALL

STRUCT. GLAZED TILE (4"x6" x 12") LINING

CORRUGATED ANCHOR ALT. COURSES

STEEL CHANNEL @ 2'-0" O.C. SPOT WELD TO STEEL PL WALL

RAKE JOINT & POINT W/ POINTING COMPOUND (TYP.)

RAKE & CAULK

LEAD LINER

12" W.W.M. REINF.

NEW CONC. SLAB & CURB

MEMBRANE WATERPROOFING

COMPOSITION FLOORING (1/4")

LOCATE 2"⌀ DRAIN CLEAR OF EXIST. WALL AND NEW MASONRY (BY P.C.)

FORM ½" x ½" REGLET & CAULK

7"

10 ⅔"

3/8"

LEAD LINER

DETAIL   32 / A-4
3" = 1'-0"

This fine example of line work has added demands, for several items of material are very thin; still they must be shown (in this case the waterproofing). The symbols and the leader lines also function well without distracting from the body of the drawing.

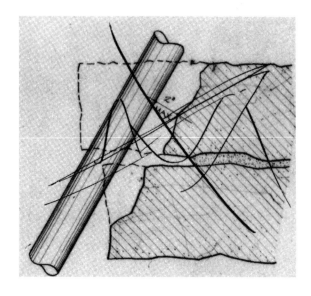

Control of line, both in weight and quality, is noticeably good. The symbols are properly related in intensity to the object lines.

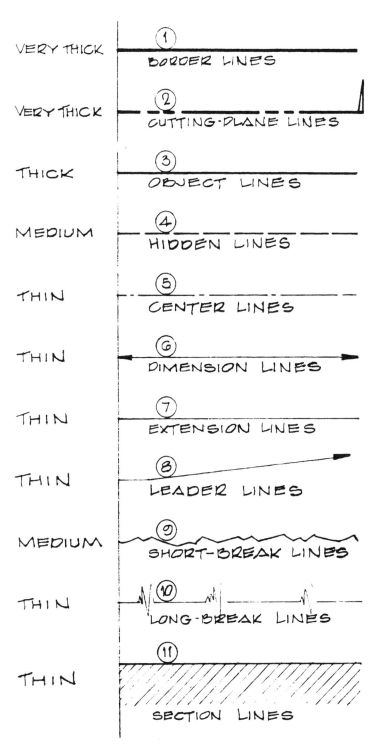

VERY THICK — ① BORDER LINES

VERY THICK — ② CUTTING-PLANE LINES

THICK — ③ OBJECT LINES

MEDIUM — ④ HIDDEN LINES

THIN — ⑤ CENTER LINES

THIN — ⑥ DIMENSION LINES

THIN — ⑦ EXTENSION LINES

THIN — ⑧ LEADER LINES

MEDIUM — ⑨ SHORT-BREAK LINES

THIN — ⑩ LONG-BREAK LINES

THIN — ⑪ SECTION LINES

Manually drafted lines with different meanings, and different line weights.

———————————————————————————— 0

———————————————————————————— 1

———————————————————————————— 2

———————————————————————————— 3

———————————————————————————— 4

———————————————————————————— 5

———————————————————————————— 6

———————————————————————————— 7

———————————————————————————— 8

———————————————————————————— 9

———————————————————————————— 10

———————————————————————————— 11

———————————————————————————— 12

———————————————————————————— 13

———————————————————————————— 14

———————————————————————————— 15

A small palette of the numerous lines that MicroStation can utilize [whole numbers designations].

Line Weight = 0

Leader lines for text notes
Floor patterns (brick, carpet, tile)
Stair tread lines [1]
Column grid centerlines [1]
Elevators and shafts- **walls [1]; elev. Car [0]**
Casework/millwork [1]
Door swings
Beam edges [1]
Beam centerlines [1]
Break lines
Centerlines (symbol) [1]
Slab edges/opening [1]
Curtainwall edges [1]

Line Weight = 1

Wall edges [2]
Written text/notes/room numbers/dimensions
Column designators/text [2]
Plumbing fixtures
Structural steel **[depends on view]**
Curtain wall edges
Room number designators
Line under room name
Poche/hatching- **all mat'ls incl., [2]**
    Concrete
    Concrete masonry units
    Brick
    Rigid insulation
    Blanket insulation
Window designators
Door designators
Accessories, devices, anchors, reinforcing

Line Weight = 2

Plan detail indicators [and leader lines- **no**]
Plan elevation designation and arrow
Elevation Targets **and** lines
Poche-earth; **grade line** [3]
Section designators **[see below]**
Curtain wall mullions **[in plan]**

Line Weight = 3

Plan detail designator/area enclosure
Building/wall section designator/path
Doors
Section designators/paths
Drawing titles
Edges of all materials cut in section

Line Weight = 4

Sheet Border
Match lines
Addenda/bulletin/revision "bubbles"

The chart noting which line weight is used for the listed work items is a suggested list from the program creator; author's suggested changes in bold typeface, follow the "three line" system for better separation of the information.

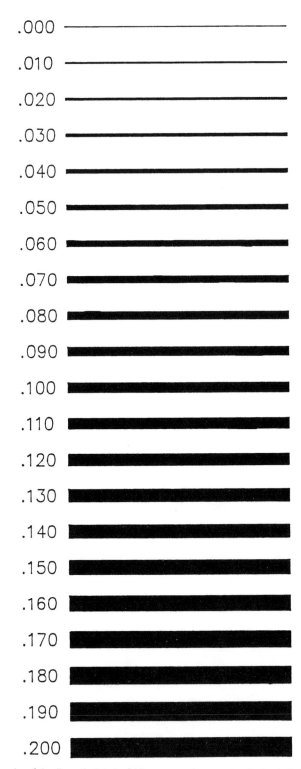

An example of the lines that AutoCAD can produce; note decimal designations.

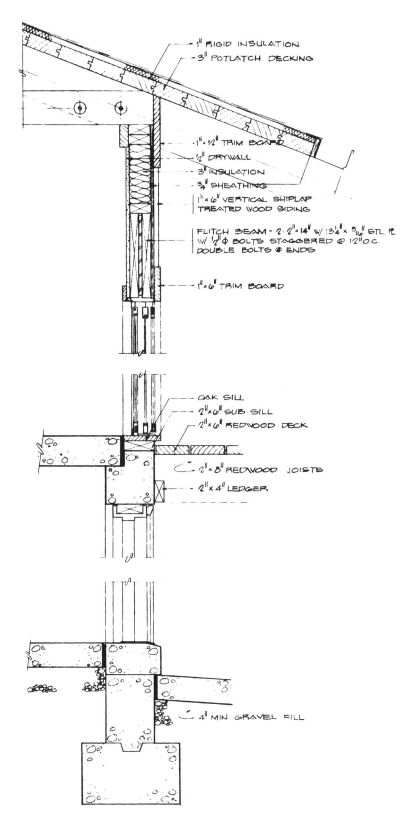

A wall section showing line variation. Note also that the material symbols are a tone or so lighter than the object lines but are still easily read.

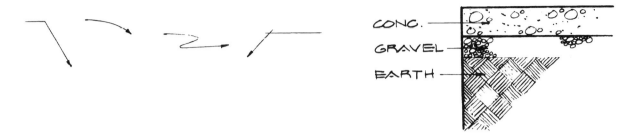

LEADER TYPES

Leader lines are essential in working drawings but must be kept under control. They should lead to and touch the material illustrated (i.e., never just point to it). The lower drawings show various methods that can be used to dimension circular objects and curves.

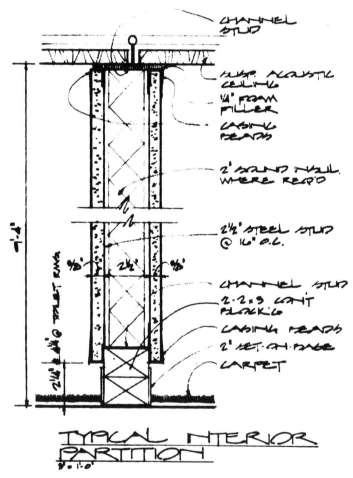

A detail in which the leader lines are fully under control and completely in character with the rest of the drawing. No other pattern of lines is created. The information is transmitted clearly. Note also that this detail is labeled "TYPICAL" and thus repeated throughout the building. In addition, break lines are used in the center of the drawing where repetitive construction has been deleted.

148

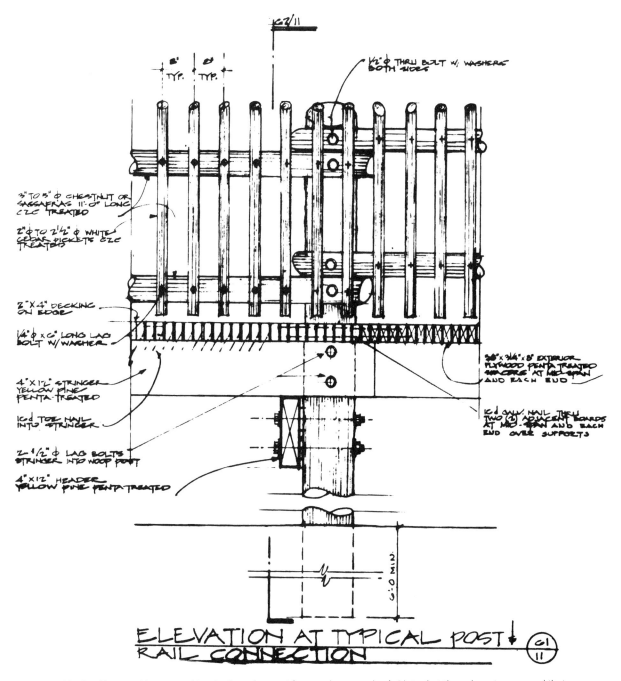

This detail is saved by curved leader lines (except for very long reaches). Note that they do not cross and that they complete their function without obscuring the drawing.

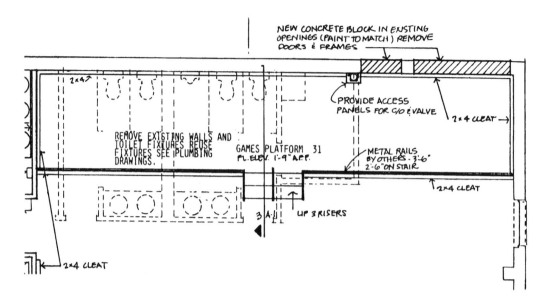

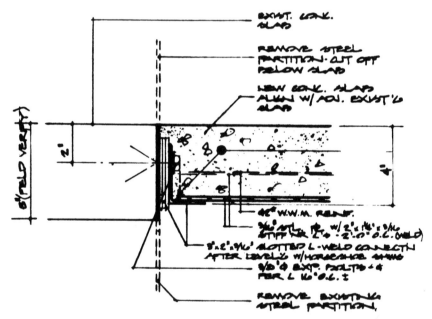

Examples of the interface between new and old (existing) work. Note the very distinct contrast in line work between existing work (work to remain) and new work (work to be executed). Dashed line work indicates existing work to be removed. Plan and detail above; elevation on next page.

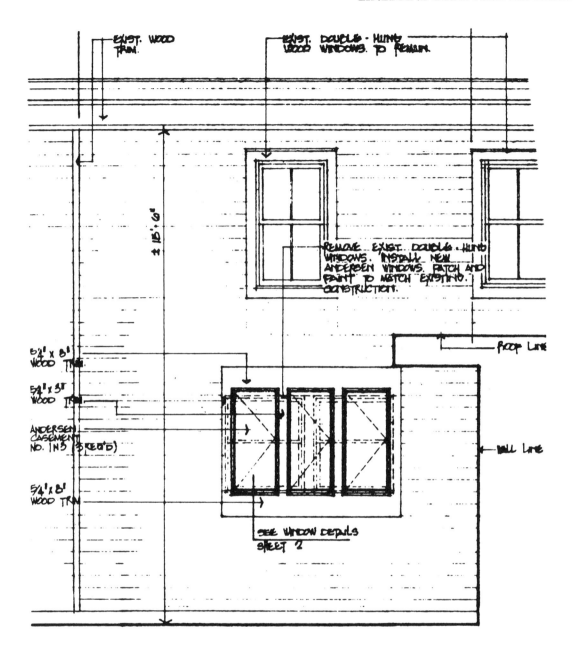

EXIST. WOOD TRIM.

EXIST. DOUBLE · HUNG WOOD WINDOWS. TO REMAIN.

± 15'·6"

REMOVE EXIST. DOUBLE · HUNG WINDOWS. INSTALL NEW ANDERSEN WINDOWS. PATCH AND PAINT TO MATCH EXISTING. CONSTRUCTION.

ROOF LINE

5½" X 8" WOOD TRIM.

5½" X 3" WOOD TRIM.

ANDERSEN CASEMENT NO. 1N5 (3 REQ'D)

5½" X 8" WOOD TRIM

WALL LINE

SEE WINDOW DETAILS SHEET 2

EXTERIOR ELEVATION
SCALE : ½" = 1'·0"

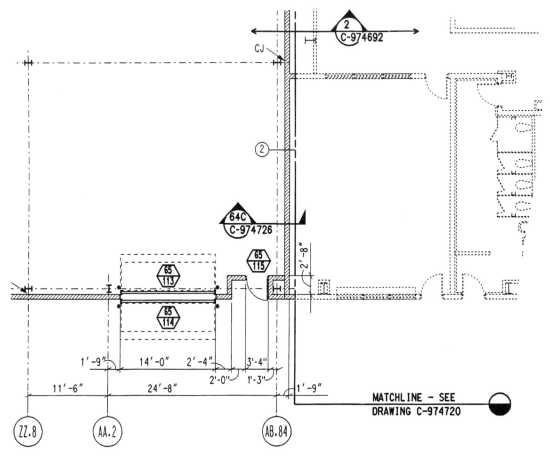

An example of the use of a match line on a floor plan. Notice that work to the right of the match line is dotted indicating that the work is required but is shown on another sheet.

It often happens that projects are of such size or extent that their floor plans and other views will not fit, in their entirety, on the drawing sheets. Although the scale of the drawings can be adjusted, there may still be inadequate space on the sheets.

In this instance, the use of "match lines" is advised. This is a drafting process whereby the project is divided into portions that will fit onto the standard drawing sheets. This divisioning should occur at logical locations on the plans—that is, at offsets in the building, at the faces of major walls, or at column lines. This can be done vertically and/or horizontally, resulting in several portions being created if necessary. The lines can be offset slightly along their route to align with walls, for instance, so as to prevent adverse effects such as dividing particular areas or creating confusion with the layout. Because there is no set rule or standard involved, the

building floor plan(s) may be reoriented to better fit on the sheets and reduce the number of match lines required. This is a decision of the project architect in cooperation with the drafter(s). Of course, the best presentation of the information is the foremost consideration; reorientation may affect several other sheets. Because this is drafting manipulation, the layout should be strictly for the benefit of the drafter, the reader of the drawings, and clear documentation.

The illustration, opposite, shows match line locations at (1), (2), and (3). The (1) location is valid and usable, but the drawing remains crowded on the sheet, with too little space for other work. The (2) location is better; more workable and beneficial to the documentation process. The (3) location is a logical break point, but similar points may be used, if more advantageous. In fact, any layout or number of match lines can be used.

Because the use of these lines is a drafting procedure, the lines are invisible and cannot be established in the field in the same way property lines and building corners are located. Therefore, no dimensions should end at match lines. Dimension through or across these lines to actual points on the new building; do this on both of the adjacent sheets, so as to cross-reference the dimensions.

Match lines should be displayed on all appropriate floor plans. They should appear as very heavy and distinctive lines, fitted with unique designators and notes identifying them; for example, MATCH LINE "Q." These lines must appear in pairs; one on each of the drawings, which, in theory, could be cut on the match lines and placed together to make up the complete plan. It is necessary that the match lines be used, consistently, on all appropriate drawings that are associated with the floor plan(s), exterior elevations, major sections, interior elevations, and so on. Take care that they always occur in the *same* location(s) as those on the floor plan(s).

It is also helpful in the coordination of the adjacent sheets to show some of the walls or partitions that lie close to the match line. On the sheet showing most of the plan, add appropriate notes and hatching to the walls near the match line(s). Where walls and other features occur on the smaller portion of the plan that extends just beyond the match line(s), just draw them in, lightly, in their correct locations and connected to the other plan where they are continuous.

There is one added requirement in using match lines. This is the use of a Key Plan, similar to that used for exterior elevations. A small drawing (need not be to scale) of the entire floor plan should be shown in the lower right of the drafting area on the sheet. On this plan, the approximate location(s) of all the match line(s) should be noted. Then the area of the plan that is shown on the sheet should be noted or, preferably, crosshatched. The other areas not shown on the sheet should be left blank (they are hatched on the sheet on which they are displayed). This plan acts as an index and is important because it orients the reader/user and prevents misunderstandings.

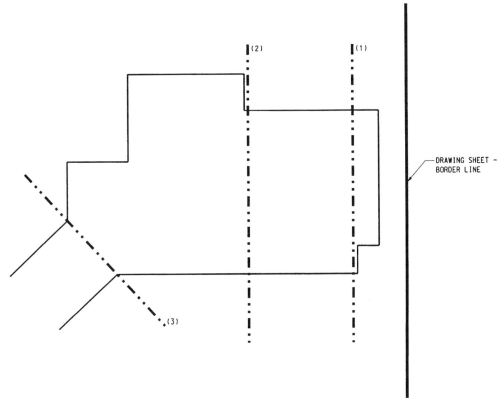

An example of the use of a match line on a floor plan. Notice that work to the right of the match line is dotted indicating that the work is required but is shown on another sheet.

11

Symbols and Conventions

As mentioned in Chapter 8, on lettering, we often rely on abbreviations to convey items of information. These abbreviations, of course, must be commonly accepted throughout the industry or defined in legends on the drawings. They can take the form of symbols, which are patterns of lines, or be incorporated directly into the lines themselves. This is done because all structures are combinations of many different materials, and methods of showing them graphically must be simplified.

It is important to understand that the use of symbols is preferred in architectural drawing. Here a small, simple designation is used to represent a larger or more complex item. One must understand that the symbol itself must be simple, direct, easily read, and devoid of detail (for the most part); better to conceive this as showing a principle, rather than an actual object.

In addition, the symbol must be adjusted in size and complexity in relationship to the scale of the drawing. Obviously, a $\frac{1}{16}$-inch scale drawing requires much less from the symbol than does $\frac{1}{4}$-inch drawing; yet in both cases a symbol is still ap-

propriate and should be used. Accuracy in architectural working drawings is not carried to the extreme of showing every possible minute detail of an item or portion of work. Larger-scale details are for that; the symbols must adjust to the situation.

A note of caution is necessary in regard to computer-aided drafting (CAD) production. There is no value in trying to show every brick or concrete block, although this is very easy to accomplish. Modify the total area of the symbols to properly show the work, but do not overwhelm the drawing needlessly.

Discussed here is a system of conventional architectural symbols which is new in that some universality has been attempted. The American Institute of Architects (AIA) recently commissioned a task force to produce these symbols, and it is generally agreed that a good draftsman will commit to memory those that are most widely used; for example, the symbols for brick, concrete, earth, rough and finished wood, concrete blocks, insulation, glass, doors, and frames. It must be remembered, however, that the symbols shown in a plan or section are not necessarily the same as those shown on an elevation. Therefore, we must take

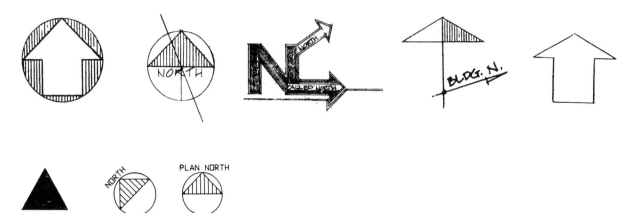

A variety of North arrows can accompany the site plan and also appear on the floor plans. It is often helpful to lay out the drawings so that the North arrow points upward. This is not always possible, however, but it is important that all sheets on which plans are drawn be oriented in the same direction to avoid confusion. In some situations "BUILDING NORTH" is added, particularly when there is considerable variation from true North. Each area in the building will then have a wall facing a major compass point to help in schedules and elevations.

into account all the meanings of a particular symbol. Whenever there is one that is less well known, it must be shown on the drawings in legend form to give the viewer a frame of reference. Basically, all symbols are indicative of the materials they represent; if we invent our own, we must be sure that the information they convey is not misleading. Material symbols, or, in other words, hatching, crosshatching, and poché, need not be indicated by extra-heavy lines. Symbols are required primarily in sectional drawings, wall sections, and floor plans, in which the most important lines are those that represent the actual object. A symbol is shown among them to clarify the construction of a particular item. When a symbol must apply to a rather extensive area, a more contemporary approach is to enter it over only a small portion of that area or to produce a fade-out near the center that would give the impression of a highlight on the surface. This, of course, will emphasize the edges of the object.

Contrast of the various materials is most important, particularly in sectional views; it is always good practice to crosshatch adjacent materials in opposite directions. It is also a good idea to make a distinction between the crosshatching intervals.

If notes or dimensions are to be entered in a hatched area, some of the symbols should be deleted to allow for their insertion. This is important to the readability of the drawing. It is also important when using drawings from other sections of the country to remember that regional variation in symbols can lead to confusion and should be kept in mind. Unnecessary repetition of hatching should also be avoided. Useful devices include a center line to divide a hatched area from a nonhatched area or a light diagonal line that does not conflict with any of the building lines to limit the hatching to one portion of the drawing. Often the symbols are backed up by some sort of clarifying note to which a dimension such as

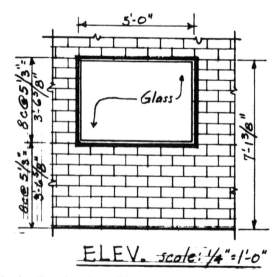

This elevation, though small in size, is an excellent example of placing too much emphasis and spending too much time on the wrong work. There is no need to show each concrete block in this elevation; nothing is gained by this useless, time-consuming effort.

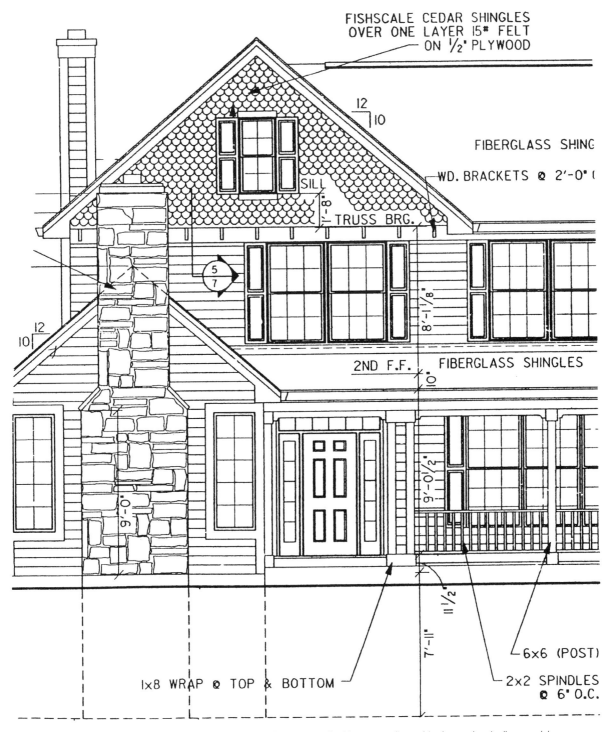

FISHSCALE CEDAR SHINGLES
OVER ONE LAYER 15# FELT
ON ½" PLYWOOD

12
10

FIBERGLASS SHING

WD. BRACKETS @ 2'-0" (

SILL

1'-8"

TRUSS BRG.

5
7

8'-1⅛"

2ND F.F.   FIBERGLASS SHINGLES

10"

9'-0½"

12
10

9'-0"

11½"

7'-11"

1x8 WRAP @ TOP & BOTTOM

6x6 (POST)

2x2 SPINDLES
@ 6" O.C.

This CAD-produced drawing simply tries to do too much. Not every line, shingle, and spindle need be shown. This problem is easily created with CAD if one does not evaluate how complex or murky the drawing has become.

depth or overall size may be added. If there are repetitive items, a symbol may be applied to only one feature, a duplicate note to the others. Again, some consideration must be given to avoiding the time-consuming labor of hatching every item on a drawing.

Some symbols are really outlines or silhouettes of the objects to be illustrated. Templates in the shape of plumbing fixtures, electrical outlets, kitchen equipment, circles, and many irregular forms that may be required in the drawings for one reason or another, are available to facilitate their reproduction. This must be done with as much care as any other drafting procedure, but, again, it is a quick, shortcut method that precludes the need to draw or dimension extremely small objects or to take the time to do more than outline them.

In many instances, particularly in the mechanical trades, symbols take the form of lines; for example, in piping or duct work. A gas line can be indicated by a long dash, a "G," and another long dash; similarly, a hot water line can be designated "HW," cold water, "CW." Each line can be distinctive in describing its own function. When a complex industrial job is laid out on the working drawings, there could conceivably be myriad lines in every direction: gas, water, steam, compressed air, various liquids for processing, and so on. Piping is most often combined in racks, and even on the drawings the lines would be in proximity. Rather than a notational system and leaders, symbology allows us to show the functions of the various elements with a minimum of effort.

Each of the mechanical trades, of course, has its own graphic symbols.

The following charts illustrate a system of abbreviations and symbols devised by the AIA Task Force for nationwide adoption in much the same manner as the CSI Standard Format for Specifications.

ARCHITECTURAL WORKING DRAWING ABBREVIATIONS

SYMBOLS used as abbreviations:

L	angle	BW	both ways	CIRC	circumference
℄	centerline	BRG	bearing	CLR	clear (ance)
c	channel	BPL	bearing plate	CLS	closure
d	penny	BJT	bed joint	COL	column
⊥	perpendicular	BM	bench mark	COMB	combination
PL	plate	BEL	below	COMPT	compartment
φ	round	BET	between	COMPO	composition (composite)
		BVL	beveled	COMP	compress (ed). (ion). (ible)

ABBREVIATIONS:

		BIT	bituminous	CONC	concrete
ABV	above	BLK	block	CMU	concrete masonry unit
AFF	above finished floor	BLKG	blocking	CX	connection
ASC	above suspended ceiling	BD	board	CONST	construction
ACC	access	BS	both sides	CONT	continuous or continue
ACFL	access floor	BOT	bottom	CONTR	contract (or)
AP	access panel	BRK	brick	CLL	contract limit line
AC	acoustical	BRZ	bronze	CJT	control joint
ACPL	acoustical plaster	BLDG	building	CPR	copper
ACT	acoustical.tile	BUR	built up roofing	CG	corner guard
ACR	acrylic plastic	BBD	bulletin board	CORR	corrugated
ADD	addendum	CAB	cabinet	CTR	counter
ADH	adhesive	CAD	cadmium	CFL	counterflashing
ADJ	adjacent	CPT	carpet (ed)	CS	countersink
ADJT	adjustable	CSMT	casement	CTSK	countersunk screw
AGG	aggregate	CI	cast iron	CRS	course (s)
A/C	air conditioning	CIPC	cast-in-place concrete	CRG	cross grain
ALT	alternate	CST	cast stone	CFT	cubic foot
AL	aluminum	CB	catch basin	CYD	cubic yard
ANC	anchor, anchorage	CK	calk (ing) caulk (ing)	DPR	damper
AB	anchor bolt	CLG	ceiling	DP	dampproofing
ANOD	anodized	CHT	ceiling height	DL	dead load
APX	approximate	CEM	cement	DEM	demolish, demolition
ARCH	architect (ural)	PCPL	cement plaster (portland)	DMT	demountable
AD	area drain	CM	centimeter(s)	DEP	depressed
ASB	asbestos	CER	ceramic	DTL	detail
ASPH	asphalt	CT	ceramic tile	DIAG	diagonal
AT	asphalt tile	CMT	ceramic mosaic (tile)	DIAM	diameter
AUTO	automatic	CHBD	chalkboard	DIM	dimension
BP	back plaster (ed)	CHAM	chamfer	DPR	dispenser
BSMT	basement	CR	chromium (plated)	DIV	division
		CIR	circle	DR	door

DA	doubleacting	FND	foundation	LAB	laboratory
DH	double hung	FR	frame (d), (ing)	LAD	ladder
DTA	dovetail anchor	FRA	fresh air	LB	lag bolt
DTS	dovetail anchor slot	FS	full size	LAM	laminate (d)
DS	downspout	FBO	furnished by others	LAV	lavatory
D	drain	FUR	furred (ing)	LH	left hand
DRB	drainboard	FUT	future	L	length
DT	drain tile	GA	gage, gauge	LT	light
DWR	drawer	GV	galvanized	LC	light control
DWG	drawing	GI	galvanized iron	LP	lightproof
DF	drinking fountain	GP	galvanized pipe	LW	lightweight
DW	dumbwaiter	GSS	galvanized steel sheet	LWC	lightweight concrete
EF	each face	GKT	gasket (ed)	LMS	limestone
E	East	GC	general contract (or)	LTL	lintel
ELEC	electric (al)	GL	glass, glazing	LL	live load
EP	electrical panelboard	GLB	glass block	LVR	louver
EWC	electric water cooler	GLF	glass fiber	LPT	low point
EL	elevation	GCMU	glazed concrete masonry units	MB	machine bolt
ELEV	elevator	GST	glazed structural tile	MI	malleable iron
EMER	emergency	GB	grab bar	MH	manhole
ENC	enclose (ure)	GD	grade, grading	MFR	manufacture (er)
EQ	equal	GRN	granite	MRB	marble
EQP	equipment	GVL	gravel	MAS	masonry
ESC	escalator	GF	ground face	MO	masonry opening
EST	estimate	GT	grout	MTL	material (s)
EXCA	excavate	GPDW	gypsum dry wall	MAX	maximum
EXH	exhaust	GPL	gypsum lath	MECH	mechanic (al)
EXG	existing	GPPL	gypsum plaster	MC	medicine cabinet
EXMP	expanded metal plate	GPT	gypsum tile	MED	medium
EB	expansion bolt	HH	handhole	MBR	member
EXP	exposed	HBD	hardboard	MMB	membrane
EXT	exterior	HDW	hardware	MET	metal
EXS	extra strong	HWD	hardwood	MFD	metal floor decking
FB	face brick	HJT	head joint	MTFR	metal furring
FOC	face of concrete	HDR	header	MRD	metal roof decking
FOF	face of finish	HTG	heating	MTHR	metal threshold
FOM	face of masonry	HVAC	heating/ventilating/air conditioning	M	meter (s)
FOS	face of studs	HD	heavy duty	MM	millimeter (s)
FF	factory finish	HT	height	MWK	millwork
FAS	fasten, fastener	HX	hexagonal	MIN	minimum
FN	fence	HES	high early-strength cement	MIR	mirror
FBD	fiberboard	HC	hollow core	MISC	miscellaneous
FGL	fiberglass	HM	hollow metal	MOD	modular
FIN	finish (ed)	HK	hook (s)	MLD	molding, moulding
FFE	finished floor elevation	HOR	horizontal	MR	mop receptor
FFL	finished floor line	HB	hose bibb	MT	mount (ed), (ing)
FA	fire alarm	HWH	hot water heater	MOV	movable
FBRK	fire brick	INCIN	incinerator	MULL	mullion
FE	fire extinguisher	INCL	include (d), (ing)	NL	nailable
FEC	fire extinguisher cabinet	ID	inside diameter	NAT	natural
FHS	fire hose station	INS	insulate (d), (ion)	NI	nickel
FPL	fireplace	INSC	insulating concrete	NR	noise reduction
FP	fireproof	INSF	insulating fill	NRC	noise reduction coefficient
FRC	fire-resistant coating	INT	interior	NOM	nominal
FRT	fire-retardant	ILK	interlock	NMT	nonmetallic
FLG	flashing	INTM	intermediate	N	North
FHMS	flathead machine screw	INV	invert	NIC	not in contract
FHWS	flathead wood screw	IPS	iron pipe size	NTS	not to scale
FLX	flexible	JC	janitor's closet	OBS	obscure
FLR	floor (ing)	JT	joint	OC	on center (s)
FLCO	floor cleanout	JF	joint filler	OP	opaque
FD	floor drain	J	joist	OPG	opening
FPL	floor plate	KCPL	Keene's cement plaster	OJ	open-web joist
FLUR	fluorescent	KPL	kickplate	OPP	opposite
FJT	flush joint	KIT	kitchen	OPH	opposite hand
FTG	footing	KO	knockout	OPS	opposite surface
FRG	forged	LBL	label	OD	outside diameter

159

OHMS	ovalhead machine screw	**RVS**	reverse (side)	**TV**	television		
OHWS	ovalhead wood screw	**REV**	revision (s), revised	**TC**	terra cotta		
OA	overall	**RH**	right hand	**TZ**	terrazzo		
OH	overhead	**ROW**	right of way	**THK**	thick (ness)		
PNT	paint (ed)	**R**	riser	**THR**	threshold		
PNL	panel	**RVT**	rivet	**TPTN**	toilet partition		
PB	panic bar	**RD**	roof drain	**TPD**	toilet paper dispenser		
PTD	paper towel dispenser	**RFH**	roof hatch	**TOL**	tolerance		
PTR	paper towel receptor	**RFG**	roofing	**T&G**	tongue and groove		
PAR	parallel	**RM**	room	**TSL**	top of slab		
PK	parking	**RO**	rough opening	**TST**	top of steel		
PBD	particle board	**RB**	rubber base	**TW**	top of wall		
PTN	partition	**RBT**	rubber tile	**TB**	towel bar		
PV	pave (d), (ing)	**RBL**	rubble stone	**TR**	transom		
PVMT	pavement	**SFGL**	safety glass	**T**	tread		
PED	pedestal	**SCH**	schedule	**TYP**	typical		
PERF	perforate (d)	**SCN**	screen	**UC**	undercut		
PERI	perimeter	**SNT**	sealant	**UNF**	unfinished		
PLAS	plaster	**STG**	seating	**UR**	urinal		
PLAM	plastic laminate	**SEC**	section	**VJ**	v-joint (ed)		
PL	plate	**SSK**	service sink	**VB**	vapor barrier		
PG	plate glass	**SHTH**	sheathing	**VAR**	varnish		
PWD	plywood	**SHT**	sheet	**VNR**	veneer		
PT	point	**SG**	sheet glass	**VRM**	vermiculite		
PVC	polyvinyl chloride	**SH**	shelf, shelving	**VERT**	vertical		
PE	porcelain enamel	**SHO**	shore (d), (ing)	**VG**	vertical grain		
PTC	post-tensioned concrete	**SIM**	similar	**VIN**	vinyl		
PCF	pounds per cubic foot	**SKL**	skylight	**VAT**	vinyl asbestos tile		
PFL	pounds per lineal foot	**SL**	sleeve	**VB**	vinyl base		
PSF	pounds per square foot	**SC**	solid core	**VF**	vinyl fabric		
PSI	pounds per square inch	**SP**	soundproof	**VT**	vinyl tile		
PCC	precast concrete	**S**	South	**WSCT**	wainscot		
PFB	prefabricate (d)	**SPC**	spacer	**WTW**	wall to wall		
PFN	prefinished	**SPK**	speaker	**WH**	wall hung		
PRF	preformed	**SPL**	special	**WC**	water closet		
PSC	prestressed concrete	**SPEC**	specification (s)	**WP**	waterproofing		
PL	property line	**SQ**	square	**WR**	water repellent		
QT	quarry tile	**SST**	stainless steel	**WS**	waterstop		
RBT	rabbet, rebate	**STD**	standard	**WWF**	welded wire fabric		
RAD	radius	**STA**	station	**W**	West		
RL	rail (ing)	**ST**	steel	**WHB**	wheel bumper		
RWC	rainwater conductor	**STO**	storage	**W**	width, wide		
REF	reference	**SD**	storm drain	**WIN**	window		
RFL	reflect (ed), (ive), (or)	**STR**	structural	**WG**	wired glass		
REFR	refrigerator	**SCT**	structural clay tile	**WM**	wire mesh		
REG	register	**SUS**	suspended	**WO**	without		
RE	reinforce (d), (ing)	**SYM**	symmetry (ical)	**WD**	wood		
RCP	reinforced concrete pipe	**SYN**	synthetic	**WB**	wood base		
REM	remove	**SYS**	system	**WPT**	working point		
RES	resilient	**TKBD**	tackboard	**WI**	wrought iron		
RET	return	**TKS**	tackstrip				
RA	return air	**TEL**	telephone				

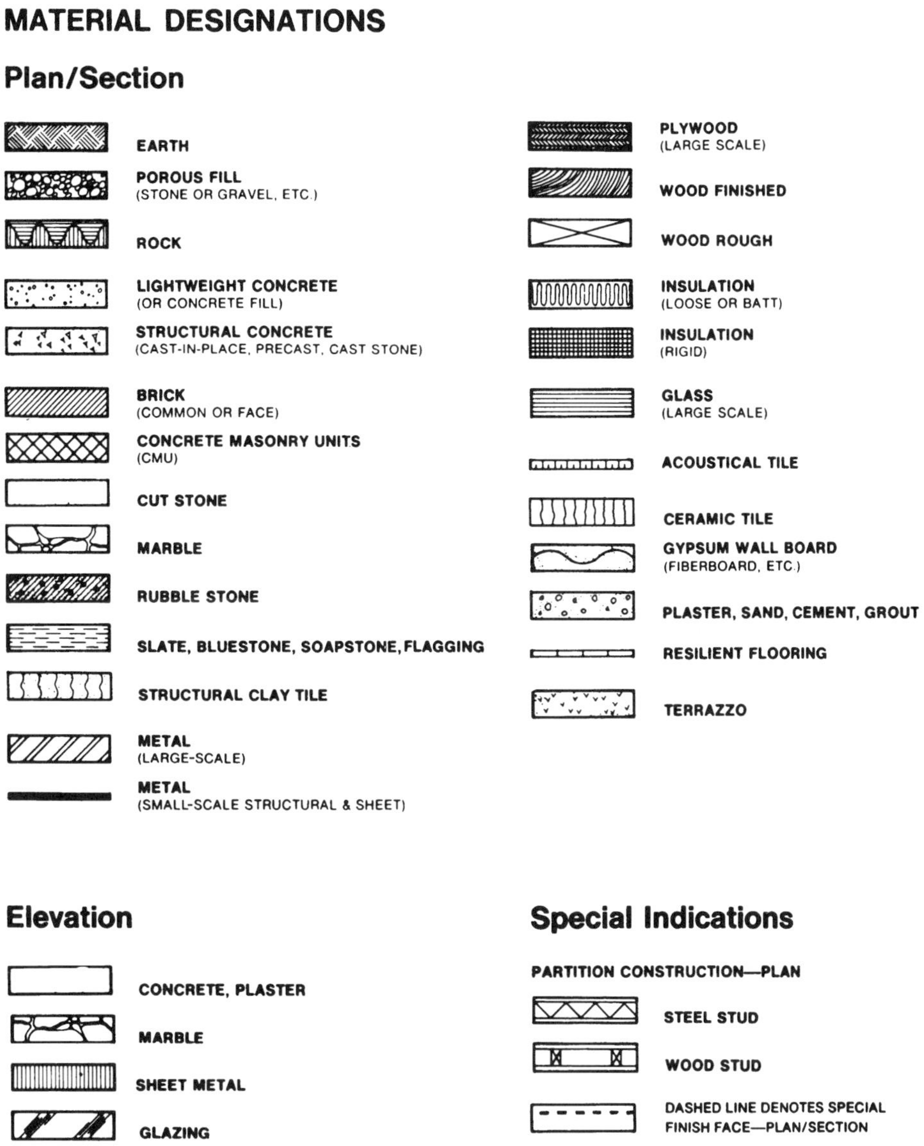

MATERIAL DESIGNATIONS

Plan/Section

EARTH

POROUS FILL
(STONE OR GRAVEL, ETC.)

ROCK

LIGHTWEIGHT CONCRETE
(OR CONCRETE FILL)

STRUCTURAL CONCRETE
(CAST-IN-PLACE, PRECAST, CAST STONE)

BRICK
(COMMON OR FACE)

CONCRETE MASONRY UNITS
(CMU)

CUT STONE

MARBLE

RUBBLE STONE

SLATE, BLUESTONE, SOAPSTONE, FLAGGING

STRUCTURAL CLAY TILE

METAL
(LARGE-SCALE)

METAL
(SMALL-SCALE STRUCTURAL & SHEET)

PLYWOOD
(LARGE SCALE)

WOOD FINISHED

WOOD ROUGH

INSULATION
(LOOSE OR BATT)

INSULATION
(RIGID)

GLASS
(LARGE SCALE)

ACOUSTICAL TILE

CERAMIC TILE

GYPSUM WALL BOARD
(FIBERBOARD, ETC.)

PLASTER, SAND, CEMENT, GROUT

RESILIENT FLOORING

TERRAZZO

Elevation

CONCRETE, PLASTER

MARBLE

SHEET METAL

GLAZING

Special Indications

PARTITION CONSTRUCTION—PLAN

STEEL STUD

WOOD STUD

DASHED LINE DENOTES SPECIAL
FINISH FACE—PLAN/SECTION

The AIA system of architectural symbols and a hand-drawn representation. Some slight variation is apparent, but the symbols remain basically the same.

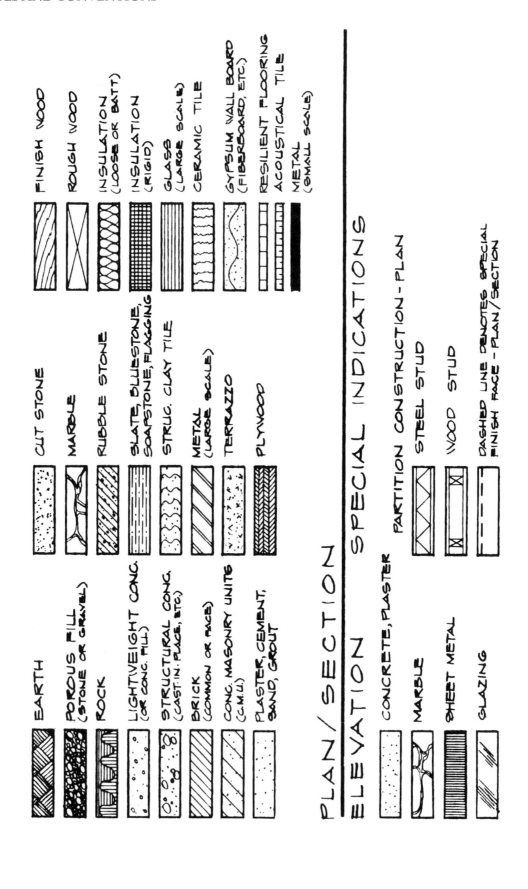

PLAN / SECTION

FINISH WOOD

ROUGH WOOD

INSULATION (LOOSE OR BATT)

INSULATION (RIGID)

GLASS (LARGE SCALE)

CERAMIC TILE

GYPSUM WALL BOARD (FIBERBOARD, ETC.)

RESILIENT FLOORING

ACOUSTICAL TILE

METAL (SMALL SCALE)

CUT STONE

MARBLE

RUBBLE STONE

SLATE, BLUESTONE, SOAPSTONE, FLAGGING

STRUC. CLAY TILE

METAL (LARGE SCALE)

TERRAZZO

PLYWOOD

EARTH

POROUS FILL (STONE OR GRAVEL)

ROCK

LIGHTWEIGHT CONC. (OR CONC. FILL)

STRUCTURAL CONC. (CAST-IN-PLACE, ETC.)

BRICK (COMMON OR FACE)

CONC. MASONRY UNITS (C.M.U.)

PLASTER, CEMENT, SAND, GROUT

ELEVATION

SPECIAL INDICATIONS

PARTITION CONSTRUCTION - PLAN

STEEL STUD

WOOD STUD

DASHED LINE DENOTES SPECIAL FINISH FACE - PLAN / SECTION

CONCRETE, PLASTER

MARBLE

SHEET METAL

GLAZING

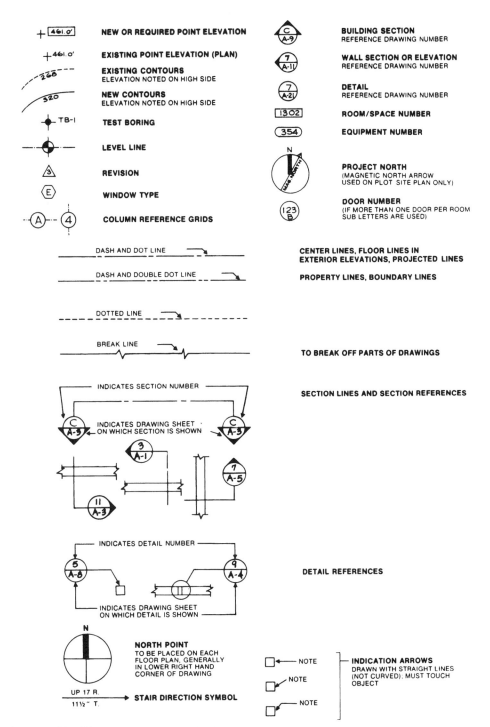

Another part of the AIA system proposes symbols in various areas. Again, it appears that standardization would greatly benefit contractors and all other users of architectural drawings. Each office, however, would have to convert from its present system, a time-consuming proposal.

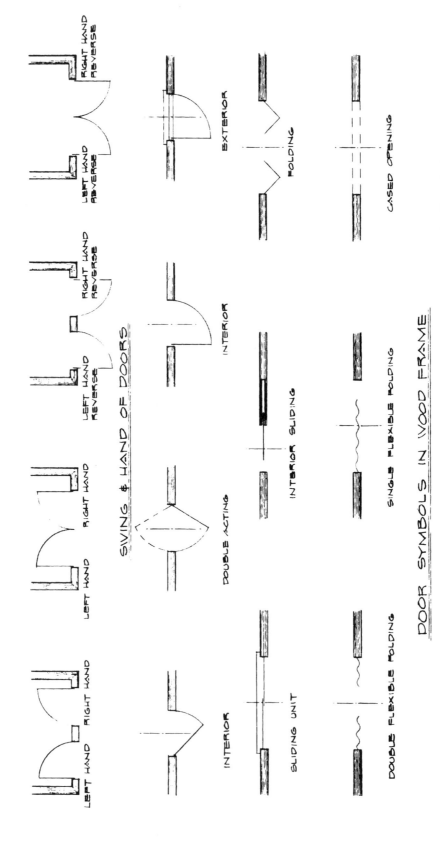

DOOR SYMBOLS IN WOOD FRAME

Door symbols used on working drawings. Although wall construction and office standards may vary, these symbols will remain the same.

WALL AND PARTITION INDICATIONS

CONCRETE

TYPICAL FURRING, 2-1/2''
UNLESS OTHERWISE NOTED

CHASE WALL

2-HR, FIRE RATED

2-1/2'' SOLID PLAS,
2-HR, FIRE RATED

2-HR FIRE RATED SMOKE
PARTITION

1-HR FIRE RATED SMOKE
PARTITION

TYPICAL PARTITION

SOUND RETARDANT

2-HR SOUND RETARDANT

1-HR SOUND RETARDANT
SMOKE PARTITION

LEAD-LINED PARTITION WITH
2-1/2 LB. SHEET LEAD U.O.N.

2-HR LEAD LINED

2-HR LEAD LINED SMOKE
PARTITION

1-HR LEAD LINED SMOKE
PARTITION

2½' SOLID PLASTER

GLAZED PARTITION

Stone, Marraccini and Patterson Self-adhering tapes can now be used for symbols to indicate various types of partitions. The tape is very adaptable to the linear pattern of walls and partitions and is much quicker than hand-drafting material symbols.

CONVENIENCE OUTLETS

⊢⊖ DUPLEX OUTLET

⊢⊖ₘₚ WATERPROOF OUTLET

⊢⊖ᵣ RANGE OUTLET

⊢⊖ₛ SWITCH & DUPLEX OUTLET

⊢⊖₃ TRIPLEX OUTLET

▲ SPECIAL PURPOSE OUTLET

(•) FLOOR OUTLET

⊢⊖ᵍᵣ DUPLEX OUTLET FOR GROUND

SWITCH OUTLETS

⊦ₛ SINGLE POLE SWITCH

⊦ₛ₂ DOUBLE POLE SWITCH

⊦ₛ₃ THREE WAY SWITCH

⊦ₛ₄ FOUR WAY SWITCH

AUXILIARY

◁ INTERCONNECTING TELEPHONE

◀ OUTSIDE TELEPHONE

▢ BUZZER

▢⊃ BELL

▣ PUSH BUTTON

Ⓜ MOTOR OUTLET

O_{a,b,c} SPECIAL AUXILIARY OUTLETS
(SUBSCRIPTS REFER TO NOTES)

▬ LIGHTING PANEL

GENERAL OUTLETS

⊢○ WALL OUTLET

⊢○ₚₛ LAMP & PULL SWITCH

Ⓕ FAN OUTLET

◯ CEILING OUTLET

SWITCHING ARRANGEMENTS

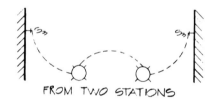

FROM TWO STATIONS

FROM THREE STATIONS

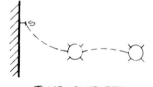

TWO OUTLETS   DUPLEX OUTLET   FLUORESCENT FIXTURE   FLOODLITE

Shown are the symbols used by the electrical trades in collaboration with architectural working drawings. These symbols must be as familiar to the architect and the architectural draftsman as they are to mechanical engineers. Some may be produced with templates; others are more quickly drawn with standard triangles and parallel bars.

LAVATORY	HOT WATER
OVAL LAVATORY	COLD WATER
DOUBLE SINK	GAS LINE
TUB	SPRINKLER LINE
SHOWER	SOIL OR WASTE LINE
SHOWER HEAD	VENT LINE
SQUARE TUB	HOT-WATER HEATING SUPPLY
WATER CLOSET	HOT-WATER HEATING RETURN
WALL HUNG W.C.	PIPE ELBOW
WATER HEATER	CLEAN OUT
KITCHEN RANGE	GATE VALVE
SOIL STACK - PLAN	WARM AIR SUPPLY DUCT
HOSE BIBB	COLD AIR RETURN DUCT
	SECOND FLOOR SUPPLY
	SECOND FLOOR SUPPLY
	WALL SUPPLY OUTLET
	WALL RETURN OUTLET
	CEILING SUPPLY OUTLET
	RADIATOR
	THERMOSTAT
	CONVECTOR

Symbols for mechanical trades as used on architectural working drawings.

12

Dimensions, Notes, and Titles

Before dimensions, notes, and titles can be applied to a drawing some overall sheet planning is necessary. Sheet composition must be considered because the three elements to be added contribute a great deal to the complexity of any given drawing. These elements play as great a part in the legibility of the total sheet as any other line or mass of lettering.

Notes and dimensions should not be placed in a helter-skelter manner merely to fill gaps; they must be done in a methodical way with due thought given to their placement and extent.

A draftsman needs only basic knowledge of dimensioning to do a good job. Sometimes, however, it will appear to be complex and the draftsman may have to struggle to meet unfamiliar situations. This is no time for guesswork or for wading through with a minimum of effort. The major controlling elements have frequently already been set, and it is the draftsman's responsibility merely to complete the job. Therefore, the only requirements are the basic reason for the dimensions and a certain arithmetic skill.

The purpose of dimensioning is to define size and location of the various materials and components. The most effective way to show these data is directly on the drawings; the specifications will list the methods and materials to be employed. The amount of measuring, cutting, and fitting that must be done on the job is based on basic dimensioning. As a general rule intermediate drawings of a similar nature are produced for use in the shops of the various suppliers.

Overall readability, conciseness, completeness, and accuracy must be foremost in any dimensional system. Perhaps the easiest way to break down the requirements is in a series of brief notes on a particular phase.

1. Dimensions should be read across the sheet and are usually placed at the bottom; vertical dimensions must be readable from the right-hand edge.
2. Dimension lines should be set apart from the object lines by spacing and line weight so that the chance of their being mistaken becomes minimal; extension lines are taken perpendicularly from the building lines out to the dimension lines. Extension and dimension lines

should be kept light in value but should have enough density to reproduce in their entirety.

3. All dimensions are written in above the dimension lines and should always be given in feet and inches; the exception to this rule applies to dimensions of less than 12 inches. The drafter must decide whether to use 12", or 1'-0". Although this is the accepted break point, when referring to particular items we may sometimes speak, for example, of a 12-inch wall, a designation that may be more easily read than the shorter symbols. It is a hard and fast and widely accepted rule, however, that anything larger than 12-inches be referred to in feet and inches; even 1'-01/2" [use the zero when the fractional dimensions is less than one full inch].

However, all dimensions less than 12" should be shown in inches, only; use 9", and not 0'-9", for example.

4. Fractions should be shown with a diagonal slash by which the numbers are separated for greater clarity. Too much space is taken vertically by the horizontal bar and the chance of misinterpretation by deleting it altogether is too great.

5. In surveys, site plans, or other engineering-oriented drawings dimensions may be shown in feet and decimal parts of a foot, usually carried to two places; for example, one foot and seven inches would appear as one point five eight feet ($1'\text{-}7'' = 1.58'$). The draftsman should be fully prepared to make these conversions.

6. Basically, there are three dimension lines: the line closest to the building should describe its small elements—for example, piers, door widths, and window openings; the second lines should carry some of the small dimensions and reflect major features such as a wing, section, or offset; the third line (farthest from the building line) should be an overall dimension that will show the total distance from outside face to outside face of the building. It must be remembered that various types of construction, as shown in the example, will demand slight changes in dimensioning; for instance, wood frame dimensioned from face of stud to face of stud. This also applies to brick veneer walls, although dimensions are usually given from face of stud to the outside face of the veneer.

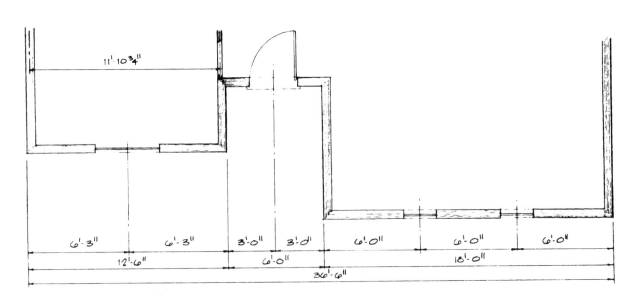

In the correct method of dimensioning, three lines are required, each of which measures a successively larger portion of the building. The inner line includes all openings and corners, the center line reflects the major features of the building, and the outer line represents the overall measurement of the building. It is important that these lines be well spaced away from the plan of the structure.

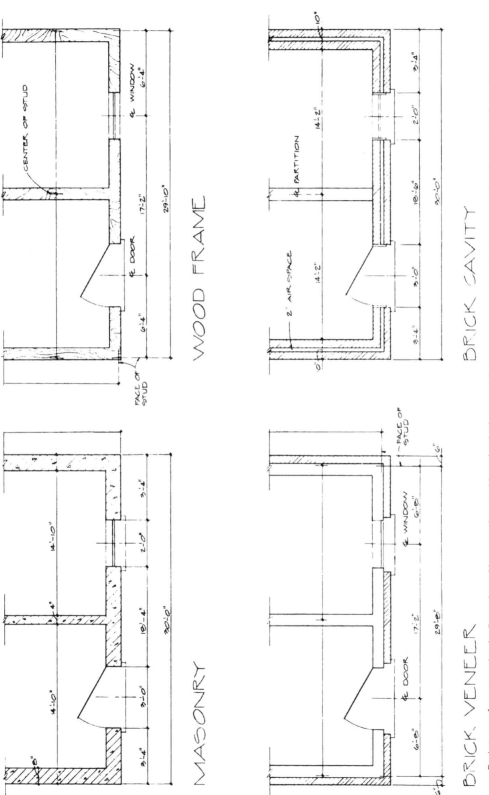

WOOD FRAME

MASONRY

BRICK CAVITY

BRICK VENEER

Each type of construction is dimensioned in a certain way. Note that in these variations masonry construction is measured to the outside face of the wall, whereas frame construction is measured to the face of the studs. In some cases interior partitions are carried to the centerline. This practice is disappearing because the centerline system is hard to use. As a rule, these dimensions are also taken to the face of the studs. In this way the finish material can be varied, whereas the structure remains the same.

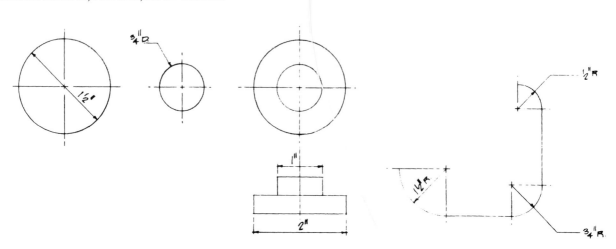

DIMENSIONS ON CIRCLES, CYLINDERS, & ARCS

Methods of dealing with the dimensioning of circles and other curved surfaces.

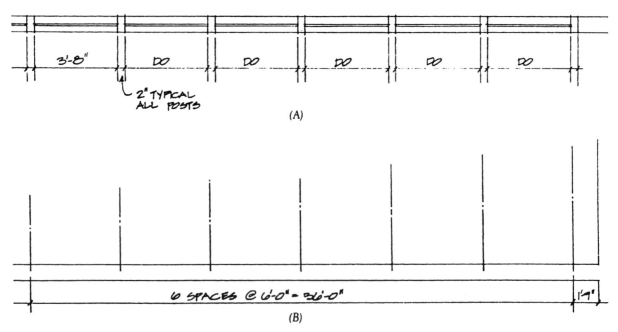

Two methods of repetitive dimensioning. (A) the 3'-8" panel size is constant and the note "DO" (do-oh) transmits the repetitive message. The note about the post is another way of indicating a repetitive situation. The notation "TYPICAL" indicates that all such items are the same. This note can be used as well for larger details that are also repetitive. (B) shows items that repeat or are equally spaced. The width of the item is of no consequence, but the spacing is important. Thus, the spaces are sized and labeled with one note. Any peculiar situation must be given its own dimension.

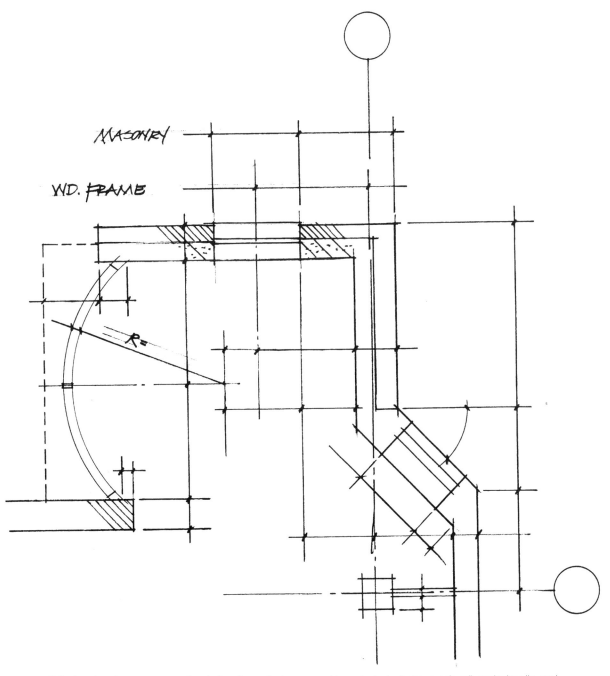

MASONRY

WD. FRAME

R=

This drawing shows some methods for dimensioning unusual layouts, including curved wall, angled walls, and isolated columns

DIMENSIONING OF ARCHITECTURAL PROJECTS

The "school solution" for architectural dimensioning is to anticipate the use of at least three (sometimes four) lines of dimensions, on the perimeter of the building.

First, extend extension lines out, perpendicularly, from the face of the building (starting about $1/8$" from the building face); Establish the first line of dimensions perpendicular to the extension lines (**never dimension in any manner except parallel to a building face, no manner what it's profile may be**), and run a "string" of dimensions which locate the building corners, all openings (door, windows, etc.) and any offset or jobs in the face of the building. It should also include the width of the exterior walls. This and ALL dimension lines should run CONTINUOUSLY, without any breaks, to or slightly passed the end extension lines (this principle also applies to interior "strings" of dimensions).

Next about $1/2$" further out from the building, establish a second line of dimensions. This, too, goes corner to corner, but this "string" only dimensions the major wal segments, offsets, wings, recesses, courts, jogs, extent of angled wall from start to end, and angle used (don't dimension parallel to angled wall), radius walls (dimension the spring points, and show radius used, and locate by dimension(s) the center point of the radius), or other changes in the line of the building, or the "footprint" profile. NOTE: where the building face has no such changes in alignment, THERE IS NO NEED FOR THIS LINE OF DIMENSIONS!

The third line, about another $1/2$" out is for the overall building dimension; this is ONE dimension which shows the entire, overall size or length/width, of the building.

A fourth line of dimensions may be used where the structural grid for columns (a series of columns lines) is used. Here this fourth line is placed just under the column designators, (it need not be directly related to the other building dimension lines) and runs a "string" of dimensions from one column centerline to the next, and ends by tying the last column centerline(s) to the overall dimension (the face of the building).

7. Dimension lines should be defined by an arrowhead or some other device, as noted in the example. There are many systems, but the only one in which the designator has significance is the modular dimensioning system used in some architects' offices. The arrowhead or other designator should point to an exact extension line, neither overrunning it nor pulling up short of it. Dimensions are definite measurements from one point to another, and showing them in a positive way can forestall the contractor's questions.

8. Currently, two methods of dimensioning are employed: one calls for lines to be continuous; the other more modern method shows only those dimensions that are vital to the placement of the various elements. Both systems are acceptable, although the current office procedures must be kept in mind. The more modern, or streamlined, version has one disadvantage, in that in showing only key dimensions the draftsman may be forcing the contractor to build in a certain sequence. This sequence may not be acceptable, and the contractor may then ask a number of questions that may be difficult to answer.

9. Similar dimensions or, indeed, the same dimensions may be required several times on different drawings. It is important that these entries be checked and coordinated. Similar dimensions, however, should never be duplicated on the same drawing. Although continuity is desired, needless repetition should be avoided.

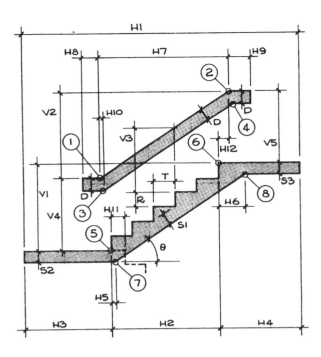

1. $\Theta = \text{ARCTAN} \ (R/T)$

2. IF V4 = V5; THEN H2 + T = H7,
    AND Θ = ARCTAN (V2/H7),
    AND V1 = V2

3. XR = V1/R

Hellmuth, Obata and Kassabaum, Inc.
A standard sheet for the office drafting standards manual, showing all of the dimensions necessary to properly define the construction of a stairway. This helps to ensure that all of the information is included on the drawing and thus eliminates questions from the field.

10. The clarity of the drawing can be improved if extension and dimension lines do not cross. In some instances crossed lines cannot be prevented, but placement should be made with the greatest care possible to avoid confusion.

11. Dimensioning of architectural drawings involves actual sizes, regardless of the scale employed. A note may contradict the dimensions given; for example, a 2 x 4 stud may show a measurement of three and five-eighths inches (3 5/8").

12. Obvious dimensions may sometimes be eliminated. A door placed in a narrow hallway does not necessarily have to be dimensioned, the inference being that the door will be centered.

13. To avoid needless dimensions or crowding, door and window sizes are often eliminated by the use of marks and a scheduling system; the

contractor can then apply the correct size to any given opening.

14. Beams and columns are located by their center lines. A column, for instance, would have a center line running in both directions.

15. Overall dimensions should never be crowded and no fussy or fancy work should accompany them. They must be legible to the casual as well as the highly interested viewer and stand out without being obtrusive.

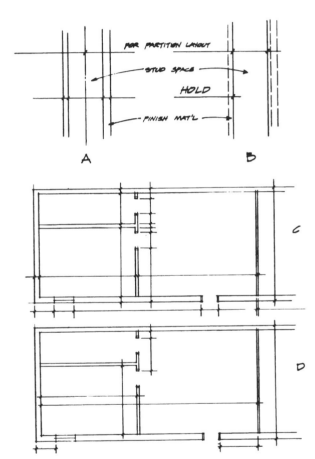

Drawing (A) shows the traditional method of dimensioning; partition layout was difficult when using centerline dimensions, and a number of dimensions were used. In (B), the more modern dimensioning is to the face of the stud for ease of layout; note the finish material information is provided elsewhere as it is not critical to the dimensioning. Drawing (C) shows the traditional dimensioning layout for several rooms, openings, and partitions. Although a good deal of information was provided, not all of it was necessary to build the work. (D) shows the "streamlined" principle of dimensioning, utilizing only those dimensions necessary for layout; all other information is available through other notes, etc., that would be added to the drawing.

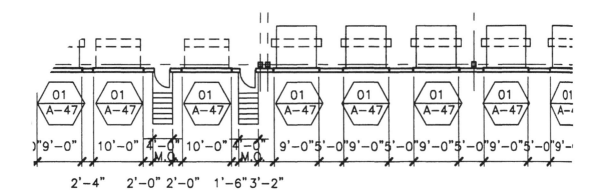

FLOOR PLAN
1/16"=1'-0"

Two portions of floor plans (above, opposite). Note in particular the location and display of dimensions where the spaces are narrow; also, note where CAD has run the line of dimensions and symbols together and over each other, so reading is difficult.

16. To increase legibility, identical units, spaces, or solids should be dimensioned at one element of the series and, by a note in a specific area, should be shown as repetitive. This will eliminate the need to repeat each unit from start to finish of the series. Items that are repetitive, meaning that they are all the same, may be noted as typical characters and not dimensioned in each of the scattered sections in which they may occur. The limits of any series should be marked by showing their extension and dimension lines and arrowhead designators.

17. The dimensional system cannot be left hanging in limbo; it must be tied to tangible, usable items apparent in the construction. The building line, or perimeter of the structure, can be used for this purpose. Items are often referenced one to another. Therefore, it is important to see the item being referenced; the item being used as a reference should be installed before the item being referenced to it. This is especially true in using imaginary lines such as centerlines or in using joints in floor slabs and similar items. Construction can sometimes be held up because of a question about the reference point.

18. Overall dimensioning can clutter a drawing with too much detail, which can lead only to difficulty. It takes experience to determine how to use dimensions to the best advantage and where to place them for the best results.

19. Many office standards address the dimensioning that is to be used. In most cases, dimensions are not required to be carried to very small increments. Particular attention must be paid when dimensioning is being accomplished via computer-aided drafting (CAD) operations. One must be watchful to see that the program does not produce dimensions that are inappropriate for construction work. For example, the automatic dimensioning in CAD may yield dimensions like $7'\text{-}5\,^{13}/_{16}''$. Rarely does architectural work utilize such "tight" or finite dimensioning; most construction work does not have to meet such fine tolerances. Here, it is necessary to apply human determination to avoid impropriety in dimensions. This should be done by inserting proper dimensions that are consistent with what is expected of the work. In addition, this allows for variations in the dimensions as well as in the actual construction. Often one or more dimensions in a line of dimensions can be noted with a "±" (for example, $1'\text{-}4\,^1/_2''\pm$) to indicate that a slight variance is permitted, either less or more the number shown. For the most part, this will not adversely affect the project, as the variation

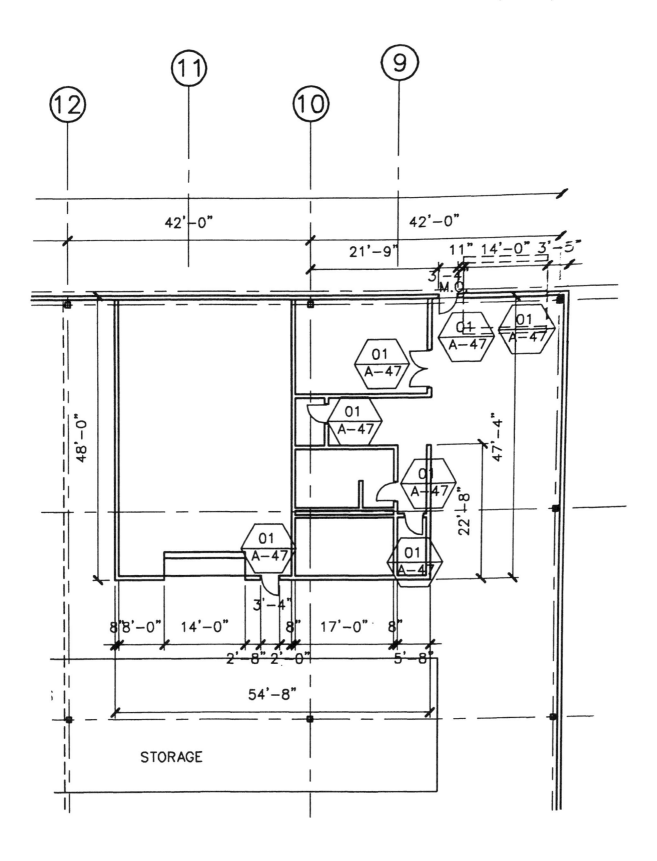

DIMENSIONS, NOTES, AND TITLES

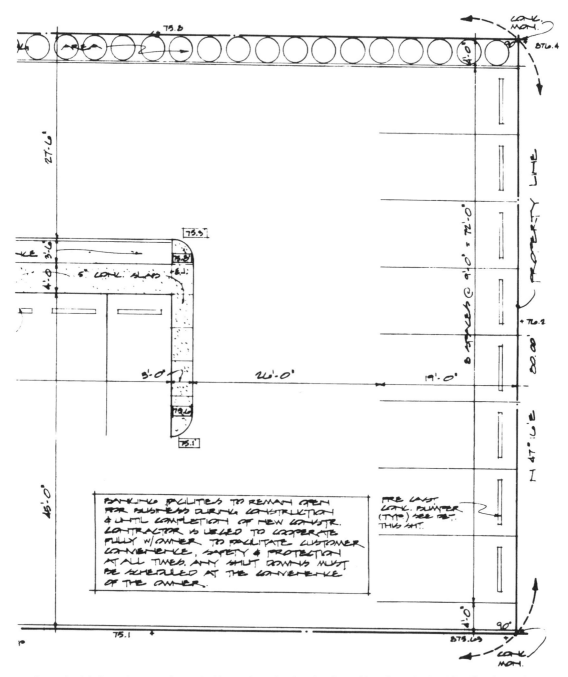

Several odd dimensions are shown in this portion of a site plan. Repetitive dimensioning identifies the parking spaces. Note that large curved arrows are used at the corners to show the dimensions of the property. Dimensions are entered on the property line to show the distance between the curved arrows.

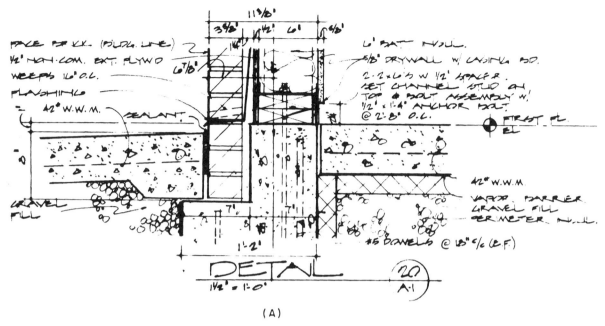

(A)

Both (A) and (B) show the paragraphing required in good notation. The lettering is fitted into neat paragraphs, which carry the complete information. The leader lines start from the beginning or end of each paragraph. Observe how the notes are fitted to the drawing on (A) without disrupting the detail. In (B) the notes are held outside the dimension line and are more widely spaced (if space allows). Moreover, one item is "flagged" for particular emphasis with the addition of the word "NOTE" in bold lettering (note error where leader line starts at the middle of a note).

is virtually undetectable in the overall project work. However, if close dimensioning is necessary, use it; for crucial dimensions, mark the dimension "HOLD." This indicates to the workers that the dimension must be exact and true; if something must vary, it should be something other than the item with a "hold" dimension.

There is no hard and fast rule that decides whether notes should follow dimensions or vice versa. The two must be planned together so that one will not obscure or interfere with the other. Long leader lines between notes and their points of application should be avoided. Notes are properly located inside the dimension lines, that is, between the dimensions and the object drawn. Extension lines that regulate the distance from the object can be adjusted as required without any detrimental effect.

Notational systems include a number of items: room names, identification of materials, reference marks for scheduling, and titles for complete drawings and their parts. Notes that stand by themselves must be given some kind of label

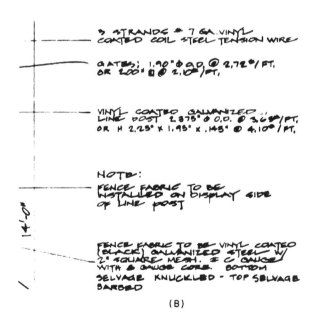

(B)

or explanation. They may also show specific locations or references. Some notes are used in direct connection with other designators such as material symbols. It is this combination of words

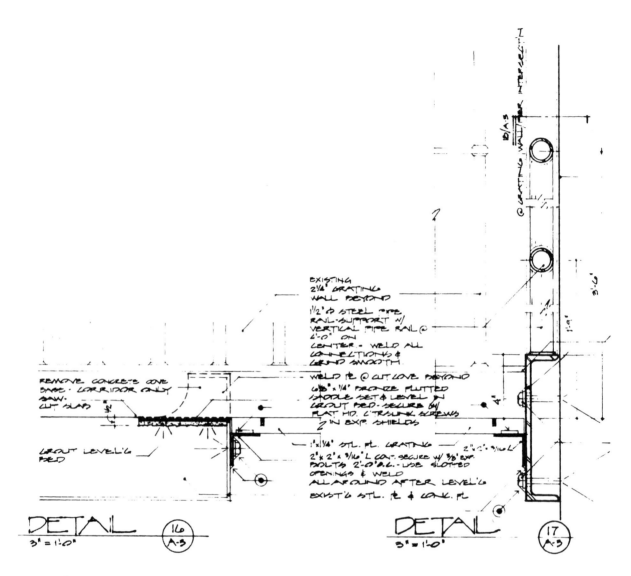

This example is included with some reservations. It is not the best practice to start a sheet with the intention of using a set of notes for more than one detail. However, the example shows that it can be done when tight situations warrant it. Note also that some of the lettering overlies the drawing, which, again, can be done (ever so carefully) if only minor items are affected.

and lines that must be carefully planned so that the legibility of the drawings is not impaired.

Notes in general should be organized and never left to chance. It is good practice to group those that apply around the construction to which they refer. This can be illustrated best in a wall section: all notes that have reference to the floor slab should be placed in one general area close to that section; notes that apply to the wall construction above the slab should be grouped else-where to avoid being mistaken or interchanged. Notes can sometimes be placed close together. The spacing between the notes must be greater than the spacing between the individual lines. The minimum should be a full line height or half the height of the lettering. However, depending on the judgment of the experienced draftsman, this space is adjustable. Punctuation marks are easily obliterated, and better readability can be attained with good spacing and arrangement.

Use	Not
accordion	accordian
acrylic sheet	Plexiglas; Lucite
batt	bat
batt insulation	Fiberglas
bituminous paving	blacktop
calking (in small joints with no movement)	caulking
cellular (foam) insulation	Styrofoam
cellular glass insulation	Foamglas
cement asbestos board	Transite
column	post
concrete masonry units (CMU)	name of units from local mfr. block; conc. blk
fascia	facia
footing	footer
furr	fur
gage	gauge
gypsum block	Pyrobar
gypsum wallboard	Sheetrock; gyp board
hardboard; pressedboard	Masonite
heat-reducing glass	Solarbronze
insulating glass	Thermopane
masonry wall reinforcement	Dur-O-Wal
mineral board insulation	Celotex board
mirror glass	one-way glass
note specific items or construction	per code; as req'd by local code
particleboard	Novoply; flakeboard
place (concrete)	pour
plastic laminate	Formica
plies	plys
porous fill	gravel
rod back-up	Ethafoam
sealant (in large joints with movement)	calking
self-weathering steel	Cor-ten steel
steel beam	I beam
story	storey
tempered glass	Herculite
type X gypsum wallboard	code drywall
welded wire	fabric mesh
wired glass	wire glass

It is most important to be consistent in the use of terms and to use terms of generic nature, i.e., do not use trade, product, or nicknames. Suggestions here are only part of the list possible.

For greater legibility and neatness notes can be aligned at the left to present an even margin. This is not a hard and fast rule, but it is a dependable one. Notes may also be staggered along a slanted imaginary line. Nevertheless, the overriding purpose that should be kept in mind is getting the notes as close to the point of application as possible; for example, the topmost note directed to a floor slab should describe the topmost material in the floor slab construction and so on down the line. This method will result in an uncomplicated system of leader lines. Leader lines may be drawn freehand in sweeping curves or drafted in some sort of angle (skew to the drawing). Another accepted method allows the freehand leader line to be quite distinguishable from any of the object lines and is thus preferable. The angle does not always have to be constant, but neither should it be allowed to become haphazard. Leaders should point away from the first or last line of a given note, never from the center, and should connect with the material to which the note refers.

When notes contain nomenclature, it is important that the same terminology be used throughout. What appears on the plans should appear on elevations, wall sections, and so on. All drawings should agree—most of all with the specifications. It is good practice for the specifications writer to decide what nomenclature will be used in all documents, unless, of course, it has been predetermined in the office manual. If there is no office policy, the drafter should take the responsibility for checking the specifications to ensure that his or her work conforms. Lack of uniformity in nomenclature (e.g., *concrete block* as opposed to *concrete masonry units*) can only lead to confusion, confusion that is compounded if sundry unstandardized abbreviations are mixed in. Some agencies (mostly governmental) require standard nomenclature, and the office will be judged on how well it conforms. Nomenclature for identifying notes is important in that it eliminates the need for repetitious lines; it is far easier to letter the word "brick" on an elevation with only a small amount of symbology than to show the wall's entire coursing system.

Some note of instruction is often a necessity; it will not always relate to a specific kind of material but it will let the contractor know that a certain condition must be met. It is best, however, to make it a mandatory statement; for example, it can order a projection of brick in a panel beyond the face of the normal masonry line—in other words, a 1-inch projection—or it can instruct a contractor working on a renovation project to "match existing wall construction." A note can also clarify intention; a good example is "Slope floor to drain." It should be concisely phrased to make a point that could be difficult and cumbersome to display in a drawing. Most notes are merely simple labels.

Effective communication is basic in the construction industry and the drafter must learn to make his or her requirements clear to all. Some notes involve identification or location; room names or room numbers are examples. It is important that each space be identified for specific purposes, such as scheduling or reference.

(A)

ALTERNATE BID PLAN
WALK-IN REFRIGERATOR
BUILT-IN CONSTRUCTION

(B)

FLAGPOLE DETAIL
SCALE ½"=1'-0"

(C)

DETAIL
3"=1'-0"

(D)

DETAIL
2"=1'-0"

A variety of titles used in detail of limited range. (A) was produced with bold LeRoy lettering to call attention to the alternate pricing required. (B), (C), and (D) are arrangements of scale indicators, lettering, and layout. The cross-reference system is included (detail numbers).

TYPICAL SECTION THRU DISPLAY
½"=1'-0"

A title for a large section. The simple layout reflects the general character of the drawing. The lettering height and spacing have been adjusted to the length available. A small, tightly spaced note here would be completely wrong.

183

13

Building Codes and Standards

Building codes chiefly safeguard the health, safety, and welfare of the general public. By establishing safe building practices, both in design and execution, they endeavor to reduce all possible hazards faced by potential occupants of buildings. Ideally, strict adherence to the ultimate building code would eliminate all elements of danger normally inherent in any building; that this ideal may never be attained is no reason to deny the value of its underlying principles.

The earliest humans, dwelling in caves or beehive huts, had only themselves and their immediate families to consider as they planned and built their shelter. They learned from experience how much space they needed, what degree of permanence a shelter should have, and what materials would combine to satisfy their requirements. Two factors of their gradual evolution altered the primordial nature of early humans: the discovery of fire and the use of communication. Soon they became part of a community formed for mutual protection and preservation.

People's attempts to provide adequate shelter have been limited by their technological knowledge and the availability of building materials. From one world area to another there is wide variation in building techniques and materials. Indeed, in the United States we have learned that dwellings remarkably suitable to prevailing conditions in New England are a ridiculously poor choice in the Southwest.

For the same reasons (climatic conditions, community practices and economy, and native material resources) a building code written to protect public safety in Boston, Massachusetts, will be largely without application in El Centro, California. Certain generalities, which pertain equally well in all areas of the country, are based on common sense and, strangely enough, have been learned by unfortunate experience, only to be incorporated in building codes too late to prevent the first loss. Such generalities stipulate regulations for fire exits, maximum capacity for various rooms, and requirements for installation of panic hardware.

Many contractors and builders, some architects, and sometimes manufacturers of building materials object to the restrictions imposed by building codes. Often these objections reflect

BB-35-19.05. Masonry, engineered brick, general design and construction requirements.

The design, construction, and use of load-bear-brick masonry construction shall conform with accepted engineering practice. Conformity with SCPI standard titled: "Recommended Building Code Requirements for Engineered Brick Masonry," under the conditions of section BB-35-03 OBC, is prima-facie evidence of conformity with accepted engineering practice under the conditions of section BB-35-19 OBC, in the design and construction of engineered brick masonry of clay or shale or mixtures thereof.　　(Eff. 7-3-67)

BB-35-19.06. Masonry, load-bearing concrete.

The design, construction, and use of load-bearing concrete masonry construction shall conform with accepted engineering practice. Conformity with N.C.M.A. Specification entitled "Specification for the Design and Construction of Load-Bearing Concrete Masonry" under the conditions of Section BB-35-03 OBC is prima-facie evidence of conformity with accepted engineering practice, under the conditions of section BB-35-19 OBC, in the design and construction of load-bearing concrete masonry.　　(Eff. 4-1-70)

BB-35-20. Masonry walls, lateral support above grade.

Lateral support shall be provided for masonry walls to insure their stability as affected by all of the forces acting on said walls. Lateral support may be provided by either horizontal or vertical members. Unless acceptable test data shows that a wall is safe and stable under conditions of its construction and support, lateral support shall be provided at intervals not greater than those specified in TABLE BB-35-20.

TABLE BB-35-20
MAXIMUM INTERVALS FOR LATERAL SUPPORT OF
MASONRY WALLS ABOVE GRADE

Construction of wall	Type mortar used	Maximum intervals for lateral supports based on nominal wall thickness
Solid masonry walls of solid masonry units	*M, S N, or O K	20 times wall thickness** 12 times wall thickness**
Walls of structural-clay tile, hollow-concrete masonry units, and hollow walls of masonry	*M, S, N, or O	18 times wall thickness**
Cavity walls	*M, S or N	14 times wall thickness**

*See TABLE BB-35-18.01 for types of mortar required.
**For one-story buildings the maximum intervals shown in TABLE BB-35-20 for lateral supports for masonry walls may be increased from 20 to 23, 18 to 21, and 14 to 15 respectively.

The maximum spacing of lateral supports for a wall constructed of a combination of different kinds or types of materials shall not exceed the maximum spacing specified in TABLE BB-35-20 for walls constructed of the material in the wall which required the least spacing of lateral supports. For nonbearing masonry partitions, see section BB-35-25.

For one-story buildings made up of solid masonry units the intervals may be 23 times the wall thickness.

For one-story buildings made up of hollow masonry units the intervals may be 21 times the wall thickness.

BB-35-20.01. Masonry walls, means of lateral support.

Lateral support may be obtained by cross walls, columns, piers, or buttresses, when the limiting distance is measured horizontally, or by floors and roofs when the limiting distance is measured vertically. Sufficient bonding or anchorage shall self-interest and, if allowed, would inure to the detriment of the public. Steel manufacturers and fabricators have argued that adequate safety factors are incorporated in their products, making additional design regulations excessive and wasteful. Writers of codes know that people are all too fallible, and manufactured products can demonstrate this fallibility. The old adage "It is better to be safe than sorry" justifies the extra ounce of precaution. Some designers would welcome the opportunity to utilize a structural steel member to its maximum capacity, as stated by the fabricator, if the building code failed to impose specific design limitations. The collapse of a bridge with its normal traffic load because one structural member of the span proved inadequate is reason enough to suspect the "built-in" safety factors in all steel components.

Building codes are written and adopted to protect everyone. The codes are legal compilations of minimum standards, set forth to establish a consistent level of public health, safety, and welfare. However, they guarantee nothing. They are part of a complex legal network that concerns design and construction of projects. The codes are the law of the jurisdiction, and as such, deserve the full and complete attention of each design professional. Every young professional must learn, early, that adherence to the law [i.e., the rules and regulations of the governing code(s)] is mandatory; it is necessary to the continuation of a successful practice.

The codes are neither conceived nor intended to be prohibitive documents that "force" designs and designers into set, or predetermined, scenarios. There are options, and usually there will be several ways to achieve the required compliance. The designer who is fully conversant with the codes will understand, know, and utilize these options to the greatest benefit of the client and the project. One must be alert to react properly to various levels of regulation. From the federal to the state, to the county, and hence to the municipality, usually the more stringent regulations will take precedence. In some instances, however, the regulations of one level of government will preempt those of the lower jurisdictions.

Moreover, it is necessary to understand that the codes are not "consumer advocate" documents, complete in every aspect and in minute detail. The authority of the code(s) and code officials is restricted and does not involve items or conditions of workmanship, fit, nonstructural maladies, and so on. The code is seeking properly constructed, structurally sound buildings that create no hazard or threat to public health, safety, and welfare. Minor and cosmetic details that may be problems pose no such threat and hence are not covered by the code nor regulated by the official. Generally, the codes seek to do for the general public what it cannot do for itself collectively, nor what each of us can do individually—that is, to match risk with commensurate protection. What is allowable in Brown County, Ohio, may well be illegal practice in Dade County, Florida. The average restrictions in force in a small midwestern town with its broad streets and low-rise buildings will be more relaxed than the "musts" and "must nots" of a large eastern metropolitan center in which the population is dense and buildings soar 70 stories into the sky. The applicable code offers protection to the designer, the client, the insurers, and all users of the facility. No designer, architecturally trained or otherwise, can be sure of the implied reliability of the materials used in his or her building; the designer relies on the product's reputation and the accountability of the manufacturer. If for any reason a material built into a structure in accordance with the code stipulation fails, the designer is absolved in the ensuing litigation. More than this, the designer's conscience can remain clear; the designer has performed his or her task and has adhered to the building code. If a failure causes bodily injury, the client is freed of blame in the final analysis, for again the design complied with the prevailing code. When reason for failure is determined, the cause is noted, responsibility affirmed, and the code modified to reflect the newly discovered facts. Awareness of code requirements and restrictions has saved the professional careers of many architects.

"Public health, safety, and welfare," as an umbrella term, takes under its protective cover all manner of related subjects. The density of a given neighborhood, controlled by zoning laws, is further protected by the building codes. A zoning law will designate an area as single-occupancy residential and, further, specify "setbacks" and yard areas. A building code governing the same residential neighborhood requires a building permit, which will notify the authorities that a new building is about to be erected. Building, plumbing, and electrical inspectors must certify the construction for its adherence to the codes' mandates and for overall adequacy, thus ensuring that the minimum standards have been met. Properly executed, this procedure serves to maintain structural integrity and produces sound buildings. Because humans are subject to corruption, the result may not be so optimistic as envisioned, yet the system can serve us well. Violations are the exception, not the rule.

Building regulations (codes) are the result of civilization's imposing itself on the individual. The codes now afford protection for both the individual and the structure as a result of the tragic history of unregulated construction in developing communities. Poorly constructed buildings, built very close together, were susceptible to collapse and fire, and easily could involve adjacent structures in a short period of time. History has recorded many such disasters, the most notable being the fires in Rome, London, San Francisco, and Chicago. All started small, only to rage rapidly through the city, not only devastating property but causing peril to citizens. It should be apparent that some regulation is vital to the continued safe and orderly development of urban areas. However, such regulation in rural areas usually meets with a good deal of resistance because the hazards seem negligible; buildings on a farm may be hazardous to each other, but they pose a minimum threat to other farms in the area owing to the distance separating them.

In the building code of Hammurabi, perhaps the most famous of the ancient codes, it was ruled that if a building collapsed and killed the owner, the builder was to be killed; if a child was killed, a child of the builder was killed, and so forth. Drastic? Yes, yet this was a direct reaction to substandard construction that was beginning to mar a developing civilization. It also emphasizes the basic premise of the codes: laws adopted to govern construction and to provide penalties for violation of the minimum standards.

As technology and methods of construction changed, more and more building regulations were enacted. As civilization refined itself, the hazards increased. Although early civilizations, which built by trial and error, were replaced by more studied construction, the introduction of fire into the buildings presented an entirely new array of hazards. The potential disasters posed by these hazards caused governments to regulate the construction of such things as thatched roofs, fireplace construction, and space between buildings, in an effort to restrict and confine the hazards. However, hazards are inherent in everything we do; hence they have become part of our way of life. We accept this situation in an effort to gain both personally and financially. Each new aspect of life contains some risk, but people are anxious to use new methods and materials in an attempt to make life better. This is particularly true in the construction industry. Many officials, particularly in the fire service, opt for a very tightly regulated, basically "hazard-free" construction, which is simply neither practical nor feasible. So a balance within the building and fire codes has been struck, whereby certain hazardous uses, methods, equipment, or materials are allowed, but they are controlled, restricted, and protected so the threat of loss (of both life and property) is minimized.

The first of the "modern-day" building codes was developed by the insurance industry. Basically, it was aimed at reducing property loss because the industry was vulnerable for payment resulting from loss of property. Further, early in the twentieth century, in an age of weekly wages of $1, the value of the materials used far outweighed the value of the labor involved. In essence, labor was fairly cheap, whereas the building represented a substantial investment.

As the years passed, people's values changed, and so did their priorities. This is particularly true in countries where human life is held in the highest esteem. The codes reacted accordingly, and now the major thrust of the building codes is the protection of the public using the structure or facility; this is followed by the protection of fire fighters, the surrounding properties, and finally the structure itself. There is no attempt to abort, or negate, the value of the building or other property (and the codes provide adequate protection here), but the first "thought" of the codes is human life and its protection.

Building codes are sets of legal documents that set forth minimum standards and which, when adopted, are converted into the prevailing law of the jurisdiction. That adoption also "locks" the local enforcing agency (and officials) into a fixed system with very little discretionary power. It is the wise design professional (and his or her staff) who recognizes these factors and reacts to them. This should take place in the earliest portion of the design phase, where the code should be met "head-on"; any problems or impingements should be evaluated, and proper solutions worked out with the enforcement agency. The building codes should be perceived as a vital part of the design process. They should be considered an integral part of the basic program for the construction and should be addressed like any other portion of the "problem-seeking" programming phase of the work. They should carry the same weight as any program requirement of the owner. The codes are "additional parameters" within the design process and are not a hindrance to good design or budget control; a beautifully designed, elegant, award-winning structure can still be a patently hazardous building if it does not meet the provisions of the codes. The elements of good design, unfortunately, neither negate nor remove unsafe and hazardous conditions.

The national Codes and Standards Committee of the American Institute of Architects (AIA) openly decries the fact that "many architects find the code documents baffling, and their administration frustrating. At the very least, most architects find the interrelationship between codes and the design process a dull business." This most unfortunate situation is very counterproductive and can lead the professional directly to a liability-threatened problem. To counteract this trend, the Committee is advocating emphasis on more education (at all levels from student to fully experienced practitioner, it is hoped), closer relationships with code-producing agencies and code change procedures, and increased (and, we hope, continuous) "codes and standards" communication to the practitioner. Furthermore, efforts toward increased awareness regarding "risk-conscious" design (which involves all life-safety elements—fire and smoke control and prevention, flood damage prevention, seismic design, dysfunctional design, air quality, etc.) will strive to reinforce the Committee's contention that "a quality building depends totally on risk-conscious design."

Moreover, it should be recognized that the use and occupancy of a building will have a continual detrimental effect on the structure; poor housekeeping, ignored maintenance cycles, improper uses, and abuse of the building will add to the hazards and fire loading and will further imperil the occupants. Much of this will be done without the knowledge, much less the approval, of the design professional or the code agency. Therefore, the codes try to ensure that the initial construction is safe and provides, at the very least, the minimal protection required.

It is common belief that the building officials are the parties solely and totally responsible for code compliance and enforcement. However, in most states the registration laws for design professionals impose the burden on those professionals; they are to meet the provisions of the codes to protect public health, safety, and welfare. In some states they are even required to report to the building officials any acts they observe that are in violation of the codes! This surely reflects the will of the legislative powers who deem code compliance to be a major necessity. It clearly requires a cooperative, coordinated "joint effort" between design professionals and the building officials. The antiquated view, still held by some individuals, that these two factions are constantly in adversary positions, should be immediately and quickly forgotten. For a complete discussion of building codes, standards, and the interface between them and the design professional, and the relationship of both to the code official, see the author's book *Construction Regulations Handbook*, listed under "General Practice" in the Suggested Reading List.

The "commitment to comply" begins with a valid and in-depth code search during the design phase of the project. All factors must be researched, options chosen where available, and a general pattern of compliance established. In the best spirit of cooperation, the building official should be utilized early in this stage as a "consultant"; he or she will most always be willing to discuss approaches, options, and proposed solutions and perhaps reveal some subtle, obscure provisions that may aid the project or may restrict some element of it. Just as the umpires and managers gather at home plate before each baseball game to review the ground rules, so too should the professionals gather to review the full parameters of the codes. There is no doubt that the codes are extremely complex and involved documents and are becoming more complex as innovations in the construction industry force constant revision. Surely, though, it makes good sense to find out early in the design stage that, for example,

TABLE A : GENERALLY APPLICABLE STANDARDS - PRINCIPAL BUILDINGS ON INDIVIDUAL LOTS

DIST.	MAXIMUM HEIGHT	LOT AREA (SQ. FT.) MINIMUM LOT AREA	MIN. LOT AREA PER D.U.	MINIMUM FRONT YARD	MINIMUM SIDE YARDS — STORIES	LEAST WIDTH	SUM OF LEAST WIDTHS	MINIMUM REAR YARD	MINIMUM COURTS
R-1 A, R-1 A(T)	3 stories or 35 ft. (Whichever is less)	20,000	20,000	1 & 2 stories: 30 ft.	1 & 2 stories	10	20 ft.	35 ft.	**Outer Court:** (a) Courts where 2 or more sides abut a public street, parkway, alley or park. Minimum court width, at any level, of not less than 3 inches for each foot of court height, but not less than 4 feet. (b) All other courts: minimum court width, at any level, of not less than 4 inches for each foot of court height, but not less than 4 feet. **Inner Court:** Minimum court width, at any level, of not less than 4 inches for each foot of court height, but not less than 8 feet, and a minimum cross-sectional area of not less than the square of its minimum court width.
R-1, R-1(T)		10,000	10,000	Over 2 stories: Additional 2 ft. per story above second	Over 2 stories	Additional 5 ft per story	Additional 10 ft. per story	Additional 5 ft. per story	
R-2, R-2(T)	3 stories or 35 ft. (Whichever is less)	6,000	6,000	1 & 2 stories: 25 ft. / Additional 2 ft. per story above second	1 story / 2 stories / Over 2 stories	6 ft. / 7 ft. / Additional 5 ft. per story	14 ft. / 16 ft. / Additional 10 ft. per story	30 ft. / 35 ft. / Additional 5 ft. per story	
R-3, R-3(T)	Same as R-2	5,000	4,000	1 & 2 stories: 25 ft. / Additional 2 ft. per story above second	1 story / 2 stories / Over 2 stories	5 ft. / 6 ft. / Additional 5 ft. per story	12 ft. / 14 ft. / Additional 10 ft. per story	30 ft. / 35 ft. / Additional 5 ft. per story	
R-4, R-4(T)	45 ft.	5,000	Efficiency 2,000 / Intermediate 2,000 / Regular 2,500	1 & 2 stories: 20 ft. / Additional 2 ft. per story above second	1 story / 2 stories / Over 2 stories	5 ft. / 6 ft. / Additional 3 ft. per story	12 ft. / 14 ft. / Additional 10 ft. per story	30 ft. / 30 ft. / Additional 5 ft. per story	
R-5, R-5(T)	2 times the distance from building line to center line of street	5,000	Efficiency 800 / Intermediate 1,100 / Regular 1,500	Same as R-4	1 story / 2 stories / Over 2 stories	5 ft. / 6 ft. / Additional 5 ft. per story	12 ft. / 14 ft. / Additional 10 ft. per story	30 ft. / 30 ft. / Additional 5 ft. per story	
R-6, R-6(T)	Same as R-5	5,000	Efficiency 600 / Intermediate 800 / Regular 1,000	Same as R-4	1 & 2 stories / Over 2 stories	5 ft. / Additional 4 ft. per story	12 ft. / Additional 8 ft. per story	25 ft. / Additional 4 ft. per story	
R-7, R-7(T)	Same as R-5	5,000	Efficiency 400 / Intermediate 550 / Regular 550	Same as R-4	1 & 2 stories / Over 2 stories	5 ft. / Additional 3 ft. per story	12 ft. / Additional 6 ft. per story	25 ft. / Additional 3 ft. per story	
R-V, R-V(T)	Same as R-5	5,000	Efficiency 800 / Intermediate 1,100 / Regular 1,500	1 & 2 stories: 20 ft. / Additional 3 ft. per story above second	1 & 2 stories / Over 2 stories	20 ft. / Additional 3 ft. per story	40 ft. / Additional 6 ft. per story	20 ft. / Additional 3 ft. per story	Inner Courts prohibited in R-V District.
RF-1	35 ft. above 65-foot flood elevation	10,000	10,000	25 ft.	1 & 2 stories / Over 2 stories	5 ft. / Additional 3ft. per story	12 ft. / Additional 6 ft. per story	5 ft. per story 10 ft. min.	

This chart is part of a zoning code. Here the various zoning designations place certain requirements on the owner and/or designer. Setbacks (yard requirements), lot size, and other items are defined. Note that R1 (single family residential) is the most restrictive. Classes are less restrictive down through R7 (multifamily residential) and thus allow higher densities and different construction conditions.

another exit stair is required. In this preliminary work the stair is incorporated much more easily, as it will not disrupt fixed design features, program parameters, final estimates, firm bids, or issuance of the building permit. Drastic changes may be necessary, but major disruption of the project design or construction is avoided. Disruption is not the intent of any code, but without prior knowledge the enforcing agency can only apply the code when the documents are submitted for permit.

Working drawings should be viewed as an extension and a refinement of the commitment to the comply. The requirements of the codes should be constantly checked, and the addition of pertinent and proper details of the requirements should be included progressively in all of the project documents as well as during the construction cycle. It is true that a great many of the code provisions must be considered or incorporated in the basic design of a building. Certain analyses, conclusions, and determinations must be made and the results accounted for in the basic planning (such as the number of exits, placement of stairs, number of plumbing fixtures, use and placement of fire walls, location of rated construction, etc.) so that proper facilities, construction, relationships, and area sizes can be established.

In the working drawing phase of the work, the minute detail of the code provisions must be accounted for. Some code features used or incorporated in a broad manner must be refined and detailed properly to reflect precisely what is required by the code, and what the design professional has chosen as a response to the requirement. (It should be noted that most model codes are performance oriented with several possible solutions to any requirement, as opposed to specification codes whereby only one solution is permitted.) Rated assemblies, for instance, must reflect the assembly that was used to establish the rating. The construction must match exactly the construction of the test assembly. No variations should be allowed, or the rating is nullified. No longer can a partition be labeled merely as having a "one-hour rating." Now the detailed construction of the wall must be determined, and the detail depicted on the drawings. Further, the location of the wall must be shown, and the proper information also incorporated in the specifications. Most building departments now require that any notation for a rated assembly should include the listing number of the assembly that is assigned by the testing

4703-1-06 CODE OF CONDUCT

(A) Competence

(1) In practicing architecture, an architect shall act with reasonable care and competence and shall apply the technical knoledge and skill which is ordinarily applied by architects of good standing, practicing in the same locality.

(2) In designing a project, an architect shall take into account all applicable state and municipal building laws and regulations. While an architect may rely on the advice of other professions (e.g., attorneys, engineers and other qualified persons) as to the intent and meaning of such regulations, once having obtained such advice, an architect shall not knowingly design a project in violation of such laws and regulations.

(3) An architect shall undertake to perform professional services only when he or she, together with those whom the architect may engage as consultants, are qualified by education, training and experience in the specific technical areas involved.

(4) No person shall be permitted to practice architecture if, in the board's judgment, such person's professional competence is substantially impaired by physical or mental disabilities.

(B) Conflict of interest

(1) An architect shall not accept compensation for his or her services from more than one party on a project unless the circumstances are fully disclosed to and agreed (such disclosure and agreement to be in writing) by all interested parties.

(2) If an architect has any business association or direct or indirect financial interest which is substantial enough to influence his or her judgment in connection with his or her performance of professional services, the architect shall fully disclose in writing to his or her client or employer the nature of the business association or financial interest, and if the client or employer objects to such association or financial interest, the architect will either terminate such association or interest or offer to give up the commission or employment.

(3) An architect shall not solicit or accept compensation from material or equipment suppliers in return for specifying or endorsing their products.

(4) When acting as the interpreter of building contract documents and the judge of contract performance, an architect shall render decisions impartially, favoring neither party to the contract.

(C) Full disclosure.

(1) An architect, making public statements on architectural questions, shall disclose when he or she is being compensated for making such statement.

(2) An architect shall accurately represent to a prospective or existing client or employer his or her qualifications and the scope of his or her responsibility in connection with work for which he or she is claiming credit.

(3) If in the course of his or her work on a project, an architect becomes aware of a decision taken by his or her employer or client, against the architect's advice, which violates applicable state or municipal building laws and regulations and which will, in the architect's judgment, materially affect adversely the safety to the public of the finished project, the architect shall:

(a) Report the decision to the local building inspector or other public official charged with the enforcement of the applicable state or municipal building laws and regulations.

(b) Refuse to consent to the decision, and

(c) In circumstances where the architect reasonably believes that other such decisions will be taken notwithstanding his objection, terminate his services with reference to the project.

An excerpt from the code of conduct for architects issued by a state licensing board. Note the responsibility to meet the codes (Par. A2) and to see that all work is performed properly (Par. C3).

agency. In this way the proposed construction can be compared easily with the test data. So, too, the inspector easily can check the actual construction against the design "commitment."

The codes tend to lag behind technology and thus evoke cries of restrictiveness, obsolescence, and design inhibition. However, it should be understood that most modern building codes are "consensus" documents. These codes are changed regularly to reflect the opinions and views gathered from many sources in the industry. A majority vote of the code group's members incorporates into the code those changes that are deemed proper. Delays in testing, evaluation, and establishing criteria for safe and proper use of new materials and methods of construction are constant. If a new material is going to be used in a project, it is wise to check with the building official so progress will not be stalled later while approvals are collected. Be prepared to submit test data about the material and do this as early as possible. There is an active, and intense, program of approvals in the industry, but physical and economic factors have a hard time keeping pace with the 5,000 new materials coming on-line each year. Moreover, there is usually an appeals procedure that can be utilized if the building department is unwilling, or unable, to approve a material or system. An established board within the jurisdiction can hear the case, evaluate the submitted data, and issue a ruling supporting the denial, allowing the use of the material, or allowing the use with conditions. Here, again, there is a time factor that may have an adverse effect on the progress of the design or construction.

Another complicating factor is the massive array of information and requirements contained in the various standards merely referenced in the codes. Often a small code provision will refer to a standard that introduces hundreds of pages of data that may have an impact on the project. Although the information is not written directly into the code book, the requirements are bona fide code provisions and must be met. The need for research, resolution, and understanding is again quite apparent.

New, or substitute, materials should never be introduced directly into the field; the inspector, almost without exception, will not allow it and may stop the work until proper information and test data are submitted and approved. It should be understood that the field inspector is required to check the actual construction against the approved documents. Therefore, the solutions or options must be resolved with the plans examiner and the building official *before* the project is approved and the permit issued. Furthermore, any noncode elements in the project that are changed should be coordinated with the building department as they occur, or the inspector may question the change.

In the year 2000, publication and adoption will begin for the newly written International Building Code, [IBC] and its companion documents. Previously, there have been three model code organizations in the United States; Building

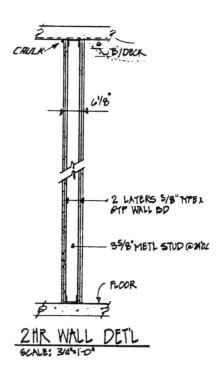

BASE LAYER 5/8" TYPE X GYPSUM WALLBD. OR VENEER BASE APPLIED PARALLEL TO EA. SD. OF 3 5/8" METAL STUDS SPACED 24" O.C. W/ 1" TYPE S DRYWALL SCREWS 8" O.C. TO EDGES & 12" O.C. TO INTERMEDIATE STUDS. FACE LAYER 5/8" PLAIN OR PREDECORATED TYPE X GYPSUM WALLBD OR VENEER BASE APPLIED PARALLEL TO STUDS OVER BASE LAYERS WITH LAMINATING COMPOUND COMBED OVER ENTIRE SURFACE, METAL BASE & TOP RETAINER CHANNELS. STAGGER JOINTS 24" O.C. EA. LAYER & SIDE.

THICKNESS 6 1/8"   APPROX WGHT 10 PSF
LIMITING HGT. 19'-5"   FIRE TEST UL RB 19-31, 32
SOUND TEST-RAL TL 61-213   DESIGN U411, 6-2-60
      7-6-61

The detail of a fire-rated partition, with all of the necessary construction requirements, the note showing the test, and the design number assigned by the testing agency.

```
3.03  SCHEDULE:

      See Drawings for types and locations of exterior wall insulation, partitions, and
      ceiling assemblies and systems:

      a.   Typical Exterior Walls:  Apply single layer foil-backed gypsum drywall over
           wall insulation blankets and Z-furring channels.  (Note:  Insulation shall
           extend above gypsum wallboard height or in some conditions insulation is
           applied only to walls; see Drawings.)

      b.   Other Interior Partitions:  Apply single layer gypsum drywall both sides
           (thickness indicated) to metal studs.

      c.   Fire-rated assemblies:

           1. Two (2) hour rated wall shall comply with U.L. Design U411.

           2. Two (2) hour rated ceilings shall comply with U.L. Design G503.
```

```
1.02    QUALITY ASSURANCE

    A.   Fire-rated assembly:  Where specific fire-tested assembly is
         called for on the drawings or in the specifications, all
         materials, installation procedures,  and other requirements of
         specific test shall supercede any conflicting requirements
         specified herein.  Fire-rated assembly for church stair enclosure
         shall be U.L. Des U301.
```

Two excerpts from specifications noting the design data for a rated partition to be used on the project. Data shown here need not be repeated on the drawings.

Officials and Code Administrators, International, Inc. [BOCA], The International Conference of Building Officials, International [ICBO], and the Southern Building Code Congress, International [SBCCI]. The groups and their members represented portions of the United States, but no building code set covered the entire nation. Each group promulgated and modified their own version of the codes; and the three varied one from the other. The single new code will eliminate the variations, as more and more jurisdictions adopt the new codes. The target is to have the IBC applicable to all of the same 20,000 individual jurisdictions in the United States, and to as much of the entire world as possible. The three current groups will no longer publish and amend their codes. The timing and cycle for changes in the IBC has not yet been determined, but it is certain that changes will occur as technology changes, or as differing code-related situations arise.

In any event, it is the design professionals who are responsible for reviewing the code [as applicable to their project], and for creating a design and documentation that complies with the code provisions on (or "as of") the day the application for permit is submitted. The professional, therefore, must be aware of the latest changes. This further points up the benefit of working with the building official as a consultant early in the project; it is the official's job to stay current and be conversant with the very latest changes and additions. After a strong initial code search by the design professional, it is far less time-consuming if he or she consults with the building official to determine whether the conclusions drawn, and the design developed, are valid, than to correct errors later. Under the model code system, and with local codes, the local authority is the final word and holds the responsibility for final interpretation of the code and final approval of the project. This provides for the incorporation of local law into the model codes and may cause variances from the "pure" model code provisions. In essence, no code should be taken for granted just because it is based on a model code. Therefore, the code and code official should be checked several times during the production of the working drawings to ensure that all current provisions are met and to see how any changes, or variations, may have an impact on the project in unexpected ways.

SECTION 01080 - APPLICABLE CODES AND STANDARDS

1.01 GENERAL

A. As applicable to the work, the codes and standards listed herein and produced by the associations, societies and agencies listed herein compromise the minimum requirements for work not otherwise specified by more detailed or more stringent requirements. In case of conflicting standards applicable to the same work, the Architect shall designate which governs, based upon which is recognized to be most closely associated with the work and, in general, the most stringent requirements shall govern. This provision, however, shall not relieve the Contractor of his responsibility to comply fully with the requirements of governing authorities and the Contract Documents.

AAMA	Architectural Aluminum Manufacturers Association
AASHO	American Association of State Highway Officials
ACI	American Concrete Institute
AGA	American Gas Association
AGC	The Associated General Contractors of America
AI	The Asphalt Institute
AIA	The American Institute of Architects
AISC	American Institute of Steel Construction, Inc.
AISI	American Iron and Steel Institute
ANSI	American National Standards Institute
APA	American Plywood Association
ASAHC	American Society of Architectural Hardware Consultants
ASHRAE	American Society of Heating, Refrigerating and Air Conditioning Engineers, Inc.
ASRE	American Society of Refrigerating Engineers
ASTM	American Society for Testing & Materials
AWI	Architectural Woodwork Institute
AWPI	American Wood Preservers Institute
AWSC	American Welding Society Code
AWWA	American Water Works Association, Inc.
BIA	Brick Institute of America
CLFMI	Chain Link Fence Manufacturers Institute
CRSI	Concrete Reinforcing Steel Institute
CS	Commercial Standard of NBS
CSI	The Construction Specifications Institute, Inc.
FGMA	Flat Glass Marketing Association
FIA	Factory Insurance Association
FM	Factory Mutual Engineering Corp.
FS	Federal Specification
FTI	Facing Tile Institute
MIL	Military Standardization Documents
NAAMM	The National Association of Architectural Metal
NBFU	National Board of Fire Underwriters
NBS	National Bureau of Standards
NBC	National Electrical Code by NFPA
NEMA	National Electrical Manufacturers Association
NEMI	National Elevator Manufacturing Industry
NFPA	National Fire Protection Association
N.F.P.A.	National Forest Products Association
NPCA	National Paint & Coatings Association
NSC	National Safety Council
NSF	National Sanitation Foundation
NWMA	National Woodwork Manufacturers Association
OBC	Ohio Building Code
ODTS	Ohio Department of Transportation Specification
OSHA	Occupational Safety & Health Administration
SDI	Steel Deck Institute
S.D.I.	Steel Door Institute
SJI	Steel Joist Institute
SMACNA	Sheet Metal & Air Conditioning Contractor's National Association, Inc.
SPR	Simplified Practice Recommendation of NBS
SSPC	Steel Structures Painting Council
SWI	Steel Window Institute
TCA	Tile Council of America, Inc.
UL	Underwriters' Laboratories, Inc.

A specification section in which all standards applicable to the project are listed. This list removes the obligation of reproducing them individually, for by this reference their provisions are made part of the contract and are binding on the contractors.

In the last few years, building disasters, both major and minor, have been attributed to a wide range of causes, and there is no clean, clearly defined way to reduce or eliminate them. In most structure fires, ignoring the basic code provisions in the design stage has led to death owing to lack of sufficient exiting facilities, rapid expansion of the fire via combustible materials, and toxic poisoning from burning materials and furnishings. In other situations, the building was found to be in keeping with the codes when it was built, but the addition of flammable decorations and other fire loading (furniture, carpeting, etc.) led to the loss of life. In still others, the initial code-abiding construction was negated by blocking exits, cutting holes in fire walls, and other such "conveniences" that helped the owner meet his or her needs, or facilitate easier operation, or sadly, save a few dollars in remodeling. Again, lives were lost and property was heavily damaged—tragic cost from all points of view.

In some cases, disaster resulted from poorly conceived details, faulty changes of details, or work that was not executed according to approved drawings. The common factor in all of the examples seems to be time. Time is not taken to conduct a thorough code search; time is not taken to resolve code problems with the code professionals; time is not taken to obtain a permit and proper inspection; time is not taken to research and detail construction properly; time is not available for complete, objective checking of documents before they are "put on the streets"; and time is not taken to be prudent in making revisions or in actually building the project. No doubt it takes a nearly superhuman effort to produce a modern structure on time, within the budget, and in the safest, most code-abiding manner, but such effort must be the daily endeavor of the construction industry.

Within this effort, though, the working drawings serve as a very distinct, precise, all-encompassing, and poignant checkpoint for compliance, *if* they are approached in the proper manner from the outset. Day by day more time-saving production techniques are being discovered, refined, and adopted in the professional office, but there still must be that human decision and commitment by the design professional to do the job right from beginning to end. The time saved in production should be diverted, at least in part, to the cause of prudent, life-saving design and construction.

Copies of all pertinent codes can be found on the shelves of drafting offices or centrally located in a design library. Each person delegated even the most minute drafting assignment on a sheet of working drawings should become familiar with the governing code and should be aware of any violation or infraction of the code stipulations so that a damaging error will not reach the contractor. The more office personnel trained to search out code transgressions, the more likely the office will engender a reputation for competency and thoroughness, two qualities requisite to good work. This is increasingly true, because, as noted in Chapter 3 "A Perspective on Working Drawings," code compliance on the part of the design professional is virtually nonnegotiable. Court decisions have placed a tremendous and meaningful emphasis on the professional's obligation to perform code searches and to meet the applicable provisions. The following is a list of code discrepancies compiled by a building department [OBBC is the Ohio Basic Building Code; HCBC is the Hamilton County Building Code]. The list contains the discrepancies/problems which are seen most frequently. This listing was made prior to the department being computerized, but still served the purpose for notifying applicants in response to a permit application. With computerization, now, it is much easier to utilize this listing, via Word Processing or other programs, when the Plan Reviewers compose response letters. It serves to show the type of items "missed" and the type of detailed information that is required. Following the list are examples of code search forms that expedite the code search for each and every project.

BUILDING CODES AND STANDARDS

INTRODUCTION

1. The referenced plans and specifications have been examined and found to have conditions which do not comply with the OBBC.
2. The referenced plans and specifications have been examined and additional information is required to conform with the OBBC.
3. The revisions to the referenced plans and specifications have been examined and the following items still do not comply with the OBBC.

INSUFFICIENT INFORMATION

4. Article I Administration Section *4101:2–1-19* requires the documents submitted for a permit to contain sufficient information for the Plan Examiner to conduct a meaningful critique.

ESTIMATED COST

5. Specify cost of architectural and structural work only (total project cost less HVAC [heating, ventilation and air-conditioning], electric, and plumbing) on building application form.

SURVEY

6. Please show the location of the building relative to the property lines and adjacent buildings on the same site, complete with dimensions and the stamp or seal of the surveyor (HCBC Sec. *A-18(H)(6)*].

CONSTRUCTION TYPE & USE

7. Please indicate the type of construction claimed in accordance with Article 4 and the Use Classification in accordance with Article 3 (Section *4101:2–1-19*).

NAME, ADDRESS

8. Documents submitted for a building permit are not valid unless each sheet has the name, address, and telephone number of the preparer (HCBC Section A-18-G).

PER CODE

9. In no case shall the Code be cited ("as per Code") or the term "legal" or its equivalent be used as a substitute for specific information (HCBC A-18-G).

ADDITIONS

10. Article 1 Administration *4101:2–1-11(C)*. If the structure is increased in floor area or the number of stories, the entire structure shall be made to conform with the requirements of OBBC in respect to means of egress, fire protection, light, and ventilation. Additional information on the existing structure must be furnished with regard to the requirements listed above, including all building dimensions and construction details. Section 908.0 offers the alternative of a fire wall.

USE CHANGE

11. Section *4101:2–1-11(A)* in "Administration of the OBBC—Change of Use": The use of a building shall not be changed unless or until the building and the building service equipment therein conform to the requirements of OBBC for buildings of the proposed new use group classification.

PART USE CHANGE	12. Article 1 Administrative *4101:2–1-11(B)* "Existing Buildings or Structures" states, "Part change in the use of a building shall be permitted if the portion of the building being changed is separated from the remainder of the structure with the required vertical and horizontal fire separation assemblies complying with the fire grading in Table 902.
GROSS AREA	13. The gross area of the building exceeds that allowed by Table *501*. Section 502 must be addressed in total for exceptions to Table *501*, i.e., Section 502.2. This must be shown on the site plans and approved by the local fire prevention officer having jurisdiction. Section 502.3 is second alternative.
HANDICAPPED	14. All buildings open to the general public must comply with Section *512.0*. Notable omissions from the drawings are Parking, Entrance Ramps, Doorway Grading, Toilet Rooms and Plumbing Fixtures, Drinking Fountains, etc. for the handicapped. Please submit manufacturers literature or detailed drawings for verification. Buildings and facilities required to be accessible by this section must comply with ANSI A117.1 1986.
FIRE WALLS	15. Section *908.1* requires fire walls to be self-supporting with structural stability under fire conditions to allow collapse of construction on either side without collapse of the wall. Strength and stability shall comply with the provisions of Articles 11 and 21.
	16. Adjacent construction may not tie into the fire wall. Lateral walls and roof structures abutting fire walls must be separated by nonstructural joint seal or caulk to allow the adjacent construction to fall clear of the fire wall.
	17. Section *908.5* requires fire walls to be continuous from foundation to 2′-8″ above the roof surface. The wall may terminate at the underside of the roof deck where the roof is of noncombustible construction or fire retardant treated wood for a distance of 4′ on either side of the wall.
	18. Fire walls must be continuous from the outer face on one side of the building to the outer face on the opposite side.
FIRE SEPARATION WALLS	19. Section *910.6* requires all fire separation walls to extend from the top of the fire resistance rated floor to the underside of the roof sheathing continuously.
UL NUMBERS	20. All rated assemblies, walls, floor/ceiling, beams, columns, etc. must have the appropriate assembly number from an approved testing agency shown on the drawings or contained in the specifications.
EXTERIOR WALLS	21. Fire resistance rating of exterior walls shall comply with Table *906.2*.

BUILDING CODES AND STANDARDS

OPENING PROTECTIVES

22. Section *906.5* requires approved protectives be provided in every opening which is less than 15' vertically above the roof of an adjacent structure within a horizontal distance of 15'. An alternate is to rate the adjacent roof/ceiling construction for not less than 1 hour.

STAMP OR SEAL

23. Please submit all calculations for sizing all structural members for the building, design loading, strength, etc. or have the Architect or Engineer responsible for the design stamp or seal the drawings per Section *4101:2–1-22(C)*.

VEHICULAR OPENINGS

24. Buildings with overhead doors or other vehicular access openings are required to comply with Section *609.0* unless the owner submits a letter stating that no vehicles will be allowed in the building at any time. (Significant requirements of Section *609.2.4* involve floor drains with grease interceptors and an exhaust system.)

STORY BELOW GRADE

25. Section *807.3.1* requires the floor/ceiling assembly and all supports below the grade level be protected by providing a fire resistance rating of not less than one hour. An alternate is to provide an approved fire suppression system for that floor below the grade level.

STORY ABOVE GRADE

26. The definition of a "story above grade" is as explained in Article 2, i.e., any story having its finished floor surface entirely above grade, except that a basement shall be considered as a story above grade when the distance from the grade to the finished surface of the floor above the basement is more than 6' for more than 50% of the total perimeter or more than 12' at any point.

20 SQ. FT.

27. Section *1002.15* requires an approved fire suppression system in every story or basement of all buildings where there is not provided at least 20 sq. ft. of opening entirely above the adjoining ground level in each 50' of exterior wall in the story or basement on at least one side of the building. The minimum dimension of the opening is 22".

CEILING HEIGHT

28. Section *708* requires the lowest projection in an occupiable room or habitable space to be not less than 7'–6". Show a cross section through the basement indicating the ceiling height to the lowest projection.

PLUMBING

29. Section *915.4* requires that all vertical pipes arranged in groups of two or more which penetrate two or more floors and which occupy an area of more than 1 sq. ft. and vertical ducts which penetrate two or more floors, shall be enclosed by construction having the fire resistance rating specified in Table *401*. Section *915.4.1* permits a shaft alternative using approved through-penetration firestop devices or systems.

30. Section *915.4* requires that all combustible pipes and ducts which penetrate two or more floors (including the slab on grade) be enclosed in construction having the fire resistance rating specified in Table *401*. Section *915.4.1* permits a shaft alternative using approved through—penetration firestop devices or systems.

ANCHORS
31. Section *1704.8* requires top plates to be anchored to walls min. 1/2" diameter anchor bolts embedded in poured-in-place concrete not less than 8" and in unit masonry construction not less than 15" (two block courses). There must be a minimum of two anchor bolts per section of plate which shall be placed a maximum of 12" from the ends of each section. Intermediate bolts must be spaced a maximum of 8' on center. This must be shown on the plans.

8" ABOVE
32. Section *1704.9* requires all frame construction to be a minimum of 8" above finish grade. This must be shown on a typical wall section.

PRESSURE-TREATED WOOD
33. Section *1712.3.1.3* requires that sleepers and sills on a concrete or masonry slab which is in direct contact with earth shall be of approved naturally durable or pressure-treated wood.

PERIMETER INSULATION
34. Section *3101.2.4* requires perimeter insulation to extend downward from the top of the slab for a distance of 24" and have a thermal resistance (R) of not less than 4.43.

FOOTINGS AND FOUNDATIONS
35. Section *1205.1* requires all footings to be a minimum of 30" below finish grade. This must be shown on a typical wall section.

36. Please refer to Section *1209* for concrete footing requirements.

37. Please refer to Section *1212.0* for mat, raft, floating, and monolithic foundation requirements.

38. Please refer to Section *1212* for pier foundation wall requirements.

39. Please refer to section *1224* for dampproofing, waterproofing, and drainage tile requirements for foundation walls.

RETAINING WALLS
40. Please refer to Section *1223* for retaining wall requirements.

TRUSS
41. When truss construction is involved in a building it is necessary to submit structural calculations or a truss loading diagram with the stamp or seal of the design engineer.

TYPE 2C CONSTRUCTION
42. This building is of 2C-type construction and no combustible construction materials may be used. This includes blocking in walls, furring strips and nailers, substrates for laminates and other decorative surfacings, and framing lumber for fixed case goods (Section *403.1*).

BUILDING CODES AND STANDARDS

DOORS	43. Section *812.3* requires all door openings to provide a free and clear width of not less than 32".
EXIT-AT-ALL-TIMES FUNCTION	44. Section *812.4* requires all egress doors (doors from occupiable rooms or spaces) to be readily openable from the side from which egress is to be made without the use of a key or special knowledge or effort. This must be shown on the plans or in the specifications. List hardware function numbers for all doors and the name of the lockset manufacturer.
KNURLED KNOB	45. Section *825.3* requires doors leading to dangerous areas to be equipped with knobs, handles, or bars that have been knurled.
ROLLING GRILLS	46. Section *812.5* requires rolling or sliding grills to have emergency manual release and lock operation from the inside without the use of a key.
TWO EXITS	47. Section *809.0* and Table *809.2* require not less than two exits from all rooms and spaces.
DEAD ENDS	48. Section *810.2* requires exit access passageways and corridors on floors required to have more than one exit to provide direct connection to such exits in opposite directions from any point in the passageway or corridor. The length of a dead-end corridor shall not be more than 20′. (See definition of "corridor.")
FIRE DOORS	49. Fire resistance rating of fire doors should comply with Table *916*.
DOORS IN SERIES	50. Section *812.2.3* requires doors in series to have a space between them of not less than 7′ measured in the closed position.
SLEEPING ROOM EXITS	51. Section *809.4* requires an emergency escape route from every sleeping room having a net clear opening of not less than 5.7 sq. ft. on the second and third floors, an 5.0 sq. ft. on the first floor (minimum height dimension—24″; minimum width dimension—20″). The sill height may not exceed 44″.
AISLES	52. For the exit route through the area, show the required aisle width (Section *805.1*).
EXIT ACCESS	53. For the exit route through the storeroom, show a 44″ wide striped aisle posted with a sign—"EXIT ACCESS—DO NOT BLOCK"—to comply with Section *807.2.1*.
OCCUPANT LOAD	54. With reference to Section *806.0*, specify the occupant load for this building.
RAMPS	55. Section *815.0* "Ramps" must be complied with, specifically *815.4*. Landings are required on both sides of doors and all landings must have a minimum length of 60″.

EXIT ENCLOSURES

56. Section *816.0* "Interior Exitway Stairways" must be complied with where applicable and, specifically, subsection *816.9.2* "Enclosures." All interior exit stairways must be enclosed in fire separation assemblies of a fire resistance rating in accordance with Table *401*. Section *910.6* requires these walls to extend to the underside of the roof above.

STAIRS

57. Section *816.2.2* requires the minimum headroom in all parts of a stairway to be not less than 6′–8″.

58. Section *816.3.1* requires the least dimension of a landing to be not less than the required widths for the stairway.

59. Section *816.4.1* requires all stair risers to be not more than 7″ and all treads to be not less than 11″.

GUARDS

60. Section *827.0* requires guardrails to be at least 42″ high with intermediate rails, balusters, or other construction such that a sphere with a diameter of 6″ cannot pass through any opening. Stair guardrails may be not less than 30″ high.

HANDRAILS

61. Section *828.2.2* requires handrails to be 34″ to 38″ high. Handrails that form part of a guardrail may be 34″ to 42″ high. Section 828.2.3. requires handrail ends to extend at least 12″ beyond the top riser and at least 12″ plus the width of one tread beyond the bottom riser.

EXTERIOR STAIRS

62. Section *819.0* "Exterior Stairways" must be complied with where applicable.

63. Section *819.1* requires exterior exitway stairs to be protected from accumulation of ice and snow.

ROOF ACCESS

64. Please refer to Section *817.0* "Access to Roof."

EXIT SIGNS

65. Show exit signs complying with Section *823.0*. Exit signs, supplemented by directional signs, are required in all buildings, rooms, or spaces required to have more than one exit.

NIGHT LIGHTS

66. Section *824.1* requires that all means of egress shall be equipped to provide one footcandle of illumination continuously during the time of occupancy. Lighting shall be controlled from a location inaccessible to unauthorized persons. Night lights shall be wired on a circuit independent of all other building circuits except emergency or exit light circuits.

EMERGENCY LIGHTS

67. Section *824.4* requires emergency egress lighting with an intensity of not less than 1 footcandle at floor level along all corridors, aisles, passageways, and stairwells in all buildings, rooms, or spaces required to have more than one exit.

LIGHTS

67A. Documentation (photometric chart) must be furnished showing the intensity of illumination and the light distribution pattern for the emergency egress lighting fixtures specified. Manufacturers literature is sufficient documentation, provided this information is furnished.

BUILDING CODES AND STANDARDS

INTERIOR SURFACES

68. All interior surfacing materials must have their fire behavior characteristics documented in accordance with Section *922.0* and Tables *922.5* and *922.7*. Manufacturers literature is sufficient documentation, providing the flame spread rate, smoke developed, and fuel contributed information is furnished.

FIRE SUPPRESSION SYSTEM STORAGE (Applicable Use Group)

69. Section *1002.14* requires an approved fire suppression system in all portions of use group (A, B, E, I, R1, R2) occupied for storage or workshop purposes. A layout of the fire suppression system and a properly executed "M" application must be submitted.

FIRE SUPPRESSION SYSTEM FURNACE

70. Section *1002.18* requires an approved fire suppression system in all furnace rooms, boiler rooms, and utility rooms with fuel fired equipment (other than electric).

LIMITED AREA SPRINKLER

71. Section *1005.0* requires that a layout of the limited area fire suppression system and a properly executed "M" application must be submitted. The layout shall locate the heads and supply piping.

PULL STATIONS

72. Sections *1017.3.1* and *1017.4* require a manual fire alarm system be installed in all A4 and E structures with pull stations not more than 5′ from each exit. The height of the manual pull station boxes shall be a minimum of 42″ and a maximum of 54″ from the floor to the activating handle.

ZONES

73. Section *1017.7.4* requires each floor to be zoned separately.

SMOKE DETECTORS

74. Section *1018.3.5* must be complied with. When more than one automatic fire alarm (smoke detector) is required to be installed, the detectors shall be hard-wired in such a manner that the activation of one alarm will activate all the alarms in the building.

HAZARDOUS STORAGE

75. Please identify materials, if any, to be stored in the proposed building in accordance with NFPA Vol. 3, Chapter 1, "Definitions" for "Combustible Liquids" and "Flammable Liquid" listing the appropriate subclassification (Classes I through III) (Table *306.2*).

76. Determine the maximum quantities of each class of liquid to be stored and list the unit of volume for each size of storage vessel. If single unit tank storage is proposed, so state and list the capacity (Table *306.2*).

77. Please identify storage areas for explosive gases or fire-enhancing materials (oxygen, nitrogen, hydrogen, etc.) (Table *306.2*).

78. Inside storage rooms must comply with all the appropriate requirements of NFPA Vol. 3, Chapter 4, Section 4.4. Some significant requirements of this section are: fire-rated construction, automatic fire suppression systems, explosion-proof electric wiring and equipment, and mechanical exhaust ventilation systems.

SPRAY BOOTHS	79. Please refer to Section *622.0* for requirements for paint spraying, spray booths, and fire protection.
FIRESTOP	80. Section *921.6* "Firestopping" must be complied with, specifically, *921.6.5* through *921.6.7*.
DRAFTSTOP	81. Section *921.7.1.1* "Draftstopping" in Use Groups R-1 and R-2 is required to be in line with the tenant separation walls when the walls do not extend to the floor sheathing above.
	82. In the attic and concealed roof spaces, draftstopping is required so that any horizontal area does not exceed 3000 sq. ft., per Section *921.7.2.2*.
CORNICE	83. Please refer to Sections *921.6.5* and *926* for exterior trim and fire-stopping requirements.
WALK-IN COOLERS	84. Section *2002.1* provides that documentation must be furnished on the fire behavior of all insulated walk-in boxes or coolers. Manufacturers literature is sufficient documentation, providing the flame spread rate, fuel contributed, and smoke developed data are provided for the finished panel, not for separate components alone.
	85. Section *2002.3.3* allows a maximum thickness of 4″ of foam plastic in freestanding walk-in freezers or coolers less than 400 sq. ft. in areas to be covered by not less than 0.032″ thick aluminum or 0.016″ thick corrosion-resistant steel.
GLAZING	86. All glazing must comply with the requirements of Section *2203.2* (tempered or safety glass). All doors and adjacent (within 12″) sidelights and all glazed panels within 18″ above a finished floor must comply.
	87. On non-egress doors, all mirrors on doors and adjacent side areas within 12″ must be tempered glass or glued 100% to solid backing.
	88. Section *807.2.4.1* does not permit mirrors on egress doors.
GLASS ROOFS	89. All glass roof structures, skylights, etc. must be shown to comply with the required live and snow loads in accordance with Article 11. Glass roof structures must also be shown to comply with Section *2204.0*.
ROOF	90. Please refer to Section *2301* roof classification and use requirements.
FIREPLACE	91. Please refer to Section *2402* for masonry fireplace construction requirements.
SERVICE SINKS	92. Section *4101:2–28-08* (C) See each Use Group table for requirements for toilet fixtures, service sinks, and drinking fountains.
TOILETS AND HEAT	93. A letter from the owner is required attesting to the existence of toilet and heat facilities under his ownership on this property with a maximum distance of travel from the proposed building to the facilities not to exceed 300 feet (Section *4101:2–28-08*).

MEZZANINE

94. Please refer to Section *605.0* for requirements for mezzanine.

MALL

95. Please refer to Section *601.0* for requirements for covered mall buildings.

SIGNS

96. Section *601.13.4* requires all edges and backs of plastic mall signs to be fully encased in metal.

97. Please refer to Sections *2901* and *601.13* for general sign requirements.

DRAINAGE

98. Please show rain-carrying equipment on the building discharging into a storm drainage system or natural swale.

TEMPORARY

99. Please refer to Section *626.0* for requirements for temporary structures.

DEMOLITION

100. Please refer to Section *3007* for precautions during demolition and excavation.

CLOSING

101. Please submit three copies of any new or revised drawings to this office. Revisions to drawings should be clouded, pochéd, crosshatched, transparent felt pen, or in some other manner differentiate between the original and the revisions.

MEES, STYLLS and PENDER, Architects/Planners
Ft. Archer, OH

DATE: REV:

CONTRACT NO.:   PO NO.:   BY: REVIEWED:

PROJECT DATA:

Project Location:

Client Representative:

Client Address:

Project Architect: Design Supervisor:

Geotechnical Engineer: Soils Report Complete: _____ Yes _____ No

LEGAL DESCRIPTION:

Lot: Block: Tract:

SITE DESCRIPTION:

Lot Size: Lot Area:

Assessor's Parcel No.:

Fire District: Seismic Zone: Wind Exposure:

FACILITY DESCRIPTION:

Building Use:

Building Area:

No. of Stories: Height of Building:

Occupancy Classifications: Construction Type:

ZONING REGULATIONS:

Applicable Zoning Ordinance:

Existing Zoning Classification: Required Zoning Classification:

No. of Parking Stalls Required: Regular Stall Size:

                                              Compact Stall Size:

No. of Handicapped Parking Stalls Required: Handicapped Stall Size:

No. of Service Vehicle Stalls Required: Service Vehicle Stall Size:

Yards: Front: Side: Rear:

Conditional Use Permit Required: _____ Yes _____ No

Special Landscape Requirements:

Special Lighting Requirements:

Buildable Area Allowed On Lot: Special Setbacks:

Construction Signs Permitted: Sign Limitations:

BUILDING HEIGHT LIMITATIONS (Stories / Feet):

According to Zoning Restrictions:

According to Occupancy Group:

A combination form incorporating both code analysis and project information; a good form for use when applying for the building permit—the code official is aware of the analysis and the personnel responsible.

MEES, STYLLS and PENDER, Architects/Planners
Ft. Archer, OH

According to Construction Type:

According to Federal Aviation Contactity:

Allowable Height Increase:

Other:

APPLICABLE BUILDING CODES:

City: Edition:

County: Edition:

State: Edition:

Federal: Edition:

Other: Edition:

Agency Responsible For Enforcing Codes:

REGULATIONS OTHER THAN BUILDING CODES:

Fire Prevention Code: Edition:

Fire Exit Code: Edition:

Elevator Code: Edition:

Institutional Code: Edition:

Industrial Code: Edition:

Hazardous Use Code: Edition:

Electrical Code: Edition:

Heating and Ventilating Code: Edition:

Plumbing Code: Edition:

Handicap Code: Edition:

Others: Edition:

                                         Edition:

ENVIRONMENTAL IMPACT REPORT REQUIRED: _____ Yes   _____ No

Prepared By:

Approval Agency:

BUILDING PERMIT:

Project Valuation:

Plan Checking Fee: Permit Fee:

Permit No.:   Date:

Variance:

Responsible Party For Obtaining Permit (Contractor, Owner, or Architect):

MEES, STYLLS and PENDER, Architects/Planners
Ft. Archer, OH

BUILDING AREA LIMITS BY OCCUPANCY GROUP:

Basic Allowable Area For 1 Story ....

Increase For 1 Hour Fire Resistance ....

Increase For Fire Zone ....

Increase for Separation 2, 3, or All Sizes ....

Increase For Fire Suppression System ....

Total Allowable For 1 Story ....

Area For Buildings Over 1 Story (Not to Exceed 200%) ....

Note!!! Attach Calculations.

OCCUPANCY SEPARATIONS IN AREAS OF MIXED OCCUPANCIES:

Group: _____ to: _____ Hours: _____

Group: _____ to: _____ Hours: _____

ASSEMBLY ROOM:

_____ Yes _____ No   Located on _____ Floors

Seat Spacing: _____   Aisle Widths: _____

MINIMUM REQUIRED TOILET FIXTURES:

	Total	Men	Women
Water Closets			
Urinals			
Lavatories			
Percent Handicapped			
Other Required Fixtures			

SPECIAL HAZARDS:

Areas and Requirements: _____

List of Hazardous Materials: _____

HELIPORTS OR HELISTOPS:

WALLS AND OPENING PROTECTION BASED ON:

	Occup.	Const.	Hazard Occup.	Fire Dist.
Fire Resistance of Exterior Walls				
Openings in Exterior Walls				
Enclosure of Vertical Shafts				

FIRE RESISTIVE REQUIREMENTS BASED ON CONSTRUCTION (RATING IN HOURS):

Exterior Bearing Walls:	Permanent Partitions:
Interior Bearing Walls:	Floors:

BUILDING CODES AND STANDARDS

MEES, STYLLS and PENDER, Architects/Planners
Ft. Archer, OH

Exterior Nonbearing Walls:	Roofs:
Structural Frame:	Exterior Doors and Windows:
Shaft Enclosures:	Parapet Required:
Smoke Tower Required:	Ceiling:
Other:	

FIRE SUPPRESSION SYSTEMS:

Automatic Fire Sprinklers:	Fire Hose Cabinets:
Fire Extinguishers:	Standpipes: _____ Wet _____ Dry
Minimum Distance Between Fire Hose Cabinets:	

ROOF REQUIREMENTS:

Construction Materials:	Slope:
Drainage System Requirements:	

EXIT ANALYSIS:

Level	Occupancy	Area (Sq. Ft.)	Sq. Ft. / Person	No. Persons	Exits Required	
					Number	Width

Total No. Persons ....

Number of Exits Required, Total Building:	Width of Exits:
Minimum Distance Between Exits:	Dead End Corridor Limit:
Exit Signs Required: Illuminated:	Nonilluminated:
Horizontal Exit Requirements:	
Exit Enclosure Requirements:	
Exit Court Requirements:	
Exit Passageway Requirements:	
Smokeproof Enclosure Requirements:	

Note!!!
1. Level exit widths = level occupied divided by 50 = Answer in feet.
2. Multiple level exits use 50 percent of level above and below added to occupants.

STAIRWAY REQUIREMENTS:

Minimum Width:	Maximum Rise:	Minimum Run:
Exceptions:		
Minimum Headroom:		Handrail Height:
Guardrail Height:		Landing Requirements:

PROJECT DATA
AND CODE ANALYSIS
FORM 220- F10 (29Jun96)
Page 5 of 5

MEES, STYLLS and PENDER, Architects/Planners
Ft. Archer, OH

HANDICAPPED RAMP REQUIREMENTS:

Minimum Width: ______ Maximum Slope: ______

Handrails: ______ Landing Requirements: ______

Door Intrusion: ______

LIST SPECIAL HANDICAPPED REQUIREMENTS:

VARIANCE / WAIVERS:

REMARKS:

OHIO BASIC BUILDING CODE
CODE REVIEW OUTLINE

PROJECT NAME _____

PROJECT LOCATION _____

BUILDING DEPARTMENT JURISDICTION _____

FIRE LIMITS _____

    RELATED AGENCIES

☐ ZONING   USE _____   SIGNS _____

        YARDS (FRONT)_____ (SIDE)_____ (REAR)_____

        EASEMENTS _____   LIGHTING _____

        HEIGHT _____   PARKING _____

☐ ENGINEER   PERMIT REQUIRED

    A.   LOCAL   DRIVEWAYS _____   ☐
    B.   STATE   CURBS _____   ☐
               SIDEWALKS _____   ☐
               CUT & FILL _____   ☐

☐ BOARD OF HEALTH   LOT CLEARANCE _____   ☐

☐ SEWER DISTRICT   STORM _____   ☐
                      SANITARY _____   ☐

☐ FIRE DEPARTMENT   CODE (403) _____   ☐

☐ NURSING HOMES   STATE AGENCY _____   ☐

ARTICLE 2 (4101:2-2)

* **USE GROUP** (202) Refer to Sections 203 thru 211 for descriptions

A-1A ☐	A-1B ☐	A-2 ☐	A-3 ☐	A-4 ☐	A-5 ☐	
B ☐	F ☐	H ☐	I-1 ☐	I-2 ☐	M ☐	
R-1 ☐	R-2 ☐	R-3 ☐	R-4 ☐	S-1 ☐	S-2 ☐	T ☐

(NOTE: 203.1 requires all assembly areas with occupancy load of less than 50 to be classified as B)

David S. Collins, FAIA
The Preview Group
A code search form that should be utilized by all design professionals. The sample here is specific to one code, but a more standard form can be developed for office use and for various codes that may be encountered.

* <u>MIXED USE</u> (213.0 & 414.2.3)

1. ☐ MOST RESTRICTIVE REQUIREMENT
   MOST RESTRICTIVE HEIGHT & AREA LIMITS APPLY

2. ☐ SEPARATED PER (902) BY FIRE SEPARATION WALLS (909).
   EACH AREA RESTRICTED BY ITS CLASSIFICATION

3. ☐ SEPARATED PER (902) BY FIRE WALLS (907 & 908)
   213.2   INCIDENTAL USES
   414.2.3   PUBLIC GARAGES & OTHER OCCUPANCIES
   905.4   PACKING & SHIPPING ROOMS
   ☐ ARTICLE 9 COMPLIANCE (905.0)

   ☐ SINGLE OCCUPANCY

* <u>SPECIAL OCCUPANCIES</u>   Article 4 - Indicate & Review

☐ (401) EXPLOSION HAZARDS
☐ (402) VOLATILE FLAMMABLES
☐ (405) EXISTING BUILDINGS
☐ (407) PYROXYLIN PLASTICS
☐ (408) PROJECTION ROOM CONSTRUCTION - FLAMMABLE FILM
☐ (409) COMBUSTIBLE FIBERS
☐ (410) COMBUSTIBLE DUST & GRAIN
☐ (411) PAINT SPRAYING & SPRAY BOOTHS
☐ (412) DRY CLEANERS
   ☐ TYPE 1A - HIGH HAZARD
   ☐ TYPE 1, 2 or 3 - HIGH HAZARD
   ☐ USE B - LOW HAZARD
☐ (413) PRIVATE GARAGE *
☐ (414) PUBLIC GARAGE * (See also M317.9 & M317.1.5)
   ☐ GROUP 1 (S-1)
   ☐ GROUP 2 (S-2)
☐ (415) MOTOR FUEL SERVICE STATION *
☐ (416) MOTOR VEHICLE REPAIR *
☐ (423) PARKING LOTS *
☐ (424) MOBILE UNITS *
☐ (417) PLACE OF ASSEMBLY
☐ (418) ASSEMBLY OTHER THAN THEATERS
☐ (419) AMUSEMENT PARKS
☐ (420) STADIUMS & GRANDSTANDS
☐ (422) TENTS, AIR SUPPORTED STRUCTURES & TEMPORARY STRUCTURES

☐ (425)   MOTELS

☐ (426)   RADIO & TV TOWERS

☐ (427)   RADIO & TV TOWERS (12' or higher)

☐ (428)   SWIMMING POOLS

☐ (429)   OPEN PARKING STRUCTURES *

☐ (430)   FALLOUT SHELTERS

☐ (431)   HIGH RISE BUILDINGS

    ☐   AUTOMATIC FIRE PROTECTION

    ☐   COMPARTMENTATION

☐ (432)   COVERED MALLS

☐ (316)   HISTORIC BUILDINGS

☐ (205.3) SPECIAL INDUSTRIAL USES

NOTES:

* AUTOMOBILE - PARKING/SERVICE

═══

* SPRINKLER (FIRE SUPPRESSION) SYSTEMS   1202.0

                    Where required

☐ A-1 (1202.2)

☐ A-2 (1202.3)

    ☐ > 5,000 sf

    ☐ > ONE STORY

☐ A-3 > 12,000 sf (1202.4)

☐ A STAGE (1202.5)(417.7)

☐ H (1202.6)

☐ I (1202.7) NOTE EXCEPTIONS CLAIMED _____

☐ M, S-1, F (1202.8) (205.3)

    ☐ > 12,000 sf

    ☐ > 24,000 sf (TOTAL FLOOR AREA)

    ☐ > 3 STORIES

☐ PUBLIC GARAGES (1202.9) NOTE EXCEPTION CLAIMED _____

    ☐ > 10,000 sf

    ☐ > 7,500 sf &   1 story

    ☐ > 5,000 sf &   2 stories

    ☐ > 3 stories

    ☐ UPPER STORIES DIFFERENT USE

    ☐ > 50% BELOW GRADE

☐ BUS GARAGE (1202.10)

   ☐ PER (1202.9)

   ☐ TERMINAL FOR > 3 BUSES

   ☐ STORAGE OR LOADING FOR > 3 BUSES

☐ UNLIMITED AREA BLDGS (1202.11, 205.3.3 & 307) NOTE EXCEPTION CLAIMED _____

☐ STORAGE & WORKSHIP (1202.12)

   ☐ A

   ☐ B

   ☐ I

   ☐ R-1

   ☐ R-2

☐ STORY, BASEMENT OR CELLAR (WINDOWLESS) (1202.13)

☐ PAINT ROOMS (FLAMMABLE MATERIALS) (1202.14)

☐ TRASH ROOMS & CHUTES (1202.15)

☐ FURNACE ROOMS (1202.16) NOTE EXCEPTION CLAIMED _____ BOILER ENCLOSURE
   REFER TO DEFINITION OF FURNACE O BMC M-201   1105.2

☐ UNENCLOSED VERTICAL OPENING (1202.17)

   ☐ OPEN WELLS (ATRIUM) 520.0

   ☐ COMMUNICATING FLOORS 616.10

☐ RANGE HOODS (1202.18)

☐ ALTERNATE PROTECTION (1202.19)

   ☐ SPECIFY SYSTEM _____ ☐ GENERATOR/TRANSFORMER ☐ COMMUNICATING EQPT

* SUPPRESSION SYSTEM SPECIFY _____

☐ WATER 1204.0

   ☐ LIMITED AREA 1205.0

   ☐ WATER SPRAY 1206.0

   ☐ CONNECTION 1213.0

☐ FOAM 1207.0

☐ CO_2 1208.0

☐ HALOGEN 1209.0

☐ DRY CHEMICALS 1210.0

* STANDPIPES 1211.0

WHERE REQUIRED:

☐ 1211.2 MANUFACTURING, MECHANICAL, ELECTRICAL, MERCANTILE, ART, LAUNDRING, PRINTING, TELEGRAPH, TELEPHONE OFFICE AND RAILROAD DEPOT.

☐ 1211.2.1 A-1, A-2 or A-3 > 1 STORY W/ > 300 OCCUP.

☐ 1211.2.2 3 STORIES

  ☐ A

  ☐ B > 3000 SF/FL.

  ☐ F EXCEPT PER 1211.2 > 3000 SF/FL.

  ☐ H > 10,000 SF/FL.

  ☐ I

  ☐ M > 10,000 SF/FL.

  ☐ R-1

  ☐ R-2 > 10,000 SF/FL.

  ☐ S-1 > 3,000 SF/FL.

  ☐ S-2 > 10,000 SF/FL.

  ☐ T > 10,000 SF/FL.

☐ 1211.2.3 FOUR STORIES

☐ 1211.2.4 PUBLIC GARAGES

  ☐ > 10,000 sf.

  ☐ > 7,500 sf. 1 story

  ☐ > 5,000 sf. 2 stories

  ☐ > 3 stories

  ☐ UPPER STORIES DIFFERENT USE

  ☐ > 50% BELOW GRADE

* AUTOMATIC FIRE ALARM SYSTEM & MANUAL FIRE ALARM

  WHERE REQUIRED (1216.0 & 1217.0)

  ☐ I

  ☐ R-1 NOTE EXEMPTION CLAIMED _____

  ☐ R-2 NOTE EXEMPTION FOR MANUAL FIRE ALARM

  - NOTE SECTION 1216.4 EXEMPTS SPRINKLERED BUILDINGS. MANUAL FIRE ALARMS PER 1217.0 ARE REQUIRED.

* MANUAL ALARM (1217.0)

  ☐ A-4 NEW AND EXISTING. NOTE EXEMPTION CLAIMED _____

  ☐ B > 2 STORIES. NOTE EXEMPTION CLAIMED _____

  ☐ R-2 > 3 STORIES

ARTICLE 3 (4101:2-3)

DETERMINE ACTUAL (DESIGNED) BUILDING AREA PER FLOOR

CHECK TABLES 305 & 305.4

ACTUAL AREA _____

ACTUAL HEIGHT _____

CONST. TYPE (214) _____

AREA & HEIGHT PER TABLE 305 _____

☐ ACTUAL BUILDING AREA DOES NOT EXCEED THAT PERMITTED BY TABLES 305 & 305.4
   (GO TO NEXT ARTICLE)

☐ ACTUAL BUILDING AREA EXCEEDS THAT PERMITTED BY TABLES 305 & 305.4 (CONTINUE
   WITH THIS ARTICLE)

A. Establish allowable perimeter increase (306.2) Note on drawings 18' FIRE LANE

$$\left(\frac{\text{Open perimeter (30'-0'' min. separation)}}{\text{Total Perimeter}} - 25\% \right) \times 2 = \% \text{ of Increase}$$

$$\left(\underline{\hspace{4cm}} - 25\% \right) \times 2 = \underline{\hspace{3cm}}$$

B. Establish reduction for height _____(305.4)

C. Establish increase for sprinklers _____(306.3)

D. Solve for tabular area (area permitted by Table 305)

$$TA = \frac{\text{Actual Area}}{1 + (\% \text{ increase perimeter}) - (\% \text{reduction for height}) + (\% \text{ increase for sprinkler})}$$

$$TA\underline{\hspace{2cm}} = \frac{AA}{(\underset{\text{Perimeter}}{\hspace{1.5cm}}) - (\underset{\text{Height}}{\hspace{1.5cm}}) + (\underset{\text{Sprinkler}}{\hspace{1.5cm}}) + 1}$$

E. From Table 305 determine minumum construction type _____
   Unlimited area bldg. 307

F. Check fire limit requirements - Section 302.0

Determine minimum fire resistance requirements based on minimum construction type and fire limit requirements (List UL or other approved
testing agency numbers for each component of construction per Table 214).

	AGENCY	LISTING			AGENCY	LISTING
1				7		
2				8		
3				9		
4				10		
5				11		
6						

TESTING ARTICLE 8, LOADING ARTICLE 7

CHECK SPECIAL REQUIREMENTS OF ARTICLES 4 AND 9

413.2, 905.8, 905.7.3

* DETERMINE OCCUPANCY LOAD   Article 6

- HOW DETERMINED (REFER TO TABLE 606) USE LARGEST (606.1)

☐ GROSS FLOOR AREA

☐ NET FLOOR AREA

☐ ACTUAL NUMBER OF OCCUPANTS

    ☐ FIXED SEATS (NOTE 1)

    ☐ AS DETERMINED (NOTE 2 & 606.7)

EXIT REQUIREMENTS   Article 4 & 6

- MINIMUM NUMBER

☐ 609.2 MINIMUM OF TWO EXITS (612.2)

    ☐ 609.3 ONE EXIT EXCEPTION

        ☐ R-2 (NOTE 2)

        ☐ B (NOTE 3)

☐ 405.3.2 EXISTING BUILDING

☐ 408.4   SCREENING ROOM

☐ 417.3   THEATRES

☐ 418.2   ASSEMBLY

☐ 425.3   MOTELS

☐ 431   HIGH-RISE

☐ 432.2.3 COVERED MALLS

NOTE REQUIRED EMERGENCY ESCAPE FROM SLEEPING ROOMS BELOW THE FOURTH FLOOR.

☐ 609.5   PARKING STRUCTURES

EXIT TABLES - INDICATE WIDTH & CAPACITY OF EACH COMPONENT AS DETERMINED BY TABLE 608 (Note: 608

PLACE A HEAVY LINE IN CONTRASTING COLOR BETWEEN FLOOR LEVELS

FLOOR	TOTAL OCCUPANCY PER FLOOR	INTERIOR DOOR (1)	CORRIDOR(2)	STAIR(3)	EXTERIOR DOOR (1)	RAMP (4)
		NO.	NO.	NO.	NO.	NO.
		NO.	NO.	NO.	NO.	NO.
		NO.	NO.	NO.	NO.	NO.
		NO.	NO.	NO.	NO.	NO.
		NO.	NO.	NO.	NO.	NO.
		NO.	NO.	NO.	NO.	NO.
		NO.	NO.	NO.	NO.	NO.
		NO.	NO.	NO.	NO.	NO.

(1) DOORS 612

OPERATION 612 ☐ INDICATED ON PLANS   ☐ SEE SCHEDULE ON _____

INTO STAIRWAY   616.6.2 & 616.6.3   REVOLVING DOORS 613
SEE 612.3 for size and capacity per 608

(2) CORRIDORS 610

GRADE PASSAGEWAYS 611   DEAD END CORRIDORS   610.2
FIRE SEPARATION WALL   610.4 & 909   THEATERS   417

(3) STAIRWAYS 616   NOTE 2 - PROPORTIONS (2R+1T = 24 to 25)

HANDRAILS 616.5.1   FIRE ESCAPES   621.0
GUARDS   616.5.2   COMMUNICATING FLOORS 616.10
EXTERIOR STAIRS   619.0   SOLID RISERS   616.9
ESCALATORS 620.0   NON-COMB (EXCEPT TYPE 3 OR 4 CONST.)

(4) RAMPS (615)

IDENTIFY HAZARDOUS EXITS   625.3

- MISCELLANEOUS EXIT PROVISIONS - INDICATE INTENDED USE

☐ HORIZONTAL EXITS 614
☐ EMERGENCY ESCAPE 431.3.2 & 609.4
☐ ROOF ACCESS   617
☐ HIGH-RISE BUILDINGS

    ☐ 618 - A-2, A-3, A-4, A-5, B, F, I, M, R-1
    ☐ 431 - B, R-1, R-2

EXITWAY ACCESS TRAVEL DISTANCE   607

☐ BUILDING SPRINKLERED

☐ BUILDING NOT SPRINKLERED

GENERAL AREA DESCRIPTION		TRAVEL TO EXITWAY ACCESS		TRAVEL TO EXITWAY	
NAME	NO.	AREA	DISTANCE	AREA	DISTANCE

\- SPECIALTY ITEMS

* EXIT SIGNS   623.0

☐ BUILDING OCCUPANCY LOAD LESS THAN 50

☐ BUILDING OCCUPANCY LOAD MORE THAN 50

- 6" LETTERS

- COLOR _____   BACKGROUND _____

- FOOT CANDLE _____

- POWER SOURCE (EMERGENCY) _____

* LIGHTING   624.0

☐ EGRESS LIGHTING CIRCUIT NO(S). _____

☐ POWER SOURCE (1 HR)

☐ A _____

☐ B _____

☐ I _____

☐ M _____

☐ R-1 _____

☐ R-2 > 50 _____

☐ WINDOWLESS BLDG _____

ARTICLE 15 REQUIRES ELECTRICAL TO BE INSTALLED PER NEC.

* <u>LIGHT & VENTILATION</u> - <u>MECHANICAL EQUIPMENT</u> (Articles 5 & 11)

NATURAL LIGHT 506.2 - 8% of floor area
NATURAL VENTILATION 506.2 - 4% of floor area

ARTIFICIAL LIGHT % VENTILATION 504

NOTE: 25% min. outside make up air per M-317.11.2.1

- YARDS (Required for light and ventilation)

RESIDENTIAL & INSTITUTIONAL 517.1
REAR YARD (35' min.) = (BLDG. HEIGHT - 35) x .33ft.+ 35 ft.

$$\frac{}{\text{REAR YARD}} = (\frac{}{\text{BLDG. HEIGHT}} - 35) \times .33ft.+ 35 ft.$$

ALL OTHER USES 517.2
REAR YARD (10' min.) = (BLDG. HEIGHT - 35) x .25ft. + 10ft.

$$\frac{}{} = (\frac{}{} - 35) \times .25ft. + 10ft.$$

- COURTS (Required for light and ventilation)

WIDTH 516.2
OUTER COURT
.25 ft. x HEIGHT = WIDTH (5' min.)

INNER COURT
.5 ft. x HEIGHT = Width (10' min.)

IRREGULAR SHAPES MAY BE AVERAGED W/ 5' MIN. AT ANY POINT.

AREA 516.2

__ CROSS SECTION AREA
$1\frac{1}{2}$ x WIDTH = CROSS SECTION AREA

__ LENGTH
LENGTH = 2 x WIDTH

ADDITIONAL REQUIREMENTS (516.4, 516.5, 516.6, 516.7)

- SHAFTS

__ REQUIRED VENTILATION (515, 520)

__ SPRINKLERED 1202.15

- CORRIDOR VENTILATION (519)

- ROOM SIZES (506.5)

__ MINIMUM CEILING HEIGHTS

__ MINIMUM FLOOR AREA (DWELLING UNIT)

- MECHANICAL EQUIPMENT (ARTICLE M-1 to M-11)

The building code and mechanical code are seperate documents but must
work together as integral parts of one another. It is extremely important

219

to recognise when parts of one code affects the application of another code. For example, penetrations of fire rated assemblies by ductwork or the use of plenums for make up, supply, exhaust or return air are addressed om the building code (905.10, 908.3). The construction of dampers and plenum construction are also covered in the mechanical code (M-301.11, M-300.6).

* SPECIAL CONSTRUCTION

___ ATRIUM DESIGN (520)

___ COMMUNICATING FLOOR (616.10)

___ ELEVATORS, ESCALATORS, DUMBWAITERS & CONVEYORS (ARTICLE 16)

___ ROOF ACCESS (617, M-306.3)

___ BALCONIES (625.5 BOCA)

___ RETAINING WALLS (1309, 870)

___ SWIMMING POOLS (428.2)
NOTE OTHER SPECIAL CONSTRUCTION AS APPLICABLE:

* ENERGY CODE NCS/BCS (ARTICLE 20)

___ APPLICATION TO ALL BUILDINGS
EXCEPTIONS

___ HISTORIC BUILDING

___ EXISTING BUILDING

___ ENERGY USE LESS THAN 1 WATT/SF = 3.4 BTU/SF

___ BUILDING NOT HEATED OR COOLED
DATA SHOWN

___ FORMS SUBMITTED

___ WALL SECTIONS - R & U_o VALUES SHEET NO.(s) _____

___ EQUIPMENT SPECIFICATION SHEET NO.(s)_____

* <u>HANDICAP REQUIREMENTS</u>   SECTION 315.0

    - CHECK WITH JURISDICTION FOR APPLICABILITY.

    - RESIDENTIAL

        ☐ R-1 (ONE UNIT IN TEN)

        ☐ R-2 (ONE UNIT IN TEN) ACCESS TO LAUNDRY & STORAGE

    - ALL OTHER OCCUPANCIES (AS DIRECTED)

        ITEMS CONTROLLED

        - ENTRANCES
        - PARKING FACILITIES, SPACES AND CURBS
        - INTERIOR ACCESS
        - SWITCHES, CONTROLS AND ALARMS
        - TELEPHONES
        - ELEVATORS
        - PLUMBING FIXTURES
        - SEATING IN ASSEMBLY
        - CHECKOUT LANES
        - TURNSTILES

* <u>TOILET FACILITIES</u>   ARTICLE 17

    PROVIDE THE MINIMUM NUMBER OF FIXTURES AS PRESCRIBED BY TABLE 4101:2-17-07

    NOTE:

    ☐ SEPARATE FACILITIES ARE REQUIRED FOR EACH SEX EXCEPT WITHIN INDIVIDUAL RESIDENTIAL UNITS , OR ONLY ONE FIXTURE REQUIRED (1707-B)

    ☐ SEPARATE TOILET AND LOCKER ROOMS ARE REQUIRED WHERE FEMALES ARE EMPLOYED

    ☐ PRIVACY MUST BE PROVIDED TO PREVENT DIRECT VIEW INTO TOILET ROOMS FROM OTHER AREAS.

    ☐ FLOORS AND 4" BASE MUST BE NON-ABSORBANT, LEAK-PROOF MATERIALS

    ☐ ENCLOSURES THAT DO NOT EXTEND TO THE FLOOR MUST BE 9" ABOVE THE FLOOR.

    ☐ TOILET FACILITIES FOR FOOD PREPARATION AREAS MUST NOT OPEN DIRECTLY INTO THE FOOD PREPARATION AREAS.

    - TOILETS NOT REQUIRED FOR BUILDINGS < 100 SF. IF TRAVEL TO TOILETS IS < 300 FT.

    - TOILETS <u>FOR THE PUBLIC</u> ARE NOT REQUIRED IN STORES OF < 5,000 SF.

    - SHOPPING CENTERS OR MALLS MAY HAVE PUBLIC TOILETS IN A CENTRAL LOCATION, THE NUMBER OF FIXTURES DETERMINED BY THE TOTAL SF NOT SERVED BY ANY OTHER PUBLIC TOILETS AND IF LOCATED WITHIN 500 FT AND NOT MORE THAN ONE FLIGHT OF STAIRS OF THE ENTRANCE TO ANY STORE SERVED.

    - TOILETS FOR FACULTY OR STAFF MUST BE PROVIDED SEPARATELY FROM STUDENTS, INMATES OR PATIENTS.

    - TOILETS MAY BE IN SEPARATE BUIDLINGS UNDER THE SAME OWNERSHIP IF OCCUPANTS OF ASSEMBLY AREAS NEED NOT TRAVEL MORE THAN 300 FT. AND ONE STORY (AND ACCEPTED BY BUILDING OFFICIAL) OR EMPLOYEES IN STORAGE BUILDINGS NEED NOT TRAVEL MORE THAN 500 FT.

ROOM NO.	NO. FIXTURES
1	
2	
3	
4	

ROOM NO.	NO. FIXTURES
5	
6	
7	
8	

* <u>CONSTRUCTION REQUIREMENTS</u> ARTICLE*s* 7, 8 & 13

-ARTICLE 7

__ LIVE LOADS (Table 706)

ROOM DESIG.	AREA OCCUPANCY OR USE	MINIMUM DESIGN LOAD	CAPACITY

__ ROOF LOADS (Table 710)

MINIMUM ROOF LOADS_____
(Note additional special loading in 710)

SNOW LOAD (711)

__ A, H, I, R-1 (one hundred year L-102.1c)_____ = g

__ B, F, M, R-2 (fifty year L102.1b)_____ = g

__ S, T   (twenty five year L102.1a)_____ = g

DESCRIBE ROOF CONFIGURATION AND SHOW C_s CALCULATION(s).

Use C_s from worst case per 711.3

C_s x g (from L102.1 above) = _____ .

__ WIND LOADS (Section 712, 713, 714)
INDICATE APPROPRIATE CALCULATIONS AND REFERENCE SECTIONS

__ COMBINATION LOADING (Section 717)

- NOTE 717.4 PERMITS WIND STRESS TO BE NEGLECTED
- NOTE 701.1 PERMITS WIND AND EARTHQUAKE LOADING TO BE APPLIED SEPERATELY - THE GREATER BEING APPLICABLE.

-ARTICLE 8

Regulates materials of construction

A & B Includes standards, tables and regulations for various materials

C is a general section of wall construction regulations
-PARAPETS (868, 907.7)
-GLAZING (857, 860) FEDERAL SEFETY GLAZING STANDARD
-FOUNDATIONS (869, 723 to 742)
-RETAINING WALLS (873)
-DECAY & TERMITE PROTECTION (874)
-FIRE STOPS & PROTECTION (875, 912, 922.2)
-THERMAL INSULATION (876)
-VENEER APPLICATION (861, 862, 864, 865)

* PREFABRICATED CONSTRUCTION (Article 18)

This section establishes control of industrialised units, modular unit and prefabricated components of construction. Everything so regulated is authorised by the State of Ohio and jurisdiction is limited to the authorising agencies. Individual certified departments of building departments regulating 1, 2, 3 family dwelling units do not have jurisdiction over the construction of authorised construction. Placement, foundations, andhorage and any on site construction, whether part of the authorised construction or not, does fall to the local jurisdiction for approval, permits, inspection and certificate of occupancy and use.

* SIGNS (Article 14)

— GROUND SIGNS (1408)

— ROOF SIGNS (1409)

— WALL SIGNS (1410)

— PROJECTING SIGNS (1411)

— MARQUEE SIGNS (1412)

— PORTABLE SIGNS (1415)

GENERAL REQUIREMENTS

— STRUCTURAL DESIGN (1407)

— ELECTRICAL CONNECTIONS (1414)

— CONSTRUCTION (1407)

14

Working Drawings

Communication between members of the design team must be open, free, continuous, and complete. There is no place for guesswork or thoughtless inclusions. Responsibility is imposed on everyone from the project architect to junior drafters. Working drawings are the graphic communication between the designer and the contractor. Therefore, to convey the designer's concept in full, the working drawings must be clear and concise. Their production should be aimed at an easy flow of information to the contractor on the job site. Further, because the drawings are a part of the contract documents, they are legal documents that impose various obligations on the parties to the contract—that is, the owner and the contractors. A simple diagram will help to show the proper alignment of the contract documents. This diagram charts each design team member and shows the distinct separation of information vital to the success of the documents. The design team consists of the designer, the supervisor (i.e., partner-in-charge), project architect or job captain, the consultants (structural, mechanical, and electrical engineers, landscape architect, graphic designer, interior designer, construction manager), and the drafting force, from registered architects to junior draftsmen, specification writers, and miscellaneous personnel (typists, reproduction specialists, and so on).

In addition, some part of the design team must function as quality control, governing and reviewing all work and all decisions made during production. Each member of the team must be aware that the owner can control only two of the three major factors affecting the project: scope, quality, and cost; for example, no owner can validly demand the biggest building (scope), the best of everything (quality), and the lowest price (cost). Obviously, this would be impossible to achieve, and the owner must choose the two factors that should be given priority. The design team then functions to provide the third factor and complete the project successfully. Example: if the owner requires a building of a given size and has a minimum budget, the design team must carefully evaluate the quality of the materials to be used. In this way a building can be built within the budgetary requirements. Evaluation must be done at almost all levels during the working drawings phase, because it is here that the various elements of the overall design are detailed. Although this sounds like a high-level process, it can affect the smallest items and the least significant draftsman working on the drawings. Nearly everyone makes some sort of decision along the line. However, these decisions must be consistent with the project requirements. We can no longer afford draftsmen who sit at their drawing boards eight hours a day doing mundane work on the

pick any 2!

The owner's dilemma! Although all three items noted are essential to every project, the owner has control over only two. The architect therefore must work in the third area to fill the owner's requirements. This choice affects all clients, no matter how big or small the project.

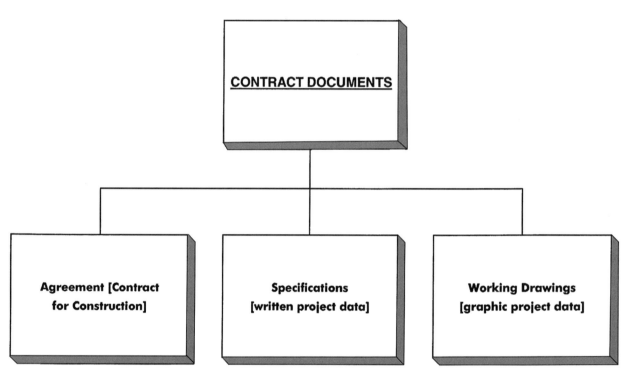

The chart shows the make-up of the Contract Documents. This set of documents encompasses the entire project work and how it will be accomplished. It is vital that there be a distinct separation between the various documents, and the information they contain, so a complete and full coordinated set of documents is achieved. The specifications should involve the "how" of the work; the drawings the "what" and "where." The agreement covers the legal obligations of all parties and, and their relationship to the project. The project architect must monitor his staff carefully to see that proper notations prevent long specifications from appearing on the drawings. These documents, when used together, should provide a complete package of information—no gaps, overlaps, contradictions, or ambiguities.

READABILITY

Technically correct information, on construction contract drawings, is better portrayed when there is distinct separation between materials, devices, and other items. Only rarely does the architect utilize an "exploded view," which in essence is an assembly or installation guide. Normally, sections and details shown the work in close proximity, as it will exist when finished.

Therefore, there is a need to be sensitive to, and to execute all drawings by:

— using variations in line weights, within a limited palate;
— treating similar edges in the same manner;
— following the principle that everything cut in section is depicted with dark lines for edges;
— distinguishing between edges of materials and thickness [of thin, sheet material such as sheet metal, floor coverings];
— understanding what the various parts are made of, and mentally visualize what they look like from an end or "cut" view;
— showing nothing on the interior of the drawings should be darker than an outer object edge; the darkest line on a section or elevation is the grade line;
— ensuring that material symbols do not even approach the line weight of the material edges;
— finding, and understanding the use, delineation and weight of other lines, such as center lines, dimension lines, extension lines, guide lines, etc.—these should never override any line within the body of the drawing.

All of this can be easily accomplished, IF you approach every drawing, from the outset, with the thought of using varied lines, and where you develop (in association with others, i.e., a fairly uniform system used by all) a single format for the lines. In this way we can direct, control, and prevent "free-lancing" which only makes for confusion and badly executed documents—none of us want this!

contract documents, never fully aware of the impact of their work. We must have an enlightened drafting force.

An experienced architect will have knowledge of about 400,000 items of construction material. Of course, this knowledge comes in varying degrees, but on any given project thousands of these items may be involved. It is easy to see that errors can become commonplace. This is a sensitive area in the practice of architecture, because each year there are thousands of disputes, claims, and lawsuits entered against professionals for their errors (see discussion in Chapter 3). A number of design professionals have found themselves on the losing end. To protect themselves, architects commonly buy costly "errors and omissions" insurance, which in reality is their liability protection. Usually there is a very high deductible in these policies, which the firm must pay before the insurance company makes its payment.

Obviously, there is a pressing need for consistency, diligence, and extreme care in the preparation of architectural documents. In this regard, there cannot be enough emphasis on the use of checklists in the preparation of working drawings and specifications. Quite often such checklists are designed to function for both the preparation of the drawings and the concurrent writing of the specifications. The basic idea is that when an item appears on the list and is incorporated into the project, both drawings and specifications must respond as necessary. This type of coordination goes a long way in reducing gaps, glitches, and other project problems.

Projects today are so complex, so legally and financially sensitive, and with so many items to be incorporated, that one simply cannot rely on memory or on others to recall all of them. Of course, we cannot always immediately apply some items, in that they are required but need other information prior to their use. In like manner, because of the lack of a direct hands-on relationship in CAD (as there is in manual drafting) drafters do not develop a feeling for the natural progression of the work. Usually they are given a direct and confined assignment, which causes them to focus on a small portion of the work, and not the ancillary items. In addition, where the drafter/CAD operator is not fully trained in the technical aspects of construction, the problem is even more imposing. However, by using a checklist, or lists, there is a much greater chance that all items will be "caught" in turn and will thereby produce a complete, uniform, proper, coordinated result.

The Victor O. Schinnerer Co., Inc., a provider of professional liability insurance, in cooperation with several professional organizations and insurance companies, has made an exhaustive study of the formal disputes, claims, and lawsuits in which design professionals have been a party. They found that almost two-thirds of the claims are directly attributable to the drawings and specifications produced by the professionals. Therefore, it is mandatory that a neat, well-organized, and complete set of drawings be the goal of any professional designer or office. These drawings constitute perhaps the most important service rendered during the design phase.

In the extensive review made by Schinnerer indications are that these errors can be categorized as resulting from the following:

1. Poor communications within the design team
2. Lack of field experience of all members of the team
3. Superficial review, or perhaps no review at all, made by a qualified supervisor

In each of these categories a breakdown in the function of the design team is the major problem.

Communication between all members must be open. Just because one person is mainly concerned with writing specifications or selecting materials rather than actively detailing the drawings does not mean that this work is less important. Perhaps the term "design team" should be emphasized to anyone entering the profession; a team, no matter whether in sports or law enforcement, can be successful only when everyone pulls equally. This most assuredly requires communication between its members.

In this day of pushing construction to the limit and minimizing time to save the cost of buying money, sometimes inexperienced personnel must be hired. This is unfortunate, for perhaps the most important experience gained by any drafter is that provided by the application of his or her own drawings in the field and the problems the drawings may have created; it would be helpful if we all had the time in our offices to ask field superintendents to show, if possible, how and why a detail had to be changed and whether it was due to a breakdown in our drawings. In fact, this information should be catalogued and reviewed whenever possible—not to undermine the draftsman's confidence but to provide constructive criticism.

Mentioning the time factor brings us to the third item. Major responsibility for any job, no matter how large or small, rests with the firm's principals, those who have their names on the door but whose time is taken up in so many activities that they may not be fully aware of all of the workings of any particular project. They are forced to delegate their responsibilities to other members of the team. Again, as the Schinnerer studies vividly show, the critical aspects of architectural drawing so commonly and grossly neglected are the use of check prints, the critical/objective eye for accuracy, completeness, and cross-referencing, and, most important, the final review. The same or additional checklist(s) used in preparing the documents should be utilized at the end of the production phase—as the documents are made ready for issue, bidding, construction, and so forth. Not only is this final and objective check required to pick up the necessities of the project, but also the nuances, the major and minor twists and turns that the project scheme requires. A project can be placed in severe jeopardy without such a check.

Yet, standardized/generalized written checklists are not all that is required. All projects have unique and special circumstances that fall beyond the scope of checklists. Human eyes and knowledge are required. Often items so slight that they are not listed on checklists will elude observation and detection. It is only the human intelligence that catches such items, by first knowing where to look and where to be cautious and on the look-out Interrelated items on a checklist may be isolated from one another. They may be checked off the list, but it is only through human knowledge that these items will be reviewed in tandem and coordinated, ensuring not only that they are present but that they are in proper order.

Checking involves much more than just seeing that a drawing is proper and complete—dimensions must add up, text spelled correctly, line work proper, and so forth. To thoroughly check, one must relate the drawing to its place of use (where it applies) and to its surroundings. Are the walls shown as they are indicated in the plan or elevation? Similarly, where a drawing references or indicates another drawing (a wall section designator on an exterior elevation, for example), the checker must look up the referenced drawing: Are the title and designation correct? Are the sheet numbers correct? Do the drawings correlate? Any failure in these or other aspects must be tracked down and resolved.

Some professionals assign time periods to checking. A sheet, they say, can be checked in 20 minutes. Maybe, maybe not! Doesn't it depend on how well, or how poorly, the drawings on the sheet are done? If cross-referencing is faulty, doesn't it take additional time to straighten it out? In reality, this makes better sense. If a project takes several months to document, should the important task of checking be confined by time restraints? Perhaps the documentation time was well used to produce a well-executed set of drawings, then checking time is reduced. But if that documentation time is misused and produces a convoluted, messy, poorly done set of drawings, wouldn't it be wiser to spend more time on checking so the documents being passed on will be better, accurate, easily used, and coordinated? The proof is in the statistics derived from Schinnerer's studies. If budgets and shortsightedness push comprehensive and objective final checking aside, the instance of claims will increase!

Perfection is an unobtainable goal, but minimizing disputes and claims is well worth the effort. It is well worth being an integral part of the time/money budget on every project.

Two words are key to good checking—*comprehensive* and *objective*. Check *everything* thoroughly, and do it in a professional and dispassionate man-

ner. No matter who executed a drawing, things must be as right as we can get them.

Continuity and completeness of the working drawings must be ensured, for they are among the most important elements of the total contract. It is vital that they be prepared carefully in order that the contractor may implement them properly. The contractor should not be expected to interpret the drawings; he or she should not be made to guess. The drawings and specifications should form a complete package—clear, accurate, and arranged in logical sequence. Experienced professionals believe that it is really their duty to provide proper coordination during the construction between the working drawings and the specifications. Care should be taken to avoid redundancy or repetition, but at the same time, it is important to recognize any point at which further communication may be needed, and to provide it. The main objectives are simply to do a good job, to protect the firm that is producing the drawings, and to render complete service to the owner by ensuring an easy, errorless, argument-free period of construction.

A few guidelines from the Schinnerer Co. are as follows:

1. Insist on neat, legible drawings.
2. Implement an office manual of working drawing standards and procedures to ensure continuity and uniformity.
3. Maintain open channels of communication between all personnel working on the project.
4. Coordinate drawings with engineering consultants.
5. Arrange drawings in logical sequence.
6. Remember to coordinate the drawings with the specifications as a means of controlling conflicts, contradictions, and ambiguities.
7. Insist on a review of all drawings by a principal or qualified supervisor.

As in any type of mechanical or critical manufacturing process, the time and effort expended by quality control can contribute to the architect's success and overall professional reputation. It will also help to prevent involvement in lawsuits that might be resolved to the detriment of his or her financial status.

In general, a few long-standing principles can be set down in regard to working drawings. These principles never change, and if the design team is aware of them decisions can be easier:

1. Try to establish the proper relation between drawings and specifications; it is most important to maintain this separation.
2. Emphasize important information: make each assembly appear as a whole unit and allude to subparts or other systems within it; everything that appears on the drawing should convey correct information within the required tolerances, whether line, letter, or numeral.
3. Avoid all forms of duplication; do not add "cute" touches, decorative detail, or unnecessary line work.
4. Coordinate all parts of the whole; any decision made for one particular item should be based on its relation to all other parts.
5. Make certain that accepted conventions and standardized items are used as required.
6. Always keep in mind, no matter how small the item, that specific action is demanded under the binding contract.
7. Perform first things first; complete one phase before starting another.
8. Insist on neatness at all times for more efficiency and effectiveness, not only in the drawings that the design team members are working on but in the notes they keep and the manner in which they communicate.

In summary, an architectural project can be compared to the human body. We have all been designed in a certain way; we have certain characteristics and physical traits. We are a certain height and weigh so many pounds. This exterior appearance would collapse into insignificance if it were not for the interior framework, the skeleton, and the various organs. This is true also of an architectural project. Surely, the essence of architecture, the basic elements of good design, must be reflected in the projects that we build so that their appearance will be pleasing to the eye and their functions satisfactory to their owners. All projects, of course, must have their own structures, their backbones and internal organs, on which to rely. So, too, can this simile be applied to contract documents. The framework of the building relies on the working drawings. Of course, the specifications give us the required guidelines. Without these two elements, no project could be conceived, no project could be built, because there would be nothing to follow. Everyone would do his or her work by whim; there would be no thought given to the end product and its coordination. In the chapters that follow we discuss each type of drawing; each is analyzed on the basis of what it is supposed to show, and some techniques are described in regard to the proper, the easiest, and the best way of achieving the purpose for which it is intended. The whole set of drawings must be kept in mind at all times, however. No drawing can stand by itself without help from the others or without helping the others.

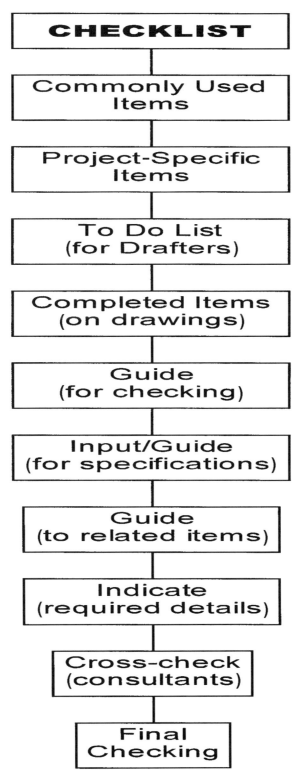

It is highly advisable that checklists be used throughout the preparation of a project's documents. The figure notes the general progression and specific uses to which the checklist should be put. Most offices have standard checklists they use consistently; there are also checklists that are published by various sources.

15

Other Construction Drawings

Although the main objectives of a project are contained in the working drawings, other drawings must be prepared before the working drawing phase, immediately after the working drawings have been issued, and as a finale to the project.

During the programming phase of any project the owner is required to supply the designer with information in regard to the tract of land and the site conditions that prevail. This information is, in effect, a survey of the property. In a remodeling project, or when designing an addition, the architect may be responsible for measured drawings of the existing structure. This represents an added service to the client, but provides the architect with reliable information and insight to the situations at hand.

In an existing structure it is difficult to judge just what effect its elements may have on later decisions in the new design process. It is necessary, therefore, to record the layout and general character of the building and to document its construction accurately. In some instances the measured drawings may be scheduled and taken in phases; for example, the initial layout and overall dimensioning of the structure may be scheduled before the programming and preliminary design phase. It may be necessary to go back to the building and measure more accurately or completely the sections that are involved in the new construction. Parts of the existing structure that are to remain intact and those that are to be removed cannot be determined initially, but they should be located on the drawings as soon as possible. In some offices the degree of accuracy of these locations is not acute, but it is generally good policy to produce a set of measured drawings to represent the existing structure and to eliminate the element of surprise in the reconstruction stage that will usually mean extra work and added costs.

Measured drawings include the structure of the building, its finishes, and all mechanical work. It takes just as much effort to relocate a steam line, a water line, or a piece of radiation equipment not recorded in the field measurements as a column, a window, or a door opening. The most important features to be picked up accurately are those elements that are to be modified by the new construction. These elements should be properly sized and precisely located.

Often the owner may have the original working drawings of the structure, in which event it is

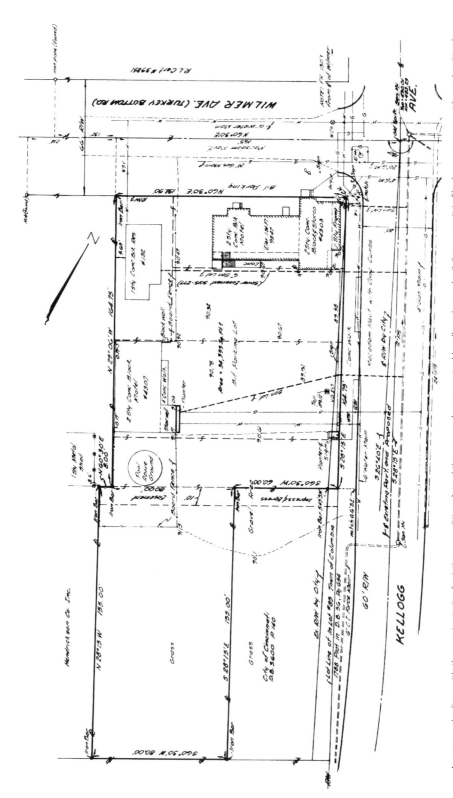

A survey dealing with the project site (existing conditions) and the owner's property. Usually, when a building permit is filed, a survey must be submitted with the building drawings. Further, all utility and zoning information and a careful drawing of all features on or adjacent to the property must be included.

necessary only to compare them with existing conditions. It should be noted that without regard for the detail of the working drawings, many factors must be considered. The project may not have been constructed exactly as the working drawings indicate, but minor variations will cause problems in the renovation.

In measuring a building some persons at times become industrious to the point of obsession. Such conscientious work pays off, but it is not always convenient or economical to return to the site to check one little item or to garner one small bit of information. If the measuring crew can be charged initially and headed by a competent design professional who knows what is needed and in what form, the return trips will be reduced and the information will be of top quality. It is always helpful, particularly if existing drawings are available, to draw a skeletal plan so that a print may be taken to the field for on-site note taking and to provide a basic form on which information can be recorded. If there are no drawings available, the profile and features of the building must be drawn in the field before being dimensioned.

In taking dimensions, small inaccuracies here and the rounding off of readings there tend to accumulate. Error is compounded; for example, if a long room with many windows and door openings is to be measured, each pier and each opening should be done separately. One full-length, overall dimension will then serve as a check against the string of smaller dimensions.

It is important also that workers directly involved in the project be equally involved with the measured drawings, for a situation once seen may be recalled and an impasse may be resolved as the drawings progress. One unfamiliar with the project will have no advantage of this sort.

Basically, the measured drawings should be thought of as a set of working drawings in reverse. Here is the building: it has doors and door swings, window swings, ceiling heights, and column locations that must be shown so that a floor plan or an elevation can be fitted together. Identify the various materials of the building: flooring, base, wainscot, walls, ceilings, and so on. If damage is observed or a peculiar condition noted, it should be detailed. As in a new building project, certain elements of the program demand that certain decisions be made by the design professional. So, too, in the measured-drawing sequence certain features of the existing structure will force certain decisions. A column may be removable, but it

must be studied first for reasons of economy. In other words, is it more economical to move the column than to realign the new structure?

Measured drawings, although taken roughly in the field without T square and triangle, should be drawn in "hard lines" (drafted) and kept on file. They should be done on good-quality paper so that they can be used, without damage, throughout the building program. In extreme conditions in which a large building, such as a steel mill, is being measured, it is more economical and convenient for the design professional to set up a team in a temporary field office in the structure itself. As the team completes the measurements, the information is fed directly to the draftsmen in the office, and as this information is being recorded the draftsmen will spot overlaps, gaps, or errors in the drawings.

In addition to the working drawings, the supplemental drawing is usually done after the working drawings are complete. The need for supplemental drawings may occur as the project is being bid or built. Supplemental, bulletin, or addendum drawings are issued for clarification, corrections, or alterations or to provide the contractor with additional information. Often in the rush of finishing the working drawings certain details may be inadvertently omitted. In fact, some details may be omitted intentionally so that there can be more study before the contractor formulates a bid. Supplemental drawings become a part of the construction contract documents, just as if they were part of the original working drawings.

A supplemental is first seen in the form of an addendum drawing. During the bidding process questions may be asked by the bidders, or in a review of the drawings the design professional may find inaccurate or incomplete information. If the change is simple, it can be described and referenced to the pertinent drawings on an addendum sheet, which is then issued to the bidders. If, however, the information is more detailed, a drawing should be made on which the information must be presented as clearly and concisely as possible. The drawing is then printed and issued to the bidders before the bidding date. It is vital that all bidders receive a copy of this addendum so that the information can be shared equally. There is ordinarily no particular area of work on which an addendum is based; it depends on the need for change.

The bulletin drawing, as it is commonly known, is the true supplemental drawing. Until the time

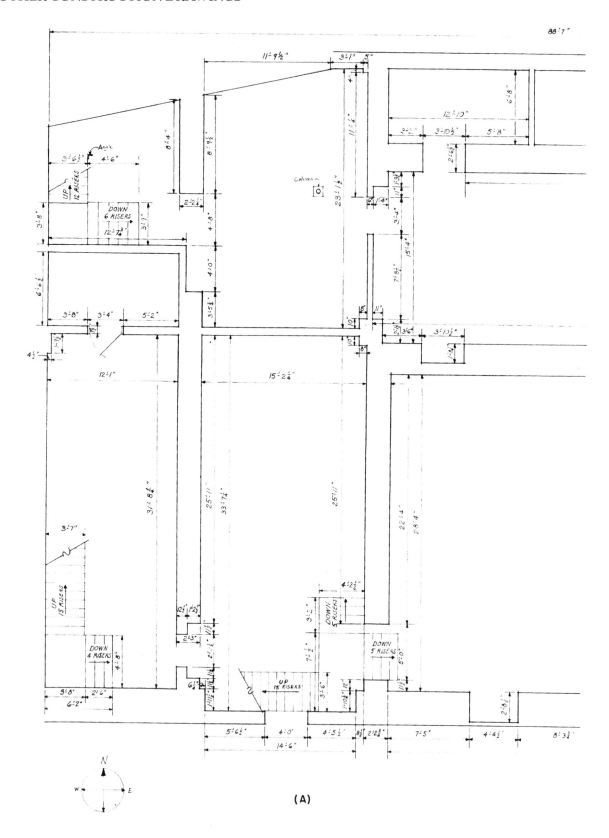

(A)

236

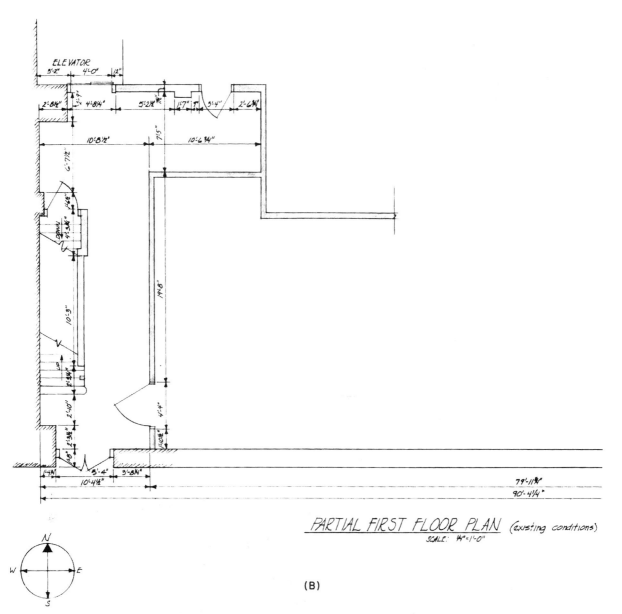

PARTIAL FIRST FLOOR PLAN (existing conditions)
SCALE: ¼"=1'-0"

(B)

These drawings are records of existing building conditions produced before starting a remodeling project. Although rough in form, they contain the necessary information. These strictly advisory drawings are for the designer and are not part of the final working drawings. (A) the full basement area. (B) The limited area to be remodeled ties the old building to the new addition.

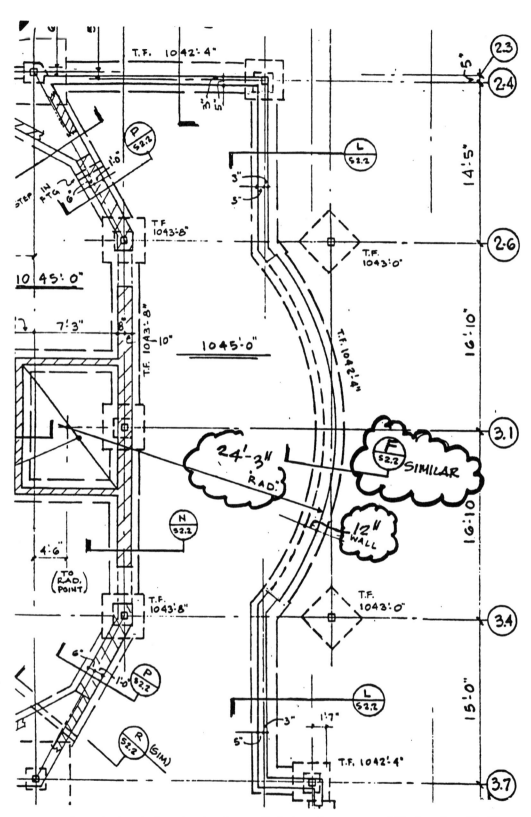

A portion of a single-sheet bulletin drawing. Can you find where the same material is given three [3] different names on this one sheet?

that a particular problem is discovered in the field, everyone has assumed that the information necessary to the total installation is on the drawings. For one reason or another, something is not fully covered. By using the supplemental drawing, or bulletin, the design professional can clarify the situation.

Various types of information may be involved: the location of an anchorage system, a special pattern of decorative material to be used on a wall, or a matter of glazing details may prompt a bulletin drawing. Perhaps a larger-scale detail than shown on the original working drawings is required. For the most part this is a clarification rather than a corrective drawing. A situation that requires correction may be remedied with the bulletin drawing.

The shop drawing that appears during the construction phase is unique because it is not produced by the design professional but by the supplier or manufacturer of a particular item, material, or system.

Shop drawings are interpretations of the work required on the working drawings. The interpretation is made by the manufacturer or fabricator of the material, product, system, or equipment in question. In essence, they are produced as instructions to the "shop" where they will be fashioned into those items required on the construction project. Actually, they are instructions to the shop; they are submitted to the design professional mainly to show what is proposed, how it will be made, and so forth. The professional can then assess whether or not the planned work is in keeping with the overall design scheme of the project.

As instructions to the shop, these drawings can be quite detailed and contain information not produced by the professional but necessary for manufacture or fabrication. They have a high "detail content" in that the producer wants to provide a good product, fully suitable for the project, but not excessive in sizing, operation, or cost. This does not signal a struggle. Rather, the manufacturer wants to sell the product, but does not want to lose money on it, nor does he or she seek to be forced to do work not explicitly shown on the professional's working drawings. *Exacting*, then, is the best description of shop drawings; thus, they have to be based on sound and good information from the professional.

Recently, shop drawings have been given a new status by design professionals. Many professionals list a minimal amount of design criteria, usually in the specifications, and then require that the contractor or fabricator for the work produce the necessary shop drawings. Unfortunately, these drawings often are required for review by the regulatory agencies before the permits can be issued. Because these drawings are produced at a time well-removed from the initial permit processing, the approval process is hampered and often forestalled. Roof trusses and fire suppression system drawings are excellent examples of this scenario. Although this is an open attempt to shift responsibility, it also is part of the exculpatory clause system, discussed in Chapter 3, "A Perspective on Working Drawings." Despite any other information, the professional remains involved in the processing of shop drawings and is never completely removed from it.

These drawings are submitted to the design professional, who stamps each sheet to indicate approval. On the stamp is a disclaimer that defines the responsibilities of all parties and indicates that the drawings have been checked for design compliance only. In other words, the drawings are in the configuration that the design professional has required, but the professional is not responsible for the fit of the items on the job or for their coordination with other materials, adjacent surfaces, or systems. This responsibility is the contractor's.

It is most important that contractors be totally familiar with the contents of the shop drawings. They should also be aware of their own responsibilities. To cite a case: A material may be supplied to a contractor after the manufacturer of the material has submitted shop drawings produced under his or her supervision. The drawings will be checked for fit and compliance by the subcontractor who holds the contract with the manufacturer. Once this first check is done, the subcontractor must submit the drawings to the general contractor, whose duties include rechecking for compliance. Here, again, responsibilities must be firmly set. The drawings are then forwarded to the design professional for his or her approval. A great many persons are charged with checking the drawings, and it is essential that each of them pass through as many hands as possible and be carefully examined by all. In this way the entire chain of construction command is made aware of the impact that a given material will have on the job. Each checker must know the extent of his or her own area of responsibility.

METAL GAUGES and THICKNESSES					
U.S.S. Gauge	U.S.S. Thickness [inches]	SDI/HMMA Thickness [decimal]	mm	ML/SFA-MSMA Thickness [decimal]	mils
4	0.2242	0.214	5.4		
5	0.2092	0.199	5		
6	0.1943	0.184	4.6		
7	0.1793	0.167	4.2		
8	0.1644	0.152	3.8		
10	0.1345	0.123	3.1	0.118	118
12	0.1046	0.093	2.3	0.0966	97
14	0.0747	0.067	1.7	0.0677	68
16	0.0598	0.053	1.3	0.0538	54
18	0.0478	0.042	1	0.0428	43
20	0.0359	0.032	0.8	0.0329	33
22	0.0299	0.026	0.6	0.0269	27
24	0.0239	0.02	0.5		
25	0.0209			0.0179	18
26	0.0179	0.016	0.4		
28	0.0149	0.013	0.3		

It has been common, for a number of years, to note and specify the thickness of sheet metal, and other metal items by using a gage number. This would be taken from a listing of United States Standard Gauges [U.S.S.], and was usually a simple number, i.e., 8 or 22. This number was related directly to a thickness of the material.

Now, since there is no longer a widely-held, general consensus on the exact meaning of each USS gauge designation, it is better to use a decimal thickness [for example 0.123 inches] instead of the USS gauge number. Although some variation exists between different organizations using these designations, the best policy is to note, "the minimum thickness required is...."

The illustration is one example of the type of detailed information that is necessary for the making of shop drawings. The design professional, in many cases, will need to indicate the thickness of material required; the shop is then obliged to meet that requirement, and will show it on the shop drawing.

SECTION F-109.0 FIRE PROTECTION PLAN

F-109.1 Requirement for Plan: Prior to the start of construction a fire protection plan shall be submitted to the fire department by the design professional for all new construction and all construction on existing buildings where fire protection equipment is involved or required (exception 1, 2, and 3 family residential). For all 1, 2, and 3 family residential construction a plot plan shall be submitted to the local fire official.

F-109.2 Content: The Fire Protection Plan is to contain a modified site plan of the entire complex complete with all fire protection equipment, exit signs, and emergency lighting. The site plan shall show access to the site, driveway locations and dimensions (widths and radius of curves), locations of fire hydrants and water mains, locations of trees, high tension wires, and other items that might affect or interfere with firefighting or emergency operations. The layout shall include the locations of all fire protection equipment and utility shutoffs.

An illustration of a newly emerging requirement in the fire codes. A specific plan is required for the fire service in their evaluation of a project and in their training for fighting a fire in the project. Note that an entirely new drawing is not required, simply a modified site plan.

Contractors often try to "wash their hands" of this responsibility and ignore the support that they owe one another. Frequently this attitude gives rise to unnecessary complications, a most unfortunate development when it happens; the shop drawing cycle, although not foolproof, is straightforward, and all drawings should be filed after use by each person who has any sort of responsibility for them. Copies should be kept at the office of the architect or engineer, in the field office, and in the offices of the general contractor and subcontractors.

At the job site the material or system must be in complete agreement with the approved shop drawings. These drawings frequently become a nuisance, because thousands must be processed in any busy professional office. Therefore, most offices with a large volume of work assign one checker to handle all. It may be the field superintendent or the contract administrator; sometimes, however, an entire section of the staff may be devoted to this function. If there is any question of noncompliance, the drawings can always be taken to the project designer or architect,

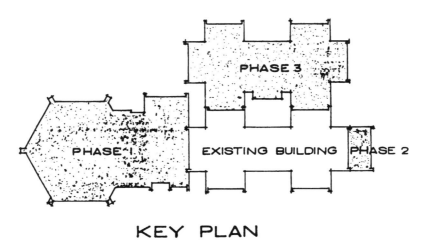

KEY PLAN

An example of a small plan denoting the various stages of a project. The same type of drawing can depict which area of the building appears on the same sheet. The key plan provides good indexing for complicated projects.

who will clarify his or her intention, thus paving the way to correct installation as designed and conceived.

One other important set of drawings is commonly required on large projects. This is the record set, or the "as built" drawings, which are usually prepared during the construction phase, although many architects tend to delay them until the end of the project. It is important that the drawings be amended as the work progresses, because they should reflect all changes from the original working drawings. It is possible, even likely, that a sewer line will be realigned because in digging the trench, workers encountered quicksand; the sewer line must be changed in direction, new fittings and a manhole must be added, and other related construction may be required. Again, a detail from the working drawings is found lacking and another must be substituted. An item of construction may be changed at the owner's request; for example, more insulation may be wanted around the perimeter of the slab. All changes must appear on the "as built" set, for the owner must know precisely where all construction items are located. It is a tragic experience when an owner is forced to tear out a large portion of a building because a sewer line is blocked and he or she must search for it under a slab. Memory becomes clouded with time, and it is difficult to recall just how far from a given wall the sewer line was laid.

The "as built" drawings are part of the contract documents on which all supplemental informa-tion is included and all field changes are marked. By using either black line or blue line prints on a white background, changes can be made with a colored pencil or marker. Explanatory notes or reference remarks should be entered directly on the drawings. Specifications are updated by changes made from addenda, change orders, and so on.

Every attempt should be made to keep the record drawings simple and concise. In an industrial plant, with its tremendous amount of piping, the drawings may be too complicated for practical use. Perhaps a layout set for nothing but gas piping and another for water piping would be a simple solution.

Not all owners are interested in these drawings and not all construction demands them. In many instances a simple project, when finished without radical changes, will negate the usefulness of the "as built" drawings. The original working drawings will be enough for maintenance and additions.

All but the shop drawings are provided by the design professional. Measured drawings may be a major decision in a remodeling project, and supplemental drawings may be necessitated by change or error. The shop drawing functions on every project, no matter how large or small. Manufacturers must know that what they are doing is correct, and design professionals must know that they are getting what they requested. The record set, which provides a planning potential, is highly recommended for all owners.

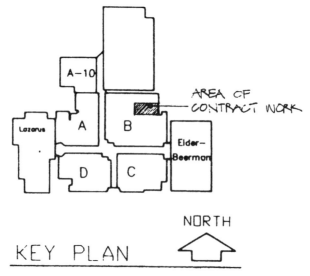

Another key plan, this denotes the area of work within a large existing complex.

16

Site Improvement Plans

lthough the terms *site plan* and *plot plan* are used frequently, the term *site improvement plan* tells a much fuller story. It describes the drawings more accurately.

This plan shows the entire scope of the project, including all its ancillary features. The drawings are executed at a small scale to incorporate the totality of the project: the site and the building and all its services.

The site improvement plan is based on a survey of the property. The information it contains should include an accurate graphic description of all property lines. The survey is furnished by the owner, and if an updated one is not available, the owner should be encouraged to have a new one made. Any competent registered surveyor can provide the necessary data. A complete list of essential survey information can be found at the end of this chapter.

A property owner is often confident that he or she knows everything about the property: where it begins, in what direction it lies, and how big it is. In reality, the owner may be quite ignorant of the facts. For instance, the owner may describe

the property as running along "that fence line" back to "about where the tree is" or "over there to that clump of bushes." These are not accurate descriptions and are not valid information for the architect who is preparing the site improvement plan. Each piece of property is shown and described in a system of books, papers, and drawings kept up-to-date by the local government. The methods may vary, but land measurement is an official function of the city or county. Each parcel of land is described and shown, no matter how large or small. A rectangular system developed by the federal government and widely applied in the United States utilizes latitude and longitude to form rectilinear townships, which are divided into sections, each 1 square mile in area. The smaller divisions are made to accommodate the smaller pieces of property. Each property owner can find his or her particular lot, parcel, or tract, regardless of its location.

Architects pay close attention to the data available to them. The prime function of the survey is to show the extent of the property lines. Each line that forms the perimeter is described by the surveyor by direction and length; for example,

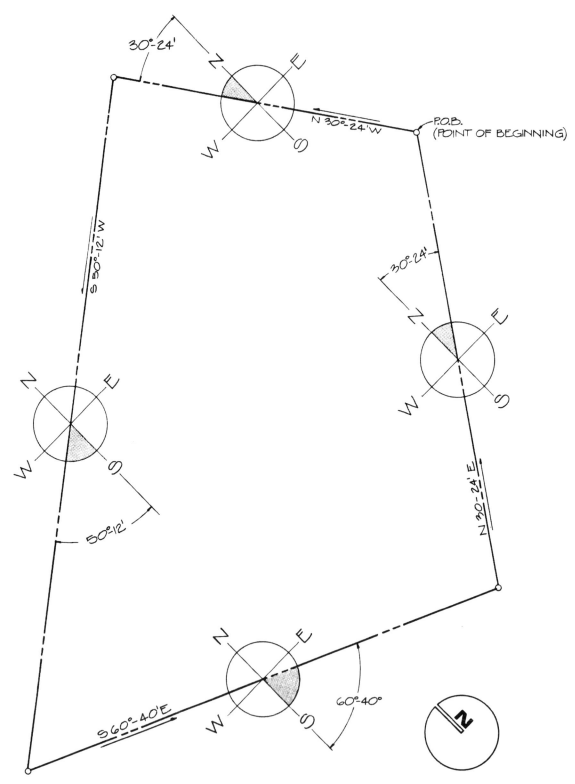

Every survey must have a POB (point of beginning) to indicate the precise direction of the lines. Angle is given to the nearest minute and bearing in relation to the cardinal points of the compass. Length of line is correct only to one hundredth of a foot.

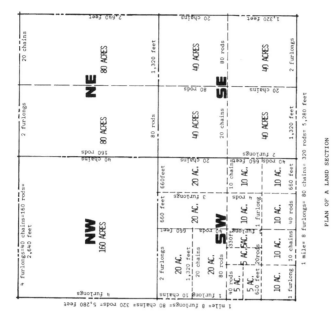

PLAN OF A LAND SECTION

SECTION= 1 SQUARE MILE= 640 ACRES   SECTIONS SUBDIVIDED BY FEDERAL ACT DOWN TO
40 ACRE-QUARTER QUARTERS

Land Acreage And Distances Within The Section Shown Here

THE STANDARD METHOD OF NUMBERING LAND SECTIONS IN TOWNSHIPS

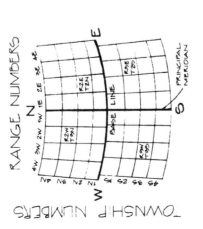

Counties in each state are divided into townships, which, in turn, are subdivided into sections. As shown, each numbered township is given individual identity. The numbered sections refer to the township. Each section can be subdivided into tracts of so many acres. This subdivision continues to the single-lot stage. Each lot, no matter how small, is identified to ensure the correct location of a building.

North 30 degrees East (N 30° E). Curved lines are given by the radius, the length of the arc, and the direction of the curve. Each lot is assigned a point of beginning (POB), which is a corner of the property located in relation to some prominent feature: a curb, a manhole, section line (which, of course, is imaginary), or centerline of the street. This point of beginning is also described and located in the deed. Angular bearings always read from north or south, and each lot line direction starting from the POBs established. The example North 30° East shows that the line is 30 degrees East of true North. This angle is called the bearing of the line; it can be taken from north or south, whichever produces an angle less than 90 degrees (90°). To complete the bearing data, a length is assigned to each line and measured in feet and decimal parts of a foot with the civil engineer's tape. At the end of the line the surveyor installs a marker, which may be a formal concrete monument, an iron pin, or a wooden stake, and which establishes permanently the exact corner of the property. By utilizing the bearing of the adjacent line, the surveyor can turn the angle at the corner.

It is then possible to show the perimeter of the lot graphically.

Other items of importance to the architect in the realm of the surveyor's work can then be located. Items of the most value are the elevations at the corners of the property and features such as hills and valleys. To obtain this kind of survey, the owner must ask for a "topographical survey," rather than a line survey, which will give only the property lines and the bearings.

A topographical survey can be made in two different ways; first, by applying a 25- or 50-foot grid over a map of the property to show the points of intersection of each elevation, and, second, by using the contour method, which connects these points with isobar lines to give an accurate picture of the slopes and ground features of the site.

The United States Geological Survey has referenced various points throughout the United States directly to sea level data. By finding one of these datum points we may establish a direct relationship between any piece of property and sea - level elevations. For convenience, local surveys usually use data in the immediate neighborhood. Elevations can be referenced to manhole

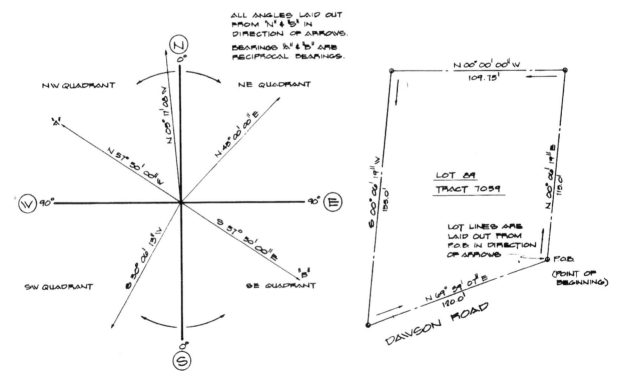

A lot survey based on a quadrant layout. The direction of traverse may be made in a clockwise or counterclockwise direction but once started must remain constant or the traverse will never close.

covers, fire hydrants, concrete pillars, or other permanent fixtures. Whatever the basic point of reference, it is assigned a zero elevation. All the elevations within the site will relate to this particular datum point, called a "bench mark."

With a little practice in reading contours, architects can easily develop a sense for the "lay of the land." They can find the high points, the depressions, the valleys and can visualize the slopes that must be dealt with in the design. On all site plans or surveys a uniform vertical distance between the contours is established. This distance will vary, depending on the scale of the survey. A small-scale map makes several feet between contour lines the standards; a large-scale map will show the contour lines one or two feet apart. Contour lines are labeled according to height so that they can be followed in length.

Contour lines that lie close together indicate a sharply rising slope; those more widely spaced show a gentler slope. The examples illustrate what can be read from these features. Consider a pail of water in which a line is drawn at the water line; some of the water is then removed so that the level is lowered, and a new line is drawn. Because the sides of the water pail are not perpendicular when viewed from above, a system of concentric rings will appear. These rings represent the contour lines of a depression.

From the contour lines, we can also draw sections through the site, to scale. These serve to illustrate the slope of the land, and the relative difference in elevation from point to point along the section. Coupled with the contour information the sections provide the information necessary to estimate the amount of cutting and filling required. In most projects, the structure will be located at an elevation somewhere between the high point, and the low point of the land. The contours reveal how much of the "high ground" must be cut [reduced in height], and how much must be filled increased in height.

A single site plan is often adequate to show the project design, but in areas in which demolition and rebuilding are planned, other drawings must be considered. It may be necessary to provide a site demolition plan that will show the features or structures to be removed. Add to this the site improvement plan of all new features and buildings. A grading plan that will combine existing conditions and the new grade may also be required. A utility plan may be added to describe extensive water, sewerage, electrical, and telephone instal-

lations, all of which are part of the site improvement. There is no perfect answer; the totality of the project will dictate the type of drawings and the number needed. In a downtown area of a major city the utility systems are extremely complicated and may lie several levels beneath the street. It is vital that the utility plan on which the existing systems must be shown be included in the set of drawings. It must also be proved that the new project, although utilizing the existing systems as required, will not disrupt or destroy them.

The surveyor, in showing the complexity of the site, will sketch in such things as trees, if they stand alone, or a clearing line at the edge of a wooded area. The survey should locate power and telephone poles and any manmade structures, such as a retaining wall, public utilities of every type, and any other features that may have legal implications. These features are called easements.

In many cases utility companies are granted easements, contained within which, usually underground, are utility lines of one kind or another. These easements are granted to provide maintenance capabilities for their installations. The agreement in general is that an easement will be open at all times, and, indeed, if there is trouble, may be torn up and repaired or replaced. The work will take place within easement, and the easement will be restored to its original condition on completion of the work.

It would be foolhardy to plan any part of a structure over an easement. This fact emphasizes the importance of showing all easements on the survey, because not only are they a practical matter but they can become decision makers in the project's initial design.

Most governmental agencies have systems that invoke restrictions on a site. The architect must be cognizant of these restrictions. In many areas of the United States zoning codes are strictly enforced. These codes are written to protect the property owner, although at times they may seem prohibitive when the owner is in conflict with their regulations. The basic purpose of zoning is to segregate, by function, the various types of property. This segregation prevents a high-hazard or nuisance type of industry from locating in a residential or a noisy manufacturing plant from being built next to a nursing home.

Zoning codes also impose restrictions relating to adjacent buildings by establishing setback or "yard" requirements; for example, front yard requirements may be in the range of 30 to 50 feet or

GENERAL CHARACTERISTICS OF CONTOUR LINES ON SITE PLANS

1. Contour lines connect points on the ground of LIKE elevation above sea-level, or a local bench mark. Every point along a contour line has the very SAME elevation.

2. Every contour closes on itself, somewhere, either within the limits of your drawing, or elsewhere on the earth's surface. In the latter case, the contours DO NOT stop, but run to the edge of your drawing.

3. A contour line that closes on itself within the scope of your drawing is either a SUMMIT (a HILL), or a DEPRESSION. Depressions are usually indicated by a "lowest spot" elevation, and small "tick" marks on the low side of the contour; a "top-most" spot elevation is noted within a summit (hill). RIDGES are elongated summits (hills).

4. VALLEYS are indicated by "V" shaped contours which point UPHILL (UPSTREAM for waterways); the contours run up the valley on one side, turn, cross the stream, or area, and run back down the opposite side.

5. Contours across CLOSELY LOCATED, or INTERSECTING streams, form an "M" shape with the outer points directed UPSTREAM.

6. The HIGHEST contours along RIDGES, and the LOWEST contours along VALLEYS always occur in pairs.

7. The water-level lines in ponds and lakes are really a form of contour line, since the water always lies LEVEL (at the same elevation) within the pond or lake.

8. Contours spaced fairly equally indicate a uniform, sloping surface. On a plane surface, the contours are straight, evenly spaced, and generally parallel.

9. Widely spaced contours indicate RELATIVELY SLIGHT SLOPES; a "more-level" condition; nearly true level occurs between contours of like elevation.

10. Contours spaced closely together indicate a STEEP SLOPE; the steepest slope occurs where these contours are the closest together (always!) as this is the shortest distance between the contours.

11. A CONVEX slope is noted by contours spaced at WIDER intervals going UP the slope; a CONCAVE slope by contours spaced farther apart going DOWN the slope.

12. Contours may appear COINCIDENT at vertical excavations, shear drops, and buildings or other structures; actually they follow along the sides of these formations, and ARE continuous.

13. Contours ONLY CROSS each other in the case of cliffs, overhangs, natural bridges, and pierced or arched rock; here the lower level contours are shown as dotted (hidden) lines of unique style.

14. Contours NEVER split in two; they occasionally occur side-by-side, and numbered the same.

****

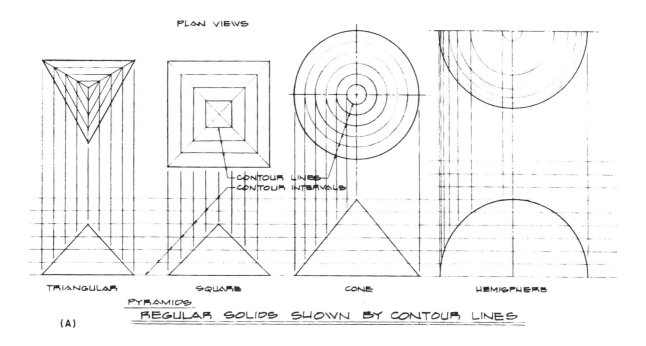

PLAN VIEWS

CONTOUR LINES
CONTOUR INTERVALS

TRIANGULAR   SQUARE   CONE   HEMISPHERE

PYRAMIDS

REGULAR SOLIDS SHOWN BY CONTOUR LINES

(A)

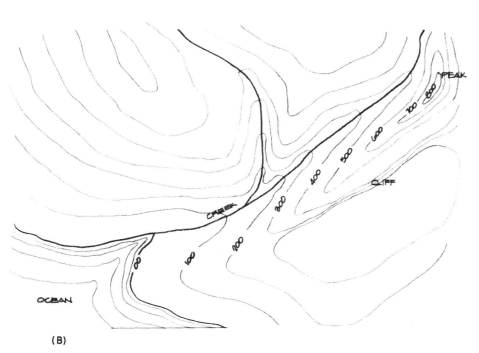

(B)

With practice, contours are easily read. The contour lines in (B) show the creek flow to the ocean by the direction of the contour's U-shaped turn. The familiar solids in (A) are seldom visualized by the contour patterns they form. Notice how readily the object can be seen from its profile or contour map.

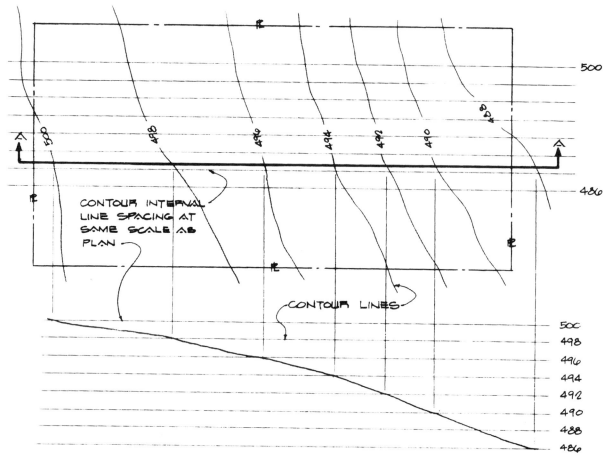

SECTION A-A

Contour lines are helpful also in the preparation of profiles of the land. By measuring the distance between the lines and showing the difference in elevation a section can be cut through the site. These profile sections can be used to locate the building properly and to determine where earth must be removed (cut) or added (fill). Other elements of the site can be analyzed: views and vistas, drainage, and the type of slope (gentle, radical, rolling, or rugged).

more back from the road on which the property fronts. This restriction means, essentially, that the building can be no closer to the street than the distance set for yard requirements. Similarly, side and rear yard requirements can be codified and usually are. The owner is restricted to a buildable area within the property lines. None of a project's major buildings or structures may be erected outside this area. Gardens, parking areas, play areas, and similar installations that are limited to surface treatment may occupy the setbacks. These restrictions should be shown in the site improvement plan. The raw survey, provided by the owner, must be converted by the architect to its proper form

before the site improvement plan can be drawn. In many areas of the country a survey is required when filing for a building permit and must accompany a set of drawings of all features. Still, however, the site improvement plan will contain much of the survey information that is adaptable to a particular project.

A site improvement plan should directly reflect the survey and can be drawn at any one of several scales. Because the survey is really an engineering drawing, the scales used are set by the civil engineer's scale; for example, 1 inch can equal 10, 20, 30, 50, or even 100 feet. This scale is used rather than the architect's. Sometimes, however,

Grade Profile	Percentage*	Ratio**	Angle***
Flat; Dead level	0	0: 1	0
	2	1:50	1
	5	1:20	3
	10	1:10	5
	20	1:5	11
	25	1:4	14
	33-1/3	1:3	18
	50	1:2	26
	58	6:10	30
	100	1:1	45
	500	2:1	64
	1,000	10:1	84
	57,000		89.9
Vertical; Straight-up		1:0	90

Slopes, gradients, and variations in grade level can be expressed in either percentage, ratio, or angle. Basically it is to establish a relationship between a horizontal distance [the "run"] and the associated change in vertical distance [the "rise"]. The chart above gives an easy reference and shows how the same slope may be noted in differing ways.

[NOTE: *=easiest to envision; change in height over a 100-foot distance which is directly the percent of change; **=calculated by dividing total run by total rise; ratios above list vertical distance first, horizontal second but unfortunately this is sometimes reversed- check when grade seems excessive; ***=seldom used to designate a natural slope- used more for mechanical or man-made features]

for one reason or another, the project demands that an architectural scale be used, but usually the civil engineer's scale provides adequate drawings, smaller in size but still legible.

The architect must necessarily have some knowledge of surveying. He or she should know what the various terms mean and be able to deal with all survey data. The architect must be able to interpret contours and to convert this knowledge to his or her own use. With this capability and a design background, the architect can produce an accurate, carefully considered, though complicated, site improvement plan.

CHECKLIST: SITE IMPROVEMENT PLANS

1. Property lines, with bearings, corner angles, and all markers; location of lot (political subdivision), street names, lot number, and all pertinent data regarding the lot
2. Building location, zoning setback lines, easements, clearing line, ground floor elevation, bench mark(s), grades at building, dimensions of building, dimensions of other features or buildings, dimensions of all overhangs or extended features beyond the

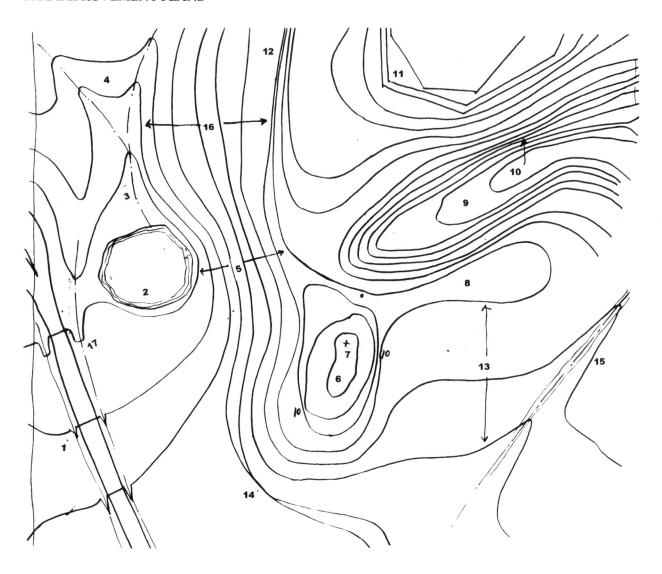

building line, and (in dotted lines) the layout of any planned additions

3. All utility lines, on the property or in the adjacent streets: electric, water, sewer, gas, and telephone

4. All existing paving, whether to remain or be removed: new paving, parking lots, parking stall bumpers, stripping, drives, walks, steps, platforms, terraces, signs, flagpoles, playfields, equipment (both mechanical and playfield), drinking fountains, light standards, and curbs or walls (decorative)

5. Fences, structural retaining walls, areaways, and pools

6. Existing structures, foundations, or cellars; trees, shrubs, both those to remain and those to be removed; structures to be relocated and any underground voids of various description

7. Storm drainage on both paved and unpaved areas; catch basins and yard drains

8. Contours, existing and new; contour elevations

9. Legend showing all symbols and materials used on the plan

10. Contract limits; note items not in contract (NIC)

11. Name and address of surveyor who supplied survey for site improvement plan

12. Location and log of test boring holes; legend of log symbols

13. Temporary facilities; roads, fences, toilets, offices, and sheds

IDENTIFYING LAND FORMATIONS BY READING CONTOURS

On the map at left, the numbers indicate the following land formations;

1. Paved roadway with swales on either side, for drainage.
2. Small pond—contour around shape at water line.
3. Stream—size may vary—"V" contours point UPstream.
4. Streams which intersect—"M" shaped contours—point UPstream.
5. Uniform slope—contours equally spaced.
6. Plateau—flat area noted by "closed" (circular) contour.
7. Summit point—highest point (spot elevation) on the hill formation.
8. Flat area between contour which returns on itself.
9. Ridge or valley—points UPhill on valley, DOWNhill on ridges.
10. Steep slope—contours closely spaced (see 13).
11. "Architectural" contouring—man-made land formation via grading.
12. Gentle slope to left (widely spaced contours); a flat area (can you find it?); and a steep slope.
13. Fairly uniform, very gentle slope—very widely spaced contours.
14. Cliff—contours one over the other—drop off—vertical slope.
15. Deep valley with larger stream—"V"s point UPstream.
16. Gentle, uniform slope—widely and evenly spaced contours.
17. Paved roadway with gully or ditch along side for drainage.

14. Material storage areas for use by various contractors
15. Areas for on-site parking

INFORMATION REQUIRED ON SURVEY

1. Surveyor's seal
2. North arrow
3. Stakes and other markers; lot dimensions and bearings
4. Adjacent lots within 200 feet; alignment, occupancy of existing building (denote vacant lots)
5. Lot area (square footage)
6. Easements
7. Street status (existing or proposed); dedicated or not, abandoned
8. Width of streets and alleys
9. Width of pavement and type of pavement
10. Location of curb; edge of traveled roadway
11. Distance to intersecting street or streets
12. Location and width of sidewalks; note if none
13. Location of street sewers
14. Location of tree branches
15. Location of building lateral
16. Sea level elevation of invert at point of connection
17. Location and size of water main and closest fire hydrant
18. Location and size of all other utilities (gas, electric, and telephone)
19. Existing elevation at each of four corners of property

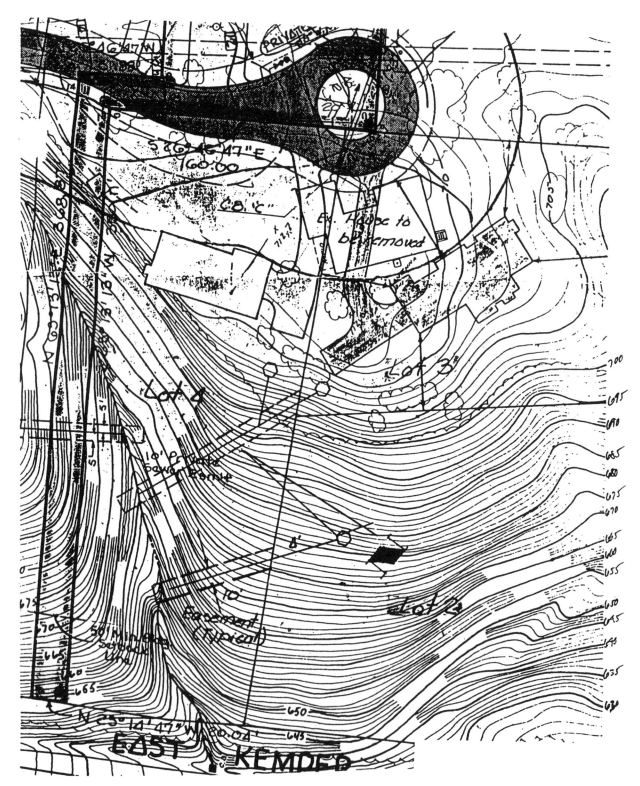

A site plan which illustrates the complexity that some projects encounter. Without these contours, the problems would be compounded in that knowledge of the site would be incomplete.

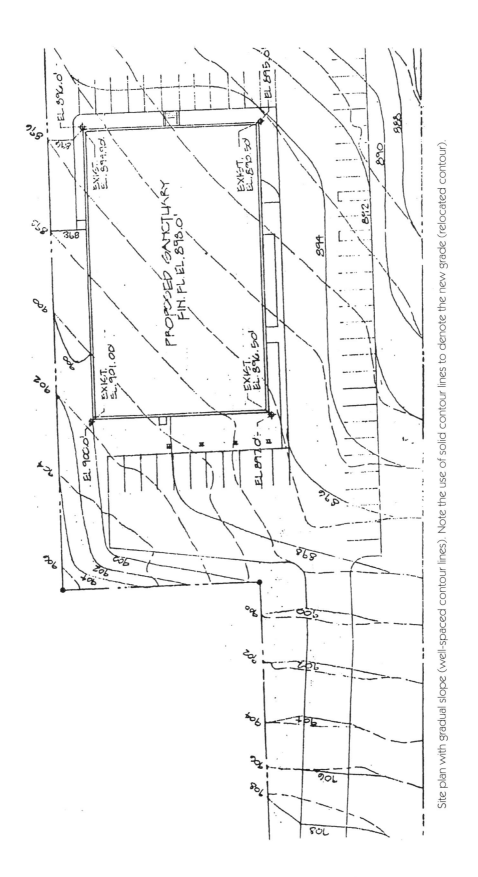

Site plan with gradual slope (well-spaced contour lines). Note the use of solid contour lines to denote the new grade (relocated contour).

255

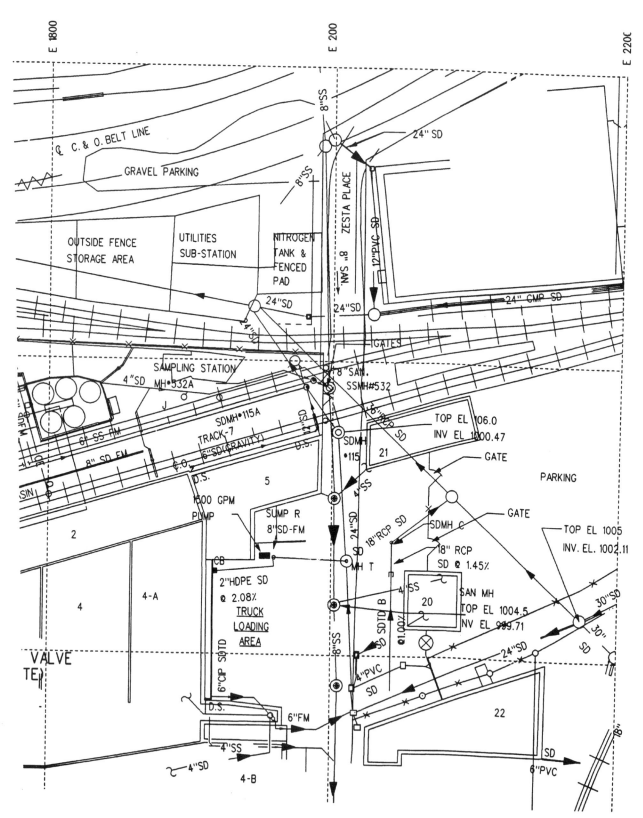

A portion of a site plan produced via CAD. Note the amount of information depicted. To do all this manually, would have been a real chore, and very difficult.

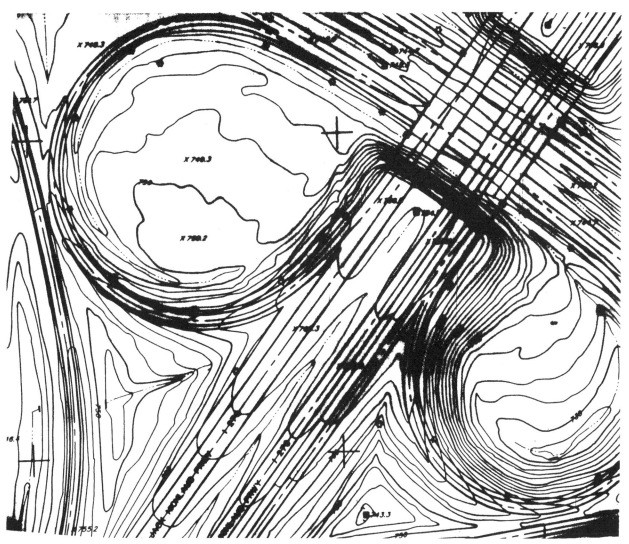

A contour plan at a highway cloverleaf. Work noted here must be done to install the roadways properly, but such complex contouring appears in nature too, and makes site planning very difficult.

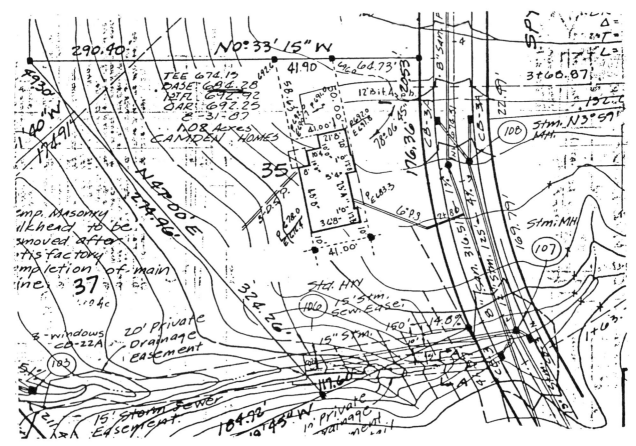

A portion of a site for a residence. Take note of the amount and type of information shown, and the line weight variations that increase the avility to clear read the information.

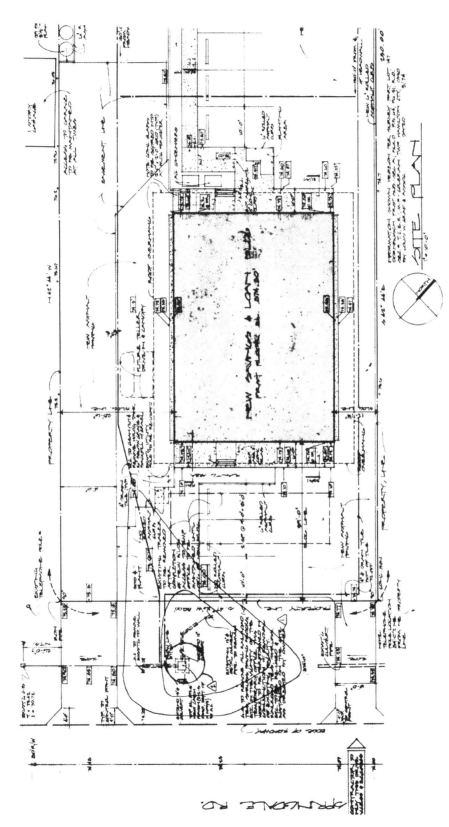

This site plan (foreshortened here because of extreme lot size) is a good example of the amount of work required. The building is small but still served by all utilities and must pass through all construction phases. It is important to have the building toned or textured so that it will read well when reproduced. It is also important to poché the concrete walks to contrast with the rest of the drawing.

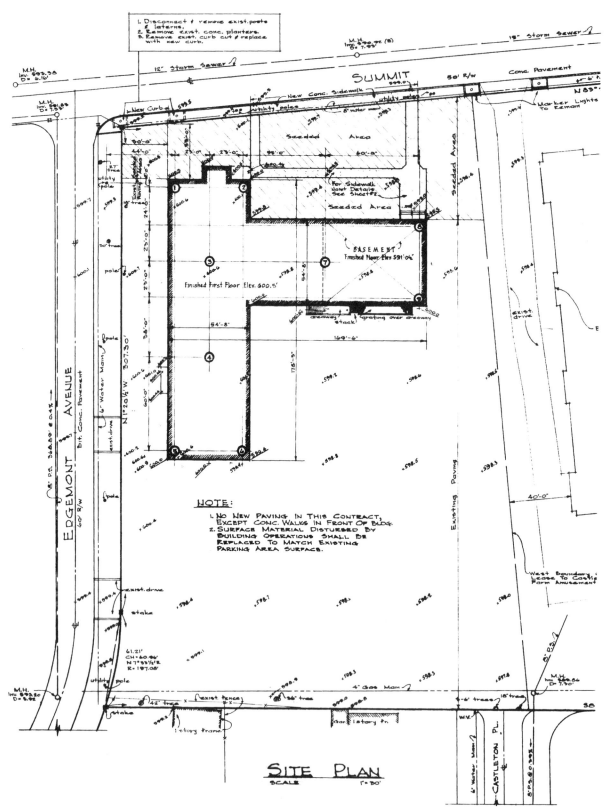

A site plan of a building erected next to an existing structure on a semipaved area. Here it is better to use "spot elevations" rather than contour lines (in general the site is flat and shows little variation). Observe the amount of survey information transferred to this plan. The circled numbers are test boring locations.

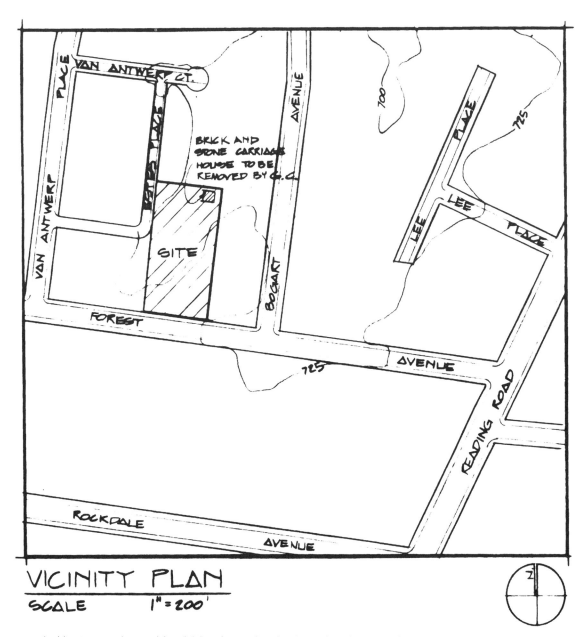

VICINITY PLAN
SCALE   1" = 200'

Architects sometimes add a vicinity plan to the drawings. This plan is helpful to everyone concerned. The general area around the project site is shown, and major traffic arteries, which make delivery of materials easier, are emphasized. It is also an aid to anyone reviewing the project and its impact on the neighborhood around it.

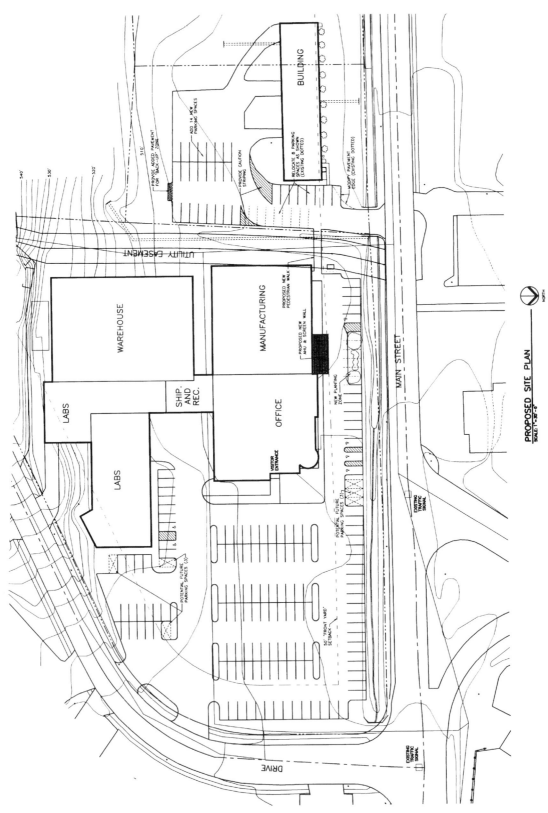

An example of a combination site improvement and key plan. Note the various, scattered work areas from new building elements to painted stripping. Also, note complexity of contour lines, street pavement lines/curbs, easements, and the zoning set-back lines on this overall plan for a large multi-building complex.

17

Lawns and Planting (Plans)

Landscaping is reasonably the province of trained specialists, namely, the landscape architects. In former years the emphasis of expertly planned landscaping was almost totally on the aesthetic enhancement it provided. Today we recognize the importance of what is planted and where it is planted as a major factor in energy consumption control. Landscape architects can contribute greatly to the total success of building projects by providing another means of reducing rising maintenance costs while meeting demands of the growing number of environmentalists, and by enhancing the basic design concept.

Considerations relegated to other members of the design team in years past properly become the initial contribution of the landscape architect today. The landscape architect should be an original member of the design team, along with the structural and mechanical engineers, to utilize his or her highly specialized knowledge to the fullest.

The profession of landscape architecture is ably represented by the American Society of Landscape Architects (ASLA), which is the result of a merger of two representative groups. This will provide for a stronger, more unified voice, solid

representation, and an organization more responsive to the needs of the profession. This should also provide for stronger financial backing and the easy achievement of more goals for more people. Overall, the group will function in a manner similar to the American Institute of Architects (AIA) and will be active in all aspects of the profession, for the good of the profession as a whole and for the individual practitioner.

Where once it was common practice simply to make a lump-sum allowance for contracting a landscape architect toward the conclusion of a project, these professionals' vital input is now so well regarded that they are contacted early to become part of the first planning stages. Their particular specifications and drawings will be developed in stages, accompanying those of the other design members. Even relatively smaller projects profit immensely by the inclusion of a landscape architect from the inception of the design.

However, should the client's budget be insufficient to permit a contractual relationship with a landscape architect throughout the design planning stages, this professional may be employed as a consultant, on an hourly basis, from the beginning. An understanding may be reached so that a satisfactory price is reached for the consulting landscape architect to provide necessary landscaping plans, details, and specifications for the finished drawings.

The landscape architect will shed a different light, another approach to the thinking of the design architect's preliminary schemes. This specialized professional adds greater dimension to paved areas, auxiliary entrances, and interior and exterior vistas by incorporating a vast experience with individual characteristics of all growing plants. The landscape architect's suggestions for use of foundation plantings, for sound abatement plantings, as well as for natural growth to provide wind and light barriers, have added a new chapter to the traditional aspects of aesthetic appeal and soil erosion controls.

Should the consultant landscape architect's service be more than the client's budget permits, services can frequently be available through seeking advice on an hourly basis, with a provision for only very general schematic drawings (the most preliminary sketches) for drafting, in the building architect's office. However, the planting schedules and details should be reviewed by the trained professional before being made a part of the completed drawings. This arrangement reduces drafting costs for the landscape architect and permits a more flexible arrangement.

Because landscape architects are registered professionals, they are held liable for all facets of their work. Accordingly, they must be permitted the same freedoms and privileges granted the other design professionals. They correctly reserve final control over their drawings and specifications. Their working drawings are as individualized as those of design architects; their schedules are more complex than the schedules design architects place on drawings. Landscape architects must incorporate the common name of every plant as well as the botanical (Latin) name to avoid confusion when the bidding process begins.

Bidding will be done by plant nurseries, ever increasing commercial enterprises, many of which are staffed by trained horticulturists, but overall expertise varies to a great degree. In all likelihood the commercial horticulturist will have far greater comprehension of the landscape architect's drawings and intent than will other members of the design team. At no time should questions about the lawn and planting drawings or specifications be directed to or fielded by any other than the original designer.

Although the drawings may contain some relatively standard details comparable to many standard details occurring on building drawings, these two are strictly within the purview of the landscape designer, and all questions should be directed to him or her. It is a fair assumption that a good working relationship exists between the landscape architect and the many commercial nurseries in any given area; such is the nature of both areas of endeavor to promote a strong interrelationship.

Drawing techniques of landscape architects, like those of other designers, exhibit wide variation. As a professional, a landscape architect may request guidance from the design team captain to correlate his or her drawings with those of the other members of the team so that the entire set of drawings will present an accomplished integration of professional skill. Although the landscape architect's drawings may be executed on the sheets printed specifically for the project, with combined names of all professionals involved in the project design, these drawings will bear his or her professional registration and seal.

Symbolism, rather than an attempt for precise depiction, has become the easiest route to good landscaping drawing. Some symbols are standard from one landscape office to another; other symbols are unique to the offices from which they emanate. A particular designator may represent a particular plant. The designator is explained fully in the drawing legend and occurs again in the schedule. Some landscape architects prefer symbols that resemble the intended plantings; for instance, a general treelike shape showing drip line or foliage brings more excitement to the drawings than does a mere dot with a number placed next to it.

It is imperative that the landscape drawing be done at a reasonable scale, eliminating small, confined areas. The outline of the building or buildings should be laid out without detail. Often the practice dictates the building outline be screened, "ghosted," or drawn on the reverse side of the sheet, permitting changes in the landscape drawing itself without constant redrawing of the major structure.

All vehicular driveways and paved areas (walks, patios, or similar site improvements) must be shown distinctly without being obtrusive. It should be remembered that strong contrast is required between landscape delineation, the building, and paved areas. Darker landscape symbols

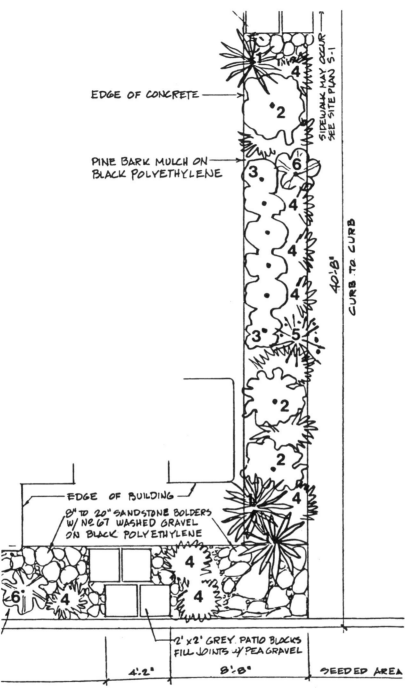

EDGE OF CONCRETE

PINE BARK MULCH ON
BLACK POLYETHYLENE

SIDEWALK MAY OCCUR
SEE SITE PLAN S-1

40'-8"

CURB TO CURB

EDGE OF BUILDING

8" TO 20" SANDSTONE BOLDERS
W/ № 67 WASHED GRAVEL
ON BLACK POLYETHYLENE

2' X 2' GREY PATIO BLOCKS
FILL JOINTS W/ PEA GRAVEL

4'-2"

8'-8"

SEEDED AREA

A plan for landscaping work denoting the specific plantings with reference, by number, to the plant schedule.

PLANTING SCHEDULE					
MARK	LATIN NAME	COMMON NAME	SIZE	QUANTITY	REMARKS
1	YUCCA FILAMENTOSA	ADAM'S-NEEDLE	24' DIAMETER	4	
2	ELÆAGNUS ARGENTEA	SILVERBERRY	24' DIAMETER	4	SUBSTITUTE JUNIPERUS VIRGINIA 'EASTERN RED CEDAR' WHEN AVAILABLE
3	TAXUS CANADENSIS STRICTA	CANADIAN YEW	18" HIGH	12 @ 18" O/C	SUBSTITUTE BUXUS SUFFRUITICOSA 'DWARF BOX' WHEN AVAILABLE
4	JUNIPERUS DEPRESSA PLUMOSA	ANDORRA JUNIPER	24" SPREAD	12	
5	VIBURNUM OPULUS NANUM	DWARF CRANBERRY	24' DIAMETER	2	
6	VACCINICUM PENNSYLVANICUM	LOWBUSH BLUEBERRY	18' DIAMETER	2	

The plant schedule, which notes type, size, and number of plants required. This schedule is formulated after study of soil conditions, the structure, and the design effect desired for the project.

will print more sharply and present a direct overview of the landscaping. Once the landscape architects confer with the design team they will devise and coordinate their technique to adjust to the major intent and technique of the team.

Drawings may attempt to suggest approximate spacing of plantings, but final resolution of these measurements rests with the schedules included with the drawings. Drawings are presented to illustrate the landscape architect's concept with greater, in-depth information carried in the specifications. Certainly, the pattern of the plantings and the location on the site are conveyed by the drawings; the specifications will demand the spacing, depth of planting, and conditions determined by the landscape architect. Schedules on the drawings will indicate the precise plants indicated by each symbol on the drawings.

Symbols and indicators used by the landscape architect seldom conflict with those of any other discipline used in the project. A preplanning session, during which principals from each discipline to be incorporated on the project become acquainted, allows the landscape architect to discuss his or her customary approach to design and presentation with those principals. Usually, each member brings representative drawings to this session and institutes a familiarity at once with his or her particular techniques. At this time any confusion of symbols can be dispelled.

In the simpler landscape drawings the number of rows of plants and some indication of their spacing may be given directly on the drawing. The symbols for these plants will be definite and distinctive, and the dimensions will be no tighter than the nearest inch with plants, and the nearest foot with large plantings such as trees and sizable shrubbery. Trees to be planted may be similar, or even of the same variety, but of differing heights; the symbols will relate one to another. The schedule will give both botanical and common name beside the symbol, the size (height, caliber, or diameter and, in some instances, age), desired spacing, total quantity on the site, and, finally, remarks, which will include information specifically for these plantings, such as a requirement for "bagged" or "balled" roots.

Some architectural projects today rely heavily on the work of a landscape architect to provide either exotic plantings for interior atria, specimen plantings in exterior courtyard displays, or, sometimes, a combination of the two. These requirements may be in addition to the requirements for his or her knowledge of environmental controls by use of natural plantings. The design team captain may become more competent to discuss the matter by reviewing documents obtainable from the United States Department of Agriculture, the Environmental Protection Agency, and, most particularly, the United States Division of Forestry. This professional may then better understand those matters of special interest to the landscape architect on the project and be better prepared to intercede on his or her behalf with other members of the design team when potential conflicts of interest arise. A more complete and readable set of drawings will be obtained when the special input of each design team member has been recognized early in the planning stages and the input coordinated and incorporated into the entire project from its inception.

Because the landscaping drawings form part of the bidding package of working drawings, these drawings should reflect the same attention to line

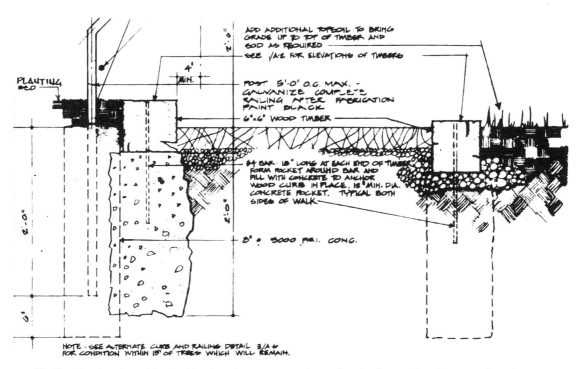

ADD ADDITIONAL TOPSOIL TO BRING
GRADE UP TO TOP OF TIMBER AND
SOD AS REQUIRED
SEE I/A-2 FOR ELEVATIONS OF TIMBERS

PLANTING
BED

4'
MIN.

POST 5'-0" O.C. MAX. -
GALVANIZE COMPLETE
RAILING AFTER FABRICATION
PAINT BLACK
6"x6" WOOD TIMBER

#4 BAR 18" LONG AT EACH END OF TIMBER -
FORM POCKET AROUND BAR AND
FILL WITH CONCRETE TO ANCHOR
WOOD CURB IN PLACE. 18" MIN. DIA.
CONCRETE POCKET. TYPICAL BOTH
SIDES OF WALK.

8" ∅ 3000 P.S.I. CONC.

NOTE - SEE ALTERNATE CURB AND RAILING DETAIL 3/A-6
FOR CONDITION WITHIN 15' OF TREES WHICH WILL REMAIN.

Working drawings in architectural landscaping are as precise as the planting requires. The more formal areas necessitate greater construction detail.

TIMBER EDGING
DETAIL   18
1/2" = 1'-0"   A-6

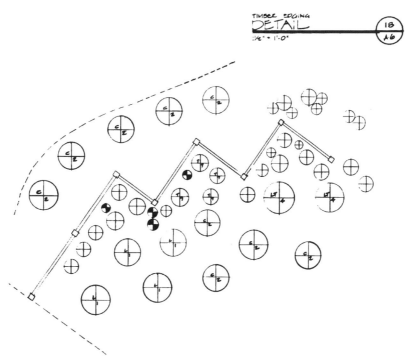

Symbols have been used to execute the landscape plan. Here some sort of coded symbol tells what sort of plant is to be placed in a given area. The symbols can also show the type and size of plant and any other pertinent data. The plant locations are approximate and can be made to fit the actual conditions.

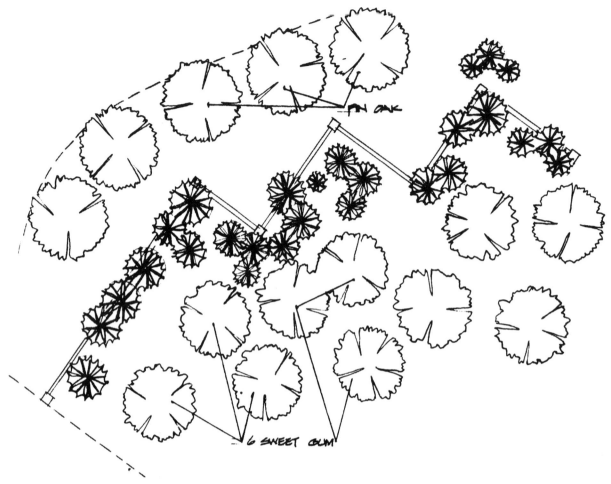

PIN OAK

6 SWEET GUM

This plan illustrates a decorative motif in varying configurations to represent the different plants. It can be carried out in great detail and used in many representations. Notes must be added to the drawings to explain the plant types.

work, clear and precise delineation, with quickly comprehended, distinct symbols that characterize all other sheets in the total working drawing set. Line variation must be observed to prevent obscuring detail and to avoid loss of emphasis.

Landscaping working drawings may be one sheet or many. The designer will select the number of sheets needed to present properly his or her intent and contribute to the overall set of drawings in proportion to need and to the cooperation he or she receives from the entire team. These drawings will reflect the landscape architect's design for the building in the proportion the design team captain has suggested.

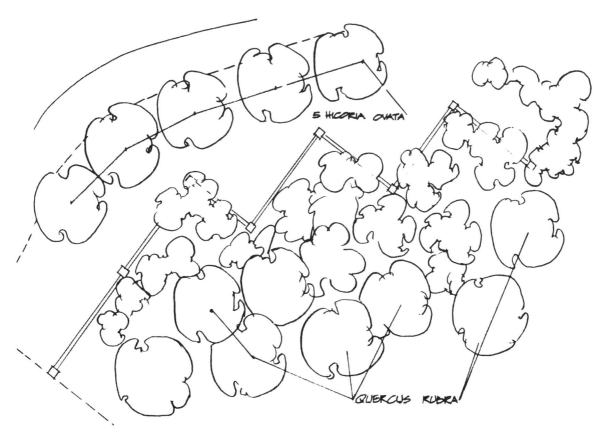

5 HICORIA OVATA

QUERCUS RUBRA

A representational landscape plan in which planting masses are suggested and botanical names are given for each area. No attempt has been made for a realistic appearance.

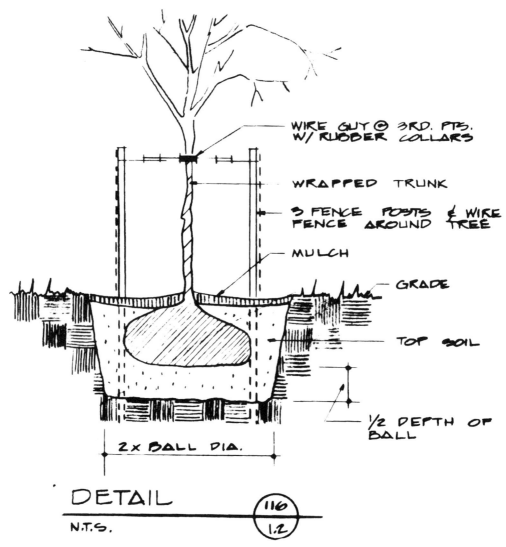

WIRE GUY @ 3RD. PTS. W/ RUBBER COLLARS

WRAPPED TRUNK

3 FENCE POSTS & WIRE FENCE AROUND TREE

MULCH

GRADE

TOP SOIL

½ DEPTH OF BALL

2 x BALL DIA.

DETAIL

N.T.S.

116
1.2

Plant materials are costly and easily damaged. The location of the various plants is established in the landscape plan; the specifications name the varieties and list other construction information. To protect the plants and bees a detail of general planting instructions is essential, particularly if uncommon or exotic plants or trees are part of the scheme.

18

Floor Plans

The most important architectural drawing is the floor plan. It contains more information than all the other working drawings and is consulted in varying degrees by almost all the tradespeople on the job at one time or another. All drawings derive at least some of the their information from it.

The floor plan represents a tremendous amount of the project designer's time spent in analyzing and meeting the needs of the client. The designer must take into account traffic patterns, working relationships, and arrangement of the rooms and must place the window and door openings. He or she must superimpose the layout of the structural members and locate the innumerable components that go into making up a complete project.

It is ironic that the amount of text in this chapter dealing with floor plans is relatively small as compared with the importance of these drawings. It is almost impossible to put into words the data that the architect and architectural draftsman must enter on them. Perhaps the easiest way is to envision the layers of information that are laid on the basic room arrangement, layers that are built up until the final plan can be presented.

Basically, the floor plan is a horizontal sectional view of the building taken about 4.5 feet above the floor line. This is done, of course, to cut through the majority of openings in the walls and to provide a view of the equipment installed inside. Nothing, from the smallest dimension to the largest component, can really escape the floor plan. The word *detail* takes on an altogether different meaning. Perhaps the best illustration is the list of items to be encountered on the floor plan of almost every project:

1. All necessary dimensions
   a. Outside walls
   b. Window and door openings
   c. Edges and thicknesses of materials
   d. Interior partitions
   e. Sizes and locations of terraces, walks and drives
   f. Special construction items
2. Window symbols and door swings
3. Window and door identification marks
4. Types of passageway through partitions
5. Stair symbols and notes showing the direction of rise, up or down, and the number of rises per run
6. Necessary changes in level occurring in areas of the building into the exterior
7. Thresholds and symbols for plumbing fixtures in the kitchens, baths, and laundries
8. Built-in cabinets, shelves, and rods in closets
9. Areas of mechanical equipment, duct space, pipe chases, vertical conduit runs, fireplace, and stacks

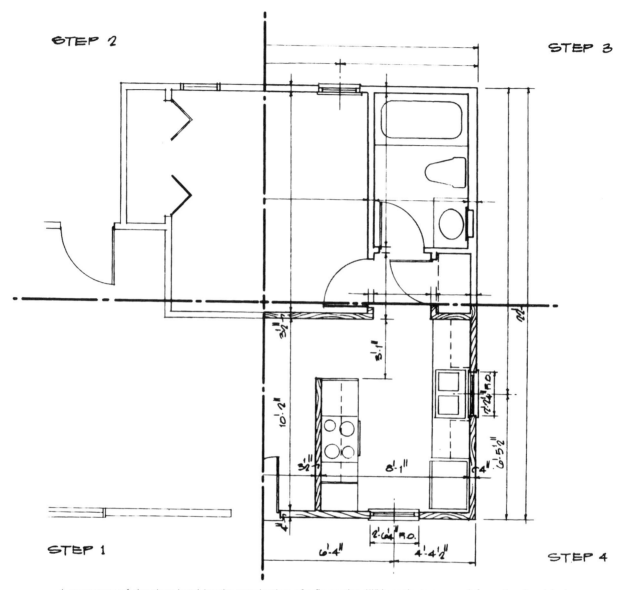

STEP 2   STEP 3

STEP 1   STEP 4

A sequence of drawings involving the production of a floor plan. With each step more information is added until the drawings are completed. There are no shortcuts in this system, although each step need not be so strictly executed as it is here. Note the light line weights and meticulous planning that must be done to place the information properly.

10. Configuration of the roof (on one-story plans)
11. Medicine cabinets and other installed accessories, fire extinguishers, fixed cabinets, and laboratory tables
12. Notes indicating the size, direction, and spacing of framing members
13. Scuttles to upper or roof areas
14. Special overhead construction
15. All structural features cut by the horizontal plane, such as columns or bearing walls

16. Symbols for various pieces of mechanical equipment, including water heaters and air handling equipment
17. Slopes in floors
18. Cutting planes, showing detailed sections
19. Titles or numbers for all rooms, spaces, hallways
20. Correct symbology for all materials cut by the horizontal section and their proper size and location

This is but a partial list, and only the requirements of the job and the experience of the draftsman can tell the full story of the floor plan.

It is important that the plan be accurately made, for so many other drawings are traced directly from it (in part or whole) or, to varying degrees, derive information from it. The plan must be constantly updated *as new information is gathered*. It is often the initial source of changes that will involve the entire project and, consequently, the other drawings.

It is essential, for instance, that error-free areas be dimensioned properly. Dimensioning has been discussed in the preceding chapters, in which we showed new and more streamlined methods. It must be done completely so that the building will tie together. Office procedures dictate different practices; in some offices actual dimensions, and in others nominal dimensions,

may be used. A drafter, of course, must be ready to meet any criterion imposed by his or her employer.

Often depending on the size of the building, a small scale one-eighth-inch or smaller floor plan will be drawn so that the entire building may be placed on one sheet. If this is done, it imposes a new set of criteria on the amount and type of information shown on that particular plan. Selected areas of the plan will have to be blown up to a larger scale and shown on other sheets; for example, an entrance complex at the front of a building may involve a large plaza, a stairway, a retaining wall, handrails, a flagpole, and similar features. To show all the construction at a one-eighth-inch scale would produce a mass of lines; it would be completely unreadable, even if it could be done. It would have to be drawn at a larger scale on another sheet on which even the handrail

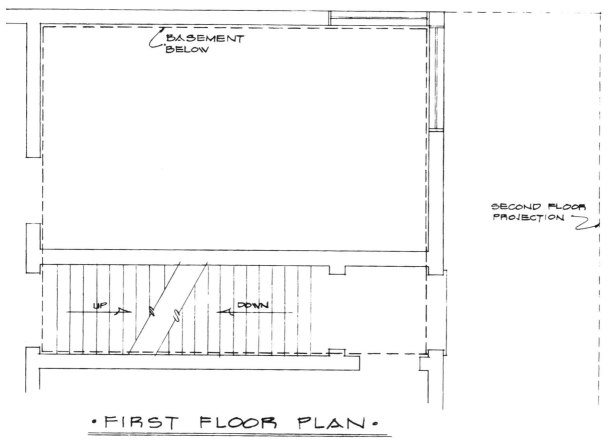

BASEMENT BELOW

SECOND FLOOR PROJECTION

UP DOWN

• FIRST FLOOR PLAN •

The first floor plan as it relates to other parts of the building. Note the dashed lines that outline the basement and second floor. The respective plans for these areas would, of course, be sized as indicated, but it is here that their relation is shown.

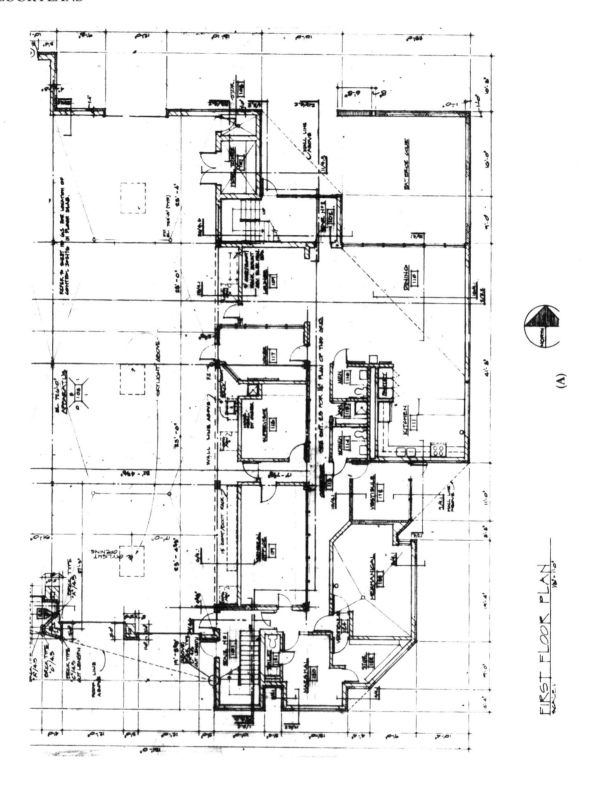

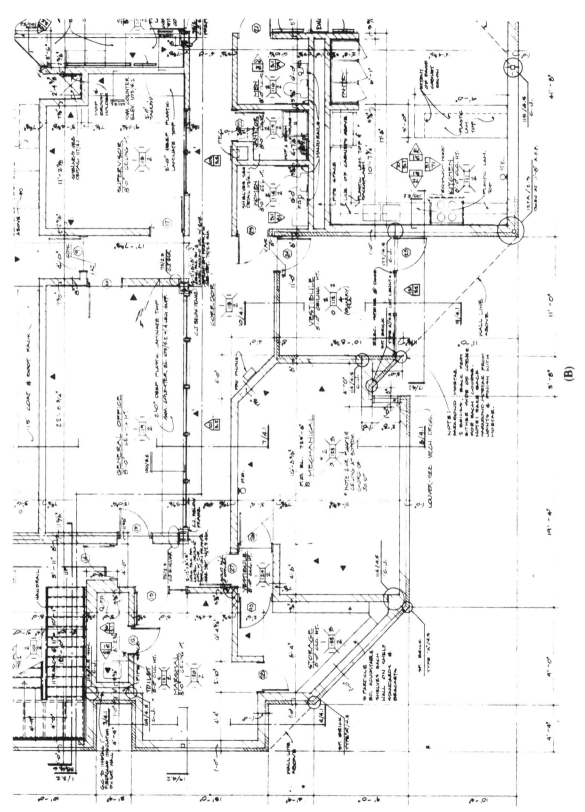

(B)

Two illustrations taken from a full set of drawings. (A) at a smaller scale is a portion of a complete floor plan (a firehouse). Because a large part of the building (where the trucks are housed) is an open area, it was necessary to provide a drawing at a larger scale. This plan (B) shows the many small areas in detail, thus providing a more useful drawing for actual construction. Both drawings, however, are needed to complete the building. Note the dimensioning of angled walls and the amount of detail in each plan.

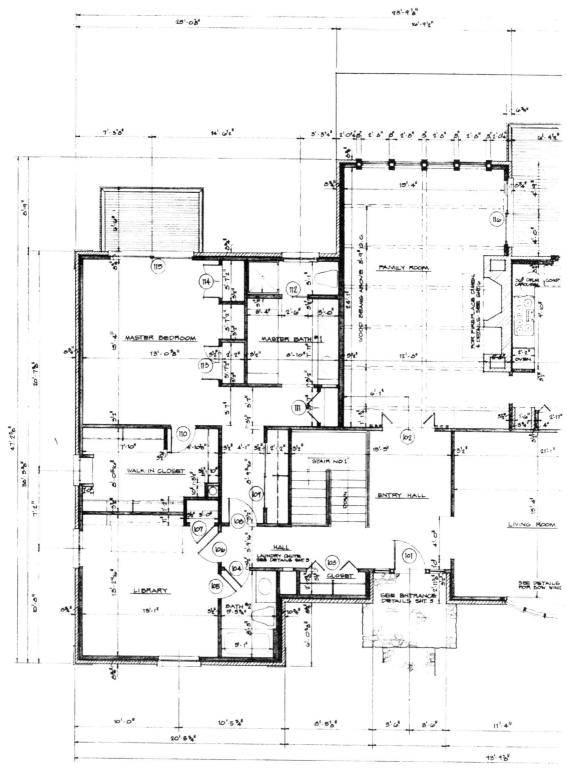

This section of a floor plan is about 90 percent complete, but still needs information about interior finishes and final coordination. It does, however, represent a well-drawn plan. The line work is clean and crisp and the dimensioning is complete and open enough not to interfere with the drawing in any way.

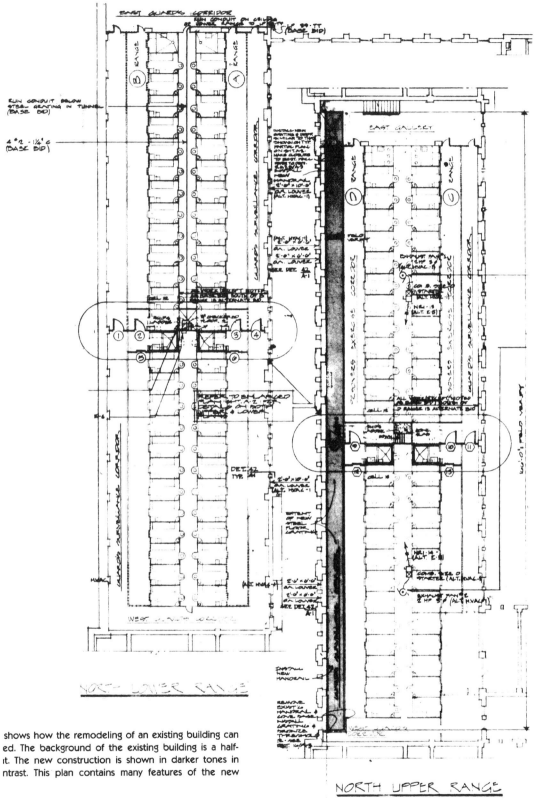

NORTH LOWER RANGE

NORTH UPPER RANGE

shows how the remodeling of an existing building can
ed. The background of the existing building is a half-
t. The new construction is shown in darker tones in
ntrast. This plan contains many features of the new

This plan shows how the remodeling of an existing building can be handled. The background of the existing
building is a half-tone print. The new construction is shown in darker tones in sharp contrast. This plan contains
many features of the new work.

brackets could be shown fairly close to scale, the stairs could be detailed, the construction and expansion joints in the concrete slab could be detailed and dimensioned, the location of the flagpole could be set, and the relation of the retaining wall, sidewalks, curbs, and other paving could be established in a clear and concise manner.

Actually, this principle applies to many areas of a building; rest rooms and locker rooms are usually drawn at larger scales. Rooms containing equipment, such as laboratories in schools or office buildings, shops, lounges, retail sales areas, office complexes, and gymnasiums, are blown up.

This is perhaps the most important lesson that the draftsman must learn about the floor plan: how to deal with scale. How much to show. Where to stop. It must be kept in mind, of course, that we cannot put out a skeletal drawing at one scale and constantly refer to other drawings. It would lead to a tremendous amount of confusion among the workers. This technique cannot be defined here; we cannot set definite parameters; we must rely on experience. In these pages we discuss techniques for approaching the working drawings and, in particular, the floor plans and how they can be developed. Only experience can take the draftsman beyond them to the production of a complete project.

CHECKLIST: FLOOR PLANS

1. Fully coordinated dimensions; overall dimensions; opening locations, features of the building, masonry, and column centerlines; make sure that each room and partition is located and sized.
2. Room names and numbers and finish information, if applicable; reference to large-scale details.
3. Floor elevations, floor covering patterns, mat recesses, changes in elevation and materials, ramps, curbs, bases, and gutters.
4. Wall material symbols, furred spaces (for pipes and ducts), recesses, openings, panels; locate wall features and attachments.
5. Ceiling heights, changes in height, breaks, bulkheads, tile patterns; locate diffusers, lights, and other ceiling appliances; include skylights and monitors.
6. Door marks and swings; show thresholds and saddles, special door features, and refer to details.
7. Windows, showing layout, swings, and mullions; interior glass in doors, partitions, and borrowed lights.
8. Show plumbing fixtures, stalls, floor drains, and reference to large-scale layouts and details.
9. Show stairs and stairwell dimensions, number of risers, and direction of travel; include handrails and references to large-scale details.
10. Fire extinguishers and cabinets, access panels, drinking fountains, expansion joints, folding partitions, gratings and pit covers, ladders, scuttles, lockers, shelving, special trenches, cornerstones, corner guards, barriers, bumpers, convector enclosures, telephone booths, roof leaders (downspouts), part-high walls, chalkboards, tackboards, folding and coiling grilles and grates, and railings.
11. Equipment and cabinet layout for laboratories, science rooms, home economics units, arts and crafts studios, and shops; equipment that requires special footings.
12. Plans for kitchen and equipment for special functions.

Reflected ceiling plans are really another form of floor plan. However, they should not be confused with floor plans, as they each show a separate and distinct view. The reflected ceiling plan utilizes the floor plan for the general layout of rooms [door opening occur under the ceiling and need not be shown]. Then the drafter must imagine that the floor is a mirror! In this view, then, looking at the floor one sees the reflection of the ceiling. This reflection must show all of the ceiling features that are planned for the various rooms and areas; ceiling support grid, light fixtures, sound speakers, etc., as noted in the following checklist.

CHECKLIST: CEILINGS (REFLECTED CEILING PLANS)

1. Remember the principle of the reflected plan (the floor is a mirror; draw the plan as if you were looking down into it).
2. Show all features of the ceiling materials, wall faces and profiles, exposed beams, and other construction.

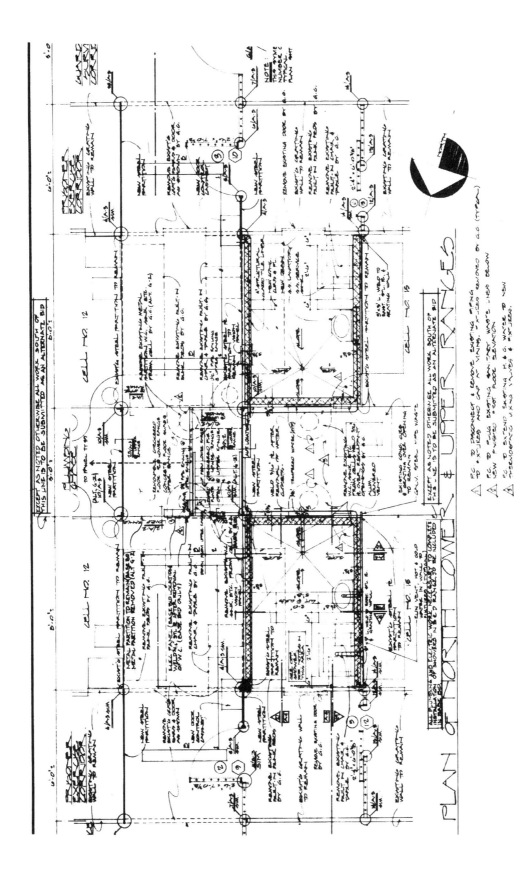

This plan was drawn at a larger scale because much of the construction is being done in a confined area. To show all necessary lines and notes at a small scale would have resulted in confusion. Obviously, if the project is small, the plan should be larger for easier reading.

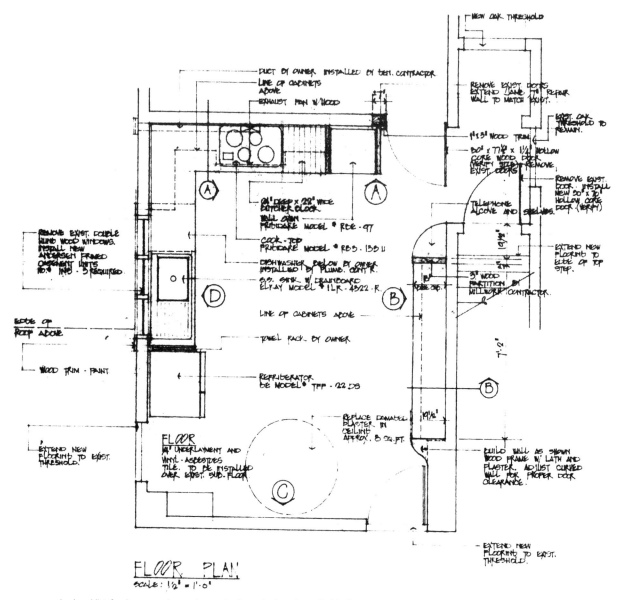

FLOOR PLAN
SCALE: 1½" = 1'-0"

A checklist for large-scale equipment plans. A drawing of a kitchen area illustrates the list:

1. Usually 1/2″ or 1/4″ plans are used.
2. Lay out such areas as classrooms, home economics labs, arts and crafts, wood, metal, and electrical shops, science labs, language labs, toilets and locker rooms, lobbies, kitchens, and monumental stairways.
3. Check all finishes with room finish schedule.
4. Check and indicate all dimensions.
5. Indicate location and size of structural members that may influence the layout or construction area.
6. Indicate details shown elsewhere.
7. Identify all items in the space for proper coordination with the specifications and equipment schedules.

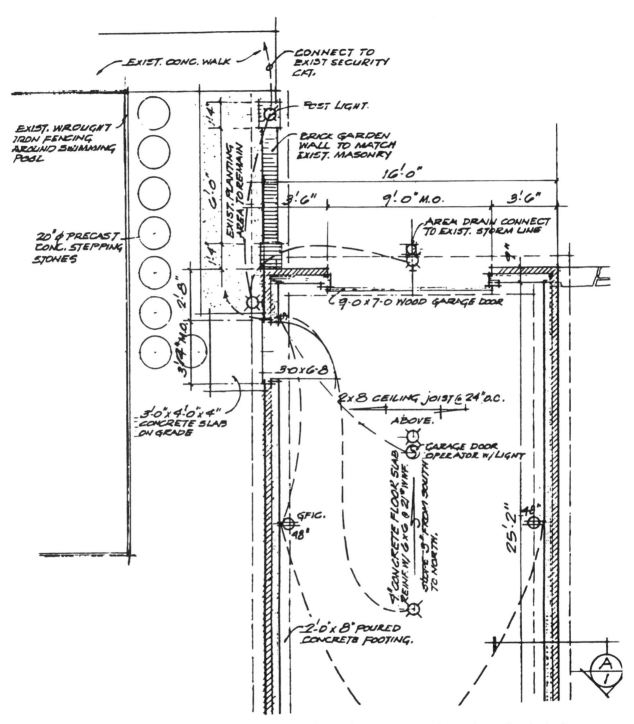

CONNECT TO EXIST SECURITY CKT.

EXIST. CONC. WALK

POST LIGHT.

BRICK GARDEN WALL TO MATCH EXIST. MASONRY

EXIST. WROUGHT IRON FENCING AROUND SWIMMING POOL

16'-0"

3'-6"   9'-0" M.O.   3'-6"

6'-0"

EXIST PLANTING AREA TO REMAIN

AREA DRAIN CONNECT TO EXIST. STORM LINE

20" ∅ PRECAST CONC. STEPPING STONES

2'-8"

3'-4" M.O.

9-0 x 7-0 WOOD GARAGE DOOR

3-0 x 6-8

2x8 CEILING JOIST @ 24" O.C. ABOVE.

3'-0" x 4'-0" x 4" CONCRETE SLAB ON GRADE

GARAGE DOOR OPERATOR W/ LIGHT

4" CONCRETE FLOOR SLAB REINF W/ 6 x 6 @ 2" W.W.F.

SLOPE 3" FROM SOUTH TO NORTH.

25'-2"

GFIC. 48"

48"

2'-0" x 8" POURED CONCRETE FOOTING.

A / 1

A floor plan of a small, simple building on which the footing/foundation system is noted as well as the basic floor plan information. Simplifies the drawings for a building with a crawl space instead of a basement, or with a slab-on-grade.

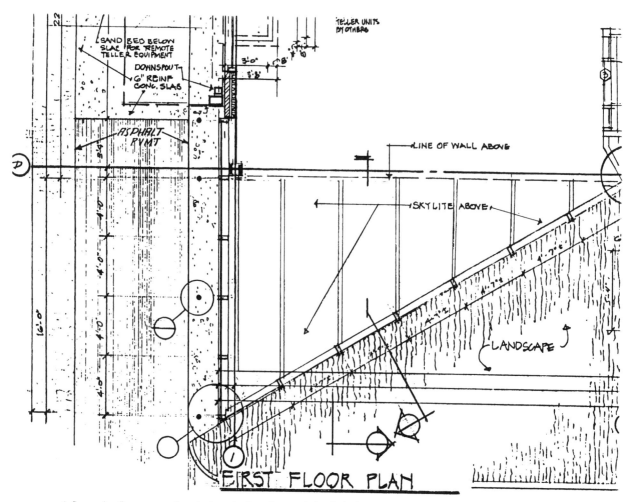

A floor plan "in progress"; note layout of section and detail designators, which will be filled in later. Also note the use of line textures to define various areas, surfaces, and materials. Care must be taken not to use the same line symbols used in sectional drawings or a pattern of lines that will confuse the user; great care is necessary, as this becomes more of a presentation drawing than a working drawing.

3. Show all light fixtures, anemostats (diffusers), access panels, scuttles, skylights, drapery pockets and tracks, trim around columns, and similar items.

4. Check clearance of structure and duct work and coordination of all mechanical items; show all borders, trim cornices, control joints,

coves, changes in ceiling height, bulkheads, structural supports, piers, columns, and sprinklers.

5. Show the ceiling pattern desired, with proper dimensioning; coordinate with building features or window mullions as desired.

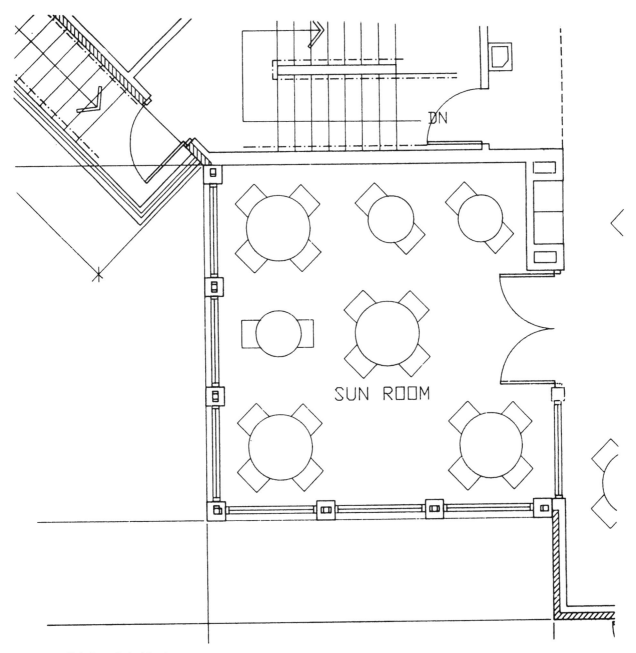

Cole/Russell, Architects
A CAD-produced seating plan. By utilizing "library" figures, the tablets and chairs are drawn quickly, in any position designated by the operator.

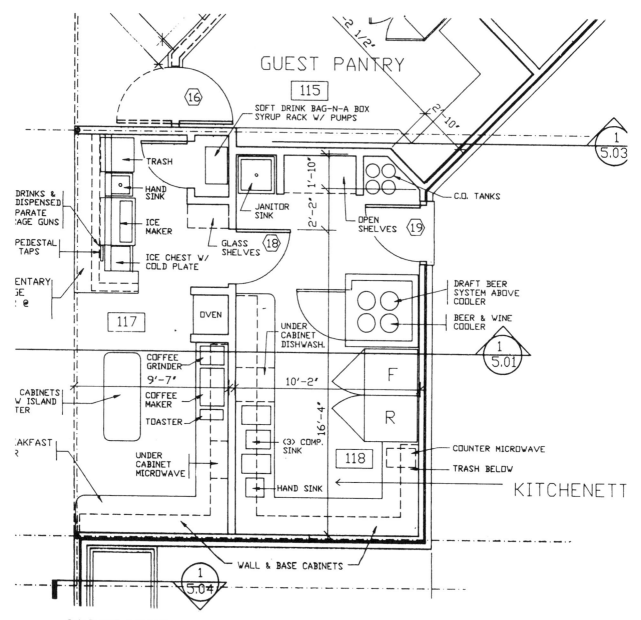

Cole/Russell, Architects
A "unique" CAD floor plan in that most of the items are distinctive (not repetitive). This shows the adaptability of CAD and also the good variation in lettering size, which is adjusted to the plan items themselves.

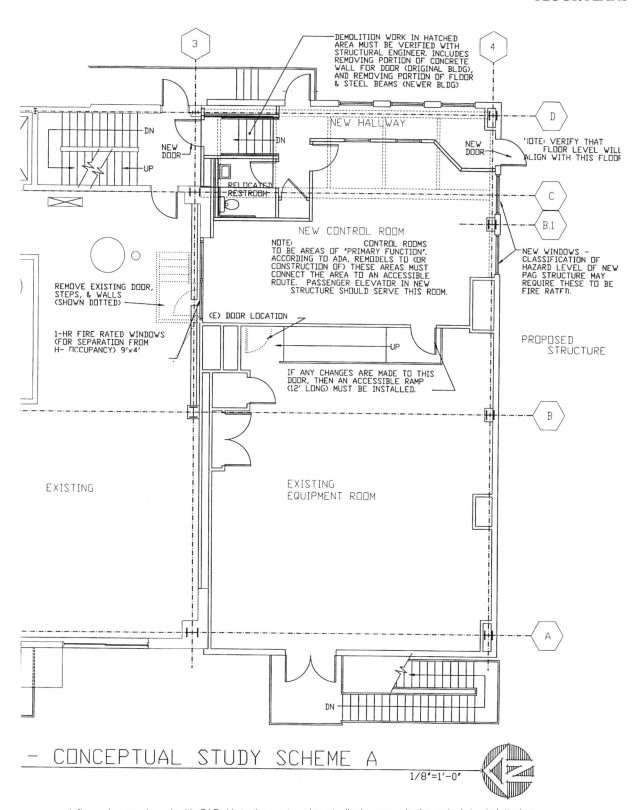

DEMOLITION WORK IN HATCHED AREA MUST BE VERIFIED WITH STRUCTURAL ENGINEER. INCLUDES REMOVING PORTION OF CONCRETE WALL FOR DOOR (ORIGINAL BLDG), AND REMOVING PORTION OF FLOOR & STEEL BEAMS (NEWER BLDG)

NEW HALLWAY

DN

NEW DOOR

NEW DOOR

NOTE: VERIFY THAT FLOOR LEVEL WILL ALIGN WITH THIS FLOOR

DN

UP

RELOCATED RESTROOM

NEW CONTROL ROOM

NOTE: CONTROL ROOMS TO BE AREAS OF 'PRIMARY FUNCTION'. ACCORDING TO ADA, REMODELS TO (OR CONSTRUCTION OF) THESE AREAS MUST CONNECT THE AREA TO AN ACCESSIBLE ROUTE. PASSENGER ELEVATOR IN NEW STRUCTURE SHOULD SERVE THIS ROOM.

REMOVE EXISTING DOOR, STEPS, & WALLS (SHOWN DOTTED)

NEW WINDOWS – CLASSIFICATION OF HAZARD LEVEL OF NEW PAG STRUCTURE MAY REQUIRE THESE TO BE FIRE RATED.

1-HR FIRE RATED WINDOWS (FOR SEPARATION FROM H- OCCUPANCY) 9'x4'

(E) DOOR LOCATION

PROPOSED STRUCTURE

UP

IF ANY CHANGES ARE MADE TO THIS DOOR, THEN AN ACCESSIBLE RAMP (12' LONG) MUST BE INSTALLED.

EXISTING

EXISTING EQUIPMENT ROOM

DN

– CONCEPTUAL STUDY SCHEME A

1/8"=1'-0"

A floor plan produced with CAD. Note the neat and controlled approach, the varied size in lettering.

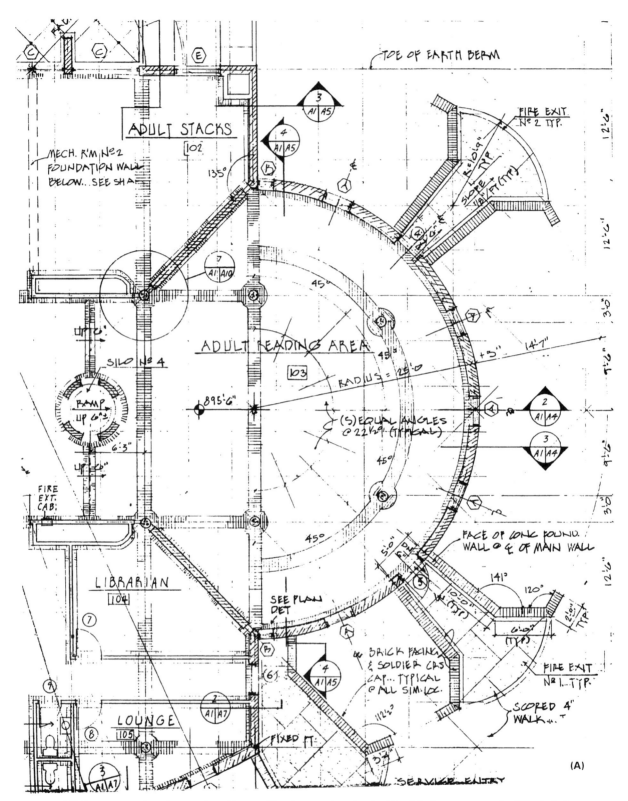

(A) A very complex plan produced by traditional, manual methods; this might be an extremely difficult CAD project. However, CAD was used in (B) to add the various items of furniture.

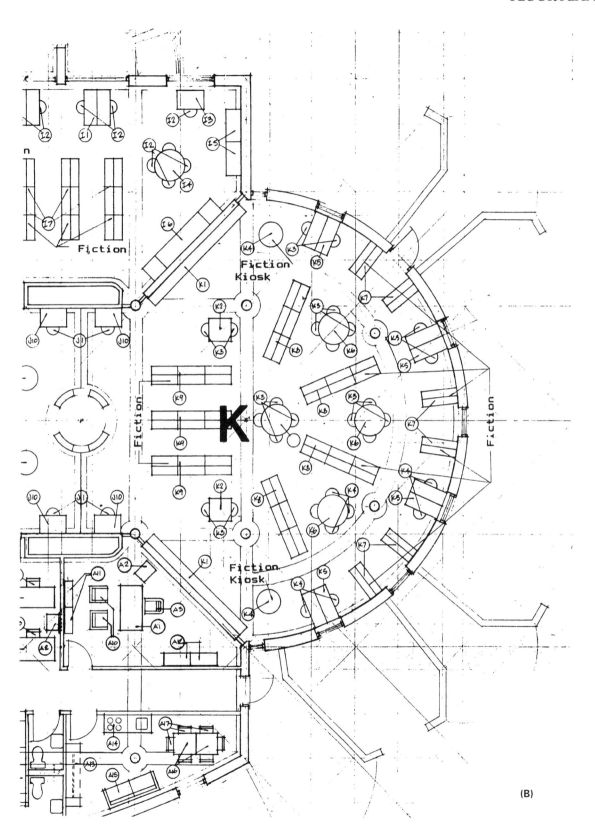

(B)

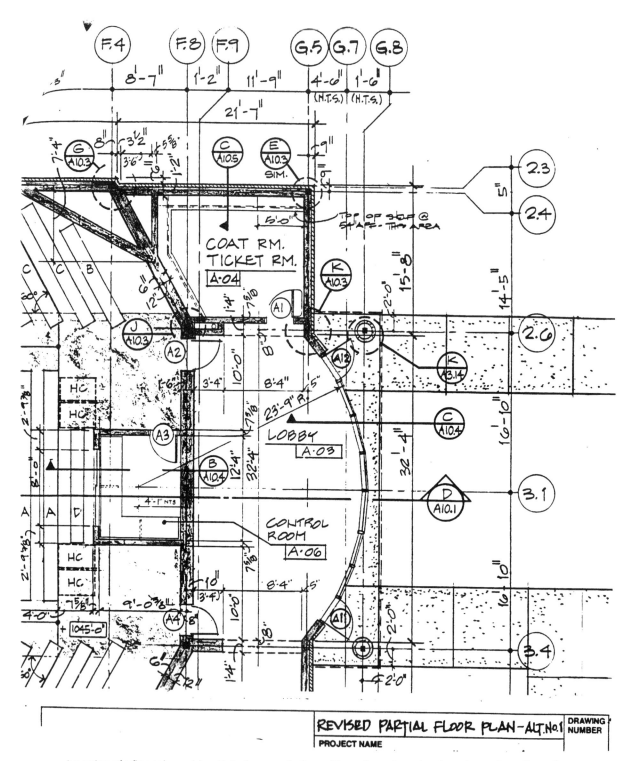

A portion of a floor plan revision. Note the complexity and the various dimensional requirements and how they are shown. This would make an interesting exercise in CAD.

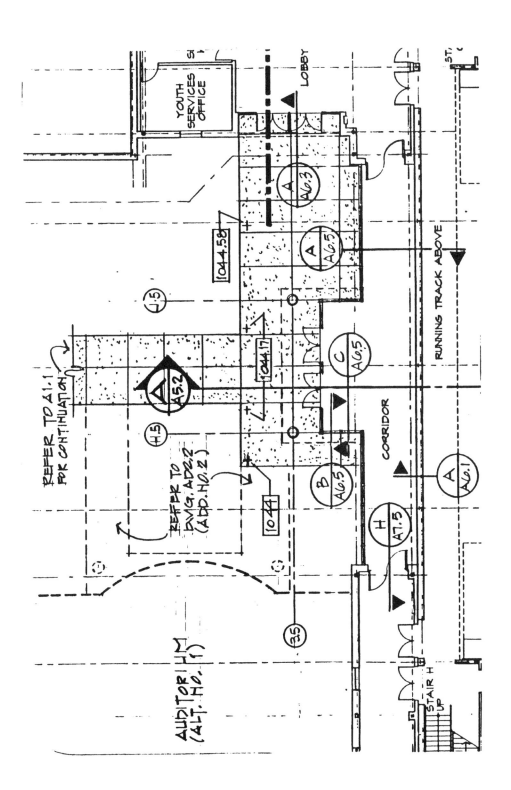

CLARIFICATION: EXTENT OF CONC. PAVING @ WEST ENTRY

PARTIAL FIRST FLOOR PLAN

1"-0" = 1'-0"

A "clarification" drawing used to show work that was not fully explained or fully clear in the contract documents.

19

Foundation Plans

Although the foundation system may entail only a small part of the total project, it must provide a firm, stable, fully designed base for the entire structure. It is responsible for the distribution of the total weight of the building and supports as well as all live loads imposed on it. The foundation must serve its purpose without uneven settling or collapse. All other systems of the building depend on it to function properly.

The foundation consists of three basic parts: the bed or soil on which it rests; the footing, which is the widened section resting directly on the bed; and the wall, which rises from the footing to a level above the ground. Before we can understand the drawing of a foundation section or foundation plan, we must be familiar with the basic foundation systems.

The foundation wall may consist of a series of columns or pedestals. If, however, a solid wall is used, it is called a continuous foundation, the system most commonly employed in lighter construction-dwellings and light industrial and commercial buildings. The building load is carried to the soil by the walls and footings. In most areas building codes will require that the footings be horizontal at the bottom and that any slopes or changes in elevation be done in steps. Stepped footings are not uncommon.

Another form of foundation, primarily residential, is the grade beam system. Grade beams are used extensively when no requirement is made for a basement and underground construction is minimal. A reinforced concrete beam at grade level surrounds the building's perimeter and is supported by a series of piers extending down into the undisturbed soil. In essence, the system is a series of piers topped by the beam, which spans from pier to pier. This type of foundation system can be used on sloping sites or when earth slippage is a possibility.

Spread foundations form another system, in which the walls above the footing are thickened to form a buttress. Spread footings are isolated one from another under the walls. This system, used beneath columns, helps to distribute the load. Spread footings are often reinforced to carry the entire load imposed on them. They can be flat, stepped, or sloped, according to the building design or the site.

The mat or raft is a heavier foundation, consisting of a stoutly reinforced concrete slab that extends under the entire building; the slab spreads the building load over the site to form a cushion on which the building rests. On uneven soil, columns rest on individual footings, some of which may settle more than others, and cracking and straining may develop. With the mat foundation, however, everything acts as a unit; the

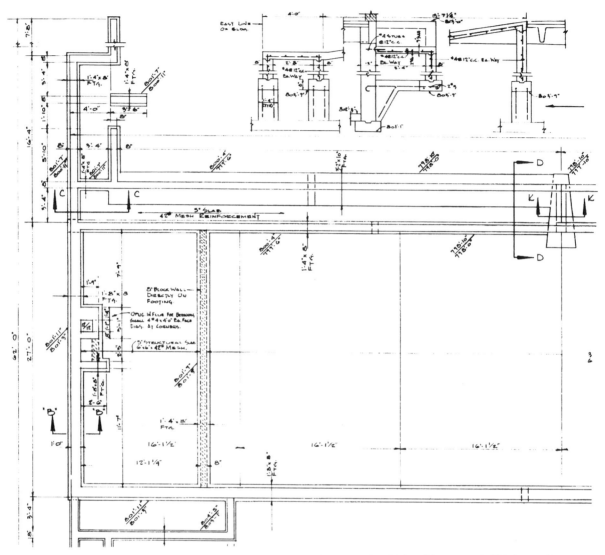

This system of continuous footings is common, and each project should be able to use it. This is not the case, however, and other systems must be provided. The footing and foundation systems lie under the entire configuration of the building. Note in the upper right the odd-shaped footing (a strap footing) that ties the two walls together. A light tone can be applied to the back of the sheet to make the walls of the foundation a little more positive.

building actually floats in its excavation. The name "floating foundation" is applicable.

Concrete piers of one type or another are used when suitable load-bearing soil lies some distance beneath the surface. The selection of piers is predicated on the cost reduction factor. To excavate the site to solid soil may incur excessive cost. By drilling or driving piers down to the load-bearing soil, the required load-bearing capacity can be provided without the ex-

tra cost. Piers come in a variety of sizes. Shafts with or without inner linings or casings can be drilled to the desired depth and filled with concrete. The drilled shaft is called the caisson, a term reserved for shafts in water or water-bearing-soil. Piers may be enlarged into a bell shape at the bottom. These bells distribute the weight of the pier over a larger area, a system employed primarily in a good load-bearing soil that is not so firm as bedrock. As noted ear-

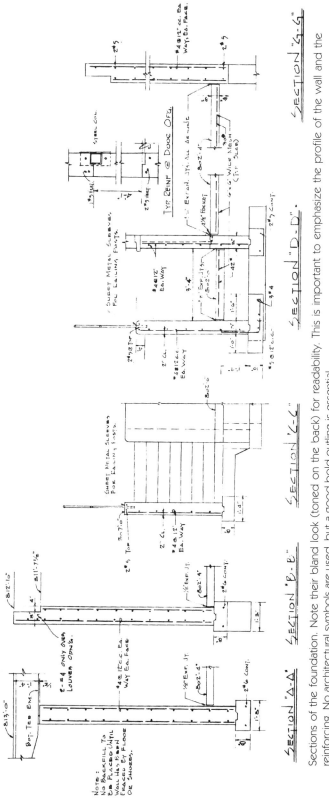

Sections of the foundation. Note their bland look (toned on the back) for readability. This is important to emphasize the profile of the wall and the reinforcing. No architectural symbols are used, but a good bold outline is essential.

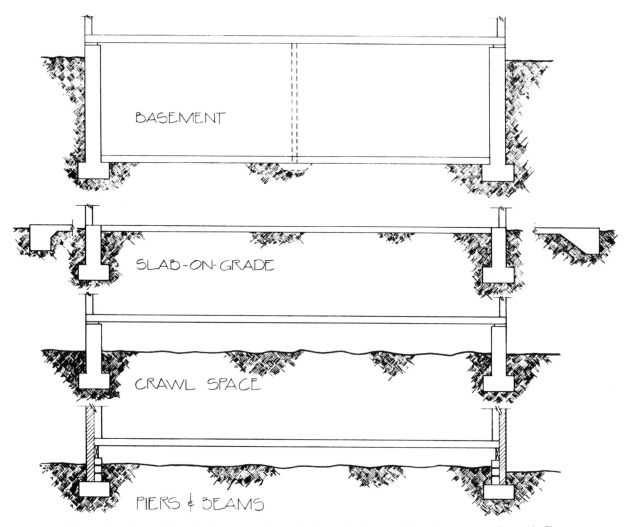

This section of several foundation systems shows their construction and how they engage the earth. These commonly used systems can be modified for more extreme soil conditions, but some provision must be made under the footings for piling and/or drilled caissons.

lier, these piers can be capped with a grade beam system.

One other system for reaching load-bearing soil employs piling. Pilings are lengths of wood, concrete, or steel that are forced or driven through the unstable strata until soil is found that can support the estimated load. Piling is a system familiar to people living in the metropolitan areas where the clang of the pile driver can be heard forcing the metal piling into the ground.

There is no set pattern and no particular criteria for choosing one of these systems over another. The choice becomes the prerogative of the structural engineers. They, of course, must study the log of soil borings made for the particular job and evaluate the total load that the building will impose. They also study the capacity of the soil. In many instances a site will contain good and bad load-bearing soil, and it is not uncommon for two foundation systems to be used in the same building. Indeed, there can be more than two systems, depending on the soil conditions.

The drawing of the foundation plan is done in two parts: the architectural plan and the structural foundation plan. In many ways the plans are similar because they are based on the same information and building configurations. They also differ radically.

The architectural foundation plan shows the entire foundation system at the point just after

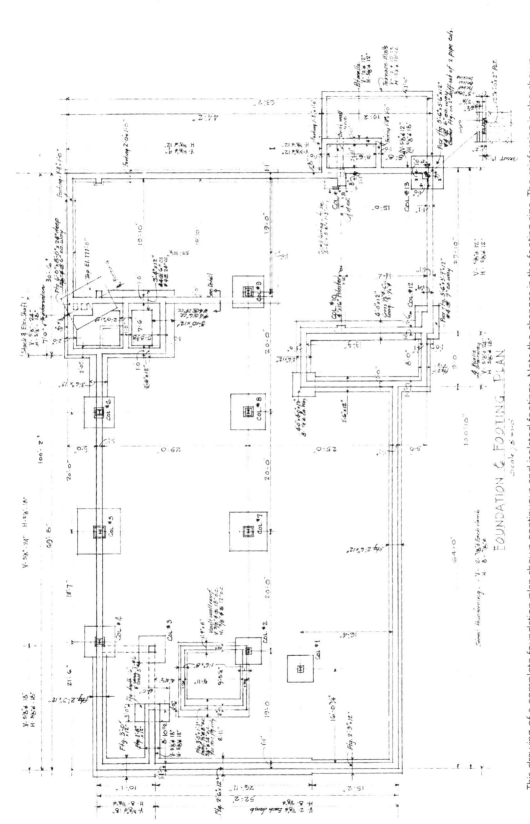

This drawing of a complete foundation plan shows continuous and isolated footings. Note the changes in the footing size. The reinforcing is also shown on the plan to eliminate the need for numerous sections. One footing has been set at an angle to compensate for poor soil conditions in the area.

the backfilling operation is completed. It also shows all components such as the foundation wall, wall footings, column footings, grade beams, caps of piles, piling, and any superstructure building (crawl space columns). This plan is drawn at the level of the basement or subbasement floor; no first floor or basement construction is shown on the architectural foundation plan. Sometimes the basement plan can be combined. The draftsman should be aware that there will often be two separate plans. It is possible in a one-story, slab-on-grade structure to incorporate the footing foundation plan if it is done carefully and precisely and each feature is clearly pointed out on the drawing.

The foundation plan locates all foundation features horizontally. The building rests securely on the foundation; therefore, it is important to show the sizes and locations of its walls, grade beams, ledges, pockets and recesses. It is equally important to determine the location of footings and columns for the building's superstructure. To feed information to other drawings, , the bottoms of the wall footings are located vertically; the critical sizes of the foundation features are given. The foundation plan is singular because no other plan drawing gives vertical dimensions.

The foundation plan is the basis of the design of the structural framework of the building. The grid is laid out for all columns extending through the building and applies as well to the footing foundations beneath the columns. The grid system is discussed at length in "framing plans".

The foundation plans reflects the overall character of the building, for the building's visible elements must be carried down and firmly attached to the earth underlying the structure. With this fact in mind, we know that the plan must account for all elements, for from it the features of the foundation are developed in minute detail.

A basic, but different, philosophy relates to the two types of structural detail shown on any set of drawings. The features of the foundation show the general configuration of the architectural elements, but the most important concept, illustrated in considerable detail, is how the foundation engages, holds, and supports these features. The reinforcing steel and other structural elements are not included.

In diametrical opposition, the structural drawings contain all these details. Each reinforcing bar in a concrete structure is delineated with brackets, stirrups, ties, and the other elements of good design. In steel frame, of course, the anchor bolts,

welding symbols, and all construction features required in column and footing connections are meticulously drawn.

At first glance, the foundation drawing appears to be extremely simple. Neither material nor structural symbols are employed. A wall is merely two parallel lines, properly scaled to indicate its thickness.

Some firms use colored pencils on the reverse side of the sheets to tone the structural elements. This tone, made with a yellow pencil or hard lead in a standard lead holder, is dark enough to distinguish between the element and the white background of the paper but not dark enough to obliterate the structural detail. The tone is not indicative; it merely emphasizes.

The foundation plan must be complete and minutely detailed. Although many features of the building will be tied directly into the foundation system, other elements (such as brackets, offsets, ledges, or decorative motifs) may create a different profile. The foundation plan is not always just a tracing of the first floor plan; for example, a basement vault will require a larger and more complicated foundation.

Foundations must also reflect the building loads to be imposed. For larger and taller buildings architects will design lighter structural systems and select lighter interior materials so that a disproportionate amount of the budget money will not be devoured by the understructure.

The foundation system is caught between conflicting requirements: the building above it must support itself and all live loads it must carry. This requirement, as translated to the base, forces a certain configuration. Underneath the foundation is the bearing soil, which may have an excellent bearing capacity, such as rock or shale, or may be poor load-bearing sand or old fill. The foundation system must react to the load above and the footing beneath; if necessary, it must be expanded over a wider area to accommodate the load, which cannot be more than the soil itself can support. If the design is faulty, the building will fail or its parts will be irreparably damaged.

The design of the parts is something that cannot be slighted. The foundation must be a unified whole, for nowhere is the old saw about the weakest link more applicable than it is here.

From time to time the architectural draftsman may have to deal with the structural drawings. To keep consulting fees to a minimum, an

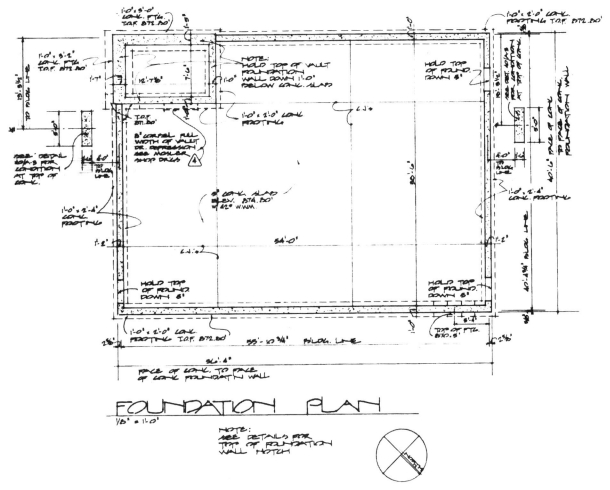

A foundation plan for a fairly simple building. Note, however, that it contains all the elements of a larger structure. This building is a slab-on-grade and has no basement. Note how the foundation changes when the loading is increased (at the vault in the upper left). Isolated piers support decorative sections and no large loads are present.

architectural firm sometimes engage a structural engineer to design the foundation; the drafting is done by architectural personnel. It is more important that the draftsman understand that every note must be accurately transcribed and that every element must be accounted for strictly according to design. This work calls for absolute caution and demands clear, concise information. Further, if there is any question in the drafter's mind, it is vital that he or she have access to a superior for an immediate solution.

The lines that define the various structural features must be black and heavy so that all features can be readily distinguished. A wide variety of line weights will characterize the complicated details of the various elements. The foundation plan, in particular, will contain extremely small items for which the line work is crucial. Clear, concise lettering will eliminate confusion between letters and structural symbols. Careful proofreading is essential.

The foundation plan follows the design of the building, both literally and figuratively. As the heaviest part of the building, the foundation carries all the upper load. Walls on the upper floor of the building are thinner. Walls nearer ground level become wider as the load from above increases.

The system design terminates in the foundation. After the upper building requirements have

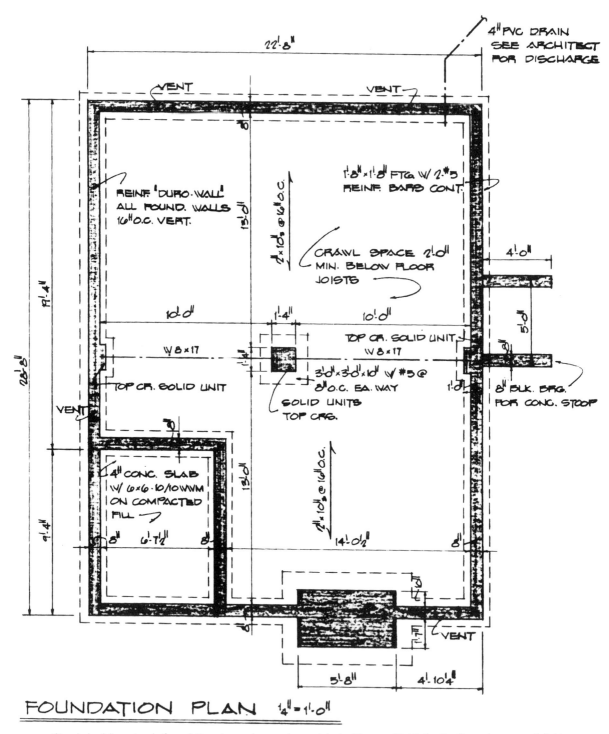

4" PVC DRAIN
SEE ARCHITECT
FOR DISCHARGE

22'-8"

VENT
VENT

REINF. "DURO-WALL"
ALL FOUND. WALLS
16" O.C. VERT.

15'-0"

1'-8" × 1'-0" FTG. W/ 2-#5
REINF. BARS CONT.

2 × 10's @ 16" O.C.

CRAWL SPACE 2'-0"
MIN. BELOW FLOOR
JOISTS

4'-0"

19'-4"

5'-0"

10'-0"

1'-4"

10'-0"

26'-8"

W 8 × 17

TOP CR. SOLID UNIT
W 8 × 17

VENT

TOP CR. SOLID UNIT

3'-0" × 3'-0" × 10" W/ #5 @
8" O.C. EA. WAY
SOLID UNITS
TOP CRS.

1'-0"

8" BLK. BRG.
FOR CONC. STOOP

15'-0"

4" CONC. SLAB
W/ 6×6-10/10 WWM
ON COMPACTED
FILL

2 × 10" @ 16" O.C.

14'-0½"

9'-4"

8"   6'-7½"   8"

8"

VENT

5'-8"

4'-10¼"

FOUNDATION PLAN ¼" = 1'-0"

Simple building, simple foundation. A crawl space is provided with wood joists for the floor above, and slight variations are required to provide correct configuration.

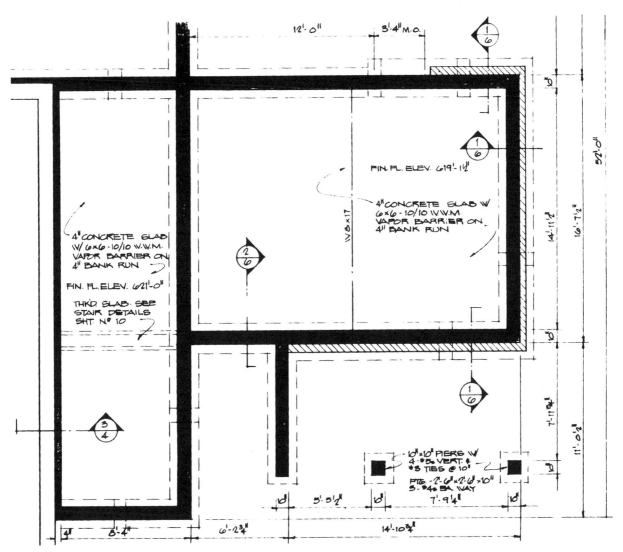

Isolated piers with footings in another section of a foundation plan. Also shown are the markers that refer to the foundation sections. Observe the notations at various points in the drawing.

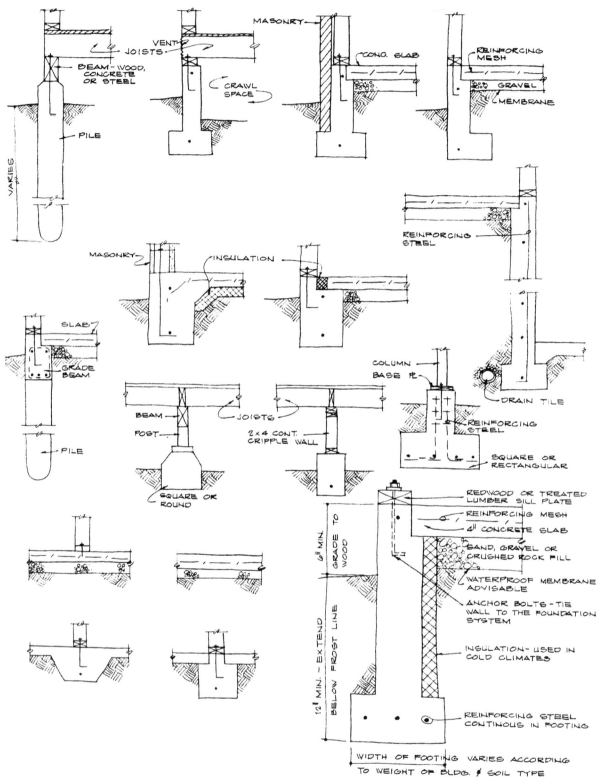

A general overview of foundation systems, each of which can be applied as required. In bad soil some type of piling is essential, whereas under normal conditions the standard footing is adequate. In some areas, and with light loads, the thickened wall or grade beam is used, and in others simple piers suffice. In many projects the slab is thickened to provide for masonry partitions.

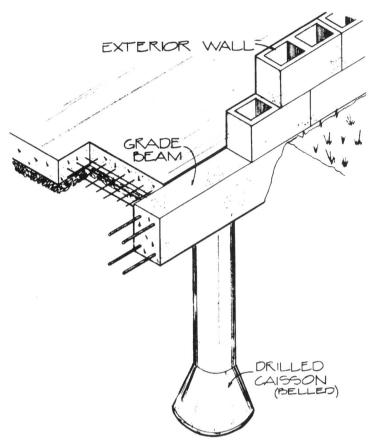

EXTERIOR WALL

GRADE BEAM

DRILLED CAISSON (BELLED)

A detail of the grade beam under a masonry wall. This beam is supported, in turn, by drilled caissons which bore into the earth until good bearing soil is found. The grade beam must be designed to span from caisson to caisson.

been determined and the plans laid out, the foundation system can be designed and drawn.

The "fast-track" method of construction, frequently used now, requires that the foundation system be designed early in the project sequence. Fast-track is a method of construction, which reduces the total time for design, and construction. Usually these phases are done one after the other [the design/documentation is fully complete before construction is started]. However, a significant amount of time can be saved by starting construction while final design and documentation is still in progress. Documents are issued as completed to allow a continuation of the construction. However, the foundation system must be in place in order for other work to be installed. This requires that the foundation be designed prior to the upper superstructure of the building; and while every design load and answer has not been resolved. Astute professionals can work in this fashion utilizing experience-based analysis and computations for their design. This procedure may seem impossible to implement, but the fast tracking system demands it. The foundation system is contingent on the preliminary architectural drawings. Once the foundation structure is imbedded in the earth (and hardened, in the case of concrete), there is no way to make changes without tremendous expense. Therefore, early decisions must be made that will affect later design considerations. Architects and consulting structural engineers must learn to adapt to this new process, for the fast tracking system is an overall time saver.

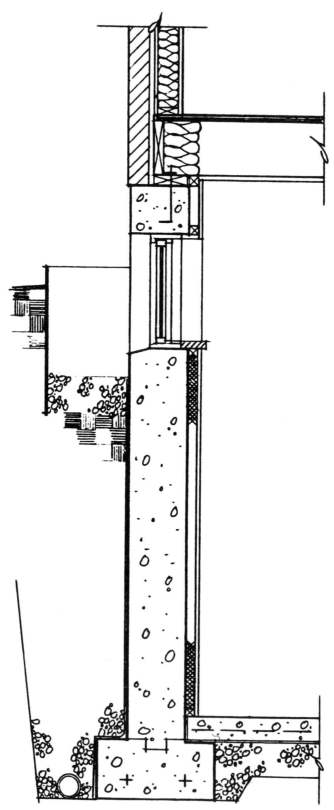

A typical foundation section for a residence with a brick veneer upper wall system. Good definition of materials, and good variation of line work.

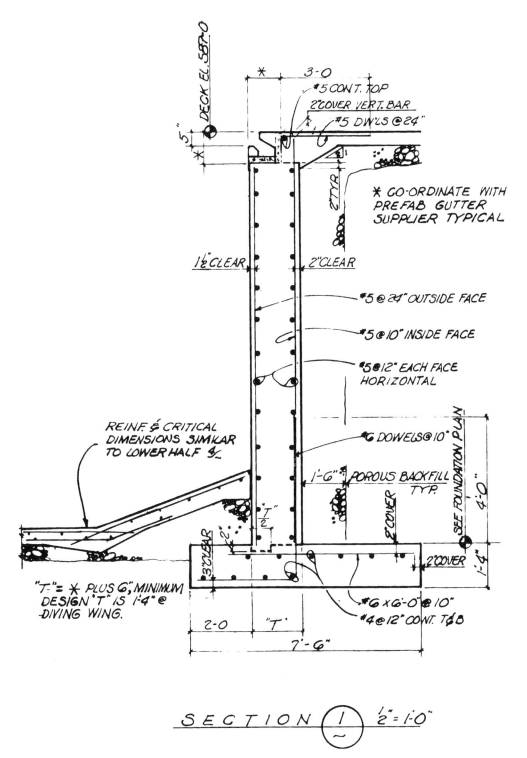

DECK EL. 58'-0

* 3-0

#5 CONT. TOP
2"COVER VERT. BAR
#5 DWLS @ 24"

5"

2" TYP.

* CO-ORDINATE WITH
PREFAB GUTTER
SUPPLIER TYPICAL

1½" CLEAR

2" CLEAR

#5 @ 24" OUTSIDE FACE

#5 @ 10" INSIDE FACE

#5 @ 12" EACH FACE
HORIZONTAL

REINF. & CRITICAL
DIMENSIONS SIMILAR
TO LOWER HALF ½

#6 DOWELS @ 10"

1'-6" POROUS BACKFILL
TYP.

SEE FOUNDATION PLAN

4'-0"

2" COVER

T/2

3" CLEAR

2"

2" COVER

1'-4"

2" COVER

#6 × 6'-0" @ 10"

"T" = * PLUS 6", MINIMUM
DESIGN "T" IS 1'-4" @
-DIVING WING.

2'-0" "T"

#4 @ 12" CONT. T&B

7'-6"

S E C T I O N ⊘ ½" = 1'-0"

Detail of a concrete wall for an indoor or outdoor swimming pool shows the type and amount of detail in the
foundation wall. Note the dark outline and lack of tone in the wall drawing.

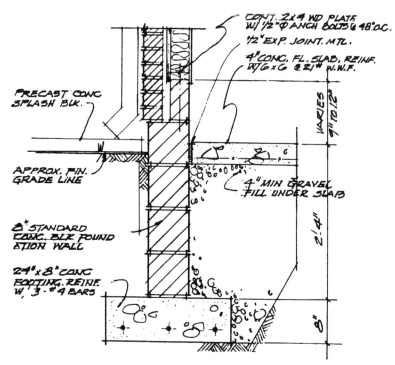

CONT. 2x4 WD PLATE
W/ 1/2" Ø ANCH BOLTS @ 48" O.C.

1/2" EXP. JOINT. MTL.

4" CONC. FL. SLAB. REINF.
W/ 6x6 @ 21# W.W.F.

PRECAST CONC
SPLASH BLK.

VARIES
9" TO 12"

APPROX. FIN.
GRADE LINE

4" MIN GRAVEL
FILL UNDER SLAB

8" STANDARD
CONC. BLK FOUND
ATION WALL

2' 4"

24" x 8" CONC
FOOTING. REINF.
W. 3 - #4 BARS

8"

Good example of a simple residential foundation detail using concrete masonry units; well executed.

20

Framing Plans

Framing plans for floor and roof construction can be derived directly from the floor plan and must incorporate all information that deals with the configuration of the building. Further, the framing plan shows the layout of the supporting features such as bearing walls, columns, beams, and girders. In preparing plans for framing, the outline of the building should be drawn on the back of the sheet, so that in the event of erasures or changes in the framing system it will not be necessary to redraw the entire building plan.

The basic building plan should show all walls without window and door openings to indicate a level of horizontal section, or plan, above the openings, at which the supporting member would rest. In drawing the backup for the framing plans, it should be kept in mind that in these particular drawings the overall building plan is a subordinate to the framing system. Therefore, a change in line weight to a lighter tone is in order. A darker, heavier tone is used for the framing-system members. Halftone printing, or screening, is another method in which framing members are shown on the correct surface of the drawing sheet.

The framing plans are meant to complement the architectural plans. These are strictly structural drawings intended for the location of all the structural members and features and should show such things as floor slabs on grade, framing members installed integrally with the floor, and framing members installed separately. In regard to these matters, some basic framing systems that require specific drawings are suggested; for example, a building framed in wood or steel is shown with isolated structural supports (columns) and individual beams, joists, girders, and purlins. A reinforced concrete building may have a system of flat slabs that span between column points or a monolithic floor system poured in one piece that would require a slab and a joist and beam system.

With concrete, which arrives on the job in plastic form, the entire system would be poured at one time. Thus, the requirements for concrete framing plans are different from those for wood or steel. Although the same types of members are shown, they must be presented in a different way. Refer to the examples and the various framing systems illustrated.

Framing plans must include all the building's structural components: horizontal and sloped slabs, stairs and ramps, and the framing members themselves (foundation walls and columns, bearing walls, and so on). It is not necessary to show nonbearing walls or partitions on the framing plan. Such extraneous matters tend to complicate the drawing. If a wall has no structural value in the building system, it need not be shown.

There are a great many components in any roof or floor framing system. The systems are similar;

for example, openings may occur in both floor and roof for penetration by components of architectural and mechanical systems. It is important that not only the major structural elements be shown, but also those that may be of a minor structural nature that would frame openings. These members are sized by the structural engineer and should be noted by the system by which various materials are designated. Wood is called out in the nominal sizes of available lumber or timber, such as 2 x 4 and 4 x 8. Steel members must be called out by their correct designation and by their depth and weight per foot.

In concrete structures the framing plans must indicate individual floor slabs, whether on grade or suspended between columns. Each floor must be delineated because the reinforcing of the slabs may change from bay to bay, depending on the superimposed load in the bay. Other variants such as recesses, stairs, pits, ramps, grade beams, or openings affect the slab's design.

Sometimes structural members are isolated from the total system. A case in point is the loose lintels that support the walls above any openings. They must be shown correctly in their proper location and size on the architectural elevation, again giving their location, type of member, amount of end bearing at both ends, or the symbol designator that cross references them to the lintel schedule.

The framing plans really become a function of the complexity of the building. If a building is composed of arches, trusses, heavy girders, and beams that support the floors and roof, the system becomes complicated. On a residential plan it is possible merely by the use of a doubleheaded arrow to indicate the size of the members and their proper spacing. Following this thought, we arrive at heavier joists, bar joists, and steel lumber, all used in lighter commercial construction. Again we indicate the size of the joists and the spacing; a modified residential indication will suffice for simple spans (beam to beam or wall to beam) or joints bearing on opposing walls. A more complex system of heavier members, used to collect smaller members, to carry the total weight of the building requires a more elaborate framing plan with more intricate indications. In some offices the entire structural system will be laid out to show all members, their spacing, and accessories

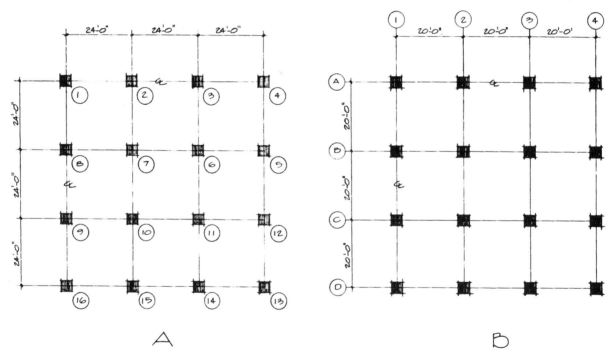

In (A) the structural grid is set up to give each column a designation that is separate from other information and can be readily adapted to any off-line columns. In (B), however, the designators mark the column lines, and the individual column is denoted by the "names" of its two centerlines (C3, for example). Here the system is tied in with dimensioning.

(bridging, anchors, headers at openings, and so on) in their correct locations and to scale with their appropriate designators. This is a conservative approach, time-consuming, but a safe course to take. The complete layout ensures that all members are shown and nothing is left to guesswork; the entire system can be plotted and studied.

The framing plan is usually drawn at the same scale as the floor plan. As stated earlier, the framing plan outline can be traced. Commonly, if there is a system of columns, a structural grid will be set up to mark the centerlines of the columns both ways. By using letters of the alphabet along one line and numerals along the other, each column can be given an individual name; for example, C-3 or r-7. This nomenclature facilitates referencing other information to a particular column.

Architectural symbols are usually not entered on the framing plans, an obvious effort to keep them simple. Section symbols are shown because the structural framing plans require that a number of sections and details be given. These details are connections, bearings, anchorage, and other related matters. The framing plans can become complicated and confusing unless interested concern is displayed on the drafted sheet.

Concrete construction presents much more of a challenge because of the opaque nature and the integral characteristics of the concrete system.

When members stand apart from one another, as in wood or steel, the drawing is greatly simplified. Here individual members are shown by a centerline designation, be they steel or wood. In concrete, however, the beam width is indicated by a double line. If there is a series of joists, it must be shown because the joists will be constructed with pan-type forms and the spacing must be laid out to show their width and the voids between them. The slabs must be individually designated so that the reinforcing can be specifically designed for each bay. The columns and connections of the flat slab system to the columns must also be detailed on the framing plan.

Many more sections are required in a concrete system because of the diverse situations; few are typical. This is not to discourage the young architect from designing in concrete. Each building must be evaluated on the requirements of the project and the system that will work best for it. It would be foolish to space steel bar joists 6 inches apart merely to make it easier to draw the framing plan when perhaps a concrete system, even with its more complicated drawing, would function better for the client who needs maximum load-bearing capacity in a building. This chapter points out the variations between systems, and, again, the system must be chosen by the structural engineer. His or her selection must fill the requirements of the building project.

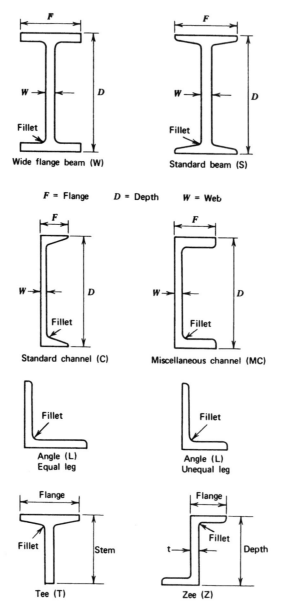

F = Flange   D = Depth   W = Web

Wide flange beam (W)

Standard beam (S)

Standard channel (C)

Miscellaneous channel (MC)

Angle (L) Equal leg

Angle (L) Unequal leg

Tee (T)

Zee (Z)

(Above, opposite) Details, names, and proper designations for structural steel shapes; to be used on framing plans and structural details. Consult steel handbook for complete listing of sizes, weights, shapes, and design details.

HOT-ROLLED STRUCTURAL STEEL DESIGNATIONS

New Designation	Type of Shape	Old Designation
W 24 × 76 W 14 × 26	W shape	24 WF 76 14 B 26
S 24 × 100	S shape	24 I 100
M 8 × 18.5 M 10 × 9 M 8 × 34.3	M shape	8 M 18.5 10 JR 9.0 8 × 8 M 34.3
C 12 × 20.7	American Standard Channel	12 C 20.7
MC 12 × 45 MC 12 × 10.6	Miscellaneous Channel	12 × 4 C 45.0 12 JR C 10.6
HP 14 × 73	HP shape	14 BP 73
L 6 × 6 × ¾ L 6 × 4 × ⅝	Equal Leg Angle Unequal Leg Angle	∠ 6 × 6 × ¾ ∠ 6 × 4 × ⅝
WT 12 × 38 WT 7 × 13	Structural Tee cut from W shape	ST 12 WF 38 ST 7 B 13
ST 12 × 50	Structural Tee cut from S shape	ST 12 I 50
MT 4 × 9.25 MT 5 × 4.5 MT 4 × 17.15	Structural Tee cut from M shape	ST 4 M 9.25 ST 5 JR 4.5 ST 4 M 17.15
PL ½ × 18	Plate	PL 18 × ½
Bar 1 ◻ Bar 1¼ φ Bar 2½ × ½	Square Bar Round Bar Flat Bar	Bar 1 ◻ Bar 1¼ φ Bar 2½ × ½
Pipe 4 Std. Pipe 4 X - Strong Pipe 4 XX - Strong	Pipe	Pipe 4 Std. Pipe 4 X-Strong Pipe 4 XX-Strong
TS 4 × 4 × .375 TS 5 × 3 × .375 TS 3 OD × .250	Structural Tubing: Square Structural Tubing: Rectangular Structural Tubing: Circular	Tube 4 × 4 × .375 Tube 5 × 3 × .375 Tube 3 OD × .250

AMERICAN INSTITUTE OF STEEL CONSTRUCTION

WELDED JOINTS
Standard symbols

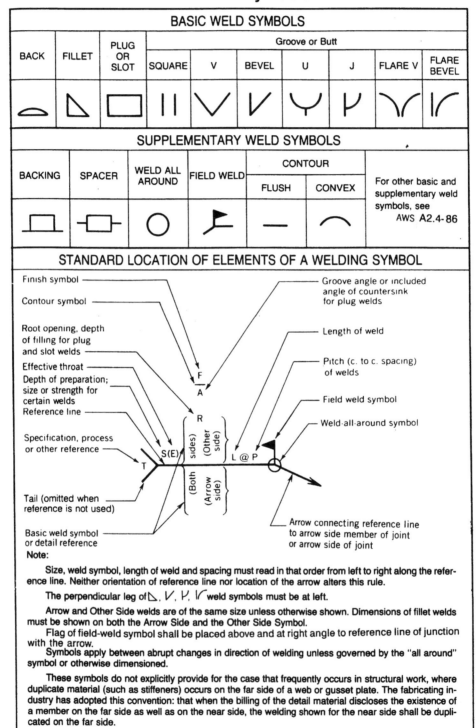

BASIC WELD SYMBOLS

BACK	FILLET	PLUG OR SLOT	Groove or Butt						
			SQUARE	V	BEVEL	U	J	FLARE V	FLARE BEVEL

SUPPLEMENTARY WELD SYMBOLS

BACKING	SPACER	WELD ALL AROUND	FIELD WELD	CONTOUR		For other basic and supplementary weld symbols, see AWS A2.4-86
				FLUSH	CONVEX	

STANDARD LOCATION OF ELEMENTS OF A WELDING SYMBOL

Finish symbol

Contour symbol

Root opening, depth of filling for plug and slot welds

Effective throat

Depth of preparation; size or strength for certain welds

Reference line

Specification, process or other reference

Tail (omitted when reference is not used)

Basic weld symbol or detail reference

Groove angle or included angle of countersink for plug welds

Length of weld

Pitch (c. to c. spacing) of welds

Field weld symbol

Weld-all-around symbol

Arrow connecting reference line to arrow side member of joint or arrow side of joint

Note:

Size, weld symbol, length of weld and spacing must read in that order from left to right along the reference line. Neither orientation of reference line nor location of the arrow alters this rule.

The perpendicular leg of weld symbols must be at left.

Arrow and Other Side welds are of the same size unless otherwise shown. Dimensions of fillet welds must be shown on both the Arrow Side and the Other Side Symbol.

Flag of field-weld symbol shall be placed above and at right angle to reference line of junction with the arrow.

Symbols apply between abrupt changes in direction of welding unless governed by the "all around" symbol or otherwise dimensioned.

These symbols do not explicitly provide for the case that frequently occurs in structural work, where duplicate material (such as stiffeners) occurs on the far side of a web or gusset plate. The fabricating industry has adopted this convention: that when the billing of the detail material discloses the existence of a member on the far side as well as on the near side, the welding shown for the near side shall be duplicated on the far side.

AMERICAN INSTITUTE OF STEEL CONSTRUCTION

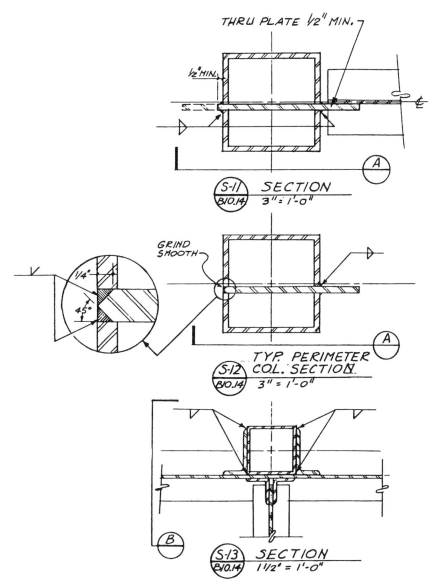

Examples of details utilizing the standard weld symbols to indicate what is required in the various connections.

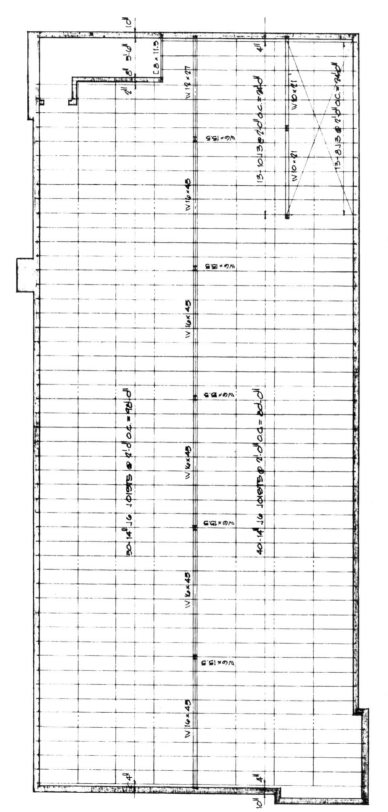

·FIRST FLOOR FRAMING PLAN· ⅜"=1'-0"

This framing plan, which consists of two spans from the outer walls to the center beam, was designed for a simple building. Its columns are few, and no system was necessary. Note how the steel joists, columns and beams are indicated.

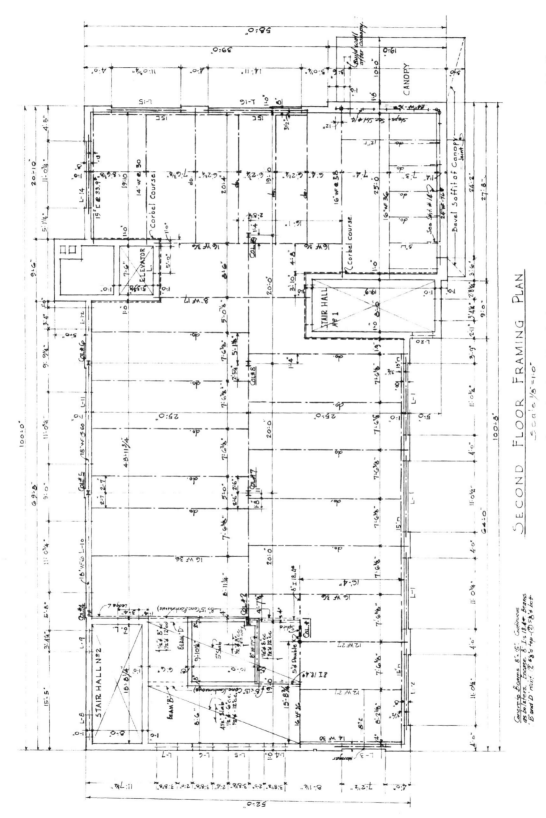

The framing plan for the second floor of a building with slab-on-grade for the first floor. Here the beam system was used to support a concrete slab. The designators are the old system. Note the dimensioning and the identification of the columns.

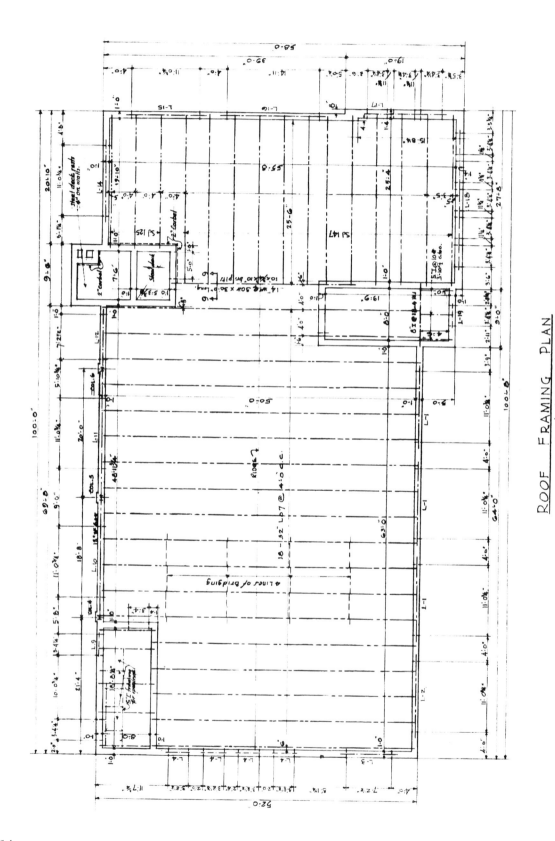

ROOF FRAMING PLAN

Scale 1/8"=1'-0"

This roof framing plan is the companion of the second floor plan. Long span joists are used from wall to wall in the main area. No columns support the roof.

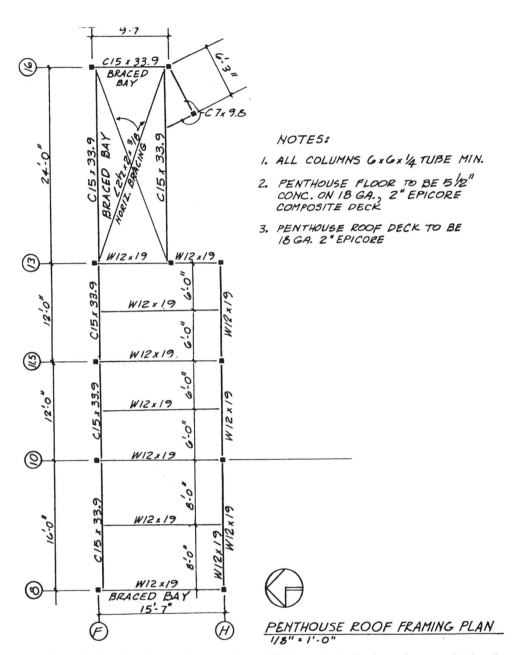

NOTES:

1. ALL COLUMNS 6 x 6 x ¼ TUBE MIN.

2. PENTHOUSE FLOOR TO BE 5½" CONC. ON 18 GA., 2" EPICORE COMPOSITE DECK

3. PENTHOUSE ROOF DECK TO BE 18 GA. 2" EPICORE

PENTHOUSE ROOF FRAMING PLAN
1/8" = 1'-0"

A limited-area framing plan for a rooftop penthouse. Well executed with clean, clear coordination, lines, and notes.

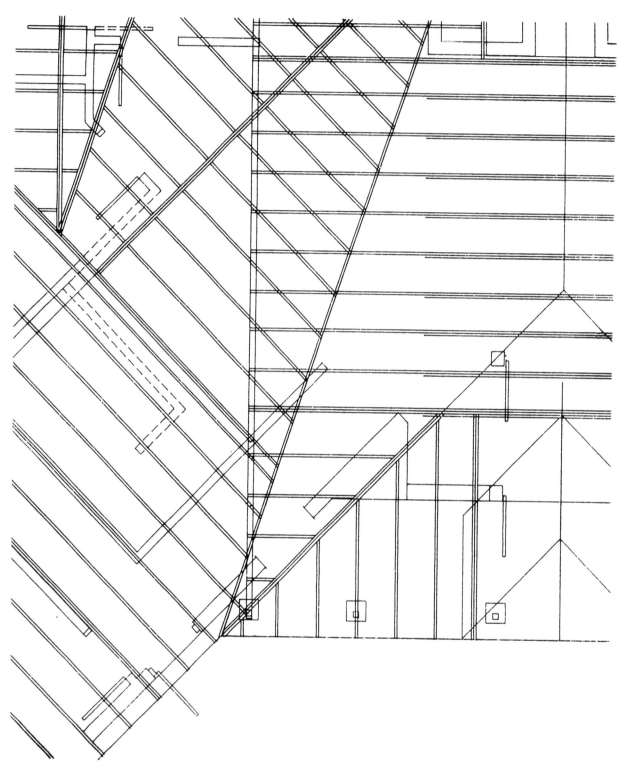

A portion of a large-scale framing plan executed using CAD equipment. Note the angles which require extensive changes in the coordinates of the lines depicting the members.

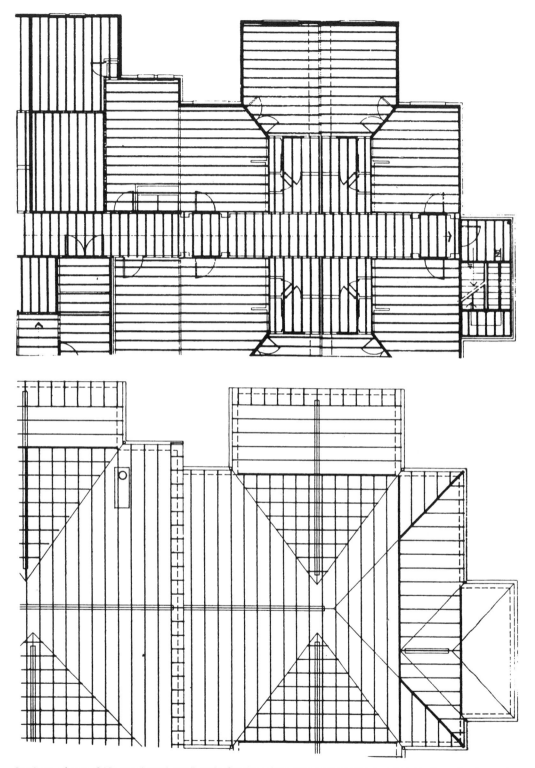

Portions of two CAD-produced small-scale framing plans. The upper plan is a floor system; the lower is a roof system.

21

Roof Plans

The roof plan explains the overall configuration of the roof and the elements that rest on, or penetrate, the roofing membrane. That every project must include a roof plan is not a hard and fast rule. Usually, a roof plan is justified only when additional construction data are needed; for instance, a roof plan is seldom required in residential work. A section through the building may show the trusses or the structural framing members, and the framing plan as well will carry some of this information. Not many elements in residential work penetrate the roof—there may be vents in the attic, plumbing vents, and a chimney or flue; however, the number of items found in roof plans of commercial, industrial, or institutional projects is shocking.

A roof plan is tantamount to a bird's-eye view of the building, similar in some respects to that shown on the site plan. It is, however, drawn at the same scale as the floor plans. The drafter should prepare an orthographic projection to show the tops of the walls and wall caps or copings. He or she will enumerate and, indeed, locate in size such things as scuttles, chimneys, drains, skylights, stacks, roof-mounted mechanical equipment, scuppers, gutters, and the pattern of slopes that may be built into the roof's surface.

The roof plan is simple in concept, if one adheres to the principle that there should be positive drainage or slope in all roof systems. No roofing contractor or manufacturer will give any kind of guarantee on a dead level roof that allows water to pond on it. Ponding forces the water to seek any opening through which it can leak into the building.

Many odd terms are used in building up the sloped portions of a roof. Pointed out in the example, they include frogs, crickets, and saddles. It is important, of course, to design the roof plan with the floor plan and to coordinate roof drains and roof leaders with the vertical runs carried down through the building without being obtrusive or destroying any of the design features. It is also important to locate the various pieces of equipment mentioned, in coordination with the other systems in the building. In some instances protection pads may be required to protect the roofing against foot travel. This is especially true when insulation is installed above the roofing membrane and is susceptible to crushing.

The roof plan can reflect the structural grid; the contractor, viewing the drawings, will immediately recognize column points and structural features in the roof structure. Everything that is roof-mounted, such as flagpoles, radio and television antennas, air-handling units, condensers, exhaust fans, atmospheric reliefs, and fire dampers, must be shown.

Each of these items or systems and their components must be properly related from the roof plan to the roof framing plan. Most of the items will require some sort of support or support frame, which in turn must be supported by the roof framing. Other items require openings in the roof, for access by personnel, or for duct work, or equipment. These openings (and their curbs, housing, etc.) also must be supported by the roof framing; obviously one cannot create a usable opening which crosses roof framing members. Coordination is vital to the success of properly installing all of these items. The roof and all openings must be made watertight by the roofer. He or she must provide adequate insulation and diagonal cant strips to facilitate easy installation of the roofing without cracking it. The roofer must have some indication of the extent of the work and must be informed of all its features.

It is helpful in some instances to show section markers on a roof plan. The type of roofing required, the dimensioning of the various features, and some indication of the slope, the high and low points, and the valleys and drains are essential and must be shown. Meticulous drafting is worth the time; the overall size of the building's configuration, the offsets, widths of copings and walls penetrating or surrounding the roof and the location of all equipment are required.

Here, again, absolute coordination with the roof framing plan must prevail. Although a roof plan is not required, it is of great value in competitive bidding. The contractor needs to know as much about the building as is humanly possible. The drawings are not complicated, although in some cases, if not carefully executed, they can be misleading.

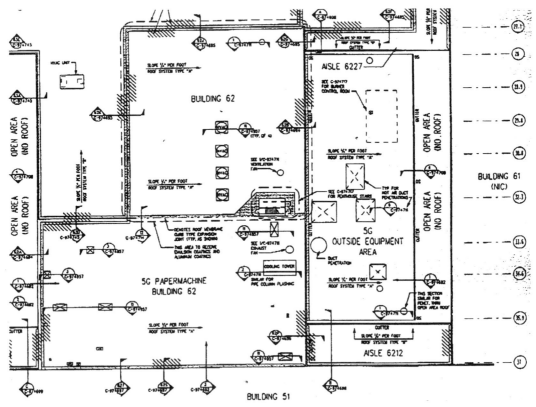

It is not unusual for roof plans to be quite complex and involved (unlike some examples in this chapter). Above is a portion of a roof plan for an industrial building. In general, such buildings have a good array of equipment, piping, ductwork, vents, hatches, etc. located on the roof, in an effort to free space inside the building for more productive functions. The roof plan becomes complicated not only because of the number of objects mounted, but also because of the size of equipment, rooftop walkways (for maintenance access), numerous vents, and other piping, exhaust fans; and in addition, roofing information such as changes in roof coverings, slopes, drains, edge conditions, etc.

CHECKLIST: ROOF PLANS

1. All necessary building dimensions; overhangs, canopies, and roof surfaces.
2. All dimensions to walls, column centerlines, or other permanent features.
3. References to large-scale details.
4. Indicate drainage of roof; slopes to drains, high and low points, saddles, frogs, and crickets; drains and leaders, scuppers, and gutters.
5. Indicate materials of roof and cornices as well as parapet walls; note type of coping on walls.
6. Show all roof-mounted mechanical equipment, scuttles, smoke vents, access panels and doors, and vents.
7. Show special paved areas, fences, railings, stacks or chimneys, bulkheads, and fire walls that extend above the roof surface.
8. Locate and properly reference ladders, splash blocks, stairs, penthouses (for equipment and elevators), ridges, valleys, eaves, special lighting, flagpoles, snow guards, and lightning rods.

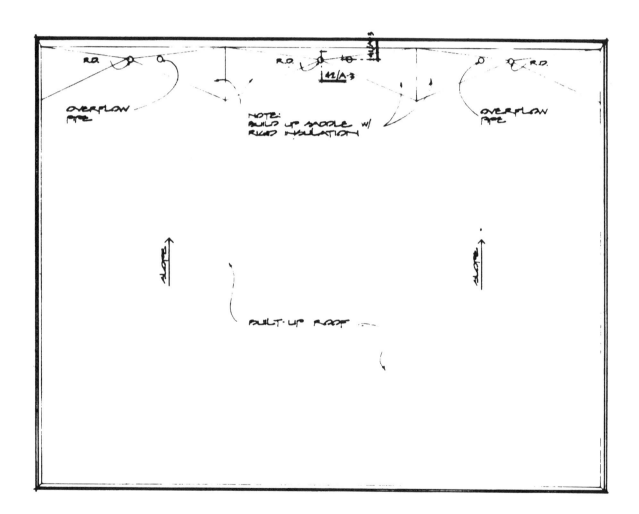

A simple roof plan in which roof saddles and drainage system are clearly denoted.

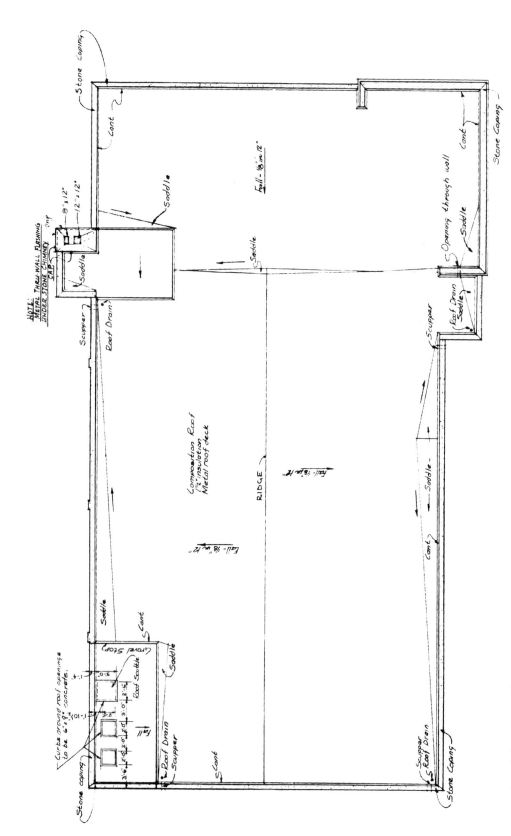

A roof plan with saddles, slopes in several directions, scuppers, and curbed roof openings. All roof-mounted features of a small commercial building are illustrated. If roof-mounted air handling had been utilized, it would have appeared on this plan.

22

Exterior Elevations

When preparing exterior elevations, it is important to keep in mind that these drawings revert to orthographic projection. All plans mentioned in preceding chapters are horizontal sectional views. The elevations are exterior views of the completed project. In a remodeling job the exterior elevations may show existing conditions with the changes or additions that are to be made. However, some knowledge of the wall sections, their construction and the layout of their openings, is essential before the elevations can be completed.

Elevations can also be projected directly from the floor plan. The layout of windows and doors, the location of offsets, and other features of the overall design can be taken directly from the floor plan. Exterior elevations are usually drawn at the same scale as the floor plans to facilitate this projection.

Normally it is good practice to use the common reference symbols for elevations; these symbols include reference symbols for windows, column lines and elevations, section "flags," and detail markers. It is important to account for all major components of the building.

Vertical dimensioning of the elevations should be continuous. The footings and foundation walls can be located horizontally by plan, but their depths are shown on the elevations. Perhaps the easiest and clearest way of recording height elevations is to show them as projected lines outside the building configuration on one or both sides of the drawing. In this way vertical dimensioning and elevation marks (e.g., First Floor Slab, elevation 101'-4") can be applied on each of the levels. The most important thing to remember is consistent dimensioning; if dimensions are shown to the top of the masonry, the dimensions should be given to that point on all elevations. Any point may be chosen, of course, but the same reference must be used on all drawings.

If additional floors are planned for some later date, they can be shown on the present drawings. The vertical control that the elevations provide is most important to the completed project, whether done in one phase or several.

With reference to orthographic projection, the length and width of the project are clearly indicated on the plan, but it is not until the elevations are made that height is indicated. As in orthographic drawings of a simple block shape, we must have all available information before building can begin. Until now the project has, to a large degree, been graphical. Perspectives and renderings have been drawn as the eye sees them. In the working drawings and, in particular, the exterior elevations it is important that we draw what we know, not what we see. Everything should be done exactly to scale; the distance between floors should be exact and there should be no introduction of

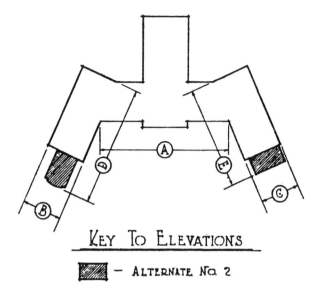

KEY TO ELEVATIONS

▨ — ALTERNATE No. 2

Another form of key plan utilized to show where the various elevations on this complicated building are located. Excellent innovation to clarify the drawings. Note the large number of elevations required to depict this building properly.

the principles of perspective—no foreshortening, for instance, that would give a false impression of the true dimensions of the building.

Just as perspective is based on the horizon line, the elevations are based on the grade line. Most of the elevations and dimensioning should begin at this line and progress upward or downward from it. It is important to show the height of the windows and any other openings that occur in the building's exterior walls. These dimensions cannot be shown on any other drawings. On a building that has some sort of pitched roof much of the roofing information, which includes everything from the materials to the slope diagram to the height of the ridge and the width of the overhang, is entered on the elevations. Also shown are the depth of the fascia, the gutter system, and the various pieces that compose the trim. As a rule it is important that a minimum of four elevations be drawn so that the building can be completely described, but the actual number required must be evaluated on a project-by-project basis. If the building is angular or complicated in plan, any number of elevations may be needed. As many as 12 or 14 are not uncommon. Perhaps the basic element of the elevations should be discussed here. The elevation should be taken at 90 degrees to the surface of the wall at which the draftsman is

looking. If an adjacent wall is at a slightly different angle, it will require its own elevation, and so on around the building. If a wall is at an angle to the plane of the elevation, there will be natural foreshortening, thus getting back to the principle of perspective which, again, will only lead to confusion and perhaps errors in the field. To understand fully the use of elevations a short review of the drawing requirements may be helpful.

1. All necessary dimensions: floor to ceiling heights, window heights, stack heights, tower heights, footing depths, roof overhangs, height and depth of all special features
2. Grade line, floor lines, and ceiling lines
3. Correct identification of windows, doors, louvers, or any other wall penetrations
4. Footing and foundation lines, which are shown by broken lines below the grade line to indicate that they occur out of sight
5. Roof slope, if applicable
6. Exterior material symbols as well as the notation accompanying them
7. Attic, crawl space, or roof configuration
8. Notes that indicate special features
9. Indicators of sections, wall sections, or details
10. Exterior steps, stoops, roofed-over areas, and railings
11. Columns and shutters
12. Dormers
13. Flashings, gutters, and downspouts
14. Proper title and scale

Elevations are more properly identified by a directional title such as north or south rather than left or right, which is elementary for viewing the building. Left and right are applicable only when no directional information is given on any of the drawings.

In an attempt to expedite the drawing of elevations some offices have been utilizing the procedure of only partial poché of the building elevation. If the building is symmetrical, the center line can serve as the dividing line. For a building that is not symmetrical it is correct to establish a diagonal line on the elevation as a demarcation for the material indicators. The building's poché, which defines the materials, occurs only on the one side of the demarcation line, whereas the other side of the building is shown only in outline form. Line weights also play a most important role in poché. It is good practice to put down a heavy grade line extending well beyond the building to illustrate

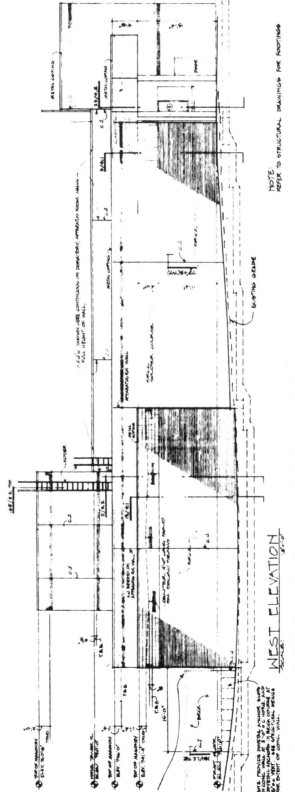

A larger commercial building that lends itself to a simple drawing because of its large masses of masonry. The elevation should directly reflect the general character of the building. Note the use of elevation markers instead of vertical dimensions, not a bad system when the construction becomes a little complicated. Good line work and symbols (masonry in elevation).

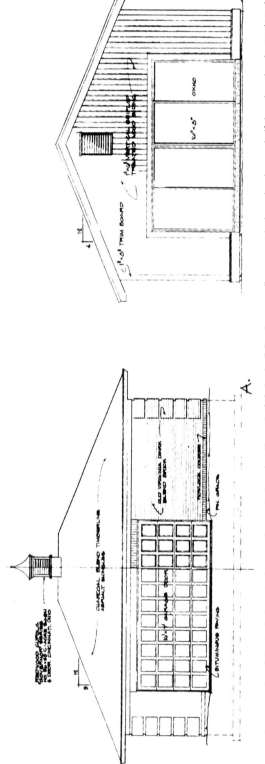

An example of the technique to be used on exterior elevations. In (A) the building is generally symmetrical, and only one-half the elevation is rendered (using the detail and symbols of its various features). In (B) an angled line (set at random) was used to confine the poché to only part of the elevation. Complete rendering is rarely done because of the time involved, and the final effect of the drawing is not greatly changed.

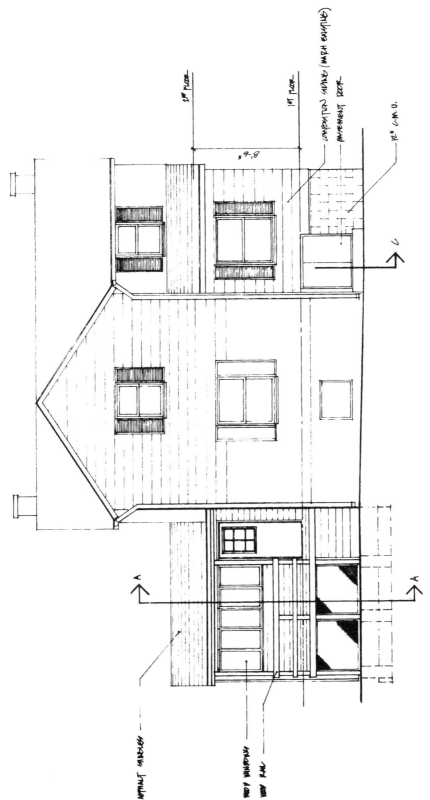

The elevation of this residence indicates the level of the first and second floors; the siding is both noted and illustrated. The draftsman has shown a primary section, A-A, which informs the viewer of the direction in which the section is made. For all purposes the elevation is incomplete; for the window and door symbols have not been applied.

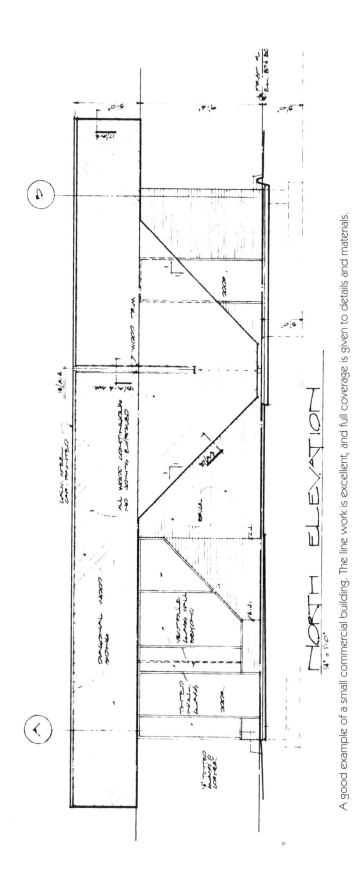

NORTH ELEVATION

A good example of a small commercial building. The line work is excellent, and full coverage is given to details and materials.

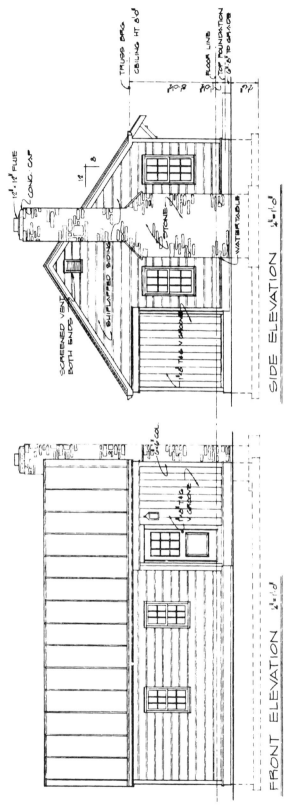

SIDE ELEVATION ¼" = 1'-0"

FRONT ELEVATION ¼" = 1'-0"

A well-delineated set of elevations, not sufficiently complete to be included in the working drawings. The line variations and the material indications promise readability.

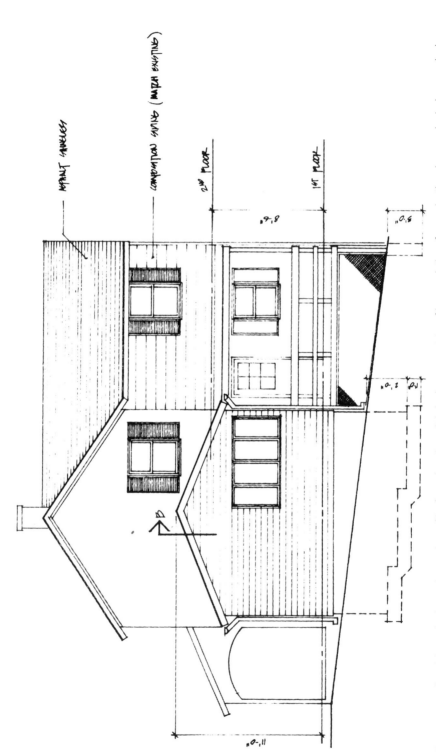

The same small residence is shown in another of its four elevations. It is in the same state of incompletion, for, again, the door and window symbols are lacking. Note the stepped footing beneath the foundation. The note "Match Existing" indicates without benefit of a title that this is a remodeling job.

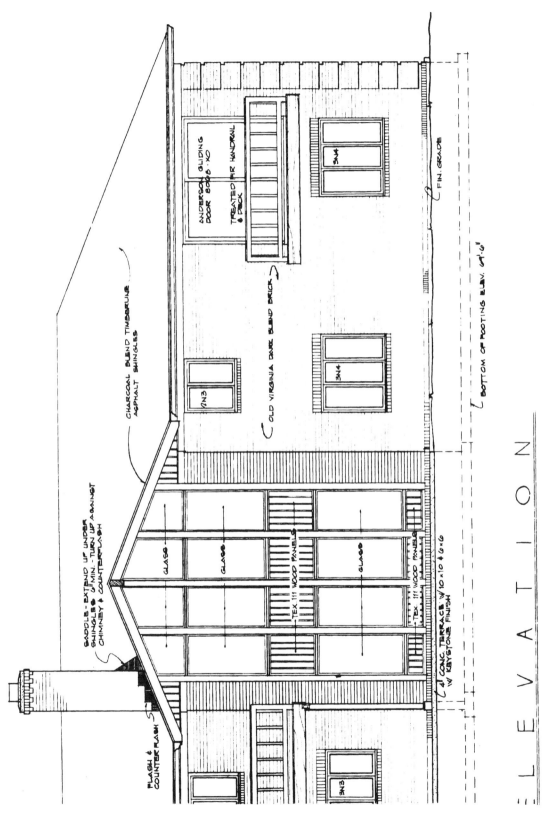

ELEVATION

The elevation of this residence defines the exterior surfacing to be employed. It also indicates the required window units. Note the footing shown as a hidden element to give the elevation level at the bottom.

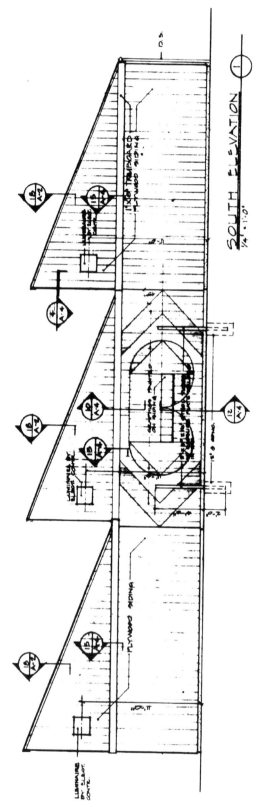

An excellent example of exterior elevation. Line variation is good. Note particularly the "punchy" wall section designators. The wall graphics are an unusual feature. They are, of course, fully detailed elsewhere, but here the owner and contractor can get a complete "picture" of the finished building.

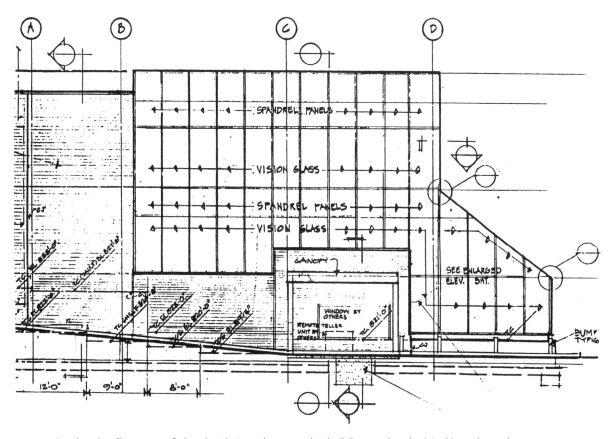

An elevation "in progress" showing that a rather complex building can be depicted in a clean, clear manner with some innovations in notation, and in carefully planned locations of cross-referencing markers.

what happens to the grade outside the building's perimeter. The dark outer line of the buildings's elevation, which divides the building from its surroundings, is properly just a shade lighter than the grade line. This is the outline of the building from the ground, up the sides, over the roof, and back down the other side; it takes in the eaves or fascia offsets as well as all penthouses. Openings in the walls, particularly masonry walls, should be given a darker tone than the coursing of the masonry. This is not meant to add interest to the drawings but is a matter of emphasis, a means of getting away from monotone drafting. Not many symbols are involved on the elevations, but if the planes and the edges of the building are made to read with high contrast, the drawings can be successful. Perhaps the easiest way to consider elevations is as drawings that show the work of the rest of the building. Until the workers see the elevations, they will be working with only two dimensions of the building; the elevations give them an exterior

view and the third dimension. It is interesting to note the contrast between the rendered elevation and its working drawings and to compare them with photographs of the completed building. This sequence is exactly what the elevations provide; they make the building come alive by bringing it from the design idea to reality.

CHECKLIST: EXTERIOR ELEVATIONS

1. Key plan, if necessary, to indicate North arrow and locations.
2. Materials; notes and indications.
3. Show all window and door openings; dimension heights that relate to floor line; type of opening by correct designator: do not draw in every detail of similar openings; operable portions of windows (casement, hopper, or projected).

333

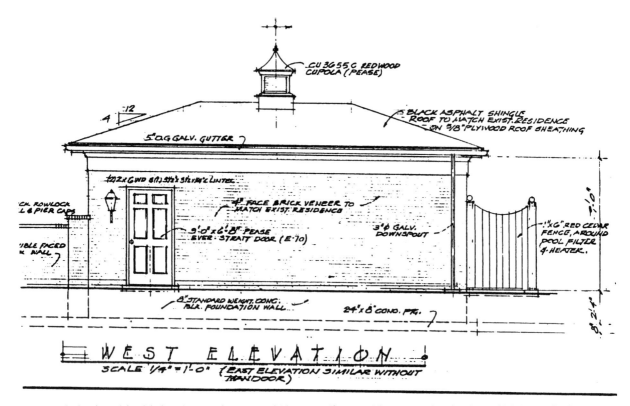

A simple residential elevation, neatly executed. Note specific material notes on the drawing, which is standard practice where no separate specification booklet will be used.

4. Indicate column lines, floor lines, horizontal brick courses (do not include vertical brick jointing), and grade elevations.
5. Show ladders, louvers, railings, vents, roof slope diagrams, downspouts, boots, access openings, splash blocks, gutters, chimneys, sidewalk levels, curbs, ramps, ridges, eaves, decks, and penthouses; also parapet walls, trenches (to be left open), beams, footings (dotted line below the grade line), finished grade line (heavy line weight) showing the ground adjacent to the building; water outlets (hose bibbs, siamese connections, and firehydrants), fresh air intakes, meter boxes, section lines (for wall sections), projections or recesses in the building, and raised or sunken areas; panels, pilasters, columns, signs, cornerstones, awnings, electrical fixtures and outlets, dormers, gables, hoods, canopies, balconies, flashing, counterflashing, roof scuttles, roof features (skylights, crosses, ventilators, snow guards, flagpoles), gates, fencing, parking blocks, bumpers at loading docks, clocks, and plaques.
6. Check dimensions thoroughly with plan, finish grade with site plan, details with their reference system, and all similar features of the building; indicate fascia cover spacing and any other special features that must be included.
7. Describe foundation system's isolated footings, stepped footings, and so on.
8. Give dimension spacing for control and expansion joints in all materials requiring it (which can be seen in the elevation).
9. Show the profile of the building; materials that overlap and project beyond wall surfaces; also items above the roof line.

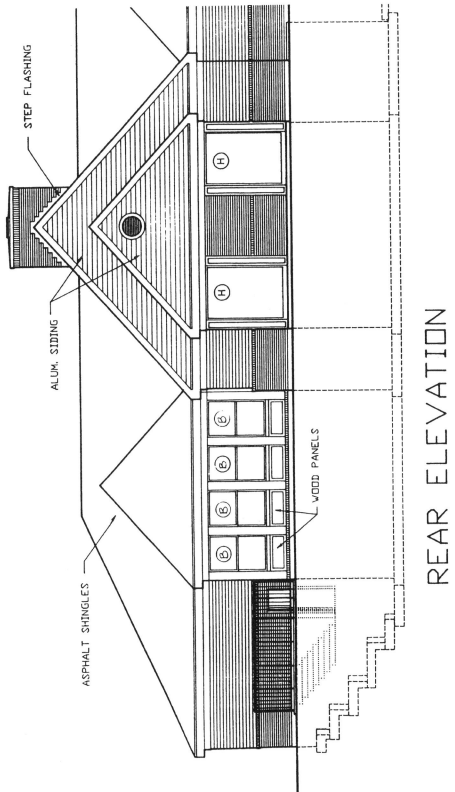

REAR ELEVATION

STEP FLASHING

ALUM. SIDING

ASPHALT SHINGLES

WOOD PANELS

Cole/Russell, Architects
A portion of a CAD-produced elevation. Good line weight variation makes this an easily readable drawing (one area of multiple overlay is a little murky). Lettering is good.

335

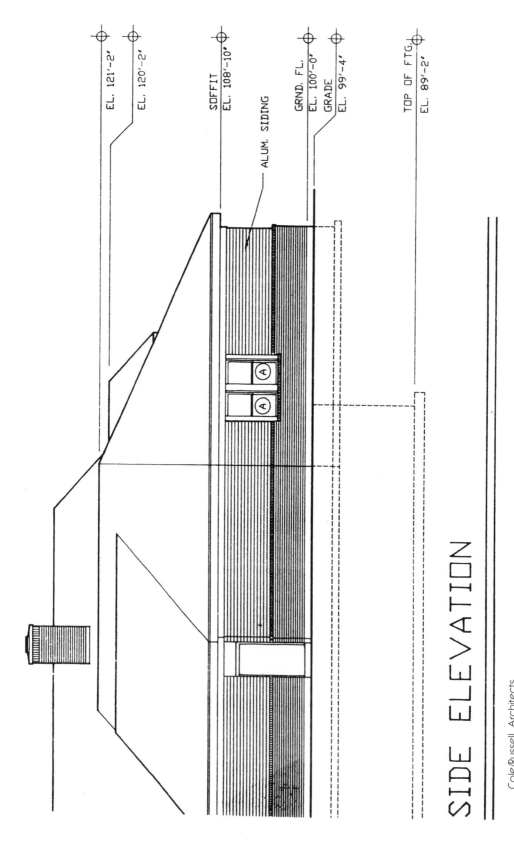

EL. 121'-2'

EL. 120'-2'

SOFFIT
EL. 108'-10"

ALUM. SIDING

GRND. FL.
EL. 100'-0"

GRADE
EL. 99'-4'

TOP OF FTG.
EL. 89'-2'

SIDE ELEVATION

Cole/Russell, Architects
Note that CAD easily added the grade elevation notations at the right; good drawing overall.

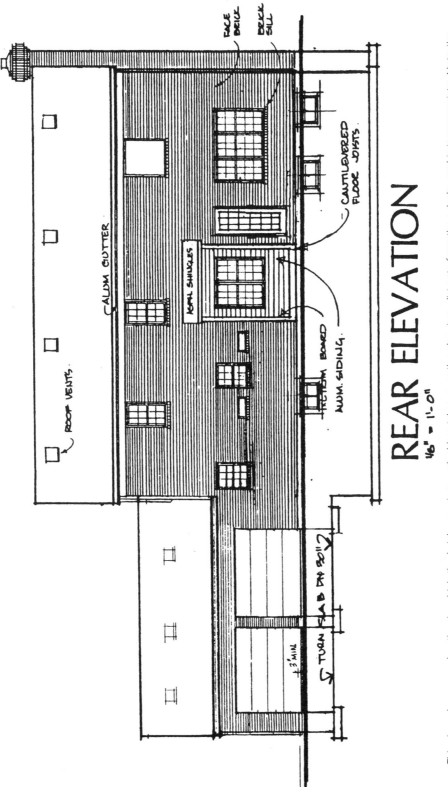

REAR ELEVATION
1/16" = 1'-0"

Labels on drawing:
- FACE BRICK
- BRICK SILL
- CANTILEVERED FLOOR JOISTS
- ALUM GUTTER
- ASPH. SHINGLES
- ROOF VENTS
- FRICTION BOARD
- ALUM. SIDING
- 3" MIN.
- TURN SLAB DN 90"

This view shows an elevation in which the brick coursing symbol has taken over the drawing, distracts from the whole, and is inappropriate. Note the overall lack of line variation in this manually drawn example.

Would you choose to produce this drawing using CAD? No doubt it could be done, but the need for complex and numerous coordinates and the use of nonstandard items make it difficult.

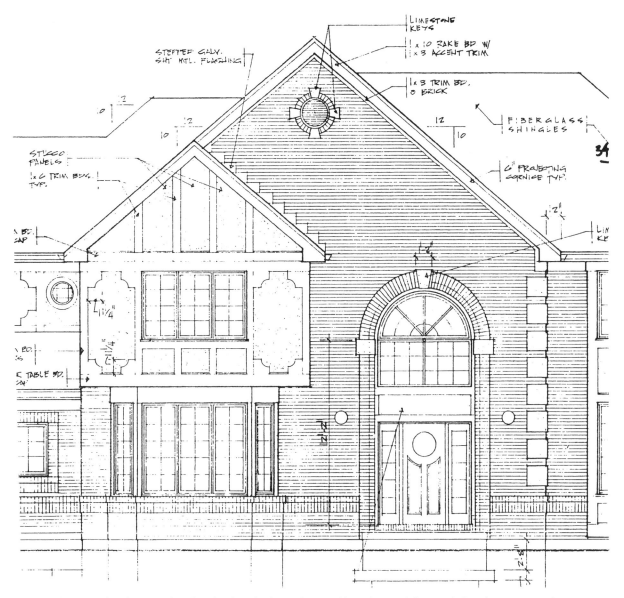

LIMESTONE KEYS

STEPPED GALV. SHT MTL. FLASHING

1 x 10 RAKE BD W/ 1 x 3 ACCENT TRIM

1 x 3 TRIM BD. 0 BRICK

FIBERGLASS SHINGLES

34

STUCCO PANELS

1 x 6 TRIM BRD. TYP.

6" PROJECTING CORNICE TYP.

LIN KE

An example of a complex elevation hurt by inconsistency. Note the weak line work, but the very complex details. CAD could aid this effort in many respects; some details just need better manual techniques.

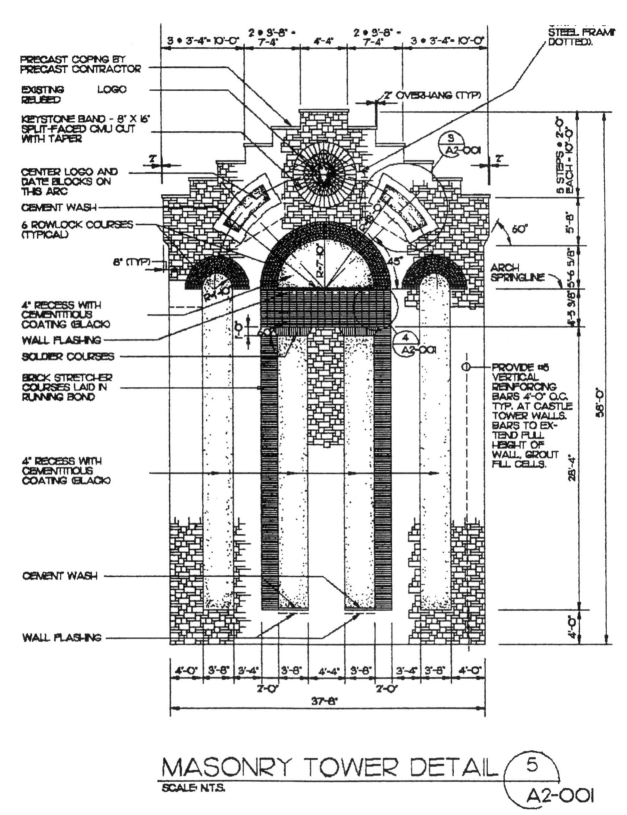

PRECAST COPING BY PRECAST CONTRACTOR

EXISTING LOGO REUSED

KEYSTONE BAND - 8" X 16" SPLIT-FACED CMU CUT WITH TAPER

CENTER LOGO AND DATE BLOCKS ON THIS ARC

CEMENT WASH

6 ROWLOCK COURSES (TYPICAL)

8" (TYP)

4" RECESS WITH CEMENTITIOUS COATING (BLACK)

WALL FLASHING

SOLDIER COURSES

BRICK STRETCHER COURSES LAID IN RUNNING BOND

4" RECESS WITH CEMENTITIOUS COATING (BLACK)

CEMENT WASH

WALL FLASHING

STEEL FRAME DOTTED).

2" OVERHANG (TYP)

60°

ARCH SPRINGLINE

45°

PROVIDE #5 VERTICAL REINFORCING BARS 4'-0" O.C. TYP. AT CASTLE TOWER WALLS. BARS TO EXTEND FULL HEIGHT OF WALL. GROUT FILL CELLS.

MASONRY TOWER DETAIL ⑤
SCALE: N.T.S.

A2-001

An excellent example of the use of CAD for a very complex and intricate drawing. Note changes in line weight, dimensioning, and notations.

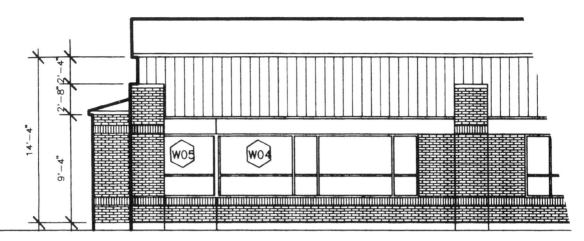

The illustration, above, is a reduction of the actual drawing. The reduction, here, begins to show the need for care in making the drawing, in line weight variations, and the number of lines, i.e., leaving areas open and free from material symbols such as masonry course lines. What may be clear and distinct on an original, even a CAD drawing, may become murky and indistinct when reduction occurs.

This is a key point, especially for CAD drawings. If the drawing is to be reduced, for any reason and to any degree, the linework will be effected. The drafter then must exercise great care and discretion in making the original so any subsequent reduction does not render the drawing unreadable. For example, the illustration above could become quite blurred and murky, when reduced, because of the small scale of the brickwork, and the numerous lines shown. Drawings today are commonly reduced in size to lower reproduction costs and to facilitate distributing of documents for review and non-construction activities. Care and forethought, therefore, are in constant need of consideration, even on the part of the originating drafter, operator, or designer.

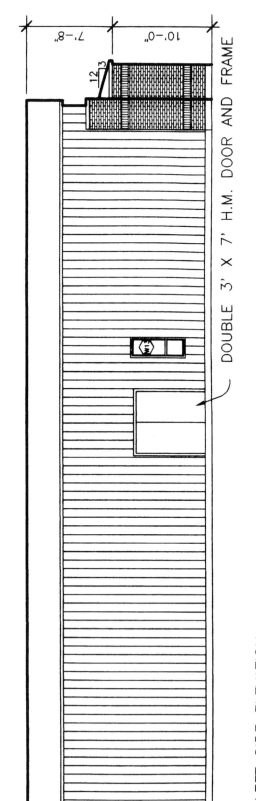

7'-8"

10'-0"

12
3

DOUBLE 3' X 7' H.M. DOOR AND FRAME

LEFT SIDE ELEVATION

Portions of CAD produced exterior elevations. Note the depiction of materials, which also could have been shown to a lesser extent [limited areas], made their point and reduced the amount of linework.

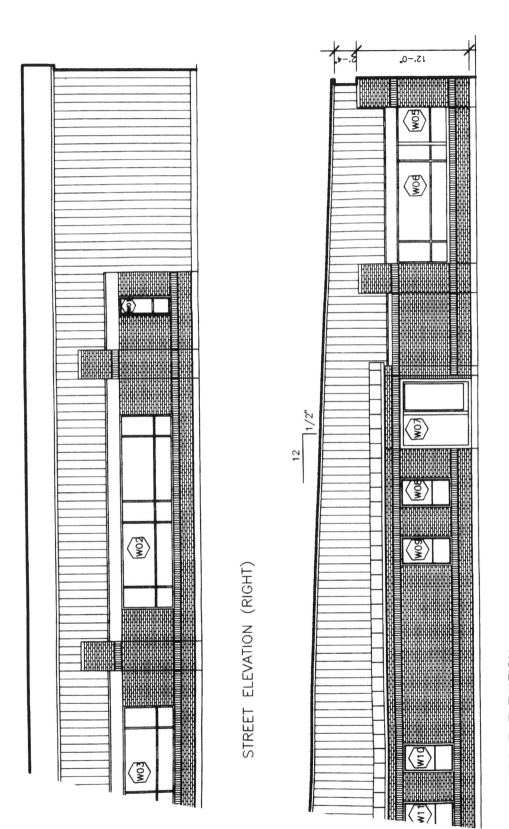

STREET ELEVATION (RIGHT)

FRONT ELEVATION

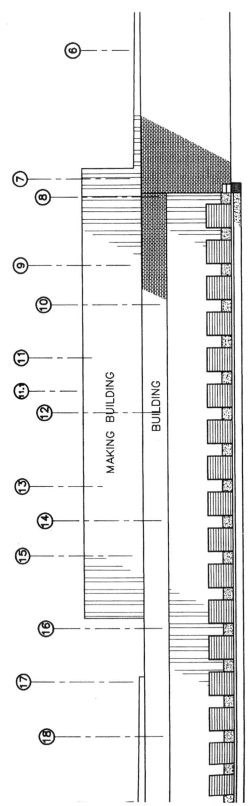

Note how the material symbols were spotted in this example. It makes it clear where the materials change, but without an abundance of needless line work.

MAKING BUILDING

BUILDING

23

Interior Elevations

Interior elevations are designed to reveal the interior features of a building, particularly the finishes and equipment. They are basic orthographic views of various room walls and are simple drawings meant only to inform bidders and contractors of the finishes, configurations, dimensions, and anything else applicable to these walls.

In an effort to give some instruction regarding every type of drawing that may possibly be utilized in a set of construction contract drawings, training in some academic arenas devotes an excessive amount of time, effort, credence, and emphasis to *interior elevations*. Often this is carried to the extent that the student thinks that these particular drawings are (1) necessary in every set of drawings and (2) required, no matter how little they contribute to the passage of information regarding the project.

Of course, both of these premises are faulty. First, and perhaps foremost, it must be remembered that the production of a set of architectural working drawings is for the basic purpose of conveying all of the *necessary* information in the clearest, most complete, and *most concise* manner possible. There is absolutely no need to provide drawings just for the sake of following tradition, meeting some unnamed requirement, or performing an old academic function—that is, to keep performing a function that aids learning

but is not necessarily required to depict a project. Interior elevations are *not* required in every set of working drawings.

Second, in today's world, where it is increasingly necessary to produce proper working drawings in ever shorter periods of time, needless drawing is counterproductive, even if rapidly produced via computer-aided drafting (CAD). In addition, where inadequate or contradictory material is included, it only adds to the liability exposure of the design professional. For example, to produce elevations of toilet rooms (a notorious "necessity") where common, standard, stock-item installations of toilet compartments (partitions) and fixtures are used, is sheer nonsense.

What is there to show, in that instance, that is new and different from the catalog "cuts" of numerous partition manufacturers? The size of the doors, pilasters, and panels, the location of hardware, the spacing and vertical heights—all are standard. In addition, all of this information will be shown on the shop drawings submitted for the specific installation. These are reviewed by the design professional to ensure general compliance with the design concept and the area dimensions shown (field verification by the supplier/contractor). Unless there is a unique or "new" configuration, the elevations are without rationale.

345

To carry this further, there may be "unique" toilet room installations and features (layouts, equipment, accessories), that provide some rationale for limited elevations. Often, even these can be eliminated, as the "blown-up" details (sections, perhaps) of the vanitories could be made to show all of the necessary detail and locations. These include, in part, soap dispensers, paper towel dispensers/receptacles, mirrors, hand dryers, and light coves. The locations and mounting heights of other items can be noted on the plan(s) or included in schedules (graphic or written). Certainly, if there is a unique pattern of decoration—ceramic tile pattern on the walls, for example—then the elevation(s) again would prove of value.

The key point a student should learn is that interior elevations should be used *where they clarify or provide information not readily available elsewhere*. This use, however, must be very judicious. It is a judgment call, which the student professional should be prepared to make or to inquire about. Moreover, there is also an obligation to ensure that these drawings are fully coordinated and cross-referenced with all other components that deal with the same information (in different views, at different scales, etc.).

The number of interior elevations directly reflects the complexity of the job. In the set of working drawings for a modest building project there will be few interior elevations, for only minimal equipment will be required by contract. These elevations are often used to show typical equipment, such as metal toilet partitions, which are standard, stock items; the detailing of these items should be conscientiously avoided.

Because of the many and varied forms of building today, interior elevations are helpful to all concerned. This is especially true when room configurations, the lines of the structure, or the finished elements (walls, ceiling, built-in features) occur at an angle or in some way differ from a flat or perpendicular surface. Such deviations should be included as part of the outline of the interior elevation.

Exploring further, we find that we are concerned with only one wall in each view. The limiting lengths between opposite walls and the floor and ceiling lines are shown. The finished ceiling line is usually shown without duct work or piping above it . The elevations are intended to identify the finishes and equipment, and structural features are omitted. If a beam projects into the room, it is shown only as part of the outline of the elevation.

Interior elevations are drawn at a larger scale than floor plans and exterior elevations. Many of the accessories and items of equipment are small and require the clarification provided by a larger scale. Although some offices draw these elevations at $\frac{1}{4}'' = 1''\text{-}0''$, $\frac{1}{2}'' = 1''\text{-}0''$ is preferable. At this scale such items as mirrors, paper towel dispensers, and wall containers may be located and dimensioned in proper relation.

The symbology used on these elevations is, of course, similar to that of the exterior elevations. If tile work or a distinct masonry bond is used, it is reflected in these drawings, as are all windows and doors. Any built-in or freestanding equipment is located on the elevations with names, designators, or model numbers that apply. Door swings, hardware, shelving, and cabinetry are indicated. The examples show how the profiles of cabinetwork appear in the drawings.

These elevations delineate many small details and specific areas of the building. After vertical dimensioning, horizontal dimensioning and the notes that describe the finishes are added as needed. It is important to show all supply grilles, wall-mounted light fixtures, or other mechanical features in their proper location.

In some instances the elevations become complicated when elaborate cabinetwork or equipment is shown. Their function, however, is to make it clear to the contractor and to provide a basis for other detailing on a larger scale. The details are "flagged" by whatever type of symbology is standard procedure. Notation should be extensive only to the point of including all appropriate features. All moldings or other trim should be located correctly.

The interior elevations, as drawings, are somewhat decorative. Although nothing in the way of color is used, the drawings can be applied to color planning and location later in the project. The drawings are not intended to be illustrations; they are bona fide working drawings and should be presented as such. The information they contain is important, depending again on how complex the area is in regard to cabinetwork and equipment.

The interior elevations are often used in conjunction with large equipment plans. They can also be directly beneficial to the interior decorator or architect in the selection of wall coverings, finishes, and color schemes. The interior

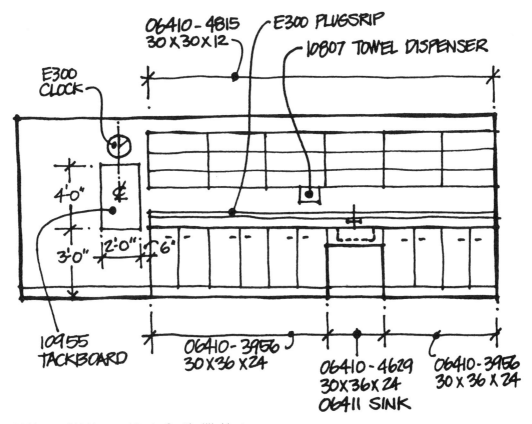

Mahlum and Mahlum, architects, Seattle, Washington
Example of interior elevation which depicts the planned work, in freehand form; for use by draftsman and the specification writer. Well-executed time-saver.

elevations are an essential part of the complete package of drawings. Their primary purpose is to show all items too small to be entered on the floor plans, but they are also a bridge between the actual construction of the building and its decoration.

CHECKLIST: INTERIOR ELEVATIONS

1. Items of concrete and masonry; height and width of bases, sleepers, facings; mat recesses in slab size, depth, and edge strips; all exposed construction with correct profiles referenced to floor and column lines and other major features.
2. Wood and millwork; except when stock items are used, the following should be fully detailed: cabinets, countertops, doors, drawers, shelving, chalkboards (complete with tray, tack strips, map hooks), display cases, lockers, recesses for telephones, wardrobes, and all items of trim.
3. Metal catwalks, ladders, handrails, nosings, pass windows, shutters (rolling).
4. Rolling, folding, or coiling partitions; special equipment of all types that may be included in the contract.

347

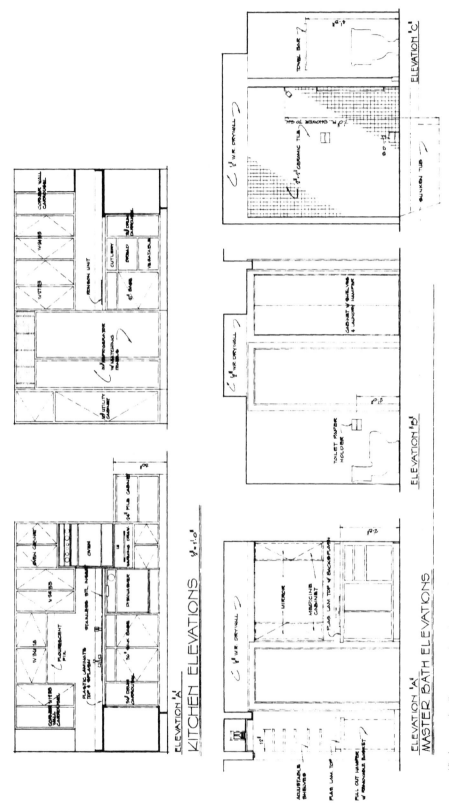

Kitchen and toilet room elevations are the most common interiors shown in architectural working drawings. Standard elements, such as water closets and other bathroom fixtures, kitchen equipment, cooking units, refrigerators, ovens, and dishwashers, are drawn with templates to obscure patented features of any one manufacturer. The particular element may carry a unit number, mentioned in the specifications, to indicate the level of quality to be obtained in the bidding process.

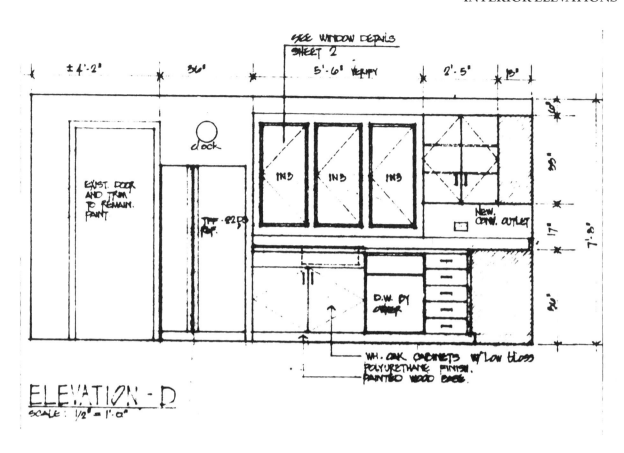

ELEVATION - D
SCALE: 1/2" = 1'-0"

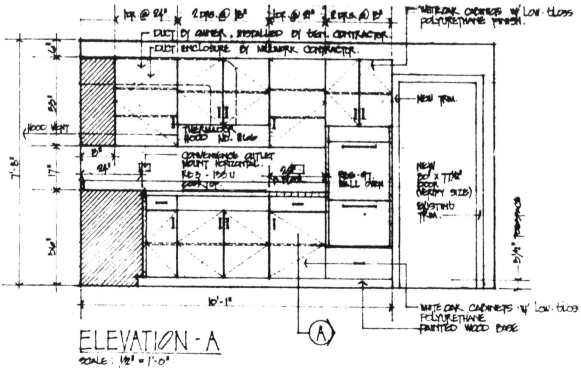

ELEVATION - A
SCALE: 1/2" = 1'-0"

This elevation displays the cabinetwork in a kitchen area. The door swings are shown, and the electrical outlets are indicated along the splashboard area. This drawing also shows the division of labor by related trades.

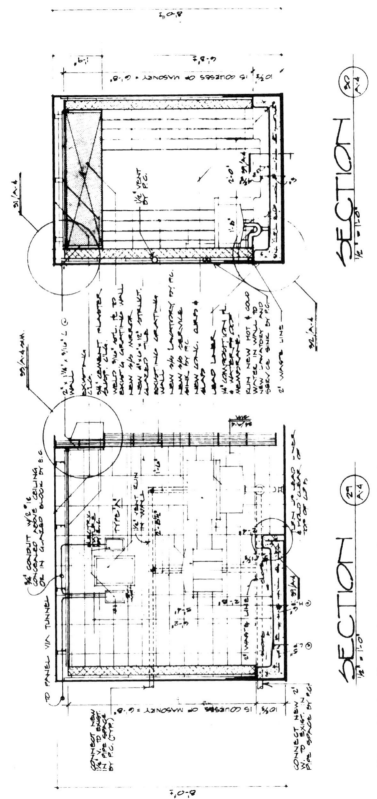

This combination of interior elevations and wall sections describes the distinctive nature of the materials and construction.

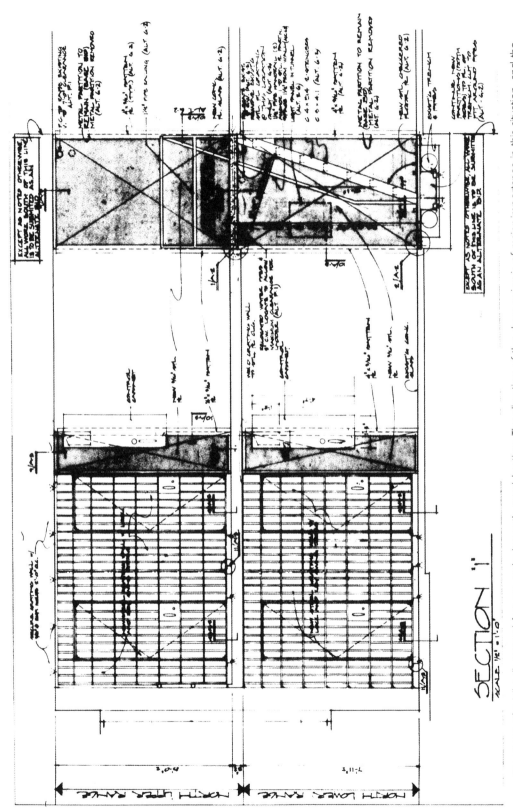

Elevations of a jail cell; unusual features make it worth consideration. The direction of the door swing is of major importance in this situation, and the delineation of the cell grating requires expert draftsmanship. The section markers are clearly drawn but remain unobtrusive.

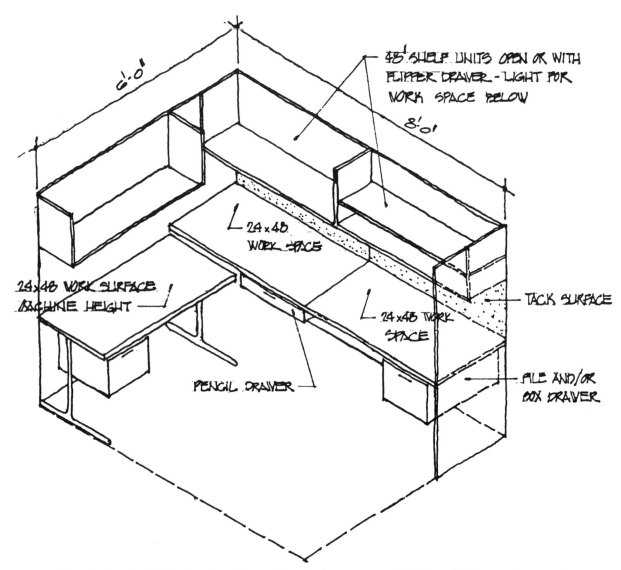

6'·0"

8'·0"

48' SHELF UNITS OPEN OR WITH
FLIPPER DRAWER - LIGHT FOR
WORK SPACE BELOW

24 x 48
WORK SPACE

24 x 48 WORK SURFACE
MACHINE HEIGHT

24 x 48 WORK
SPACE

TACK SURFACE

PENCIL DRAWER

FILE AND/OR
BOX DRAWER

Example of an "extra" drawing, done in isometric projection to more quickly show all of the requirements of this workstation complex. The one drawing here easily, and properly, replaces several drawings by showing all pertinent surfaces and equipment.

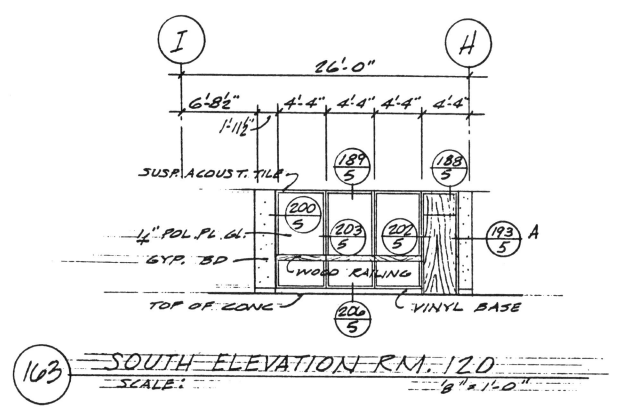

$$\textcircled{163} \quad \underline{SOUTH\ ELEVATION\ RM.\ 120}$$

SCALE: ⅛" = 1'-0"

Interior elevation of one small area of a project, but with very good cross-referencing to the details that apply. In addition, this wall is tied very nicely to the column lines, i.e., its proper position.

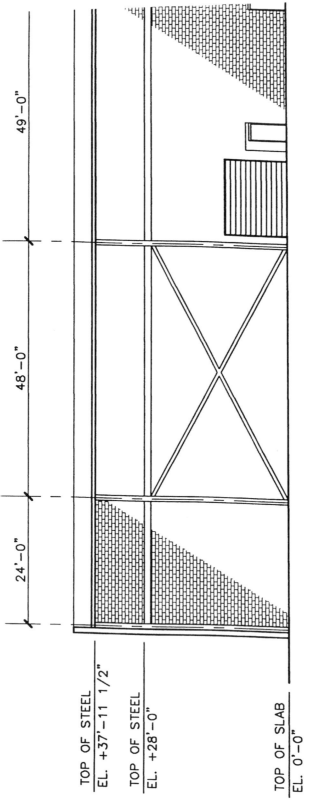

TOP OF STEEL
EL. +37'-11 1/2"

TOP OF STEEL
EL. +28'-0"

TOP OF SLAB
EL. 0'-0"

24'-0"

48'-0"

49'-0"

Interior elevations with limited use of material symbols. Note the lack of notations, limiting the value of the drawings, and the information they convey.

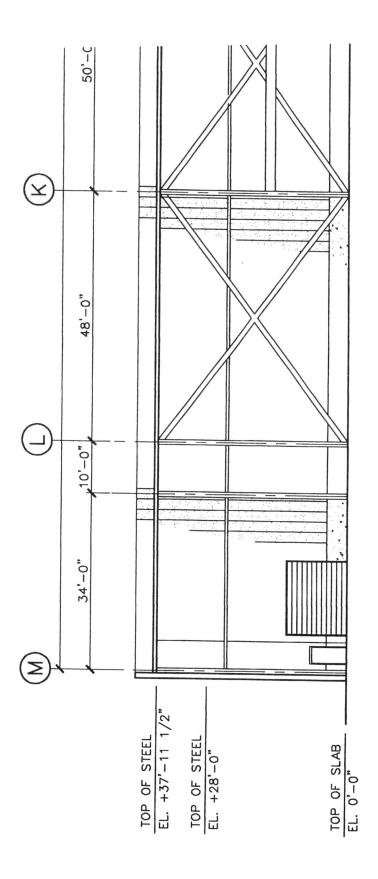

24

Cross-Referencing

All information on a set of working drawings becomes valueless if it is not properly coordinated and cross-referenced. This system is time-consuming but necessary to the success of the project. A great number of definitions, neither in alphabetical order nor cross-referenced, would be useless in a dictionary. To find a definition would be nearly impossible, as impossible as the proverbial needle in a haystack.

On architectural working drawings a totally coordinated and complete system of cross-referencing begins on the individual sheet layout. Every working drawing set contains any number of sheets, depending on the complexity of the job, each of which should have individual identification, commonly known as the sheet number. Every office has its own system of numbering, beginning with the simple numerical. Some offices separate the drawings into categories: architectural sheets are prefaced with an A, mechanical sheets with an M, electrical sheets with an E, and so on, through the various divisions of work. This system of identification speeds up the location of information; it is helpful in searching through the drawings to find a particular category.

Many offices with more complex projects use a series of catalog, or category, numbers: one series of drawings will be strictly site plans, details, and related site work; the second series will be floor plans for all levels of the building; the third will contain the elevations and building sections; the fourth will be wall sections and details; the fifth will be stair drawings; the sixth, the interior layouts, reflected ceiling plans, and similar drawings; the seventh, interior details. Categories may be omitted; for instance, the next category may be the tenth, which will contain the structural drawings; the eleventh, the mechanical; and twelfth, the electrical drawings. The unused categories may be filled later, if required. Any logical sequence can be set up; there is no formal format.

A system may be set up by which the drawings are cataloged according to the Construction Specifications Institute (CSI) format of 16 divisions. Some divisions can be aligned; for example, division 16, electrical, would be given category 16 on the drawings, and division 12, which is furnishings, would include all movable furniture in the building. Many of the other categories, however, become too complex; the divisions cover material that will be used in a number of areas around the building and involve many different trades.

In any numbering system it is important that the number be permanently affixed, in bold characters, in a prominent position on the sheet. More and more offices are going to one of two formats for sheet layout: a vertical title block along the right-hand margin or a horizontal title block along the bottom edge. In both cases the sheet

357

number appears in the lower right-hand corner. In this position the number can be readily located. These two formats, incidentally, allow a clear rectilinear area on the sheet into which the individual drawings can be fitted. In days gone by a small title block, perhaps 4 or 5 x 6 inches, placed in the lower right-hand corner, always left a rather oddly shaped drafting area. It sometimes seemed that the draftsman had cut off the drawing to accommodate the title.

Once the sheet numbering system has been established, it is easy to begin the cross-referencing system. One simple method keeps a running account of detail numbers for each job. Each drawing is given a number in sequence as it is drawn. It may be that a particular drawing will not appear among the final working drawings, having been voided during the drawing sequence or changed

or combined with others. All numbers need not appear as long as those that do are consecutive. In this way a detail drawing has an individual identity from the outset. This system also obviates the use of long, elaborate titles for each detail.

Tying the information together now commences. The sequence can be simplified as the building is simplified. On a residence drawing there may be one typical wall section and perhaps one or two other partial sections, which can be simply designated (e.g., A, B, C,). Obviously, only one or perhaps two sheets are required for these sections; they, in turn, can be easily cross-referenced by note. When the building becomes complex, it is a much better idea to combine the section or detail number with the sheet designation, preferably the sheet number on which the detail appears; for example, we may have detail

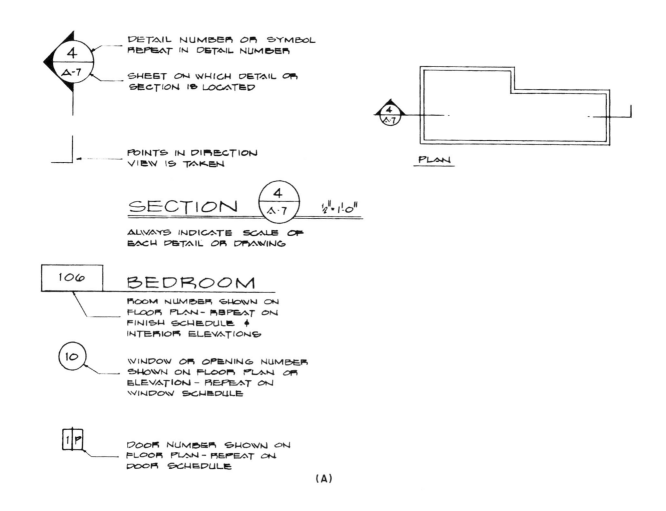

(A)

358

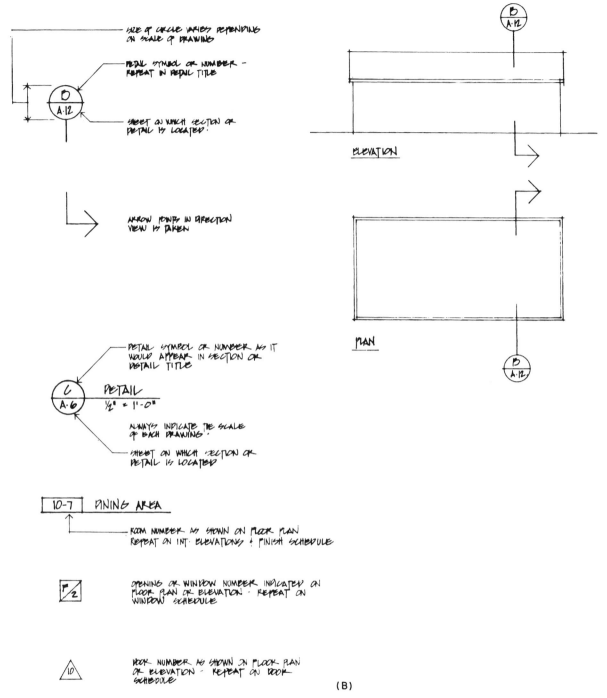

(B)

Two drafted sheets, (A) and (B), display the different techniques of two draftsmen used in the formulation of a system of symbols for cross-referencing. The viewer may decide which of the two systems is preferable; these systems could become the basis for another original approach to the essential matter of cross-referencing.

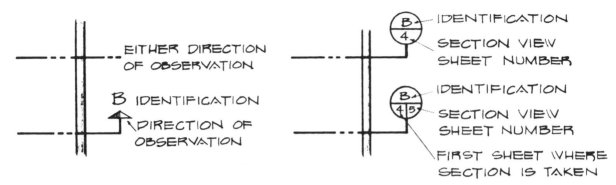

Cross-referencing requires that all sections and the exact points at which they are cut be clearly identified. The section is referenced to that point on the structure, or through the structure. The sheets on which the drawings appear are shown (as noted in the examples).

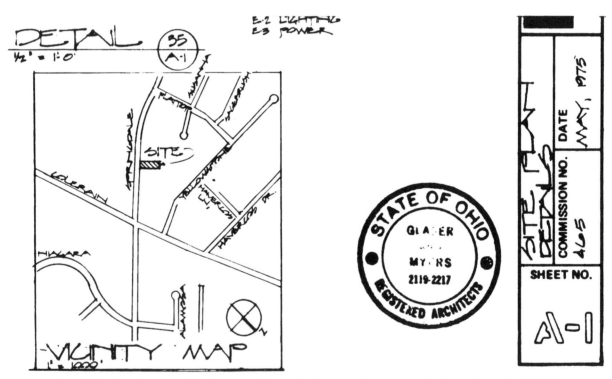

The title block carries the architect's seal and the seals of any engineering consultants employed for the job. The sheet number should be easy to read. On large or obscurely located projects the use of a vicinity map is advised.

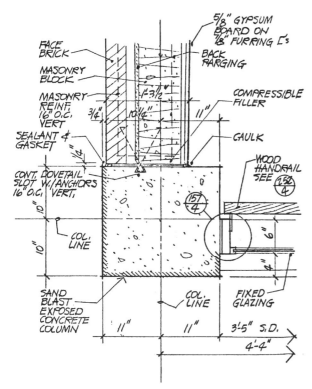

Hellmuth, Obata and Kassabaum, Inc.
Good example of isolated detail, cross-referenced properly to other work nearby. Good, clean lettering, but some notes (about spacing of ties, etc.) not proper on a drawing; should be placed in the specifications.

No. 6 located on sheet No. A10 (see page 372). The designator is then the title of that particular detail/section when referenced on the drawings. A similar designator is used on sheet No. A14 where the No. 6 detail is applied to the work for a simple, full, direct cross reference for users.

Some offices argue that this system has one distinct disadvantage. A section of interest may be found that is not referenced to the sheet from which it was taken. This valid criticism has given rise to a system of section markers to denote the name or number of the section, the sheet from which it is taken or cut, and the sheet on which it appears. This system requires more elaborate designators but eliminates the gap in the information. More care must be taken to make sure that the complete designator is always used. Again, there is no standard system.

Designators may be any shape; a simple arrow, a filled-in arrow, an arrow and circle combination, a simple circle, an ellipse, a hexagon, a segmented circle, or a double underscore. It is most impor-

tant that the designator appear on the plan or elevation at the spot where the section is cut. Proper reference must be given to its location on a particular drawing of the set. The system can be modified by adding titles or informative notes near the section designators.

The system chosen should be straightforward; there should be no possibility of confusion. Experience will show that some systems work better than others, and nothing short of trial and error can teach this lesson. The foregoing is a catalog of ideas to be adapted as necessary.

Many coordinating systems have been tried. Some offices bind the structural foundation drawings in the set immediately after the site plan. The latter is used for excavation and grading. Foundation drawings are followed by the architectural drawings that approximate the sequence in which the building will be constructed. When the floor plan is inserted, it should be followed by the roof plan, with the roof framing plan (another structural drawing) in between. The appropriate mechanical drawings should directly follow the architectural drawings. This system does tend to confuse, however, for various divisions of labor are scattered throughout the set. Unless there is a consistent policy of tight coordination, it does not work well.

The most conventional system depends on no particular sheet numbering or category. In other words, any set of categories can be used. The site drawings are normally placed first and

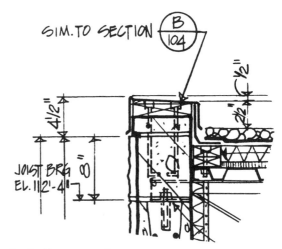

A detail with a cross-reference to another drawing; used in lieu of repeating the same information which is available elsewhere. A time-reduction technique, to be used with care (refer only to notes nearby).

361

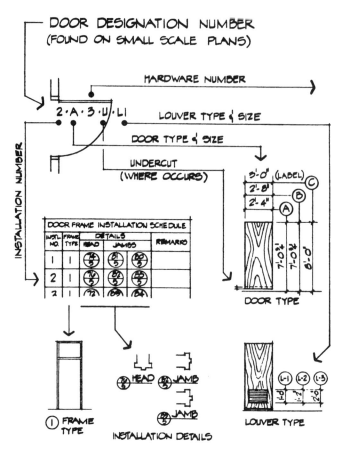

Hellmuth, Obata and Kassabaum, Inc.
Drawing that "disects" the door designator and shows how each symbol is related to the proper information.
Good sheet for inclusion in the office drafting standars manual.

are followed by the architectural and structural drawings. Plumbing, heating, ventilating, and air-conditioning, and electrical drawings are next. The title sheet should carry the name of the project, all symbols used, and the legends of the designators. General information about the project, its location (perhaps by vicinity plan), and the technical data for office filing and client's identification should be included. Some projects demand other drawings, for example, for special piping, fire protection, or sprinkler systems, which should be placed in the category with which they are most closely associated.

The title block will show the title and location of the project, the names of the architect, structural engineer, and consulting engineers, the names and addresses of their firms, and the name of the construction manager if one is employed. It also has space for a list of revisions. Drawings are often reissued over a period of time, and the dates on which they are reissued or completed are important, for they may be the deciding factor in any subsequent court action. Scales used can be listed in, or near, the title block; required licensing seals (those of the architect and engineers), with accompanying registration numbers, and the sheet title all must appear in the title block.

In addition, the telephone number of the architectural office and the name of the owner of the project should be clearly stated on each sheet. This is mandatory for individual distribution.

Most offices have established this method of communicating a project's essential data. One system mentioned earlier in the chapter, that of categories, allows the insertion of extra sheets without drastic interference in the numbering

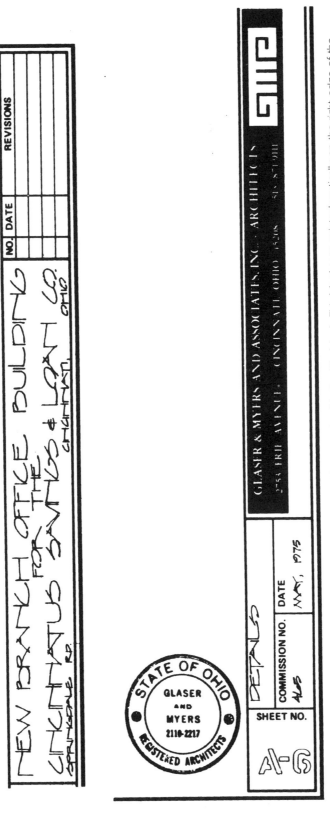

This example shows the full range of information that should be contained in the title block. This block was printed vertically on the right edge of the drawing sheet.

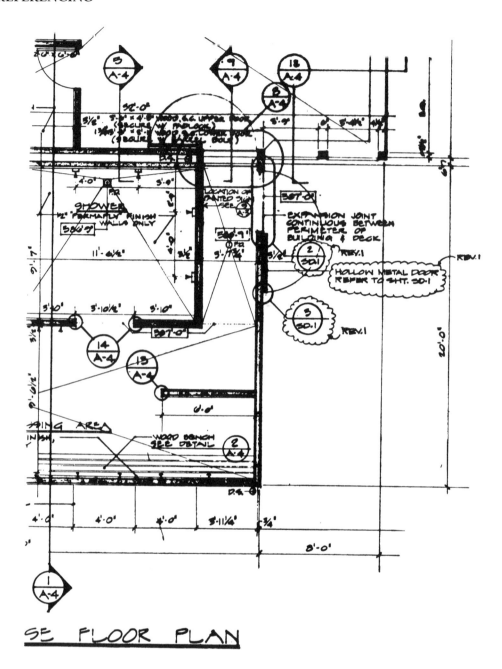

SE FLOOR PLAN

system. The decimal system (1.1, 1.2, 1.3, etc.) is a good choice. Another sheet can always be added at the end of the category simply by employing the next number. The category number is to the left of the decimal. If an added sheet logically fits between 3 and 4 in the consecutive numbering system, it must be given the label 3-A or some other means of identification must be introduced.

It can be seen that even this coordination of drawings should be kept simple, direct, and unconfused.

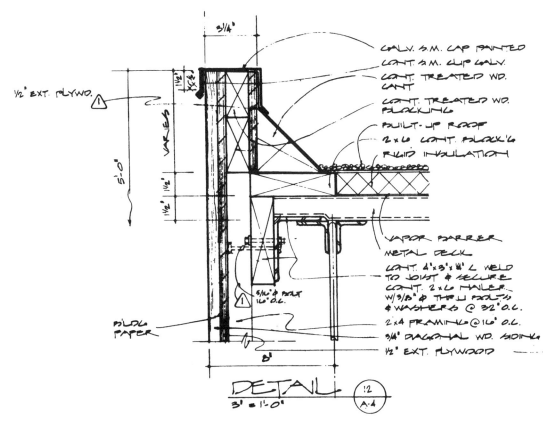

(Above opposite) Examples of drawings revised after initial issue. The notes in balloons or indicated by a numbered triangle have some information in them that has been revised and, hence, changes the work involved. Very important item of cross-referencing the job control.

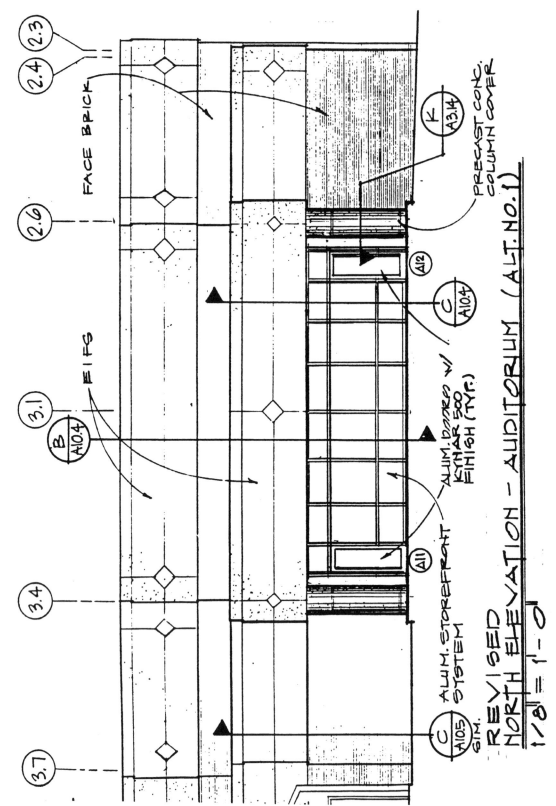

Cross referencing a portion of an elevation to a detail-elevation [note the C/A10.4] designator.

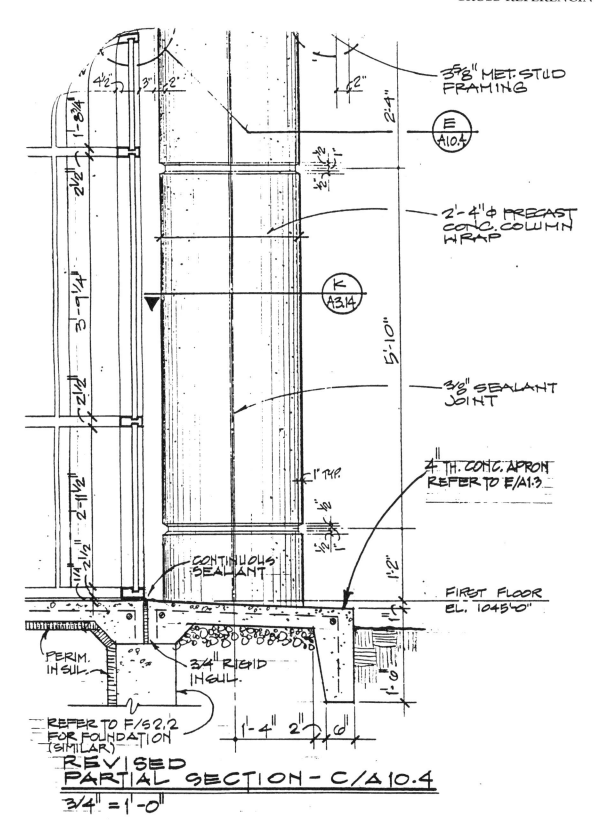

3⅝" MET. STUD FRAMING

E / A10.4

2'-4" ⌀ PRECAST CONC. COLUMN WRAP

K / A3.14

⅜" SEALANT JOINT

4" TH. CONC. APRON REFER TO E/A1·3

1" TYP.

CONTINUOUS SEALANT

FIRST FLOOR EL. 1045'-0"

PERIM. INSUL.

¾" RIGID INSUL.

REFER TO F/S2.2 FOR FOUNDATION (SIMILAR)

1'-4" 2" 6"

REVISED PARTIAL SECTION — C/A10.4
¾" = 1'-0"

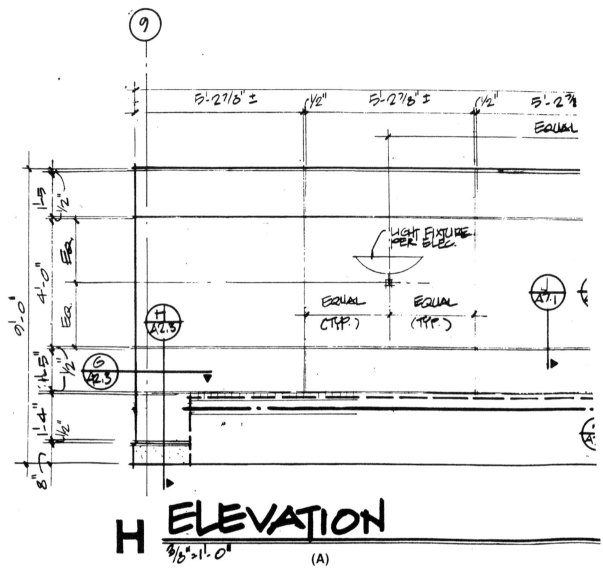

H ELEVATION
3/8" = 1'-0"
(A)

This is an example of an unfortunate problem created within the documents. Note the reference in [A] to detail G/A2.3; that detail is [B] and shows the layout of the corner of the wall and a $3/4''$ joint at the reference to K/A7.1. [C] is an elevation of the return wall, and also indicates K/A7.1, but also a $1/2''$ dimension for the joint. Looking at [D] which is detail K/A7.1, we find that the joint is noted as $1/2''$. What is the correct dimension?

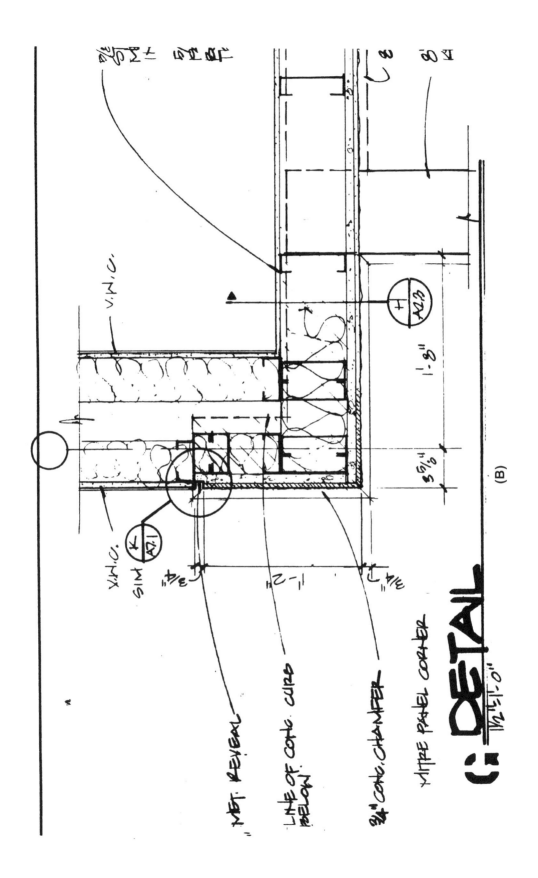

G DETAIL
1½"=1'-0"

(B)

MTL. REVEAL

LINE OF CONC. CURB BELOW.

¾" CONC. CHAMFER

MITRE PANEL CORNER

V.I.W.C.

SIM

V.I.W.C.

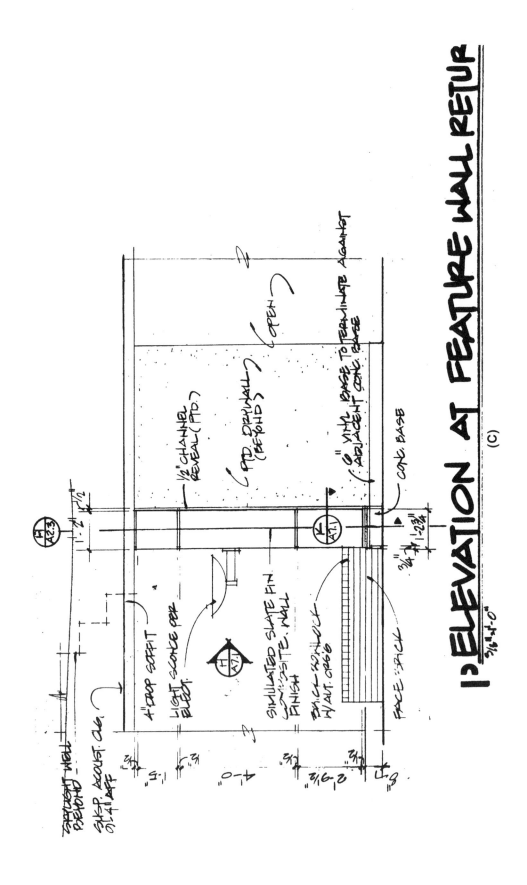

1 ELEVATION AT FEATURE WALL RETUR

(C)

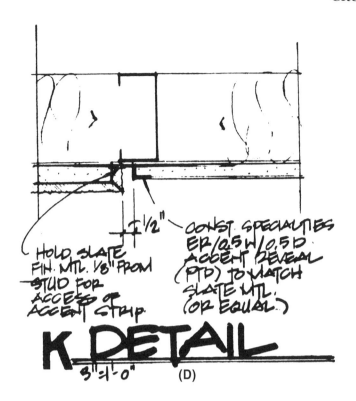

1/2"

HOLD SLATE
FIN. MTL. 1/8" FROM
STUD FOR
ACCESS OR
ACCENT STRIP.

CONST. SPECIALTIES
EP/0.5 W/0.5 D
ACCENT BEVEL
(PTD) TO MATCH
SLATE MTL.
(OR EQUAL.)

K DETAIL
3"=1'-0"   (D)

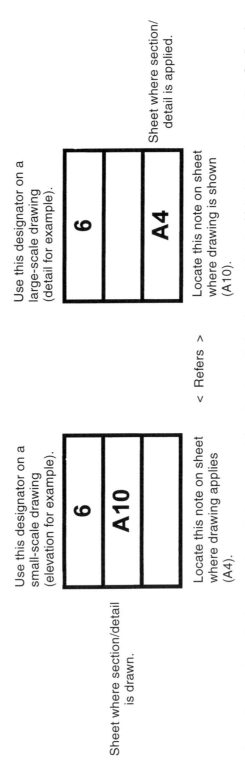

Use this designator on a small-scale drawing (elevation for example).

6

A10

Sheet where section/detail is drawn.

Locate this note on sheet where drawing applies (A4).

< Refers >

Use this designator on a large-scale drawing (detail for example).

6

A4

Sheet where section/detail is applied.

Locate this note on sheet where drawing is shown (A10).

Cross-referencing is an absolute necessity, so that the correct information is applied at the correct location(s) in the actual construction. Small-scale drawings become an index that show where other details and sections (large-scale drawings) apply. In like manner, the large-scale drawings refer back to the drawing sheet to which they apply. By using designators similar to those shown here (but smaller, of course, and in different shapes), proper coordination is achieved.

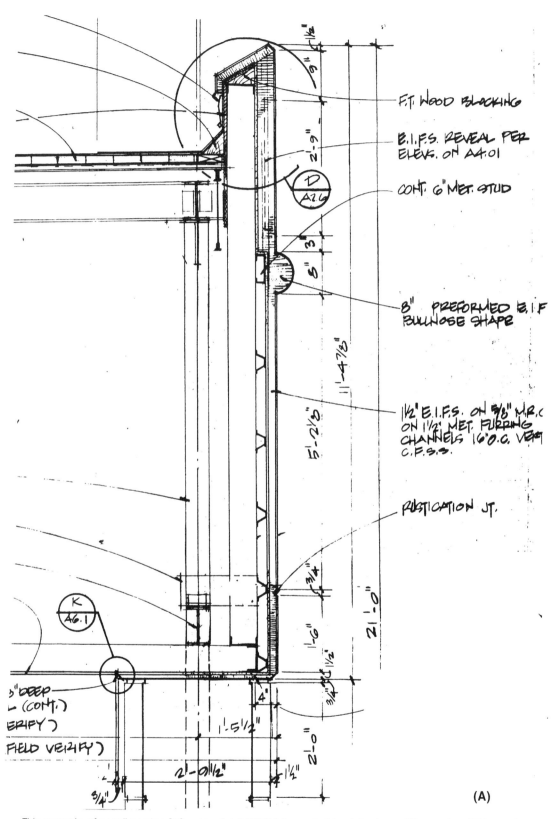

F.T. WOOD BLOCKING

E.I.F.S. REVEAL PER ELEVS. ON A4.01

CONT. 6" MET. STUD

8" PREFORMED E.I.F BULLNOSE SHAPE

1½" E.I.F.S. ON ⅝" M.R.C ON 1½" MET. FURRING CHANNELS 16"O.C. VERT C.F.S.S.

RUSTICATION JT.

D / A2.6

K / A6.1

3" DEEP
∟ (CONT.)
ERIFY)
FIELD VERIFY)

(A)

This example of a wall section [A] notes detail D/A2.6 is applicable at the top of the section. [B] is another section that indicates that work "similar" to D/A2.6 is required at its top. [C] is Detail A/A2.6; compare it with the others to see how it can be applied to them, or how it is different.

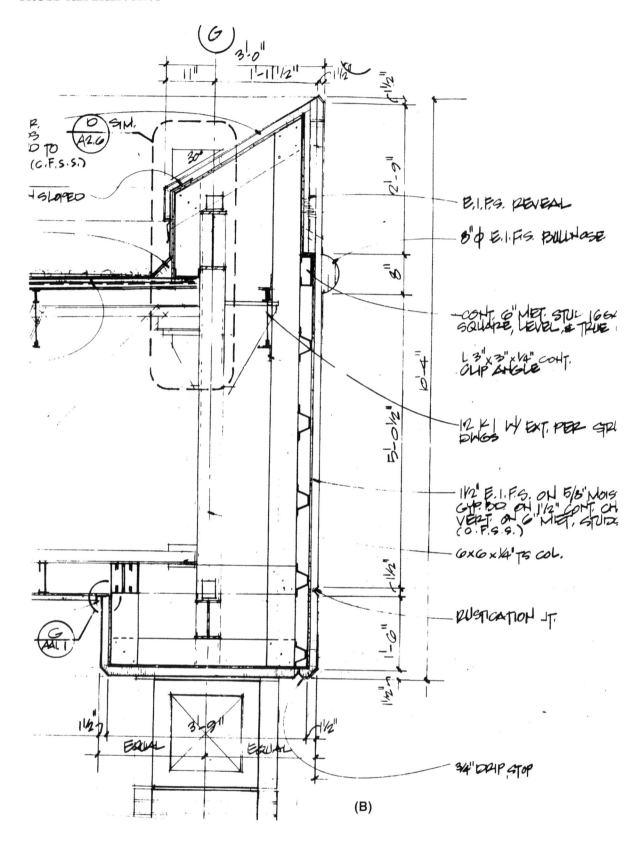

E.I.F.S. REVEAL

8" ⌀ E.I.F.S. BULLNOSE

CONT. 6" MET. STUD 16 GA
SQUARE, LEVEL, & TRUE

L 3" x 3" x 1/4" CONT.
CLIP ANGLE CONT.

12 K 1 W/ EXT. PER STRL
DWGS

1 1/2" E.I.F.S. ON 5/8" MOIS
GYP. BD. ON 1 1/2" CONT. CH
VERT. ON 6" MET. STUDS
(O.F.S.S.)

6x6 x 1/4" TS COL.

RUSTICATION JT.

3/4" DRIP STOP

(B)

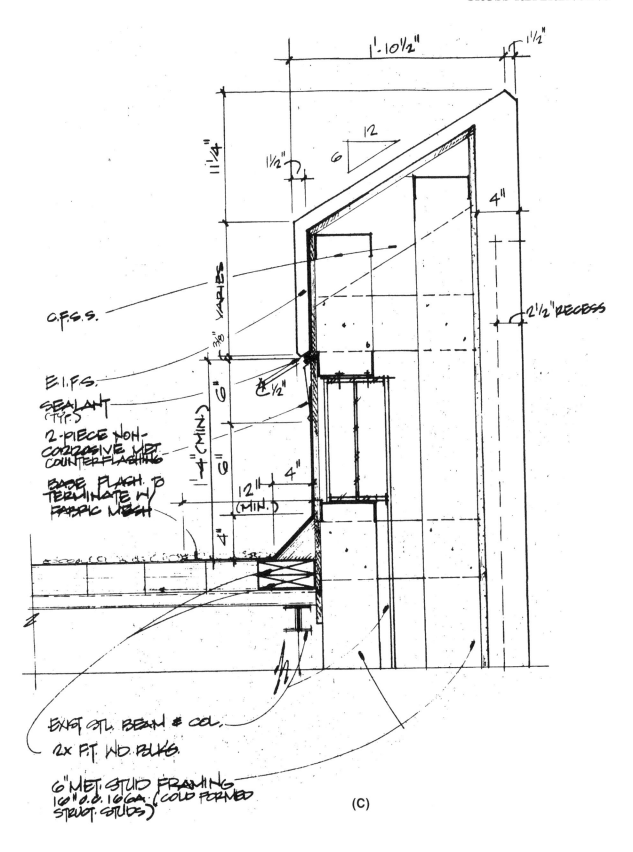

O.F.S.S.

E.I.F.S.

SEALANT (TYP.)

2-PIECE NON-CORROSIVE MET. COUNTERFLASHING

BASE FLASH. TO TERMINATE W/ FABRIC MESH

1'-10½"

1½"

12

6

11¼"

1½"

VARIES

⅜

6"

4½"

4" (MIN.)

6"

12" (MIN.)

4"

4"

4"

2½" RECESS

EXIST. STL. BEAM & COL.

2x P.T. WD. BLK'G.

6" MET. STUD FRAMING 16" O.C. 16 GA. (COLD FORMED STRUCT. STUDS)

(C)

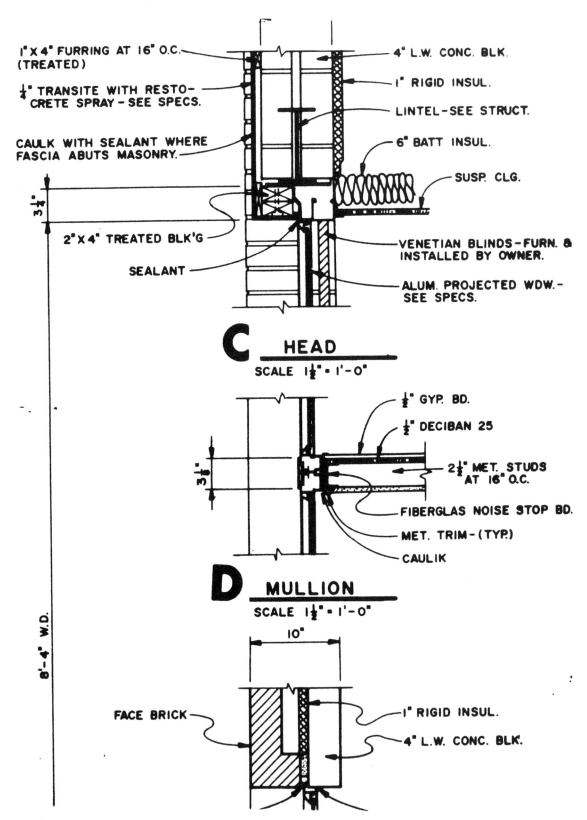

1" X 4" FURRING AT 16" O.C. (TREATED)

½" TRANSITE WITH RESTO-CRETE SPRAY – SEE SPECS.

CAULK WITH SEALANT WHERE FASCIA ABUTS MASONRY.

2" X 4" TREATED BLK'G

SEALANT

3¼"

8'-4" W.D.

4" L.W. CONC. BLK.

1" RIGID INSUL.

LINTEL – SEE STRUCT.

6" BATT INSUL.

SUSP. CLG.

VENETIAN BLINDS – FURN. & INSTALLED BY OWNER.

ALUM. PROJECTED WDW. – SEE SPECS.

C HEAD
SCALE 1½" = 1'-0"

3⅛"

½" GYP. BD.

½" DECIBAN 25

2½" MET. STUDS AT 16" O.C.

FIBERGLAS NOISE STOP BD.

MET. TRIM – (TYP.)

CAULK

D MULLION
SCALE 1½" = 1'-0"

10"

FACE BRICK

1" RIGID INSUL.

4" L.W. CONC. BLK.

Compare the drawings; they occur side-by-side, the same wall, but one drawing is through the wall, the other through the window unit in the wall. Note the 1″ × 4″ furring [upper left on the first drawing]. Where is that furring in the second drawing? Is there furring shown properly?

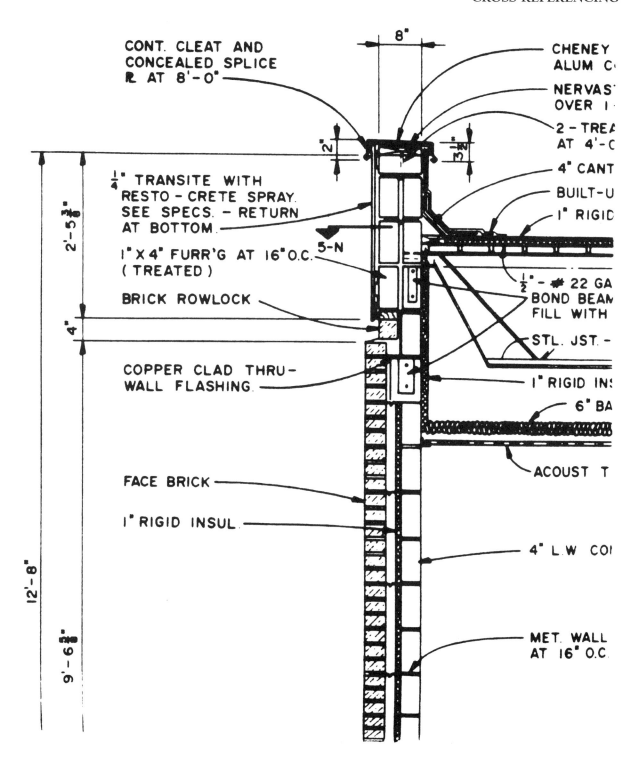

CONT. CLEAT AND
CONCEALED SPLICE
ℝ AT 8'- 0"

8"

CHENEY
ALUM C

NERVAS
OVER I

2 - TREA
AT 4'- C

2"

3½"

4" CANT

BUILT-U

¼" TRANSITE WITH
RESTO - CRETE SPRAY.
SEE SPECS. – RETURN
AT BOTTOM.

I" RIGID

5-N

1" X 4" FURR'G AT 16"O.C.
(TREATED)

½" – # 22 GA
BOND BEAM
FILL WITH

BRICK ROWLOCK

4"

STL. JST. –

COPPER CLAD THRU-
WALL FLASHING.

I" RIGID INS

6" BA

ACOUST T

2'-5 ¾"

FACE BRICK

I" RIGID INSUL.

4" L.W COI

12'- 8"

9'- 6 ⅝"

MET. WALL
AT 16" O.C.

377

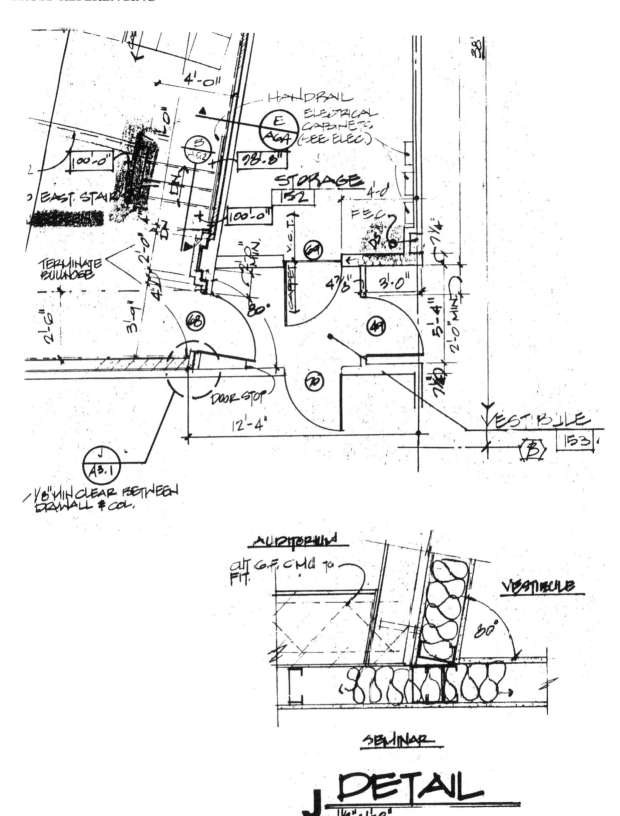

There is not always the opportunity to place your referenced detail so close to the reference. Here Detail J/A3.1 is right below, and very handy for use, reading and explaining what occurs in the small-scale plan.

25

Wall Sections

As noted before, floor plans contain a wealth of information usable by all trades engaged in any building project. These plans show the position and construction of all walls and partitions. However, because the scale of the plan is small, wall construction details cannot be shown. It is important, therefore, that even the simplest project contain at least one drawing known as the "wall section."

The wall section is a vertical cut through and perpendicular to the outer face of the exterior wall. It need not be extensive; detailed information about the inside of the building is not necessary in this drawing. The wall section is aimed at detailing the construction of the wall itself. It is vital that it appear in every set of drawings, even those of a modest residence, to illustrate the joining together of the various parts. Items as minute as a guttering system, downspouts, moldings, vents, and small nailers or blocking required in the construction are shown,

Different offices approach wall section drawings in different ways. The more conventional method is a large-scale drawing, perhaps as large as $1\frac{1}{2}'' = 1'-0''$. In some offices the section may be produced at $\frac{3}{4}'' = 1'-0''$, or slightly smaller, accompanied by a series of large-scale details taken from the section. Neither system can be faulted, because large-scale drawings are presented in both. The choice rests with the degree of complexity

of the building and how thoroughly the construction information should be conveyed.

The advantage gained from wall section drawings is twofold: exact construction details are clearly illustrated and large details need not be repeated. If a concrete warehouse is being detailed, it is unnecessary to show the entire 20-foot concrete-block wall. Of course, it is essential to show its intersection with the roof, floor slab, and foundation and those systems that depend on it. In the total vertical rise of the wall there may be as many as 10 or 12 feet that are nothing more than block laid on block, the drawing of which adds no information for the contractor. Many offices, with the assistance of a pair of break lines, eliminate this section of the wall and provide a system of details properly aligned with one another to serve instead. In this simple warehouse example we have a detail that shows the footing and foundation complex, another at the sill (or where the floor, the top of the foundation, and the wall intersect), and still another at the cornice where the roof system and wall intersect. Vertical alignment is mandatory in these drawings.

Just how a particular material is carried from the sill to the underside of the roof system should be instantly apparent. Correct drafting and material indications denote the simplicity of the construction. In more complicated work it becomes a matter of showing the details involved. A high-rise building, which frequently has multiple basements, is a good example. The basement walls may vary in detail; therefore, whenever a variance occurs it should be shown on the wall section. In most high-rise buildings the first, or main, floor is unique in function and construction and proper detailing is a must. The second floor may also be unique as the upper extension of the main entrance, but above it the floors become repetitive. From the second floor upward the wall section may be termed typical and, once properly delineated, may be eliminated from the drawings. The interjection of a typical floor necessitates additional detailing, and so on, until the meeting of the roof system and walls is reached. When many atypical floors are added, the wall section may grow long and complicated and have to be placed sideways on the sheet to be shown in its entirety. For many jobs a sheet 30 or 36 inches wide will suffice; the wall section can be drawn at a large scale, properly aligned, and still fit into this measurement.

When only large details are prepared, there is no question that some continuity is lost. Nevertheless, the project architect may elect to use the large-scale detail system because of its specific design advantages. It is also possible to draw sections at large scale ($\frac{1}{2}''$ or $\frac{3}{4}'' = 1'\text{-}0''$) to show the wall sections. These sections, in turn, act as an index for the large-scale drawings mentioned earlier. So we have still another system. The building section introduces a new element into the system of drawings, as we show in Chapter 26.

It is possible to build a simple structure with one wall section, for the construction is the same throughout the building. However, this is often neither true nor desirable. Again, experience must dictate the number of wall sections and where and why they are to be cut. Yet too many sections should not be cut, and special attention should be given to ensure against repetitive drawing and garbled information and to reduce the opportunity for error.

The first wall section in any project should be labeled "typical" to indicate that it appears frequently and is the most common to the building. Once this has been established, there is a norm of construction and we can begin to evaluate the necessity for other details and wall sections by variance from it. In the example it can be seen that the high element of the building, a simple block shape, has one detail—one wall section used exclusively in its construction. The low element of

the building has two distinct systems; one is the curtain wall (panel wall) and the other, stone veneer. The criterion for wall sections is clean-cut. Each type of construction should be detailed in a wall section. As seen in other views, the typical section appears in the main building block on all four sides; the other wall sections do not apply so extensively. The decision to draw a detail rather than a wall section is governed by whether a one-time or limited area (detail) or a condition that occurs frequently and over a large area (wall section) is to be shown. The difference between the detail and wall section is not serious, but we usually try to main the separation between them.

In the wall section any material that is cut should be strongly outlined to indicate a cut section. Proper architectural symbols should be drawn in the cut areas. Notice that in wood framing a stud with sheathing on one side and wall finish on the other will have a strong black line around it. The stud is not cut, however; it is shown in elevation as the section is cut between the studs. The top plates are cut because they run horizontally. Joists and rafters are seen in elevation and only one in each case is shown. Most of the materials, which are continuous along the wall rather than intermittent (e.g., the framing members), are cut. To produce readable, concise drawings we must identify the materials with correct architectural designations. If the symbols are inconsistent or indistinct, the section will be worthless. We must be able to recognize a particular molding as finished wood as opposed to wall sheathing, which may be a plywood panel. It is equally important to identify metal items, such as flashing, gutters, and other thin materials, by a heavy black line. Structural members of varying size must be shown, the larger with the standard steel symbol and the smaller members blackened.

Careful drawing guarantees the demanded elements of construction. Nothing should be left to the whim of the contractor. All parts should be studied and put together as the design dictates. All items, even of a minor nature, should be considered carefully. A piece of blocking may be required to attach a cabinet to a wall. *If it is required, show it!* In brick veneer the top of the brickwork, under the soffit, must be closed. How is this to be done: with a simple molding or with a supplemental trim board?

Brick coursing should be indicated on the wall section. How many courses of brick are to be laid from the top of the foundation wall to the underside of the soffit and the top of the brickwork should be indicated accurately. We state unequivocally the number of courses required and the point at which the brickwork ceases.

Although it is not necessary to illustrate how the pieces are nailed together and with how many nails (this is usually a specification item, and a widely used workbook, *Manual for House Framing, Nailing Schedule,* is specified), the inclusion of extraordinary construction may require this intricate detailing. In general we rely on contractors to provide substantial construction, properly nailed, for they are familiar with the technique of nailing and the types and sizes of nails. Again, however, the design professional is responsible for the design concept; how do we want the building put together? Often, sitting in the office, we can think of methods that may or may not work well and may have to be modified in the field.

There should be no reluctance to put down any system of construction that is workable. No one can be entirely familiar with all materials or the requirements for their connection, but we can offer suggestions that, to the best of our knowledge, will work.

When we need break lines we must remember to place them in pairs to indicate that the wall section has been broken and that part of it has been removed. The break lines should fall at intervals along the height of the wall where no important detail occurs and no construction of substance will be obscured. In the wall section we must become intimately aware of the "nuts and bolts." In fact, we are concerned with showing reinforcing bars, anchor bolts, and items of small size and minute detail that must appear in order to meet the requirements of the job. We must ensure that they are not obscured or deleted.

As already stated, notations on wall sections should be entered on the drawings in a clear and concise manner, properly placed and marked by accurate leader lines. The wall section should be dimensioned vertically and horizontally to give the exact requirements of the particular construction. Wall sections should be titled individually for clear differentiation. In cross-referencing, the wall sections must be shown on the exterior elevations with some type of unique flag or indicator.

The plans will show us the configuration and extent of the building; the elevations will show us how the outside face of the building will appear. The wall sections are a vital part of the construction information because they show us what the wall is made of and how the various pieces and parts are put together.

CHECKLIST: WALL SECTIONS

1. Show all materials in their proper location and thickness, all "cut" material strongly outlined.
2. Indicate proper symbology for all materials; standard or noted symbols; symbols must be clear even at small scale.
3. Identify all materials and use proper notes and no specification wording; use the same terminology as the specifications for each item.
4. Fully dimension sections vertically and horizontally; use complete dimensions from bottom of footing to top of section; dimension to easily recognized locations (top of masonry, etc.).
5. Coordinate section with column lines or building lines whenever possible.
6. Use a scale adequate to provide the information required; a small scale can destroy communication.
7. If one section is similar to another, with only slight changes, do not redraw the entire section; use a similar outline, add the new features, and refer by note to the other section.
8. Tie the section into the cross-reference system by number or designator; use descriptive titles when necessary.

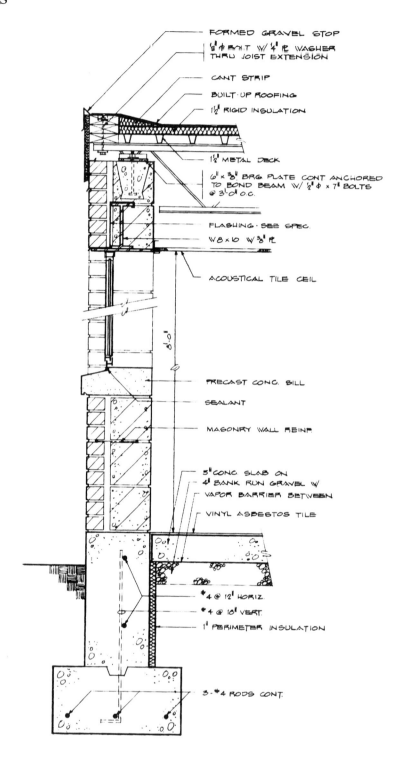

FORMED GRAVEL STOP

½"⌀ BOLT W/ ¼" ℞ WASHER THRU JOIST EXTENSION

CANT STRIP

BUILT-UP ROOFING

1½" RIGID INSULATION

1½" METAL DECK

6" x ⅜" BRG PLATE CONT ANCHORED TO BOND BEAM W/ ½"⌀ x 7" BOLTS @ 3'-0" O.C.

FLASHING · SEE SPEC.

W 8 x 10 W/ ⅜" ℞

ACOUSTICAL TILE CEIL

8'-0"

PRECAST CONC. SILL

SEALANT

MASONRY WALL REINF.

5" CONC SLAB ON 4" BANK RUN GRAVEL W/ VAPOR BARRIER BETWEEN

VINYL ASBESTOS TILE

#4 @ 12" HORIZ.

#4 @ 18" VERT.

1" PERIMETER INSULATION

3 - #4 RODS CONT.

BRICK & BLOCK ¾"=1'-0"

A full wall section from the bottom of the footing to the topmost reach of the roof gravel stop. The wall section shows in meticulous detail the construction, change of materials, and systems incorporated in the solid masonry wall. The drafting is excellent and the information of first-rate architectural quality.

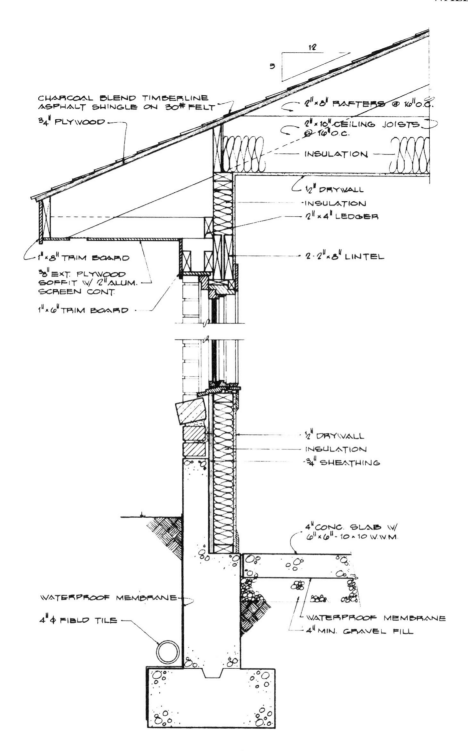

CHARCOAL BLEND TIMBERLINE
ASPHALT SHINGLE ON 30# FELT

3/4" PLYWOOD

2"x8" RAFTERS @ 16" O.C.

2"x10" CEILING JOISTS
@ 16" O.C.

INSULATION

1/2" DRYWALL

INSULATION

2"x4" LEDGER

2·2"x8" LINTEL

1"x8" TRIM BOARD

3/8" EXT. PLYWOOD
SOFFIT W/ 2" ALUM.
SCREEN CONT.

1"x6" TRIM BOARD

1/2" DRYWALL

INSULATION

3/4" SHEATHING

4" CONC. SLAB W/
6"x6"-10x10 W.W.M.

WATERPROOF MEMBRANE

4"φ FIELD TILE

WATERPROOF MEMBRANE

4" MIN. GRAVEL FILL

BRICK VENEER 3/4" = 1'-0"

A full wall section showing light construction from the bottom of the footing through the slope and overhang of the roof system. Brick veneer on the frame construction backup is detailed at 3/4" = 1'0". The draftsmanship and materials indication are explicitly clear. Vertical dimensions are neglected, for this wall section is meant to be "typical."

383

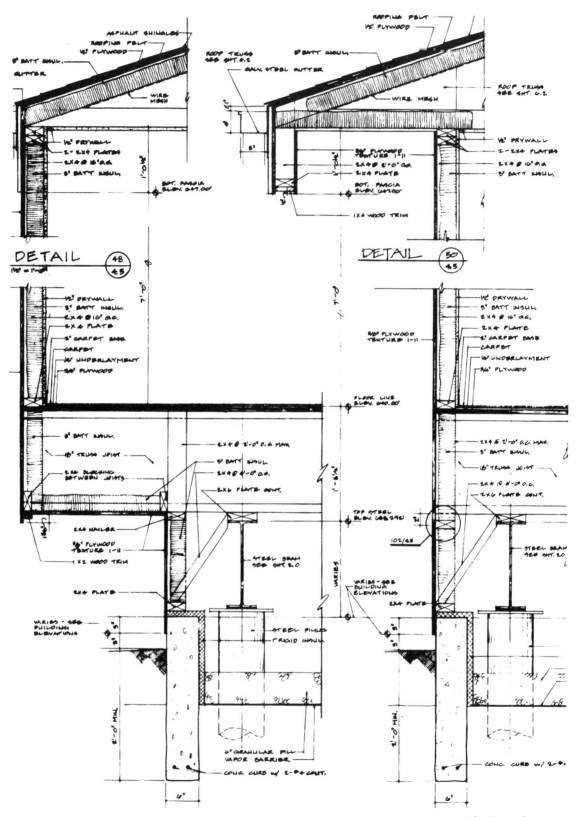

These carefully cross-referenced wall details become partial wall sections. The details speak for themselves. Material indications, section markers, dimensions, and construction notes are the finest in quality and clarity.

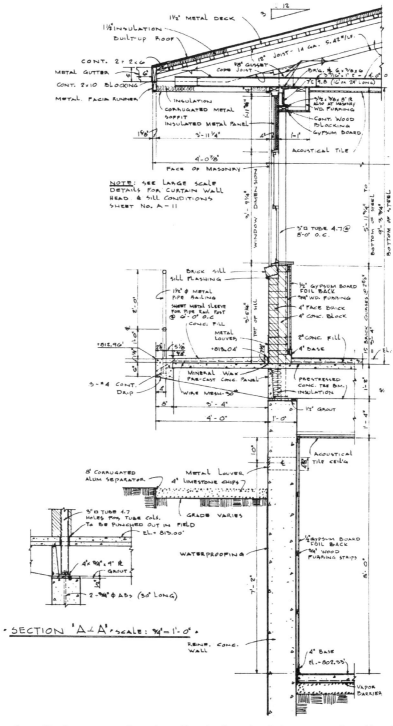

- SECTION "A⊥A" scale: ¾"=1'-0".

A full wall section with all necessary dimensions. The detail section is from a set of working drawings; the practice of breaking continuous elements where no changes of major import occur, has been ignored. It is usual to break areas of pure repetition rather than spend time drafting no additional information. The material indication is good, and confusion is minimal. The drawing may be considered typical of wall sections produced in the standard architectural offices of the past forty years.

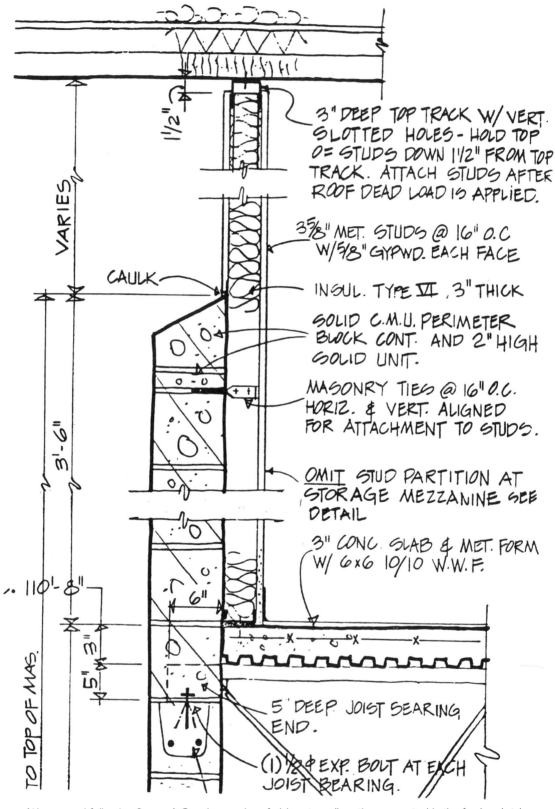

3" DEEP TOP TRACK W/ VERT. SLOTTED HOLES - HOLD TOP O= STUDS DOWN 1½" FROM TOP TRACK. ATTACH STUDS AFTER ROOF DEAD LOAD IS APPLIED.

3⅝" MET. STUDS @ 16" O.C W/ ⅝" GYPWD. EACH FACE

INSUL. TYPE VI, 3" THICK

SOLID C.M.U. PERIMETER BLOCK CONT. AND 2" HIGH SOLID UNIT.

MASONRY TIES @ 16" O.C. HORIZ. & VERT. ALIGNED FOR ATTACHMENT TO STUDS.

OMIT STUD PARTITION AT STORAGE MEZZANINE SEE DETAIL

3" CONC. SLAB & MET. FORM W/ 6x6 10/10 W.W.F.

5" DEEP JOIST BEARING END.

(1) ½"∅ EXP. BOLT AT EACH JOIST BEARING.

VARIES

CAULK

3'-6"

110'-8"

TO TOP OF MAS.

1½"

6"

5" 3"

(Above, and following 2 pages) Good examples of elaborate wall sections executed in the freehand style. A grid underlayment helps keep lines straight and in scale, but care and skill are nonetheless required. Good time-reducing technique when mastered properly.

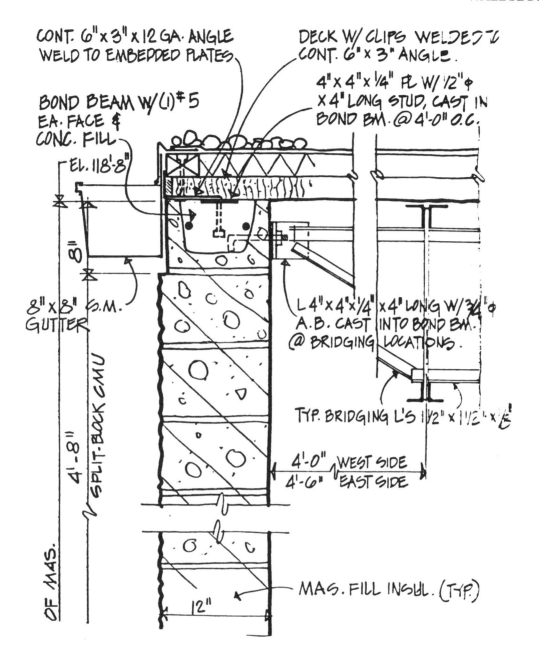

CONT. 6" x 3" x 12 GA. ANGLE
WELD TO EMBEDDED PLATES.

BOND BEAM W/ (1) #5
EA. FACE &
CONC. FILL

EL. 118'-8"

8"

8" x 8" G.M.
GUTTER

4'-8"

SPLIT-BLOCK CMU

OF MAS.

12"

DECK W/ CLIPS WELDED TO
CONT. 6" x 3" ANGLE.

4" x 4" x 1/4" PL W/ 1/2"ø
x 4" LONG STUD, CAST IN
BOND BM. @ 4'-0" O.C.

L 4" x 4" x 1/4" x 4" LONG W/ 3/4"ø
A.B. CAST INTO BOND BM.
@ BRIDGING LOCATIONS.

TYP. BRIDGING L'S 1 1/2" x 1 1/2" x 1/8"

4'-0" WEST SIDE
4'-6" EAST SIDE

MAS. FILL INSUL. (TYP.)

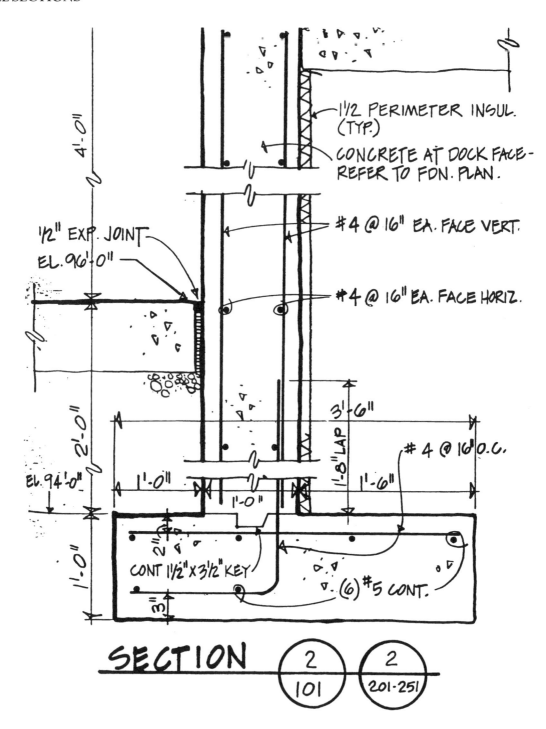

4'-0"

1½ PERIMETER INSUL. (TYP.)

CONCRETE AT DOCK FACE- REFER TO FDN. PLAN.

#4 @ 16" EA. FACE VERT.

½" EXP. JOINT EL. 96'-0"

#4 @ 16" EA. FACE HORIZ.

3'-6"

2'-0"

1'-8" LAP

#4 @ 16" O.C.

EL. 94'-0"

1'-0"

1'-0"

1'-6"

1'-0"

2"

CONT 1½" X 3½" KEY

3"

(6) #5 CONT.

SECTION   2 / 101   2 / 201-251

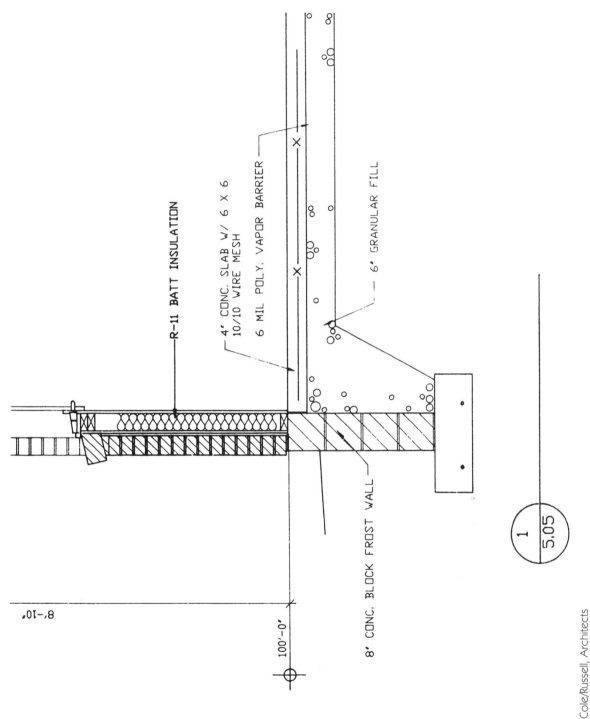

R-11 BATT INSULATION

4' CONC. SLAB W/ 6 X 6
10/10 WIRE MESH

6 MIL POLY. VAPOR BARRIER

6' GRANULAR FILL

8' CONC. BLOCK FROST WALL

8'-10'

100'-0'

1
5.05

Cole/Russell, Architects
The lower section of a CAD-produced wall section. Good line weight variations help to separate visually the different materials.
Lettering is well adjusted to the drawing.

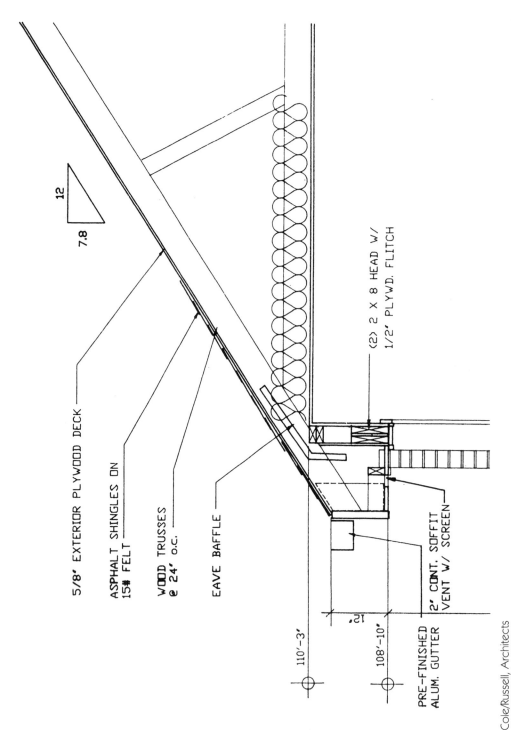

5/8" EXTERIOR PLYWOOD DECK

ASPHALT SHINGLES ON
15# FELT

WOOD TRUSSES
@ 24" o.c.

EAVE BAFFLE

(2) 2 X 8 HEAD W/
1/2" PLYWD. FLITCH

2" CONT. SOFFIT
VENT W/ SCREEN

PRE-FINISHED
ALUM. GUTTER

12

7,8

12"

110'-3"

108'-10"

Cole/Russell, Architects
The upper portion of the wall section shown opposite. Note how CAD has adapted to shingle designation and small wood blocking. Also note how insulation symbol could easily just be a CAD-expanded version of that used in the other drawing (note the consistency).

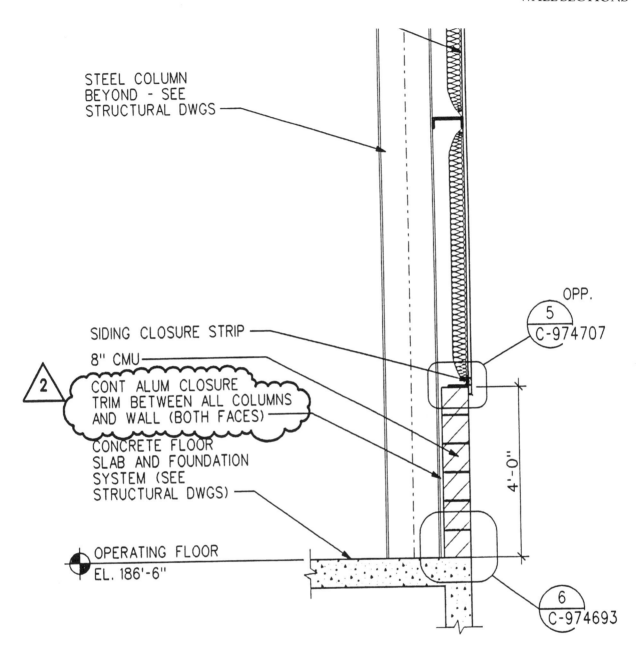

STEEL COLUMN
BEYOND - SEE
STRUCTURAL DWGS

OPP.

5
C-974707

SIDING CLOSURE STRIP

8" CMU

2 CONT ALUM CLOSURE
TRIM BETWEEN ALL COLUMNS
AND WALL (BOTH FACES)

CONCRETE FLOOR
SLAB AND FOUNDATION
SYSTEM (SEE
STRUCTURAL DWGS)

4'-0"

OPERATING FLOOR
EL. 186'-6"

6
C-974693

WALL SECTION
SCALE: 1/2"-1'-0"

Portion of wall section drawn via CAD.

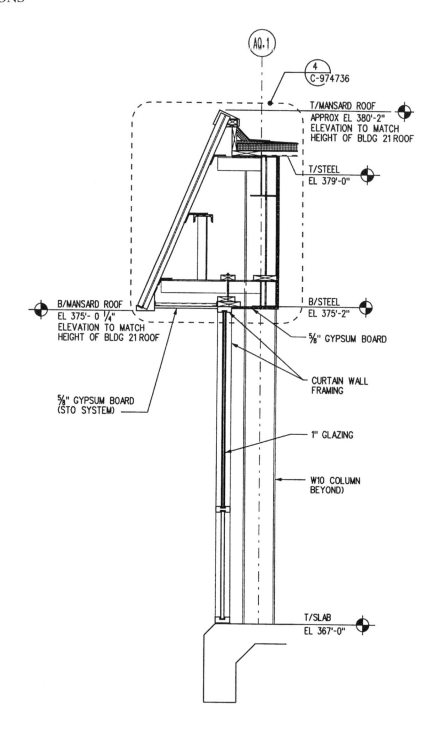

AQ.1

4
C-974736

T/MANSARD ROOF
APPROX EL 380'-2"
ELEVATION TO MATCH
HEIGHT OF BLDG 21 ROOF

T/STEEL
EL 379'-0"

B/MANSARD ROOF
EL 375'- 0 1/4"
ELEVATION TO MATCH
HEIGHT OF BLDG 21 ROOF

B/STEEL
EL 375'-2"

5/8" GYPSUM BOARD

CURTAIN WALL
FRAMING

5/8" GYPSUM BOARD
(STO SYSTEM)

1" GLAZING

W10 COLUMN
BEYOND)

T/SLAB
EL 367'-0"

NEW WALL SECTION
SCALE: 3/4" - 1'-0"

50N
C-974727

Full height wall section produced via CAD; opposite, the top portion of the wall section at a larger scale, to better explain the construction required.

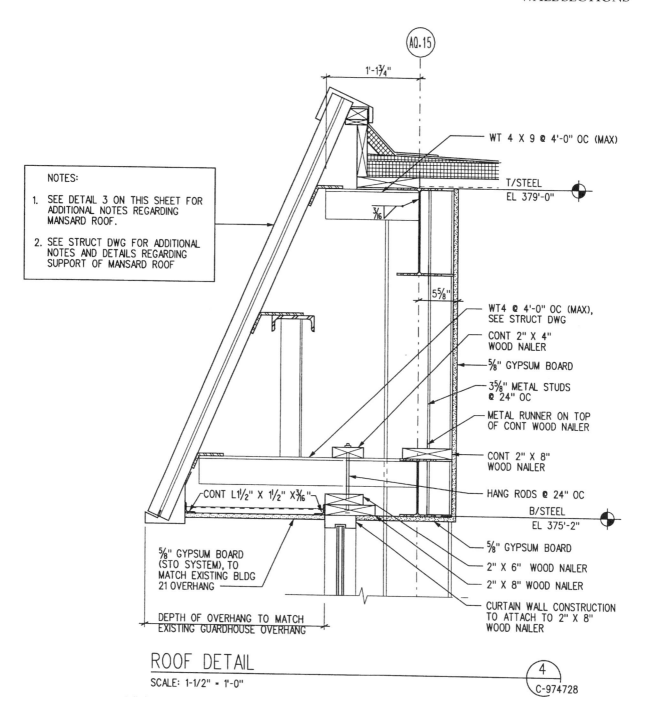

NOTES:

1. SEE DETAIL 3 ON THIS SHEET FOR ADDITIONAL NOTES REGARDING MANSARD ROOF.

2. SEE STRUCT DWG FOR ADDITIONAL NOTES AND DETAILS REGARDING SUPPORT OF MANSARD ROOF

AQ.15

1'-1¾"

WT 4 X 9 @ 4'-0" OC (MAX)

T/STEEL
EL 379'-0"

3/16

5⅝"

WT4 @ 4'-0" OC (MAX), SEE STRUCT DWG

CONT 2" X 4" WOOD NAILER

⅝" GYPSUM BOARD

3⅝" METAL STUDS @ 24" OC

METAL RUNNER ON TOP OF CONT WOOD NAILER

CONT 2" X 8" WOOD NAILER

HANG RODS @ 24" OC

B/STEEL
EL 375'-2"

⅝" GYPSUM BOARD

2" X 6" WOOD NAILER

2" X 8" WOOD NAILER

CURTAIN WALL CONSTRUCTION TO ATTACH TO 2" X 8" WOOD NAILER

CONT L1½" X 1½" X3/16"

⅝" GYPSUM BOARD (STO SYSTEM), TO MATCH EXISTING BLDG 21 OVERHANG

DEPTH OF OVERHANG TO MATCH EXISTING GUARDHOUSE OVERHANG

ROOF DETAIL
SCALE: 1-1/2" = 1'-0"

4
C-974728

393

26

Building Sections and Section-Elevations

It is true that between the floor plans and the exterior elevations we are able to acquire full comprehension of a building project. The floor plan is a horizontally cut section that provides us with a layout of the rooms and the openings into them. The elevations show us the floor-to-floor heights in their correct dimensions, but these floors are revealed to us only in the form of a single line on the elevations, and we are unable to recognize the full complexity of the building construction. In an effort to provide the contractors with more exact information and to explain the construction to them fully, the architect will provide sections cut vertically through the entire building. These sections generally fall into two classifications: longitudinal, on the long axis of the building, and cross or traverse sections across its narrower dimension. The indicators for these sections are applied to the floor plan sheet and properly cross-referenced. The sections go through the building from left to right to the exterior walls on either side, to the bottom-most part of the basement or foundation system, and to the top of the roof.

The section line need not be entirely straight; we can sometimes indicate an offset if we want to show a particular feature or other conditions at another location in the building, although there should not be a great many offsets in any particular section. In other words, there should be good reason for showing them; even so, the deviation should be a matter of only a few feet. Referred to as small-scale sections because they will be produced at the same scale as the floor plans and the exterior elevations, they are used primarily to locate and measure the floors, roof, and the exposure of critical intersections between floors and walls. The sections may also expose edge conditions at openings. Basically they are oriented vertically to reveal information not shown on other drawings. They will usually show features that appear on other large-scale details and, in a sense, are an index of these details. They can be used to pinpoint the application of a particular detail. In a simplified manner they show all the features of the building, wall openings, wall projections, suspended ceilings, partitioning, wainscots, cabinetwork, chalk and tack boards, borrowed lights, doors, and frames, once again to provide total information. The concept of the building section is to cut the building with all details in place, to look in a particular direction as denoted by the designator, and show everything in front of the cut line. Many items are cut. If there is cabinetry and the section marker passes through it, it will be shown in section, like the walls, ceiling, and floors. If there is a door in a partition beyond the cutting plane, it will be shown in its correct location, but in elevation. Corridor openings, columns, and any feature of the building that can be seen from the section line will be shown. In high-rise construction these particular drawings are sizable. They can in some instances be the same size as the elevations and must be worked out in basically the same way. It is obvious to all that an elevator shaft must be continuous, without offsets or jogs, from top to bottom. This shaft is incorporated into the drawings merely to show what happens when the floors intersect it and how the detail is treated, for in every job the treatment may be different. So it becomes a verification process for the contractor; it also fully meets the requirement for total information. We try to go in two directions with building sections if at all possible, at 90 degrees to each other to reinforce complete information. Framing systems for roofs and floors are often basically oriented in one direction, and a section of this construction, which shows the elevation of the joists, is really not very informative. However, a section at right angles to the joists, which would show their number and spacing, is much more informative. Therefore, the two-section complex, cross and longitudinal, is most important in any project, no matter how large or small. In some offices the concept is slightly different. They carry the idea of the sections being a catalog of details a few steps further. Rather than producing them at the same scale as the plans and elevations, they give them a larger scale, perhaps $\frac{1}{2}'' = 1'\text{-}0''$, to show more detail in the way in which the pieces are fitted together. Generally, these sections do not stand alone; it is impossible to draw them large enough to tell us everything we want to know. If the building has many unusual details, the larger scale is justified, but we must still draw large-scale drawings to show all the varied parts. Again it becomes a matter of concept. What can we show and what is the best way to show it? Backed by experience and correct office procedure we can formulate rea-

sonable answers. Of course, architectural symbols must be used as in wall sections; a material that is cut must be marked by the appropriate symbol.

Column lines (perhaps interior elevation markers) and section markers are also shown. These drawings in many instances will appear to lack interest as compared with other drawings in the set, but the facts they contain are important, and in spite of their bleakness they can clear up a question, verify a condition, or be generally helpful to the contractor.

Sometimes it is hard to visualize a project in its completed form when only beams, joists, and columns are apparent. Therefore, the more complete information we can transmit to the various trades, the greater the likelihood of realizing the project as it was conceived. These building sections help to complete the package.

In some projects the configuration of the building is such that it may be advantageous to cut a section through one part, which, however, may reveal another. In practice this drawing known as a section-elevation. Here we can cut through part of the building as a building section, extend the drawing as needed, and show the appropriate elevation adjacent to the section. It is not always possible to show the complete project on four or five elevations, but if we continue them with sections we can show the lines of the roof ridges, gutters, and trim as they are carried through. These elements are then reflected in the sections. What is under that line? What is being joined together and why? This information can be correlated on the building section-elevation. Here, again, is a means of gathering the facts the contractor needs. It is not an ambiguous device so long as it is clearly labeled and its location and function are clearly presented on the plan.

CHECKLIST: BUILDING SECTIONS AND SECTION-ELEVATIONS

1. Show complete vertical dimensions; tie major features of the building together.
2. Identify the section and coordinate with the cross-referencing system.
3. Because of lack of scale and complete data, indicate materials only in general terms; that is, concrete block, concrete, brick, wood beam, steel column.

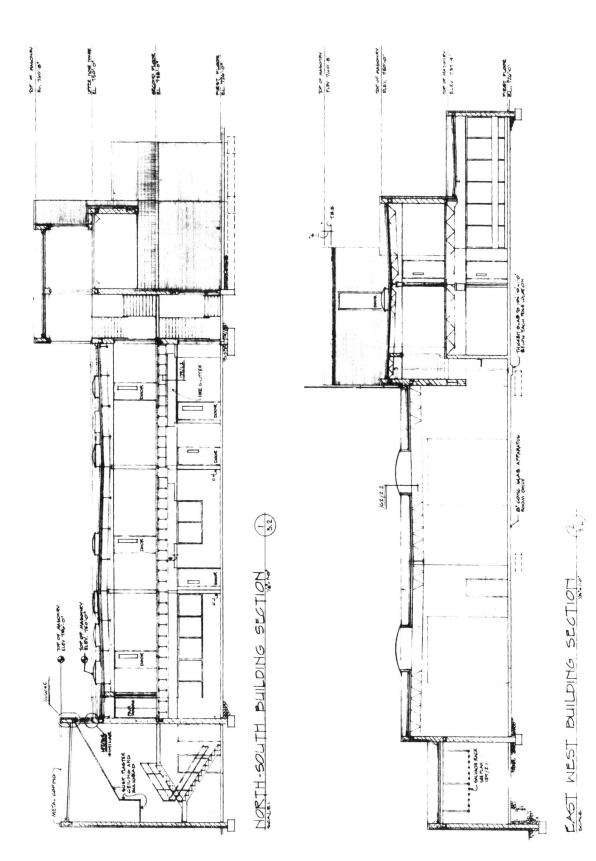

NORTH-SOUTH BUILDING SECTION

EAST WEST BUILDING SECTION

These two full-building elevation sections, although at small scale, give complete information for the structural requirements of the total building. The section markers distinguish the structural elements detailed at larger scale. The overall concept of the structure is well defined.

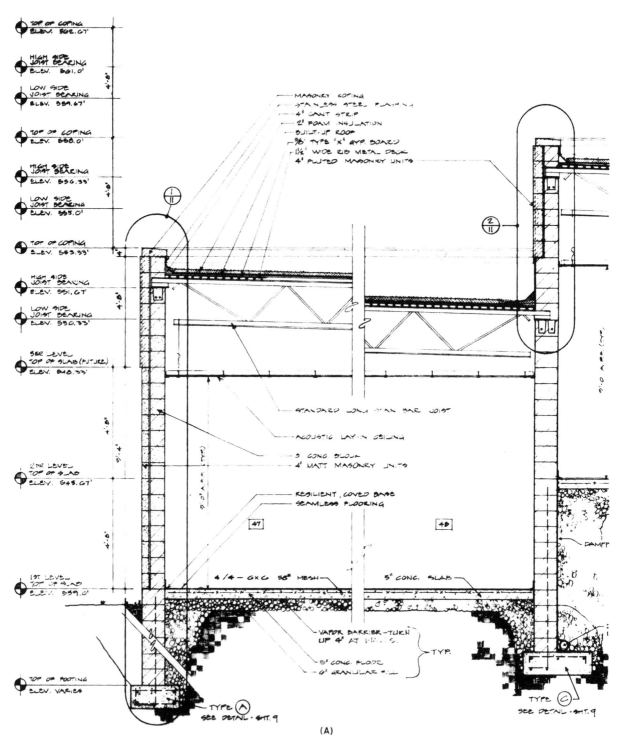

(A)

(A) This section was drawn at an unusually large scale to accommodate a multilevel building that needed to be clearly defined. Rather than trying to enter all the information on this drawing, the designer included some material data, but the walls were referenced to large-scale wall sections as shown in (B). The project requirements were specific or another technique could have been employed to produce these drawings in this manner.

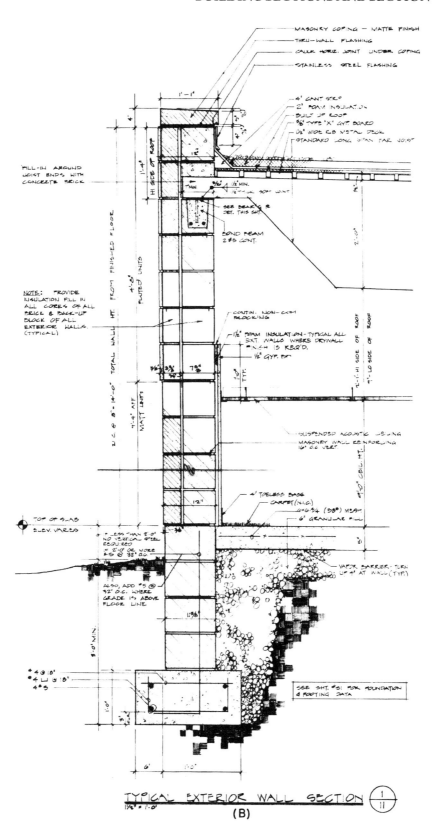

TYPICAL EXTERIOR WALL SECTION

(B)

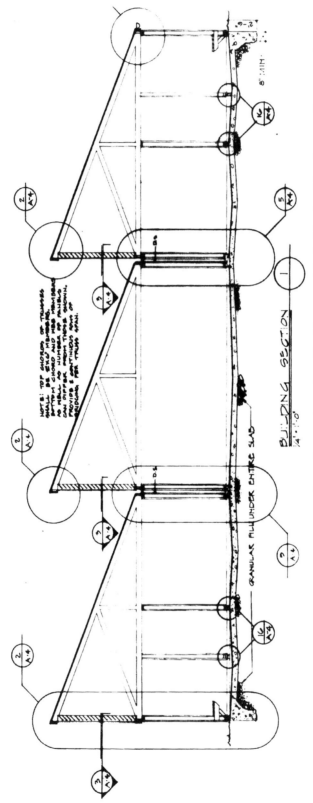

Another example of a small-scale building section that refers to large-scale sections. The full scope of the building is evident, but specific construction information is shown on the wall sections.

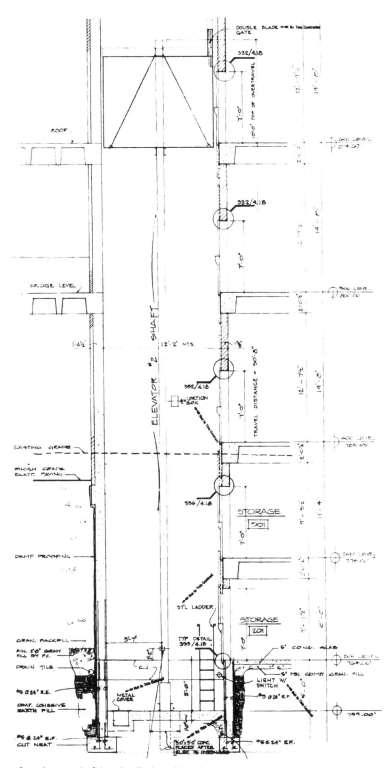

This full section of an elevator shaft is a detailed working drawing. Note the stamped imprint "Not in this contract," which precludes false bids. The information represents the total picture, but any doubt about its position in the work to be done is removed by the note. Sections have been detailed at all the crucial points along the shaft wall. The cross-referencing and dimensioning are well done.

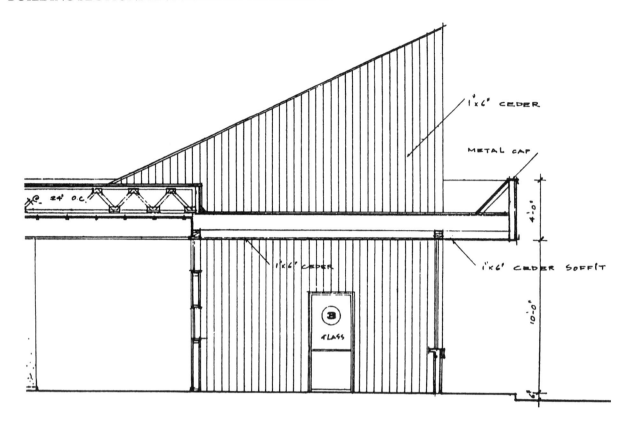

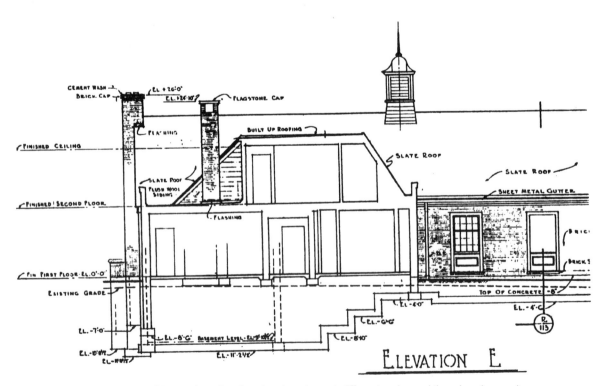

Two good examples of the section-elevation drawing, done at different scales and thus showing varying areas of the buildings. Helps workers relate a large portion of the building to another, rather than totally using isolated details. While fairly conceptual, these drawings can provide a wealth of detailed information.

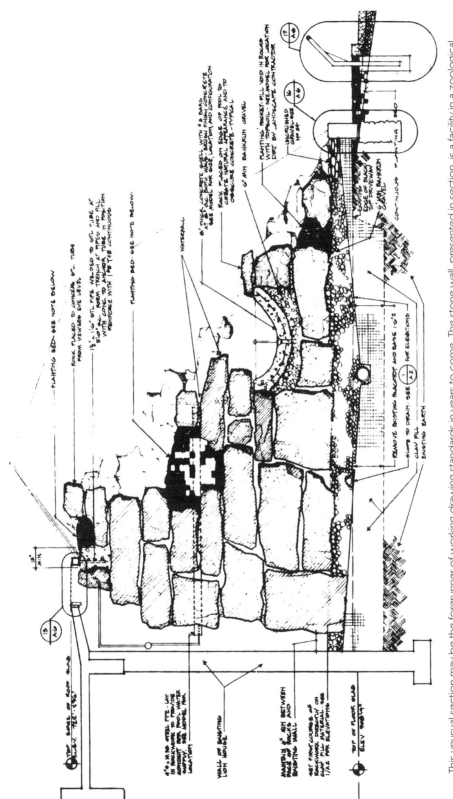

This unusual section may be the forerunner of working drawing standards in years to come. The stone wall, presented in section, is a facility in a zoological setting. The drawing shows an addition to an existing structure. It has exceptional drafting quality and design concept. Full information is given for the construction.

4. Show interior features, lightly and in general terms (not a lot of detail); indicate all wall outlines, doors and frames, cabinetwork, and similar items.

5. Locate mechanical items: water coolers, louvers, fire extinguisher cabinets, and so on.

6. Check all finishes with room finish schedule.

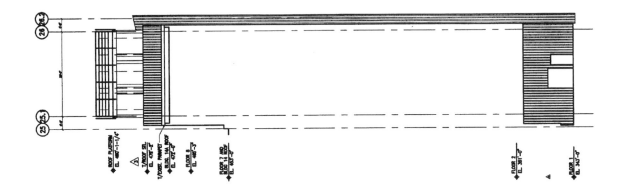

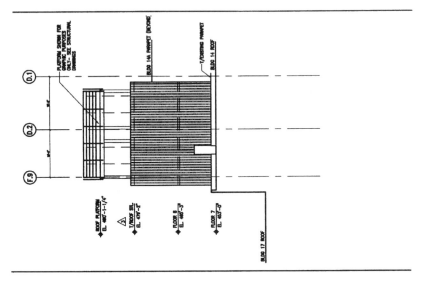

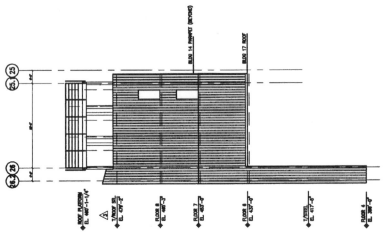

Exterior elevations where construction occurs over, aside and beneath existing work

404

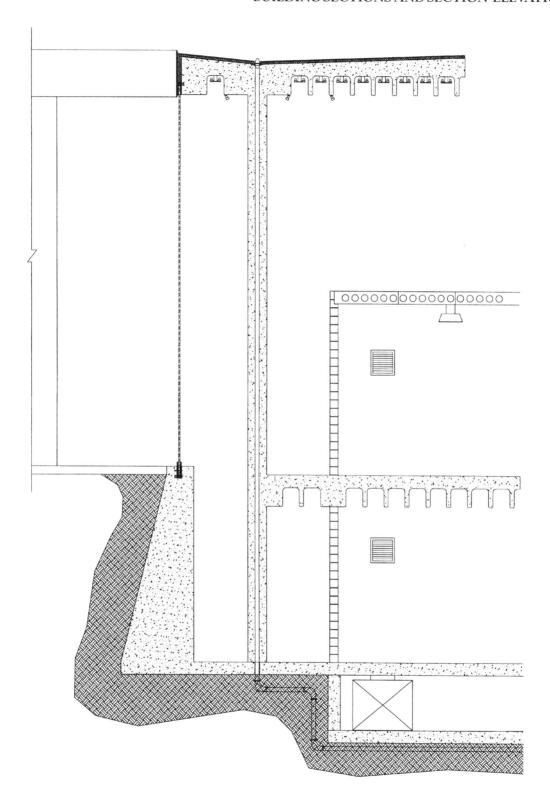

WALL SECTION
SCALE: 1/2" = 1'-0"

Partial building section drawn with CAD

27

Schedules

Much of the information required on the drawings can be organized in schedules. Because of the volume of the data, the schedule presents an easy and convenient format for delivering information to the contractor without obliterating the drawings. A schedule is much more concise, yet totally efficient.

The extensive information contained in the schedules can be lettered in a smaller space than the notes that must be entered on the drawings near their point of application. To describe a single door requires a number of lines of lettering; by scheduling, the door's more descriptive information can be provided in a very concise manner.

Although schedules have already been in use for many years, they are becoming increasingly popular with architects and contractors, particularly in view of the number of formats and automated methods available. The schedules need not appear on the drawings. Many offices add them to the specifications. This makes sense because legend items can be typed on the schedule form and reproduced as part of the specifications booklet. Typing, of course, does away with the need for hand lettering, which is inordinately time-consuming for the draftsman.

Some offices type their schedules on clear decals that can be applied directly to the drawings. Again, this method eliminates hand lettering. No matter what the presentation, the data must be complete, concise, and clear.

Schedules contain numerous facts about the building materials; some include room finishes, windows, doors, lintels, footings and columns, beams, borings, louvers, fans, and diffusers. Other schedules are needed for radiation, fixtures and appliances, cabinets, equipment and furnishings, and trees and bushes. From this list it can be seen that the schedules are not necessarily confined to one particular set of drawings or trade.

Schedules can be as detailed as the job requires; this chapter presents several examples. Individual offices have set procedures, or outlines, into which such schedules fit, and their formats and texts vary considerably. Perhaps a new system will be suggested or, at least, the overall approach to schedules from differing sources may be considered.

In general, if the schedules are hand lettered on the sheets, their lines should be spaced about $1/4$ inch apart and, utilizing $1/8$-inch lettering, centered in this space. The drafter will complete the lines of information in the separate columns. If there is need for a smaller, more compact schedule, $3/16$-inch spaces with $1/16$-inch lettering are adequate.

The schedule should be properly titled with title-sized lettering, larger and bolder than the lettering used in the schedule itself. A heavy border around the entire schedule distinguishes it from other work on the sheet.

Most schedules contain two columns on the left-hand side. One column will be for the same marks or designators used on the drawings to indicate the materials to which the schedule entries refer. The next column may carry the names of the items or some other means of identifying them. From here the schedules vary widely, as seen in the examples. We touch on each one only briefly so that the examples themselves will be more effective.

The room finish schedule is, perhaps, the most extensive and the most important. There is some latitude of approach to its presentation, but possibly the best method is to place it on the right-hand side of another sheet if it does not fit on the floor plan. Reference between floor plan and the room finish schedule can be facilitated by turning the right-hand edge of the drawing sheet over far enough to make the schedule visible. If the schedule is placed toward the left-hand side (or in the center of the sheet), the set will have to be opened wide or the sheets turned back completely to expose the schedule.

Each area (room) of the project is assigned a number. This is the designator to which we refer in the room finish schedule. It is also helpful, since a great many persons, including the owner, will handle the drawings, to identify these areas by name or function. In this way a lay person, unfamiliar with the numbering system and caring more about the data contained in the space, will be able to recognize them instantly. As shown in the example, the room finish schedule, which progresses from the floor upward, lists the type of flooring, the base or baseboard installed to seal the juncture of floor and walls, and the finish on the walls.

Common practice enumerates the four walls by the cardinal points of the compass (east, west, north, and south). If a building is placed askew to compass north, a plan north, grid north, or building north is indicated; each room will have a north wall in the orientation. Ceiling material and height are also given. If wainscoting is included, it is listed separately between the base column and wall entries.

A large "Remarks" column, in which specific items may be called to the attention of the contractor or a specific dimension or finish may be noted, is a wise addition. As some of the examples show, equipment may be included in the room finish

schedule and there may be notes on trim or millwork. Schedules may be presented in many ways. One example enters the headings and abbreviations of the materials used in each block of each applicable column. This means that a legend must be added to the room finish schedule to explain the abbreviations. A more extensive schedule lists all types of materials used on the job; this format is shown in another example. The room finish schedule is, to some degree, simplified by a dot or circle placed in the materials column applicable to the area. The type of finish (natural, stained, painted) can then be added.

Basically, this is the prime function of any finish schedule; to point out the areas that are to be painted or finished.

Other examples show a variety of room finish schedules that may be adapted for use; other nomenclature and designators are the choice of the office or designer. It becomes a matter of knowing what basic materials to include in the room finish schedule.

The window and door schedules, although never combined, are similar. Again, each opening, whether window or door, is marked by a distinctive designator or mark, which should be recorded in the left-hand column of the schedule and followed by the size of the unit. Another column should show door thicknesses, for these dimensions may vary from unit to unit. A column headed "Type" applies to both door and window units and explains the functions and construction of each. Some practitioners choose to include the manufacturer's name and catalog number, a practice that is frowned on because this information is properly stated in the specifications and should not be repeated on the drawing.

The window schedule may include such information as type of glass (glazing) and the material from which each unit is to be fabricated. The door schedule lists the basic material of the doors, their details, the finish to be applied, and any labeling (fire rating) that may be required. The Remarks column is appropriate in both cases.

Frequently the presentation of window and door schedules is graphic rather than tabular. The graphic presentation is accomplished by drawing simple elevations. The designators may be applied to the elevations and the function of each door spelled out with its size and construction and other pertinent information. Either type of schedule may be used; it is important that a distinction

| WALL THICKNESS | BAR SIZE & SPACING EACH MAT | | REMARKS |
	HORIZ. BARS	VERT. BARS	
4"	#4 @ 18"	#4 @ 18"	SINGLE MAT
4½" TO 6"	#4 @ 13"	#4 @ 13"	SINGLE MAT
6½" TO 8"	#5 @ 15"	#5 @ 15"	SINGLE MAT
8½" TO 10"	#4 @ 16"	#4 @ 16"	DOUBLE MAT
10½" TO 12"	#5 @ 18"	#5 @ 18"	DOUBLE MAT
12½" TO 14"	#5 @ 18"	#5 @ 18"	DOUBLE MAT

NOTES:
1. THE ABOVE SHALL BE MINIMUM REINF'G. FOR ALL CONCRETE ELEMENTS.
2. SINGLE MAT REINFORCING SHALL BE IN CENTER OF WALL UNLESS OTHERWISE DETAILED

MINIMUM CONCRETE WALL REINFORCING SCHEDULE

Martin & Cagley, Structural Engineers
A schedule recommended for use where the project has a number of varied-sized walls scattered throughout the project. Information is combined and depicted more easily in a schedule, rather than being repeated in each applicable location on the drawings.

be made between the designators so that a door cannot be mistaken for a window.

Every opening that appears in the building must be supported by a lintel to carry the weight of the wall above it. Here, again, a proper designator is applied; in simple fashion it could be L_1, L_2, L_3, and so on. If the lintel is composed of several items (steel angles placed back-to-back), its schedule will include a small detail. The unit is described, and the sizes of the separate members are given with a notation of the overall length of the full member, which includes the required bearing (that part of the lintel that extends into the wall at both ends of the opening). This schedule need not be extensive, but all necessary information should be readily accessible to provide for the fabrication and installation of the units.

The footing schedule shows the sizes and depths of the footings, the reinforcing, and the strength of the concrete. It may also include the column piers that project from the footings. This information may be combined with the column schedule. The examples show two types of column schedule: one that indicates the steel members, which show where the bottoms of the columns occur and how high certain members must extend before changing size (in relation to the floor elevations). We must also show the overall sizes of concrete columns, their reinforcing, ties, and any changes along their lengths.

The beam schedule follows the column schedule by showing sizes, reinforcing, ties, and any individual peculiarities. In many instances beams with differing designators are actually the same size. The procedure depends on the office. In practice, a schedule may contain beam marks (designators) that indicate consecutive numbering; therefore, any number of beams may have exactly the same configuration and reinforcing. Only their location will differ. In other schedules beams that are similar will have similar designators. The schedule can be written either way.

The log of test borings is a form of schedule; valuable information is shown partly by graphic means and partly by notation, usually on the site plan or on one of the front drawings of the set. The test boring log is a graphic and written display of the underlying earth strata—the soil beneath the proposed structure. This information is essential to the contractor in the bidding procedure; the contractor must be familiar with the type of soil to be excavated and built on.

The rest of the schedules listed above follow the same format. The idea is to place a simple designator on the drawing that refers to the item's data in the schedule. The plan drawings locate the items; the elevations show the items in their proper location. All terminology, nomenclature, model numbers, sizes, and finishes are listed in the schedule.

ROOM FINISH SCHEDULE

NO.	SPACE NAME	FLOOR	BASE	WALLS MAT'L	WALLS FIN.	CEILINGS MAT'L	CEILINGS HT.	CEILINGS FINISH	REMARKS
1	VESTIBULE	Q.T.	NONE	QL./D.W.	V.FAB.	WD. DECK	±10'-0"	STAIN	
2 & 2A	ENTRY + ALCOVE	CARPET (N.I.C.)	VINYL	D.W.	PAINT	WD. DECK	±10'-10"	STAIN	
3	OFFICE	CARPET (N.I.C.)	VINYL	BLK/D.W.	NONE/PT	WD. DECK	±10'-10"	STAIN	
4	CLOSET	CARPET (N.I.C.)	VINYL	D.W.	PAINT	D.W.	8'-0"	PAINT	WD. SHELVES + ROD
5	WOMEN	V.A.T.	VINYL	D.W.	V.FAB.	M.F. D.W.	8'-0"	PAINT	
6	MEN	V.A.T.	VINYL	D.W.	V.FAB.	M.F. D.W	8'-0"	PAINT	
7	KITCHEN	CARPET (N.I.C.)	VINYL	D.W.	PAINT	D.W.	7'4"	PAINT	
8	DINING AREA	V.A.T.	VINYL	D.W.	V.FAB.	D.W.	8'-0"	PAINT	
9	MULTI-PURPOSE RM.	CARPET (N.I.C.)	VINYL	BLK/D.W.	NONE/PT	WD. DECK	±10'-10"	STAIN	
10	STAIR	CARPET (N.I.C.)	NONE	BLK/D.W.	NONE/PT	WD. DECK	VARIES	STAIN	STAIR TO HAVE 2 HR RATING
B1	EQUIP. ROOM	CONC.	NONE	BLK.	NONE	D.W. (2 HR.)	9'-10"	PAINT	2 HR. RATED CLG.
B2	AMBULANCE PARKING	CONC	NONE	BLK.	PAINT	D.W. (2 HR.)	9'-10"	PAINT	2 HR. RATED CLG.

(A)

Three types of room finish schedule are shown. In (A) the information is written in for each area. These data can also be transmitted by symbol (e.g., C for carpet), and it is often convenient to list all four walls of the room (finish materials may vary).

ROOM FINISH SCHEDULE

RM. NO.	ROOM NAME	Carpet	Thin Set Ceramic Tile	Exposed Concrete	Sheet Vinyl	4" Rubber Straight Wall Base	4" Rubber Cove Base	5/8" Drywall	Plaster	Thin Set Ceramic Tile	Exposed Concrete Block	5/8" Texture 1-11 Plywood	5/8" Firecode Drywall	Chair Rail	1/2" Drywall	Plaster	CLG HGT	REMARKS
		FLOORS				BASE		WALLS							CEILING			
65	KITCHEN							●							●		8'-0"	
66	ENTRY							●			●				●		8'-0"	
67	DINING ROOM	●						●							●		VARIES	
68	LIVING ROOM	●						●	●						●		VARIES	
69	VESTIBULE	●						●							●		8'-0"	
70	LAUNDRY		●					●							●		8'-0"	
71	TOILET		●							●					●		8'-0"	
72	BEDROOM	●						●	●						●		8'-0"	
73	CORRIDOR	●						●	●						●		8'-0"	
74	SHOWER		●							●					●		8'-0"	
75	TOILET		●							●					●		8'-0"	
76	TOILET		●							●					●		8'-0"	
77	VESTIBULE		●					●							●		8'-0"	
78	BATH		●							●					●		8'-0"	
79	TOILET		●							●					●		8'-0"	
80	SHOWER		●							●					●		8'-0"	
81	DOUBLE BEDROOM	●						●	●						●		8'-0"	
82	DOUBLE BEDROOM	●						●							●		8'-0"	
83	BEDROOM	●						●							●		8'-0"	
84	BEDROOM	●						●							●		8'-0"	
85	BEDROOM	●						●							●		8'-0"	
86	CORRIDOR	●						●						●	●		8'-0"	
B2	MECH. EQUIP. ROOM			●									●			●	8'-0"	

(B)

In (B) all materials entered in the heading and the dot indicator is placed in the correct material square for each area. This schedule can become rather bulky because of the large number of materials required on the job. Extra care must be taken to place the dot in the proper locations. Readability is sometimes difficult if the schedule is lengthy.

ROOM FINISHES

LOCATION	ROOM NO.	ROOM NAME	FLOORS MATERIALS	BASES MATERIALS	WAINSCOTS MATERIALS	WAINSCOTS HT	WALLS MATERIALS	CEILINGS MATERIALS	CEILINGS MTG	SUSP HT	COLOR SCHEME	REMARKS
FIRST FLOOR	101	STORAGE	4	4			2 / P	P	C		B	
	104	OFFICE	4	4			2 / P	3	F		B	
	105	UNASSIGNED	1		P		1	1	C		A	
	110	DAY CARE CENTER	2	1			2 / P	4	S	9'-0	C	
	115	NURSERY	4	4			2	3	S	8'-0	D	
	117	WOMEN'S TOILET	3		2		3 / P	5	P		E	
	118	JANITOR'S CLOSET	1				1 / P				F	
	119	MEN'S TOILET	3		2		3 / P	5	P		G	

Note: The numerical material designation takes precedence over the column location box.

ROOM FINISHES   KEY

① FLOORS		② BASES		③ WALLS		④ CEILINGS		⑤ CS	
A	CONCRETE	1		A	CONCRETE UNIT MASONRY	1		A	A
B	TERRAZZO	2	TERRAZZO	B	PLASTER	2	CONCRETE	B	B
C	CERAMIC TILE	3	WOOD	C	KEENE'S CEMENT	3	PLASTER	C	C
D	VINYL ASBESTOS TILE	4	CERAMIC TILE	D	5'-0 VINYL WSCT/PLASTER	4	FURRED ACOUS. TILE A	D	D
E	CARPET	5	VINYL	E	5'-4 CERAMIC TILE WSCT/PLASTER	5	SUSP. ACOUS. TILE A 9'-0	E	E
F		6		F		6		F	
G		7		G		7		G	
H		8		H		8		H	
J		9		J		9		J	

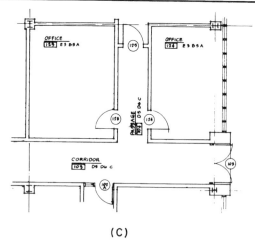

(C)

The two schedules in (C) were developed by the AIA Task Force.

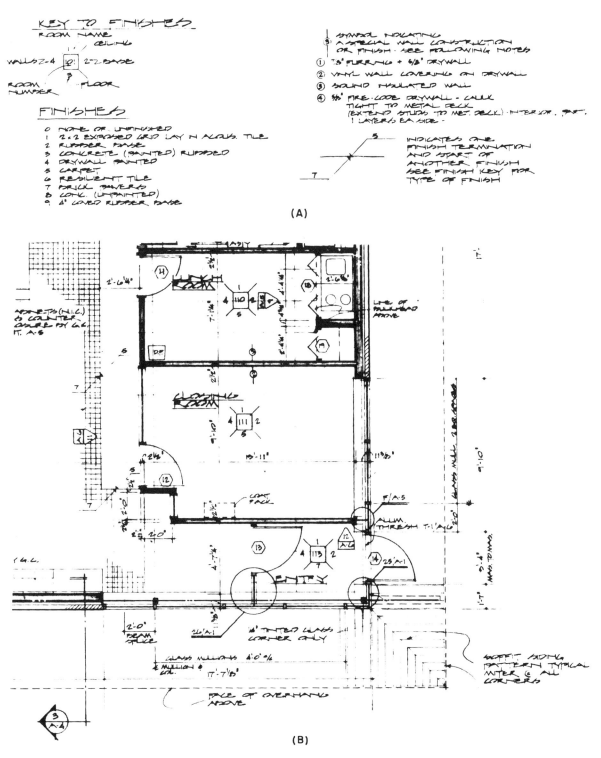

(A)

(B)

This example is a newer form of room finish schedule. It is really an adaptation of the old residential method of writing the finish data on the floor plan. This refinement uses a coded designator, as shown in (A), which is then placed in each area of the building. The code numbers are filled in as they apply. This is a simple and direct method of denoting finishes on a small project (B).

KITCHEN EQUIPMENT SCHEDULE

ITEM NO.	DESCRIPTION	ITEM NO.	DESCRIPTION
1	1 - PRESENT STEAMER, 3 COMPT., TO BE RESET.	37	1 - LOT FREEZER REFRIGERATOR SHELVING - PORTABLE
2	2 - PRESENT KETTLE, 50 GAL., TO BE RESET.	38	1 - VENT HOOD ABOVE DISHWASHER
3	1 - FLOOR DRIP PAN - PART TO BE REMOVED. ADD NEW END FC.	39	1 - SERVICE SINK, BY FC. TOWEL DISP. & WASTE CAN BY GC
4	1 - ROAST OVEN, 2 COMPT. CONVECTION TYPE	40	1 - LOT (4) SECTIONS STORE ROOM WIRE SHELVING
5	1 - RANGE - FOUR BURNER - CABINET BASE	41	SPARE NO.
6	2 - FRYERS - AUTO LIFT BASKETS W/TIMERS & DRAIN BETWEEN		
7	1 - GRILL ON STAND	42	1 - PLATE DISPENSER (4 STACK 10½" DIA.)
8	1 - COFFEE URN - TWO 6 GAL. JARS	43	2 - BOWL DISPENSERS (BOWLS IN D. W. RACKS)
9	1 - URN STAND	44	1 - CART FOR BEVERAGE DISPENSERS & BREAD
10	1 - PRESENT HOOD - ADD NEW FILTERS W/FRAMES & LIGHTS 14,000 CFM VEL, 2243 FPM	45	2 - CUP DISPENSERS (CUPS IN DISH W. RACKS)
11	1 - MIXER - 60 QT. W/VEG, SLICER	46	1 - PRES. MILK DISPENSER ON PORT. STAND
12	3 - CLEAN POT & PAN STORAGE CABINETS - PORTABLE	47	3 - COUNTER SERVING SECTIONS - PORTABLE
13	1 - DONUT FRYER W/DROPPER	48	1 - SPOON DISPENSER W/6 CYLINDER HOLDERS
14	1 - DONUT FRYER TABLE - PORTABLE	49	3 - COFFEE DISPENSERS - 5 GAL. EACH (THERMOS)
15	2 - CARTS - TWO SHELF	50	1 - CREAM DISPENSER - 2 QT., PUSH DOWN PUMP MODEL
16	3 - INGREDIENT BINS - ROLL UNDER COOKS TABLES	51	1 - CONVEYOR TOASTER, 1200 SL. PER HR. CAP., ELEC.
17	2 - COOKS TABLES	52	1 - STEAM TABLE - 2 PAN SERVING SHELF W/BREATH GUARDS - PORT.
18	1 - POT SINK W/DRAINBOARDS	53	1 - STEAM TABLE - 3 PAN SERVING SHELF W/BREATH GUARDS - PORT.
19	1 - SANITIZER FOR SINK COMPT. - ELECT.	54	1 - CART W/DISH BOXES FOR COLLECTION OF SOILED TABLEWARE
20	1 - DISHWASHER BOOSTER W/36 BOWL & CUP RACKS AND 6 PLATE RACKS	55	1 - CONDIMENT TABLE (BY OWNER)
21	1 - PRESENT DISPOSER, RESET IN TABLE AND NEW RINSE SPRAY O.M.	56	SPARE NO.
22	1 - SET SOILED & CLEAN DISH TABLES	57	SPARE NO.
23	2 - HAND WASHING LAV. BY F.C. TOWEL DISP. & WASTE CAN. BY GC.		
24	2 - TRAY TRUCK (CELL INMATES) W/COFFEE, SOUP & CREAM DISP.	58	1 - RANGE - ONE OVEN
25	2 - POT FILLER SWING FAUCETS W/SUPPORT BRACKETS	59	1 - HOOD W/FILTERS AND LIGHTS - (FAN AND DUCT BY VENT. CONT'R.)
26	1 - WORK TABLE - PORTABLE	60	1 - HAND WASHING LAV. BY F.C. TOWEL DISP. & WASTE CAN BY .....
27	1 - VEG. PEELER W/DISPOSER	61	1 - REFRIGERATOR - NORMAL TEMP.
28	1 - VEG. SINK AND DRAINBOARD	62	1 - WORK AND SERVING TABLE W/SNEEZE GUARD
29	1 - PRESENT ICEMAKER	63	1 - PRESENT TOASTER, 4 SLICE
30	1 - OFFICERS REFRIGERATOR	64	1 - WORK TABLE
31	1 - PRESENT SLICING MACHINE	65	1 - UTILITY SINK W/DRAINBOARD
32	1 - PREPARATION TABLE	66	1 - BEVERAGE TABLE W/CABINET BASE
33	1 - WORK TABLE	67	1 - CREAM DISPENSER - 2 QT. - PUSH DOWN PUMP MODEL
34	1 - TWO COMPT. WALK-IN REFRIGERATOR/FREEZER	68	1 - COFFEE DISPENSER - 3 GAL. (THERMOS)
35	1 - LOT COMPRESSORS AND REFRIGERATION EQUIP. FOR WALK-IN	69	1 - CART W/DISH BOX FOR SOILED TABLEWARE
36	1 - LOT REFRIGERATOR SHELVING - PORTABLE		

* SEE DRAWINGS & SPECIFICATIONS FOR ALTERNATE 'K-1'

(A)

Although the example is a kitchen equipment schedule (A), the principle can be applied in general. A large-scale plan (B) is used, and each item of equipment is numbered. These numbers on the plan refer to a line item in the accompanying schedule. Note also that the schedule was typed on special paper, which was then applied to the back of the drawing sheet.

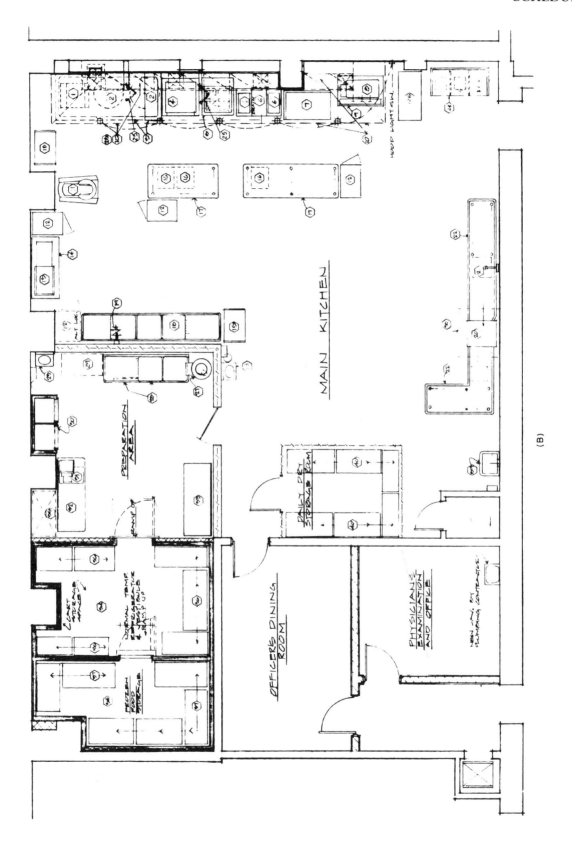

(B)

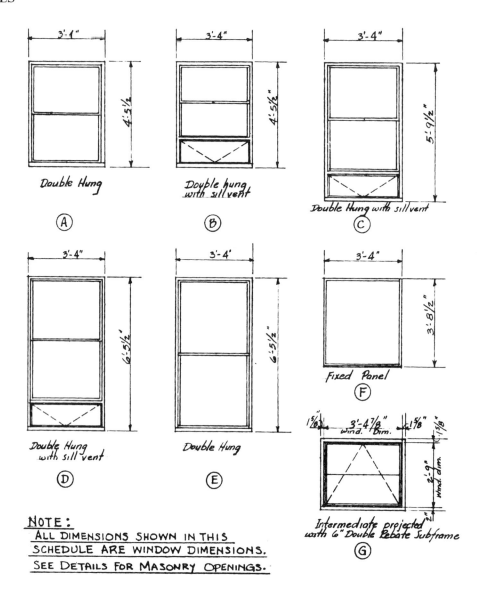

A — Double Hung — 3'-4" × 4'-5½"

B — Double hung with sill vent — 3'-4" × 4'-5½"

C — Double Hung with sill vent — 3'-4" × 5'-9½"

D — Double Hung with sill vent — 3'-4" × 6'-5½"

E — Double Hung — 3'-4" × 6'-5½"

F — Fixed Panel — 3'-4" × 3'-8½"

G — Intermediate projected with 6" Double Rebate Subframe — 3'-4⅞" wind. Dim. × 2'-9" wind. dim.

NOTE:
ALL DIMENSIONS SHOWN IN THIS
SCHEDULE ARE WINDOW DIMENSIONS.
SEE DETAILS FOR MASONRY OPENINGS.

WINDOW SCHEDULE
Scale: 3/8"=1'-0"

This graphic window schedule shows the elevation and size of the units as well as the operating and fixed sections. The designators are drawn on the building elevations and in some cases, especially when standard units are used, the model numbers of the units are listed.

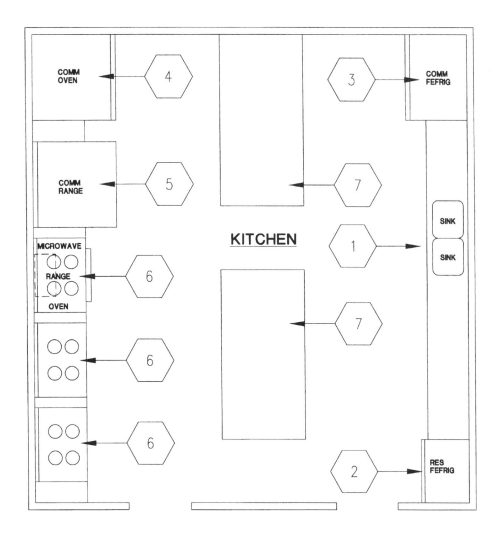

CAD drawing of a commercial kitchen, with equipment list.

NO.	QTY.	DESCRIPTION
1	1	DOUBLE BOWL SINK
2	1	RESIDENTIAL REFRIGERATOR
3	1	COMMERCIAL REFRIGERATOR
4	1	COMMERCIAL OVEN
5	1	COMMERCIAL RANGE
6	3	RES MICROWAVE/RANGE/OVEN
7	2	STAINLESS STEEL TABLE

DOOR SCHEDULE

DOOR NO.	TYPE	MATERIAL	DOOR SIZE W	H	T	DOOR FINISH	DOOR BUCK MAT'L	TYPE	THRESHOLD	REMARKS
1	A	H.M.	36"	80"	1¾"	PAINT	H.M.	C	ALUM.	'B' LABEL
2	A	H.M.	36"	80"	1¾"	PAINT	H.M.	C	ALUM.	'B' LABEL
3	B	WOOD-S.C.	36"	80"	1¾"	PAINT	WD.	B	NONE	
4	C	WOOD-H.C.	88"	80"	1⅜"	PAINT	WD.	A	NONE	BI FOLD
5	B	WOOD-S.C.	30"	80"	1⅜"	PAINT	WD.	B	NONE	
6	B	WOOD-S.C.	30"	80"	1⅜"	PAINT	WD.	B	NONE	
7	D	WOOD-S.C.	30"	80"	1⅜"	PAINT	WD.	D	NONE	
8	S.D.	ALUM.	90"	80"	-	BK. ENAMEL	-	-	ALUM.	SLIDER W/ ⅛" INSUL. GL.
9	B	H.M.	36"	80"	1¾"	PAINT	H.M.	C	NONE	'B' LABEL
10	B	H.M.	36"	80"	1¾"	PAINT	H.M.	C	NONE	
11	O.H.	ALUM.	192"	120"	-	NONE	WD.	-	NONE	OVERHEAD DR. W/ MOTOR OPR.
12	O.H.	ALUM.	132"	120"	-	NONE	WD.	-	NONE	OVERHEAD DR. W/ MOTOR OPR.
13	D	H.M.	42"	84"	1¾"	PAINT	H.M.	C	ALUM.	

(A)

(A), (B), and (C) are three types of door schedule. Basically, the same information is given in all, although the titles and numbers of columns vary. The first is rather complete for a fairly simple project. The second and third are similar; one is the CSI standard, the other is supplied by the AIA Task Force. All are fine examples of moderate-to-large projects. (D) is an example of a graphic schedule in which the door symbol on the plan refers directly to an elevation. The written schedules can also utilize the graphic elevations, usually by showing "type" of door.

CSI STANDARD DOOR SCHEDULE FORMAT

1	2	3	4	5	6A	6B	6C	7	8	9	10	11A	11B	11C	12	13
OPENING NUMBER	TYPE	MATL	CONSTR	LOUVER	DOOR — NOMINAL SIZE WIDTH PER LEAF	HEIGHT	THICKNESS	SPECIAL DETAIL	SILL DETAIL	TYPE	MATL	FRAME SECTIONS — HEAD (at wall)	JAMB (at wall)	SPECIAL	HARDWARE GROUP	REMARKS
101	A	WD			3'0	7'0	1¾		30/17	1	WD	1/17	2/17		1	
102	B	TG			3'0(4)	8'0	½	34/17	35/17	2	AL	4/17	5/17		2	Continuous Threshold
103	C	HM	A		3'6	7'0	1¾		36/12	3	CI	6/17	7/17		3	
104	D	Fab			12'0	8'0			37/17	1	WD	8/17	9/17		4	Folding Door
105	F	WD		A1	2'6	7'0	1¾	38/17	38/17	1	WD	1/17	2/17		5	Dutch Door
106	F	HM		B2	3'6(2)	8'0	1⅞	39/17	31/17	4	HM	10/17	11/17		6	
107	A	WD	HC		2'8	6'8	1⅞		30/17	1	WD	12/17	13/17		7	Transom Bar
108	C	HM			3'0	7'0	1¾		36/17	4	HM	14/17	13/17	14/17		Cased opening
109									30/17	5	HM	15/17	16/17		8	
110	A	WD	B	C4	3'0	7'0	1¾		38/17	4	HM	17/17	16/17			
111	G	WD	Spec		3'4	8'0	2¼	40/17	30/17	6	W	19/17	18/17		9	Sound proof
112	H	AL			3'0	8'0	2		35/17	7	AL	19/17	20/17	21/17	10	Relito

Column numbers are for reference only.

1. Opening Number
Number all openings individually. Numbering sequence should reflect floor number if possible.

2. Door Type
Use alphabetical designation for door types shown in elevations. Door elevations should show lights, configurations, or any other information.

3. Door Material
Indicate material from which door is constructed. HM-Hollow Metal, WD-Wood, AL-Aluminum, TG-Tempered Glass, K-Kalamein, P-Plastic Faced.

4. Construction
Designate information relating to core of door such as fire rating, sound rating or hollow core.

5. Louver
Indicate type with alphabetical designation and size with numerical designation.

6. Nominal Size
List nominal door sizes. Indicate head and jamb clearances in the specifications. Cover sill clearances by detail in column 8. ANSI clearances should be used if special conditions do not exist: 1/8" at head and jamb, 3/4" at sill.

7. Special Detail
Reference number for unusual door construction details such as dutch door shelf or panel over.

8. Sill Detail
Reference number for details of all sill conditions. Caution should be used in coordinating hardware and floor material specifications to this detail.

9. Frame Type
Use numerical designation for frame types.

10. Frame Material
Indicate construction material in the same manner as used in column 3 for door material.

11. Frame Sections
Show detail number of frame sections as conditions exist at the wall for both head and jamb. Indicate special detail numbers for conditions such as transom bars or special frame reinforcement.

12. Hardware Group
Indicate hardware by numerical designation.

13. Remarks
Use to bring attention to detail or special problem for contractor or supplier to coordinate, construct and install all doors and frames.

(B)

DOORS AND FRAMES

LOCATION	DOOR NO.	DOOR SIZE W	H	T	MAT	TYPE	GLASS	LOUVER W	H	FRAME MAT	TYPE	DETAILS JAMB	HEAD	SILL	FIRE RATING LAB	CON	HARDWARE SET NO.	KEYSIDE ROOM NO.	REMARKS
	101A	3-0	7-2	1¾	HM	N	¼ TEMP			AL	C	5/6	5	12			4	EXTERIOR	SIDE LITE ¼" TEMP. GLASS
	102A	3-0	7-2	1¾	HM	F		2-0	1-0	HM	A	1	1		B		6	107	
	102B	3-0	7-2	1¾	HM	F				HM	A	¼	1		B		6	107	
	103A	2-10	7-2	1¾	HM	V	¼ WIRE			HM	A	2	2			B	21	101	
	104A	3-0	7-2	1¾	HM	F				HM	A	3	3		C		22	108	
	104B	6-0	7-2	1¾	HM	G	¼ WIRE			HM	B	7/8	9	12			16	EXTERIOR	PAIR

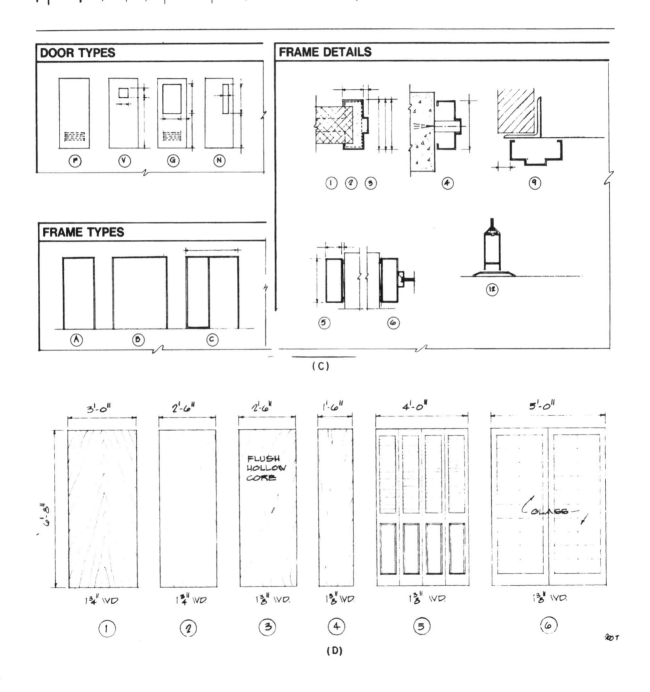

DOOR TYPES

F   V   G   N

FRAME TYPES

A   B   C

FRAME DETAILS

1 2 3   4   9

5   6   12

(C)

3'-0"   2'-6"   2'-6"   1'-6"   4'-0"   5'-0"

6'-8"

FLUSH HOLLOW CORE

GLASS

1¾" WD.   1¾" WD.   1⅜" WD.   1⅜" WD.   1⅜" WD.   1⅜" WD.

1   2   3   4   5   6

(D)

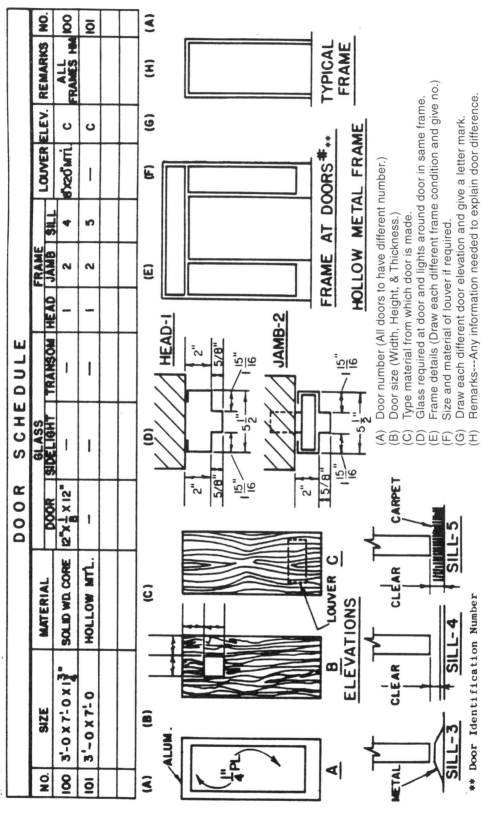

DOOR SCHEDULE

NO.	SIZE	MATERIAL	DOOR	GLASS SIDELIGHT	TRANSOM	FRAME HEAD	FRAME JAMB	FRAME SILL	LOUVER	ELEV.	REMARKS	NO.
100	3'-0 x 7'-0 x 1¾"	SOLID WD. CORE	12"x 1⅛ x 12"	—	—	1	2	4	8"x20 MTL.	C	ALL FRAMES HM	100
101	3'-0 x 7'-0	HOLLOW MTL.	—	—	—	1	2	5	—	C		101
(A)	(B)	(C)								(G)	(H)	(A)

(A) Door number (All doors to have different number.)
(B) Door size (Width, Height, & Thickness.)
(C) Type material from which door is made.
(D) Glass required at door and lights around door in same frame.
(E) Frame details (Draw each different frame condition and give no.)
(F) Size and material of louver if required.
(G) Draw each different door elevation and give a letter mark.
(H) Remarks---Any information needed to explain door difference.

HEAD-1

2" 5/8" 1 5/16" 5½"

JAMB-2

1 5/16" 5½"

2" 1 5/8" 1 5/16"

FRAME AT DOORS ✱✱

HOLLOW METAL FRAME

TYPICAL FRAME

LOUVER C

B
ELEVATIONS

A

ALUM.

¼"PL

CARPET

CLEAR

SILL-5

CLEAR

SILL-4

CLEAR

METAL

SILL-3

✱✱ Door Identification Number

Another format for a door schedule, both written and graphic.

421

FOOTING SCHEDULE

MARK	A	D	C	FTG. REINF.	BOT. ELEV.	COMMENTS
1	5'x5' FDTN	24"#	12"	6#4 E.W.	751'-0"	
2	10" WALL	22"	12"	5#5 CONT.	VARIES-SEE PLAN	
3	4' STL. PIPE	24"#	12"	NONE	750'-0"	
4						

· COLUMN · SCHEDULE ·

MARK	FTG. SIZE	REINF. (EA.WAY)	COL. SECT. TO FLR. SLAB	REINF. CONC. COL. TO ROOF	STL. COL. TO ROOF	BASE PL	ANCHOR BOLTS	CAP PL	REMARKS
1A	36"x36"x12"	6#4	12"x12"	4#5- TIES #2@12"	3½"x3½" □	4"x8"x½"	2'-12"x½"	4"x8"x¼"	4#5 DOWELS-10" ABOVE FLR
2A	50"x50"x15"	7#5	12"x12"	4#6- DO	4"x4" □	DO	DO	DO	4#6 DOWELS- DO
3A	DO	DO.	DO	4#5- DO	DO	DO	DO	DO	DO

· BEAM SCHEDULE ·

MARK	SIZE	REINFORCING		STIRRUPS (#3) SPACING	REMARKS
		ST. BARS	BT. BARS		
B1	12"x18"	2#5	–	–	NOTCH FOR MASONRY
B2	12"x24"	4#6	3#10	10.3", 2@7", 3@9", 3@12"	DO
B3	13½"x18"	2#5	–	–	DO
B4	12"x27"	4#9	3#9	2@5", 10.7", 3@9", 10.12"	

· LINTELS ·

MARK	NO. ON JOB	PROFILE	MEMBER(s)	BRG EA. END	REMARKS
L-1	7	⌐	L 5"x3"x5/16"	6"	
L-2	2	I	W8"x17-¼"R ON BOT.	8"	R-7½" WIDE
L-3	1	T	2L-⅛"x4"x3/8"	6"	
L-4	3	II	4"x8" PRECAST CONC.	8"	

LOG OF TEST BORINGS

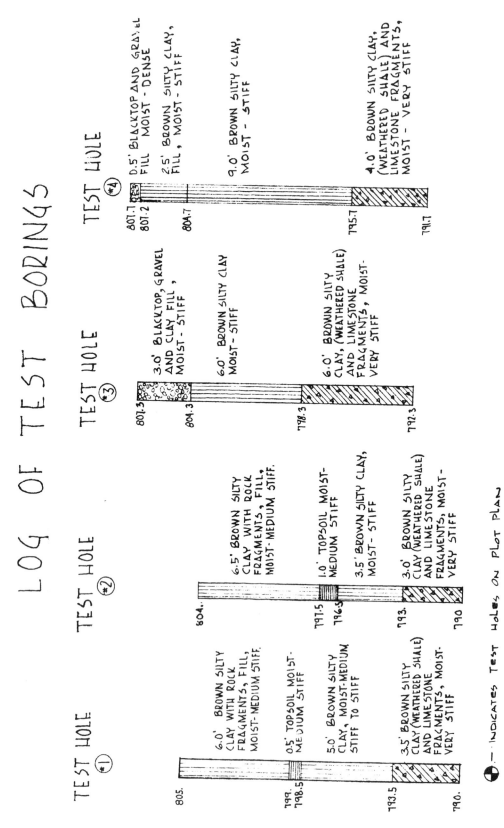

TEST HOLE (1)

- 805.
- 799. / 798.5
- 793.5
- 790.

6.0' BROWN SILTY CLAY WITH ROCK FRAGMENTS, FILL, MOIST- MEDIUM STIFF.

0.5' TOPSOIL MOIST- MEDIUM STIFF

5.0' BROWN SILTY CLAY, MOIST-MEDIUM STIFF TO STIFF

3.5' BROWN SILTY CLAY (WEATHERED SHALE) AND LIMESTONE FRAGMENTS, MOIST- VERY STIFF

TEST HOLE (2)

- 804.
- 797.5 / 796.5
- 793.
- 790

6.5' BROWN SILTY CLAY WITH ROCK FRAGMENTS, FILL, MOIST- MEDIUM STIFF.

1.0' TOPSOIL MOIST- MEDIUM STIFF

3.5' BROWN SILTY CLAY, MOIST- STIFF

3.0' BROWN SILTY CLAY (WEATHERED SHALE) AND LIMESTONE FRAGMENTS, MOIST- VERY STIFF

TEST HOLE (3)

- 807.3
- 804.3
- 798.3
- 792.3

3.0' BLACKTOP, GRAVEL AND CLAY FILL MOIST - STIFF

6.0' BROWN SILTY CLAY MOIST- STIFF

6.0' BROWN SILTY CLAY, (WEATHERED SHALE) AND LIMESTONE FRAGMENTS, MOIST- VERY STIFF

TEST HOLE (4)

- 807.7 / 807.2
- 804.7
- 795.7
- 791.7

0.5' BLACKTOP AND GRAVEL FILL MOIST - DENSE

2.5' BROWN SILTY CLAY, FILL, MOIST - STIFF

9.0' BROWN SILTY CLAY, MOIST - STIFF

4.0' BROWN SILTY CLAY, (WEATHERED SHALE) AND LIMESTONE FRAGMENTS, MOIST - VERY STIFF

⬤ - INDICATES TEST HOLES ON PLOT PLAN

A log of test borings is considered a schedule. The log gives the contractor the information necessary for bidding purposes and the structural engineer the data needed to design the foundation of the structure.

SCHEDULE OF LIGHT FIXTURES

MARK	MANUFACTURER	CAT. NO.	WATTS	FINISH	REMARKS
LF-1	LIGHTOLIER	7892C	200	ALUM.	
LF-2	DO	7893	300	WALNUT	
LF-2A	DO	7893T	300	–	TRIMLESS
LF-3	STONCO	4711-31	2@150	ALUM.	

(Above, following pages) These are examples of the type of information that will appear on the drawings and how it can be scheduled. The information can be presented much more easily in this form.

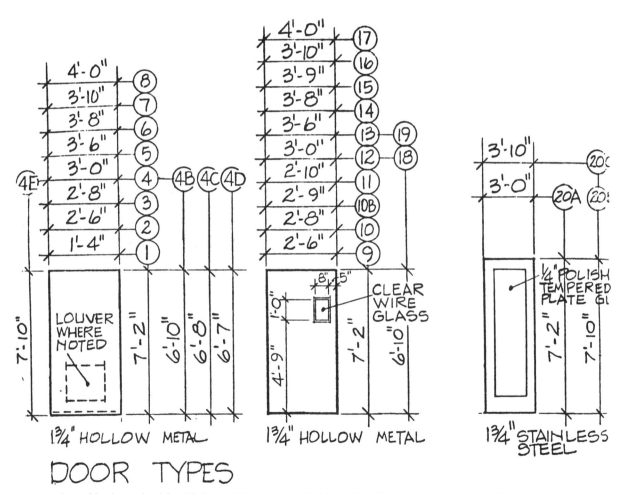

DOOR TYPES

A graphic door schedule with the variations in sizes depicted rather than placed in a written schedule; system is adequate for a small to moderate-sized project, but could prove problematic on a very large project with a great many variations.

PANEL BOARD SCHEDULE

M.D.P. 120/240 V, 1φ   SURFACE MTD.   600A BUS

Qty	Pole	Amp	Type	Description
3	1P	15A	CIR. BKR.	CIR. #4,12,13
4	2P	20A	CIR. BKR.	CIR.#8,9,10,11
2	2P	30A	CIR. BKR.	CIR.#6,7
1	2P	50A	CIR. BKR.	CIR.#1 LP"EM" CONNECT AHEAD OF MAIN C.B.
2	2P	225A	CIR. BKR.	CIR.#2-LPA,C; #3-LP"B"
1	2P	600A	CIR. BKR.	MAIN CIRCUIT BREAKER
3	2P	20A		SPACES

CONNECTED LOAD 101. KW

LP"A" 120/240 V, 1φ   SURFACE MTD.   225A BUS

Qty	Pole	Amp	Type	Description
18	1P	20A	CIR. BKR.	CIR'S #1 THRU 16, 19,20
2	2P	20A	CIR. BKR.	CIR. 17,18
6	1P	20A	CIR. BKR.	SPARE
2	1P			SPACE

CONNECTED LOAD 21.3 KW

LP"B" 120/240 V, 1φ   SURFACE MTD.   225A BUS

Qty	Pole	Amp	Type	Description
31	1P	20A	CIR. BKR.	CIR'S #1 THRU 31
3	2P	30A	CIR. BKR.	CIR. # 32,33,34
5	1P	20A	CIR. BKR.	SPARE

CONNECTED LOAD 52.4 KW.

LP"C" 120/240 V, 1φ   FLUSH MTD.   225A BUS

Qty	Pole	Amp	Type	Description
20	1P	20A	CIR. BKR.	CIR'S #1 THRU 18, 20,21
1	2P	50A	CIR. BKR.	CIR.# 19
6	1P	20A	CIR. BKR.	SPARE
2	1P			SPACE

CONNECTED LOAD 22.8 KW

LP"EM" 120/240 V, 1φ   SURFACE MTD.   100 A BUS

Qty	Pole	Amp	Type	Description
6	1P	20A	CIR. BKR.	CIR'S #1 THRU 6
1	2P	20A	CIR. BKR.	CIR #7 FIRE ALARM
2	1P	20 A	CIR. BKR.	SPARE
2	1P			SPACE

CONNECTED LOAD 6.8 KW

HEATING SYMBOL SCHEDULE

—H—	HOT WATER
—HR—	HOT WATER RETURN
ER	EXHAUST REGISTER
OA	OUTSIDE AIR
FTR	FIN-TUBE RADIATION
RR	RETURN REGISTER
UV	UNIT VENTILATOR
CD	CEILING DIFFUSER
(valve)	GATE VALVE
(valve)	BALANCING COCK
(valve)	THERMOSTAT CONTROLLED VALVE
(symbol)	THERMOMETER
T	THERMOSTAT, PNEUMATIC
Te	THERMOSTAT, ELECTRIC
TM	THERMOSTAT, DUAL, DAY-NIGHT PNEUMATIC
G	PRESSURE GAGE
RG	RETURN GRILLE

PLUMBING SYMBOL SCHEDULE

— - —	(CW) COLD WATER
— ·· —	(HW) HOT WATER
— — —	(V) VENT PIPING
————	(W) WASTE PIPING
— — — —	FOOTING DRAIN
————	STORM DRAIN
— — —	(HWR) HOT WATER RETURN
—G—	GAS PIPING
(valve)	CHECK VALVE
(valve)	GATE VALVE
(valve)	GLOBE VALVE
CO	CLEAN OUT
FD	FLOOR DRAIN
BWV	BACK WATER VALVE
VTR	VENT THRU ROOF
DS	DOWNSPOUT
RD	ROOF DRAIN
HB	HOSE BIBB

PLBG. FIXTURE CONNECTION SCHEDULE

FIXT NO	DESCRIPTION	W	V	CW	HW
P-1	WATER CLOSET	4"	2"	1¼"	-
P-2	WATER CLOSET	4"	2"	1¼"	-
P-3	URINAL	3"	1½"	1"	-
P-4	LAVATORY	1¼"	1¼"	½"	½"
P-5	SERVICE SINK	3"	1½"	½"	½"
P-6	WATER COOLER	1½"	1¼"	½"	-
P-7	SINK *	1½"	1¼"	½"	½"
P-8	SINK *	1½"	1¼"	½"	½"
P-9	SINK *	1½"	1¼"	½"	½"
P-10	SINK *	1½"	1¼"	½"	½"
P-11	KITCHEN SINK *	1½"	1¼"	½"	½"

* BY GENERAL CONTRACTOR

Area	Color	Prime Coat (1 Coat)	Finish Coat (1 Coat)
8.4 Interior - Toilet Rooms (above Ceramic tile), Locker Rooms, Lunch Room and Corridor			
1. Concrete block & concrete walls	Lime	P-3	F-3 (2 Coats)
2. Drywall walls	Lime*	P-4	F-3 (2 Coats)
*Note: Lime = Pratt & Lambert 3023, Sherwin-Williams BW-462, Glidden AC-399, PPG P-403, Foy-Johnston 11C11, Benjamin Moore 1-18.			
3. Ceiling	White	P-3	F-3
4. Piping	Match Adjacent Surface	P-5	F-3
5. Duct Work	Match Adjacent Surface	Spec. Etch. P-2	Wash & W-1, E-1 F-3
8.5 Interior - Back Rooms			
1. Produce prep area exposed col and downspouts Meat preparation room doors (except aluminum)	White	P-5	F-3
2. Ladders, handrails, stairs, and other metal (except aluminum)	K-750 Black	P-5	F-3
3. Stair risers to compressor room	Yellow	P-6	F-6
4. Bottle storage - Block walls	White	P-3	F-3 (2 Coats)
- Plywood walls	White	P-4	F-3 (2 Coats)
5. Fire exit lanes: Define lanes with a border each side of 3" lines spaces 44" apart (outside dimension). For location see Floor Covering Layout sheet.	White	---	F-6 (2 Coats)
6. Inspection stripe: 8" stripe on floor and 8" stripe on wall at base corner. For location see Floor Covering Layout sheet.	White	---	F-3 (2 Coats)

PARTITION SCHEDULE

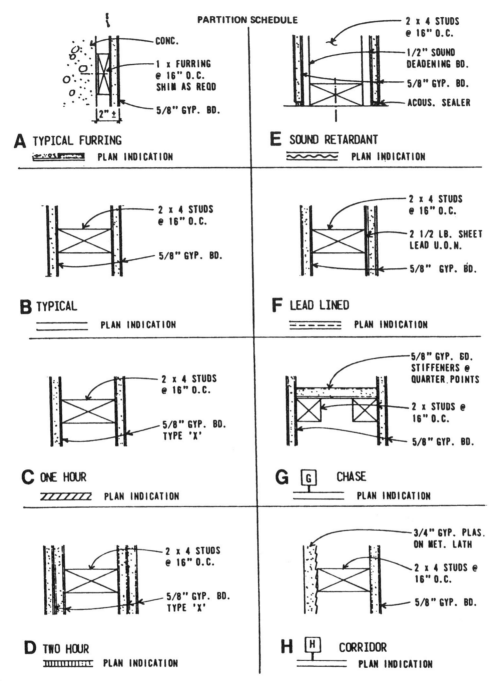

A TYPICAL FURRING — PLAN INDICATION

CONC.
1 x FURRING @ 16" O.C. SHIM AS REQD
5/8" GYP. BD.
2" ±

B TYPICAL — PLAN INDICATION

2 x 4 STUDS @ 16" O.C.
5/8" GYP. BD.

C ONE HOUR — PLAN INDICATION

2 x 4 STUDS @ 16" O.C.
5/8" GYP. BD. TYPE 'X'

D TWO HOUR — PLAN INDICATION

2 x 4 STUDS @ 16" O.C.
5/8" GYP. BD. TYPE 'X'

E SOUND RETARDANT — PLAN INDICATION

2 x 4 STUDS @ 16" O.C.
1/2" SOUND DEADENING BD.
5/8" GYP. BD.
ACOUS. SEALER

F LEAD LINED — PLAN INDICATION

2 x 4 STUDS @ 16" O.C.
2 1/2 LB. SHEET LEAD U.O.N.
5/8" GYP. BD.

G CHASE — PLAN INDICATION

5/8" GYP. BD. STIFFENERS @ QUARTER POINTS
2 x STUDS @ 16" O.C.
5/8" GYP. BD.

H CORRIDOR — PLAN INDICATION

3/4" GYP. PLAS. ON MET. LATH
2 x 4 STUDS @ 16" O.C.
5/8" GYP. BD.

Stone, Marraccini and Patterson
The partition schedule is a good way to preclude the use of large wall sections to show fairly simple partition construction. The small details are sufficient, and the addition of the applicable symbol is very handy.

- - - - - SCHEDULE OF HARDWARE SETS - - - - -

The following Notes apply where indicated in the SCHEDULE Chart below

a. Flushbolts installed on inactive leaf only
b. Flushbolts- manual type
c. Astragal only at double-egress doors
d. Astragal only required
e. Pivots required in lieu of butts
f. Double-acting closers required
g. Set shown is required for each leaf
h. Sound seals per door schedule
i. Lockset; Classroom function type- on active leaf
j. Dummy trim required inactive/narrow leaf
k. Surface bolts on room/interior side

1	2	3	4	5	6	7	8	9	10	11	12	13	14	15	16	17	18	19	20	21	22	23	24	25	26	Set Number
P	P	P	S	P	S	P	P	P	P	S	S	S	P	P	S	P	P	S	S	S	S	S	S			Single/Pair
HM	HM	HM	HM	HM	HM	HM	HM	HM	HM	HM	HM	HM	HM	HM	HM	HM	HM	HM	HM	HM	HM	HM	HM			Material
		X		X												X	X			X		X				Label
PAIR OF DOORS; NONLABELED	SHOP DOORS; NON-LABELED	SHOP DOORS; LABELED	EXIT DOORS; RIM DEVICE	CORRIDOR DOORS; LABELED	DOUBLE-ACTING DOORS	EXTERIOR PAIR; 2 EXIT DEVICES	EXTERIOR PAIR; ONE EXIT DEVICE	CONFERENCE ROOM; PAIR	EXTERIOR PAIR; NO EXIT DEVICES	EXTERIOR DOORS; NO EXIT DEVICE	NONLATCHING/LOCKING DOORS	NON-LATCHING DOORS	EXIT DOORS; EXPOSED VERT ROD	EXIT DOORS; CONCEALED VERT. ROD	EXIT DOORS; CONCEALED VERT. ROD	UTILITY ROOMS; NO LABEL; PAIR	UTILITY ROOMS; LABELED; PAIR	UTILITY ROOMS; LABELED	UTILITY ROOMS; NO LABEL	LABELED DOORS; NON-LOCKING	DOORS; NON-LOCKING	OFFICE DOORS; WITH LABEL	OFFICE DRS	ENTRANCE ASSEMBLIES	ENTRANCE ASSEMBLIES	Function
																							X	X	X	Hdwe by Dr/Mfr.
																									X	Cylinders Only
X	X	X	X	X	X*	X	X	X	X	X	X	X	X	X	X	X	X	X	X	X	X	X	X			Butts
	X	X						1	1	X						X	X	X	X			X	X			Lockset
																					X	X				Latchset
2		2	X	2		2	2	2	2	X	X	X	2	2	X	2	2	X		X	X	X	X			Door Stop[s]
X	X	X	X	X				X				X	X	X	X	X	X	X	X	X	X	X	X			Silencers
2	2	2	X		2*	2	1	1	1	X	X	X	2	2	X	2				X		X				Closer[s]
													X					X	X							Mop Plate
2					2																					Kick Plate
	2	X					1	1*	1*							X	X*									Flushbolts
								X*								X*	X*									Sound Seals
			X	2		2	1						2	2	X											Exit Device[s]
		X		X		*	*					.		1	1*											Astragal/Coordin
2					2							X														Push/Pull Set
						X	X		X	X																Weatherstrip'g
						X	X		X	X																Threshold
				X				1																		Hold-opens
2*																										Surface Bolt[s]
k	i	i			e. f, g	d	d	b, j, h	a				c			h	a, h									*- See notes above as listed at left

With most specifications being produced via computerized word processing, Finish Hardware Schedules, like the above and following, can be inserted directly into the Project Manual. The amount of information required in this schedule and the ease of revision, in a specifications format, is a great advantage over trying to produce this schedule by hand, or even as a schedule on the drawing sheet.

SCHEDULE OF FINISH HARDWARE MANUFACTURERS

Hardware Item	Manuf. Specified	Accept. Substitutes
Hinges	Hager	McKinney; Stanley
Lockset/Latchsets	Yale	Corbin-Russwin; Sargent; Schlage
Keying Systems		
Exit Devices	Yale	Von Duprin; Sargent Corbin-Russwin
Closers	Yale	LCN; Norton; Rixson
Stops; Holders; Bolts; Strikes	Ives	Glynn-Johnson; Trimco
Overhead Stops	Corbin	
Thresholds; Astragals; Weatherstripping;Drips	National Guard	Pemko; Zero Reese;
Coordinators	Glynn-Johnson	---
Push/Pull Plates; Bars Kick, Mop, Armor Plates	Trimco	Hiawatha; Brookline
Flushbolts [Head/Foot]	Ives	
Automatic Flushbolts	Hager	
Surface Bolts	Hager	
Hold-Open Devices [magnetic]	Rixson	----
Magnetic Locks	Security Engrg	---
Rain Drip	National Guard	---
Door Seals	Zero	---
Auto. Door Bottoms	National Guard	
Silencers	Glynn-Johnson	---

28

The Matter of Detailing

The detailing of a construction project must be properly done, neither short-changing nor overwhelming the work and the personnel involved. Detailing is a method of control—control by the design professional over exactly how the project will be constructed. Remember, everything shown on the contract drawings and included in the specifications become contract obligations of the contractor. The owner, in turn, is obligated to pay only for work done "according to the plans and specifications." Control, then, is essential.

Where detailing is lax, ambiguous, or nonexistent, the contractor(s) will attempt to fill in the information required, often without consulting the design professional. At this point control of the work is taken from the professional and is exercised by the contractor. This scenario is one that causes a good number of disputes, and even lawsuits. The lack of information, filled in by improper contractor decisions that are not consistent with the needs or requirements of a project, is the root source of such problems. In many cases, a design professional's attempted imposition of additional work to fill in the information gap, which usually involves a "discussion" of cost (who pays—the contractor or the owner?), leaving neither happy, is a cause of adversity on the project. This is not a good situation, nor should it be tolerated.

Whereas the professional is specifically prohibited from directing or advising about the construction means, methods, techniques, sequences, and procedures, the contractors carry the responsibility in those areas and are obligated, contractually, to construct the project as shown/described. Where the plans and specifications prove inadequate to their task, a contractor will move ahead as best he or she can in an effort to fulfill the contract. Hence, there is an inherent onus on the professional to produce not only proper but complete contract documents. This ensures the proper level of control over the project, as the client expects of the professional.

The basic function of detailing is to isolate restricted areas of the work and to depict them, usually at an enlarged scale, so that specific work area or item is revealed and the intended construction, requirements, and methods are noted. The details are extracted from smaller-scale drawings, which show their locations, but not the degree of specific information required to construct the work. This is in full accord with the construction

433

axiom "The specific rules the general; detail rules concept."

Fundamentally, detailing entails (1) what to show, (2) how to show it (as to scale and scope of the drawing), and (3) where to stop. The last determination is difficult because it is a learned process and something that cannot be taught. Actually, only field experience and knowledge will allow one to stop detailing at the appropriate point and permit workers to provide the minute, final "how-to" to complete the detailed work. For example, rarely is every nail shown on the drawings; usually nails are shown only where their placement and number are critical, as in the gusset plate joints of trusses. Sizes and numbers of fasteners are not included *unless* they are so vital to the success of the detail that a selection must be made by the design professional. Here, for example, custom cabinetwork may be detailed in general because a subsequent shop drawing will be submitted review. The contractor and supplier, however, are responsible for the correct size, fit, and construction of the work involved (as per the General Conditions), which includes selecting and using the proper fasteners.

The knack of "stopping" is something one must learn, as going too far may confuse, add unnecessary cost (by requiring extraordinary understanding, change of procedure, and/or effort), and increase the liability of the professional. The more that is shown, the greater the risk to the professional; where such "showing" is faulty, the professional will find added responsibility and need for remedy on his or her part.

Trade workers, in the main, are trained and taught to perform their work. No contracting firm will purposely risk the cost of ineffective and poor workmanship by its personnel. Yet too often workers are made into "do-it-alls," whereby they are told to perform varying tasks from day to day, often outside their basic expertise. Of course, many persons can perform a multitude of tasks, but not necessarily up to the standards required on a construction site. The more the workers are so directed, the greater the risk involved (for the contractor) and the greater the need for accurate detailing (control) by the professional. In larger communities, however, the trades are rather distinctly defined, and workers work only within their own fields of expertise and prescribed duties. In this case, they know the correct methods to be employed to produce quality and proper work and are usually supervised by competent persons who are knowledgeable and experienced in the work. Moreover, they know where and when to seek help if necessary. Neither the contractor nor his or her superintendent will ever try to do more than required; some will try to do less. For the most part, however, they will perform as required by contract, as this is in their best interest overall. Likewise, the design professional's personnel must also work within their fields of expertise. They should not seek to control the project by detailing to such a finite degree that the project is stifled, progress is impaired, costs are inflated, and the project imperiled in other ways. There is no need for any architectural drawing to show doorknobs, hinges, pulls, fasteners, decorative features, or similar items, except where some very specific requirement is involved. Then only general depiction is required, not detailed drawings of the fittings.

Correct or proper detailing is not so much the showing of everything as it is the showing of the essential elements of the construction. Most professionals acknowledge and respect the expertise of the contractors' personnel and use this as the line of departure—the juncture at which further detailing is suspended. The contractor must be permitted the opportunity to incorporate his or her expertise, methods, means, and procedures into the work. Hence, the professional is not involved in the size, placement, and proper installation of every item. Quite often the contractor will use methods of construction or installation that are not what the professional envisioned. However, this does not necessarily make them wrong per se, but simply another way of doing things. More often than not, these methods are equal to, or even superior to, those the professional might use or anticipate; there are usually many ways to solve a given problem. However, where the professional believes that a distinct and specific methodology is required, this must be conveyed to the contractor—that is, detailed. This interplay is not, and should not be perceived as, the professional's "giving up" authority or control, but rather as the meshing of the expertise of both professional and contractor to the benefit of the client's project. At best, it will foster a conversation that benefits the project; it brings the parties to a common ground and understanding. With the vast number of materials, systems, devices, equipment, apparatus, and so forth, on the market for construction use, this combining of expertise is really crucial to a successful project. Usually it will produce the best possible solution.

There is also interplay between the professional and the manufacture of a material, system, or device. This is usually effected through the manufacturers' representatives or sales personnel and the time, literature, and knowledge that is given the professional regarding a specific product and its use on the project. Sources such as Sweet's Catalogs provide a passive array of information, and a product often entails a number of installation possibilities. These may all be valid and correct, but are usually not universal (for every installation); in the main there is one good and proper method for the condition under consideration. Here the professional must seek out this information, possibly through personal contact, assess its impact on the project, adjust where necessary or advisable, and then proceed to detail the installation in a method deemed to be "correct" in the view of the professional. This is the point at which the professional's expertise and experience come into balance with the liability risk.

This is also the point at which the professional engages the prevailing standard of care: "Is this the right thing to do? Is this what the prudent person would do?

In many cases, "overdetailing" arises directly from this procedure. The professional, in "making sure," will add extra work, devices, products, or other items to ensure proper and lasting installation and workability of the product, construction, or equipment detailed. Here, often, needless cost is added for no real return, except added peace of mind and assurance. Not every sales "pitch" should be accepted outright; the professional must make very judicious decisions concerning any additions that are required and give them consideration only where the perceived installation appears to be marginal or outright faulty in the professional's view. This interplay is particularly important today given that new materials and products appear on the scene almost daily; just keeping up is a difficult task. Some of the new product lines are not well thought out nor engineered to meet the variety of conditions they may encounter. In addition, mass-produced materials and systems are not intended to fit every project situation exactly. Professional expertise and experience are the key (and only) factors in assessing, adjusting, coordinating, incorporating, and resolving this situation; "making things better" is a professional function.

Where that function is deemed necessary, it is incumbent upon the professional to detail, precisely, what is required; this includes appropriate adjustments in the specifications where necessary. All this must be done carefully, inasmuch as the professional too has not been exposed to "every condition" and can therefore create problems by unwittingly overlooking the good features of a product or material. Although the effort to make things better is sincere, the result can be disastrous. Obviously, this is but one place where the professional fully "earns his or her money."

Generally, contractors are aware of most of the materials and products presented to them via the contract documents. Of course, they too are not omnipotent and often encounter unfamiliar constructions and installations. Here they must forego any hint of egotism and seek the expertise and help they need. This also means that the superintendent on the job must accept the fact that he or she cannot always know and do everything; seeking help, here, is not a sign of weakness. Following instructions is vital and necessary particularly where the details vary from the manufacturer's printed instructions. And many times materials are merely shipped to a job site for installation by inexperienced personnel—a situation that bears watching. More and more manufacturers are requiring that their products be installed by licensed or franchised personnel who have been "factory-trained" and have a stake in correct installations.

Both professional and contractor must take great care that their determinations do not deteriorate into off-hand comments such as, "I don't like that," "I wouldn't do it that way," or "That'll never work." Such untested assertions cannot substitute for a good-faith effort on the part of the manufacturer to achieve good and predictable results, especially where calculation and/or testing has ensued. Good practice dictates that all project personnel (professional and contractor) consult with the manufacturer where changes in the detail or installation seem prudent.

Although the final results on the contract drawings may belie the fact, detailing is a very involved process. It is actually an ongoing event that continues even during the actual construction activity. In the following text, this concept (and the resulting process) is analyzed and depicted in its entirety. Its pervasive nature is quite apparent, as well as the fact that detailing is not a "busywork" chore that has relatively little impact on a project. To

To demonstrate the type and level of information required in construction documents (drawings and specifications), let us assume that we have $25 to spend. We can enter a clothing store, for example, and act in any of the following ways:

- Ask the clerk to give us $25 worth of merchandise, without asking for anything specifically (the choice is left to the clerk).
- Ask for some type of shirt or top (nothing specific about type, style, material, etc.).
- Ask for a sports shirt (again, nothing about material, type, sleeve, color, etc.).
- Ask for a long-sleeved sports shirt with a regular collar (better, but several features still missing).
- Ask for a long-sleeved, regular collar, cotton, plaid sports shirt (still more is required).
- Ask for a long-sleeved, regular collar, cotton, red plaid sports shirt, size medium.
- Ask for a long-sleeved, regular collar, cotton, red plaid sports shirt, size medium, by Arrow, Van Heusen, or Manhattan.

Need we ask anything more?

Notice that we retain the right to make the final decision about the cost of the shirt. There may be several such shirts, and some may exceed $25 in cost. In that event what do we do?

This example may seem simplistic, but it gives us a good idea of what can happen when information is lacking and decisions are left to other people. There can be a lack of control, dissatisfaction with the final choice, or added cost for no particular good reason.

Imagine now that the $25 is your client's, and you, by virtue of being hired as the architect, are in a position to go out and spend that money. Can you see how giving up control and not providing enough information can lead to your client's dissatisfaction with the result—and with your services!

the contrary, the best of design concepts will fail where detailing is not faithful, proper, and adequate. Even where the design concept's overall appearance survives and is reasonably achieved, the "close-up view" and working life of the project will likely suffer where detailing is ill-conceived, inappropriate, faulty, or deteriorated.

Perhaps the most important element of the working drawings concerns the detailing of the construction parts. The construction documents form a framework and, in general terms, exercise control. They also define the work to be done. Details, however, are necessary to provide the individual tradesperson with special information regarding his or her own part in the project. In many other areas of the working drawings it is the

creativity of the designer that is paramount, but nowhere is the actual construction more involved than in the details, in which the various pieces of material are fitted together to complete the design concept.

Many different sources trigger the need for details. The scope of the work is one, although the general items will dictate some of the detailing. Another important source is field observation and experience. Here a knowledge of what will and will not work is helpful. Of course, the details must reflect the latest product changes and the latest technology that concern construction and testing programs.

The detail cycle begins with the project itself, and the details originate with the execution of the design. The design is a major generator of details. How can this building or project be fitted together to reflect the design? The field work and the actual construction changes caused by unknown field conditions also call for details. We must start a design with a concept and a definition of a detail which, in turn, will produce some basic rules for development.

In the development stage we put these rules into action and begin to recognize the factors that will control the details. It is vital that we coordinate them with the specifications. It is also vital that we coordinate the activities of the structural and mechanical engineers, the field supervisor, and other consultants. This coordination means not only the collection of information but its collation and, at some point, its evaluation.

The final stage is the actual documentation and the confirmation of the details. Their formats must be discussed: how will the interplay between methods work, and how can the cycle contribute to a retrieval system?

Breaking down each of these parts is comparable to analyzing a diagram. The diagram may be simple, but each component that forms the whole is composed of many facets. Between concept and definition we must come to grips with methods and materials to be used in the project. We must be concerned with the new products, assemblies, and components that are constantly being introduced on the market. Every office must be aware of new construction techniques and of the revisions that occur almost daily. It is important that the project be detailed in such a way that

The Detail Cycle

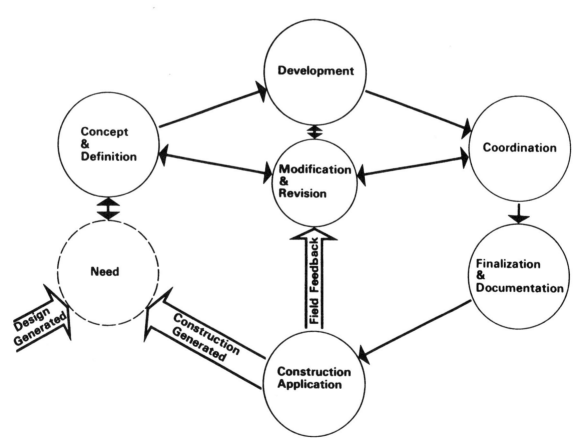

The Detail Cycle, as devised by D. R. Roggenbach (see Preface), shows the entire process that must be resolved in order to detail a project. Other illustrations in this chapter describe the finite parts of the several elements presented here.

prevailing local practices will not preclude good execution of the work. While attending to the new items that come along, we must consider current conditions. Changes are ongoing; coding agencies may be testing certain materials and methods or perhaps exercising prohibitions against them. The liability for the detailing should be considered: What can we do safely? What is currently being done, and how can we modify it?

The key to concept and definition is acquired by experience. Experience teaches a pattern of solutions to problems that have occurred in earlier projects. A poor choice of materials or the selection of an inferior method provides a background for future choices and selections. Here the professional must consider selection of new materials as opposed to reusing an existing system. There

is always a risk in using new materials. Complete test results and a full range of information are not always available. Expertise goes hand in hand with experience to evaluate the durability of a product and its impact on the total design concept. How does this particular material test out in projected longevity? And, of course, how does the material stand up under a cost analysis?

The final factor in the concept is a constant that joins the design and the development of detailing. Field feedback must be recognized. The detail under contemplation must really prove to be worthy as well as efficient. This knowledge is gained only by experience in the field. Arguments are expounded to prove the value of a product or technique, but both rationale and product can fail when applied in the field. A fast and factual

Concept & Definition

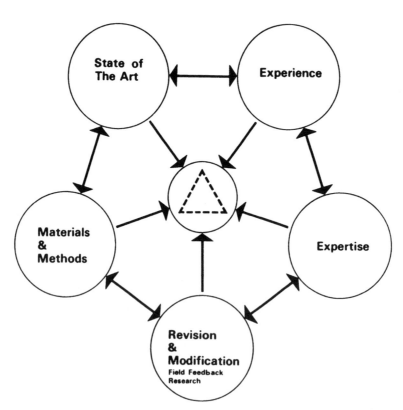

The Detail Cycle

The process here is involved with the concept and definition of detailing. The basic design of the project coupled with the other parts begins to define type and scope. Also included are the current-practice factor and element of experience (feasibility of the details).

performance analysis is needed to evaluate the detailing. This need suggests a reporting system by which everyone concerned with the project will be reached. It will inure to the benefit of all. If the information on the contribution of a particular detail is fed back from the field to the designer, its inherent faults and the necessary changes can be categorized.

In the development of the design cycle the various factors of the project begin to appear. How does the detail fit into the aesthetic quality of the project? What does the designer want this particular detail to accomplish? How suitable and how compatible are the materials? Are extreme care and excessive amounts of time required to make these materials work together? Are they, indeed, capable of working together easily?

Climate is a constant consideration. What is the setting for the project? Are there extremes of heat and cold? Wetness and dryness? Will the detail be heavily affected by weathering?

Another parameter is the coding agency. What is the current status of the materials? Have they been approved? What stipulations, if any, accompany the approvals? Are waivers or variances required?

The feasibility of the detailing must also be examined. What are the tolerances of the materials? Do they present a complicated fabrication problem? Can the detail be unitized to make a larger assembly possible? Will the detail be costly because of complicated fabrication?

Finally, there is the body of uncodified knowledge derived from experience. Are there skilled workers available to execute this detail? This consideration, in fact, governs one aspect of the

Development

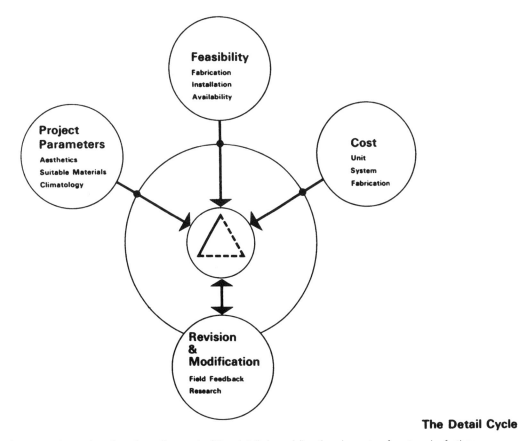

The Detail Cycle

The development phase describes the refinement of the details by adding the elements of cost and a further investigation of how a detail works within the project requirements.

CONSTRUCTION ADMINISTRATION FEEDBACK TO DESIGN/SPECIFICATIONS

DATE: _____

PROJECT: _____

CHANGE TO: (Design) (Specifications) (Other _____)

                (Standard Detail) (Special Detail, No. _____)

ITEM DESCRIPTION: _____

_____

_____

_____

_____

PROBLEM: _____

_____

_____

RECOMMENDED CORRECTION (Attach sketches as necessary): _____

_____

_____

_____

_____

_____

_____

_____

_____

_____

_____

Distribution: Design Coordinator – 2 copies
               Specifications Department
               Construction Administration

_____
                         Signature

Ahern, MacVittie, Hofmann & Goodwin, Ltd.
A sample form that should be in every office manual, as it provides for feedback on any aspect of a project. This is vital in use of standard detailing and is an asset in every phase of work, as it can document the mistakes or problems encountered on a project and can help prevent them in the future.

entire project design. Many towns are known as concrete or steel towns. Over the years the contractors in these towns, as well as the design professionals, have produced much of the design work by one particular construction method; most of the buildings are concrete or steel frame. Sometimes, when a new project comes along, out-of-town contractors will be called in, thus upsetting the sequence. Are we prepared to have projects subjected to additional steps of coordination? The labor market must be given thought in the course of detailing.

For installation we must take into account the size and shape of the materials the project can accept. In regard to access, how approachable is the job site? Will the required handling devices have the necessary room to work? What types of construction methods are involved? Will the contractors and workers know the tolerances with which they must work? And, most important of all, is there an adequate explanation of the detail? This is not to say that a paragraph must be written to clarify the designer's intentions, but there should be enough information available to forecast the result. The workers must know exactly how to approach the work and how they are to execute any particular part of the construction.

A recurring problem is the availability of materials and possible delays in delivery. Both availability and delay change frequently in short time frames. It may be that a material in low demand with a fast delivery status only six months ago has now become critical, with a long delay for promised delivery. The base materials reflect the market in cost and supply. It is often necessary to order structural steel even before the drawings are complete. The lead time for delivery to the site can then be evaluated and coordinated.

Cost becomes a factor in development. Can a particular unit be used in place of an entire system? Frequently one method or another is more valuable than the detail. The cost of materials directly influences their selection. Again, individual expertise must be used to advantage in the choice of materials and the control of costs. Runaway fabrication costs can destroy that choice. All workers are reluctant to attempt new or different processes with familiar materials, much less with unfamiliar items; to create either situation promises a nasty construction problem.

Revision and modification are constant, resulting from both field feedback and construction research. Until this point in the project draftsmen, designers, or project architects have been detailing the pieces of construction without much input from the other disciplines. Coordination must be ongoing! Filed feedback reports and construction research are an immediate input. If a process or technique does not work, the information must be sent back to the drafting room, so that other projects may use a different system of detailing or different materials and techniques.

The architect is the key to the design team and really its leader. Therefore he or she must organize the activities of all other consultants on the project; for example, the mechanical engineer may have large machinery to handle and a mammoth amount of ductwork and piping. The routing of these items and their positioning must be taken into account in the overall design and detailing. Sufficient space, though never overabundant, must be provided. How does the mechanical work influence the detailing? What must be done if a building is to be electrically heated? The choice of heating system will guide wall detail selection, for more insulation will be used. Orientation of the area is also a consideration; vapor barriers may be required.

The same investigation is made for details employed in sound control. What type of building does the owner want? A building with greater than normal sound control? What rooms must be kept private? The answers to these questions will dictate what can be done in the detailing as well as in the mechanical trades. Therefore, there is no avoiding coordination.

The same thing happens in the electrical system. What does the owner want? What kind of electrical equipment? Audiovisual? What type of illumination and at what lighting levels? How does this affect the detailing? The answer can influence the selection of paint; lighter colors are better light reflectors. What type of special lighting? Emergency? Control in the choice of fixtures should be exercised for practical and aesthetic reasons. If we do not coordinate, we may never know until the fixtures are delivered that a choice was inappropriate.

Structure must go hand in glove with the other elements. A column cannot be allowed to rise in the middle of a private office! Sometimes systems must be juggled. New column lines may be added to improve the overall design. It would be helpful if all structural systems could take the form of a grid: a column at each intersection and rectangular or square bays. Most of the time, however this is not the way it is.

The design professional must remain flexible to meet any situation. There could be a need for other consultants in varying fields, from roofing to acoustics, food service, material handling, and radiation. The project and its details must be clearly worked out and must be coordinated with all the other disciplines.

It is most important to understand that in a complicated building the coordination problem is acute. It makes no sense at all to have a well-designed, well-conceived building, only to fail functionally because coordination was lacking. At this point, the architect must look back at the project and at his or her own staff. The architect must review the scope of the job, its definitions and limitations, and examine the budget and the projected costs. He or she must remain within the contract's bounds of liability. This looking-within is important. It is a system of checks and balances on the producing office and must extend to the offices of the numerous consultants.

After all this has been done, still more of the architect's attention is required. He or she must ensure that drawings, details, and specifications have been properly coordinated. Do the specifications include the materials detailed? Do the specifications discuss the materials in the same context as they appear on the drawings? Do the documents

Coordination

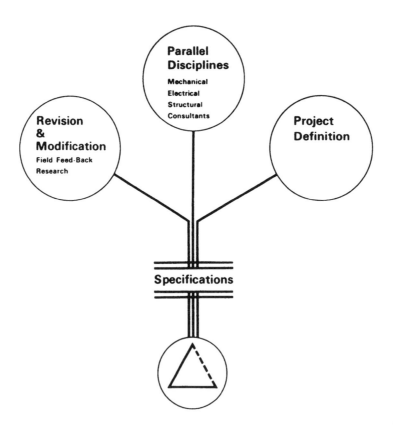

The Detail Cycle

No detail stands or works in total isolation. Coordination is most important to ensure that every detail works with its surroundings, and with the work of other disciplines. Also, the work and requirements of the detail must be reflected and incorporated into the specifications, in a proper manner.

Finalization & Documentation

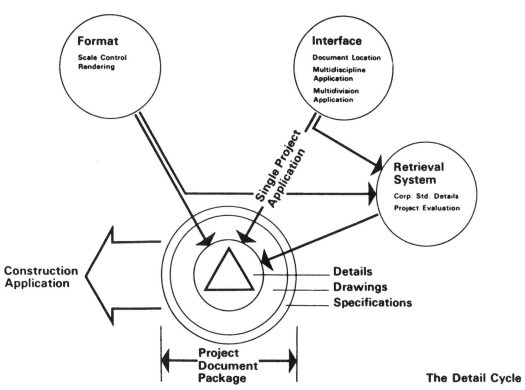

The last element in the cycle incorporates finalization and documentation. Thought must be given to the presentation of the detail its placement in the document package, its value to future projects, and its qualifications for a place in the retrieval system.

indeed parallel one another? One should provide information that the other does not, without overlaps, contradictions, or confusion.

The project architect must also be aware of standard details. Is there a retrieval system, either manual or automatic? Are computer graphics available? All of this is coordination! As much time can be devoted to coordination as to detailing, but it is time well spent.

In documentation the initial step is the format, which incorporates several decisions. Are the details to be hard-lined (drafted) or freehanded? What are the advantages and disadvantages of each method for this particular project? If the details can be projected in sufficient size, freehanding will work. Again, in an office that lacks freehand background experience it is difficult to work a job without handling the drawings. This

could be a definite penalty; it deserves evaluation.

What about dimensioning? How much dimensioning? How much do we show? How much do we rely on standard components? How much control do we need over fabrication? In some instances we will be detailing standard systems. To give special attention to standard items coming from the factory is a foolish practice. At the same time, enough information must be provided to allow complete installation.

Once the details have been analyzed and brought to this point, we must determine how they are fitted into the construction documents. Will there be a series of drawing sheets to show the details, or will they be reproduced on $8\frac{1}{2} \times 11$ sheets and bound in a "detail book" or project manual? It is important that this format be worked out ahead of production so that it is not re-

443

duced to a helter-skelter situation. Indecision leads to further problems throughout the job. We must also look for multidisciplined development, in which more than one operation is concerned with a particular detail. The retrieval system has a tremendous impact on finalization. What about standard details? Will they be transparencies pasted to the sheets? Is some kind of photography to be used? What is the system, and how are the sheets composed?

We must learn to identify details with some sort of numbering system. Shall we use a system from the Construction Specifications Institute (CSI)?

We can have our own basic sequence; details can be numbered consecutively throughout the project.

Again, it is important that costs be considered. For the retrieval system we must determine whether a detail can be employed in other projects. If so, it must become part of the system as input.

The design cycle is not simple; it is usually the heart of the project. It must be considered in the design concept within the capabilities of the office. Details must be cross-referenced with all trades to produce a well-executed project.

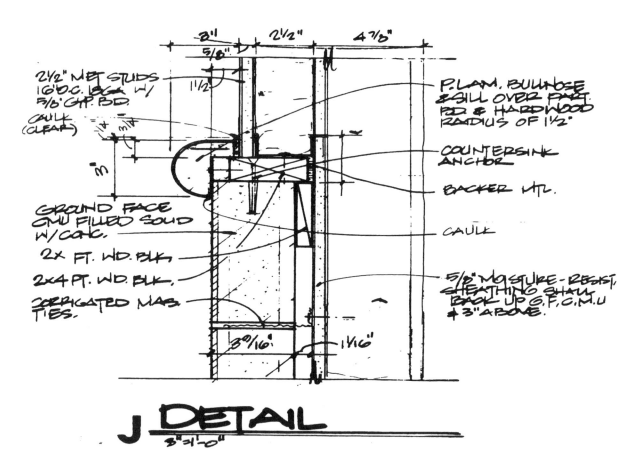

CONSIDER: 1. How is the radius trim attached to the wall?
2. How and when is the plastic laminate applied to the wood radius trim?
3. Can you identify and note the use of the items not described in this detail?
4. What alternative(s) can you offer for this detail to clarify these issues and to make a more workable detail?
5. Do you understand the notes, etc. on this detail?

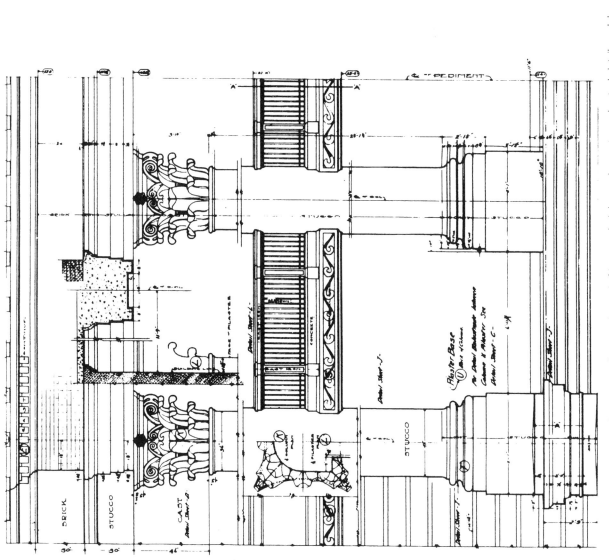

An interesting set of drawings (above, next) to see how drafting needs, job requirements, and actual detail work has changed. CAD, of course, would add another exmaple in yet another format.

445

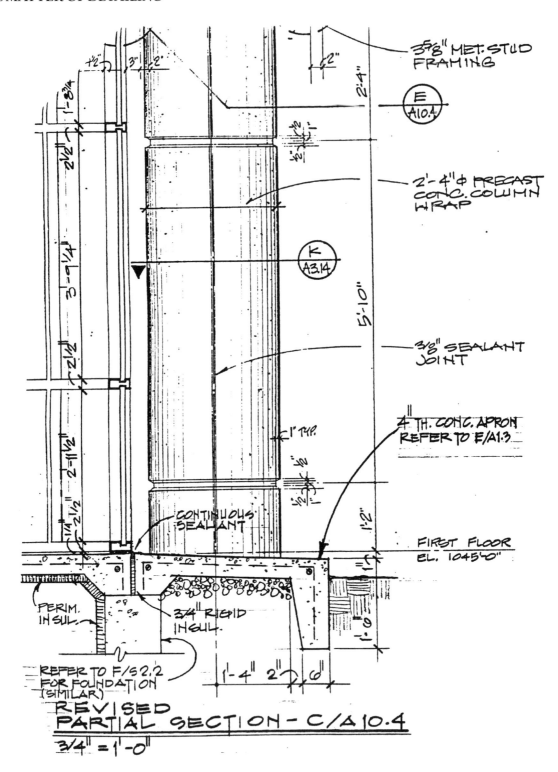

REVISED
PARTIAL SECTION - C/A10.4
3/4" = 1'-0"

446

DETAILER NOTES

*1. GIVE DIMENSION – VERIFY AMOUNT OF
     DEFLECTION W/ STRUCTURAL DEPARTMENT

*2. GIVE INSUL. TYPE OR NUMBER FOR CLOSURE
     MATERIAL AT TOP OF WALL AND AROUND JOIST
     (OR REMOVE FROM DETAIL IF NOT REQUIRED)

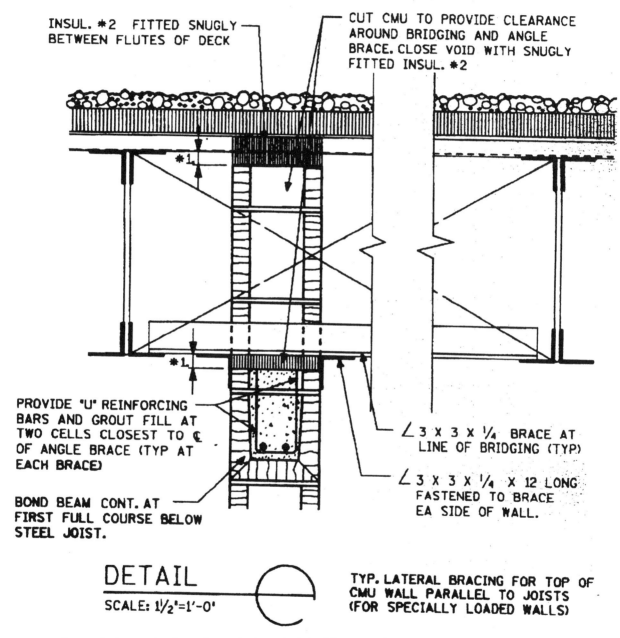

INSUL. *2 FITTED SNUGLY
BETWEEN FLUTES OF DECK

CUT CMU TO PROVIDE CLEARANCE
AROUND BRIDGING AND ANGLE
BRACE. CLOSE VOID WITH SNUGLY
FITTED INSUL. *2

PROVIDE "U" REINFORCING
BARS AND GROUT FILL AT
TWO CELLS CLOSEST TO ℄
OF ANGLE BRACE (TYP AT
EACH BRACE)

BOND BEAM CONT. AT
FIRST FULL COURSE BELOW
STEEL JOIST.

∠ 3 X 3 X ¼ BRACE AT
LINE OF BRIDGING (TYP)

∠ 3 X 3 X ¼ X 12 LONG
FASTENED TO BRACE
EA SIDE OF WALL.

DETAIL

SCALE: 1½"=1'-0"

TYP. LATERAL BRACING FOR TOP OF
CMU WALL PARALLEL TO JOISTS
(FOR SPECIALLY LOADED WALLS)

An excellent example of a well-executed standard detail from a professional office. This depicts a condition that occurs often, and thus the detail is well suited for repetitive use. Note the attention given the Detailer by pointing out questions must be asked, before using the detail. These address project conditions that will vary. This approach ensures proper application of the detail and adapts it specifically to the conditions of the project at hand.

447

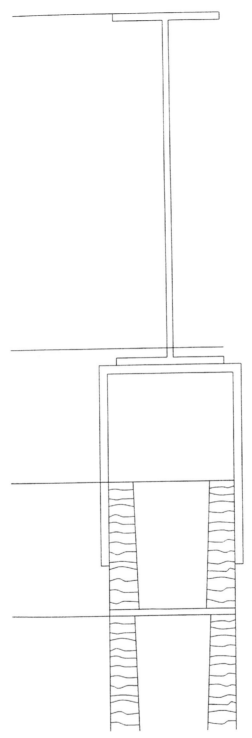

The new CMU wall is centered under the existing steel beam. It is necessary to laterally brace the top of the wall which is overly high. The continuous U-shaped bracket would be welded to the bottom of the beam and would merely touch the wall on either side, but would not be attached to it. The beam could deflect up and down as necessary, without crushing or disturbing the new wall. The wall, though, would be restrained from any sideways movement.

The designer admits to sketching up this detail [in a rushed, weak moment]. The problem is . . . it cannot be built! Why? What would you do to make it buildable?

29

Door and Window Details

The most efficient way to deal with doors and windows on working drawings is to assign some symbol or mark to each type of opening. These designators are then incorporated into a schedule that provides complete data about the openings in question and the products to be used in them. Although a lot of information may be contained in the schedule, it still remains for the draftsman and project architect to describe the window or door products. It is not enough to give the size, model number, or other discriminating feature. The units must be shown in relationship to the walls.

This relationship necessitates additional specific details for doors and windows. These details may be separate from the schedules, or perhaps a more coordinated system will result if they are incorporated into the schedules. Having found the proper designator, a person using the drawings may go from the schedule information directly to the pertinent details.

To show how the units, whether doors or windows, fit into the openings, a series of sections must be cut, which should provide three major pieces of information, namely, head, jamb, and sill conditions. It is important that all three be

shown, the total opening detailed, and all surrounding construction noted. In this system it is possible to outline the clear, or rough, openings between the structural members. The fitting of a typical unit is shown and, finally, of course, the type of finish closure wanted between the rough wall materials and the units themselves.

Many types of windows and doors, and as may methods by which the units can be built into the walls, are available. The possible wall conditions are also beyond enumeration. In addition, the combinations present a problem. By the time window and door detailing appears in the construction sequence, the wall systems will be known; it then becomes a matter of adapting the units to the wall conditions.

This, then, is the reason for the three detail sections: head, jamb, and sill. With only two, the head and sill, there is a gap in the information needed. How must we treat the side (jamb) of the opening? The jamb details are usually repetitive; only one need be shown. The sequence in drawing these details is from top to bottom, vertically: the head detail, the jamb, and, finally, the sill. The details should be properly aligned, as in a wall section, so that the lines between the various drawings can be read. Details are usually drawn at a larger scale, either $1\frac{1}{2}'' = 1'\text{-}0''$ or $3'' = 1'\text{-}0''$. The larger the scale, the more detail allowed.

The complete detail should be shown so that critical questions may be answered. How does the door frame or window section fit into the wall? How is the unit flashed against the penetration of air and water? How are the pieces fitted together with other construction, perhaps even by other trades? There may be a need for additional details if a transom, impost, muntin, or mullion is specified. The detailing must be adapted to the particular job, and, again, if a detail is peculiar to the standard system (which is being built up by the project architect for his or her own use), it must be fully detailed.

In many instances it is helpful to show even standard details directly from the manufacturer's catalog to describe what is wanted and how it is to be incorporated into the building. There is little chance that a window will be installed in the wrong opening, but if this information is not related properly, then ragged, incomplete, and indecisive detailing in the field will be the result. What does the architect intend here? How is it supposed to be done? A guess is made that the detail will work one way or another, and even though the job may be well supervised, on-the-job control is beginning to disintegrate.

If we do not detail correctly, if we do not show precisely what is to be done in the window and door details, we are not going to get what we want. It will be difficult to prove that the contractor's worker is wrong in the work that has been performed. Wrong in regard to what? We cannot say a detail is wrong because its performance differs from our intent. Whatever our intention, it must be clearly shown in every case.

To combine the details with the schedules is a good idea. It may not always be possible as the set is constituted, but it is helpful if it can be accomplished. Determination of the number of sheets devoted to door and window schedules and drawings depends on the size of the project. The details can be drawn on letter-size sheets and bound into the specifications booklet. Even though we are dealing with stock items, the stock units must coincide with the design. They must fit into the construction as specified; there should be no doubt of the ultimate intention in anyone's mind. All pieces of the stock items as well as any necessary trim must be shown.

Problems of coordination are common; for instance, if a particular closure angle is designed to seal a gap between a window section and a wall, it must be specified that the trim will be supplied by the window manufacturer, who can furnish an aluminum angle in exactly the same finish as the window unit to prevent discoloration or change in finish detrimental to the detail itself. However, another trade could be required to supply the closure.

We cannot explain how every piece will fit into the construction (experience is the governing factor) or by whom this piece will be supplied, but in a large measure we can control the detail and the supplier. In custom work (the window and door frames are specially built), it is important that every item be detailed.

We must be careful to detail in correct sequence. We do not ask for the impossible because this will only tend to run up the cost, but we should detail within the scope of our project for the effect we want and, going back to the design cycle, according to practice and the state of the art. Customizing does increase the cost; the manufacturer must change his or her method of production for a special size to meet a particular order. The owner, of course, will have to pay for this specialization. This is not to say that we must forget about "specials" entirely. If there is a valid need for an unusual window or door unit, it should be installed. If an item must be oversized or specially constructed to meet the owner's need, it should be ordered. However, to demand minimal changes in stock items for the sake of variation is not reasonable. The total concept of the project must be kept in mind.

It seems odd that a project's drawings must include windows and doors; everyone knows how to put them in! There is a tremendous fallacy in this statement. A skilled worker knows how to install a window or door, but not every skilled worker is familiar with the project at hand and its requirements. It is true that we can walk into a store and select clothing from the racks that will fit and look reasonably well, and we can buy this way. In construction we must be better than close; we must be exact. It is not that we have to be exclusive or to incur unnecessary cost; we can use stock items similar to those bought from the racks. At the same time, we are special and so must our details be special. The complete door and window story is told in good details.

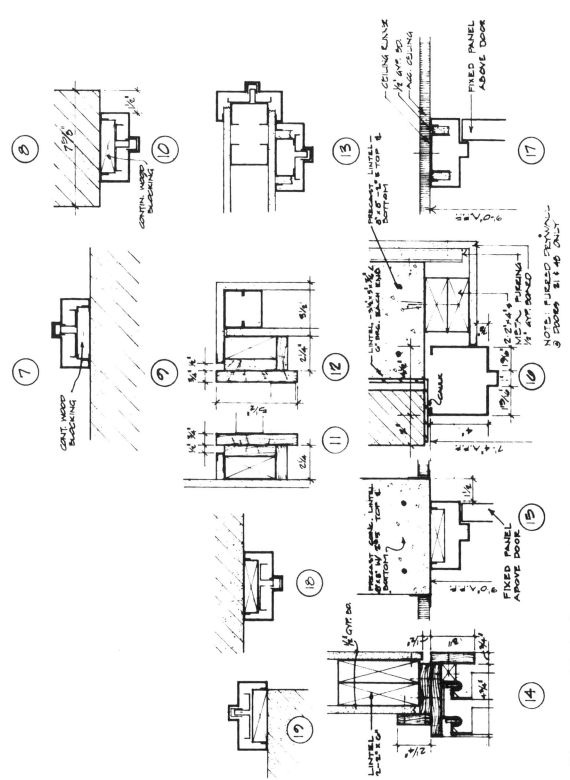

This common set of drawings illustrates door frame details. The door, of course, fits into the frame and is adjusted to it. The frame, however, requires more attention, for it must be fitted into the walls of the project. This set of details often becomes bulky, but it must cover every situation.

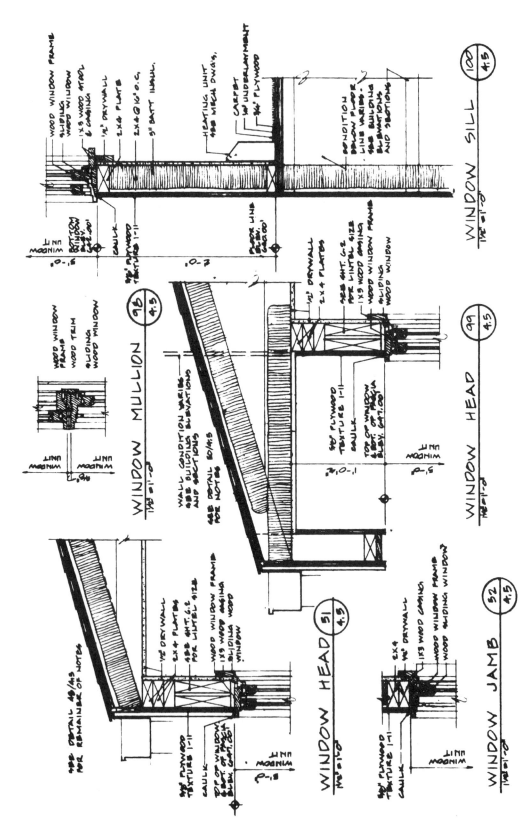

Typical examples of window details (above; opposite) show how the units are fitted into a wall. Basically, stock window units are used and just a small amount of detail is required to describe the general method of installation.

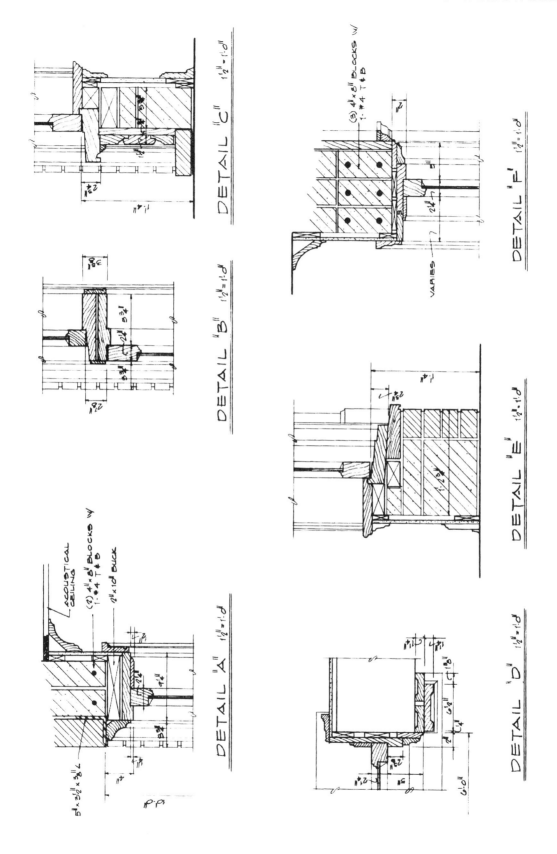

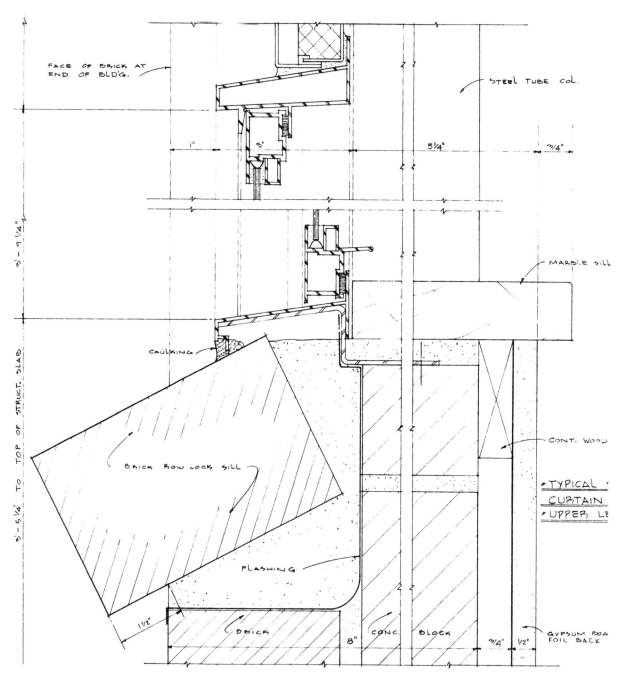

FACE OF BRICK AT
END OF BLD'G.

STEEL TUBE COL.

1"   3"   5¼"   ¾"

MARBLE SILL

CAULKING

BRICK ROW LOCK SILL

CONT. WOOD

TYPICAL
CURTAIN
UPPER LE

FLASHING

1½"   BRICK   8"   CONC. BLOCK   ¾"   ½"   GYPSUM BOA
FOIL BACK

5' - 9¼"

3' - 5¼" TO TOP OF STRUCT. SLAB

It is sometimes beneficial to show window details at full scale. This is true when a new system is being devised or a complicated wall section is needed. It is not the norm and is not done for every project.

CHECKLIST: WINDOW DETAILS

1. Show all sizes and elevations; operable portions; head, jamb, and sill details.
2. Detail actual installation of windows; coordinate by drawing the window with all applicable wall conditions.
3. Consider the need for the following: screens, frame reinforcing, washer bolts, shades, access for washing, fit of adjacent equipment inside the building.
4. Indicate weatherstripping, thickness and type of glass (in general terms).
5. Finishes of frame material, caulking and sealing, interior closures and trim.
6. Include all necessary blocking and construction that makes the opening ready for the unit.

"When I went to graduate school at Harvard, I was the only one of 30 classmates who could detail a building. On the other hand, the others knew who Proust was."

– Michael Graves, Internationally-known architect, commenting on his undergraduate grounding in architecture at the University of Cincinnati (OH)

DETAILS

1. Depict limited area(s) of work.

2. Chose a scale appropriate for clear presentation of the construction involved.

3. Utilize "good" drafting techniques (IMPORTANT!!!!!)

      linework   notes   line weight
    symbols   lettering

4. Correlation; Coordination; Labelling; Reference(s)

5. Is resulting detail; Re-usable?   Unique?   a Modified standard?

6. Location   – on drawing(s); what in the format of the set?
             – in the specifications, or just augmented there?

30

Miscellaneous Details

In almost every set of drawings, for a building of any size, myriad details are necessary for a complete and finished project. Many are not easily categorized but instead reflect a need or gap in the drawings that must be filled.

The best solution to the problem (to show or not to show a given detail; what detail to show; how many details to be shown) is a mental analysis of the processes of building the particular complex. The conclusion will be that more information is needed or that all the information required is at hand. A number of facts can then be adjusted. First, the number of details to be shown can be determined; second, the scale of the details can be set, for by showing a particular assembly at a larger scale more can be shown, more information can be provided, and the need for more detailing precluded. This procedure of evaluating needs (how much is needed and when) comes with experience. Total knowledge cannot be gained in an office atmosphere because the architect cannot properly analyze the facts if he or she has not been in the field and does not know at least a little about the actual construction work. It would be marvelous if all students could work in the construction trades in one capacity or another during their learning period. Unfortunately, this is seldom possible.

Although it is necessary to fill the gaps with complete information, there is danger at the other end of the scale. This is overdetailing! By overdetailing we often succeed in getting a stranglehold on the particular project.

The construction costs, the complexity of the building process, the relations between contractor and owner, and, above all, the entire project can be greatly influenced by the type of relationship that is set up in the drawings. Many architects and draftsmen have differing views; some regard the mentality of contractors as bordering on idiocy and think that they must detail every last item in order to hold the contractors in an iron grip that will force them to perform exactly as the drawings indicate. There are others who do not share this view of the contractors' mentality and produce their drawings in a different context.

The more data shown on the drawing, the more knowledge and experience the architect must have. In fact, an architect must be sure of his or her systems and methods or this professional will effect a drastic change in the cost of the project. Perhaps the best catch phrase is that the architect should know what he or she does not know! Applying this maxim to detailing, the architect must know when to stop. Certainly, if an assembly has many pieces from many sources, it must be detailed for the contractor. On the other hand, it is not necessary to tell a contractor to spike two

457

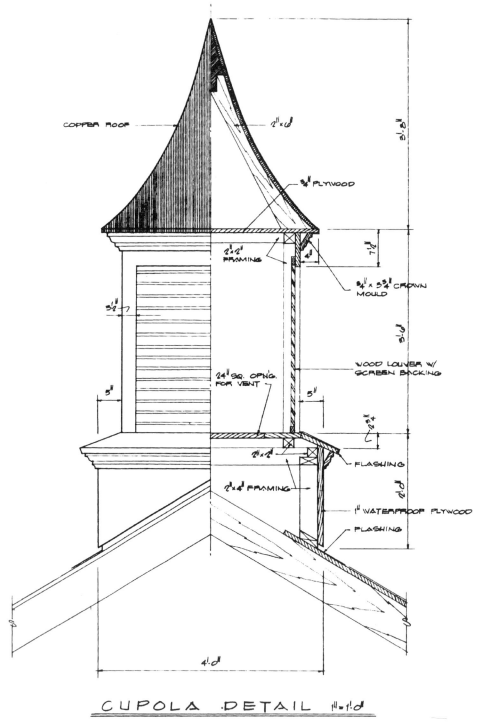

COPPER ROOF

2" x 6"

3/4" PLYWOOD

2" x 2" FRAMING

4"

3/4" x 3 3/4" CROWN MOULD

3' - 0"

7 1/2"

3 1/2"

3' - 0"

WOOD LOUVER W/ SCREEN BACKING

24" SQ. OPNG. FOR VENT

5"

5"

2 3/4"

2" x 2"

FLASHING

2" x 4" FRAMING

1" WATERPROOF PLYWOOD

1' - 0"

FLASHING

4' - 0"

CUPOLA DETAIL 1" = 1'0"

This detail, although uncommon, shows the use of another technique in which the elevation section represents the outer surface and contour of the steeple and at the same time reveals the construction, a most valuable "tool" that eliminates additional costly drawing.

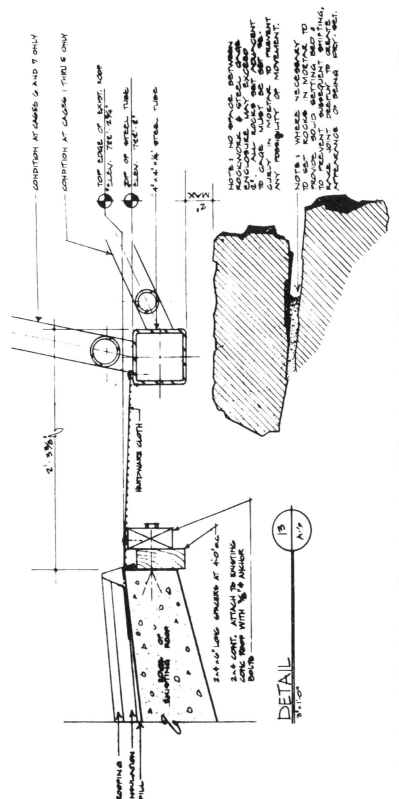

DETAIL

A good example of the detail required in a small area of a project. The various parts must be fitted together, however. (see top of drawing on p. 403).

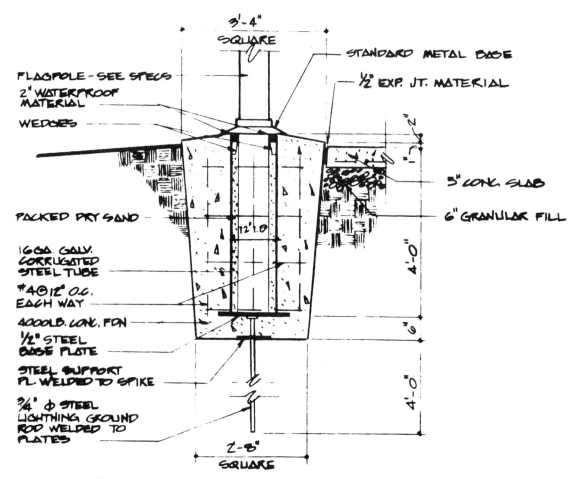

Labels (left side):
FLAGPOLE - SEE SPECS
2" WATERPROOF MATERIAL
WEDGES
PACKED DRY SAND
16 GA. GALV. CORRUGATED STEEL TUBE
#4 @ 12" O.C. EACH WAY
4000 LB. CONC. FDN
1/2" STEEL BASE PLATE
STEEL SUPPORT PL. WELDED TO SPIKE
3/4" Ø STEEL LIGHTNING GROUND ROD WELDED TO PLATES

Labels (top and right side):
3'-4" SQUARE
STANDARD METAL BASE
1/2" EXP. JT. MATERIAL
5" CONC. SLAB
6" GRANULAR FILL
12" I.D.

Dimensions: 2", 4'-0", 6", 4'-0", 2'-8" SQUARE

Three very different details (above and following), each of which provides the project with essential information. They vary in size, scale, and impact, but are typical of miscellaneous details. All cover the small items that can "make or break" any project.

2 × 4s together by driving four 16d nails through the face of one 2 × 4 into the other. Many specification writers refer to a workbook called *Manual of House Framing, Nailing Schedule*, which lists the various criteria for proper nailing, the number of nails, their sizes, spacing, and so on, the use of which eliminates a vast amount of detailing in the drawings.

However, if trusses are to be made from wood members, it may be necessary to show the pattern of nailing in the gusset or nailing plates. It may also be necessary to show the number of nails on each side of the connection, but, again, the architect and his or her consultants, because of their superior knowledge and experience, will know what to show and when to show it.

Often one of the biggest areas of conflict will develop when cabinetwork is called for. The ar-

chitect sits at the drawing board and designs this casework in architectural form. However, current shop practice or good workmanship may dictate otherwise. Again, the situation varies from office to office, but in many instances a design concept is what is shown: the height and width of the cabinet, the materials, the thickness of the top, type of doors, type of base, number of shelves, and the hardware. The basic elements of putting it together are left to the specifications or the contractor's workmanship.

A check on the manufactured items is provided by the shop drawings discussed in a later chapter. Shop drawings show us what the manufacturer has in mind, how he or she proposes to put the item together, and other special elements of the unit. At this point we can compare our own ideas with what is being used.

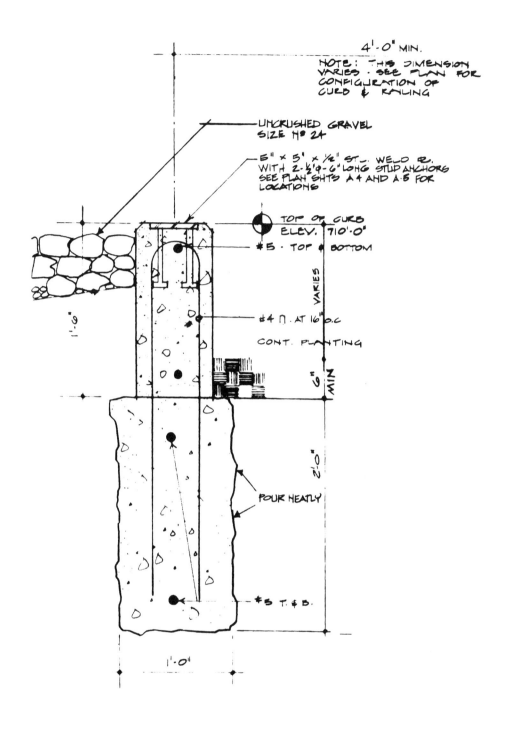

4'-0" MIN.

NOTE: THIS DIMENSION VARIES. SEE PLAN FOR CONFIGURATION OF CURB & RAILING

UNCRUSHED GRAVEL SIZE N° 24

5" × 5" × ½" ST. WELD R. WITH 2-½"⌀-6" LONG STUD ANCHORS SEE PLAN SHTS A·4 AND A·5 FOR LOCATIONS

TOP OF CURB ELEV. 710'-0"

#5 - TOP & BOTTOM

#4 ∏ AT 16" O.C

CONT. PLANTING

VARIES

1'-0"

6" MIN

2'-0"

POUR NEATLY

#5 T. & B.

1'-0"

CURB & FOOTING
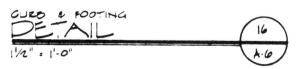
DETAIL

1½" = 1'-0"

16

A·6

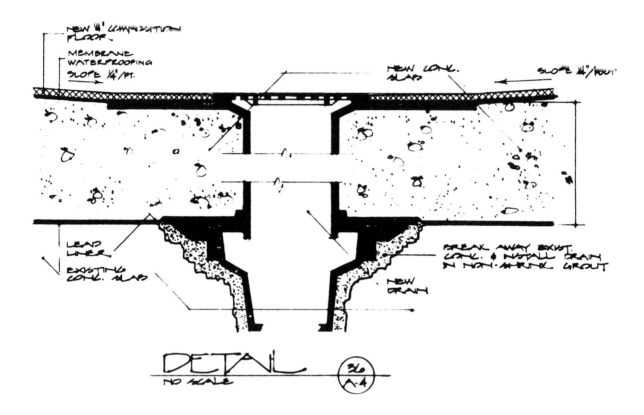

Detailing is important. Looking through a set of drawings, we may find seemingly minute items that may be vital to the success of the project. They are so vital that we need to be intimately concerned with the project to understand the part the details contribute. The details should not be sheet fillers or mere time killers for the draftsman; they should be well thought out, well planned, completely cross-referenced, and professionally executed. In this way we will not serve up redundant miscellany that will be of no value to the contractor or the owner.

Although relevancy is one of the prime considerations in detailing, another is the time consumed in *properly* detailing a project. Three factors come into play: underdetailing, overdetailing, and redundancy. The project will run into a great deal of trouble if the detailing is inadequate and does not properly or completely depict the construction required. Experience is a big factor, inasmuch as one must have a feel for what information is required and how much information is necessary.

To provide inadequate information leaves the work to the contractor, who may perform as intended or who may use experiences from previous projects to build the work in some way that is not in keeping with the architect's intent in the current contract. The remedy for such work is almost impossible, and very expensive if work must be razed and rebuilt. Draftsmen should get used to questioning their own work, asking, "Is there enough information here for me to build this work?" In addition, checking with others in the drafting room will expose gaps or inaccuracies in the detailing.

On the other end of the scale is overdetailing, whereby the professional literally imposes a death grip on the work. He or she details the threads on the screws, odd-sized washers, and other such items, to the point that the work is either impossible to build or extremely expensive. And if the contractor is "forced" to perform exactly as detailed, costs will jump even further. Simply, one must know when to stop detailing; again this comes from experience. Some architects feel comfortable only when they control every feature of the work, down to the finite detail; care must be taken that such an attitude is not counterproductive.

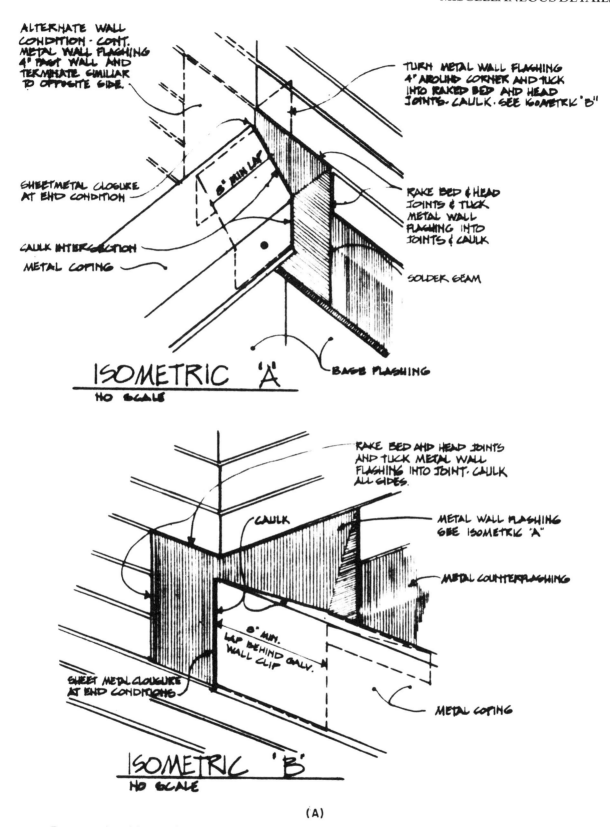

ALTERNATE WALL CONDITION - CONT. METAL WALL FLASHING 4" PAST WALL AND TERMINATE SIMILIAR TO OPPOSITE SIDE.

TURN METAL WALL FLASHING 4" AROUND CORNER AND TUCK INTO RAKED BED AND HEAD JOINTS. CAULK. SEE ISOMETRIC "B"

SHEETMETAL CLOSURE AT END CONDITION

RAKE BED & HEAD JOINTS & TUCK METAL WALL FLASHING INTO JOINTS & CAULK

CAULK INTERSECTION

METAL COPING

SOLDER SEAM

8" MIN LAP

BASE FLASHING

ISOMETRIC 'A'
NO SCALE

RAKE BED AND HEAD JOINTS AND TUCK METAL WALL FLASHING INTO JOINT. CAULK ALL SIDES.

CAULK

METAL WALL FLASHING SEE ISOMETRIC "A"

METAL COUNTERFLASHING

8" MIN. LAP BEHIND GALV. WALL CLIP

SHEET METAL CLOSURE AT END CONDITIONS

METAL COPING

ISOMETRIC 'B'
NO SCALE

(A)

Two examples of the use if isometric drawings that add to readability. (A) is a complex flashing detail, which would not be well shown in two dimensions. In (B) the special brick comes through much more clearly than in a multiview presentation. Not commonly used, this process in some instances is a valuable tool.

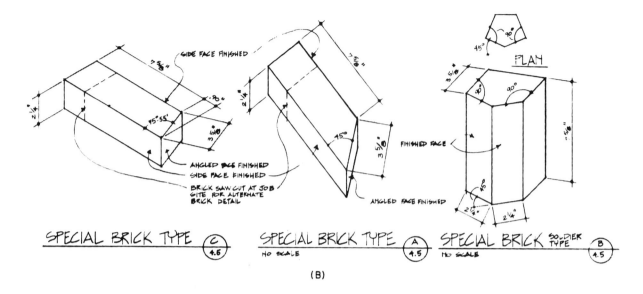

SPECIAL BRICK TYPE (C 4.5)

SPECIAL BRICK TYPE (A 4.5) NO SCALE

SPECIAL BRICK SOLDIER TYPE (B 4.5) NO SCALE

(B)

Redundancy has been addressed in the last few years, summarized in the question, "Does this detail need to be drawn again?" The point here is that a great number of very similar details are incorporated in work, even though the projects involved may vary considerably. Flagpole, curb, and roof drain details come to mind quickly; do they vary or, rather, *must* they vary from job to job when conditions are similar? Should time be spent on each project to detail this work? Should this time be expended again and again? The current answer is a resounding No!

Although considered the height of unprofessional practice in the 1950's, standardized detailing is now a viable and legitimate production technique. The reuse of details is not only advocated, but is recommended, encouraged, and widely practiced. More and more offices are developing systems of standard details, drawn once, retained in retrieval systems, and reused when appropriate. The keys to such a system are proper input, a studied detail free of peculiar features, neatly and properly drawn in a standard format, and placed into a coherent filing system, completely indexed for future retrieval and use.

Do not try to approach this system by having each drafter keep "some details he (or she) draws in the drafting table drawer." The system varies from office to office. Some still retain a manual system of simply filing the details neatly, and others use microfilm or computer-aided drafting (CAD) and retrieval systems that produce the detail in self-adhering decal form. It is the concept of standard detailing that is important, not the system that is utilized. Some offices, of course, have moved from very primitive systems to rather involved, sophisticated systems as their needs changed.

The most recent approach has been the establishment of a detail bank. This is a commercial venture whereby one can subscribe to, or actually buy details from, a central source (not another office) that has an excellent background in this work. The cost is moderate when considered with the cost of redrawing the same work over and over. Moreover, in utilizing the bank, one buys the highest level of expertise and can therefore raise his or her level of work.

To make any of these systems work there must be a way for the field personnel to comment on the details. This feedback is a vital part of the detailing system. Here, problems in the field caused by the standard details can be recorded on the file copies, so that in the future adjustments can be made to avoid repeating the problems. Of course, if too many problems occur or drastic changes are required, the detail should be reevaluated and redrawn as required.

The use of standard details is also discussed in Chapter 35.

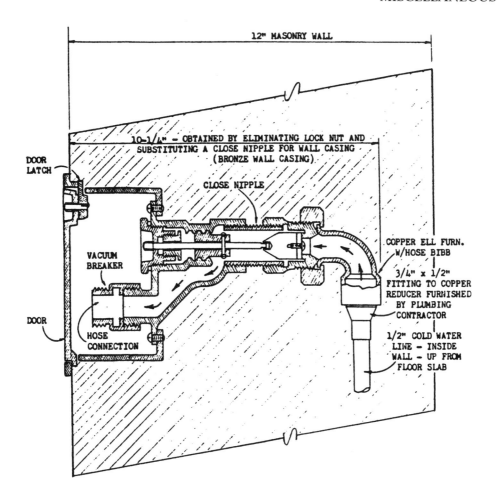

12" MASONRY WALL

10-1/4" – OBTAINED BY ELIMINATING LOCK NUT AND
SUBSTITUTING A CLOSE NIPPLE FOR WALL CASING
(BRONZE WALL CASING)

CLOSE NIPPLE

DOOR
LATCH

VACUUM
BREAKER

DOOR

HOSE
CONNECTION

COPPER ELL FURN.
W/HOSE BIBB

3/4" x 1/2"
FITTING TO COPPER
REDUCER FURNISHED
BY PLUMBING
CONTRACTOR

1/2" COLD WATER
LINE – INSIDE
WALL – UP FROM
FLOOR SLAB

(Above, following) Good examples of "overdetailing" of an item that is ordered as a unit by stock or model number. Since it is not unique to the project, it does not require the extensive time used for this detailing.

465

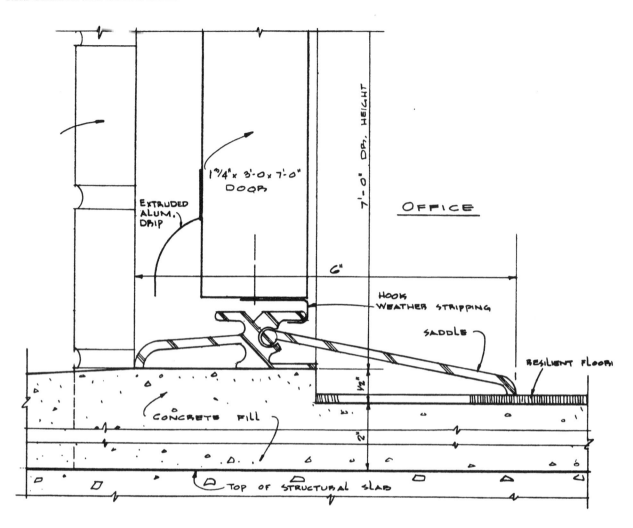

1³/4" x 3'-0 x 7'-0" DOOR

EXTRUDED ALUM. DRIP

7'-0" DR. HEIGHT

OFFICE

6"

HOOK WEATHER STRIPPING

SADDLE

RESILIENT FLOOR

1½"

2"

CONCRETE FILL

TOP OF STRUCTURAL SLAB

466

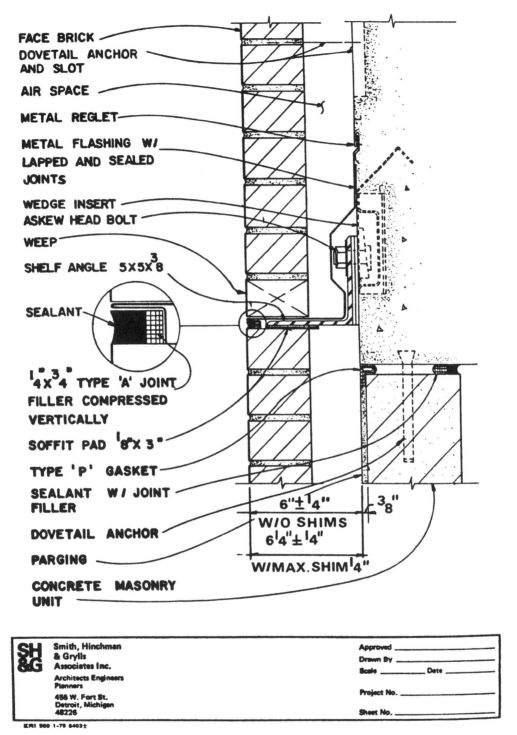

FACE BRICK

DOVETAIL ANCHOR AND SLOT

AIR SPACE

METAL REGLET

METAL FLASHING W/ LAPPED AND SEALED JOINTS

WEDGE INSERT
ASKEW HEAD BOLT

WEEP

SHELF ANGLE 5X5X$\frac{3}{8}$

SEALANT

$1\frac{1}{4}$X$\frac{3}{4}$ TYPE 'A' JOINT FILLER COMPRESSED VERTICALLY

SOFFIT PAD $\frac{1}{8}$X 3"

TYPE 'P' GASKET

SEALANT W/ JOINT FILLER

DOVETAIL ANCHOR

PARGING

CONCRETE MASONRY UNIT

6"±$\frac{1}{4}$"

$\frac{3}{8}$"

W/O SHIMS
6$\frac{1}{4}$"±$\frac{1}{4}$"

W/MAX.SHIM$\frac{1}{4}$"

SH&G   Smith, Hinchman
& Grylls
Associates Inc.

Architects Engineers
Planners

455 W. Fort St.
Detroit, Michigan
48226

ERI 900 1-79 8403±

Approved _____
Drawn By _____
Scale _____ Date _____
Project No. _____
Sheet No. _____

An excellent example of a standard detail utilized by an office. There is absolutely no need to redraw this widely applicable detail. Note insert detail of a very small portion of work to clarify exactly what is required.

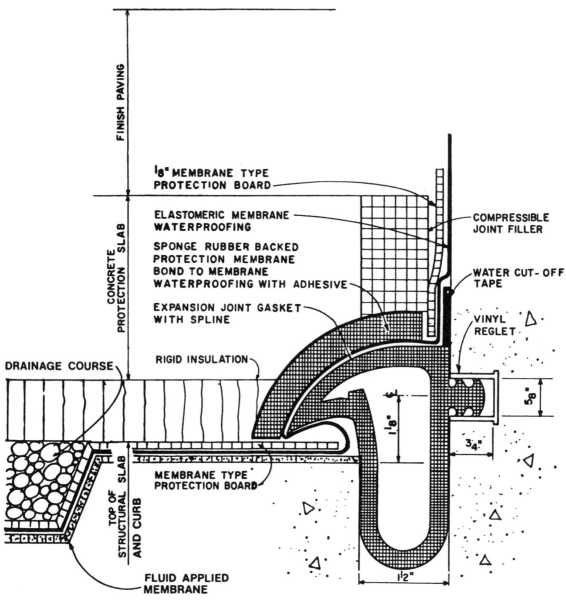

FINISH PAVING

CONCRETE PROTECTION SLAB

$\frac{1}{8}$" MEMBRANE TYPE PROTECTION BOARD

ELASTOMERIC MEMBRANE WATERPROOFING

SPONGE RUBBER BACKED PROTECTION MEMBRANE BOND TO MEMBRANE WATERPROOFING WITH ADHESIVE

EXPANSION JOINT GASKET WITH SPLINE

DRAINAGE COURSE

RIGID INSULATION

TOP OF STRUCTURAL SLAB AND CURB

MEMBRANE TYPE PROTECTION BOARD

FLUID APPLIED MEMBRANE

COMPRESSIBLE JOINT FILLER

WATER CUT-OFF TAPE

VINYL REGLET

$\frac{5}{8}$"

$\frac{3}{4}$"

$1\frac{1}{8}$"

$1\frac{1}{2}$"

Copyright, ASTM, 100 Barr Harbor Dr., West Conshohocken, PA 19428. Reprinted with permission. Well-executed standard detail of a small portion of work. Clear definition of materials; borders on an "exploded" view, which separates line work to show each material distinctly apart from its substrata.

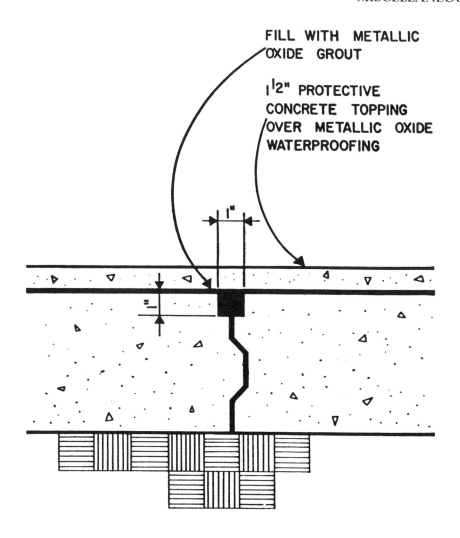

FILL WITH METALLIC
OXIDE GROUT

1½" PROTECTIVE
CONCRETE TOPPING
OVER METALLIC OXIDE
WATERPROOFING

1"

METALLIC OXIDE WATERPROOF'G
FLOOR CONSTRUCTION JOINT

DATE   SPEC. REF.

10 - 1 - 70

TYPE   STD. DET. NO.

Smith, Hinchman and Grylls Associates

Standard details of a very minute, but nevertheless important, item of work. Note basic concrete slab is not dimensioned, which allows this detail to be utilized in numerous cases, while the slab thickness may vary.

469

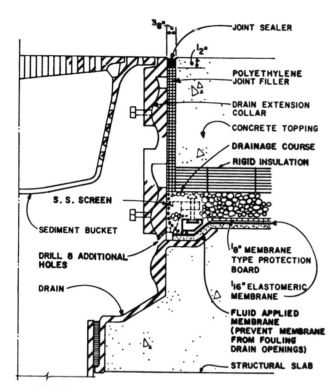

ELASTOMERIC MEMBRANE WATERPROOFING
(BONDED SHEET SYSTEM)

PLAZA DRAIN

DATE   SPEC. REF.
3-1-72   7A14
TYPE   STD. DET. NO.

— Important standard detail at the interface between some mechanical trade's work and some architectural work. The drain is a standard, stock unit, but its incorporation into the work requires involved detailing and careful work to provide a waterproof, nonleaking installation.

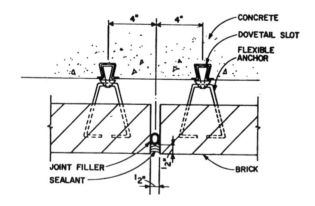

CONTROL JOINT - BRICK FACING AT CONCRETE

DATE   SPEC. REF.

TYPE   STD. DET. NO.

Brick Industries of America
A simple standard detail. Note that no specific material information is used; dovetail slot, anchors, filler, etc., will all be described fully in the specification manual.

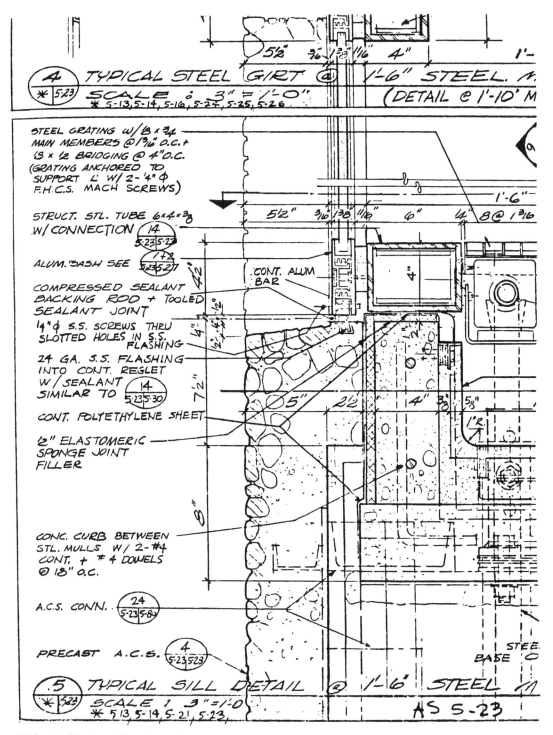

4 TYPICAL STEEL GIRT @ 1'-6" STEEL. M.
✳ 5-23 SCALE ; 3" = 1'-0" (DETAIL @ 1'-10' M
✳ 5-13, 5-14, 5-16, 5-27, 5-25, 5-26

STEEL GRATING W/ 18 x 34
MAIN MEMBERS @ 1³/₁₆" O.C. +
⅛ x 12 BRIDGING @ 4"O.C.
(GRATING ANCHORED TO
SUPPORT L W/ 2-¼" ∅
F.H.C.S. MACH SCREWS)

STRUCT. STL. TUBE 6 x 4 x ⅜
W/ CONNECTION ⟨14 | 5-23|5-23⟩

ALUM. SASH SEE ⟨1+2 | 5-23|5-27⟩

COMPRESSED SEALANT
BACKING ROD + TOOLED
SEALANT JOINT

¼"∅ S.S. SCREWS THRU
SLOTTED HOLES IN S.S.
FLASHING

24 GA. S.S. FLASHING
INTO CONT. REGLET
W/ SEALANT
SIMILAR TO ⟨14 | 5-23|5-30⟩

CONT. POLYETHYLENE SHEET

½" ELASTOMERIC
SPONGE JOINT
FILLER

CONT. ALUM
BAR

CONC. CURB BETWEEN
STL. MULLS W/ 2-#4
CONT. + #4 DOWELS
@ 18" O.C.

A.C.S. CONN. ⟨24 | 5-23|5-8?⟩

PRECAST A.C.S. ⟨4 | 5-23|5-23⟩

STEE.
BASE C

.5 TYPICAL SILL DETAIL @ 1'-6' STEEL M
✳ 5-23 SCALE : 3" = 1'-0
✳ 5-13, 5-14, 5-21, 5-23,

AS 5-23

Hellmuth, Obata and Kassabaum, Inc.
An extremely complicated detail like this requires very careful planning, good line work, and disciplined
execution. Sloppy, haphazard work would destroy this detail, and possibly the actual work.

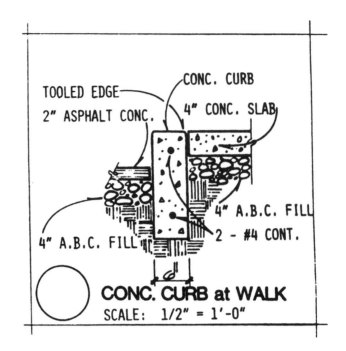

remarks:

Ahern, MacVittie, Hofmann & Goodwin, Ltd.
Example of a standard detail on an office format sheet. There is no need to redraw this detail ever again, and on this sheet it fits easily into the office filing system for future retrieval.

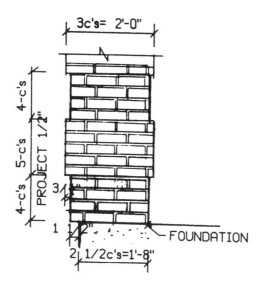

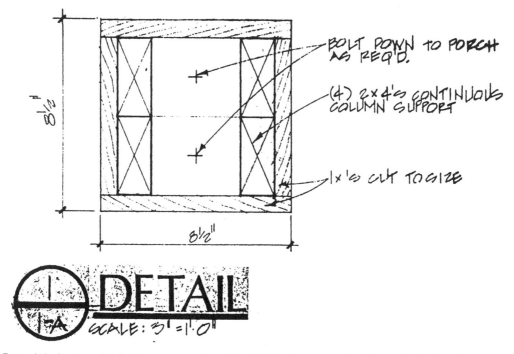

Two relatively minor details, the upper produced by CAD, the lower produced manually. Both are shown here for comparative purposes. Note that each could be produced in either format.

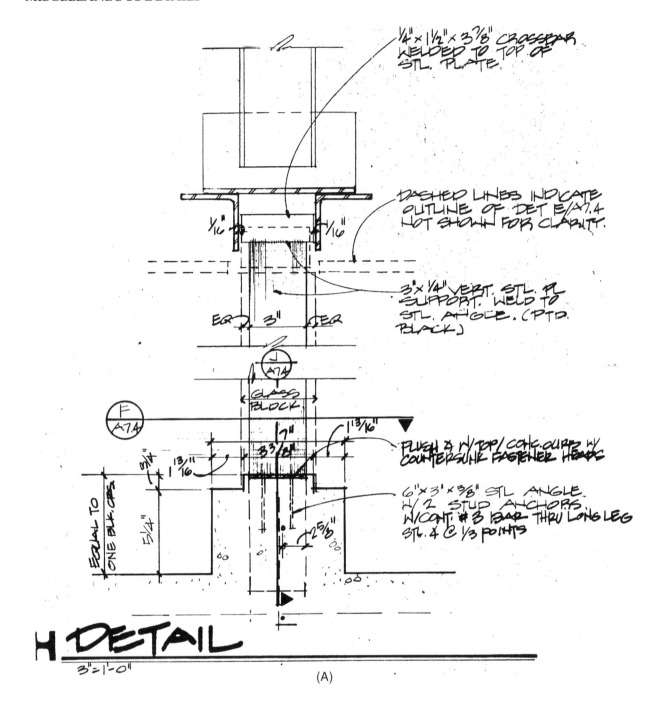

1/4" x 1 1/2" x 3 7/8" CROSSBAR WELDED TO TOP OF STL. PLATE.

DASHED LINES INDICATE OUTLINE OF DET E/A7.4 NOT SHOWN FOR CLARITY.

3" x 1/4" VERT. STL. PL SUPPORT. WELD TO STL. ANGLE. (PTD. BLACK)

FLUSH & W/ TOP/ CONC. CURB W/ COUNTERSUNK FASTENER HEADS

6" x 3" x 3/8" STL ANGLE. W/ 2 STUD ANCHORS W/ CONT. # 3 BAR THRU LONG LEG STL. 4 @ 1/3 POINTS

1/16"   7/16"

EQ   3"   EQ

GLASS BLOCK

1 3/16"

7"

3 3/8"

1 3/16"

3/4"

5 1/4"

EQUAL TO ONE BLK. CRS.

2 5/8"

H DETAIL

3" = 1'-0"

(A)

The structural support detail for a glass block wall [A]. The other [B] is the architectural detail for installing the glass block. Check the depiction, validity, and correctness of this head detail [packing material and sealant shown at same location, along with 4"CMU?; why an expansion strip when nothing abuts it?]

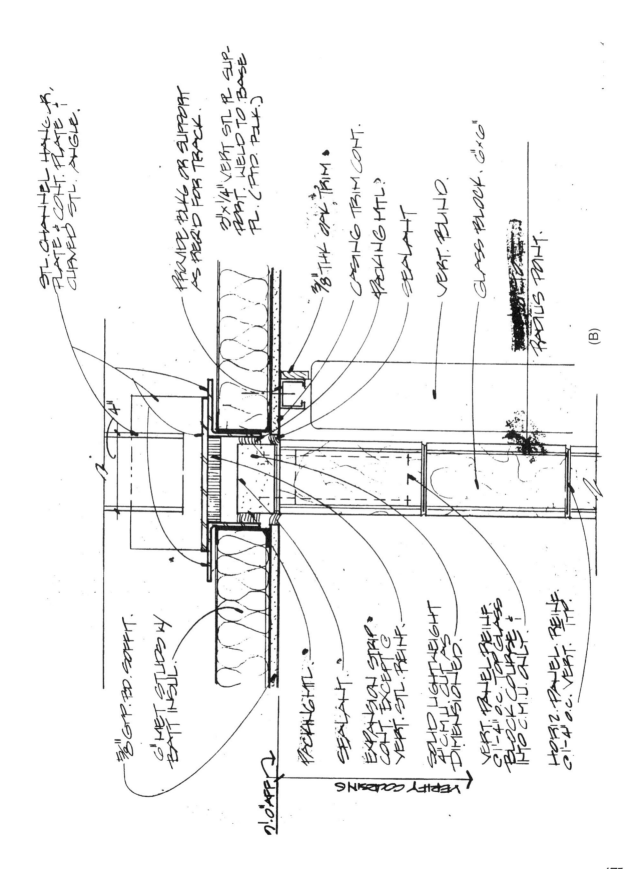

(B)

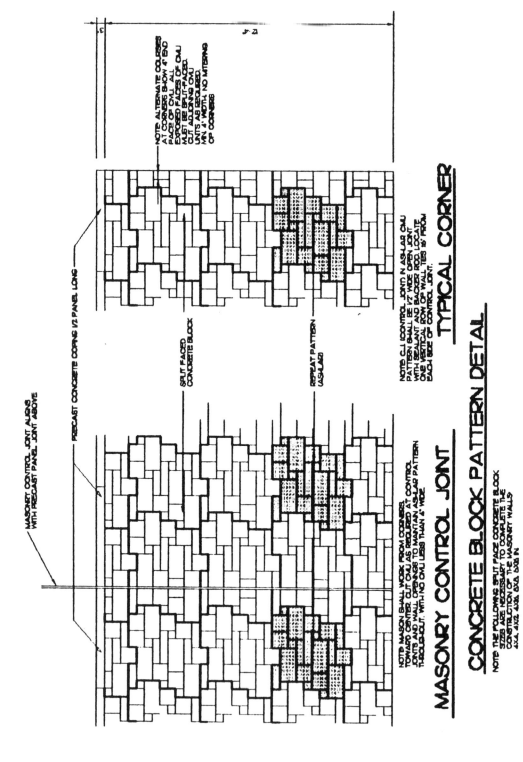

CONCRETE BLOCK PATTERN DETAIL

MASONRY CONTROL JOINT

TYPICAL CORNER

An interesting detail, via CAD, showing control joint layout, and the use of the same ashlar pattern of concrete masonry units, on a repetitive basis

476

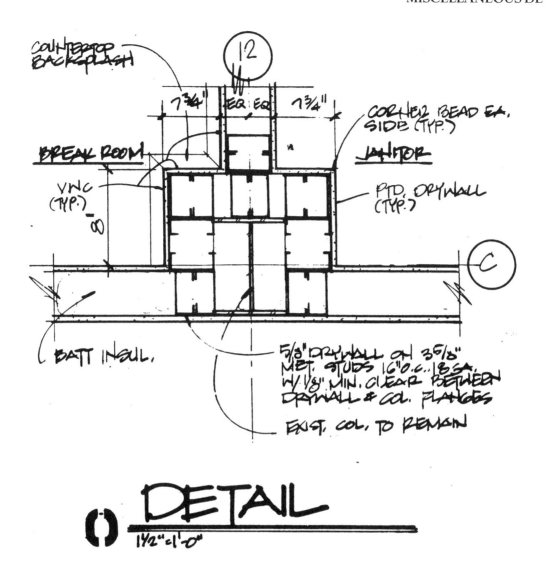

COUNTERTOP BACKSPLASH

12

7¾" EQ EQ 7¾"

CORNER BEAD EA. SIDE (TYP.)

BREAK ROOM

JANITOR

VINC (TYP.)

PTD. DRYWALL (TYP.)

C

BATT INSUL.

5/8" DRYWALL ON 35/8" MET. STUDS 16" O.C., 18 GA. W/ 1/8" MIN. CLEAR BETWEEN DRYWALL & COL. FLANGES

EXIST. COL. TO REMAIN

DETAIL
1½"=1'-0"

How many studs do you count in this detail? Can you detail this situation using a lesser number of studs? [Might check a drywall installation resource]

31

Freehand Detailing

Freehand detailing has become part of the profession in a unique evolution. It has helped to speed the production of working drawings and has, in the same measure, improved the quality of the documents.

One of the first firms to advocate freehand detailing was Hellmuth, Obata and Kassabaum of St. Louis, Missouri. Some of the firm's personnel, under Vice President Robert Stauder, developed this system after it became apparent that the office was redrawing too much material. A study of the existing procedure showed that the project architect would sketch a detail, which was then refined and passed to a draftsman. The draftsman would convert the sketch into a hard-line drawing and apply it to the construction tracings. This procedure was time-consuming and subject to compounded error and confusion. Every time the detail was redrawn more information, both written and visual, was added and given to various draftsmen, each of whom would take liberties or supply unnecessary, even confusing, elements to the drawing. Because the study made these facts apparent, more time was spent after the detail was drawn hard-line, in checking to ensure proper execution.

In further study of the system it was found that the project architect's initial sketches were usually adequate for the final documents with only minor modifications. Often the details were drawn to scale and, of course, contained most of the information that the project architect wanted. Obviously, some of the work steps taken were redundant. The realization was the beginning of the freehand system. It was not, however, adopted overnight; its use required some adjustment to the firm's overall policy.

Basically, the system dictates the use of lightweight tracing paper over a grid sheet of $1/4$-inch squares. The detail can then be drawn on the tracing paper, usually at 3" = 1'-0", without the use of an architect's scale. In many instances the tracing paper is not even taped down, thus allowing some flexibility in the drawing process. With a little training, the drafter can produce line work of high quality. As shown later, this quality is most important to the success of the system.

Other adjustments must also be made. One-eighth-inch lettering (minimum) is required, and the poché textures must be more widely spaced.

These tracing paper sketches can then be applied with clear tape to a linen backing sheet that has been preprinted with the title block and the other standard information. The sheet is then reduced to one-half size photographically, a reduction that gives reason for the minimum-size lettering and the more open poché. It is also responsible for the required improvement in line work quality, which is increased and becomes more reproducible.

The overwhelming advantage of freehand detailing rests in the amount of time that can be saved. Estimates vary widely from a minimum of approximately 20 to as much as 35 percent. Time saving is the life's blood of any office. If good working drawings can be produced at a 20 percent saving of work hours, the system can be a success. The money saved can be appropriated for the preliminary design phase. Although this system looks encouraging, and for many offices has been successful, it is not necessarily the total answer. To tell all students or new architects that this is a must as far as their professional advancement is concerned, would be a serious mistake. In many offices this system is not employed at all. Even the pioneer Hellmuth, Obata and Kassabaum had to make a major adjustment, for many of the older staff members lacked the expertise for freehand detailing. A major revision was accomplished in an easy and orderly manner in that freehand detailing became exactly that: the detailing. Floor plans, elevations, building sections, and other drawings normally included in the working drawings, were continued in production at the smaller scales ($\frac{1}{8}$ and $\frac{1}{4}$ inch). These drawings are still hard-line. With this separation Hellmuth, Obata and Kassabaum was able to divide its staff according to individual skills. The older draftsmen stayed with their work on the hard-line, small-scale drawings, whereas the newer staffers, competent in freehand detailing, were assigned to the details and larger sections. Nevertheless, Hellmuth, Obata and Kassabaum has adopted a policy of hiring only persons with freehand capabilities.

Freehand detailing utilizes a new reproduction system, which, however, may not be advantageous or money saving in all cases. It is a photographic process that is convenient and interesting because of its newness. But it is not necessarily the entire answer. A small office, engaged in designing a residence or a small commercial building, would never even entertain the idea of using photographic reproduction. Not many prints would be required, and the cost break would be intolerable.

The cost factor shows the value of freehand photographic systems. Various offices have reported that thousands of dollars can be saved by using photographic reproduction processes, but it implies a multimillion dollar project—for example, a project with a stack of working drawings with as many as 200 sheets in each set and perhaps a requirement of 150 sets.

There are many ramifications to the system. To state that it should be used exclusively is plainly wrong. Freehand detailing has, indeed, turned many offices around. Wherever the system has been adopted it seems to have worked extremely well, but some adjustments had to be made in staff and budgeting. Some larger offices have completely converted by acquiring not only their own cameras for in-house reduction and reproduction, but their own offset printing plants. This, of course, is not possible for every office in practice. The American Institute of Architects (AIA) tells us that the major city of offices in the United States employ 10 or fewer persons. Some offices, however, maintain as many as 800. The challenges of practice are different, the requirements are different, but freehand detailing does give us another tool for the production of working drawings. Beyond that, freehand detailing allows us to place our work force where it really counts. By being able to transfer money from the "nuts and bolts" working-drawing phase of the contract back into the preliminary phase, the system can be made more complete and more involved in better design.

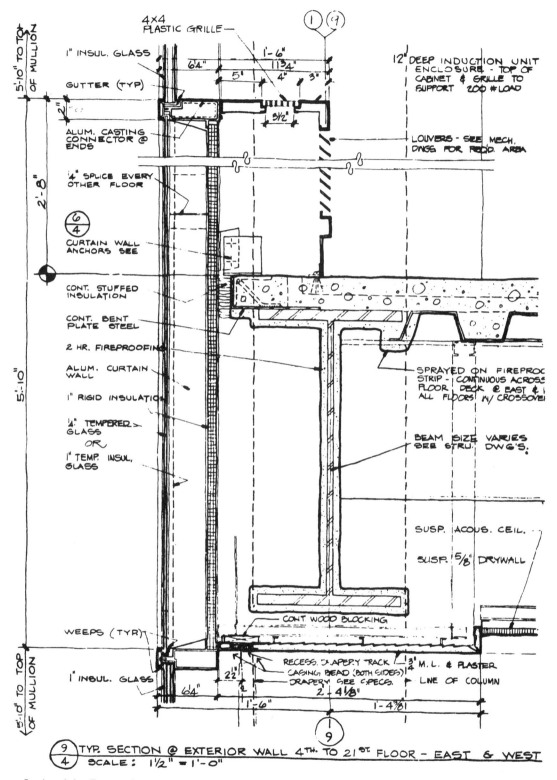

4×4 PLASTIC GRILLE

1" INSUL. GLASS

GUTTER (TYP)

ALUM. CASTING CONNECTOR @ ENDS

4" SPLICE EVERY OTHER FLOOR

6/4

CURTAIN WALL ANCHORS SEE

CONT. STUFFED INSULATION

CONT. BENT PLATE STEEL

2 HR. FIREPROOFING

ALUM. CURTAIN WALL

1" RIGID INSULATION

4" TEMPERED GLASS
OR
1" TEMP. INSUL. GLASS

WEEPS (TYP)

1" INSUL. GLASS

5'-10" TO TOP OF MULLION

2'-8"

5'-10"

5'-0" TO TOP OF MULLION

1-6"
6/4"
11 3/4"
5'
4"
3"
5 1/2"

12" DEEP INDUCTION UNIT ENCLOSURE - TOP OF CABINET & GRILLE TO SUPPORT 200 # LOAD

LOUVERS - SEE MECH. DWGS FOR REQ'D. AREA

SPRAYED ON FIREPROOF STRIP - CONTINUOUS ACROSS FLOOR DECK @ EAST & ALL FLOORS W/ CROSSOVER

BEAM SIZE VARIES SEE STRU. DWG'S.

SUSP. ACOUS. CEIL.

SUSP. 5/8" DRYWALL

CONT WOOD BLOCKING

RECESS. DRAPERY TRACK
CASING BEAD (BOTH SIDES)
DRAPERY SEE SPECS.
3/4" M.L. & PLASTER
LINE OF COLUMN

2 2 1/2"
2-4 1/8"
1-6"
6/4"
1-4 3/8"

9/4 TYP. SECTION @ EXTERIOR WALL 4TH. TO 21ST FLOOR - EAST & WEST
SCALE: 1 1/2" = 1'-0"

Freehand detailing requires practice. This drawing is a typical section in which the technique has been so highly developed that it permits the study drawing to become part of the working drawings.

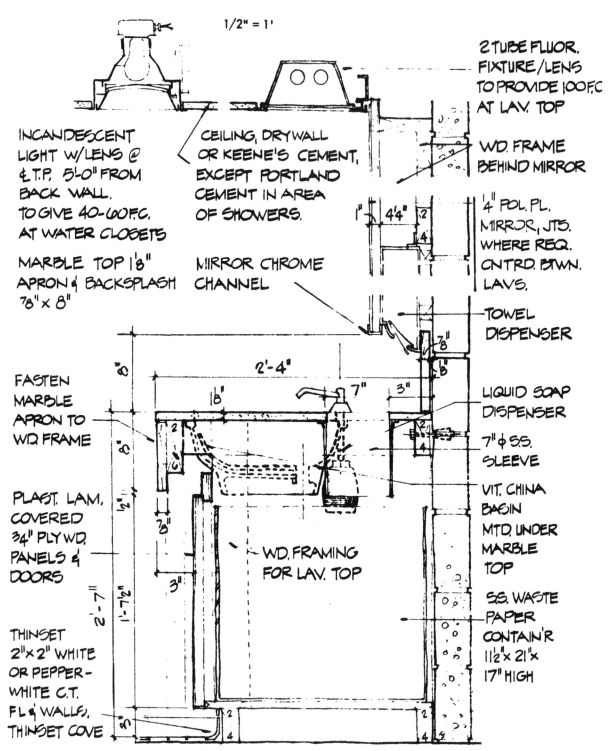

1/2" = 1'

2 TUBE FLUOR. FIXTURE/LENS TO PROVIDE 100 F.C. AT LAV. TOP

INCANDESCENT LIGHT W/LENS @ ¢ T.P. 5'-0" FROM BACK WALL. TO GIVE 40-60 F.C. AT WATER CLOSETS

CEILING, DRYWALL OR KEENE'S CEMENT, EXCEPT PORTLAND CEMENT IN AREA OF SHOWERS.

WD. FRAME BEHIND MIRROR

MARBLE TOP 1⅛" APRON & BACKSPLASH ⅞" x 8"

MIRROR CHROME CHANNEL

¼" POL. PL. MIRROR, JTS. WHERE REQ. CNTRD. BTWN. LAVS.

TOWEL DISPENSER

FASTEN MARBLE APRON TO WD FRAME

2'-4"

LIQUID SOAP DISPENSER

PLAST. LAM. COVERED 3⁄4" PLY WD. PANELS & DOORS

WD. FRAMING FOR LAV. TOP

7"φ S.S. SLEEVE

VIT. CHINA BASIN MTD. UNDER MARBLE TOP

THINSET 2" x 2" WHITE OR PEPPER-WHITE C.T. FL & WALLS, THINSET COVE

S.S. WASTE PAPER CONTAIN'R 11½" x 21" x 17" HIGH

This freehand detail explains the architect-designer's intention and is sufficiently detailed to serve as a construction drawing. Although a sketchy appearance seems to dominate it, the viewer will note that all of the essential information accompanies legible lines and the design is clearly understood.

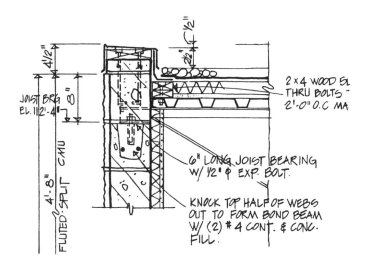

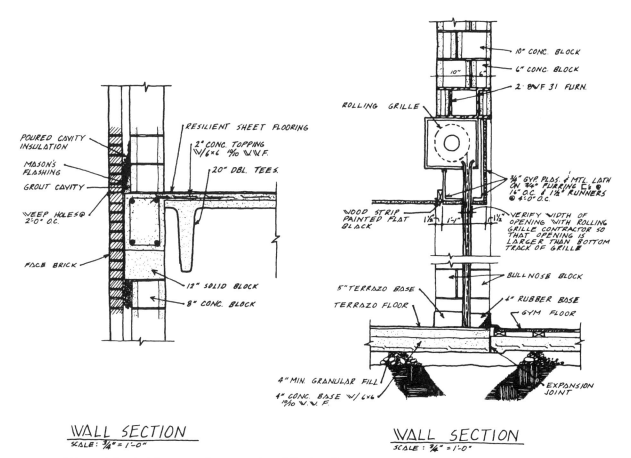

2 X 4 WOOD SL
THRU BOLTS -
2'-0" O.C MA.

6" LONG JOIST BEARING
W/ 1/2" φ EXP. BOLT.

KNOCK TOP HALF OF WEBS
OUT TO FORM BOND BEAM
W/ (2) #4 CONT. & CONC.
FILL.

JOIST BRG
EL.112'-4"

FLUTED SPLIT CMU

POURED CAVITY
INSULATION

MASON'S
FLASHING

GROUT CAVITY

WEEP HOLES @
2'-0" O.C.

FACE BRICK

RESILIENT SHEET FLOORING

2" CONC. TOPPING
W/ 6 x 6 19/10 W.W.F.

20" DBL. TEES.

12" SOLID BLOCK

8" CONC. BLOCK

WALL SECTION
SCALE: 3/4" = 1'-0"

ROLLING GRILLE

WOOD STRIP
PAINTED FLAT
BLACK

5" TERRAZO BASE

TERRAZO FLOOR

4" MIN. GRANULAR FILL

4" CONC. BASE W/ 6x6
19/10 W.W.F.

10" CONC. BLOCK

6" CONC. BLOCK

2 · 8 W F 31 FURN.

3/4" GYP. PLAS. & MTL. LATH
ON 3/4" FURRING CL @
16" O.C. & 1 1/2" RUNNERS
@ 4'-0" O.C.

VERIFY WIDTH OF
OPENING WITH ROLLING
GRILLE CONTRACTOR SO
THAT OPENING IS
LARGER THAN BOTTOM
TRACK OF GRILLE

BULLNOSE BLOCK

4" RUBBER BASE

GYM FLOOR

EXPANSION
JOINT

WALL SECTION
SCALE: 3/4" = 1'-0"

(Above, following) Some excellent examples of "freehand" details. Extreme care and a good deal of skill are required to execute in this manner. It is best to work over a grid that serves as a guide for the line work.

483

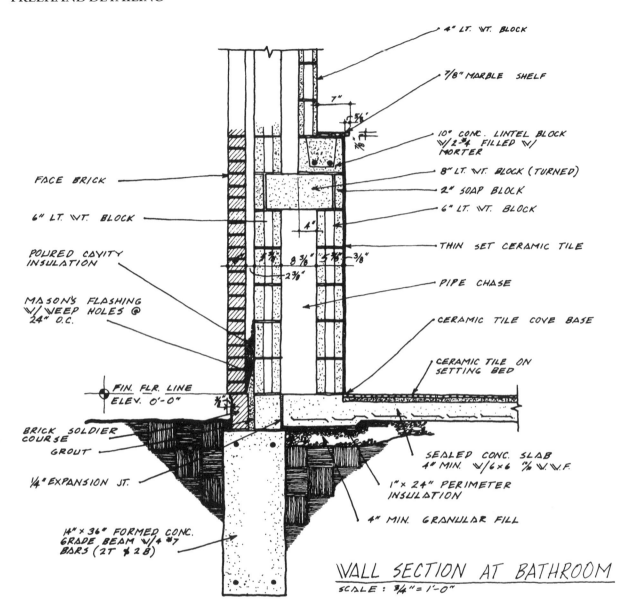

4" LT. WT. BLOCK

7/8" MARBLE SHELF

10" CONC. LINTEL BLOCK W/ 2-#4 FILLED W/ MORTER

8" LT. WT. BLOCK (TURNED)

2" SOAP BLOCK

6" LT. WT. BLOCK

THIN SET CERAMIC TILE

PIPE CHASE

CERAMIC TILE COVE BASE

CERAMIC TILE ON SETTING BED

SEALED CONC. SLAB 4" MIN. W/ 6×6 10/10 W.W.F.

1" × 24" PERIMETER INSULATION

4" MIN. GRANULAR FILL

FACE BRICK

6" LT. WT. BLOCK

POURED CAVITY INSULATION

MASON'S FLASHING W/ WEEP HOLES @ 24" O.C.

FIN. FLR. LINE ELEV. 0'-0"

BRICK SOLDIER COURSE

GROUT

1/4" EXPANSION JT.

14" × 36" FORMED CONC. GRADE BEAM W/ 4 #7 BARS (2T & 2B)

7"

8 3/8"

2 3/8"

3/8"

4"

WALL SECTION AT BATHROOM

SCALE : 3/4" = 1'-0"

32

Composite Drafting

F reehand drafting has made a major contribution to the development of composite drafting. Freehand details are produced on lightweight tracing paper and attached by transparent tape or rubber cement to a backing sheet, a drafting medium of medium or heavy weight, such as linen or mylar film. As long as all details on a particular sheet are made on the same type of tracing paper (to provide a similar background), there will be no problem. The "pasted up" sheet can be photographed, imperfections caused by the edges of paper or tape eliminated with eradicator, and the sheet made ready for further production.

With freehand detailing the sheets are usually "shot down" to one-half size. The negatives resulting from the photographic process become the basis for printing plates. The actual working drawings that are sent to the contractors for bids are produced by offset printing, which is more stable than ozalids or diazos. There is less fading, the images are sharper, the paper heavier, and the reduced size handier for use in the field.

The combined effects of freehand detailing and the reduced-size working drawings are a real boon to many major projects. It is no longer necessary to carry large sets of drawings containing many hundreds of sheets into the field. Neither do marginal drawings (as far as readability is concerned) have to be used.

The ramifications of the composite drafting concept are many, however. For years the architecture professional practiced within an "ivory tower" philosophy. Many architects turned arty and their drawings were masterpieces, but as a direct result of World War II rapid production became a necessity. This necessity gave birth to the original idea of freehand detailing; freehand detailing reduces the amount of time spent on a particular project and maximizes profit. Architects, like any other business people, are in business for profit. Time reduction is money saved.

Composite drafting has other inputs beyond freehand detailing. Several years ago it became apparent that many mundane items were being repeated on the drawings, some of which were North arrows, professional seals, graphic scales, title blocks, and half-toning. It was found that these items could be produced in the form of stick-on decals, which could then be applied directly to the sheet in a manner that would permit reproduction on the final prints. This discovery led to a form of composite drafting known as scissors drafting, the basic concept of which has opened new horizons. If we are to accept the idea of scissors drafting, we must also accept the idea that anything that has been drawn once need not be drawn again.

With the photographic process any type of material may be applied to the backing sheet

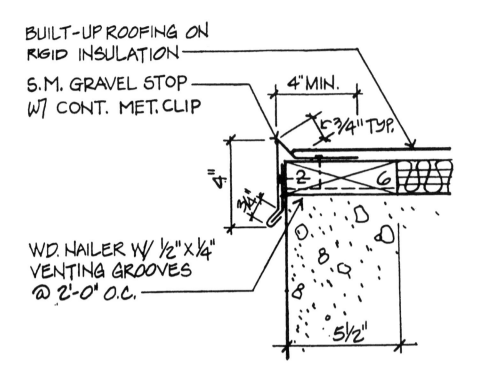

BUILT-UP ROOFING ON RIGID INSULATION

S.M. GRAVEL STOP W/ CONT. MET. CLIP

4" MIN.

3/4" TYP.

4"

3/4"

2

6

WD. NAILER W/ ½" X ¼" VENTING GROOVES @ 2'-0" O.C.

5½"

SHT. MET. GRAVEL STOP
SC. :

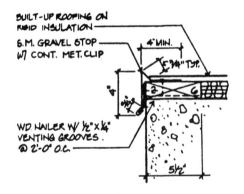

BUILT-UP ROOFING ON RIGID INSULATION

S.M. GRAVEL STOP W/ CONT. MET. CLIP

4" MIN.

3/4" TYP.

4"

2

6

WD. NAILER W/ ½" X ¼" VENTING GROOVES @ 2'-0" O.C.

5½"

SHT. MET. GRAVEL STOP
SC. :

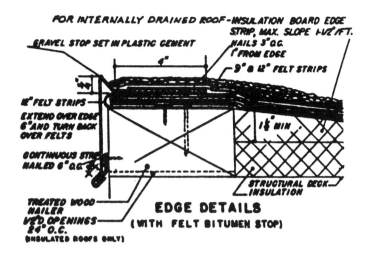

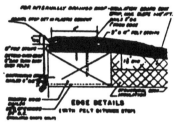

Chapman, Cobeen, Desai, Sakota, Inc.
Architecture, Planning, Interior Design, Graphic Design
These examples illustrate the problem that must be avoided if original drawings are to be reduced in size.
Lettering must be sized properly (oversized) and the drawing made to a larger scale than usual. If any of the
work is too small, the detail lines will merge and smear when reduced, rendering the detail useless.

photographed, doctored with eradicators, have new lines added, and be converted to a negative, a printing plate, and, finally, a half-size drawing. There is no need to copy directly from a manufacturer's catalog onto the working drawing tracings. Merely take the catalog, cut out the applicable details, paste them on a sheet, and presto! the working drawings. This practice does not inhibit the bidding process because, in general, a particular system is usually detailed, and the specifications allow for a range of bidders whose systems are similar to that detailed on the drawings. Printed matter in the form of specifications or large notes can now be cut from catalogs or typed on translu-

cent decal paper that transfers to the backup sheets. This procedure avoids hours of laborious hand lettering and copying or tracing. Again, time saved is money saved, but be cautioned: quality must be maintained.

Other ideas related to composite drafting have crept into professional practice in the last few years. Sheets of drafting media with preprinted border lines and title blocks are now available. At one time these standard features represented long dreary hours of drudgery for some poor soul in the office; to get the title block on correctly by using LeRoy lettering, to space the letters and words perfectly, to avoid ink blots while including all essential information, and to apply the border lines around each sheet and then cut or trim lines beyond the borders has been a task no one welcomed.

Composite drafting opens other new vistas. In remodeling or renovation projects it is possible for photographs of the actual building, in its present state, to be mounted on the backing sheet and reproduced photographically. By applying notes to the backing sheet and leader lines, certain conditions can be pointed out and remedies offered. Color can be added to show the new or existing features; it can also be used to separate the work of the mechanical engineers from the structural and architectural on drawings reproduced by the offset method. Beyond this, the scale of the photographs can be changed accurately as desired. This system does not inhibit design ability; it is another means to an end.

Much of the time that is spent in redoing, copying, and tracing can be eliminated; for instance, a basic floor plan that shows the structural grid of a complicated building can be reproduced photographically as the basement plan, first floor plan, second floor plan, and so on up to the roof plan. It would be futile for someone to copy the plan each time it is needed. The photographic process also allows us the use of various "screens," which can change the intensity of the lines. The plan laid out for the architectural plan can be muted and used as a mask or backup by the structural and mechanical engineers. The engineers' equipment, beams, ductwork, and conduits, can be drawn with a drafted line that will contrast well with the muted background of the building.

Some of this work can be done in-house at the architectural office, but the amount of equipment and the number of work hours that can be devoted to this process are usually limited. Most reproduction companies have a variety of processes to offer their clients. Experts employed by them are frequently asked for advice, which they extend as part of their services. Often systems that involve varying costs will come into play. One sheet may cost $1.65 to produce, whereas by another system the same sheet may cost $7.50. The factor of cost must be weighed. What is the value of one system as opposed to another? What is the life of one of these sheets? How often will the sheet be used?

We must remain open-minded to these methods. If a draftsman can be freed from the drudgery of tracing work, the mistakes that so often occur in copying can be eliminated, and with the more error-free methods combined with cheaper reproduction methods we most certainly will end with a more profitable project. In the meantime none of these elements reduces the efficiency or quality of the drawings. With these two factors in play, the system of composite drafting is something that each architect or firm should consider. The system will not work for everyone; it is not something that should be absorbed automatically. It should be noted that within the last few years firms have researched many systems, and it would be a safe statement that no two firms at this point do exactly the same things in exactly the same way. The techniques are available, however, as are the experts. It is left only to seek them out and select the proper one for a given situation.

Composite drafting is discussed further in Chapter 35.

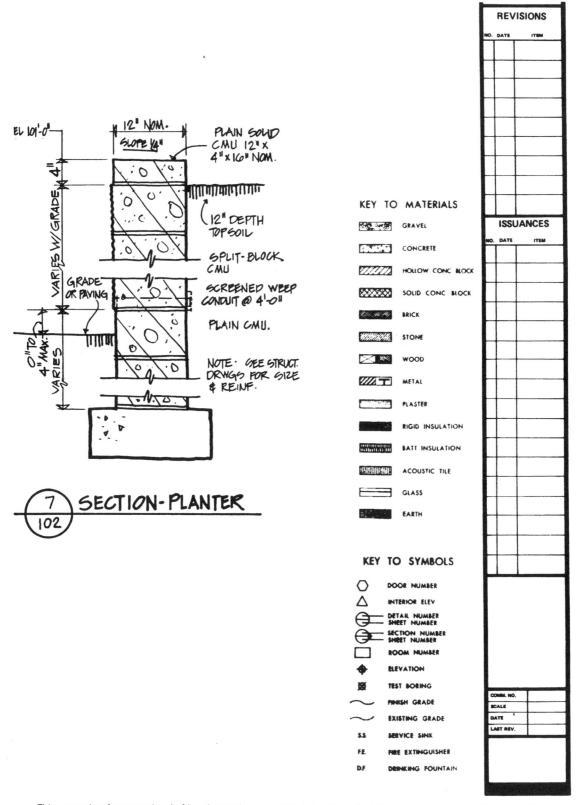

EL 101'-0"

12" NOM.
SLOPE 1/4"

PLAIN SOLID
CMU 12" X
4" X 16" NOM.

4"

VARIES W/GRADE

12" DEPTH
TOP SOIL

SPLIT-BLOCK
CMU

GRADE
OR PAVING

SCREENED WEEP
CONDUIT @ 4'-0"

PLAIN CMU.

0" TO
4" MAX.
VARIES

NOTE· SEE STRUCT.
DRWGS FOR SIZE
& REINF.

7
102

SECTION-PLANTER

KEY TO MATERIALS

GRAVEL

CONCRETE

HOLLOW CONC BLOCK

SOLID CONC BLOCK

BRICK

STONE

WOOD

METAL

PLASTER

RIGID INSULATION

BATT INSULATION

ACOUSTIC TILE

GLASS

EARTH

KEY TO SYMBOLS

DOOR NUMBER

INTERIOR ELEV

DETAIL NUMBER
SHEET NUMBER

SECTION NUMBER
SHEET NUMBER

ROOM NUMBER

ELEVATION

TEST BORING

FINISH GRADE

EXISTING GRADE

S.S.   SERVICE SINK

F.E.   FIRE EXTINGUISHER

D.F.   DRINKING FOUNTAIN

REVISIONS

NO.	DATE	ITEM

ISSUANCES

NO.	DATE	ITEM

COMM. NO.	
SCALE	
DATE	
LAST REV.	

This example of composite drafting shows the preprinted sheet to which the tracing paper detail is taped. The many preprinted decals include scale, standard symbols, and transfer lettering. The time-saving character of this drafting technique recommends it highly, but many offices have not yet adopted it.

G E N E R A L   N O T E S

CODES AND SPECIFICATIONS
OHIO BUILDING CODE
ACI 318-71
ACI 301-72 SPECIFICATIONS FOR STRUCTURAL CONCRETE FOR BUILDINGS

FOUNDATIONS
FOOTINGS ARE DESIGNED TO BEAR ON EXISTING NATURAL GROUND OR NEWLY PLACED FILLS. BEARING MATERIAL AT FOOTING SUBGRADE MUST BE APPROVED BY THE SOILS ENGINEER PRIOR TO PLACEMENT OF FOUNDATION CONCRETE.

CONCRETE
CONCRETE STRENGTHS:
    4000 psi A.E. CHEM COMP – POOL BOTTOM SLABS AND POOL WALLS
    4000 psi A.E.   – SIDEWALKS AND POOL DECK SLAB
    4000 psi REGULAR   – ALL OTHER BUILDING CONCRETE

REINFORCING STEEL
STIRRUPS, TIES AND BARS INDICATED
    FIELD BENT - - - - - - - - - - - - - - - - - 40 KSI YIELD
    ALL OTHER BARS - - - - - - - - - - - - - 60 KSI YIELD
REINFORCE ALL SIDEWALKS WITH 6×6 – 4/4 MESH UNLESS OTHERWISE NOTED.
PROVIDE COMPRESSION SPLICES FOR ALL SPLICES UNLESS OTHERWISE NOTED.
CLEARANCES BETWEEN REINFORCING BARS AND CONCRETE SURFACES ACI MINIMUM
    UNLESS OTHERWISE NOTED.
PLACE NO OPENINGS, SLEEVES, INSERTS, ETC. IN CONCRETE WORK UNLESS INDICATED
    ON STRUCTURAL DRAWINGS OR APPROVED BY THE ENGINEER.

COORDINATION
REFER TO ARCHITECTURAL AND MECHANICAL DRAWINGS OR ADDITIONAL EMBEDDED
    ITEMS, SLEEVES, FLOOR PITCHES, FILLS AND DEPRESSIONS.

CONSTRUCTION
POOL WALLS AND POOL SLAB TO BE PLACED IN ONE COMPLETE POUR UNLESS OTHERWISE
    PERMITTED BY THE ARCHITECT.
BRACE ENTIRE STRUCTURE AS REQUIRED TO MAINTAIN STABILITY UNTIL COMPLETE AND
    FUNCTIONING AS THE DESIGNED UNIT.

SAFETY
IN ACCORDANCE WITH GENERALLY ACCEPTED CONSTRUCTION PRACTICES, CONTRACTOR WILL BE SOLELY AND COMPLETELY RESPONSIBLE FOR CONDITIONS OF JOB SITE INCLUDING SAFETY OF ALL PERSONS AND PROPERTY DURING PERFORMANCE OF THE WORK. THIS REQUIREMENT WILL APPLY CONTINUOUSLY AND NOT BE LIMITED TO NORMAL WORKING HOURS. THE DUTY OF ENGINEER TO CONDUCT CONSTRUCTION REVIEW OF CONTRACTOR'S PERFORMANCE IS NOT INTENDED TO INCLUDE REVIEW OF ADEQUACY OF CONTRACTOR'S SAFETY MEASURES IN, ON, OR NEAR CONSTRUCTION SITE.

Use of the composite drafting technique allows notes to be typed directly on the sheet at the point of application or on decal paper and attached to the sheet. The example represents a set of general notes that is to be attached by tape to the sheet for final photographic processing.

33

Stairs and Fireplaces

The title of this chapter seems to have combined two diverse subjects. There is a basic lesson to be learned in these two particular categories that can be incorporated into the total building.

The need to detail is inherent in architectural working drawings. Pieces of construction must be literally taken apart and drawn at large scale to show how they are to be fitted together. This is indeed a major part of the architect's drawings.

Piecing together exactly how much detail is needed in his or her conception of a project is a very hard lesson for the average young architect. If showing a unique item that does not involve standard procedures or standard materials, the architect must, of course, detail minutely to describe exactly what he or she wants and how he or she wants it. By so doing the architect is telling the contractor that he or she accept no other way. This system presents the contractor with a problem, and talks or negotiations may be required. Young architects, however, should be aware of the fact that minute detailing (to the point of overdetailing) can be dangerous. First of all, it is impossible for one person to know everything about all construction systems. The contractor will often see, or know of, a better way to put a series of materials together. The architect, seeing it another way, may introduce more cost by virtue of more

elaborate equipment or material needed or more time required. The project budget will suffer.

Here appears that particular point, similar to the finite line between love and hate, at which the young architect must learn to stop detailing. It must be said that underdetailing is even more dangerous, because assumptions will be made by the contractor. The client may be shortchanged by shoddy work that cannot be rectified without additional cost, usually to the architect, who did not do his or her job properly. This is the experience factor in architectural practice, not only to know what to show but how to show it and where to stop.

The categories of fireplaces and stairs are prime examples of this dilemma of detailing. For many hundreds of years people have been trained as masons or bricklayers. Part of their training has been concerned with the totality of the masonry system—not only walls and corners but such details as corbeling, decorative bonds of brickwork, tying walls together, and fireplaces. Many years ago fireplaces constituted the heating system; masons became experts in building them, and even today some of the older masons may still be specializing.

A good fireplace is, of course, architecturally pleasing, but it is also one in which the draw (the operation of the fireplace) is excellent. It makes no difference what the exterior shell of the fireplace may be. Primarily it can be paneled or brick-faced; it can have a metal hood over the opening or any number of other motifs. The configuration can be varied: a single opening, an open corner exposed to two sides at right angles,or two openings through which one can look from room to room. Some fireplaces are open on three sides, and some are freestanding.

No matter what the system, the basic detailing remains the same. A fireplace must have a properly proportioned opening and should be pleasing to look at (a rectilinear opening is much more desirable than a square). Some have openings in which a person can stand upright. Once the size is determined, the firebox itself must be properly shaped, usually tapering toward the rear, and lined with high-temperature firebrick. (Common brick will not withstand the excessive heat and will crack and spall.)

The next important factor is the height of the chimney and the size of the flue. The chimney should extend at least 2 feet above the high point of the roof. The orientation of the building and the prevailing winds must be considered for both the height of the chimney and the placement of the fireplace. Flue size can be adjusted if a height problem affects the draw. Generally speaking, the higher the fireplace, the greater the draft speed involved. The wind and the surrounding buildings must be taken into account. A flue that is too large is better than one that is too small. (If it is undersized, the flue will not provide sufficient draw for the smoke, which will pour back into the room.) In the preferred method a vitrified clay lines the chimney mass up into the flue. Without this lining, cracking has a tendency to appear that will allow seepage of water into the masonry and thus facilitate deterioration.

The architectural detail of the fireplace requires a number of dimensions; here, again, overdetailing should be avoided. A plan should show a section and its dimensions to make sure that the chimney is properly designed. An elevation is particularly helpful to show the client the decorative form of the fireplace.

In studying the section of the fireplace, we note that the firebox slopes upward to the damper. The throat above the damper slopes back and up into the smoke chamber and then to the flue. A good mason will know how to place the brickwork and will also be familiar with the correct dimensions and angles even though they are not shown. The mason should be held responsible for providing an operable fireplace.

Here it can be seen that if we begin to put in what we think would be a "good" shape for a smoke chamber, it is conceivable that the chamber will not work. Dampers of steel and cast iron come in stock sizes. On the various charts available all dimensions of the fireplace have been figured out and proved workable, in which event it is not necessary to detail every feature of the fireplace, for again some misinformation could cause failure.

Many general rules of thumb may also be applied. Sloping walls immediately above the damper are usually set at 60 degrees above the horizontal. The rear wall is built vertically and the front wall is corbeled or splayed out to form the angle back to the flue. Various configurations can be made for the ash dump; if there is space below, the dump can be installed in the bottom of the firebox. It can also be built into the rear wall to the outside of the room. In some instances when no access can be had to an exterior wall or to the fireplace floor, the dump becomes a pan that must be emptied through the firebox opening.

It is most important in fireplace design that a hearth of noncombustible material be provided for approximately 18 inches in front of the firebox. A material such as quarry tile, brick, slate, flagstone, or similar masonry materials is a common choice. One other factor that must be seriously considered is the amount of heat generated. This heat must be prevented from superheating any adjacent wood framing, and starting a fire. Various fire codes prohibit direct contact between the fireplace construction and the framing members. Usually a 2-inch air space must be allowed between the two. In some instances this air may be filled with a noncombustible insulating material. The masonry construction of the chimney offers some insulation, but the wood members will still be warmed by the tremendous heat in the firebox.

Various specialty fireplaces are available, particularly in the more contemporary styles. They include a hooded type of fireplace screen, but the basic masonry construction is still provided even though the hood is merely a decorative element. No matter what the system, no matter what the motif or type of fireplace, the client is not going to be satisfied if the fireplace operates poorly. If the flue is too small, the damper throat too narrow, the chimney too low, and other exterior conditions inhibit the proper flow of air around

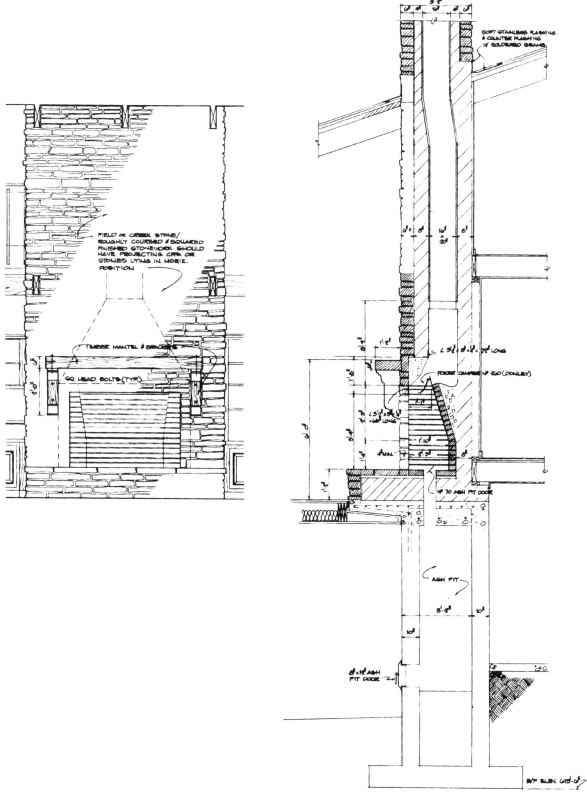

A full section and elevation of a fireplace. The basic construction and the proportions of its vital aspects will remain static no matter how many variances occur in its design. The example shows how carefully dimensioned and detailed the working parts of a fireplace must be.

Size Category	Width of Opening W	Height of Opening H	Depth of Opening D	A	B	Nominal Flue Size
Single faced						
Very small	2'-0	2'-0	1'-5"	6"	1'-0	8" × 12"
Small	2'-8"	2'-3"	1'-8"	6½"	1'-2"	12" × 12"
Medium (most common)	3'-0	2'-5"	1'-8"	6½"	1'-2"	12" × 12"
Medium large	3'-4"	2'-5"	1'-8"	6½"	1'-2"	12" × 16"
Large	4'-0	2'-8"	2'-0	9"	1'-4"	16" × 16"
Very large	5'-0	3'-1"	2'-0	9"	1'-4"	16" × 20"
Double faced, corner						
Small	2'-8"	2'-3"	1'-8"		1'-2"	12" × 16"
Medium	3'-0	2'-5"	1'-8"		1'-2"	16" × 16"
Medium large	3'-4"	2'-5"	1'-8"		1'-2"	16" × 16"
Large	4'-0	2'-5"	2'-0		1'-2"	16" × 16"
Double faced, opposite sides						
Small	2'-8"	2'-5"	3'-0			16" × 16"
Medium	3'-0	2'-5"	3'-0			16" × 20"
Medium large	3'-4"	2'-5"	3'-0			16" × 20"
Large	4'-0	2'-8"	3'-0			20" × 20"
Three-faced						
Small	3'-4"	2'-3"	3'-0			20" × 20"
Medium	3'-8"	2'-3"	3'-0			20" × 20"
Medium large	4'-0	2'-3"	3'-0			20" × 20"
Large	4'-8"	2'-3"	3'-0			20" × 24"

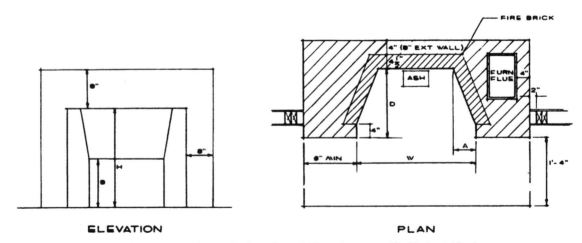

The design of a fireplace requires the application of special formulas, as codified in the table shown.

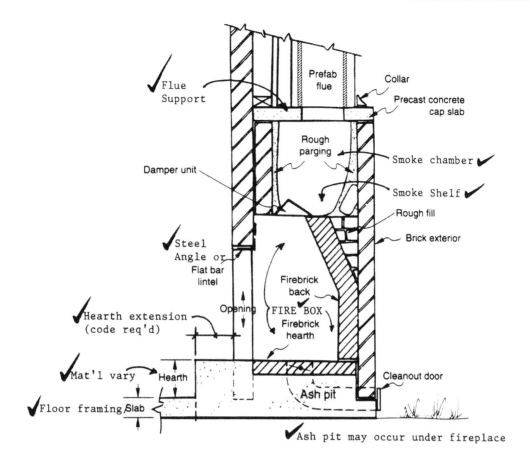

Fireplace design is a highly developed masonry specialty. The relationships between the hearth opening, the vent shaft, the damper, the smoke shelf, and cleanout features are critical.

Other than sizing and proportioning the firebox of a fireplace and the flue, it is very hazardous to do any more detailing, particularly for the damper installation, the smoke shelf, and the smoke chamber. This includes the slant, warp, slope, etc. of these items.

Where all of these items are detailed and installation is made per the drawings, and the fireplace does not work, the fault lies with the designer/drafter.

Conversely, if the designer details only the sizes of items (as previously noted), the responsibility to provide a working fireplace lies with the contractor or builder. Where that installation fails to occur, it is then the responsibility of the contractor/builder to remedy the situation, at his or her cost—not at an added cost to the owner or to the designer/drafter.

the top of the chimney, the draft will not evacuate the smoke from the chamber. Freestanding fireplaces or open-backed fireplaces tend to allow smoke into the room, and it becomes more important that room drafts be prevented by the installation of glass sides or screens. Freestanding fireplaces present another sort of problem: there is usually no masonry enclosure (for these are packaged units) unless it is properly designed by the architect.

Steel fireplace boxes can be covered with masonry or other material to provide ducting for warm and cool air, the warm air being produced by the fireplace and the cool being returned to assist in combustion. These are stock units and all sizing is done by the manufacturers.

The main point is that numerous systems and numerous fireplace styles are available, all of which must be carefully detailed. Moreover, the manufacturer's data must be incorporated to make sure that the fireplace will operate.

In the same vein, stair building is a highly specialized trade. A great variety is available: wood, steel, aluminum, open tread, open riser, closed riser, decorative, and utilitarian, but a few basic principles apply to all. Here, again, a team of factory experts will be better equipped than the architect to supply complete detailing. The overall design criteria can be shown by the architect, but it may be wise to allow the actual completion of the detailing and construction to be done by the workers in the factory.

In most instances the architect will demand, in the specifications, that the stairs carry a certain load; for example, 100 pounds per square inch. These calculations can be made by the manufacturer and checked by the structural engineer.

Most important to the young draftsman is the layout of the stairs and a knowledge of the various types. Stair design depends on the amount of space expendable for vertical access. Stairs are really sometimes a necessary evil. If at all possible, a minimum area should be used. In decorative or monumental types the reverse is true. The idea of stairs primarily for public use is that they be safe and comfortable. Often stairs that look easy

---

Fireplace openings. The opening in the face of the wall; it may be a single-face, two-face, or three-face opening, depending on the design.

Hearth. Fireproof masonry floor in front of the opening, usually raised.

Mantel. An extension from the face of the fireplace above the opening; can be wood, brick, or stone.

Combustion chamber. The area within the opening that is lined with firebrick; also called fire box.

Throat. The narrow area just above the combustion chamber leading to the flue.

Damper. A steel or cast-iron door directly over the throat to control the draft through the fireplace opening.

Smoke shelf. The horizontal projection just above the inclined back wall of the chamber prevents downdrafts through the flue from putting out the fire or blowing smoke into the room.

Smoke dome. The tapered cavity above the smoke shelf and at the bottom of the flue.

Flue lining. Vitrified clay units that line the flue shaft.

Chimney pots. Extensions of the flue lining above the top of the chimney; must be made watertight around top of chimney.

Cap. Stone or concrete cap at the top of the chimney for the purpose of waterproofing the masonry; its sloping top surface sheds water; sometimes known as a "cement wash."

Ash dump. Small door in floor or rear wall of the fireplace for removal of ashes.

Ashpit. Cavity below the fireplace from which ashes can be removed through a basement or exterior door.

Hood. Metal covering (usually copper) above the fireplace opening, attached to the face of the brick and forming a smoke dome.

Certain terms apply specifically to fireplaces and their construction. The vocabulary is included to help the draftsmen and designer to speak the language of the trade.

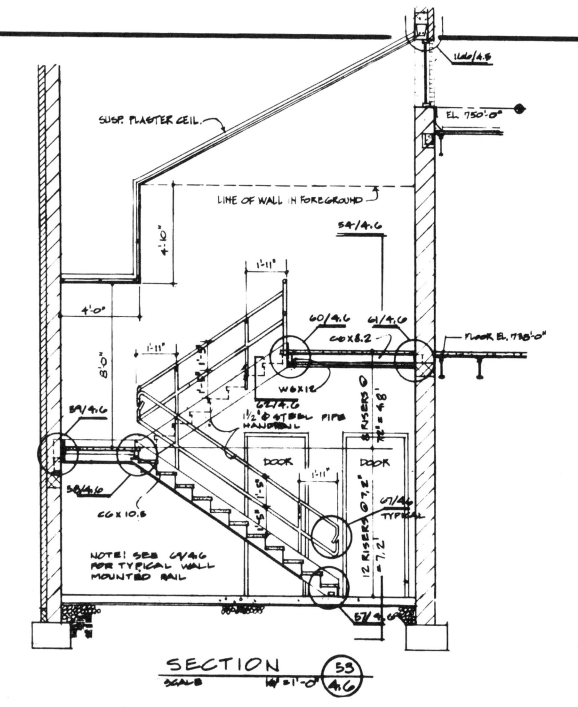

SECTION (53/4.6)

Note the number of detail references shown in these two stair sections. Because they have been drawn at a small scale, the details must be larger to show the construction of the stairs. Note the overall type of dimensioning that gives the full requirements.

497

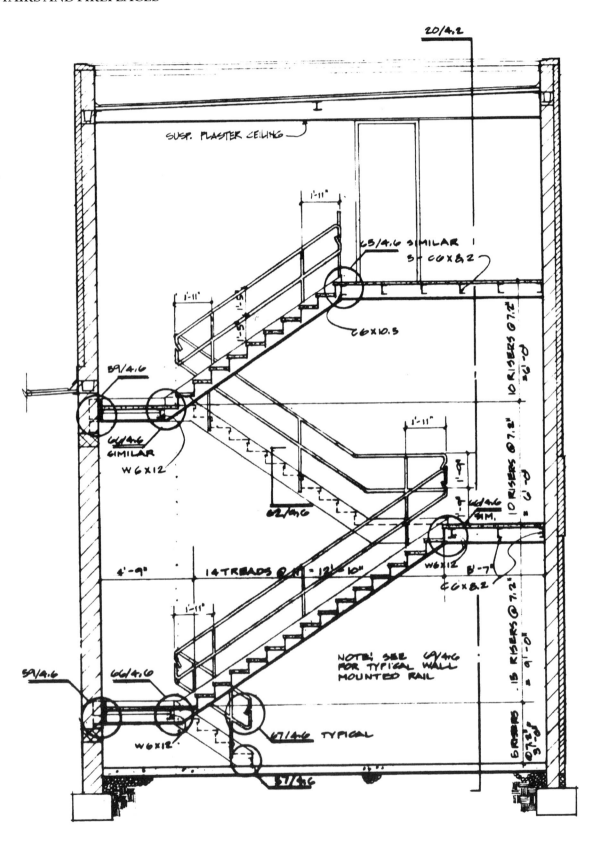

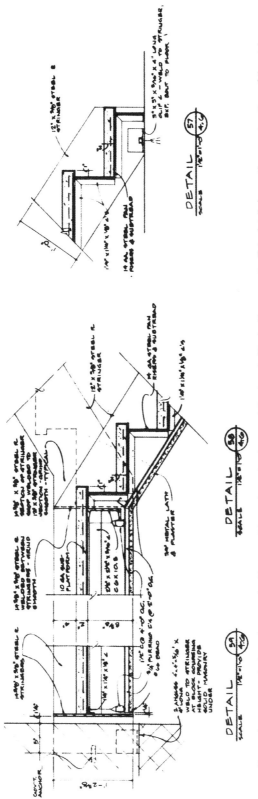

Shown here are typical steel pan stairs. The metal frame is set in place and the treads filled with concrete. This detail shows the construction of the stairs in the preceding drawings.

499

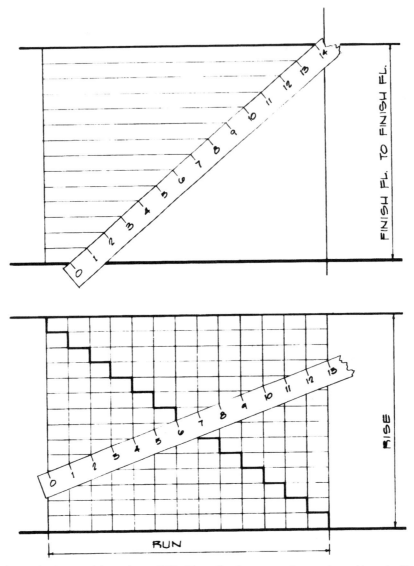

This chart shows the layout of the stairway. With this method even spacing can be achieved without scaling errors. Scaling would be extremely difficult, for the riser dimensions are often odd fractions of an inch. The layout would follow the calculation of the number of risers for the floor-to-floor height.

to climb, such as those with low risers, will have wide treads that make the normal rhythm of ascent or descent impossible, and become difficult to climb.

An established proportion of the riser to the tread must be followed. Over the years risers have fallen within a range of 7 to 7 ½ inches in height, a comfortable rise, although in some instances service stairs (not for public use) employ 8-inch risers. For public use the 7 to 7 ½ inch riser is a must, in conjunction with which most coding agencies will demand some relation between the

height of the riser and the depth of the tread. There are three basic formulas:

1. One riser plus one tread should be 17 to 17½ inches.
2. Two risers and one tread should be between 24 and 25 inches.
3. One riser multiplied by one tread should be between 70 and 75 inches.

Therefore, if we choose a 7-inch riser, we will automatically go to a 10- or 10½-inch effective tread width. The effective tread does not include the nosing or overhang of the tread.

Again, some treads are as narrow as 9 inches for utility stairs, and some have gone to 12 inches and more for the monumental. The stair angle is usually between 30 and 35 degrees. As the chart shows, nay radical departure from this norm is more like a ladder and anything less than 30 degrees resembles a ramp.

Many codes prohibit fewer than three risers in a run of stairs. Similarly, they prohibit more than 18 risers in any run unbroken by a landing. This prevents the public, particularly the aged or handicapped, from having to work at climbing a set of long stairs. Here, at least, in every 18 risers there is a place to rest before undertaking the next run. One- and two-step risers are extremely dangerous. Many injuries are caused because people are unaware of them, and many lawsuits have resulted. If the designer finds a situation in which one or two risers are needed, another means of making that level change should be investigated.

The layout of the stairs begins with a calculation of the number of risers and treads. The first dimension to be determined is the floor-to-floor. The number of risers can be determined by dividing by the 7-inch riser. We often find that a fractional answer is the consequence; for example, an 8-foot ceiling plus a floor construction of 11 inches and a 2 X 10 joist, adds $9\frac{1}{2}$ inches, plus 2 layers of $\frac{3}{4}$-inch flooring, for $1\frac{1}{2}$ inches, when divided by 7 produces a quotient of something around 15.25 inches. Of course, it is impossible to produce a quarter of a riser, and either 16 risers at a height lower than 7 inches or 14 risers with something more than 7 inches in each rise must be provided.

Once the number of risers is determined the number of treads is established, for there is always one less tread than riser. By going through the proportioning formulas we can see what the width of the treads should be.

Because of the odd fractional dimensions for risers, it is difficult to scale the drawing when trying to produce a detail of the stair profile. The best means is to scale the floor-to-floor height and draw in the lines. Then take the number of risers; for example, 14. Any of the architectural scales can be used. By placing zero on one floor line and a multiple of the number of risers on the other (14, 28, or 42) the space between the two floor lines is then divided into the proper number of spaces equal to the number of risers.

By knowing the number of treads and their width, the run (total of tread widths) can be calculated and established by two vertical lines equal to the total run. This total can be properly divided into the correct number of risers just as the treads were determined. With the production of the grid the stair profile can be developed and the details added as necessary. Although the basic layout does not change, there is a requirement of 6 feet 8 inches to 7 feet of headroom between the stairs and the construction above as one walks up or down the stairs. This headroom can locate the header in the floor framing and the sloped ceiling over the stairs. Whether they are concrete, steel, concrete-filled pans, or wood, the layout system is the same. The detailing becomes different in the actual construction, not in the configuration of the stairs.

Many helpful booklets have been published about the various methods of stair construction. Concrete stairs, for instance, are basically slabs that span from one floor to another, with a triangular-shaped riser-tread profile added to form the stairs. All the accouterments of landings and railings are easily added, depending on the demands of the building.

Stairways are also classified in the codes by width, type, and construction. Egress from a building is most important. In an emergency situation the building should be evacuated in the most direct and efficient manner possible. The stairs should be easily negotiated; there should be handrails, and the stairs should be "easy" so that one person or a group of persons will have no trouble leaving the building in an emergency. Stairs should ordinarily be kept to a minimum size. In some cases, however, they must be oversized because of the number of persons in the building. Winders (risers and treads placed diagonally at a turn) are prohibited because it is easily seen that the winder-tread near the inside becomes too narrow to function as a step. It is dangerous and can cause serious harm.

The overall concept, the basic layout of the stairs, is similar to that of the fireplace. We do not necessarily have to detail every single connection or even every item in the construction of the stairs. The architect must be so familiar with the layout, codes, and requirements of the building that he or she can determine what the stairs must do and how they must serve. Architectural detail can be added to them to make them whatever the architect wants them to be. In most instances the

TO CALCULATE STAIR DIMENSIONS

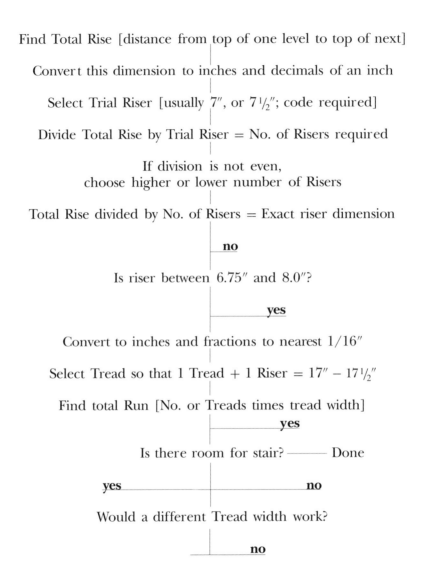

Find Total Rise [distance from top of one level to top of next]

Convert this dimension to inches and decimals of an inch

Select Trial Riser [usually 7″, or 7½″; code required]

Divide Total Rise by Trial Riser = No. of Risers required

If division is not even,
choose higher or lower number of Risers

Total Rise divided by No. of Risers = Exact riser dimension

no

Is riser between 6.75″ and 8.0″?

yes

Convert to inches and fractions to nearest 1/16″

Select Tread so that 1 Tread + 1 Riser = 17″ − 17½″

Find total Run [No. or Treads times tread width]

yes

Is there room for stair? ——— Done

yes   **no**

Would a different Tread width work?

no

final shop drawings and construction of the stairs will be left to the fabricators.

CHECKLIST: STAIRS

1. Check building requirements.
2. Check required loading, dimensions, and clearances.
3. Material indications, width of tread, number of risers, height of risers, direction of travel, handrails and trim, grade elevations of landings (and floor or levels served), structural coordination, and features of the stairs, railing anchorage, and general stair construction.
4. Extra attention should be given to the following for exterior stairs: pitch of tread (to drain water), side walls and buttresses, ramps, tread finish (nonslip), watertight handrail anchors, tight jointing for veneered stairs (stone-on-concrete, etc.).

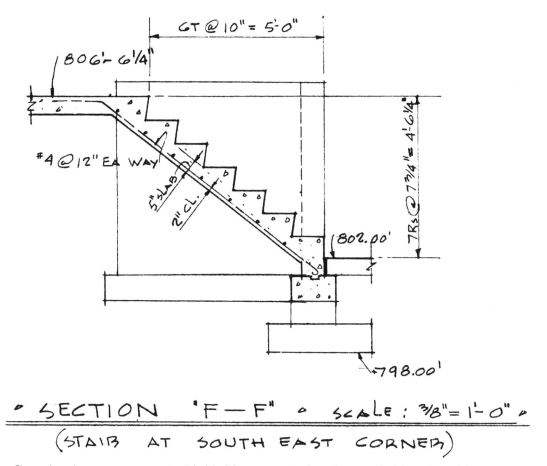

806'- 6 1/4"

6T @ 10" = 5'-0"

#4 @ 12" EA WAY

5" SLAB

2" CL.

7 Rs @ 7 3/4" = 4'-6 1/4"

802.00'

798.00'

° SECTION "F—F" ° SCALE : 3/8" = 1'-0" °

(STAIR AT SOUTH EAST CORNER)

Shown here is a common concrete stair slab. It is necessary to show the overall height and run of the stairs and the reinforcing for the slab.

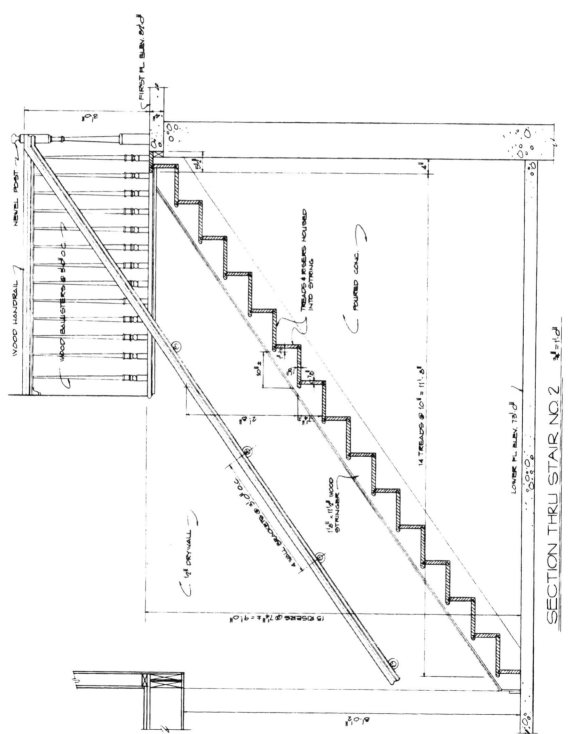

SECTION THRU STAIR NO. 2

The construction of this typical stair may vary, but the basic elements are shown with the correct dimensioning.

Balusters. Vertical supports for the handrail of open stairs.

Carriage. The rough structural support for treads and for risers of wood stairs, sometimes called a stringer.

Closed stringer. The visible member of the stairs that abuts the risers and treads but is not cut to show the profile of the stairs.

Handrail. The member of a railing that is grasped with the hand.

Headroom. The narrowest distance between the surface of a tread and any construction above.

Housed stringer. The stringer that has been grooved to receive the ends of the risers and treads.

Landing. The floor at the top or bottom of a flight of stairs; can also be located between flights.

Newel. The main post of the railing at the bottom of the stairs or where they change direction.

Nosing. The projection of the tread beyond the face of the riser.

Open stringer. A stringer that has been cut to fit the profile of the stairs.

Platform. The intermediate landing between stair flights.

Railing. The handrail and baluster.

Rise. The total floor-to-floor height of the stairs.

Riser. The vertical face of the step.

Run. The total horizontal length of the stairs, including platforms and stairs.

Stairwell. The enclosure in which the stairs are built.

Step. The combination of one riser and one tread.

Stringer. The inclined member supporting the risers and treads.

Tread. The horizontal surface member of each step, usually hardwood.

Winder. The wedge-shaped treads at a turn of the stairs (usually illegal).

Riser heights and tread widths are planned so that the stairs will have uniform steps throughout the flight, making it comfortable to ascend or descend from one floor to another.

Stairway drawings employ special terminology, and for the sake of easy construction the draftsman will do well to use the correct terms for all items and all construction. The most common references to stairs and stairways are listed.

34

Environmental Control Systems

In addition to architectural drawings, every project needs a number of environmental systems (plumbing, heating and ventilating, air-conditioning, and electrical), added to which are the life-safety systems (sprinklers, alarms, detectors, and others of a mechanical nature; e.g., telephones and pneumatic tubes). The sequence in which these drawings are done has a different orientation than the architectural drawings.

In these systems, drawings show the building, and the various room areas, as shells in which the various environmental system equipment and devices are located. The complete array of systems must be included and fully delineated. The outline of the building and rooms are shown lightly, so they can be differentiated from the systems work. They still must be reproducible and readable. In the past, the building lines were drawn on the backs of sheets and were known as masks, ghosts, or backups. In this way, any erasure on the front of the sheet would not necessitate redrawing the building. Today many offices use halftone prints or photographic methods, which screen out the intensity of the building lines. Now,

of course, the building lines can be most easily varied in weight and intensity, via CAD settings.

As a rule no building openings (doors, windows, etc.) were shown, since the systems be shown are usually located in the plenum space above the ceilings and the openings below. Mechanical designers should be fully aware of these and similar features, but they usually have no direct bearing on the layout of the systems.

Basically, mechanical systems show a schematic layout. More often than not a particular waste line in a plumbing drawing or a conduit in an electrical drawing will not be built in the exact position shown. This is not to say that the installation is wrong or that it should be changed, although some inspectors may view it that way. It is a matter of fitting the system together and of running the lines to facilitate not only that system but to prevent conflict with others. The latter is an especially knotty problem on any construction job. There must be a tremendous amount of coordination between the mechanical trades, and good mechanical drawings will to a large degree remove all sources of friction. If the engineers and designers who produce these drawings are aware of one another's responsibilities, they will

507

not plan a light fixture for the same location as an air diffuser. This coordination is usually rather hard to come by even in the same office and much more so in dealing with several consultants.

The plumbing drawings are produced primarily in a single line context—basically a centerline. A number of symbols are entered in the lines for proper identification, to show the vertical risers and vents as well as the horizontal runs, the interconnections of the fixtures, and, most important of all, where the pipe sizes change. The schematic drawing will not contain every fitting or every length of pipe, for this is left to the person in the field. Locations and interconnections are the crux of the plumbing drawings, shown in the plan for each floor. Even if there is only a single floor drain, there must be a plan to show its connection with the building drainage. The plumber must also be informed of the architectural features; he or she cannot run a pipe past a window opening. The plumber must be concerned with the materials used in the walls as well as their thicknesses. A 4-inch cast iron plumbing line cannot be hidden in a 4-inch cast iron partition. The 4-inch partition built of wood studs is smaller than the nominal 4 inches. The pipe itself has a bell-shaped fitting at one end that is larger than 4 inches. The plumbing engineer must work hand in hand with the architect to produce drawings and construction details that are workable.

Along with the plan the plumbing drawings have schematic isometric drawings that show the risers in the third dimension and also the location of all the fixtures.

In heating, ventilating and air-conditioning work the system is a little more complicated. Although used in some cases, a single line drawing (where one line represents a duct of any size) is not sufficient in all cases. More often than not a double line drawing (accurately showing the width of the ducts) will be needed to show the full configuration of the ductwork, and the relationship between the ducts and other features of the work (piping, light fixtures, structural elements, vertical risers and penetrations, etc.) The double line drawing may appear to be more complex, but it provides a much clearer display of actual sizes and relationships. This is especially important to the installers. Usually piping can use just single line drawing, since pipe diameters are generally small, as compared to some ducts. The double line drawing can display any type of reduction fittings, any turns in the runs and outlets; it can show the various diffusers and grilles and their capacities. Here again the designer must consider the building openings. It is far better to center a diffusing grille above a door than to allow it to be off-center. In a paneled conference room the duct outlet will look better centered on a panel or joint than in a haphazard position. Duct work can become intricate. In some buildings it is not uncommon to find ducts that are 60 to 68 inches wide, depending on the necessary volumes of air. Ducts must reach from the air-handling machinery to each room that requires air, either heated or cooled. If other systems that supply heating (hot water, steam, or electric) are present, they must also be laid out to show the appliances in the areas to be heated. Here again the mechanical systems should utilize dark line weights. There can be some tone in the line work, but the building lines should be in halftones. The mechanical trades must be cognizant of the overall configuration, materials, and layout while working with them. All drawings are done to scale so that the project may be seen in complete context and no one will be fooled into thinking that there is more area available above the ceiling than exists.

Mechanical systems, the two-duct system in particular in which air is not only supplied but returned through ducts, can become extremely complicated. These ducts must cross each other, and depth becomes a critical matter. Diagrammatic drawings will show the dampers, thermostats, and other controls. There may also be schedules of equipment; air-handling units, distributors, diffusers, and exhaust fans. Also to be incorporated in the architectural layout of the floor plans are areas in which the ducts can rise vertically (duct spaces, shafts, chases, and recesses). This can sometimes be a problem: to provide sufficient space so that any chases or recesses involved can contain a large amount of mechanical equipment.

Drawings of the electrical ways follow the other types closely. Here the scaling of the drawing may be neglected; fixtures are seldom laid out and dimensioned individually, but the number and general layout must be shown. This allows for variance in the field. It is important to note that electrical contractors may attempt to scale the drawings, a practice that is to be discouraged as much as possible. The contractor should be warned that the layout must in general follow the drawings; the specifics must be worked out to meet field conditions. Fixtures are usually circuited together with

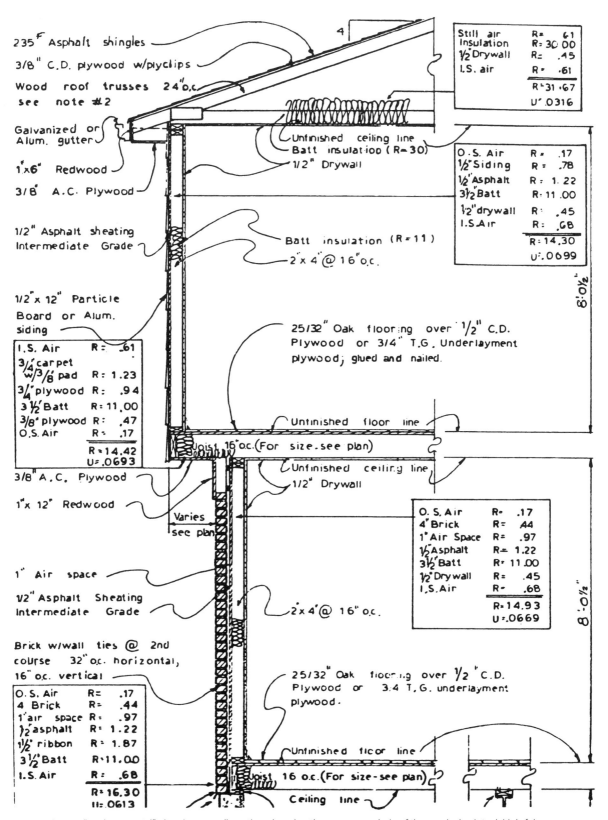

235^F Asphalt shingles

3/8" C.D. plywood w/plyclips

Wood roof trusses 24"o.c. see note #2

Galvanized or Alum. gutter

1"x6" Redwood

3/8" A.C. Plywood

1/2" Asphalt sheating Intermediate Grade

1/2" x 12" Particle Board or Alum. siding

Still air	R =	.61
Insulation	R = 30.00	
1/2 Drywall	R =	.45
I.S. air	R =	.61
	R = 31.67	
	U = .0316	

Unfinished ceiling line
Batt insulation (R=30)
1/2" Drywall

O.S. Air	R =	.17
1/2 Siding	R =	.78
1/2" Asphalt	R =	1.22
3 1/2 Batt	R =	11.00
1/2" drywall	R =	.45
I.S.Air	R =	.68
	R = 14.30	
	U = .0699	

Batt insulation (R=11)
2"x4" @ 16"o.c.

25/32" Oak flooring over 1/2" C.D. Plywood or 3/4" T.G. Underlayment plywood; glued and nailed.

I.S. Air	R =	.61
3/4 carpet w/3/8 pad	R =	1.23
3/4" plywood	R =	.94
3 1/2 Batt	R =	11.00
3/8" plywood	R =	.47
O.S. Air	R =	.17
	R = 14.42	
	U = .0693	

3/8" A.C. Plywood
1"x 12" Redwood

Varies see plan

Unfinished floor line

Joist 16"o.c.(For size.see plan)

Unfinished ceiling line
1/2" Drywall

1" Air space

1/2" Asphalt Sheating Intermediate Grade

O.S. Air	R =	.17
4" Brick	R =	.44
1" Air Space	R =	.97
1/2 Asphalt	R =	1.22
3 1/2 Batt	R =	11.00
1/2" Drywall	R =	.45
I.S.Air	R =	.68
	R = 14.93	
	U = .0669	

2"x4" @ 16"o.c.

Brick w/wall ties @ 2nd course 32" o.c. horizontal, 16" o.c. vertical

O.S. Air	R =	.17
4 Brick	R =	.44
1" air space	R =	.97
1/2 asphalt	R =	1.22
1 1/2 ribbon	R =	1.87
3 1/2 Batt	R =	11.00
I.S. Air	R =	.68
	R = 16.30	
	U = .0613	

25/32" Oak flooring over 1/2" C.D. Plywood or 3.4 T.G. underlayment plywood.

Unfinished floor line

Joist 16 o.c.(For size-see plan)

Ceiling line

A new "environmental" drawing; a wall section showing the energy analysis of the work depicted. Helpful way of showing compliance with energy code provisions without producing extra documents.

an arrow pointing in the direction of the lighting panel that supplies power; this is called a "home run," and is entirely schematic. The curvilinear pattern of lines merely shows where connections are to be made. The actual conduit is not shown, but the location of switches, wall devices, fixtures, and other electrical appliances is given. Because of the complexity of these systems many offices have been separating lighting from power drawings; lighting fixtures and other appurtenances are laid out on one sheet, the various types of outlets on another. This separation provides simpler drawings that are more easily read. Here, again, we have details: meter and panel setups and different types of circuits (emergency lighting and alarm systems).

Imposition of the energy conservation codes has required the various engineering disciplines to submit data about their systems which heretofore was retained in their office calculations. These codes document the ratings and efficiencies of the equipment and the total energy requirements of the entire system. Many have taken the approach that most of these data can be placed on the drawings, although others utilize the specification booklet or even separate submittals.

When utilizing the drawings, it is essential that the data be complete, legible, accurate, and very well referenced. Much of the data can be placed close to the feature being explained, whereas other information can be scheduled elsewhere. Some professionals have incorporated separate sheets designed wholly for energy code provisions. Whatever the motif, the information should follow the "clear, concise, and complete" criteria of all work on the drawings.

The mechanical engineer's approach to drawings is entirely different in orientation, method, and impact than that of the architect. It is most important that there be a high degree of line differentiation between the architectural features and those of the mechanical systems; it is not satisfactory to interpret a wall line as the edge of a piece of equipment or the run of a conduit.

Mechanical drawings contain a vast number of symbols; it is much easier to use a symbol to indicate a minute piece of equipment, perhaps 4" x 4" junction box, than to try to draw it at small scale. The whole idea is to show principles; certain items must appear in certain places. The exact details must be worked out by the people in the field, although much of their equipment will not need detailing. An air-handling unit is designed by the manufacturer, and it becomes a matter of assembling the pieces at the project in the proper sequence with the proper connections. A light fixture is manufactured and wired in a certain way and remains only to be wired into the building system. If there are particular features of the architect's work, such as a light cove, it is important that they be detailed by the mechanical trade.

Cooperation between the architect's project leader and the mechanical engineer should be complete in order that each can meet the other's requirements for a thorough job. Mechanical drawings in a large measure become complicated. In the last 15 years the cost of mechanical systems has increased from about 33 percent of the total cost for a project to approximately 50 percent. The drawings have become more involved because at this point more equipment is being used, as reflected in the amount spent on the mechanical systems. Therefore, the drawings must be complete, just as complete as the architect's drawings; the impact on the pocketbook is just as important. If not done correctly, costs can escalate. No matter how the drawings look, the systems must work. Good drawings go far in ensuring a good installation. It is most important that the architect's project leader, as head of the design team and selector of the consulting engineers, monitor the drawings that are being done. The same criteria that hold for the architectural drawings should be applied to the mechanical drawings: good, crisp line work and neat, precise lettering done with well-sharpened leads against a straightedge.

Many engineers today are field workers who have become involved in design. For the most part they are well trained in the mechanical systems, knowing what they must do and how to put them together, but it is also important that they produce workable drawings. This is not to downgrade the engineering profession, but often in their haste engineers place speed above the overall high quality that the drawings require and end by casting a bad light on the entire set of working drawings.

It must be remembered that the architect has a contract with the owner; the engineer has not. The engineer's contract is with the architect. Control must be exercised so that no one's reputation can be hurt by a poor performance.

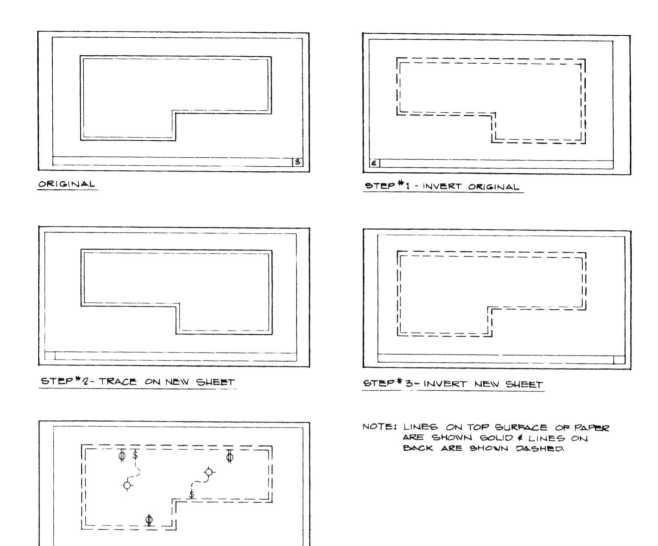

ORIGINAL

STEP #1 - INVERT ORIGINAL

STEP #2 - TRACE ON NEW SHEET

STEP #3 - INVERT NEW SHEET

NOTE: LINES ON TOP SURFACE OF PAPER ARE SHOWN SOLID & LINES ON BACK ARE SHOWN DASHED.

STEP #4 - PLACE DESIRED INFORMATION

The correct sequence in the production of mechanical drawings.

ITEMS FREQUENTLY OVERLOOKED AND LEFT UNCOORDINATED

1. Ensure combustion air for fuel-burning appliances.
2. Establish walls of sufficient thickness to provide space for pipes, pipe chases, hose cabinets, or electric panels.
3. Provide lights and power receptacles in the pits of elevators and dumbwaiters; provide ladders also.
4. Provide electric outlets in attics as required by code.
5. Architectural drawings should locate hose cabinets, electric panels, standpipes, hose bibbs, and so on.
6. Provide fresh air, through mechanical ventilation, for toilet rooms and janitors' closets.
7. Locate all access panels on architectural drawings.
8. Establish and provide street numbers at front entrance.
9. Provide mail drop or box; also, door and/or night bells.
10. Check height of receptacles and thermostats with fixtures, counters, cabinets, and other built-ins.

511

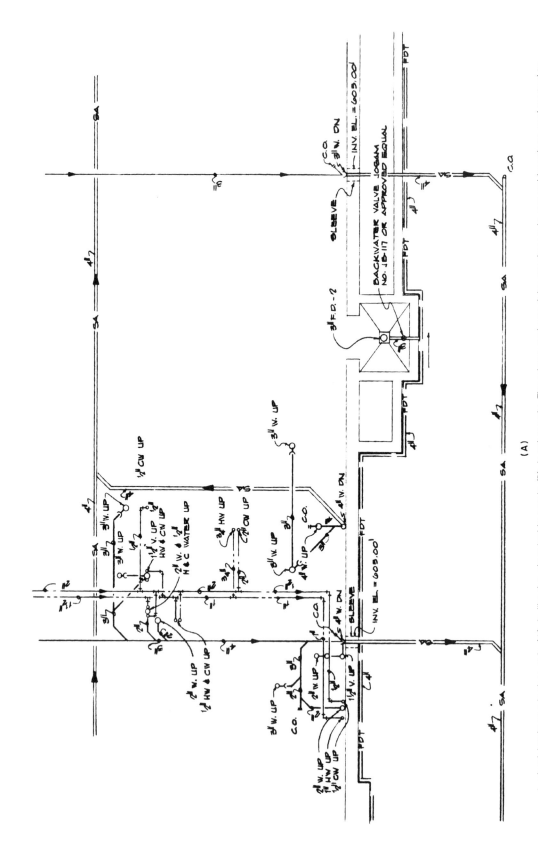

(A)

A plumbing layout is shown in (A). It, like the electrical layout in (B), is schematic. The pipes and conduits are shown in general locations and routed to their proper sources. In the actual building they will vary to meet the conditions.

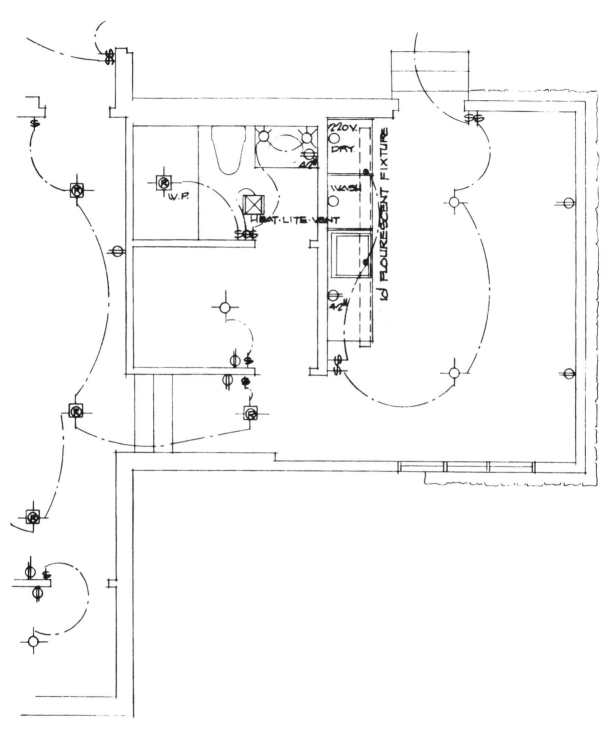

220V.
DRY.

WASH

HEAT-LITE-VENT

W.P.

 w FLOURESCENT FIXTURE

BASEMENT PLAN $\frac{1}{4}" = 1'-0"$

(B)

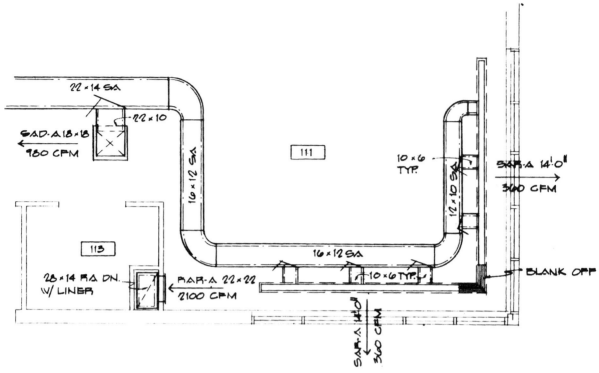

A portion of a duct drawing where notes refer to the features of the system; size of duct, amount of air being delivered, and the like.

11. Ensure proper installation of fire alarm systems and boxes.
12. Ensure proper posting of all areas requiring same.
13. Provide properly for waste receptacle or dumpster.
14. Ensure proper installation of emergency lighting system.

15. Check drawings with all other disciplines for proper coordination as often as possible; prevent errors from reaching the field.

Although not all-inclusive, this is an interesting list of items that are all too often overlooked on the drawings and thus may not be included in the contract.

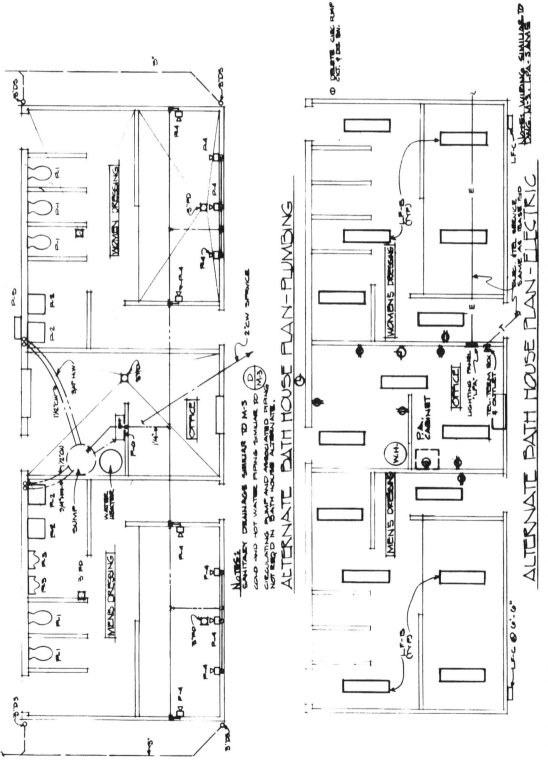

In this example it can be seen how the same floor plan is used in two different mechanical disciplines. Each serves its purpose but also meets the requirements of the building.

515

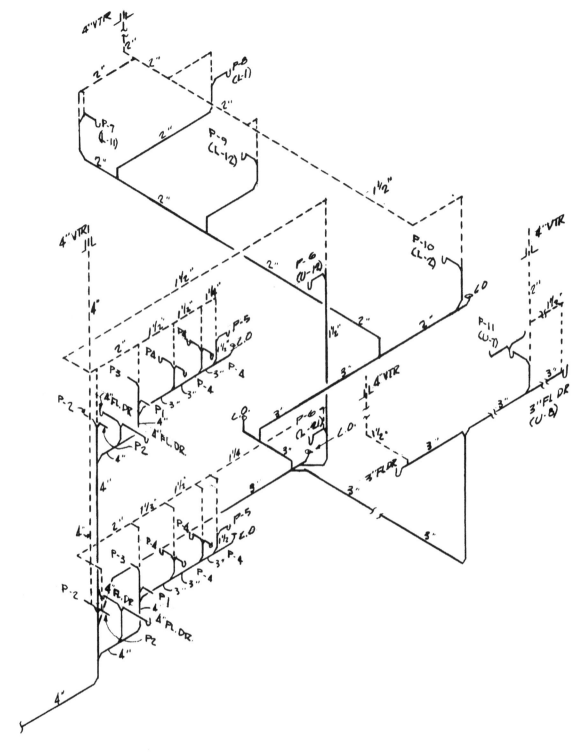

PLUMBING ISOMETRIC
NOT TO SCALE

A typical plumbing isometric, used to show the general run of the piping. Note that the drawing is not done to scale.

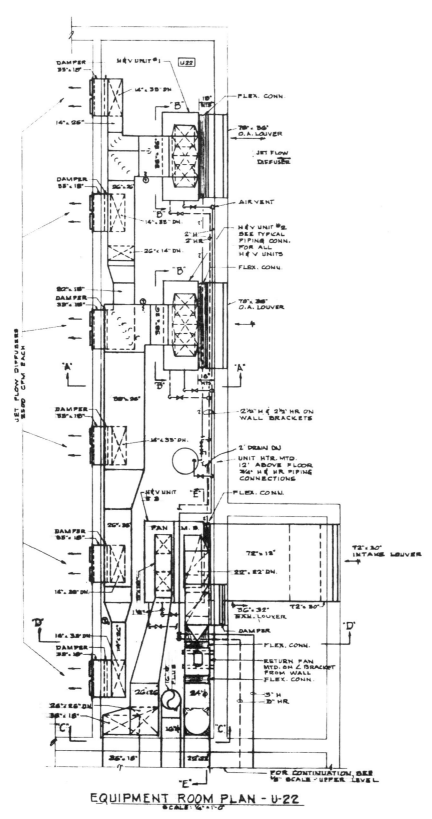

EQUIPMENT ROOM PLAN – U-22
SCALE: ¼" = 1'-0"

A rather complicated layout of duct work for a gymnasium. Note the connections and the "under and over" routing of the ducts. A large amount of detail is also shown.

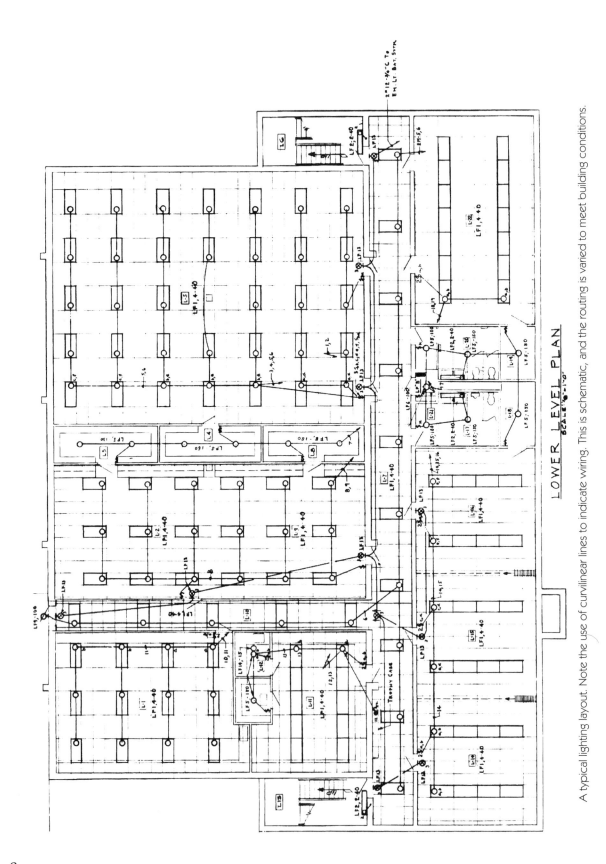

LOWER LEVEL PLAN

A typical lighting layout. Note the use of curvilinear lines to indicate wiring. This is schematic, and the routing is varied to meet building conditions.

35

Production Formats

Down through the years architects have been searching for ways of improving the quality and efficiency of the production of working drawings. Shortcuts, as with all things done in haste, are always risky, although they do increase productivity by expediting drafting. Shortchanging the time devoted to working drawings can result in errors, omissions, and confusion that may creep into the drawings to endanger the project both structurally and economically. This is further compounded by the lack of time allotted for complete, objective review and checking of the drawings before they are put into the hands of the contractors for bidding and construction.

Although the architect has been characterized as more artist than engineer, and more master builder than draftsman, today an architect is assumed to be a professional first, and a business person second, with an array of other functions following. No longer is the profession replete with dilettantes. At the turn of the century, working drawings were unlike those produced today. Full-sized wall sections were common, and these were produced on opaque manila drafting paper. They were cumbersome, time-consuming, and virtually unusable, but in many instances necessary. Owing to the lack of standardized products and stock materials, basic construction, ornamentation, and decorative details were individualized for each project and thus required extensive drafting following the initial design. These required meticulous and minute detailing showing, for instance, the ever changing radii and myriad of curvilinear patterns.

In this early era, working drawings, with their full array of minute detail, demanded, mind-boggling amounts of time and "grind-it-out" work that was an excruciating experience for both architect and draftsman. The drawings were usually produced in ink on linen; each drafter was known for his or her characteristic penmanship; lettering, more flowery than legible, overdecorated the drawings; and final drawings became works of art, beautifully executed, very complete and accurate. The goal of accuracy has never changed, but the formats, procedures, techniques, and methods of production have undergone dramatic change.

Through the years offices and individual professionals have come to realize that different formats can produce excellent working drawings with much greater speed and ease. Only a few years ago an office using details on a repetitive basis was frowned upon as being a "factory" and almost totally unprofessional (not the most praiseworthy virtues). The idea persisted that a client would not get his or her money's worth unless every detail of the project was individualized, either by being original or by being redrawn. Further, it was thought that surely the "artistic" quality of architecture was somehow diminished by these suspect procedures.

There is a strongly emerging concept that should not be characterized as a technique; it is a new overall approach to drafting for construction, as well as other purposes. This concept is vitally important to a segment of the design professionals in practice now, but its full emergence will take more time because of lack of understanding and training. Moreover, not every office has the need or the financial resources to incorporate this system into its practice. To properly discuss the virtues of computer-aided design and drafting (CADD) in the context of this book, we will not address the use or adaptability of the system in the design process. Obviously, the intent in that process is much different from the uses and the mechanics used in drafting mode. So the following is directed totally toward computerization in drafting.

Computer-aided drafting (CAD) carries the use of standardized material to its ultimate, in that the computer's memory banks can be crammed full of library figures, data, information, and other input vital to any project. From the smallest piece of wood blocking to full unit plans, the computer can retrieve and "spit out" any information stored in it. Of course, the memories must be programmed and filled initially and over a period of time, in order for the office to call forth what is needed. With the proper input, the programmer/architect (why not?) can call forth the necessary items, program their rearrangement, and integrate them into details or other desired contexts. The computer will reproduce them with unerring accuracy, and when attached to a "slave" plotter will produce the basis of the working documents (reproducible for the best immediate use). These basic documents then can be enhanced, if necessary, by the other techniques. CAD, then, is a system of storage, retrieval, and reproduction that is quite similar to the paper, pencil, and file cabinet crammed full of standardized drawings and details. The system is also just as passive. Even though an automatic timer could be used to energize, or start up, the CAD equipment, the system has no ability to "think" of its first task, or what to do, or produce, nor for which project. In addition, CAD is totally dependent on hardware and software capabilities, or what is programmed into it by the operator. With a specific database encased in its memory, the system can "spit out," on command, that which the operator calls up. It is here, then, that CAD begins to come into its own: rapid, reliable retrieval of stored data. Next, that data can be easily and quickly modified as desired by the operator and for the project at hand. The original data can be retained (and re-stored in the memory), while the new configuration is carried forth for use.

If, however, there is no appropriate base information in the system, it will not and cannot generate that data. Data entry techniques can introduce such data into the system, as required, for immediate or future use. Thus, it is fairly easy to see that very complex "drawings" *can* be done via CAD, but they may (almost assuredly) involve extensive programming of the system. This calls for a "human" determination as to the acceptability or advisability of CAD use for a particular drawing; normal manual techniques may be preferable, and perhaps even quicker, in some cases.

CAD, then, is a "tool" that functions in a highly responsive and inordinately rapid manner; it is not a panacea for all situations. It should not be considered, or viewed, as a replacement for staff members, but rather as another instrument with which staff can produce the necessary work. It adds a level of reliability and flexibility that enhances the rapid production of good, accurate, and clearly presented working drawings.

Fundamentally, CAD is a different way of communicating the necessary information for a project. It varies from manual drawing in two primary ways; it is a different process for doing things, and is different in content, in that some CAD aspects cannot be accomplished by manual drawing. CAD, however, is more precise, more reliable, and draws much more rapidly; it is "mechanical" and not subject to the foibles of the human. Very quickly, it is evident that CAD really is a tool that is an aid to, not a replacement for, the regular drafting functions. This is the primary consideration that must be kept in mind from the outset and at all times. Let us first compare the advantages of the manual and the computerized systems.

CAD Outperforms Manual Techniques In:

Dimensioning: rapid, automatic calculation and recalculation

Formatting: location or data on drawing

Editing (global or local): rapid changes without erasing

Erasure: easily accomplished in whole or in part

Translation: moving elements around—reorienting

Changes: rapid conversion to a new scale, size, type, or orientation

Stretching: increase or decrease portion of drawing in any direction

Duplication: reproduce all or part of drawing any number of times

Substitution: replacement of incorrect entries

Consistency uniformity: data repeated without error

Layerings: ability to overlay several segments of data, one on another

Looping: repeat a specific task several times, rapidly

Standard tasks: performance repeated—mundane work

Calculation: automatic answers when new parameter set into program

Manual Techniques Outperform CAD In:

Creating: design of drawing—use of imagination—selecting data

Flexible analysis: exploration for correct answer/method

Decisiveness: application of firm thinking

CAD can be relied upon for a good deal of work, a good portion of which is very repetitive. Programs for structural analysis and plans of standard units (motel rooms, workstations, equipment complexes, and the like) are common in many offices and generally reflect the work done by the office in the mainstream of its practice. The more specialized the practice, the more support can be offered by the computer. Of course, there is a large area of commonly used items that could be computerized in any office, but the move to computerization is still a decision of the office.

Perhaps the overriding attribute of the CAD system is the speed with which it performs its functions. This, however, should not be established as a point of competition or comparison with the manual process; CAD will far outdistance the manual. No effort should be expended to match the speed;

it would be fruitless. Rather, the system's speed should be used as a positive resource whereby the CAD system can be utilized to meet the deadlines set forth by the manual methods; they should be finished together. Moreover, where a quick source of input to the manual process is necessary or some additional manual work can be reduced or deleted, surely the CAD process should be used.

CAD also tends to bring a new discipline to the drafting process. Heretofore, office drafting standards have been established more as general guides than anything else. Often, neither adoption nor consistent use (enforcement) of the standards is required. However, with CAD, standards for symbology, line weights, layering, text fonts and sizes, and so on, *must* be established and set into the system. This is a fundamental process that underlies the system, and it necessary to bring it on-line properly. Certainly, because it is quite impossible for the manual drafter to match the CAD product, it is best to establish the CAD standards close to the manual standards. The two then become combined, and usually it is the ultimate client who establishes the level of acceptability. Obviously, a uniform document is a valuable and proper goal; neither CAD nor the manual process should be allowed to "outshine" the other.

Once one has accepted the tool/aid concept for CAD, the next most important consideration is the output that is desired from the system. In fact, this is the prime consideration in the purchase of the system. Preplanning and evaluation are critical to a sound investment. Few, if any, installations will be used solely for drafting purposes. Therefore, there must be a determination as to what design output is necessary and another separate determination as to what drafting output is desired or required. The following is one scenario that could be used in making this determination. This is not set forth as a "norm," inasmuch as different firms will see the list in many different ways. So, too, project requirements will also dictate, to some degree, how the list should be revised or adjusted. Therefore, this list is a guide or a starting point for the consideration of CAD use. The list is incomplete, as it does not contain all the different types of documents. Although it is possible for CAD to produce all of the drawings listed, it will usually be assigned only those in the left-hand column.

Documents Produced by CAD	Documents Produced Manually
Basic modules (floor plan)	Complete floor plans
Site plan (footprint)	Forging blank configurations
Preliminary plans	Elevations (exterior and interior)
Spatial diagrams (blocking)	Single-line flow diagrams
Development in phases	Tooling standard limits
Adjacency layouts (plans)	Material flow patterns
Standard/repetitive details	Primary sections
Perspcetive views	Perspective views
"Intelligent drawing" database(s)	Excavation and fill (site work)
Area and materials reports	Various schedules
Orthoghographic views	Isometric views (schematics)
General notes	Process flow diagrams
Critical path charts	Electrical line tabs
	Piping diagram
	Project title sheet
	Special-condition details (nonrepetitive)

One must then ascertain how the CAD drawings will be integrated with the manual drawings to form a coherent and complete set of drawings. Optimal use of the CAD system must be determined early in the assimilation of the system into the entire office scenario. Producing documents in a shorter time frame, for instance, may not be a consideration worth developing. A 1988 survey showed that firms with CAD are not realizing the highest possible returns in either productivity or profitability. This outcome is tied directly to the lack of optimization of the system. It appears that there is an inherent and quite widespread difficulty in bringing the systems on board and that full utilization is still a coming event. On the other side of the situation, some firms use CAD very heavily, but usually have cheaper, less sophisticated systems that they utilize, according to policy, for longer terms and by more personnel. The survey showed at least one professional who indicated that it is cheaper to use pencils than

CAD, if drafting is the sole or prime function of the system. Yet the same survey showed that the greater number of firms utilize the computer for CAD operations than for both drafting and design purposes. There is also a question of paying for the systems and their annual operating costs (for both computerware and personnel). Firms bill anywhere from 100 to 0 percent of their CAD costs. This appears to depend more on the philosophy of the office and the acceptable market (their clients) open to them. Although these costs really stress overhead allocations, one professional observed that owners are unwilling to pay added costs for something (CAD) that does not necessarily produce a better product for them; CAD then is simply a "production-enhancing device."

Perhaps one of the harder issues that the human mind has to resolve in the consideration of CAD, is that the end product will look somewhat different from a manually produced drawing. There is much more of a no-nonsense, utilitarian look, with none of the unique, embellishments, individualized flair, or other lively aspects of the line work and lettering. In fact, although they are distinctive, some CAD drawings run counter to what many hold as good architectural drafting principles: no line weight variations, overall weakness for good reproduction, blandness, and so on. CAD hard copies (plotter drawings) tend to be "expressionless" if the operator does not incorporate the full variant capability of the system. They will be clear, accurate, and fully communicative, but could concern some professionals who pride themselves in more artistic, hand-crafted working drawings. The more "engineered" look is striking when compared with some traditional-technique documents.

Even this glitch in CAD is now being addressed, as some software programs are capable of producing "architectural" lettering, which simulates the more traditional, stylized hand lettering, so distinctive from office to office, and from drafter to drafter. In addition, different types of lines and different line weights are available, but their quality relies on astute operators who see a value in distinct and differentiated linework.

The choices involved are basic and obvious: is format, style, or appearance more important than speed, unerring accuracy, and amazing ability and flexibility? Perhaps a better standard for comparison is "desirability" instead of importance. The quandary is similar to using the telephone (in lieu of fact-to-face conversation), the sewing machine (in lieu of hand needlework), or listening to verbal pictures on radio (in lieu of watching television). Here just as in CAD, each pair of options are viable and have a good range of appropriate usage; but at times, one choice stands far above the other. In CAD, the end result, even though "flawed" in the eyes of some, is by far overshadowed by the capacity of the system itself and the service it can provide to the professional and the client. CAD fits very neatly into the prevailing and increasing need for more rapid production of higher-quality documents. If we must sacrifice the aesthetics of the traditional drawings, chances are that no harm will come to the project. It is more a matter of changing the traditional mindset of the professional(s); this is simply a better way of doing things overall. Initial training will not establish a fluent operator, nor will it begin to optimize the system's use. It appears that a continuing process of experimentation and exploration will take place (and should) to improve use and to move into ancillary uses that will eventually prove of value. Conversion to CAD, then, is really a continuous process, not a one-time gesture. Simply, your investment in this rather costly venture can be justified only if you see substantial savings in production, as well as in the design processes.

An increasing number of firms are finding that they are hiring "computer wizardry" in their new staff members; some flatly require it. As more and more design schools offer greater exposure, opportunity, and advances in the CADD computer science as part of their architectural curriculums, the graduates will come "CAD - or CADD-equipped." Their impact can be immediate. Although there will be some restricted views or opinions in these persons (depending on their experience and breadth of knowledge), they do offer enthusiastic, on-board computer expertise and can aid in the purchase or update of CAD systems. They will be more able to reflect office procedure, policy, and philosophy in their selections, but may come up a little short in knowledge of "all" available computerware combinations. Outside computer expertise must help. Subsequently, the new hires will almost without exception, be bent toward continuous experimentation and extension of the system into new and innovative ventures. This will aid optimization and cost-effectiveness of the CAD system.

Of course, we are addressing a system that is in a very competitive, evolving, and, hence,

rapidly changing mode. New computer equipment (hardware) is coming on line in a most rapid fashion. The introduction of new technology is constant, to the point that obsolescence is nearly a daily occurrence. Even this, however, is far outperformed by the introduction of new programs (software) on what seems to be an hourly basis. These include both new programs covering expanded or new areas of work and newer versions of old programs with greatly increased capabilities. The selection of software is the driving force in establishing a CAD system. There is a direct relationship between software and hardware, of course, but it must be remembered that not all software is compatible with all hardware and, hence, is not interchangeable. Obviously then, one could purchase a computer system (hardware) and find that the software needed to meet the requirements of the office is not available for the hardware purchased. There can be some conversion and adaption, but this requires a computer expert and, of course, added funding. It is better to purchase software appropriate to the needs and then a computer system either by the same manufacturer or with full compatibility.

There is little, if any, opportunity for trial-and-error experimentation in selecting CAD equipment or even trying to determine whether such a system is right for a particular office. There is, of course, a certain degree of status and fadism in the use of CAD, but the system has well proved its worth over the last 20 years where properly implemented. Its use continues to grow and its functions become more and more innovative. It is just that the financial commitment is deep and operating costs imposing; one cannot simply discard the system if it proves unworkable, inappropriate, or nonprofitable. Like every new medium, CAD must pass through a period of experimentation and evaluation (remember mylar films and grease leads?) before an office can comfortably commit to continued use. There must be wide-ranging discussions of functions, hardware and software, output capabilities, costs, and specific items such as the value or difference between laser and electrostatic printers.

In CAD, because of the dollars involved, one must be sure of the selection before the purchase is finalized. It appears to be virtually impossible to determine, at any given time, what to purchase in this accelerating kaleidoscope of developing technological advances. To address "now," locking in a given scenario, leads directly to obsolescence tomorrow, one must be innovative and imaginative, with a rather wide and clear view of the future. At the same time, one must be very prudent. Here in-depth study, critical analysis, pragmatism, and full discussion are imperative. This is crucial to the success of the purchase and the use of system over the long term. Here is where one must engage in an in-depth evaluation and study of needs and costs, versus available technology. A computer expert or consultant is essential (far beyond advisable). This should *not* be just a salesperson, but one who has a knowledge of the array of sources, manufacturers, suppliers of hardware, software, and allied equipment, and the myriad of possible combinations for any one installation. Otherwise, one can easily be lead into a dead-end where the system purchased is limited in scope and incompatible with new and eminently helpful software. Granted, there is a risk in any purchase in such a rapidly changing field, but certain paths are much more preferable than others.

Operationally, the CAD system works very much like the manual process. Input, be it verbal, written, or sketched/drawn, goes to the operator, who must reshape it into a computer-acceptable form (command, options, or digitizing). This could merely be a command calling forth some "library figure" or other data already part of the database. Otherwise, the instruction may be something that must be fully programmed into the system. Drawings and sketches usually will be "digitized," whereby the input material is traced onto a digitizer pad using a "mouse" or other cursor instrument. Here each line is given its coordinates (on the x-y axis); the computer responds by connecting the points with a line as directed. Each line is then drawn in the same manner—very similar to the manual process. The great value here is that changes can be made so easily (by erasing or changing coordinates), and the computer does most of the actual "drafting work" very rapidly.

The procedures maximize the attributes of CAD: precise, consistent far beyond hand methods in line and lettering quality, faster to the point that it is useless to try to manually match it, and "willing" to perform the most mundane, and repetitive work relentlessly.

CAD instruction and information are more extensive now and readily available from numerous sources. Moreover, good, solid technical information on CAD and CADD, hardware and software, flows quite continuously from good sources like *Architectural Record*, the magazine of the American Institute of Architects (AIA), *The Specifier*, the magazine of the Construction Specifications Institute (CSI), and *Engineering News Record* (which has had an extensive special supplement during the last quarter of the last several years). One is well-advised to plug into this flow of information, simply as an ongoing resource that may eventually aid in updating or changing hardware or software.

Each format discussed in this chapter, and elsewhere in this book, has as its goal the shortening of the office production phase for any given project. This, of course, provides benefit not only to the

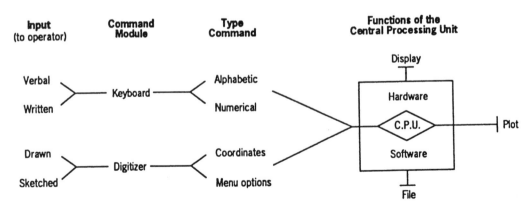

A flowchart depicting how various input into the CAD System is translated into usable form.

professional but to the client, as well as to the contractor for the project. Each format suggests a degree of simplification and standardization that can be applied to any, and indeed, all projects to do away with costly customizing (except where absolutely necessary). Items that were custom-made in past eras are now either stock items or common practice, which obviously qualifies them for minimal attention. They should be utilized to the fullest, without any fear of stigma; such use has become not voguish, but smart, prudent, intelligent business practice. Whether a project costs 20 thousand dollars or 20 million dollars, there are items that can be exactly the same. Although the quantity would naturally vary, the detailing and the installation can remain the same. Not only should such mundane work be done more rapidly, but it should be done only once.

A broad term has been applied to the new formats, namely, *systems drafting*. Although containing several very different techniques, these can be quite valuable when used individually, as well as in various combinations. The techniques can revolutionize the production phase of any product in any office, large or small. Basically, the entire system need not be employed in every case. Some combination of the following will be the benefits derived:

1. Less production time allows more time for creative work.
2. Repetitive drafting work is eliminated.
3. Better and more effective control and coordination between design professional and consultants are fostered.
4. Larger projects can be produced without an increase in staff.
5. Checking and changes can be made much easier.
6. Production will be preplanned and organization will be less of an "unknown" variable.
7. Quality of final documents will enhance and speed plan review.
8. Better documents will enhance the competitive bidding process.
9. Drafting effectiveness will be higher at lower per-unit costs.
10. More accurate and flexible drafting methods can be employed.

Sounds impressive, but there are some basic dangers in entering this system. First, the staff must be fully trained, and there must be a complete understanding of the techniques and the goals. Time must be spent in this effort. Second, there must be a deep working rapport (not simply a working relationship) with the reproduction firm. It must be brought into the picture early in the transition and must have the expertise to produce the work as required by the office. Many of these firms have a reprographics expert on staff for constant, quick consultation. There must be a commitment by the reproduction firm to meet the same goals that motivate the professional office. Failures in this system are directly attributable to weakness in these two areas.

Because there is no set pattern within the system, the following list of formats, or techniques, is offered with no inferred or intended priority. The new, rapidly expanding formats are:

1. Computer-aided drafting (CAD)
2. Standard or reference details
3. Overlay drafting
4. Appliqué drafting
5. Composite drafting
6. Keynoting/typewritten/word processed notations
7. Photo drafting

Now that computers and the tremendous array of CAD software have become the "tools of choice," the entire process of working drawing production has taken on new dimensions and aspects. Young professionals must understand that there are a host of software programs available and more coming on-line day by day. However, not all professional offices or firms are using the same programs nor do they possess the same hardware. There is such wide variation that one is simply best advised to understand general principles of CAD operations, which are or can be applied with any program. Many firms are using what may be characterized as outmoded, slow, obsolete, or inadequate programming. Others have the very latest versions and releases, such as Auto CAD 14 (issued in 1997). Still others usually larger and more active firms have programs of cutting-edge technology that, are creating revolutionary new possibilities (along with, we might add, new and unresolved problems).

It is almost impossible to capture a typical or optimal situation with CAD, inasmuch as each professional situation has been created by decisions that fitted the computerized operations to the needs and desires of the professional firm. These entail everything from the type of hardware to the software programs that will be purchased and used. The decisions made prior to purchase and initial implementation must reflect the intended uses, the amount of work projected, and the skill of available personnel. Perhaps the main driver is the financial commitment that can be made to the system and, especially, the time and money for appropriate training and orientation to bring the equipment to fully functional productivity. Obviously, a small office with limited staff will outfit itself with an altogether different equipment configuration than a major professional office of several hundred professionals. Of course, the staffing level reflects the amount of work in an office and the kind of work involved. The more complex the work, the greater the value of computerized drafting; consider, for example, massive installations of process piping in a chemical manufacturing plant.

There is also the factor of "staying power" of the particular software. With a continuing and impressive flow of new improved software, there is an inherent desire to work with the latest programs and their new, enhanced capabilities. Software producers, one must remember, have as their sole impetus the gain to be realized from new, unique and better programs; their entire effort is directed toward that end. The hazard to the professional is that the desire for the newest and best may outstrip the financial support available. Programs at initial issue are not becoming any less expensive, so the move to change programs has a direct cost increment and must be carefully weighed against the new capability and value to the professional. In addition, it must be recognized that there is a cost of training and a need to move the new program into full utilization in the work of the office. Both are time and cost factors over and above the cost of the software itself.

Offices are finding that too-frequent changes to new software are quite disruptive to the production process. There is a natural slowdown in making the transition to a new program and a necessary learning period to understand both how the program works and what it can do differently and/or better than the current program. Learning all this, while still trying to maintain production, is difficult and often produces a setback as time is lost in the change. In addition, the skill of the operators increases with the amount of time devoted to a program. To change software just

when staff is "hitting stride" on an older program is not well-advised.

There is also a level of frustration, that is reached periodically. This is best shown by the quotation, which reflects a "bad day at the office."

> **Why is it, that 10–15 years ago, we produced twice the work, with one-quarter the staff, AND no computers?**
>
> — Kaye Stabler
> registered architect

Like any machine, the computer, and its associated components, is marvelous when working, but it is a device that is subject to shutdown for one reason or another—always, it seems, when you need it most. It is not necessarily the electronics of the computer itself that breaks down, but the plotters and such ancillary equipment that are more mechanical in nature. Of course, there are also power disruption and outages and the proverbial "operator error" that still confound production at times. Although disturbing and maddening, the downside is not near enough reason to abandon the CAD process.

There is, however, a real dilemma facing students, educational curricula, and, of course, employers. CAD training, in light of all of the operating programs, is a difficult problem. One of the most prevalent software programs is AutoCAD, which now has its 14-release version in place. One of the releases fits the needs of most offices (from the smallest to the more moderate-sized), but there is then a built-in differential in that the various releases do not offer the identical attributes. The numerous other programs that can be utilized by offices further compound this problem as they choose a full array of software. Large, busier, and multidiscipline firms with high-profile clientele will embrace programs in the range of PArch, MicroStation, and so forth. These of course, are much more sophisticated, utilize 3-D modeling, and appear to underlie the strong trend toward designing in 3-D programming, tying this to a database, and extracting the required information for 2-D presentations and other documents (such as working drawings).

Because of the major inroad of such programs as AutoCAD, most educational efforts are directed toward that specific program. This encompasses the greater number of students, the greater number of offices and job opportunities, and is perceived to be a "mainstream" effort that meets the current employment market. Students, however, are well-advised to look beyond this single program and ascertain what else is now being offered that they might engage or be asked to use in a job situation. Some offices are already looking for and hiring only people with advanced CAD skills. This is noted not to compare one software program against others, but rather as a caution that CAD operations are changing rapidly, education, for the most part, is lagging behind cutting-edge software programs, and employment requirements are escalating, as are job demands.

A good many people offer the argument that CAD is not the fastest method of production in at least some categories. They argue that a manual drafter can outperform CAD in the production of a floor plan and other documents where specific, nonstandard work is required. Others note that even if CAD is perceived to be faster, the fact that someone has to create a sketch for the CAD operator/draft to convert means that some duplication of time and effort is expended. They contrast this with the person in the first instance who merely refines and finishes out the sketch into a working drawing context.

However, when it comes to revising, moving, expanding, copying, or otherwise modifying drawings, CAD has an obvious and tremendous advantage and will outperform manual work. In lieu of the erase-trace-redraw cycle, CAD can merely cut/paste, copy, rotate, and move by "click" command. Such ability is coming to the forefront as the current trend in most architectural software is toward fashioning a project in three-dimensional views and, with an associated database, directly and first-off; rather than with 2-D drawings being converted into 3-D views. This is known as "modeling." It will become more potent as more database (text) is attached to the drawings. Then they can be easily and quickly converted, as required, into the 2-D views for working drawings and the necessary specifications text. With modeling, the project is built electronically and then dissected in a manner and format (the traditional style) that can be given to contractors for the actual construction work.

In addition, other disciplines can add information to the model. This allows better coordination between trades and exposes, more readily, interference problems—for example, piping running through stairways, beams too low for passage, or conduit running through concrete beams. Needless to say, this provides much greater insight into the project and offers a tremendous advantage to the project in that most, if not all, of the problems will be seen early and in an easily remedied condition. They will not linger for discovery and resolution in the field, where more adverse situations can develop.

Well beyond the mere production of a single drawing via CAD are the many and extremely helpful capabilities the program brings to working drawings. Often the fact and principle of "layering" is lost in the analysis of CAD. In bygone days, the drafter merely added more and more information as it became available or apparent. In essence, this actually meant adding layers of information, although it was not formally recognized as such. Neither was the layering retained on a separate format or screen. CAD takes this concept to new dimensions, whereby numerous electronic layers of information can be added or superimposed to produce yet another document. This is done with a minimum of effort and with the inherent accuracy that CAD maintains. It allows any of a vast array of drawings, all different, to be produced quite rapidly.

Just as the early word processing programs for computers obviated the need for numerous retyped drafts of a document, so CAD contributes to the drawings. As in word processing, a segment of information can be moved, copied, rotated, reinstalled, reedited, and otherwise manipulated to create or contribute to a better or new document. The operator or professional of course, must take care in any of this work, but the final result will be quickly produced and will in itself become another layer if not a complete new, stand-alone document. This product can also be a combination of several portions of different documents, with a varied array of information intermixed as necessary to communicate the specific data required—completely and accurately.

The American Institute of Architects (AIA) has issued the second edition of its *CAD Layer Guidelines*. This is a refined version of the original document produced in 1990. The system seeks to maximize CAD as a tool not only for the exchange of information, but also for the production of documentation. The latter is accomplished through the organization and use of standards for files and layers (or levels) essential within CAD. The primary benefit is the greater efficiency in both communications and the work itself. As the technology of CAD changes, there is a need for such guidelines to adjust, change, and, of course, improve commensurately.

The new version expands layer designations to include remodeling projects, establishes one CAD layer as the standard format (no longer using long and short formats), addresses use by other disciplines such as telecommunications and interior design were not included before), and adds information regarding reference files. All this was done in coordination with a national CADD standard that is being developed by the National Institute of Building Sciences at the federal level. There also is coordination with the CSI's Uniform Drawing System (UDS), the Defense Department's Tri-Service CADD/GIS Technology Center, and other new international CAD layer standards.

There also is information and definition regarding manufacturers' product data as they relate to CAD layers. It appears that this will foster the use of specific product information more directly in the document production process.

Some problems can arise in this system and in the CSI's UDS. These are created mainly by the lack of compatibility between the computer programs of the various discipline users. Interoperability (the ability of one computer to "speak" to others) is an evolving technology that still has some inherent problems. Some experts project that it will take about 5 years, minimum, to work out all of the glitches. Although communication, electronically, may be occasionally disrupted, by storms, failures, or outages, the new system for drawing and layering standardization is still valid within each profession. Until the problems of interoperability are solved, some firms may have to simply talk to each other, transmit in alternative forms, maybe even exchange hard copies of CAD plots.

Owing to the large amount and wide variation in the types of data there is a growing need to control CAD operations. In even the best and most sophisticated CAD operations there is a constant need for care and protection of the system and, more important, the information it contains. Although inadvertently from time to time large caches of data have been deleted and otherwise corrupted by a careless operator, a power surge, a power outage, or other electronic mishaps. In addition to relying on in-system timed data-saving devices, there is a need to save data being worked on periodically. Of course, it is imperative to follow set procedures and not to attempt functions that are not understood in full or that are totally "experimental" for the operator.

The loss of data can be a mind-boggling event. Thousands of documents can be lost, which require hundreds of hours to recover (if that is even possible) or reproduce. This, in turn, will have a major adverse effect on operations, record keeping (for future use and resourcing), and meeting project deadlines, to say nothing of the dollar cost involved.

There is also an increasingly crucial need to provide a system of intercommunication whereby one system or program can be related and interconnected to another. Here data could be passed without extraordinary effort, great time loss, or misaligned programs (they could relate to and understand each other). Several programs have been developed or are under development to facilitate this effort. The parochial attitude held about most products is being realigned within CAD and other computerized database banks so that the information is not inhibited or subverted, but ease of access, use, and distribution are available. This is not to say that security, copyright, secrecy, or other needed aspects of propriety and protection are compromised, but rather that the ability to interrelate is so important now that no user will accept a system isolated unto itself. In the field of architecture there is a pervasive need to ease calumniation with understanding and share information with associated consultants, the client, the constructors, and other parties to the contract.

Although the concept of layering is quite simple, the amount of information involved can be formidable. Layering was one of the first attributes used to sell CAD programming to professional offices. It was not well understood at the time. Now, however, it is widely and unwittingly used on a daily basis; it is simply normal procedure. It has become necessary, however, to be wary of the layers so they are not combined or laid one upon the other in a manner or in such numbers that murky, confusing, and illegible drawings result. These, of course, serve no one well and can be problems in the field as well as affect the project progress overall, both technically and administratively (and may be a source of disputes, cost extras, etc.). For some time, several years ago (and to a limited extent even now), working drawings were printed half-size, usually 11" x 17" via offset press. Because this was a printed product, each layer, representing a different system, could

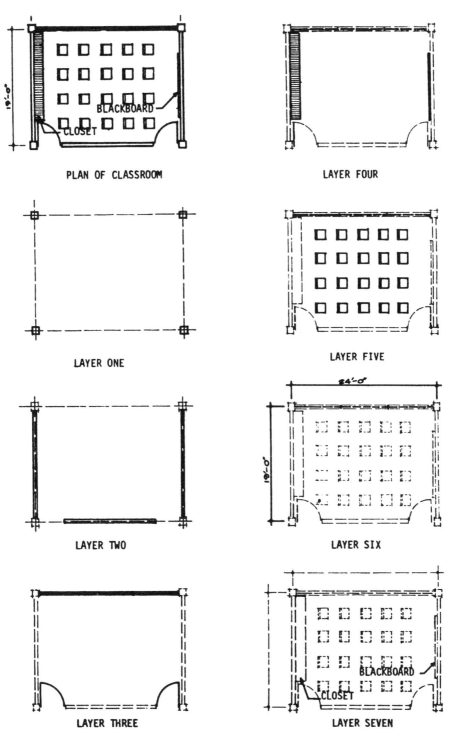

PLAN OF CLASSROOM

LAYER FOUR

LAYER ONE

LAYER FIVE

LAYER TWO

LAYER SIX

LAYER THREE

LAYER SEVEN

Dr. Kaiman Lee

A plan produced by a computer. Each "layer" of information was programmed into the unit previously, and then recalled when required. Ideal for repetitive work, such as this classroom.

529

be shown in different colored ink. Landscaping became "the green lines"; fire protection was in red; water and plumbing in blue, and so forth. This, of course, (yielded extremely useful drawings, easily read and assimilated, which were a tremendous aid to field personnel.

In a supplement published by *Cadence* magazine (August 1998) there was a rather surprising survey. In a sampling of some 250 members of the AIA across the country, there was an exact split, fifty-fifty between those who do and those who do not use CAD. More surprising was the note that "ease of use" was the primary factor in selecting new software, not the cost. In addition, some noted that nonarchitects performed the CAD operations in their offices. Obviously, there are still other methods of production being utilized by various offices and departments within offices. Professionals, themselves, may not be CAD-literate, but certainly make provisions for its use in their operations.

Of course, none of the formats for production have been as highly organized, well publicized, or marketed in a manner that similar to that used to promote CAD. The others were mostly developed or evolved out of necessity mixed with innovation, based on available resources and immediate needs. Those that followed are still in many offices and used for differing reasons. Nonetheless, their value is still intact even though their prestige, speed, end product, and utilization may not approximate those attributes in CAD. These production formats are still capable of communicating the necessary information in a clear, precise, and usable manner, so their inherent value remains despite their shortcomings. Young professionals, and students should take heed, understand everything available to them, and use what best does the job at hand. CAD may prevail in far more instances, but one should never lose sight of other approaches that may serve well for a specific need.

It is well established that working drawings containing good, clear, informative details will produce quality projects while saving money and time, and perhaps most important, eliminating negative feedback over the life of the project. Simply, effective detailing will greatly reduce or eliminate entirely the confusion in the construction process and will thus eliminate most construction errors. With this in mind, doesn't it follow that if a detail is successful in one project it will more than likely be successful in other projects if used properly? Further, doesn't it make sense to draw a detail *once*, properly, then maintain its integrity by storing it for future use? Why redraw it when you run the chance of building in an error in the new drawing? Obvious answers to these questions quickly lead to the realization that standard, or reference, details and their storage, or "banking," is a very easy, quick, and positive solution. Careful production of details in the first place eliminates customization (which is totally unnecessary in this age) and can lead to work that is reusable for similar circumstances. Here staff must understand this system and not try to force standard details into situations that are inappropriate; but there are literally thousands of instances where standard/reference details are the perfect *and proper* solution.

As with any of the new formats, though, there must be a period of preplanning before establishing a system of standard details in the office. There must be a studied approach, or there may be the establishment of several drawers full of standard details, each the property of a different draftsman. The natural flow of projects will produce details that qualify for standardization, so there is no worry about input. The worry is how do we store, and more important, how do we quickly retrieve the details we want to use? Early on, a fairly simple manual filing system filing system emerged and was formed around the 16-division format established for specifications by the Construction Specifications Institute (CSI). Obviously, this was a wise direction to take, as it placed the details in much the same context as other information going into a project, such as material selection, specification writing, and so on. Even now this is not the worst system to use initially, but the volume of details will force some decision rather quickly about a larger capacity (larger than several file drawers) and quicker retrieval (quicker than finger-walking through the entire division). Bulk can be reduced by microfilming; search can be reduced by accurate and up-to-date indexing. Further enhancement can be achieved by assigning one person to maintain the files for both intake and retrieval.

Filing and reuse will cause two other factors to emerge: quality control and standard format. Quality control is best achieved by the use of checklists, guidelines, and set procedures. Information must be gathered from draftsman, project architect, designers, and manufacturers. This data must be evaluated, formulated into details, monitored, checked, incorporated properly,

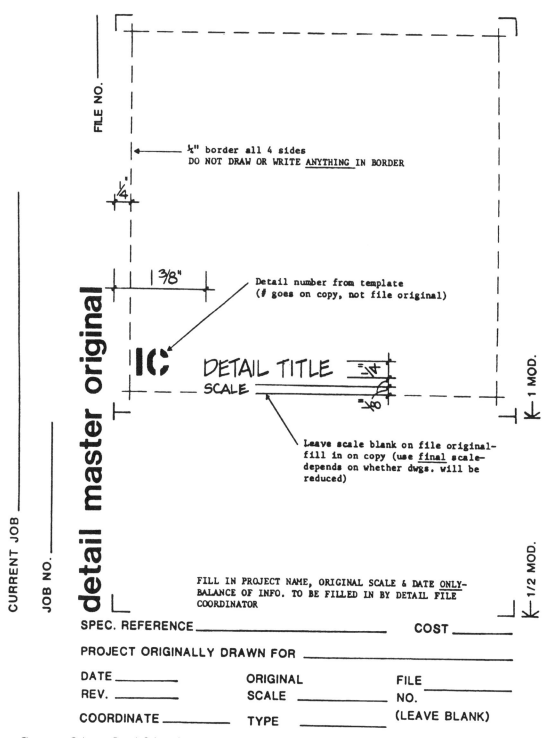

FILE NO.

¼" border all 4 sides
DO NOT DRAW OR WRITE ANYTHING IN BORDER

¼"

1 3/8"

Detail number from template
(# goes on copy, not file original)

CURRENT JOB

JOB NO.

detail master original

DETAIL TITLE
SCALE

1 MOD.

1/2 MOD.

Leave scale blank on file original-
fill in on copy (use final scale-
depends on whether dwgs. will be
reduced)

FILL IN PROJECT NAME, ORIGINAL SCALE & DATE ONLY-
BALANCE OF INFO. TO BE FILLED IN BY DETAIL FILE
COORDINATOR

SPEC. REFERENCE _____ COST _____

PROJECT ORIGINALLY DRAWN FOR _____

DATE _____   ORIGINAL   FILE _____
REV. _____   SCALE _____   NO. _____

COORDINATE _____   TYPE _____   (LEAVE BLANK)

Chapman, Cobeen, Desai, Sakata, Inc.
Architecture, Planning, Interior Design, Graphic Design
A master format sheet for standard details; can be used as a guide, as each office must determine its own requirements.

and reevaluated based on field experience and feedback. Again, the process cannot be done on a whim or at a moment's notice. It must be planned carefully and then integrated into the office. At any point a detail may be proven faulty, and this will require revision or possibly deletion, not only from the project, but perhaps from the file entirely. The system is not a static, passive activity; it is constantly under evaluation, and must be sensitive to changes around it.

Beyond the obvious cost savings in reduced drafting time, the detail bank allows the office to experiment with many other aspects of the new techniques. Any of the other techniques can be utilized, or tried on one small detail, and success then can be evaluated without ruining a large segment of the project. One can test freehand detailing, appliqués, composites, ink drafting, new media, or any new or untried reproduction system. Moreover, these small units are easily integrated into other techniques, such as composite drafting, when the office ventures into even newer production systems.

One aspect should never be forgotten or reduced in status: feedback from the files. This should be formalized by written notes attached directly to the standard detail format and kept on file for the enlightenment of future users. Although full revision may not be necessary, it certainly is wise to keep a constant watch over the detail, how it performed, and what, if any, problems it created. Again, obviously, further cost or problem reduction in the future may be the result. See also the discussion in Chapter 30.

Overlay drafting moves attention from the small detailed elements of the project to an overall view of the work. Primarily, overlay drafting is a process for use exclusively on the various plans necessary for the project. It reinforces the contention that any drawing is really the application of several layers of information onto the drafting media. Overlay drafting is the assembling, vertically, of the necessary graphic information. Simply, "layers of information" are placed on different sheets, combined by laying one on the other, and then reproduced to create a new document that contains all of the information. The first striking cost-cutting feature is the elimination of redrawing the same work several times to accommodate several functions. Case in point: How many times does the floor plan have to be redrawn (or traced) to allow the display of structural, plumbing, HVAC, electrical, ceiling,

flooring, furnishing, and other work? *Too many!* is the right answer.

However, once again what seems like a direct and simple solution must be preplanned and may involve months of research before the office can use the technique on even the smallest project. Overlay drafting is the most actively used technique in the new system. The vast majority of offices have been exposed to the system and either use it completely (for some projects) of have had just a smattering of exposure. In any event the technique will pay dividends only when carefully and completely preplanned; don't be fooled into believing anything else. This preplanning must be across the board, beginning with the staff and extending to the consultants and to the reproduction house. Many firms have created the position of production manager, or coordinator, who devotes full time to researching new systems and implementating them in the office. It cannot be done overnight or by simple memo.

After perhaps months of research and decision making, the first project should be small and should be directed by one person. The very first step is to produce a set of small, or "mini-," drawings that will serve as a guide or map for the actual production. Here, too, a more accurate budget can be prepared and assigned to the production phase, because basically the team knows where it is going. Often, the production team simply sets out to "do the job" without budgetary guidance, only to find in the end that production was the money-losing element in the whole project. Done properly, overlay drafting could reap as much as a 20 percent reduction in productions costs when fully implemented.

The set of minidrawings should then be presented to the reproduction firm. Both the staff and the reproduction firm should be brought together to understand how each functions and what their capabilities are. The best of techniques in the office will be for naught if the reproduction is inadequate. The reverse may seem true but, unfortunately, even excellent reproduction cannot save poor drafting techniques or coordination.

The first project with overlay drafting, although small, should also contain little risk of major change or revision. It should be established that the number of overlays will be kept to a minimum; the concept and theory will be present, but the staff will not be overwhelmed by numerous complicated situations that a large, complex project may require. Ease into this technique. The

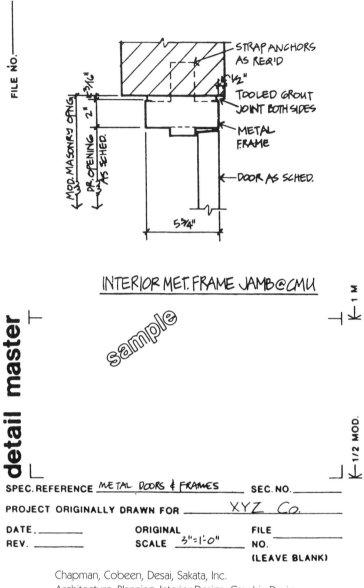

INTERIOR MET. FRAME JAMB@CMU

sample

detail master

SPEC. REFERENCE _METAL DOORS & FRAMES_____ SEC. NO._____

PROJECT ORIGINALLY DRAWN FOR ____ _XYZ Co._____

DATE._____   ORIGINAL   FILE _____
REV. _____   SCALE _3"=1'-0"___ NO.
                                     (LEAVE BLANK)

Chapman, Cobeen, Desai, Sakata, Inc.
Architecture, Planning, Interior Design, Graphic Design
Detail filled in on the sample format sheet.

consultants should be involved and also eased into the system. Remember, the consultants are not uniquely yours; they may work for many other offices and may be involved in many other, different techniques. Not only may they be a source of information to you in your new venture, they should not be ignored to the detriment of your project and system. The benefit you gain will be greatly enhanced coordination between all disciplines.

Overlay drafting begins with the base sheet depicting floor plan elements such as walls, door openings and swings, but no notations. These, including titles, designators, notes dimensions, and so on, will appear on another sheet that, when combined, or overlaid, on the other base plan sheet, will produce the final document. These base sheets (such as floor plans, site plans, sections, and elevations) although principally design drawings, can be taken directly into the production phase without change. Combined with the title block base sheet, they can create the final document.

DETAIL DATA CARD

Detail No. _____

Detail Title/Description _____

_____

DEVELOPMENT DATA

0 Developed By _____

0 Date _____

0 Approved By _____

0 Revision Dates _____

PROJECT IDENTIFICATION

0 Project No. _____

0 Location _____

0 Climate

   0 Temperature range _____

   0 Rainfall _____

   0 Wind speed _____

0 Soils _____

FIELD EVALUATION

0 Construction Period

   0 Response: ☐ Excellent   ☐ Good   ☐ Poor

   0 Field Evaluation Data Card No. _____

   0 Problems _____

   _____

0 Five-Year Evaluation

   0 Response: ☐ Excellent   ☐ Good   ☐ Poor

   0 Problems _____

   _____

0 Ten-Year Evaluation

   0 Response: ☐ Excellent   ☐ Good   ☐ Poor

   0 Problems _____

   _____

RETRIEVAL DESCRIPTORS

Phillip M. Bennett, "Establishing a Standardized Detail Bank," The Paper Plane, May 1980.
A very fine sheet for the development and evaluation of standard details. It takes in the initial and long-term value of the detail and provides a history of the detail and its use.

In the working drawing production phase the final documents required should not involve more than two or three overlays. For instance, the title block sheet overlays the base elevation sheet to produce the final document. A floor plan could require the overlay of the title block sheet, plus the sheet with the structural grid to produce a new drawing for use with all other floor plans required on the project. Adding the sheet of notes, titles, and dimensions, the floor plan becomes a final sheet.

An exact-size duplicate is made of the base plan and given to the various consultants. This duplicate is produced on a prepunched sheet (see the discussion of pin-bar registration in a following paragraph), which the consultant then overlays with a new, prepunched sheet. This work is produced on the new sheet, and the two sheets combined produce another new sheet for the project, but redrawing and/or tracing of the base information has been totally eliminated, and at a very nominal cost.

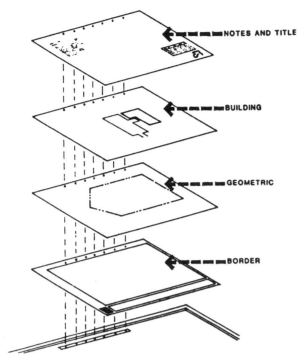

Compubase, Inc.
Example of the overlay drafting concept, manual predecessor to CAD. Note "layers" of information place one on another to create one drawing. Overlay is restricted [CAD is not] in number of layers that can be used; too many will not reproduce well. In both cases it is necessary to avoid overcrowding of data by trying to show too much on one sheet. Also, see figure, page 529.

By placing all of the overlays from the several disciplines on top of the base sheet on a light table, the architect can spot quickly and easily any conflicts between the various elements. No longer will a plumbing vent rise through a light fixture, or a sprinkler head coincide with a column, except on the light table where revision is the least costly. Note, though, that time is not only available now, but it is allotted to checking, thus enhancing coordination, eliminating errors and creating a smooth-running project. It could be that profit will rise also.

An added feature can be introduced to further help assimilation of the drawings. Background information (floor plan behind the duct work layout) can be screened, or reduced in intensity, so the separation between the linework will be more striking. Here the duct work is the important feature, and it will be displayed, to those interested, in a much more direct manner. Confusion is eliminated, and a line of a wall will not be mistaken for the line of a duct.

In the final analysis, overlay drafting yields greater accuracy, as well as greater integrity to the individual drawing and to the set of drawings as a whole. Although the general principle of overlay drafting enhances the drawings, both accuracy and integrity are products of "pin-bar registration." In lieu of trying to align sheets over each other by use of pointed pins or targets printed on the sheets, the new technique utilizes a metal bar attached to the top of the drafting board. Mounted on this bar are several (7, 9, or 11) small metal posts, which are placed to align with the holes in the prepunched drafting media. Because of the inherent weakness of paper, polyester film is usually used; this can take the abuse of being placed over and lifted from the posts. Absolute alignment is secured this way, and the reliability of the overlay is ensured, whether for checking or for final reproduction.

Appliqué drafting will add further to the integrity of the documents. Although containing some inherent problems, this technique greatly increases the impact of each drawing, as well as increasing the speed with which the various sheets can be produced. As with each of the previously mentioned techniques, the tendency toward a rather haphazard approach to appliqué drafting should be forestalled by preplanning and staff education.

Actually, this technique has been creeping quietly into the office over the period of some years. Adhesive materials were introduced and first utilized for title blocks (usually with very elaborate texts for government projects) and for the quick process of adding typewritten notes on a sheet. The material was not very compatible with excellence in reproduction, as there were ghosting and smeared tones around the decals. Much of this problem has been eliminated with more research into the products and with the need to react to increased demand.

Gradually other fixed, or repetitive, items were converted into decals and stuck on the backs of the original drawing sheets. Titles, professional seals, graphic scales, North arrows, and legends of materials were routinely considered stick-ons, but few offices recognized the trend that was facing them. Owing to the lack of thoughtful preplanning, a vast array of opportunities were passed by and the offices continued to grind out the work by hand. Only the obvious received the new technique treatment.

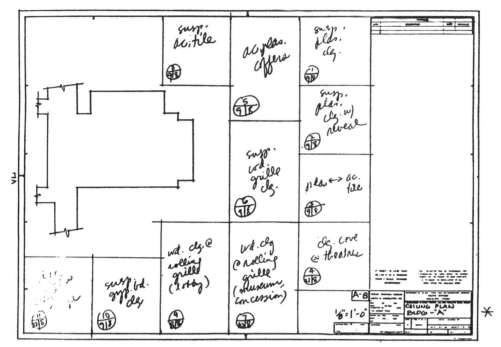

Chapman, Cobeen, Desai, Sakata, Inc.
Architecture, Planning, Interior Design, Graphic Design
The minidrawing is the planning instrument for overlay drafting and guides the production staff in how each sheet is to be developed. Reduces haphazard, misaligned information and adds better coordination to the set of drawings and the work thereon.

Sticky-back film, however, is just one of several materials now available for appliqué drafting. Also included are dry transfers, textured films, and graphic tapes. Most of the expertise in use of these items emanated from the schools of architecture and was actively brought into the offices by students and young architects. There was, of course, the remaining stigma of unprofessionalism. Not until the offices realized the cost implications did the system really take hold and the stigma disappear. Now crisp, dense titles were available hundreds of different typefaces, and they could be laid out and applied in a fraction of the time usually devoted to the title sheet. Rather than crosshatching an area with hand-drafted lines, a tone, selected from hundreds, could be applied almost instantly; reproduction was impressive, clean, and professional.

Once again, however, use outran technology, and problems began to surface in the appliqué technique. Blistering, crazing, and creep of the various items seemed commonplace as the sheets received more work and as they were reproduced by the heat-producing diazo process. Time gained by the initial application was now lost because of the instability of the products and the need to redo the work—in some cases, redoing the work several times. Quickly, it seemed, the industry produced heat-resistant products that could withstand the diazo process. Office personnel also began to plan the applications and waited until near the end of the project for their installation. Others began to overlay the sheets with clear film as they ran through the reproduction process.

Other problems plagued the process as well. Being sticky-backed, the material collected dirt; lengthy storage made the sheets lose their quality, and random, uncontrolled buying produced mountains of the material in offices. First, the system must utilize first-quality materials at all times in order to produce the best and most lasting results. Thus, there must be a quick use and a planned storage system. Surely, standardization of effort and use will preclude each drafter's buying what he or she wants to use. The office should establish what it wants, then advise staff through

536

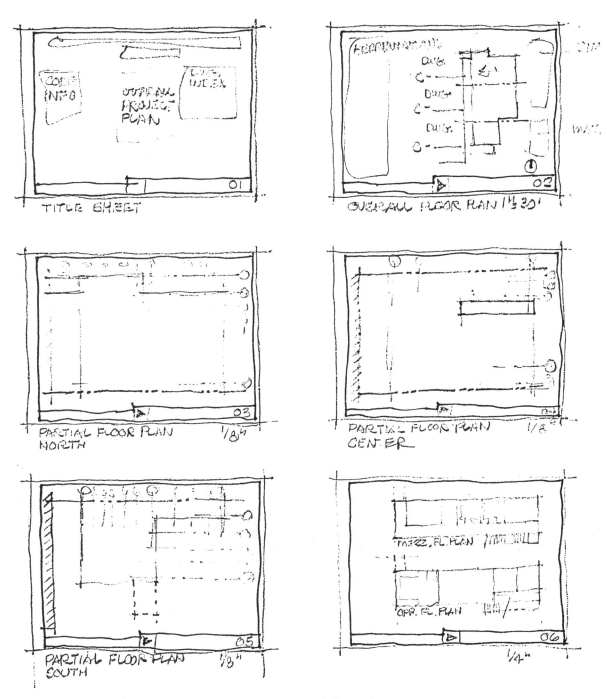

An example of the planning which aids the development of a full set of drawings. Here sheets can be compared, and proposed information moved for better correlation and coordination.

```
                        SET COMPOSITION SCHEDULE              DATE:

PROJECT                                    JOB NO.              PAGE
```

SHEET NO.	TITLE	SCALE	SCREEN	COLOR	OVERLAY NO.	TITLE	
S-36	PRESTRESSED, PRECAST MEMBERS				mbs	master border sheet	
					s49	prestressed, precast	
S-37	PRECAST MEMBERS				mbs	master border sheet	
					s50	precast members	
S=38	MISCELLANEOUS DETAILS				mbs	master border sheet	
					s51	miscellaneous details	
M-1	MECHANICAL SYMBOLS & ABBREVIATIONS	1/20			mbs	master border sheet	
					m1	mech. symbols & abbrev.	
M-2	FOUNDATION MECHANICAL PLAN SECTOR I	1/8	50% 50% 50%		mbs a8 a10 s2 m2	master border sheet sector I grids base. plan base-I fdn./base. strl. base-I foundation mech. notes-I	1/8" 1/8"
M-3	FOUNDATION MECHANICAL PLAN SECTOR II	1/8	50% 50% 50%		mbs a9 a11 s4 m3	master border sheet sector II grids base. plan base-II fdn./base. strl. base-II foundation mech. notes-II	1/8" 1/8"
M-4	BASEMENT MECHANICAL PLAN SECTOR I	1/8	50% 50% 50%		mbs a8 a10 a19 m4	master border sheet sector I grids base. plan base-I parking layout-I basement mech. notes-I	1/8" 1/8"
M-5	BASEMENT MECHANICAL PLAN SECTOR II	1/8	50% 50% 50%		mbs a9 a11 a20 m5	master border sheet sector II grids base. plan base-II parking layout-II basement mech. notes-II	1/8" 1/8"
M=6	FIRST FLOOR MECHANICAL PLAN SECTOR I	1/8	50% 50%		mbs a8 a12 m6	master border sheet sector I grids 1st fl. plan base-I 1st fl. mech. notes-I	1/8" 1/8"
M=7	PLAZA MECHANICAL PLAN SECTOR II	1/8	50%		mbs a13 m7	master border sheet plaza plan base-II plaza mech. notes	1/8"

Chapman, Cobeen, Desai, Sakata, Inc.
Architecture, Planning, Interior Design, Graphic Design
This list denotes each final sheet and the overlays required to form it. Note the "screened sheets used in those instances where muted work is desirable. This is the next step after the miniset is completed, or can be a running account of sheet development.

its office manual. Second, staff education and hands-on experience must again be planned, and the office must be eased into the system. Planning before going in will produce predictable results going out.

One more recent idea is the establishment of a graphics center in the office. Here, as with the standard detail system, one person should be assigned or, preferably, hired as the graphics expert and given full charge of the center. All of the nec-essary ancillary materials and equipment should be purchased and maintained by the center. The operator of the center more than likely will require less salary than a staff draftsman, which adds further to the overall savings from the system.

Offices now have moved to the point where they "draw" with appliqué material, namely, graphic tapes. Obviously very adaptable to linear work, the tapes are now used for borders, lines, wall symbols, fencing, property lines, utility lines,

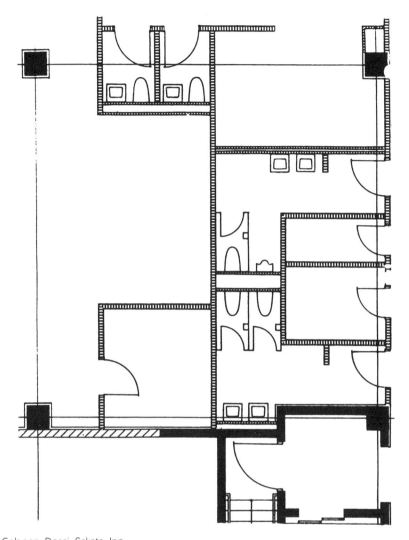

Chapman, Cobeen, Desai, Sakata, Inc.
Architecture, Planning, Interior Design, Graphic Design
Example of a plan executed totally with appliqué materials; some are stock materials, while others have been custom-made for the office.

setback lines, match lines, and cut lines. Here, too, a vast variety of patterns, types, and widths are available, eliminating any confusion that might occur in closely related work. As with any symbols, a legend explaining what each tape pattern represents is mandatory, but adds little to the cost in view of the time and cost saved by the application in the first place.

In each of the four basic materials care must be taken during application. Dry-transfer materials usually require firm attachment and then a good burnishing to ensure permanent installation. Textured films since they are usually used over fairly large areas must be applied in a manner similar to laying a carpet; start at one place and progress to the other, removing bubbles and ridges as you go. Again, firm attachment and care are needed when trimming off the excess so the basic sheet is not sliced. (Usually this material cannot be cut to size and then attached; apply it to the sheet in a size larger than necessary and then trim). Graphic tapes should be unrolled as you press the material in place; don't try to unroll and cut a long piece and then attach it. Slow, careful progress will produce accurate and attractive documents.

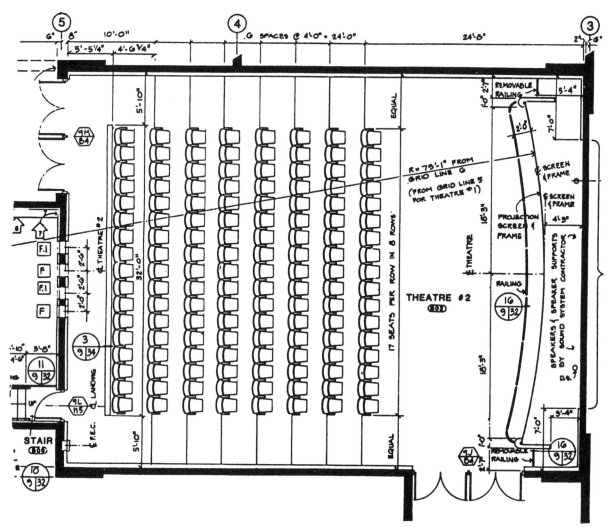

Chapman, Cobeen, Desai, Sakata, Inc.
Architecture, Planning, Interior Design, Graphic Design
In this layout for an auditorium the seating arrangement was cut from a manufacturer's catalog; using composite drafting, it required no drafting work.

Composite drafting, as described in Chapter 32, is also rapidly expanding in use and is being used in more ways. Originally conceived as "scissors" or "cut-and-paste" drafting, the technique has been refined and now solves many of the problems produced by use of the other techniques. Now termed "lay-it-down and pick-it-up" drafting, composite drafting allows, for instance, the best virtues of appliqué to be used, but eliminates the absolute need for sticky-back material. Here, the nonsticky material can be laid in place, temporarily fastened, reproduced, and then dismantled and saved for future use.

Overlay drafting is greatly enhanced by composite techniques as more non-hand-drafted material can be incorporated, and the vivid qualities will produce even crisper, sharper, and more imposing documents. Ink drafting in cooperation with printed textures and tapes and with "cuts" from catalogs will provide very impressive final documents to be used in the field. Fading, weak drafting work and poor reproduction (which burns out the drafted work) can be virtually eliminated by use of composite techniques.

If overlay work is considered vertical assembly of information, then composite is the *horizontal*

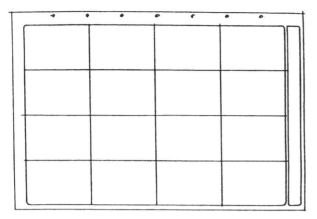

Compubase, Inc.
This is a sheet layout for composite drafting and the use of standard detail sheets. The border and title block can be produced in a number of ways, but the grid defines the limits of each detail sheet. This format may be used several times over for a project, as the need requires.

assemblage; elements can be placed, composed in any location, then repositioned or relocated for another effect. The work is in moving the material, not in erasing and redrawing, revising, or drawing. But, as with any of the techniques, preplanning is required.

It can easily be seen that a series of standard details can be attached to a backing sheet, photographically reproduced into a detail sheet, and then dismantled and returned to the file. That is composite drafting; add to this the overlay sheet containing the graphic tape border lines and the sticky-back title block, and you have three techniques involved in the production of one sheet, and not one line is hand-drawn! With development of the techniques and staff experience the combinations are endless. Each technique feeds into the other; standard details give impetus to standard decals, which further enhance the composite concept. Composite materials can now include all of the stick-ons plus any other repetitive material; legends, notes, schedule formats details, specifications. Beyond these, items that are constant from drawing to drawing can be utilized; parts of elevations floor plans, and sections may be the most effective use of the composite system. Repetitive plans of toilet rooms, storage rooms, stairs, utility cores, doors, windows, fixtures, or equipment can be assembled in varying ways. Any required change in scale can be achieved quickly and totally avoids, any redraw-

ing, the photographic process will accommodate these maneuvers very easily. Units that repeat within the building can be drawn once (or pulled from a file), reproduced in the proper number, assembled, and thus provide the overall plan required for the structure. So, too, with elevation elements and repetitive parts of sections and details. The mind boggles at the variety of items that can be produced without any drafting work at all; high-rise buildings, motels, hotels, hospitals, schools, multifamily housing units, shopping centers, parking areas, curtain or panel walls, strip windows, standardized buildings, unitized buildings, and so forth.

Composite drafting can benefit almost every project and will certainly provide better documents at a great reduction in production time. An added value is the quality of the documents if carefully executed by the staff; the materials at hand will suffer only from hurried, inept execution. Even revisions will enter the project more easily as they will not be disruptive or distracting.

The lettering on working drawings has long been a problem; it is very time-consuming if done by hand, and the quality varies tremendously. Many offices forced new employees to train themselves to letter in the "office style" so that every sheet leaving the office looked as if only one person did the lettering. Unfortunately, not everyone is capable of lettering in exactly the same fashion as another; to do so only further wastes time. Eventually, the same general type of lettering was required; basically it was vertical, capital lettering. Individual quirks were tolerated as long as the lettering was presentable, legible, and, of course, accurate in content.

Titles and other larger lettering always proved to be a problem. One could not simply increase the size of his or her normal alphabet for titles out had to use different styles and different media, and most of the time the hand-lettered title was distractive. This was a natural for dry-transfer lettering. One needed the same skill for spacing the lettering, but the letters were consistent (being printed on the backing sheet) and uniformly dense for good reproduction. The system, however, was not cost-effective for all lettering on the documents. Sticky-back material, once it was introduced, was immediately snatched up for typewritten notes. Here the fastest of lettering, uniform in style, construction, and density, could be utilized and then merely attached to the drawing sheet. Surely no other system could outdo it. As mentioned before, problems did exist and the decals were shelved for want of a more positive system. Typing units were created specifically for large drawing sheets; open-end carriages, carriage frames that fit on top of the drawing, machines that fit on the drafting table or on the drafting machine, have all come along, and many are still very active and viable today.

From its inception, of course, CAD equipment has contained the ability to overcome many of the problems with printing instructions, and other notations directly on the drawings sheets; it was merely part of the computerized attributes. However in this, even now, pre-planning and precautions must be taken to ensure that the lettering, and notes are adapted to, contribute to and properly supplement the drawings, without overwhelming the drawings; also without confusing or distracting the users.

The process of typewritten notations boils down to typing on small sheets and then somehow applying them to the drawings themselves. Of course, this fits the appliqué and composite techniques to a "tee"; but, for fear of redundancy, plan ahead. With the innovation of standard details bound into the newly emerging project manual, as much material as possible was included in these booklets: details, schedules, notes, maps, charts, sections, unit plans, and so on. Anything "small" was relegated to typed notes and placed in the manual. Projects suffered to some degree by this separation of information; the field personnel of the contracting companies now had to have the drawings and the project manual in order to "see" all of their work. It was cumbersome and not readily accepted, even when drawings were reduced to half-size and printed by offset press. Referring back and forth was not easy and not cost reducing in the final analysis. Office costs might be reduced but field costs suffered.

When the decision is made to use typewritten notations, the system should be entered gradually, with an eye toward standardization, clarity, consistency, and, eventually, speed. And more than likely this decision will be made in light of the use of another technique; this will affect the approach taken toward the type of material to be purchased and used. Some persist in the use of the sticky-back decal material, and the concept of key-noting with its massive array of notes can be handled very well with decals. Schedules also lend themselves very nicely to typing, either for insertion in the specification booklet or for appliqué to the drawing sheets. In some instances, a tremendous amount of written material is required for the legal aspects of the project; approvals by various agencies, conditions bearing on the project, and so on, and all of this, too, can be typed easily and in some fashion attached to the drawings.

In any event, typing should be preplanned and timed so that a large amount of typing can be done at one time. This provides not only for a consistent approach, but also for efficiency in the entire office operation. There is disruption only if the production team is constantly running to the typist for a one-line note or a title. Other work must be stopped, the typist must change format, typeface, and other facets of work to accommodate a tiny note. The preplanning may best take the form of "roughed-out" notes placed on a set of check prints. Time will be saved in the long run, although at first glance it seems that the preplanning negates time and cost savings.

Large decals are very hard to place on the drawings, and this must be done with extreme care. Of course, the finest virtues of the appliqué process are present, and that technique must be utilized for the typed decals. Smaller typed notes are much easier to install, and one can further ease the job by working over a grid sheet, which can act as a guide for straight and neat alignment. Some offices particularly for key-noting (the technique whereby a symbol is placed near the detail or construction and refers to a rather elaborate note description of what is intended), have utilized a notation sheet that is smaller than the drawing sheet. Here the notation sheet will easily fit a standard large-carriage typewriter and further calls attention to the drawing sheet by being undersized. Moreover, the reference back and forth is simplified, since one need not manipulate a full-sized sheet to see the sheet below.

Typing can greatly enhance the other techniques, particularly composite drafting. Obviously the typed sheet need not be sticky-backed and thus can be assembled horizontally as needed in the composite process. Consistency is the ultimate goal of typing, with speed a very nice by-product, as the office gradually integrates the typed system into standard practice.

Whereas several of the other techniques involve photographic processes, photodrafting utilizes "regular" photographs, in their pure form, for some projects. Remodeling, renovation, and restoration work can yield many dividends, including lower production costs, by using photo-

1. WALL SEPARATING STUDIO 123 FROM REST OF BUILDING TO BE COMPOSED OF TWO FULL HEIGHT 3-5/8" STEEL STUD PARTITION WITH 2 LAYERS OF 5/8" DRYWALL ON THE OUTSIDE. PROVIDE CONTINUOUS SOUND ATTENUATION BLANKETS IN BOTH PARTITIONS. CAULK BETWEEN DRYWALL PERIMETER AND ALL ADJACENT SURFACES.

2. WALLS ENCLOSING CONTROL/EDITING 121, SOUND LOCK 122, AND CLOSET 124 TO BE FULL HEIGHT 3-5/8" STEEL STUD PARTITIONS WITH TWO LAYERS OF 5/8" DRYWALL ON EACH SIDE. PROVIDE CONTINUOUS 4" SOUND ATTENUATION BLANKETS. CAULK BETWEEN DRYWALL PERIMETER AND ALL ADJACENT SURFACES.

3. PROVIDE 4" SOUND ATTENUATION BLANKETS OVER CEILING OF CONFERENCE 119, CONTROL EDITING 121, SOUND LOCK 122, STUDIO 123 AND CLOSET 124.

4. HANGING ROD AND (2) PLASTIC LAMINATE SHELVES TO BE PROVIDED IN FULL WIDTH OF CLOSET.

5. ACOUSTICAL PANELS TO BE PROVIDED ON ALL WALLS OF STUDIO. SEE DETAIL 1, SHEET A.1.

6. PAINT ALL SURFACES ABOVE ACOUSTICAL PANELS (12'-6" AFF) FLAT BLACK, INCLUDING JOISTS, DUCTWORK, PIPING, EQUIPMENT, ETC. THROUGHOUT STUDIO 123.

7. SEMI-RECESSED CABINET WITH PORTABLE FIRE EXTINGUISHER.

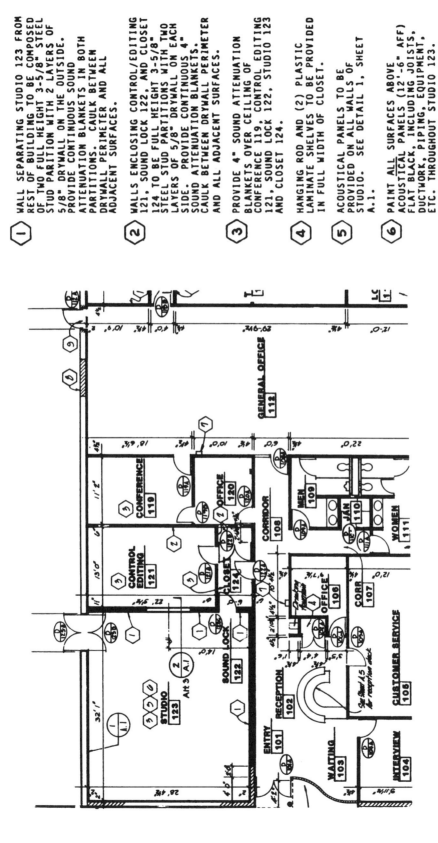

Example of keynoting on a plan; hexagonal designators with numbers refer to a note located elsewhere on the sheet. Typed notes can further reduce the time required to produce the drawing.

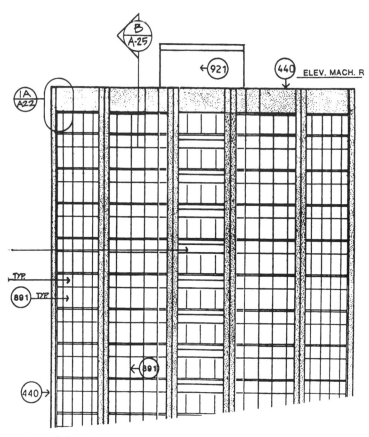

Chapman, Cobeen, Desai, Sakata, Inc.
Architecture, Planning, Interior Design, Graphic Design
Keynoting on an elevation reduces the clutter of notes, dimensions, and leader lines that may interfere with the lines of the elevation drawing itself.

drafting. Simply take black-and-white photos of the areas involved in the project and have them transferred onto large sheets of drafting media. By adding the proper notes, dimensions, titles, and so on, either by conventional drafting or by overlay techniques, the final documents can be produced easily. Note that this production does not involve the measuring and drawing of the building. Formerly, the most positive way of dealing with renovation in a building (for which there were no drawings available) was to assign a team to literally reconstruct the drawings by measuring the building and using this information to produce working drawings after the fact. These became the basis for the new work and the drawings necessary to describe that new work. This was, without a doubt, a good approach but very costly and time-consuming.

The use of photos obviously reduces the time needed to "explore" the old building, but some time must be spent to preplan the project and to determine where pictures should be taken. A good guideline is to photograph any area in which new work is contemplated, interior and exterior. Even areas in which mechanical equipment will be modified qualify for this technique, and here even more time is saved over the minute tracing of these very involved systems.

It goes without saying that some talent in photography is absolutely necessary. This is not a project for a Brownie box camera and the mere ability to trip the shutter. Usually the most successful ventures utilize a 35mm camera, with both telephoto and wide-angle lenses; you must be able to react to the conditions you encounter, and you must be able to depict them for the best advantage of the users of the documents. There may be a distinct need for a tripod, and perhaps a cable-release for time release in areas that are lighted poorly. One vital additional item is some sort of

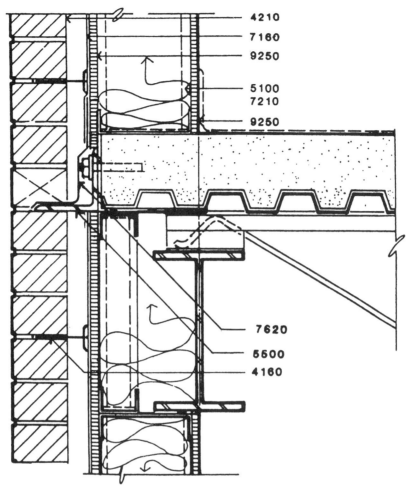

Gresham, Smith and Partners
Even details can be converted to keynoting. Here the number can be referenced to the note, and that in turn
to the section of the specification that applies. Good, coordinated system.

measuring device (scale, rule, etc.). This should be included in each shot to properly orient the work to the viewer's eye.

Some investigations should be made before the type of film is selected, and here again some planning is necessary. You cannot change films very readily, so you must plan to use a full roll for certain types of shots before going into other areas that may require a change of film, ASA rating, and so on. Such factors as weather will also play a part in the approach and just how and when the pictures will be taken. The best results are extremely sharp, clear, well-lighted, descriptive photographs. It is very helpful to include several areas of work, rather than taking a great many photos of very restricted areas or single items of work. Even a good photographer is well-advised to seek the advice of the reproduction firm before embarking on a photodrafting project. Such professionals' expertise will reveal various methods that can be used, perhaps with further cost implications. These are the people who must provide the final documents. If faulty material is sent to them, it must be understood that they cannot remedy basic mistakes. They can also give advice on the size of prints to use, intermediate prints that can be used in the office for checking, various media available, and, of course, how the entire system can be improved.

Beyond this aspect is the fact that added automation and electronic capabilities will both expand and increase in number, so the information

545

can be produced in various forms and transmitted in numerous ways. Speed of production is but one factor, perhaps becoming the second in priority to ease and timeliness of transmission. An obvious illustration of this factor is the ever increasing use of e-mail (for electronic messages) and facsimile (fax) machines (for other messages), whereby documents are transferred in seconds rather than in hours, by courier, or days, by mail and other systems.

Similarly, meetings have become multiparty teleconferences (collective telephone calls between several stations). Video conferencing is on the increase, whereby drawings and other documents can be reviewed simultaneously by several remotely located parties, through the use of a closed television system showing the various locations participating. The future of information transfer, in both the short and long term, is mind-boggling and, in many cases, not yet conceived. Even now there is use of electronics to transfer complete drawing information, eliminating the need for the reproduction of "hard copy" sets and their more voluminous and time-consuming transfer. In addition, the electronic material can be further modified at the new location if necessary. (There is some hazard in this eventuality, as the work of the design professional could be changed, without permission, increasing the professional's liability for improper or inadequate construction.)

Many may consider such insistence to be old-fashioned, conservative, or stodgy, but there is still a pervasive need for the documents—no matter their use or mode of transport—to contain proper, accurate, complete, well-coordinated, and project-pertinent information. If there is any failure to meet this need, the sophistication of the new technologies will not help to resolve the resulting problems. There is still a deep and abiding need for the professional to create and develop a well-conceived, properly documented array of project information; that charge is addressed herein; at least in a fundamental manner.

When photographic processes were introduced as a "better and faster" way to produce working drawings, the primary operation was to "shoot" drawing sheets made up of isolated sketches from various sources. One could also include printed information that greatly clarified issues, but this would require excessive amounts of time to reproduce in traditional methods. It is obvious that taking a portion of a manufacturer's catalog and attempting to use it as part of the working drawings entails either reproduction by hand or by other methods—primarily photography.

Some offices saw this as an opportunity to utilize photographs themselves as part of the working drawing set. Here was an excellent way in which to illustrate, to the contractors, actual conditions—at renovation site, for example. This did not circumvent site visits prior to bidding, but did provide a good, reliable memory of the condition for all to view, and to refresh the designers' own memories when necessary.

The photos could be augmented by applying ink (white or black, depending on the background) leader lines, from a point of reference in the photo to a drawing note outside the photo. Here "call outs," and/or instructions could be included—in a sense, making the photo a "working drawing detail" with little if any drafting.

The use of photographs was not widespread and, of course, was more viable for existing building projects than for new (bare land) projects. Computerization and the expanding use of computer-aided drafting (CAD) procedures (including plotting of drawings) all but eliminated the use of photography in the working drawing production process.

Recently, however, there has been a new development that provides for digital photography. This can be applied directly to architectural working drawing work, particularly for renovation work. Photos can be taken of existing work/conditions and processed through the computer. These can be enhanced, via computer operations, by adding notations, instructions, explanations, dimensions, and so forth. Then the enhanced photo can be made part of the drawing set, again via computer operations. Obviously, this eliminates the need for extensive field work, measuring of conditions, and other investigation to ascertain or report on existing conditions.

Quite naturally there is a growing use of computers on the job site, particularly by construction managers and contract administrators. These are either the more permanent PCs or computers of the lap-top version, as the persons involved may deem advantageous and useful. The professional, more than likely, will choose the lap-top when he or she is rotating between several projects at a time. A PC-type of setup into which the lap-top can be docked (connected) combines the best of both systems.

In addition to the obvious administrative functions—record keeping, making notes and memos, writing agendas and minutes, preparing forms, sending e-mail messages, and so on—a new and evolving function is coming into its own. This is the use of digital photography, valuable in two areas.

First, many larger projects require in-progress photos. In the past a professional photographer was employed to make periodic visits to the site and take still photos, normally 8" x 10"; usually a photo session coincided with the monthly payment request to document progress. Some sites currently have continuous video monitoring, whereby photos are taken on a timed basis (every 15 minutes, for example) to finitely note progress and procedures. These prove quite handy where there is an impending dispute or litigation over a claim for money or injury.

This process has now been developed so that pictures can reflect activity 24 hours a day if necessary, and the equipment can be computerized to tilt, zoom pan, or move otherwise in order to distinctly record what are considered to be crucial elements or operations (this capability is widely used for security systems). The data can then be transmitted to the company's server via an ISDN line and unloaded, if of advantage, to the company's Internet web site for viewing by all those interested and with compatible equipment. Being digital, these photos can be drawn from the Internet and the web by satellite, wireless, ISDN, or plain old telephone connections. Professionals, off-site, with PCs and PDAs can assess all this data for immediate use.

Perhaps more important to design professionals are the newer (and still evolving) hand-held cameras and the ability to take a picture of a limited portion of the work (for a small detail) and transmit it, almost immediately, to another person. This can be done to illustrate a problem without wordy and inexplicit communications. In addition, if properly equipped, the receiver can transmit the solution to the problem back to the field, if it is a visually adaptable situation.

There is quite an array of cameras readily available today, which are reasonably priced. Coupling this low-cost equipment with proper software has renewed interest in using photographs in the documentation process (although this process still has little value for "bare land" projects). Results are good and are improving. This technology has proved most helpful be easily showing details and conditions that otherwise may be overlooked or misinterpreted.

Cameras, of course, are of many different types, depending on what one seeks to accomplish. Those now available from such sources as Kodak, Sharp, Logitech, Canon, and Ricoh (among many others) are very reasonably priced in a range from just under $1,000 to about $1,800. Picture capacity varies from 16 to 48 shots, with many optical options that can be added if desired. Some cameras include an audio recording feature that allows verbal notation directly associated with the picture (all are digital and transmittable via the computer system- microphone straight to a file on the disk).

In addition, when a digital picture is processed through the computer software program—Word 6.0, for example—notes (in high-contract boxes or "bubble" areas), leader lines, dimensions, cropping, and the like can be added directly to the picture to further explain the visual presentation. Obviously, one must investigate the market to ascertain what is available to fulfill the needs at hand, budget, future expectations, and so forth.

Even an old-fashion photographic technique can be used by laying a rule or tape (or other *readable* measuring device) next to the work to be pictured so that actual scale and sizes can be determined. All of the features of this system are fully manipulable by the operator (the contract administrator!) and can be combined with his or her imagination to make a very distinct, specific, clear, concise but yet complete, presentation or record document—and to provide solutions to problems in a very short amount of time when necessary (a most valuable asset in contract administration).

Digital photography is also a new and excellent method for producing digitized renderings of a proposed project. This aids the owner, in particular, by showing how the existing conditions can be converted into portions of the new and completed project.

The new formats, or techniques—the full array of systems drafting—at hand for use by any and all.

Every day, refined techniques are being used or coming onto the scene to further enhance the cost-saving better-document effort. Manufacturers of all types of materials and systems are reacting and adding to their lines so the techniques can be applied even more easily and with even better results. Office after office is moving into the use, principally, of the many new capabilities of CAD; some utilize CAD exclusively. Many firms, however, still produce quality documents using a combination of the features of other formats; some may still be using a majority of "traditional" formats. Yet there is a distinct direction toward CAD, whether performed by professionals or their staffers. Not everyone is at home with CAD or the newer formats, but it is difficult to believe that there is not a format that can meet every documentation need. In the face of all the new complexities in construction, there is a definite mandate for "better documentation, in a shorter period of time, and at lower cost."

DOOR TO STAIRWAY
ON THE WEST SIDE
OF THE FA
ACID BUILDING

EXISTING ELEVATION

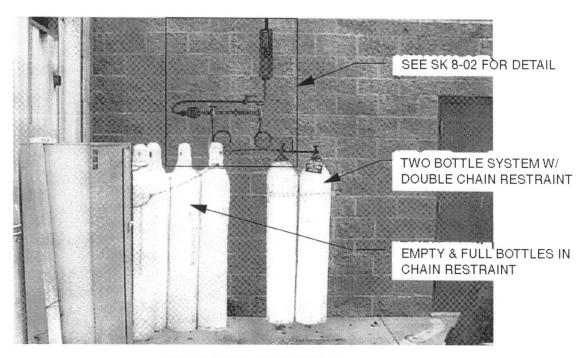

SEE SK 8-02 FOR DETAIL

TWO BOTTLE SYSTEM W/
DOUBLE CHAIN RESTRAINT

EMPTY & FULL BOTTLES IN
CHAIN RESTRAINT

PROPOSED ELEVATION

Two examples of digital photography. These photos relate; one is the existing condition and the other is the proposed installation to be placed in this outside the new building. Note the addition of notations and leader lines superimposed on the photos, via the computer.

36

Case Studies in CAD Detailing

I t seems appropriate at this juncture to provide a contrast between the details in the preceding chapters (mostly produced by manual drafting) and CAD-produced drawings. Freehand detailing, also provides another point of comparison. Much of what is contained immediately following can be reviewed and applied to the manual drafting. Points discussed are also valid for all types of drawings.

The following is a collection of details produced by computer-assisted drafting (CAD). They are all valid details that were used on projects. However, they were selected as examples because of the common presentation problems they contain and their instructive value. We are grateful to the people who graciously allowed this use of their work. All of these details were done when the operators were just beginning their CAD work; of course, through experience their work has been modified and greatly improved.

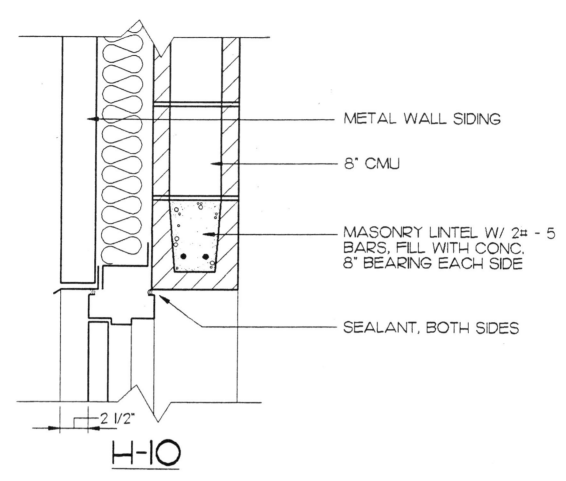

H-10

A pair of CAD details (above, opposite) that note work around a door opening. Decent line work, except the metal door frame, siding, closure pieces and flashing pieces should be heavier [to indicate metal thickness]; also there is no indication of how the door frame is attached to the wall in H-10. Some vital notes are missing.

Labels in figure:
- METAL WALL SIDING
- 8" CMU
- MASONRY LINTEL W/ 2# - 5 BARS, FILL WITH CONC. 8" BEARING EACH SIDE
- SEALANT, BOTH SIDES
- 2 1/2"

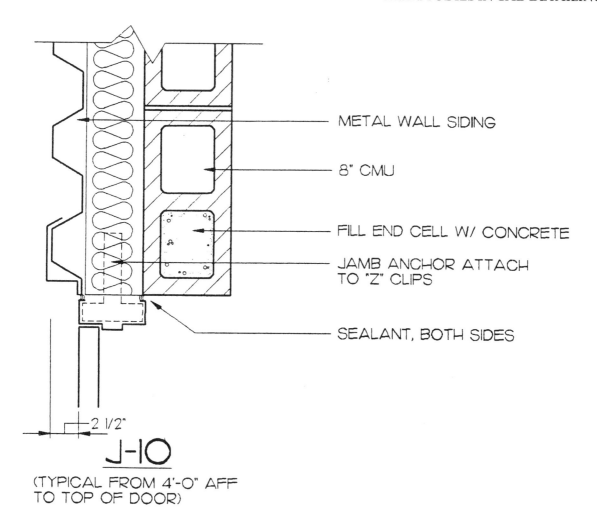

METAL WALL SIDING

8" CMU

FILL END CELL W/ CONCRETE

JAMB ANCHOR ATTACH
TO "Z" CLIPS

SEALANT, BOTH SIDES

2 1/2"

J-10

(TYPICAL FROM 4'-0" AFF
TO TOP OF DOOR)

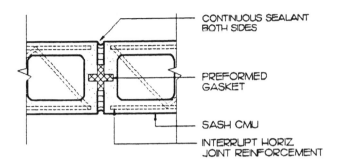

CONTINUOUS SEALANT
BOTH SIDES

PREFORMED
GASKET

SASH CMU

INTERRUPT HORIZ
JOINT REINFORCEMENT

INTERIOR VERTICAL CONTROL JOINT

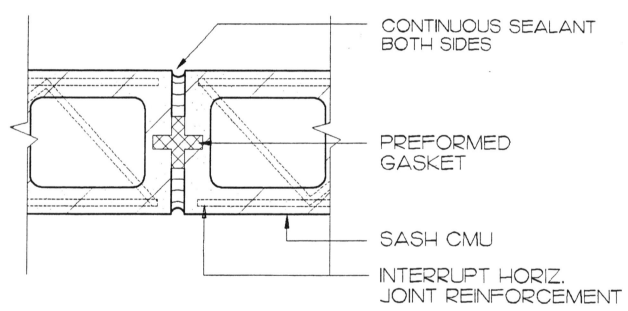

CONTINUOUS SEALANT
BOTH SIDES

PREFORMED
GASKET

SASH CMU

INTERRUPT HORIZ.
JOINT REINFORCEMENT

The same detail at different scales; compare the readability of material symbols. Note how the change in scale was also carried into the size of the letter [a very necessary change]. The preformed gasket should be in a darker line since it is "cut" in section, as is the CMU.

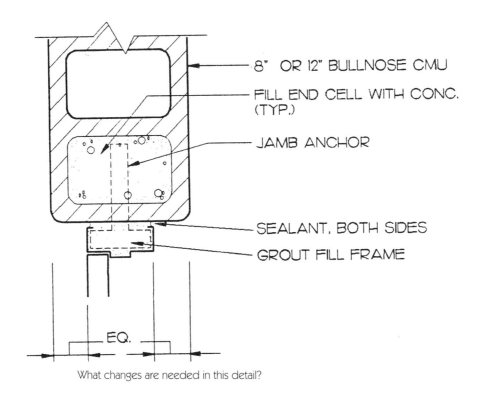

8" OR 12" BULLNOSE CMU

FILL END CELL WITH CONC. (TYP.)

JAMB ANCHOR

SEALANT, BOTH SIDES

GROUT FILL FRAME

EQ.

What changes are needed in this detail?

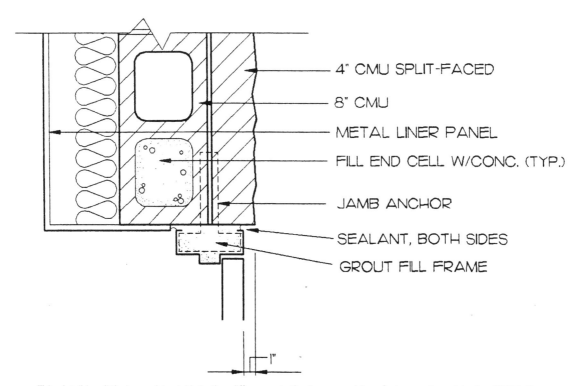

4" CMU SPLIT-FACED

8" CMU

METAL LINER PANEL

FILL END CELL W/CONC. (TYP.)

JAMB ANCHOR

SEALANT, BOTH SIDES

GROUT FILL FRAME

1"

This detail is a little inconsistent. Note the difference in the liner panel lines [where adjacent to the CMU is the correct way since both materials are cut]. Metal products should be darker [note how dark the joint between CMU and split-faced CMU reads [and this is not all that important].

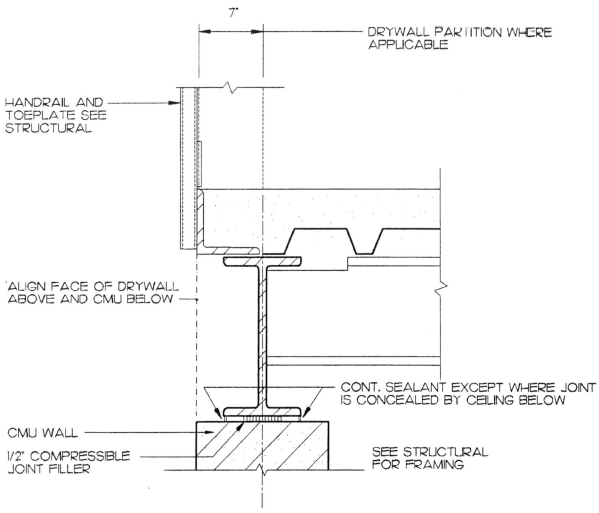

7"

DRYWALL PARTITION WHERE APPLICABLE

HANDRAIL AND TOEPLATE SEE STRUCTURAL

ALIGN FACE OF DRYWALL ABOVE AND CMU BELOW

CONT. SEALANT EXCEPT WHERE JOINT IS CONCEALED BY CEILING BELOW

CMU WALL

1/2" COMPRESSIBLE JOINT FILLER

SEE STRUCTURAL FOR FRAMING

Another pair of details (above, opposite) with differing scales. Note how difficult it is to read the work under the beam on the smaller scale drawing. Crucial notes are missing; where? If we consider the angle and the concrete slab to be continuous, how should their line work be changed, if at all?

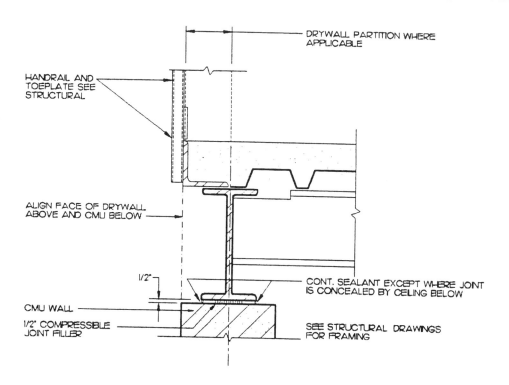

DRYWALL PARTITION WHERE
APPLICABLE

HANDRAIL AND
TOEPLATE SEE
STRUCTURAL

ALIGN FACE OF DRYWALL
ABOVE AND CMU BELOW

1/2"

CONT. SEALANT EXCEPT WHERE JOINT
IS CONCEALED BY CEILING BELOW

CMU WALL

1/2" COMPRESSIBLE
JOINT FILLER

SEE STRUCTURAL DRAWINGS
FOR FRAMING

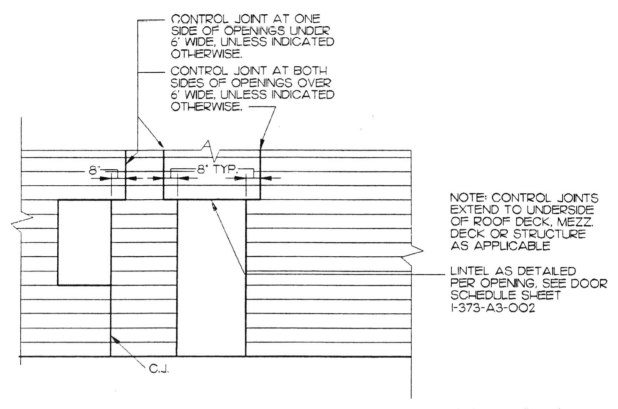

CONTROL JOINT AT ONE SIDE OF OPENINGS UNDER 6' WIDE, UNLESS INDICATED OTHERWISE.

CONTROL JOINT AT BOTH SIDES OF OPENINGS OVER 6' WIDE, UNLESS INDICATED OTHERWISE.

8"

8" TYP.

NOTE: CONTROL JOINTS EXTEND TO UNDERSIDE OF ROOF DECK, MEZZ. DECK OR STRUCTURE AS APPLICABLE

LINTEL AS DETAILED PER OPENING, SEE DOOR SCHEDULE SHEET I-373-A3-002

C.J.

Essentially the same detail (above, opposite) with slight scale changes. But notice how the larger uses linework in a better fashion [makes for a more readable drawing] and portrays the important work [control joints] much better. The heavy line work for the CMU coursing is wrong and distracts in the smaller drawing, and literally hides the important work.

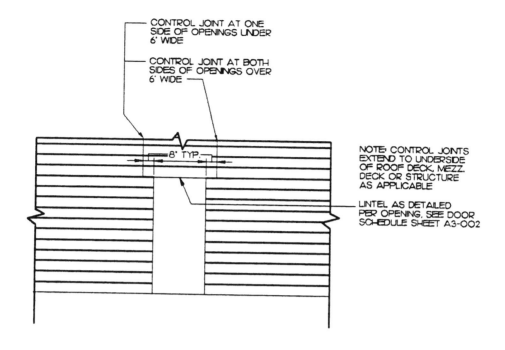

CONTROL JOINT AT ONE SIDE OF OPENINGS UNDER 6' WIDE

CONTROL JOINT AT BOTH SIDES OF OPENINGS OVER 6' WIDE

8" TYP.

NOTE: CONTROL JOINTS EXTEND TO UNDERSIDE OF ROOF DECK, MEZZ. DECK OR STRUCTURE AS APPLICABLE

LINTEL AS DETAILED PER OPENING, SEE DOOR SCHEDULE SHEET A3-002

CONTROL JOINT
AT WALL OPENING

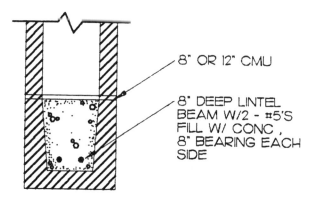

8" OR 12" CMU

8" DEEP LINTEL
BEAM W/2 - #5'S
FILL W/ CONC ,
8" BEARING EACH
SIDE

Wrong approach! The CMU and lintel are the important items, and should be depicted in the heavier line work; not the material symbol.

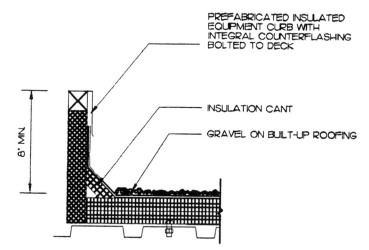

PREFABRICATED INSULATED
EQUIPMENT CURB WITH
INTEGRAL COUNTERFLASHING
BOLTED TO DECK

INSULATION CANT

GRAVEL ON BUILT-UP ROOFING

8" MIN

A detail done backwards! Obviously a detail at this scale is overwhelmed by the dark line work. In addition, the whole concept is wrong in that the darkest line are merely material symbols perhaps some of the least important information on the drawing. Metal thickness, and the principles for "cut" work in sections should be applied with an overall eye toward readability.

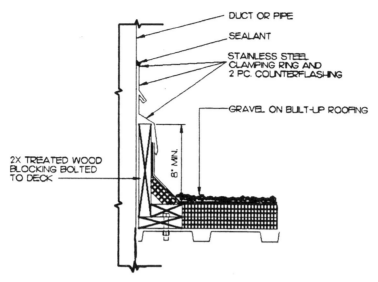

DUCT OR PIPE

SEALANT

STAINLESS STEEL
CLAMPING RING AND
2 PC. COUNTERFLASHING

GRAVEL ON BUILT-UP ROOFING

8' MIN.

2X TREATED WOOD
BLOCKING BOLTED
TO DECK

Another example of wrong line work. Here things are even more obvious; the 2x blocking has a light outline, but a heavy symbol-backwards]. The various break lines are a mystery, as to why they exist and what is readlly cut.

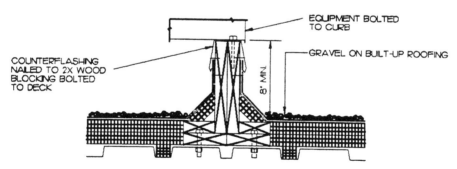

EQUIPMENT BOLTED
TO CURB

GRAVEL ON BUILT-UP ROOFING

COUNTERFLASHING
NAILED TO 2X WOOD
BLOCKING BOLTED
TO DECK

8' MIN.

Yet another "backwards" detail.

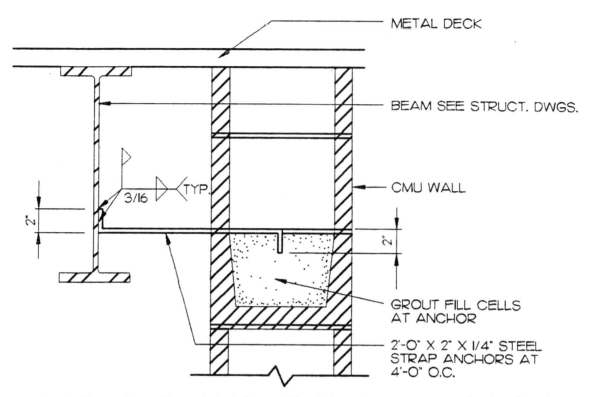

METAL DECK

BEAM SEE STRUCT. DWGS.

CMU WALL

3/16 ◁ TYP.

2"

2"

GROUT FILL CELLS
AT ANCHOR

2'-O" X 2" X 1/4" STEEL
STRAP ANCHORS AT
4'-O" O.C.

This detail has a mixture of line work. Again the material symbols are improper, as compared to the edges of the CMU and the steel beam; course lines in the CMU should be lighter and one line of the metal deck should be heavier to show the metal thickness.

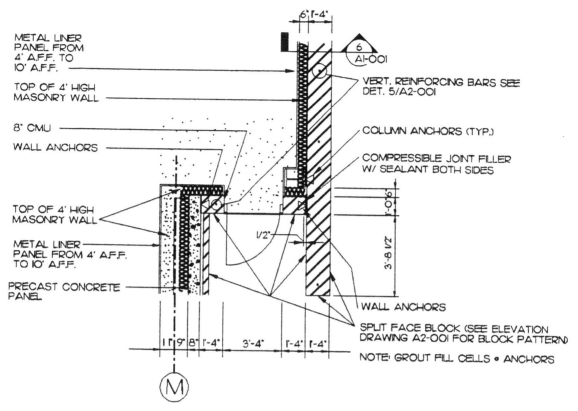

METAL LINER
PANEL FROM
4' A.F.F. TO
10' A.F.F.

TOP OF 4' HIGH
MASONRY WALL

8" CMU

WALL ANCHORS

TOP OF 4' HIGH
MASONRY WALL

METAL LINER
PANEL FROM 4' A.F.F.
TO 10' A.F.F.

PRECAST CONCRETE
PANEL

6" 1'-4"

6
A1-001

VERT. REINFORCING BARS SEE
DET. 5/A2-001

COLUMN ANCHORS (TYP.)

COMPRESSIBLE JOINT FILLER
W/ SEALANT BOTH SIDES

1/2"

1'-0"

3'-8 1/2"

WALL ANCHORS

SPLIT FACE BLOCK (SEE ELEVATION
DRAWING A2-001 FOR BLOCK PATTERN)

NOTE: GROUT FILL CELLS ● ANCHORS

1' 1" 9" 8" 1'-4" 3'-4" 1'-4" 1'-4"

M

This is a plan view that suffers because of small scale, and several different details that need to be more openly shown. Note the "spider web" of leader lines, and the length of some [maybe note should be repeated?] Of course, the material outlines are weakened by the dark symbols.

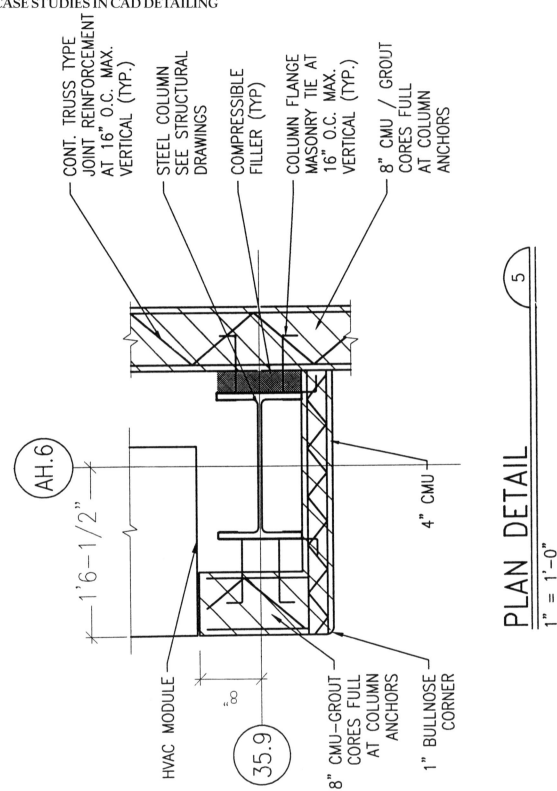

CONT. TRUSS TYPE JOINT REINFORCEMENT AT 16" O.C. MAX. VERTICAL (TYP.)

STEEL COLUMN SEE STRUCTURAL DRAWINGS

COMPRESSIBLE FILLER (TYP)

COLUMN FLANGE MASONRY TIE AT 16" O.C. MAX. VERTICAL (TYP.)

8" CMU / GROUT CORES FULL AT COLUMN ANCHORS

AH.6

1'6–1/2"

8"

35.9

HVAC MODULE

8" CMU–GROUT CORES FULL AT COLUMN ANCHORS

1" BULLNOSE CORNER

4" CMU

PLAN DETAIL
1" = 1'-0"

5

In this example, too many lines are in the same line weight; object outlines, reinforcement, anchors, etc. The object lines [CMU, steel column] should be darkest, with reinforcement and anchors lighter [but not the same as the material symbols].

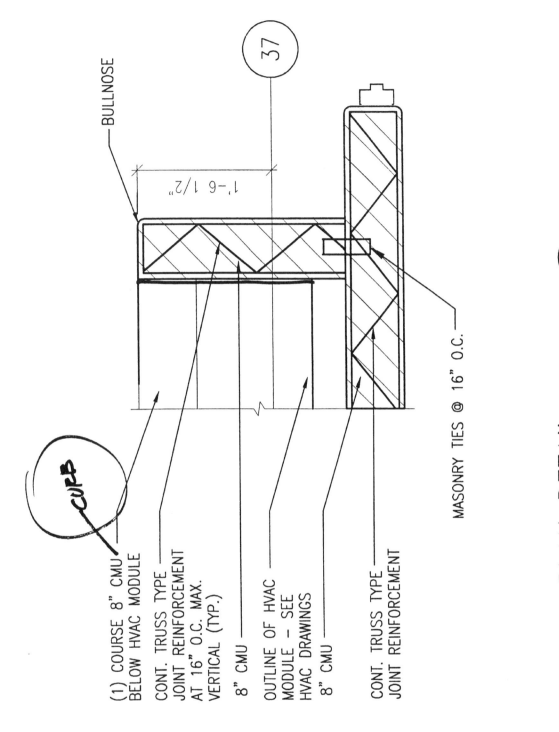

BULLNOSE

37

1'-6 1/2"

CURB

(1) COURSE 8" CMU
BELOW HVAC MODULE

CONT. TRUSS TYPE
JOINT REINFORCEMENT
AT 16" O.C. MAX.
VERTICAL (TYP.)

8" CMU

OUTLINE OF HVAC
MODULE – SEE
HVAC DRAWINGS

8" CMU

CONT. TRUSS TYPE
JOINT REINFORCEMENT

MASONRY TIES @ 16" O.C.

PLAN DETAIL
1" = 1'-0"

11
C-974

This detail is similar to the previous, but here the column centerline should use the standard centerline designation; the door frame needs to be darker [for metal thickness]. Note conflict at top leader line and the dimension line.

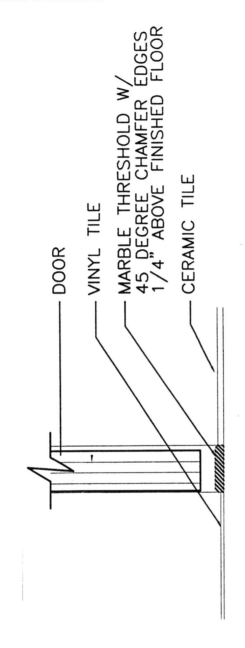

DOOR

VINYL TILE

MARBLE THRESHOLD W/
45 DEGREE CHAMFER EDGES
1/4" ABOVE FINISHED FLOOR

CERAMIC TILE

SILL DETAIL
3" = 1'-0"

The threshold is NOT the primary issue here [and should not be darkened]. The floor line needs to be darkened, along with the ceramic tile. Proper material symbols need to be used. Note leader lines with no distinct terminal point [arrowhead, etc.]

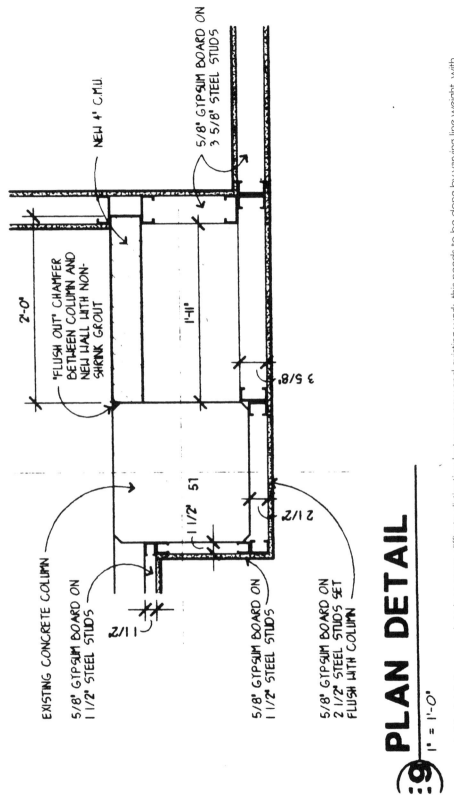

EXISTING CONCRETE COLUMN

5/8" GYPSUM BOARD ON
1 1/2" STEEL STUDS

5/8" GYPSUM BOARD ON
1 1/2" STEEL STUDS

5/8" GYPSUM BOARD ON
2 1/2" STEEL STUDS SET
FLUSH WITH COLUMN

NEW 4" C.M.U.

5/8" GYPSUM BOARD ON
3 5/8" STEEL STUDS

"FLUSH OUT" CHAMFER
BETWEEN COLUMN AND
NEW WALL WITH NON-
SHRINK GROUT

2'-0"

1'-11"

3 5/8"

1 1/2"

2/12

2/11

6 PLAN DETAIL
1" = 1'-0"

In this detail, there needs to be a more diffinate distinction between new and existing work; this needs to be done by varying line weight, with new work being the darker. Also, the note "flush out" is inappropriate. Variation in the readability and weight of material symbols is notable.

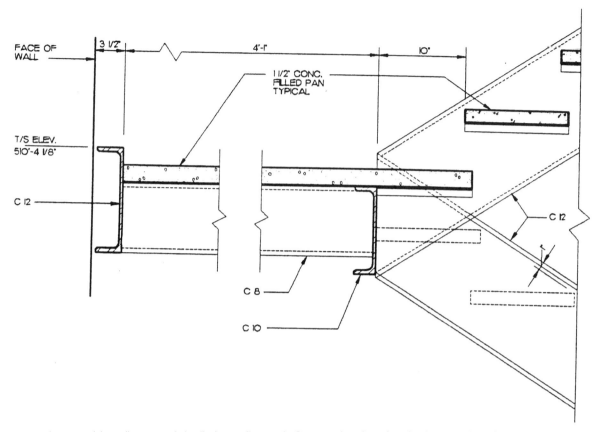

A reasonably well executed detail; decent line work. Care needs to be taken that items such as the tread and landing pans, are shown in the same line weight [since they are of the same metal thickness]. What else would you do to touch-up and improve even this good detail?

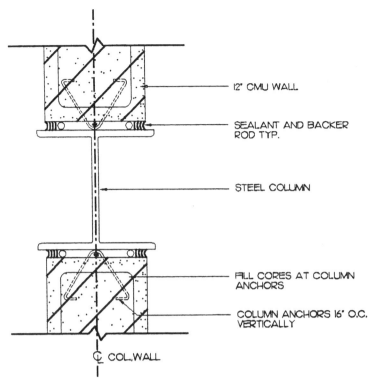

12" CMU WALL

SEALANT AND BACKER
ROD TYP.

STEEL COLUMN

FILL CORES AT COLUMN
ANCHORS

COLUMN ANCHORS 16" O.C.
VERTICALLY

℄ COL. WALL

Can you identify what the dark diagonal lines are meant to show—
— Horizontal masonry joint reinforcing?
— Material symbol for concrete masonry units?
— A bad idea?
Also, What three [3] other things would you do to improve this detail?

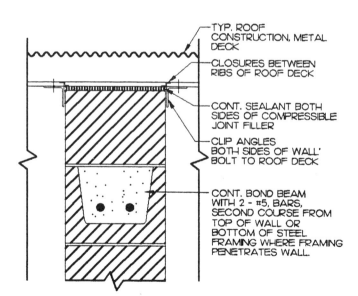

TYP. ROOF
CONSTRUCTION, METAL
DECK

CLOSURES BETWEEN
RIBS OF ROOF DECK

CONT. SEALANT BOTH
SIDES OF COMPRESSIBLE
JOINT FILLER

CLIP ANGLES
BOTH SIDES OF WALL'
BOLT TO ROOF DECK

CONT. BOND BEAM
WITH 2 - #5, BARS,
SECOND COURSE FROM
TOP OF WALL OR
BOTTOM OF STEEL
FRAMING WHERE FRAMING
PENETRATES WALL.

A detail badly hurt by, small scale; bad lines [objects, and material symbols], useless break lines, and poor readability!

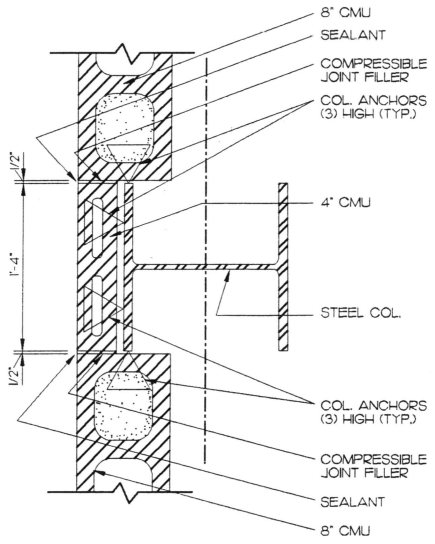

8" CMU

SEALANT

COMPRESSIBLE
JOINT FILLER

COL. ANCHORS
(3) HIGH (TYP.)

4" CMU

STEEL COL.

COL. ANCHORS
(3) HIGH (TYP.)

COMPRESSIBLE
JOINT FILLER

SEALANT

8" CMU

1/2"

1'-4"

1/2"

Can you identify at least five [5] errors in this detail? More than 5?

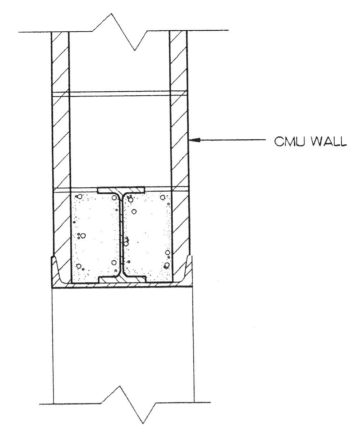

CMU WALL

Note the inconsistency in the line work for items that are cut by the section.

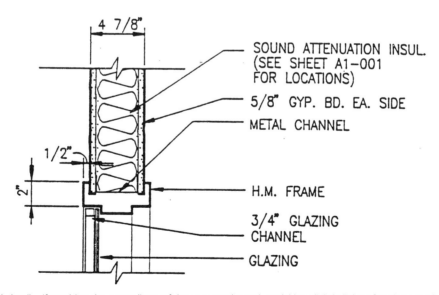

4 7/8"

SOUND ATTENUATION INSUL. (SEE SHEET A1-001 FOR LOCATIONS)

5/8" GYP. BD. EA. SIDE

METAL CHANNEL

1/2"

2"

H.M. FRAME

3/4" GLAZING CHANNEL

GLAZING

A good detail—if anything the outer lines of the gypsum board could be slightly lighter [so they don't appear exactly like the metal door frame].

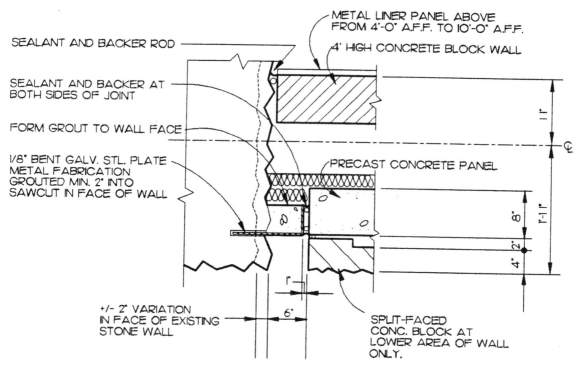

SEALANT AND BACKER ROD

SEALANT AND BACKER AT BOTH SIDES OF JOINT

FORM GROUT TO WALL FACE

1/8" BENT GALV. STL. PLATE METAL FABRICATION GROUTED MIN. 2" INTO SAWCUT IN FACE OF WALL

+/- 2" VARIATION IN FACE OF EXISTING STONE WALL

METAL LINER PANEL ABOVE FROM 4'-0" A.F.F. TO 10'-0" A.F.F.

4' HIGH CONCRETE BLOCK WALL

PRECAST CONCRETE PANEL

SPLIT-FACED CONC. BLOCK AT LOWER AREA OF WALL ONLY.

A little inconsistent in the line weights between new and existing work [new should be darkest].

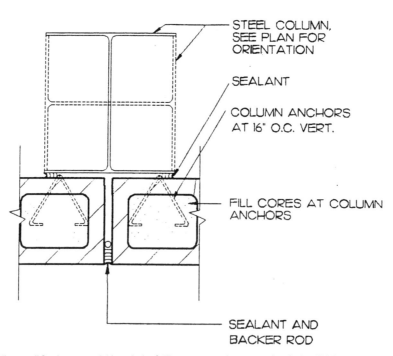

STEEL COLUMN, SEE PLAN FOR ORIENTATION

SEALANT

COLUMN ANCHORS AT 16" O.C. VERT.

FILL CORES AT COLUMN ANCHORS

SEALANT AND BACKER ROD

A good detail overall [column could be darker]. The concept here may be faulty. While trying to show that the column could be oriented either way, some confusion may occur; if may be better to show it one way, and use a note to indicate that it may be [per plan] different in other locations. Also, if the "dotted column" is in place, how do you attach the column anchors shown?

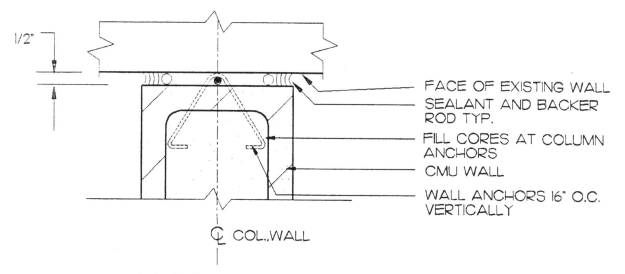

1/2"

FACE OF EXISTING WALL

SEALANT AND BACKER ROD TYP.

FILL CORES AT COLUMN ANCHORS

CMU WALL

WALL ANCHORS 16" O.C. VERTICALLY

℄ COL.,WALL

How can you make this detail better?

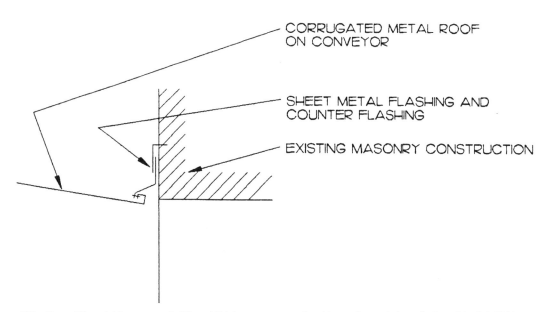

CORRUGATED METAL ROOF ON CONVEYOR

SHEET METAL FLASHING AND COUNTER FLASHING

EXISTING MASONRY CONSTRUCTION

If the three [3] metal items are of different thickness, can you [and how do you] show that on this detail? How does the wall material influence what you do?

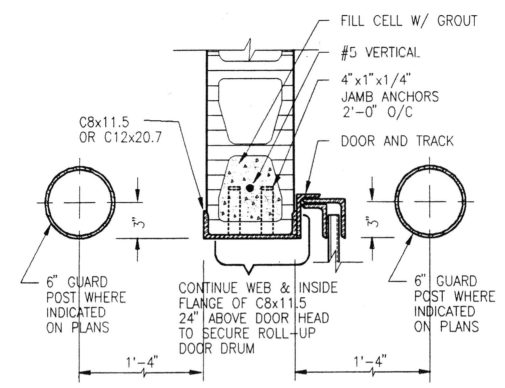

FILL CELL W/ GROUT

#5 VERTICAL

4"x1"x1/4"
JAMB ANCHORS
2'-0" O/C

DOOR AND TRACK

C8x11.5
OR C12x20.7

3"

3"

6" GUARD
POST WHERE
INDICATED
ON PLANS

CONTINUE WEB & INSIDE
FLANGE OF C8x11.5
24" ABOVE DOOR HEAD
TO SECURE ROLL-UP
DOOR DRUM

6" GUARD
POST WHERE
INDICATED
ON PLANS

1'-4"

1'-4"

A detail handled rather well; any ideas for changes or improvements?

37

Reproduction Systems

Traditionally, the blueprint has been the prime means of reproducing drawings employed in the construction industry. Even laymen referred to the architect's work as "drawing the blueprints." The blueprint system is about 150 years old, but to a large degree is no longer in use. It is actually a photographic copying method in which the following steps are required:

1. The original drawings are done on translucent tracing paper and placed over sensitized print paper.
2. The two sheets are exposed to a light source inside the blueprint machine.
3. The light, which penetrates the translucent original, burns or fades out the sensitized chemicals of the print paper.
4. The light is blocked out wherever lines appear on the original. They are then reproduced on the print paper by sensitizing chemicals.
5. The sensitized paper copy is put through the entire process after being separated from the original and exposed to various chemicals that first of all develop the sensitized lines that remain.
6. The sheet then passes through a fixing bath that completes the chemical process and fixes the printed lines permanently.

The sensitized paper in this system produces a white-lined, blue background print, from which its name is derived: the blueprint. The method has now been perfected to a point at which a modern machine can process the original and sensitized paper in one application, separate them automatically, and produce a print in little time. In addition, a roll of sensitized paper can be attached to the machine, which will run prints continuously as needed.

Perhaps the most important part of blueprinting and comparable processes is exposure. Machines have no way of knowing just exactly what is on the print or of assessing the quality or quantity of lead on the original. Whatever the advantages and disadvantages of the various reproductive processes, the system will show them as specific attributes or liabilities.

Each process, however, involves the human element in the evaluation of line work. A machine will reproduce what it sees; if there is a stain, smudge, or spot, it will be reproduced as if it were the most important part of the drawing. A faint line on the original will show up exactly as that. This is the prime reason that in all architectural offices the stress is on firm, black, consistent lines on all drawings. In most offices extreme care is taken to protect the originals and to keep them as clean as possible. While a set of drawings is worked on over a period of weeks or months, the sheets will take on an overall gray cast where lead smudging has been spread by the drafting instruments. If an erasure is made, a white spot may appear on the gray background. Again, however, it is most important that the drawings be cared for meticulously.

Although blueprints have become a tradition, they have distinct disadvantages and advantages for the users. First of all, they are economical to produce; they stand up well in sunlight or other bright light and show some resistance to aging. However, because the paper has been saturated and then dried, the prints are brittle, and in folding or rolling, or by being dog-eared or having items set down on them, have a tendency to crack and tear. The major disadvantage of the blueprint, however, is that having been totally immersed in a water bath, the paper will have shrunk and the scale of the drawing changed. This fact, although one of which the industry is well aware, is important to such a degree that prints should never be scaled. Sometimes, for a quick check, scaling is done, but if the drawings are radically out of size, faulty spacing or some misconstruction can result. Moreover, the background color makes it extremely difficult to make legible corrections or changes directly on the prints. A yellow or orange pencil is needed to write or draw on the prints, but even at best gives poor results.

The ozalid or diazode system is the most widely used today. It is similar to blueprinting, except that the paper is never totally saturated and the prints produced are the reverse of the blueprint. The background is light and line work dark, either blue or black. This direct and positive method does not utilize the reversals typical of blueprinting. The same type of paper, which is sensitive to ultraviolet light, is used, although it must be combined with a coupler to provide a permanent image. Again, the sensitized paper is placed under the original and fed through the machine. The two papers pass under a light source, and the same exposure process is repeated as in blueprinting: the lines of the original block out the light and the translucent paper without delineation allows the light to bleach out the sensitized paper coating. The exposed sheet is then separated from the original and the print passed through a vapor of alkaline ammonia. This step eliminates all remaining compound on the sensitized sheet and combines with the coupler to give a permanent image. This is known to some degree as the ammonia process or more popularly as "an ozalid."

A much more readable print usually results if the background is given a slight overall tone rather than pure white bleaching. Depending on the medium and office practice, this has been changed. Some offices require a high-contrast print: dark lines against a white background. Another drawing medium similar to mylar film produces a high-contrast print more easily than linen. The vast majority of persons, however, prefer a light, mottled background on which the line work is displayed. Sensitized paper for printing an opaque print has the ability to produce blue or black lines. Paper is also available for making intermediate prints, a process known as Van Dyke; these prints actually serve as second "originals." Van Dyke prints, or sepias, on which brown lines are produced on translucent paper, become negatives and the source of future drawings. Van Dykes are stable, high-quality prints that can be used for further reproductions if continued handling of the originals is considered undesirable. In time ozalid prints deteriorate if they are exposed to open sunlight, which turns the lines to a pale hue with a purple tinge as they gradually fade away. This will also happen, for instance, when an object is placed on a print (a book or a stack of white paper) and left there in the sunshine; the background will change and the line work will fade. The effect is similar to that of a piece of furniture whose back and top have been faded beyond recognition by the rays of the sun.

In the past, photographic reproductions have been photostats, products of a direct photographic process that focuses on sensitized paper. The scale of the drawings can be increased or reduced in a manner similar to that used in making prints or reproductions larger or smaller. This has been helpful in that small pieces of graphic information can be increased in size for use as underlays by the draftsman. By the same token, large drawings can be reduced in size to fit the requirements of a brochure or pamphlet. A negative in which white lines appear on a black background, similar to a photographic negative, is made as the first step. Any number of positives with white background and black line work can then be obtained by rephotostating it. The process is an expensive but positive way of reproducing accurately opaque material. It is used extensively with legal documents in which precise duplication is essential.

The product of another method by which an opaque drawing is reproduced photographically as a translucent original is known as an autopositive. It is usually printed in reverse, black line on white background. Although it is not highly translucent, it will produce a high-quality print if the original drawing is in good condition. Often, when remodeling a building, the owner may have a copy of the original prints, if not the original tracings. If the tracings are not available, it is a good idea to make autopositives of the prints for future use. They, too, are a bit expensive, but when we consider the alternative of having to retrace or redraw the drawings, the cost becomes relatively minor.

In the last few years a tremendous amount of photocopying machinery has been put on the market, usually aimed at serving rather small drawing sheet sizes ($8\frac{1}{2} \times 11$ or $8\frac{1}{2} \times 14$), although some can actually cut the paper to the size of the original. These machines can be divided into two basic categories: electrostatic and heat processing. To produce its copies the electrostatic copier charges the paper electronically and then sprays it with a white powder that adheres to the areas that remain sensitized. These areas are sensitized by an image on the original that prevents the background from being uncharged. Many of these copies deteriorate quite rapidly, and one must choose a system carefully and be aware of its ramifications. Some machines of a cheaper variety will produce only marginal prints. Of course, improvements have been made, and today the copy is often better than the original. Some machines reproduce color and others are capable of copying halftones, many of which can be used for bulletin or addenda drawings. Again, we should be aware of the life span of the copy. We should know a little about the extremes.

Radical changes have been made in the reproduction of regular construction documents. Project costs have been increasing, so that when we hear of a $20 or $25 million project we are not so overawed as we might have been years ago. In projects of this size the number of drawings required may be counted in the hundreds and the scope of the building may involve sheets as large as 4'-0" long by 3'-0" or 3'-6" wide.

It becomes difficult to work in the field with prints of this size, although this is not the entire problem. Once the drawings have been completed, jobs of this multimillion dollar order will draw a large number of bidders and contractors, each of whom must be accorded a fair break in bidding the project. Each will need at least one, if not more, sets of drawings on which to base his

or her estimates. A total of 200 sets of drawings, each containing a few hundred sheets of prints, is not uncommon. This can be extremely expensive, although it is a direct cost to the owner; it is not part of the architect's cost or fee. Accordingly, in preceding chapters we discussed photographic drafting techniques, including composite drafting. The idea of using half-size prints was presented. In this process a photograph is taken of each of the original sheets; the prints are reduced by one-half and printing plates are made. The drawings are then printed by offset on good-quality printing paper, black line on white at one-quarter the size of the originals. Of course, the offset printing process is quicker and the size is smaller, yet readable as well as convenient. If there were imperfections in the original, the negatives can be corrected and sharpened; results will be high-quality prints. In a job of the magnitude discussed here the savings can amount to as much as $12,000 in the reproduction of the drawings alone. This system, however, is not a cure-all for every office and every project. Surely, a job composed of 15 to 18 sheets of 24 x 36 drawings is not going to benefit by the use of half-size drawings. Many offices will reject it because the size of their projects would never allow it to be economically feasible, but many large firms find it much simpler for the people in the field to use these half-size drawings at a considerably lower cost to the owner.

Another interesting element is introduced in the use of offset printing: the multicolor print. In one system the building lines are reproduced in black on white; an overlay of red lines represents the plumbing system; on another blue lines trace the heating, air-conditioning, and ventilating systems, and green lines add the electrical system. Not all overlays are made on the same set of prints, but each trade is clearly distinguishable by color. This is a tremendous advancement because no longer will the basic structural lines be confused with those of the many services. Easier reading, fewer mistakes, and the time saved in the interpretation of drawings are enormous advantages. Again, however, is the office capable of using this method? Do the jobs demand it? This decision belongs to the principals.

Some talk has been heard of sensitized paper for use in the ozalid process that would allow color printing, but none has yet been marketed. The reproduction of drawings may seem inconsequential when, in truth, it involves only about $9,000 in a project that may cost as much as $30 million. The problem becomes one of simple reality. Why take the time, why make the effort, to produce good original tracings if their reproduction is defective? If the prints are not good, the job will suffer. If the information is faulty, the problem, of course, lies with those who supplied it, but prints that deteriorate rapidly, that are not properly reproduced in regard to line quality, exposure, and background, are a problem that must be solved. The process is not inexpensive, and whether it originates in a schoolroom exercise or an office, we should demand the best results from whatever type of reproduction system is chosen. Incidentally, the reproduction systems discussed here, particularly the simple blue and black line prints, are excellent classroom exercises. Do some drawings on tracing paper and have them reproduced. Again, demand the best print possible. The print will demonstrate how good your line work is and will point out vividly all technical drafting errors.

Film negative. Polyester film, high contrast, and true to scale; can be enlarged, reduced, rearranged, or blocked out; first step in making matte or clear positives.

Paper negative. (Camera or contact.) Most versatile of film negatives if true scale is not required; excellent for "as-built" or nondimensioned documents.

Clear film positive. Base for scissors drafting (composite); excellent media for standardized details.

Polyester matte film. Washoff type on which a reproduced line can be eradicated with moist eraser; excellent drafting surface; available for ink or pencil, with one or two matte surfaces.

Polyester matte film. Eradicating type on which reproduced line must be eradicated with solution eradicator; excellent for halftones, fine line work, photodrafting and sheet with stick-on materials.

Washoff cloth. Waterproof cloth with line eradication with moist eraser; limited popularity due to lack of versatility; requires inked changes for best results.

Shadow print. Make on washoff or eradicating film; tinted line gives a gray halftone on copies, very fine background for superimposition of other work, such as landscape, wiring, duct, plumbing, and other such systems.

Brief description of some of the reproduction mediums available for use in different ways. There are many more, and the project architect should consult the local reprographics firms for their latest methods, technology, and capabilities before engaging a new system or method of production.

38

Summary

I t seems both appropriate and desirable to summarize some of the information that has been discussed previously. An attempt to do this, at least in part, follows.

These are simply more thoughts about working drawing preparation. The suggestion is to use these frequently, whether for specific problems or simply to reorient yourself to your proper perspective for producing working drawings. Underline or highlight those items that interest you or seem to give you new and better direction and perspective.

• No matter your current station in life (graduate, degreed, bachelor, associate, master, registered, co-op, or designer/operator), the success of the project you are working on depends *directly* on how much *you* care.

• Caring has a direct impact on the project and its cost. For example, if you show a detail requiring work that is not normally done or is not normally done as you show it, the cost of the project will go up. Simply because there is a question as to what will be required if you insist on your own way, the added cost is justified to your client's detriment.

• You have to care about each line—what it does and doesn't do and, more important, what it is *supposed* to do. So, too, with each note, work, and dimension. Be aware and sensitive to conditions: Does the door open into a brick wall? Why is a door opening "hatched"? Do your dimensions add up to overalls? Do things look neat, controlled, and orderly? Be careful to avoid misspellings.

• Don't be misled by the words "architectural *practice*." The work of the profession is as serious as the "*practice* of medicine." While practice in some contexts indicates less than a fully committed effort, or something less than serous, here it means the real, actual, and dedicated work of the professionals. In plain language, giving a damn counts! Blowing things off, forgetting, "sloughing off," glossing over, and simply not understanding (and being too proud to ask) doesn't cut it. If you are charged with making changes noted on a check set, make absolutely sure that you make *all* of the changes and in a correct manner.

• *Never* consider any assignment or work on documents to be menial; the project architect knows what must be done and is looking to you to help, assist, aid, and contribute in a positive manner to their completion.

• It is your job to do the work assigned to you in the most complete, well-depicted, well-coordinated, and absolutely pertinent manner. Slopping something together is indefensible, especially with the resources and people around you who can help.

579

• Thinking does *not* hurt, but gives you a world of pride and makes you a valued employee.

• There is no such thing as a "dumb" question—ask, ask, ask! (It's only dumb to think there is a dumb question!) If you believe you have a possible solution, bring it along, but be sure to ask, ask, ask.

• You run, control, and think for the computer-aided drafting (CAD) system—*you!*

• From now on, consider CAD as nothing more than your valuable production tool. It is exactly that—a tool—it does no more than a pencil. OK, so it's faster, but that in itself is meaningless if content, intent, and clarity are not present.

• CAD is a marvelous but inanimate machine. It cannot even turn itself on without you or a timing gadget. It doesn't know what to do, when, or where; all it knows is what *you* tell it. Tell it foolishness, it produces foolishness—who then is at fault? It doesn't know how to correct your mistakes, or how to do something you failed to do.

• By the same token, CAD has great capabilities, granted, but there is nothing that says you have to use all of them, or all of any one of them. CAD will insert brick symbology until the cows come home—you give it the extent and the command for the symbol and *wow!* look at all those bricks!

But have you—and CAD— contributed anything of value to the project?

• In none of this do we consider you dumb or inadequate; you are merely unprepared and inexperienced. There is no way to overcome this except by getting field and office knowledge and guidance; by asking questions and advice; by seeking to better yourself through reading and educational courses that increase your insight to construction.

• The Intern Development Program (IDP) proves, outrightly, that architecture schools are not teaching everything they should or could within the time you spend with them. You have to engage in on-the-job-training (OJT), and you will add to your knowledge and career status by asking and finding out from others who have been "bloodied" and have also learned from those before them.

• There is a great deal to learn, but don't fear this—it comes in steps or stages, and each project will add something to your personal storehouse of details, concepts, approaches, and solutions.

• If it doesn't look right, it probably isn't!

• In the bygone days, every so often each day we looked at our drawings upside down; you'll be amazed at how easy it is to spot errors when you do this.

• Look at the drawings through half-closed eyes, and you'll see line work that is too light for proper readability and reproduction.

• Remember, a line has a beginning and an ending—it goes "from" somewhere "to" somewhere.

• Check and coordinate everything, no matter how small. If each of us "makes sure," we'll do a much better job, quicker, and at less cost.

• You will make mistakes! But make them in the office where they are easily changed. Don't let things slide, hoping they will be caught or remedied in the field—only "bad" things happen that way.

• *Keep control.* Only you can make things happen, including making the CAD machine do something. This means using the best information and the best technique(s) to get the project documented.

• Don't be afraid to use resources. Most of what we use is shown or pictured somewhere; we use a lot of standard materials or systems. Look them up in reference books, other project drawings, Sweet's Catalogs, product reference manuals. Just be sure the drawings or details you use apply completely to your work. Nothing is more distracting than a detail no one can figure out or place in the job. If you need information, talk to your supervisor and suggest that the product representative be called or a catalog sent for.

HELPFUL HINTS

1. All lettering in notes is the same size, style, and case. Titles are always larger than notes.
2. Turn on all layers, to ensure that notes, etc., do not (1) overlap each other or (2) overlap portions of the drawing.
3. Titles, section markers, door marks, wall-type designators, targets, and all other such symbols should be uniform and the same size in all locations. Door marks should *always* be within the door opening (move other "stuff" to miss them).
4. Dimension two thin, adjacent materials like this:

5. Run dimension lines *through* a wall or partition like this (CAD likes to dimension just to the face of the wall, leaving a gap):

6. Run a line of dimensions between the column centerlines. Locate walls, partitions, and other landmarks (corners, bulkheads, etc.) from the nearest column centerline. Column centerlines are just that—long dash, dot or dash, then long dash, at close intervals and continuous through the drawing, both ways.

7. Dimension lines that cross match lines require a definite termination, either to a column centerline or to a wall, with a note showing the distance from the terminus to the landmark on the other side of the match line. *Do not dimension* to the match line, as this is an invisible line that is not located on-site (it is merely a drafting technique!).

   Don't use match lines in wall sections. Think of wall sections as a series of details aligned one over the other. If the full height of a wall cannot be shown on the sheet, delete portions of the wall that just show repetitive construction (example: a brick wall) by using pairs of break lines (and keep them small too) through the width of the wall. Then merely space the detail work above and below the break lines closer together. *Do*, however, make every attempt to show the very top and the very bottom of the wall.

8. Reflected ceiling plans should show walls only, and with the same line weight for both new and existing; do not show door openings, etc. (remember that these drawings are the views we would see if we looked down at the floor and it was mirrored).

   Do not dimension borders of ceiling tiles (rooms can vary in size and alignment, so a border may be altogether different from what you show). Note spaces with no ceilings as "exposed structure," not "open"; "unfinished" spaces should be shown as unfinished.

   In laying out a ceiling grid start at the geometric center of the room with an intersection of four panels, *or* with a panel centered both ways.

9. Delete North arrows from section and detail sheets; use them on plan sheets *only*.

10. Be aware of the need to vary line weight:

new and existing work, work to be removed, materials that are "cut" in section. This adds readability to the drawings and makes things much clearer.

11. Do not rely on or "allow" auto-dimensioning to produce and control your dimensions (remember who is in control). Architectural drawings are *not* dimensioned down to $\frac{1}{16}$ and usually not even to $\frac{1}{8}$. CAD may want to do this, and some engineers tend to do it as well, but our work is too variable and there is no need for such precision in view of the normal variation in our materials and systems. If a dimension is critical or necessary, mark it "Hold"; if you are aware of a dimension that may vary several inches, add ± to the number dimension. When changes are made late in production, using "NTS" (not to scale) is permitted.

12. When adding hatching and use other material symbols, on both plans and elevations, do this work only in relatively small areas, *not* throughout entire walls. Usually it is helpful to add such indicators at opening jambs, repaired work, offsets, corners, and the like.

13. Use a "detail call out" only where a specific and unique location is involved. For example, *not every* bollard needs a "bubble," but can be noted as "See Detail 12345," or "Typical bollard." Where other typical (same item repeated), continuous, or wide-ranging work is done, use notes, *not* a call out.

14. Even though they may repeat each other, use a separate set of notes for each drawing/detail; don't use one set with merely two sets of leader lines pointing to the two drawings.

   Moreover, ensure that the same note for the same work, but on different drawings, says things identically. Do not include a lot of specification information on your drawing notes (this includes material information, installation methods, etc.).

15. Do some preliminary planning about sheet layout; never allow leader lines to cross ("linear spaghetti" will result); locate notes close to the point of application; leader lines should touch the work, not merely point to or "aim at" it.

16. Never use such large lettering that the drawing or object is obscured or made to "disap-

pear." Just as in cartoons and comics, words should be used to aid and explain the drawing.

17. Be extra careful that you never transpose or otherwise "mess up" a model number or other pertinent information. Don't misspell.

18. Periodically, ask yourself (and be as objective as you can) whether you have enough information on the drawing that you could build the work. Be careful not to assume something in your head that is not on the drawing(s).

19. By the way, *assume nothing!*

20. Never let any of the following thoughts enter your mind: I guess that's OK; Oh, that'll be all right; Who cares? No one will notice! Who knows? Let 'em work it out in the field; it doesn't make any difference what I put down.

21. Be very wary of detailing or requiring work that you do not fully understand; your concept may be not only faulty, but unbuildable; here, only experience is the remedy.

22. You've heard of the "honor system" at the military academies; there is one in architecture too, and in document production. Precious little time is available, in any office, for a complete and comprehensive review of every document, detail, and so on. What you do or don't do may be overlooked.

    You are, or will be, a professional, and with that comes the need to meet a standard of care (note: *care*), which means doing the right thing, for the right reason, at the right time. Oddly enough, the standard of care that affects you is part of the legal network that surrounds you.

    And, not to frighten you, but in this world today, you could find yourself in a witness chair in a court explaining why you drew what you did. Don't be caught having "I thought that would be OK" as your only defense. Litigation is a nasty process (I hope you never engage it!), whose sole purpose is to point fingers and establish responsibility. Following set procedures and working within the standard of care are of utmost importance.

23. Another important aspect to your professional OJT and education is your ability to understand the need to be flexible. Every office has an office standards manual, the ground rules about how the office does things or wants things done. Everything we do here is not necessarily the same way it is done by other offices.

    A basic understanding of *why* something is done is far more important than *how* or under what symbol it appears. We can best serve you, personally and professionally, by giving you some insight into this process.

24. It is very important, for your development, to think for yourself. However, understand that you cannot do this isolated from your colleagues and supervisors. What you put on the documents "commits" your firm. Therefore, take the initiative, do things, think, research, seek answers, ask questions, but at the same time keep referencing back, and keep your supervisors informed. None of us knows every way to do everything; some of us have the experience to know, a little better, what works best and what won't work—you need to gain this information through your career.

25. A lot of this is "heavy stuff," but try not to be discouraged or frightened. We all like to enjoy our work. Your satisfaction and ultimate success as a professional lies in doing things well, properly, and once!

**Welcome to the profession—
have a long, wondrous,
fruitful, and satisfying career**

> **We are what we repeatedly do.
> Excellence, then, is not an act;
> It is a habit.
> — Aristotle**

APPENDIX A

Useful Geometric Relationships

PLANE (TWO-DIMENSIONAL) FIGURES

Perimeter

The term *perimeter* means the distance around a plane surface: the direct measure of the length of the sides of the plane surface.

Polygon

A *polygon* is a closed figure bounded by straight lines. A regular polygon has all of its sides equal in length. Polygons are named according to the number of sides.

Square and Rectangle

Square   A *square* is a geometric figure having four sides of equal length and equal angles.

Rectangle A *rectangle* is a geometric figure having four sides. The opposite sides are the same length and all the angles are equal.

The perimeter of a square equals the sum of the four sides.

P (perimeter $= 4S$ (sides)

The perimeter of a rectangular figure also equals the sum of the four sides.

$$P \text{ (perimeter)} = 2L + 2W \quad \text{or} \quad P = 2(L + W).$$

Circle

A *circle* is a plane figure bounded by a single curved line, each part of which is equally distant from the center point. The perimeter of the circle is known as its *circumference*.

To determine the circumference, one of the following two factors must be known:

1. The *radius r* of the circle
2. The *diameter d* of the circle

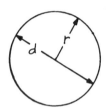

The third factor used to find the circumference is a *constant* and is called *pi* (π), the numerical value of which is 3.1416 or $^{22}/_7$.

The two mathematical formulas used to determine the length of the circumference are:

1. The diameter (d) times π ($d\pi$).
2. Twice the radius (r) times π ($2r\pi$).

The fraction $^{22}/_7$ may be used for π instead of 3.1416 for computing the circumference of a circle. However, the answer will not be quite as accurate.

The outer edge of a circle is called the circumference. A portion of this circumference is called an *arc*. The straight line that joins the ends of the arc is called a *chord*. A *segment* is the area included between the arc and the chord. A *sector* is the area included between two radii and the circumference.

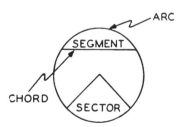

Angular Measure

Although most measurements of round surfaces are given in linear measure, many measurements are in terms of angular measure. Angular measure is based on the opening between two lines extending from a point. This point is called a *vertex*. The opening is called an angle and is measured in terms of degrees. The size of the angle depends entirely on the opening and not on the length of the sides.

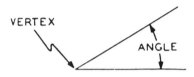

A circle is divided into 360 equal parts, each of which is called a degree. The symbol for a degree is a small zero slightly above and to the right of the number. Ten degrees would be written 10°. Usually a degree is the smallest unit used. However, when more accurate measurement is needed, the degree is broken into 60 equal parts, which are called minutes. The abbreviation for a minute is a ′ placed in a position similar to the degree sign. Example: 15 minutes = 15′. A minute may be broken into 60 equal parts which are called seconds. The abbreviation is a ″ similarly placed. Example: 15 seconds = 15″.

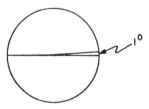

Addition and subtraction of angular measurements require the ability to reduce degrees, minutes, and seconds.

$$1° = 60'$$

$$1' = 60''$$

To reduce degrees to minutes, multiply the number of degrees by 60.

To reduce minutes to seconds, multiply the number of minutes by 60.

To convert seconds to minutes, divide the number of seconds by 60.

To convert minutes to degrees, divide the number of minutes by 60.

When adding or subtracting it is necessary to add or subtract like quantities. Therefore, degrees must be added to degrees, minutes to minutes, and seconds to seconds.

EXAMPLE. Add 3° 25′ 40″ to 6° 42′ 35″.

3° 25′ 40″	Step 1	Place the two figures over each other
6° 42′ 35″		
9° 67′ 75″		
	Step 2	Add the quantities individually.
9° 68′ 15″	Step 3	Reduce seconds to minutes. 75″ = 1′ 15″. Add the 1′ to the 67′. 1 + 67 = 68.
10° 8′ 15″	Step 4	Reduce the minutes to degrees. 68′ = 1° 8′. Add the 1′ to the 9°. 1 + 9 = 10.

EXAMPLE. Subtract 10° 19′ 35″ from 18° 10′ 25″.

18° 10′ 25″	Step 1	Place the subtrahend under the minuend.
10° 19′ 35″		
18° 9′ 85″	Step 2	Begin by subtracting the seconds.
10° 19′ 35″		Since the subtrahend is larger than the minuend, borrow one minute (60″) from 10′ and add to the 25″. This will decrease the 10′ to 9′.
50″		
17° 69′ 85″	Step 3	Subtract the minutes. Again the subtrahend is larger than the minuend. Borrow 1 (60′) from the 18° and add to the 9′. This will decrease the 18° to 17°.
10° 19′ 35″		
50′ 50″		
17° 69′ 85″	Step 4	Subtract the degrees.
10° 19′ 35″		
7° 50′ 50″		

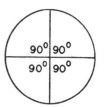

A circle is often divided into four equal parts. Each [art contains 90°, commonly called a right angle.

Angular measure is used to determine the length of the arcs of a circle. Because the whole circle contains 360°, the length of an arc bears the same ratio to the circumference as the angle included by the radii from the ends of the arc does to the 360. The formula would then be:

$$\frac{arc}{circumference} = \frac{degrees\ of\ opening}{360}$$

$$arc = circumference \times \frac{degrees\ of\ opening}{360}$$

EXAMPLE. If a circle has a circumference of 6 inches, what is the length of an arc with an opening of 60°?

$$arc = 6 \times \frac{60}{360} = 6 \times \frac{1}{6} = 1''$$

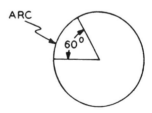

AREA MEASURE

A plane surface has two dimensions, length and width. This surface measurement is expressed in square units. The width and the length must be expressed in the same units before an area measurement may be taken. If the length is given in inches, the width must also be inches and the area will be expressed in square inches. Similarly, if the width is in feet, the length must be reduced to feet and the area will expressed in square feet.

The area will always be expressed in terms of the linear measurement used i determining the width and length.

Square

The area of a square is computed by multiplying the length of a side by itself. The formula ia $A = S^2$.

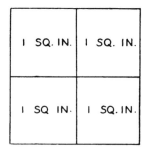

Common measurements of area are the square inch, the square foot, and the square yard. Areas are reduced to one of these three measurements in common practice.

$$1 \text{ sq ft} = 144 \text{ sq in.}$$
$$(12 \text{ in.} \times 12 \text{ in.} = 144 \text{ in.})$$
$$1 \text{ sq yd} = 9 \text{ sq ft } (3 \times 3 = 9)$$
$$= 1,296 \text{ sq in. } (9 \times 144 = 1,296)$$

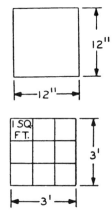

To convert square inches to square feet, divide the number of square inches by 144.

To convert square feet to square yards, divide the number of square feet by 9.

To reduce square yards to square feet, multiply the number of square yards by 9.

To reduce square feet to square inches, multiply the number of square feet by 144.

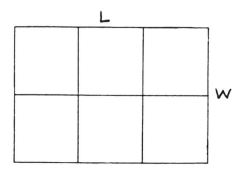

Rectangle

The area of a rectangle is computed by multiplying the length by the width. The formula is $A = LW$.

Parallelogram

A parallelogram is a four-sided plane figure whose opposite sides are parallel and of equal length. The area of a parallelogram is computed by multiplying the base times the altitude. If the shaded area A within the parallelogram were moved to the area B, a rectangle would be the result. The formula is $A = ba$.

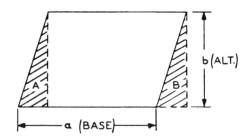

Triangle

A triangle is a plane figure having three sides and three angles. The sum of the three inside angles. The sum of the three inside angles formed by the sides equals $180°$. One side of the triangle is called the *base*. The angle opposite the base is called the *vertex* angle.

TRIANGLE

Types of Triangle

1. Acute angle triangle. All angles are less than 90°.

ACUTE ANGLE TRIANGLE

2. Obtuse angle triangle. One angle is greater then 90°.

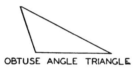

OBTUSE ANGLE TRIANGLE

3. Isosceles triangle. Two sides are equal in length and base angles are equal.

ISOSCELES TRIANGLE

4. Equilateral triangle. All sides are equal in length and all the angles are equal (60°).

EQUILATERAL TRIANGLE

5. Scalene triangle. All sides are different lengths and no angles are equal.

SCALENE TRIANGLE

6. Right-angle triangle (also called right triangle). One angle is equal to 90°. The side opposite the 90° angle is called the *hypotenuse.*

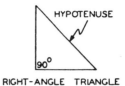

RIGHT-ANGLE TRIANGLE

The Right Triangle— Special Rules

1. The square of the hypotenuse of a right triangle is equal to the sum of the square of the other two sides. In formula form:

$$H^2 = a^2 + b^2$$

where a = altitude, b = the base, and H = the hypotenuse.

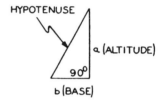

2. The diagonal of square or a rectangle may be computed by using the rule of the right triangle. The diagonal becomes the hypotenuse of the right triangle. The triangle D of a square equals the square root of the sum of the square of the two sides. In formula form:

$$D = \sqrt{s^2 + s^2} = 1.414S$$

3. The diagonal D of a rectangle with sides L and W equals the square root of the sum of the squares of the two sides. In formula form:

$$D = \sqrt{L^2 + W^2}$$

Since the area of a parallelogram is equal to the base times the altitude, the area of the triangle would be one half of the total area. In formula form it would be written as:

$$A = \frac{ba}{2} \quad \text{or} \quad A = \frac{1}{2}ba$$

where A = area, b = base, and a = altitude.

Another method of finding the area of a triangle when only the lengths of the sides are known involves the use of two formulas:

$$S = \frac{a + b + c}{2} \quad \text{or} \quad \frac{1}{2} \text{ perimeter}$$

$$A = \sqrt{s(x - a)s(x - b)s(x - c)}$$

where a, b, and c are the sides.

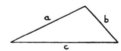

The Isosceles Triangle

A line drawn from the vertex of an isosceles triangle to the midpoint of the base forms two tight triangles and is also the altitude.

Given the length of one of the equal sides and the altitude, the formula to find the base b is:

$$b = 2\sqrt{s^2 - a^2}$$

Given the length of one of the equal sides of an isosceles triangle and the base, the formula to find the altitude a is:

$$a = \sqrt{s^2 - (b^2/4)}$$

The Equilateral Triangle

Since all sides are equal, there are some special rules that apply only to the equilateral triangle. The altitude line divides the base, which is the same length as the sides, into two equal parts and forms two 90° angles at the base.

To find the altitude of an equilateral triangle, use:

$$a = \sqrt{3s^2/4} = s/2\sqrt{3} = 0.866s$$

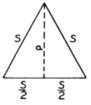

where 0.866s is a constant in solving equilateral triangles.

To find the area of an equilateral triangle, use the formula for the area of a triangle:

$$A = \frac{ba}{2} \quad b = s, a = 0.866s$$

$$A = \frac{s \times 0.866s}{2} = s \times 0.433s$$

$$A = 0.433s^2$$

Trapezoid

A *trapezoid* is a figure having four sides with only one pair of parallel sides. The parallel sides of the trapezoid are called the lower base and the upper base.

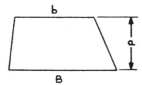

The area of a trapezoid is equal to $\frac{1}{2}$ the sum of the parallel sides times the altitude. In formula form:

$$A = \frac{B + b}{2} \times a$$

where B is the lower base, b is the upper base, and a is the altitude.

If a line is drawn from opposite corners of the trapezoid, two triangles are formed which have the same altitude but different bases.

In triangle 1, the area $= \dfrac{b \times a}{2}$

In triangle 2, the area $= \dfrac{B \times a}{2}$

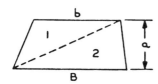

The sum of the areas of the two triangles gives the area of the trapezoid.

$$A = \frac{ba}{2} + \frac{Ba}{2} = \frac{(b + B)}{2} \times a$$

Hexagon

A hexagon is a plane figure having six sides. A regular hexagon has all six sides equal in length. Diagonals drawn as indicated form six equilateral triangle is:

$$A = 0.433 \ S^2$$

where S equals the length of a side. The area of a regular hexagon then equals six times the area of one of the equilateral triangles formed by the diagonals. In formula form,

$$A = 6 \times 0.433 \quad S^2 = 2.598 \ S^2$$

Octagon

An *octagon* is a plane figure having eight sides. A regular octagon has all eight sides equal in length. The following formula has been developed to determine the area of a regular octagon if the length of one side is known:

$$A = 4.8284 \ S^2$$

where S equals the length of one side of a regular octagon.

Circle

The formula to find the area of a circle is:

$$\text{Area} = \pi r^2 \qquad \text{where } r = \text{radius}$$

If the diameter (d) is known, the formula becomes

$$A = \frac{\pi d^2}{4} \quad \text{or} \quad 0.7854 \ d^2$$

If the area is known, the diameter and the radius can be easily calculated.

$$d = \sqrt{A/0.7854} = \sqrt{A/0.8862}$$
$$r = \sqrt{A/\pi} = \sqrt{A/1.7724}$$

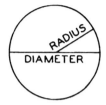

Sector

A sector is the area included between an arc and two radii. The sector is a part of the entire circle. The area of the sector bears the same ratio to the area of the circle as the angle included by

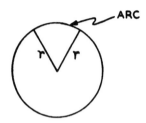

the two radii does to 360° (the degrees in a full circle). In formula form:

$$\frac{\text{Area (sector)}}{\text{Area (circle)}} = \frac{\text{angle (sector)}}{360}$$

$$\text{Area (sector)} = \text{area (circle)} \times \frac{\text{angle (sector)}}{360}$$

$$= \pi r^2 \times \frac{\text{angle } (s)}{360}$$

SOLID (THREE-DIMENSIONAL) FIGURES

A *prism* is a solid whose ends are similar, equal, and parallel and whose sides are parallelograms. The ends, both top and bottom, are called bases of the prism. The sides are called lateral faces. The altitude (height or depth) of a prism is the perpendicular distance between the two bases.

Prisms are named according to the shape of the base. For example:

A rectangular solid has rectangular bases and faces.

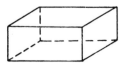

A cube is a prism whose bases and lateral faces are all equal squares.

A hexagonal solid is a hexagon-shaped prism. A regular hexagon has six equal sides.

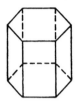

The *lateral area* of a prism is equal to the sum of the area of the faces.

The *total area* of a prism is equal to the lateral area plus the area of the bases.

The lateral area of any prism equals the perimeter of the base times the altitude.

$$A_{(L)} = P \times a$$

where $A_{(L)}$ = lateral area, P = perimeter, and a = altitude.

The total area of a prism equals the sum of the area of the bases plus the lateral area.

$$A_{(T)} = 2\,A_{(B)} + P \times a$$

where $A_{(T)}$ = total area, $A_{(B)}$ = area of the base, P = perimeter of base, and a = altitude.

The total area of a cube equals six times the area on one face. The area of a face equals the square of one side. In formula form:

$$A_{(TC)} = 6\,S^2$$

where $A_{(TC)}$ = total area of a cube, S = length of one side.

Volume is expressed in terms of cubic measure. In determining a volume, the same units of linear measurement must be used through the entire process. The basic unit of cubic measurement is the cubic inch, which is a cube with all sides 1 sq in.

The volume of a prism equals the area of the base times the altitude. In formula form,

$$V = A_B \times a$$

where V = volume, A_B = area of base, a = altitude.

EXAMPLE. Find the volume in cubic inches of a cube with sides 1 ft in length.

$$1 \text{ ft } = 12 \text{ in.}$$
$$A_{(B)} = 12 \times 12 = 144 \text{ sq ft}$$
$$V = A_{(B)} \times a = 144 \times 12$$
$$V = 1728 \text{ cu in. } = 1 \text{ cu ft}$$

EXAMPLE. Find the volume in cubic feet of a cube with sides 1 yd in length.

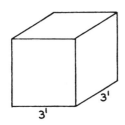

$$1 \text{ yd } = 3 \text{ ft}$$
$$A_B = 3 \times 3 = 9$$
$$V = A_B \times a = 9 \times 3$$
$$V = 27 \text{ cu ft } = 1 \text{ cu yd}$$

To convert cubic inches to cubic feet, divide by 1728.

To convert cubic feet to cubic yards, divide by 27.

To reduce cubic yards to cubic feet, multiply by 27.

To reduce cubic feet to cubic inches, multiply by 1728.

The volume of a rectangular prism equals the length times the width times the height. In formula form:

$$V = L\,W\,h$$

where L = length of base, W = width of base, and h = height (or depth) of prism.

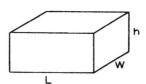

The volume of a cube equals one side cubed. In formula form:

$$V = S^3$$

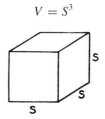

A *cylinder* is a long circular body, solid or hollow, of uniform diameter. The lateral area of a cylinder equals the circumference of the base times the height of the cylinder. In formula form:

$$A_{(lc)} = C \times h$$

where $A_{(lc)}$ = lateral area, C = circumference, and h = height.

Substituting for C, we also have the following formula to obtain the lateral area of a cylinder.

$$A_{(lc)} = C \times h$$

or

$$A_{(lc)} = \pi d \times h \,(C = \pi d)$$

or

$$A_{(lc)} = 2\pi r h \,(C = 2\pi r)$$

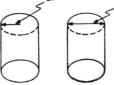

Appendix A

The total area of a cylinder equals the sum of the two bases plus the lateral area. The bases are circles. The area of a circle equals πr^2 or $0.7854d^2$. In formula form,

$$A_{(t)} = 2\pi r^2 + 2\pi rh$$

or

$$A_{(t)} = 2 \times 0.7854d^2 + \pi dh$$

$$A_{(t)} = 1.5708d^2 + \pi dh$$

The volume of a cylinder equals the area of the base times the height. The area of the base times the height. The area of the circle equals πr^2 or $0.7854d^2$. In formula form:

$$V = \pi r^2 h \quad \text{or} \quad V = 0.7854d^2 h$$

A *cone* is a figure having a circle for a base and surface (sides) which tapers evenly up to a point called the vertex. The *altitude* (*VO*) of a cone is the perpendicular distance from the base to the vertex. The *slant height* (*VS*) is the distance from the vertex to any point on the circumference of the base.

The slant height $= \sqrt{r^2 + a^2}$, where r = radius, a = altitude.

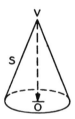

Useful Geometric Relationships

The *lateral area* of a cone is equal to one-half the circumference times the slant height. In formula form:

$$A_L = \frac{1}{2}Cs$$

where s = slant height and C = circumference of the base.

$$C = \pi D \quad \text{or} \quad 2\pi r (D = \text{diameter or } r = \text{radius})$$

The *total area* of a cone equals the sum of the lateral area plus the area of the base. In formula form:

$$A_T = \frac{1}{2}\pi Ds + 0.7854D^2 \quad \text{or} \quad \pi rs + \pi r^2$$

The *volume* of a cone equals one-third the area of the base times the altitude. In formula form:

$$V = \frac{Ba}{3} \quad \text{or} \quad \frac{\pi r^2 a}{3} \quad \text{or} \quad 0.2618 \, D^2 \times a$$

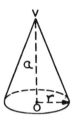

Ellipse

An ellipse is a closed oval-shaped figure that is symmetrical to two lines or axes that are perpendicular to each other.

The formulas for the area and perimeter of an ellipse give approximations that are accurate enough for general usage.

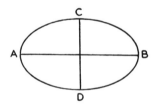

AB = MAJOR AXIS
CD = MINOR AXIS

The *area* can be found by either one of two methods:

1. Area $= \pi \times \dfrac{\text{major axis}}{2} \times \dfrac{\text{minor axis}}{2} \quad \text{or} \quad \pi ab$

   where $a = \frac{1}{2}$ major axis, $b = \frac{1}{2}$ minor axis

2. Area = (factor) $0.7854 \times$ major axis $\times$ minor axis or $0.7854 \, Mm$

   where M = major axis, m = minor axis

The *perimeter* can be found by either one of two methods:

1. Perimeter $= \pi(a + b)$ where $a = \frac{1}{2}$ major axis, $b = \frac{1}{2}$ minor axis.

2. Perimeter $= \pi\sqrt{2(a^2 = b^2)}$.

EXAMPLE. Find the perimeter of an ellipse with a major axis of 18 ft and a minor axis of 12 ft.

1. $P = \pi(a + b) = 3.1416\left(\frac{18}{2} + \frac{12}{2}\right)$
$P = 3.1416(9 + 6) = 3.1416 \times 15 = 47.124$ ft

2. $P = \pi\sqrt{2(a^2 + b^2)} = 3.1416\sqrt{2(9^2 + 6^2)}$
$P = 3.1416\sqrt{2(81 + 36)} = 3.1416\sqrt{2(117)}$
$P = 3.1416\sqrt{234} = 3.1416 \times 15.29 = 48.035$ ft

Note the variation between the answers in the two methods.

APPENDIX B

Fire Door
Selection Data

CLASSIFICATIONS

Fire door openings are classified by their location within the building. The location determines the length of exposure protection required [as stated in the building code], based on the potential fire hazard of that particular area. The five opening classifications are shown below along with the four door ratings, and the maximum glass areas allowed in each classification. The hourly ratings given doors <u>and associated frames and hardware</u> are a result of testing in fire conditions by the Underwriters' Laboratories, Inc.

UNDERWRITERS' [U.L.] LABEL DOORS

Label Classification		Use In Buildings	Max. Glass Area
A	3-Hour Rating	Openings in fire walls and division walls between buildings with a 3-hour rating	None Permitted
B	1-1/2-Hour Rating	Openings in vertical shafts with a rating of 1-1/2 hours	100 sq.in per door leaf
C	3/4-Hour Rating	Openings in corridors and room partitions with a 3/4 hour rating	1296 sq.in per lite; 54"max. dim.
D	1-1/2 Hour Rating	Openings in exterior walls with a rating of 1-1/2 hours; severe exterior fire hazard	None Permitted
E	3/4-Hour Rating	Openings to exterior fire escapes with a rating of 3/4-hour; moderate exterior fire hazard	720 sq.in per lite; 54" max. dim.

20-minute or 1/3 hour ratings- no formal classification; used when smoke control is primary concern.

In general, doors carry three-fourths of the rating of the adjacent wall. Therefore, a 3-hour fire door is used in a 4-hour wall; a 1-1/2 hour fire door in a 2-hour wall; a 3/4 hour door in a 1-hour wall.

It should be noted that it is acceptable to use a door with a higher fire rating than the opening requires. For example, a 1-1/2 hour Class "B" door maybe used in a "C" opening, so long as the glass area does not exceed the maximum allowed for the door rating.

DOOR LOCATION	PROTECTION REQUIRED	TYPE OF EXPOSURE	DOOR TYPE REQUIRED	RECOMMENDED STEELCRAFT DOORS
Apartment Suite Entrances	3/4 or 1/3 Hour	Moderate	F	L18, L20—1-3/4"
Automotive Dealer Show Room to Garage	3 Hour	Extreme	F	J18—1-3/4" (Industrial Sliding Door)
Boiler Rooms	3 Hour	Extreme	F	L18—1-3/4"
Chemical Lab. Rooms	1-1/2 Hour	Severe	F, V	L18, L20—1-3/4"
Corridors (Fire)	1-1/2 Hour	Severe	F, V	L18—1-3/4"
Corridors (Smoke)	3/4 or 1/3 Hour	Moderate	F,V,N,G,FG2,FG3	L18, L20—1-3/4", S16—1-3/4"
Doors Between Factory & Office	1-1/2 Hour	Severe	F, V	L18, L16—1-3/4", SRD—1-3/4" J18—1-3/4" (Industrial Sliding Door)
Electrical Equipment	3 Hour	Extreme	F	L18, L20—1-3/4"
Elevator Equipment	1-1/2 Hour	Moderate	F, V	L18—1-3/4"
Exits Between Buildings	3 Hour	Extreme	F	L16, L18—1-3/4"
Exits to Exterior Fire Escapes	3/4 Hour	Moderate	F	L18, L20—1-3/4"
Furnace Room in Multiple Family Dwellings	1-1/2 Hour	Severe	F, V	L20—1-3/8", L20—1-3/4"
Garage to House	3/4 Hour	Moderate	F	L20—1-3/8"
Garage to Apartment	1-1/2 Hour	Severe	F, V	L18, L20—1-3/4"
Hospital Laboratories	1-1/2 Hour	Severe	F, V	L18, L20—1-3/4"
Hospital Patient Rooms	3/4 or 1/3 Hour	Moderate	F, V, N, G	L18—1-3/4"
Kitchen Area	1-1/2 Hour	Severe	F, V	L18—1-3/4"
Legal Document Storage	3 Hour	Extreme	F	L20—1-3/8", L18—1-3/4"
Paint Rooms	3 Hour	Extreme	F	L20—1-3/8", L18—1-3/4" J18—1-3/4" (Industrial Sliding Door)
Room Partitions	3/4 or 1/3 Hour	Moderate	F, V, G	L20—1-3/8"
Stairwells	1-1/2 Hour	Severe	F, V	L18—1-3/4", T-18, T-20—1-3/4"
Storage Closets	3/4 Hour	Moderate	F	L20—1-3/8"
Storage Closets	1-1/2 Hour	Severe	F	L18, L20—1-3/4"
Warehouses	3 Hour	Extreme	F	J18—1-3/4" (Industrial Sliding Door)

F = FLUSH PANEL
V = VISION LIGHT
N = NARROW LIGHT
G = HALF-GLASS LIGHT
FG2 = TWO GLASS LIGHTS
FG3 = THREE GLASS LIGHTS

F V N G FG2 FG3

APPENDIX C

Reinforcing Steel Charts

CONCRETE REINFORCING STEEL INSTITUTE
228 NORTH LA SALLE STREET, CHICAGO, ILLINOIS 60601

ASTM STANDARD REINFORCING BARS

BAR SIZE DESIGNATION	WEIGHT POUNDS PER FOOT	NOMINAL DIMENSIONS — ROUND SECTIONS		
		DIAMETER INCHES	CROSS SECTIONAL AREA - SQ. INCHES	PERIMETER INCHES
# 3	.376	.375	.11	1.178
# 4	.668	.500	.20	1.571
# 5	1.043	.625	.31	1.963
# 6	1.502	.750	.44	2.356
# 7	2.044	.875	.60	2.749
# 8	2.670	1.000	.79	3.142
# 9	3.400	1.128	1.00	3.544
#10	4.303	1.270	1.27	3.990
#11	5.313	1.410	1.56	4.430
#14	7.65	1.693	2.25	5.32
#18	13.60	2.257	4.00	7.09

Sizes #14 and #18 are large bars generally not carried in regular stock. These sizes available only by arrangement with your supplier.

CONCRETE REINFORCING STEEL INSTITUTE

180 NORTH LA SALLE STREET, CHICAGO, ILLINOIS 60601

ACI STANDARD HOOKS

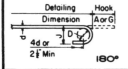

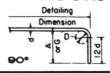

SIZES OF 180-DEG HOOKS All Grades	SIZES OF 90-DEG HOOKS All Grades
D = 6d for #3 through #8	D = 6d for #3 through #8
D = 8d for #9, #10, and #11	D = 8d for #9, #10, and #11
D = 10d for #14 and #18	D = 10d for #14 and #18

RECOMMENDED END HOOK DIMENSIONS

Bar Size	180° HOOKS All Grades		90° HOOKS All Grades
	A or G	J	A or G
#3	5	3	6
#4	6	4	8
#5	7	5	10
#6	8	6	1-0
#7*	10	7	1-2
#8*	11	8	1-4
#9*	1-3	11¼	1-7
#10*	1-5	1-0¾	1-10
#11*	1-7	1-2¼	2-0
#14	2-2	1-8½	2-7
#18	2-11	2-3	3-5

* These sizes — Grade 40 — check availability. Sizes #14-#18, check availability; no Grade 40 under ASTM.

CONCRETE REINFORCING STEEL INSTITUTE

180 NORTH LA SALLE STREET, CHICAGO, ILLINOIS 60601

REINFORCING BAR SPECIFICATIONS

U.S. standard specifications for reinforcing bars are established by the American Society for Testing and Materials (ASTM). These standards govern strength grades, rib patterns, sizes, and markings of bars.

Reinforcing bars are produced from three kinds of steel—new billet, axle, or rail—in three grades of useful (yield) strengths. The yield strength of a bar is its useful strength.

The three ASTM Bar Specifications are:
A615—Billet steel deformed bars
    Grade 40 · Sizes #3–#11
    Grade 60 · Sizes #3–#11; #14 and #18
A616—Rail steel deformed bars
    Grade 50 · Sizes #3–#11
    Grade 60 · Sizes #3–#11
A617—Axle steel deformed bars
    Grade 40 · Sizes #3–#11
    Grade 60 · Sizes #3–#11

INCHES OF LAP CORRESPONDING TO NUMBER OF BAR DIAMETERS *

Number of Diameters	Size of Bar										
	#3	#4	#5	#6	#7	#8	#9	#10	#11	#14	#18
20	—	—	13	15	18	20	23	26	29	34	46
21	—	—	14	16	19	21	24	27	30	36	48
22	—	—	14	17	20	22	25	28	31	38	50
23	—	12	15	18	21	23	26	30	33	39	52
24	—	12	15	18	21	24	28	31	34	41	55
25	—	13	16	19	22	25	29	32	36	43	57
26	—	13	17	20	23	26	30	33	37	45	59
27	—	14	17	21	24	27	31	35	39	46	61
28	—	14	18	21	25	28	32	36	40	48	64
29	—	15	19	22	26	29	33	37	41	50	66
30	12	15	19	23	27	30	34	39	43	51	68
32	12	16	20	24	28	32	36	41	45	55	73
34	13	17	22	26	30	34	39	44	48	58	77
36	1-4	18	23	27	32	36	41	46	51	61	82
38	15	19	24	29	34	38	43	49	54	65	86
40	15	20	25	30	35	40	46	51	57	68	91

Minimum lap equals 12 in.
* Figured to next larger whole inch.

SUPERSEDES CARDS ISSUED PRIOR TO JAN. 1975

APPENDIX D

The Metric System and Equivalents

The demise of the U.S. Metric Board has caused the program converting the United States to the metric system to lose all impetus. The program will continue, without governmental effort, on a voluntary basis, and as such will probably never be widely nor uniformly used. However, a good deal of reference material and material literature (primarily from corporations operating on an international basis) have been produced using both English and SI (metric) units. The architect should be familiar with the metric conversations to the degree that he or she can utilize and understand all information. Of course, an office operating in the multinational market must fully utilize the metric system, and each staff member must be quite fluent in the system.

For many years other countries have measured length with the more easily understood system of millimeters, centimeters, and meters based on units of 10 instead of our more complicated system which is divided into units of 12. As part of the American effort toward metrification, and to remain competitive in the world market, most manufacturers of construction products in the United States issue their technical literature showing both U.S. and metric sizes and dimensions. In foreign countries all business requiring any measurement is transacted in metric units.

The international vehicular roadway laws have now established that all vehicles will drive on the right-hand side of the road. All signs posted will be in an understandable graphic language, universally accepted and readily comprehensible. The more recently completed superhighways in the United States are posting mileage in miles *and* kilometers. Before too many years have passed only the kilometers will be shown on the signs. We will buy gasoline by the liter, not by the gallon, or the Imperial gallon, as we have always done. No matter where we may travel over the earth in the near future, we will employ one standard of measurement, and the understanding will be universal.

The time is approaching when we will draw our architectural plans in millimeters rather than in inches and feet. All the usual architectural drawings will be dimensioned in millimeters. Only civil engineers will employ the meter for some of the larger dimensions on large projects. This exception is not uncommon, however, for the civil

Thickness: $^7/_{16}$ inch (11.1 mm), unless otherwise indicated.
Thickness: $^1/_2$ inch (12.7 mm), unless otherwise indicated.
Thickness: Manufacturer's standard thickness, but not less than $^7/_{16}$ inch (11.1 mm), unless otherwise indicated.
Thickness: $^5/_8$ inch (15.9 mm), where indicated.
Thickness: As indicated.

Furring to Receive Plywood Paneling: Install 1-by-3-inch nominal- (19-by-63-mm actual-) size furring at 24 inches (610 mm) o.c., horizontally and vertically. Select furring with no knots capable of producing bent-over nails and damage to paneling.

Select above for IP-Size Paneling or Below if Metric-Size Paneling is Used.

Furring to Receive Plywood Paneling: Install 19-by-63-mm actual-size furring at 600 mm o.c., horizontally and vertically. Select furring with no knots capable of producing bent-over nails and damage to paneling.

Furring to Receive Gypsum Board: Install 1-by-2-inch nominal- (19-by-38-mm actual-) size furring at 16 inches (406 mm) o.c., vertically.

Select above for IP-Size Gypsum Board or Below if Metric-Size Gypsum Board is Used.

Furring to Receive Gypsum Board: Install 19-by-38-mm actual-size furring at 400 mm o.c., vertically.

Furring to receive Plaster Lath: Install 1-by-2-inch nominal- (19-by-38-mm actual-) size furring at 16 inches (406 mm) o.c., vertically.

Examples of the use of metric units (conversions) in architectural specifications. Usually both American and metric units are shown, since all American firms do not use metric units, but it is wide spread in the manufacturing industry, which services projects worldwide.

engineer has used such terminology as "mile one," "mile two," and "yards," to which the architect has been forced to adjust.

We must note at this time an apparent non sequitur. We do not employ the centimeter in any drawings for architectural or engineering use. The centimeter is applied exclusively to body measurements and as such is the standard by which clothing sizes are designated. Do not think in terms of the centimeter for drawing dimensions!

1. Architectural working drawings are dimensioned in millimeters only.

2. Site plans are drawn in meter dimensions with accuracy given only to three decimal places.
3. Kilometers or meters may be used to dimension "location plans."

A discussion of these suggestions is stated in detail in the *American Metric Construction Handbook*.

It is apparent that the advantages of the entire building world employing the same system of measurement far outweigh present conditions. We shall be able to assess costs, materials, and production without being troubled by conversions or the lack of precision built into those in present use. Certain restrictions on materials for the construction industry will be eliminated by this universal system.

Without doubt the adoption of the metric system by the United States will also mean the introduction of entirely new scales for architects and engineers. These scales will be those more adaptable to the work of both and will eliminate forever the necessity of combining two different philosophies. Once the professional practitioners have overcome the basic difficulties of "converting" from inches and feet to the metric system and begin to think in the metric measurement, new scales convenient to all will be forthcoming.

One other adjustment must be made. The British spell these terms with the ending "-tre" and not as we do. WE have had this type of variance with the British before, however, and met the difference without creating international incidents. By the same token, the British pronunciation differs from ours. Either is acceptable. These differences seem minuscule in face of the radical change we must effect in our methods.

Although some usable conversion tables appear in the appendixes of this book, the following is listed for ready reference.

$$1'' = 25.4 \text{ mm (millimeters)}$$

$$1' = 0.3048 \text{ m (meters)}$$

$$1 \text{ yd} = 0.9144 \text{ m}$$

The degree of accuracy used in rounding off to the nearest tenth, hundredth, or thousandth place is dictated by the degree of accuracy of the least accurate dimension. The measurement of 9 1/2 inches is precisely 241.3 millimeters. Obviously this figure can be rounded to 241 if no more precision than the rounded number is required. In large dimensions custom dictates that the decimal be rounded to the nearest 5 millimeters for an indication of precision; 5 millimeters is roughly the equivalent of 3/16ths of an inch. Meters are normally rounded to the nearest 5 millimeters when the dimension is no more stable than the precision accorded to long measurement. Any measurement given to the nearest 1/8 inch over a length of hundreds of feet would be suspect.

The American National Metric Council is in agreement with the councils governing the standards of measurement of other nations.

Equivalents

Inches	Decimal of Inch	Decimal of Foot	Metric (mm)
1/6	0.0625	0.0052	1.5875
1/8	0.125	0.0104	3.175
3/16	0.1875	0.0156	4.7625
1/4	0.250	0.0208	6.35
5/16	0.3125	0.0260	7.9375
3/8	0.375	0.0313	9.525
7/16	0.4375	0.0365	11.1125
1/2	0.500	0.0417	12.7
9/16	0.5625	0.0469	14.2875
5/8	0.625	0.0521	15.875
11/16	0.6875	0.0573	17.4625
3/4	0.750	0.0625	19.050
13/16	0.8125	0.0677	20.6375
7/8	0.875	0.0729	22.225
15/16	0.9375	0.0781	23.8125
1	1.00	0.083	25.40
2	2.00	0.166	50.80
3	3.00	0.25	76.20
4	4.00	0.33	101.60
5	5.00	0.42	127.00
6	6.00	0.50	152.40
7	7.00	0.58	177.80
8	8.00	0.67	203.20
9	9.00	0.75	228.60
10	10.00	0.83	254.00
11	11.00	0.92	279.40
12	12.00	1.00	304.80

(See next page for dimensions over 12″)

Metric Equivalents Commonly Used on Working Drawings

1/4″ = 6 mm	1″ = 25 mm	5″ = 127 mm	24″ = 610 mm
5/16″ = 8 mm	1 1/8″ = 29 mm	6″ = 152 mm	36″ = 914 mm
3/8″ = 10 mm	1 1/4″ = 32 mm	8″ = 203 mm	48″ = 1m 219 mm
1/2″ = 13 mm	1 1/2″ = 38 mm	10″ = 254 mm	60″ = 1m 524 mm
5/8″ = 16 mm	2″ = 51 mm	12″ = 305 mm	72″ = 2m 134 mm
3/4″ = 19 mm	3″ = 76 mm	14″ = 356 mm	84″ = 2m 438 mm
7/8″ = 22 mm	4″ = 102 mm	16″ = 406 mm	96″ = 2m 438 mm
			120″ = 3m 48 mm

The preceding chart (top) shows the accurate equivalents for English units. However, on working drawings, many people reduce the metric units as shown here (bottom), in an effort to prevent confusion and errors that may occur with rather complex decimal notations. Although they are less accurate, the construction industry has accepted the units in this form.

inches	milli-meters	ft. in.	milli-meters	ft. in.	milli-meters
12	**304.800**	3 7	1092.20	**7 7**	**2311.40**
13	330.200	3 8	1117.60	7 8	2336.80
14	355.600	3 9	1143.20	7 9	2362.20
15	**381.000**	3 10	1168.40	7 10	2387.60
16	406.400	3 11	1193.80	7 11	2413.00
17	431.800	**4 0**	**1219.20**	**8 0**	**2438.40**
18	457.200	4 1	1244.60	8 1	2463.80
19	482.600	4 2	1270.00	8 2	2489.20
20	**508.000**	4 3	1295.40	8 3	2514.60
21	533.400	4 4	1320.80	8 4	2540.00
22	558.800	**4 5**	**1346.20**	**8 5**	**2656.40**
23	584.200	4 6	1371.60	8 6	2590.80
24	609.600	4 7	1397.00	8 7	2616.20
25	**635.000**	4 8	1422.40	8 8	2641.60
26	660.400	4 9	1447.80	8 9	2667.00
27	685.800	4 10	1473.20	8 10	2692.40
28	711.200	4 11	1498.60	8 11	2717.80
29	736.600	**5 0**	**1524.00**	**9 0**	**2743.20**
30	**762.000**	5 1	1549.40	9 1	2768.60
31	787.400	5 2	1574.80	9 2	2794.00
32	812.800	5 3	1600.20	9 3	2819.40
33	838.200	5 4	1625.60	9 4	2844.80
34	863.600	**5 5**	**1651.00**	**9 5**	**2870.20**
35	**889.000**	5 6	1676.40	9 6	2895.60
36	914.400	5 7	1701.80	9 7	2921.00
37	939.800	5 8	1727.20	9 8	2946.40
38	965.200	5 9	1752.60	9 9	2971.80
39	990.600	5 10	1778.00	9 10	2997.20
40	**1016.000**	5 11	1803.40	9 11	3022.60
41	1041.400	6 0	1828.80	**10 0**	**3048.00**
42	1066.800	6 1	1854.20	11 0	3352.80
		6 2	1879.60	12 0	3657.60
		6 3	1905.00	13 0	3962.40
		6 4	1930.40	14 0	4267.20
		6 5	**1955.80**	**15 0**	**4572.00**
		6 6	1981.20	16 0	4876.80
		6 7	2006.60	17 0	5131.60
		6 8	2032.00	18 0	5486.40
		6 9	2057.40	19 0	5791.20
		6 10	2082.80	**20 0**	**6096.00**
		6 11	2108.20	21 0	6400.80
		7 0	**2133.60**	22 0	6705.60
		7 1	2159.00		
		7 2	2184.40		
		7 3	2209.80		
		7 4	2235.20		
		7 5	**2260.60**		
		7 6	2286.00		

The dimensions shown above may be modified as needed by adding the values for full inches, and fractions as shown on preceding page. For example, 11'-5 3/8" is converted to metric values in the following manner:

$$11'\text{-}0'' = 3352.80\text{mm}$$

$$\text{plus } 5'' = 127.0\text{mm}$$

$$\underline{\text{plus } 3/8'' = \quad 10.0\text{mm}}$$

which equals 3489.80 mm for 11'-5 3/8"

APPENDIX E

Conversion Table for Commonly Used Scales

Site Plans

$1/16'' = 1'0''$ corresponds to 5 mm = 1 m	
$1/8'' = 1'0''$	10 mm = 1 m
$1'' = 20'\text{-}0''$	2 mm = 1 m
$1'' = 50'\text{-}0''$	1 mm = 1 m

Architectural Drawings

$1/8'' = 1'\text{-}0''$	10 mm = 1 m
$1/4'' = 1'\text{-}0''$	20 mm = 1 m
$1/2'' = 1'\text{-}0''$	50 mm = 1 m
$1'' = 1'\text{-}0''$	100 mm = 1 m
$1\,1/2'' = 1'\text{-}0''$	150 mm = 1 m
$3'' = 1'\text{-}0''$	200 mm = 1 m

Vertical Masonry Dimensioning

(Based on common construction—3 brick + 3 joints = 8″)

Number of Courses				Number of Courses				Number of Courses			
Modular Brick	Tile	Block	Size	Modular Brick	Tile	Block	Size	Modular Brick	Tile	Block	Size
1			$2\frac{2}{3}''$	35			$7'\text{-}9\frac{1}{3}''$	68	34		$15'\text{-}1\frac{1}{3}''$
2	1		$5\frac{1}{3}''$	36	18	12	$8'\text{-}0$	69		23	$15'\text{-}4''$
3		1	$8''$	37			$8'\text{-}2\frac{2}{3}''$	70	35		$15'\text{-}6\frac{2}{3}''$
4	2		$10\frac{2}{3}''$	38	19		$8'\text{-}5\frac{1}{3}''$	71			$15'\text{-}9\frac{1}{3}''$
5			$1'\text{-}1\frac{1}{3}''$	39		13	$8'\text{-}8''$	72	36	24	$16'\text{-}0$
6	3	2	$1'\text{-}4''$	40	20		$8'\text{-}10\frac{2}{3}''$	73			$16'\text{-}2\frac{2}{3}''$
7			$1'\text{-}6\frac{2}{3}''$	41			$9'\text{-}1\frac{1}{3}''$	74	37		$16'\text{-}5\frac{1}{3}''$
8	4		$1'\text{-}9\frac{1}{3}''$	42	21	14	$9'\text{-}4''$	75		25	$16'\text{-}8''$
9		3	$2'\text{-}0$	43			$9'\text{-}6\frac{2}{3}''$	76	38		$16'\text{-}10\frac{2}{3}''$
10	5		$2'\text{-}2\frac{2}{3}''$	44	22		$9'\text{-}9\frac{1}{3}''$	77			$17'\text{-}1\frac{1}{3}''$
11			$2'\text{-}5\frac{1}{3}''$	45		15	$10'\text{-}0$	78	39	26	$17'\text{-}4''$
12	6	4	$2'\text{-}8''$	46	23		$10'\text{-}2\frac{2}{3}''$	79			$17'\text{-}6\frac{2}{3}''$
13			$2'\text{-}10\frac{2}{3}''$	47			$10'\text{-}5\frac{1}{3}''$	80	40		$17'\text{-}9\frac{1}{3}''$
14	7		$3'\text{-}1\frac{1}{3}''$	48	24	16	$10'\text{-}8''$	81		27	$18'\text{-}0$
15		5	$3'\text{-}4''$	49			$10'\text{-}10\frac{2}{3}''$	82	41		$18'\text{-}2\frac{2}{3}''$
16	8		$3'\text{-}6\frac{2}{3}''$	50	25		$11'\text{-}1\frac{1}{3}''$	83			$18'\text{-}5\frac{1}{3}''$
17			$3'\text{-}9\frac{1}{3}''$	51		17	$11'\text{-}4''$	84	42	28	$18'\text{-}8''$
18	9	6	$4'\text{-}0$	52	26		$11'\text{-}6\frac{2}{3}''$	85			$18'\text{-}10\frac{2}{3}''$
19			$4'\text{-}2\frac{2}{3}''$	53			$11'\text{-}9\frac{1}{3}''$	86	43		$19'\text{-}1\frac{1}{3}''$
20	10		$4'\text{-}5\frac{1}{3}''$	54	27	18	$12'\text{-}0$	87		29	$19'\text{-}4''$
21		7	$4'\text{-}8''$	55			$12'\text{-}2\frac{2}{3}''$	88	44		$19'\text{-}6\frac{2}{3}''$
22	11		$4'\text{-}10\frac{2}{3}''$	56	28		$12'\text{-}5\frac{1}{3}''$	89			$19'\text{-}9\frac{1}{3}''$
23			$5'\text{-}1\frac{1}{3}''$	57		19	$12'\text{-}8''$	90	45	30	$20'\text{-}0$
24	12	8	$5'\text{-}4''$	58	29		$12'\text{-}10\frac{2}{3}''$	91			$20'\text{-}2\frac{2}{3}''$
25			$5'\text{-}6\frac{2}{3}''$	59			$13'\text{-}1\frac{1}{3}''$	92	46		$20'\text{-}5\frac{1}{3}''$
26	13		$5'\text{-}9\frac{1}{3}''$	60	30	20	$13'\text{-}4''$	93		31	$20'\text{-}8''$
27		9	$6'\text{-}0$	61			$13'\text{-}6\frac{2}{3}''$	94	47		$20'\text{-}10\frac{2}{3}''$
28	14		$6'\text{-}2\frac{2}{3}''$	62	31		$13'\text{-}9\frac{1}{3}''$	95			$21'\text{-}1\frac{1}{3}''$
29			$6'\text{-}5\frac{1}{3}''$	63		21	$14'\text{-}0$	96	48	32	$21'\text{-}4''$
30	15	10	$6'\text{-}8''$	64	32		$14'\text{-}2\frac{2}{3}''$	97			$21'\text{-}6\frac{2}{3}''$
31			$6'\text{-}10\frac{2}{3}''$	65			$14'\text{-}5\frac{1}{3}''$	98	49		$22'\text{-}9\frac{1}{3}''$
32	16		$7'\text{-}1\frac{1}{3}''$	66	33	22	$14'\text{-}8''$	99		33	$22'\text{-}0$
33		11	$7'\text{-}4''$	67			$14'\text{-}10\frac{2}{3}''$	100	50		$22'\text{-}2\frac{2}{3}''$
34	17		$7'\text{-}6\frac{2}{3}''$								

Note: "Tile" denotes units 5 x 12" (nominal) x thickness required.

APPENDIX G

Construction Specifications Institute Format

The 16-division specifications format of the Construction Specifications Institute (CSI) has been established and used for a number of years. Within the Division, however, changes occur periodically to ensure the best possible information, and display of that information.

BIDDING REQUIREMENTS, CONTRACT FORMS AND CONDITIONS OF THE CONTRACT

00010 Pre-Bid Information
00100 Instructions to Bidders
00200 Information available to Bidders
00300 Bid Forms
00400 Supplements to Bid Forms
00500 Agreement Forms
00600 Bonds and Certificates
00700 General Conditions
00800 Supplementary Conditions
00900 Addenda

Note: The items listed above are not specification sections and are referred to as "Documents" rather than "Sections" in the Master List of Section Titles, Numbers, and Broadscope Section Explanations.

The technical specifications are contained in the 16-Divisions set out in the CSI format. Note must be taken though, that as of June, 1999, CSI has taken no action and anticipates taking no action to expand the format beyond the 16 Divisions currently used. However, some design firms have seen fit to expand the format, mainly for their own use, their clients in reaction to the types of project work they engage in on a continuing basis. Currently some firms are actively using Divisions No. 17, 18, 19, etc., with such titles as Communications, Control systems, Security Systems, and other limited scope work. [Readers are advised to be aware of this lack of uniformity, and the lack of official CSI action, support, and approval].

For complete and current information consult the CSI chapter in your area, or the national office.

Appendix G

Following is a general list of the work usually included in each CSI Division.

Division No.	Work Efforts Addressed
1	Specific Project conditions, procedures, interrelationships, and requirements applicable throughout the project, and by all parties; overall poject control, responsibilities, definitions, etc.
2	All activities dealing with earthwork operations and site improvements; overall site preparation, excavation, grading for walks, roads and curbs; landscaping, lawn sprinkler/irrigation system
3	All forms of concrete, which is the primarily foundation material; concrete systems and materials; also appears as a finish material both exterior and interior
4	Masonry is one of the primary enclosure material for the envelope of the building; also an interior finish and partition material and system; CMU, brick, stone, facings, pavers, etc.
5	Metals include structural steel, columns, beams, girders for main walls and supports, roof framing and decking; and light-weight, miscellaneous light-gauge framing for non-loading bearing and drywall partitions; also appear in stairs, some decorative trims
6	Carpentry covers the full range of rough and finished wood work; includes plastics and other material with a carpentry connotation; from framing to highly decorative paneling
7	Thermal and moisture concerns are addressed in roofing, insulation, caulking, fire proofing, penetration sealing, siding/cladding.
8	Elements of enclosure include doors, and windows of all kinds, glass and glazing, entrances, skylights, and other such features to augment and complement the basic material of masonry, roofing, etc.
9	Finishes including almost all exposed systems and features; paint/coatings/floor and wall coverings, ceiling, ceramic and other tile
10	Specialties is a potpourri of devices, small equipment and elements which convert a simple building into a usable and occupiable structure with proper functions; flag poles, mail boxes, rest room accessories and compartments, signage, bulletin boards, write-on boards, platforms/risers
11	Equipment includes unitized systems [usually considered "fixed"] which are designed to function for a specific purpose; bank equipment, for example includes counters, undercounter units, etc. for full outfitting and bank-type operations
12	Furnishings are everything from overstuffed furniture to office partition systems, and other movable items, which allow proper use of the building.
13	Special construction deals with modules such as "clean rooms", and other segments of a project which can built off-site, transported and installed in the building in tact; usually special and high-tech requirements which are better achieved in a factory controlled atmosphere than on a construction site.
14	Anything that moves people or material is part of conveying systems; escalators, conveyors, moving sidewalks, elevators, lifts, dumb waiters, and so forth
15	Called Mechanical, it is normally sub-divided into plumbing and heating, ventilating and air-conditioning [HVAC]; contains every elements of those systems including all necessary devices, controls, etc. as well as the basic equipment, supports, units
16	Electrical covers the full range of devices and equipment for the delivery of power and lighting to the building; again, from simple small devices to transformers, panels, cables, cable trays, and light fixtures; designed to provide the correct power to the various units requiring such anywhere in the building.

The listing below sets out the "broadscope" specifications Sections that can be contained within each Division. Broadscope means he widest advisable latitude in describing the work involved; other levels of increased detail are also available. For example, Section 02900, Landscaping [in this listing] can be broken down into a separate Section for Lawns, another for Plantings, and yet another for Outdoor Furnishings, and so forth. All this depends on the size, scope and type of project involved.

SPECIFICATIONS

Division 1 - General Requirements

01010 Summary of Work
01020 Allowances
01025 Measurement and Payment
01030 Alternates/Alternatives
01035 Modification Procedures
01040 Coordination
01050 Field Engineering
01060 Regulatory Requirements
01070 Identification Systems
01090 References
01100 Special Project Procedures
01200 Project Meetings
01300 Submittals
01400 Quality Control
01500 Construction Facilities and Temporary
      Controls
01600 Material and Equipment
01650 Facility Startup/Commissioning
01700 Contract Closeout
01800 Maintenance

Division 2 - Sitework

02010 Subsurface Investigation
02050 Demolition
02100 Site Preparation
02140 Dewatering
02150 Shoring and Underpinning
02160 Excavation Support Systems
02170 Cofferdams
02200 Earthwork
02300 Tunneling
02350 Piles and Caissons
02450 Railroad Work
02480 Marine Work
02500 Paving and Surfacing
02600 Utility Piping Materials
02660 Water Distribution
02680 Fuel and Steam Distribution
02700 Sewerage and Drainage
02760 Restoration of Underground Pipe
02770 Ponds and Reservoirs
02780 Power and Communications
02800 Site Improvements
02900 Landscaping

Division 3 - Concrete

03100 Concrete Formwork

03200 Concrete Reinforcement
03250 Concrete Accessories
03300 Cast-in-Place Concrete
03370 Concrete Curing
03400 Precast Concrete
03500 Cementitious Decks and Toppings
03600 Grout
03700 Concrete Restoration and Cleaning
03800 Mass Concrete

Division 4 - Masonry

04100 Mortar and Masonry Grout
04150 Masonry Accessories
04200 Unit Masonry
04400 Stone
04500 Masonry Restoration and Cleaning
04550 Refractories
04600 Corrosion Resistant Masonry
04700 Simulated Masonry

Division 5 - Metals

05010 Metal Materials
05030 Metal Coatings
05050 Metal Fastening
05100 Structural Metal Framing
05200 Metal Joists
05300 Metal Decking
05400 Cold Formed Metal Framing
05500 Metal Fabrications
05580 Sheet Metal Fabrications
05700 Ornamental Metal
05800 Expansion Control
05900 Hydraulic Structures

Division 6 - Wood and Plastics

06050 Fasteners and Adhesives
06100 Rough Carpentry
06130 Heavy Timber Construction
06150 Wood and Metal Systems
06170 Prefabricated Structural Wood
06200 Finish Carpentry
06300 Wood Treatment
06400 Architectural Woodwork
06500 Structural Plastics
06600 Plastic Fabrications
06650 Solid Polymer Fabrications

Division 7 - Thermal and Moisture Protection

07100 Waterproofing
07150 Dampproofing
07180 Water Repellents
07190 Vapor Retarders
07195 Air Barriers
07200 Insulation
07240 Exterior Insulation and Finish Systems
07250 Fireproofing
07270 Firestopping
07300 Shingles and Roofing Tiles
07400 Manufactured Roofing and Siding
07480 Exterior Wall Assemblies
07500 Membrane Roofing
07570 Traffic Coatings
07600 Flashing and Sheet Metal
07700 Roof Specialties and Accessories
07800 Skylights
07900 Joint Sealers

Division 8 - Doors and Windows

08100 Metal Doors and Frames
08200 Wood and Plastic Doors
08250 Door Opening Assemblies
08300 Special Doors
08400 Entrances and Storefronts
08500 Metal Windows
08600 Wood and Plastic Windows
08650 Special Windows
08700 Hardware
08800 Glazing
08900 Glazed Curtain Walls

Division 9 - Finishes

09100 Metal Support Systems
09200 Lath and Plaster
09250 Gypsum Board
09300 Tile
09400 Terrazzo
09450 Stone Facing
09500 Acoustical Treatment
09540 Special Wall Surfaces
09545 Special Ceiling Surfaces
09550 Wood Flooring
09600 Stone Flooring
09630 Unit Masonry Flooring
09650 Resilient Flooring
09680 Carpet

09700 Special Flooring
09780 Floor Treatment
09800 Special Coatings
09900 Painting
09950 Wall Coverings

Division 10 - Specialties

10100 Visual Display Boards
10150 Compartments and Cubicles
10200 Louvers and Vents
10240 Grilles and Screens
10250 Service Wall Systems
10260 Wall and Corner Guards
10270 Access Flooring
10290 Pest Control
10300 Fireplaces and Stoves
10340 Manufactured Exterior Specialties
10350 Flagpoles
10400 Identifying Devices
10450 Pedestrian Control Devices
10500 Lockers
10520 Fire Protection Specialties
10530 Protective Covers
10550 Postal Specialties
10600 Partitions
10650 Operable Partitions
10670 Storage Shelving
10700 Exterior Protection Devices for Openings
10750 Telephone Specialties
10800 Toilet and Bath Accessories
10880 Scales
10900 Wardrobe and Closet Specialties

Division 11 - Equipment

11010 Maintenance Equipment
11020 Security and Vault Equipment
11030 Teller and Service Equipment
11040 Ecclesiastical Equipment
11050 Library Equipment
11060 Theater and Stage Equipment
11070 Instrumental Equipment
11080 Registration Equipment
11090 Checkroom Equipment
11100 Mercantile Equipment
11110 Commercial Laundry and Dry
            Cleaning Equipment
11120 Vending Equipment
11130 Audio-Visual Equipment
11140 Vehicle Service Equipment
11150 Parking Control Equipment

11160 Loading Dock Equipment
11170 Solid Waste Handling Equipment
11190 Detention Equipment
11200 Water Supply and Treatment Equipment
11280 Hydraulic Gates and Valves
11300 Fluid Waste Treatment and Disposal
    Equipment
11400 Food Service Equipment
11450 Residential Equipment
11460 Unit Kitchens
11470 Darkroom Equipment
11480 Athletic, Recreational, and Therapeutic
    Equipment
11500 Industrial and Process Equipment
11600 Laboratory Equipment
11650 Planetarium Equipment
11660 Observatory Equipment
11680 Office Equipment
11700 Medical Equipment
11780 Mortuary Equipment
11850 Navigation Equipment
11870 Agricultural Equipment

Division 12 - Furnishings

12050 Fabrics
12100 Artwork
12300 Manufactured Casework
12500 Window Treatment
12600 Furniture and Accessories
12670 Rugs and Mats
12700 Multiple Seating
12800 Interior Plants and Planters

Division 13 - Special Construction

13010 Air Supported Structures
13020 Integrated Assemblies
13030 Special Purpose Rooms
13080 Sound, Vibration, and Seismic Control
13090 Radiation Protection
13100 Nuclear Reactors
13120 Pre-Engineered Structures
13150 Aquatic Facilities
13175 Ice Rinks
13180 Site Constructed Incinerators
13185 Kennels and Animal Shelters
13200 Liquid and Gas Storage Tanks
13220 Filter Underdrains and Media
13230 Digester Covers and Appurtenances
13240 Oxygenation Systems

13260 Sludge Conditioning Systems
13300 Utility Control Systems
13400 Industrial and Process Control Systems
13500 Recording Instrumentation
13550 Transportation Control Instrumentation
13600 Solar Energy Systems
13700 Wind Energy Systems
13750 Cogeneration Systems
13800 Building Automation Systems
13900 Fire Suppression and Supervisory Systems
13950 Special Security Construction

Division 14 - Conveying Systems

14100 Dumbwaiters
14200 Elevators
14300 Escalators and Moving Walks
14400 Lifts
14500 Material Handling Systems
14600 Hoists and Cranes
14700 Turntables
14800 Scaffolding
14900 Transportation Systems

Division 15 - Mechanical

15050 Basic Mechanical Materials and Methods
15250 Mechanical Insulation
15300 Fire Protection
15400 Plumbing
15500 Heating, Ventilating, and Air Conditioning
15550 Heat Generation
15650 Refrigeration
15750 Heat Transfer
15850 Air Handling
15880 Air Distribution
15950 Controls
15990 Testing, Adjusting, and Balancing

Division 16 - Electrical

16050 Basic Electrical Materials and Methods
16200 Power Generation - Built-Up Systems
16300 Medium Voltage Distribution
16400 Service and Distribution
16500 Lighting
16600 Special Systems
16700 Communications
16850 Electric Resistance Heating
16900 Controls
16950 Testing

APPENDIX H

Table of Squares and Square Roots

No.	Square	Square Root	No.	Square	Square Root	No.	Square	Square Root	No.	Square	Square Root
1	1	1.000	26	676	5.099	51	2601	7.141	76	5776	8.718
2	4	1.414	27	729	5.196	52	2704	7.211	77	5929	8.775
3	9	1.732	28	784	5.291	53	2809	7.280	78	6084	8.832
4	16	2.000	29	841	5.385	54	2916	7.348	79	6241	8.888
5	25	2.236	30	900	5.477	55	3025	7.416	80	6400	8.944
6	36	2.449	31	961	5.568	56	3136	7.483	81	6561	9.000
7	49	2.646	32	1024	5.657	57	3249	7.550	82	6724	9.055
8	64	2.828	33	1089	5.745	58	3364	7.616	83	6889	9.110
9	81	3.000	34	1156	5.831	59	3481	7.681	84	7056	9.165
10	100	3.162	35	1225	5.916	60	3600	7.746	85	7225	9.220
11	121	3.317	36	1296	6.000	61	3721	7.810	86	7396	9.274
12	144	3.464	37	1369	6.083	62	3844	7.874	87	7569	9.327
13	169	3.606	38	1444	6.164	63	3969	7.937	88	7744	9.381
14	196	3.742	39	1521	6.245	64	4096	8.000	89	7921	9.434
15	225	3.873	40	1600	6.325	65	4225	8.062	90	8100	9.487
16	256	4.000	41	1681	6.403	66	4356	8.124	91	8281	9.539
17	289	4.123	42	1764	6.481	67	4489	8.185	92	8464	9.592
18	324	4.243	43	1849	6.557	68	4624	8.246	93	8649	9.644
19	361	4.359	44	1936	6.633	69	4761	8.307	94	8836	9.695
20	400	4.472	45	2025	6.708	70	4900	8.367	95	9025	9.747
21	441	4.583	46	2116	6.782	71	5041	8.426	96	9216	9.798
22	484	4.690	47	2209	6.856	72	5184	8.485	97	9409	9.849
23	529	4.796	48	2304	6.928	73	5329	8.544	98	9604	9.899
24	576	4.899	49	2401	7.000	74	5476	8.602	99	9801	9.950
25	625	5.000	50	2500	7.071	75	5625	8.660	100	10000	10.000

APPENDIX I

Units of Measure

Linear Measure

1 inch	=	2.54	centimeters
12 inches = 1 foot	=	0.3048	meter
3 feet = 1 yard	=	0.9144	meter
5 1/2 yards or 16 1/2 feet = 1 rod (or pole or perch)	=	5.029	meters
40 rods = 1 furlong	=	201.17	meters
8 furlongs or 1760 yards or 5280 feet = 1 (statute) mile	=	1609.3	meters
3 miles = 1 (land) league	=	4.83	kilometers

Square Measure

1 square inch	=	6.452	square centimeters
144 square inches = 1 square foot	= 929		square centimeters
9 square feet = 1 square yard	=	0.8361	square meter
$30\frac{1}{4}$ square yards = 1 square rod (or square pole or square perch)	=	25.29	square meters
160 square rods or 4840 square yards of 43,560 square feet = 1 acre	=	0.4047	hectare
640 acres = 1 square mile	= 259		hectares or 2.59 square kilometers

Appendix I

Cubic Measure

1 cubic inch	= 16.387	cubic centimeters
1728 cubic inches = 1 cubic foot	= 0.0283	cubic meter
27 cubic feet = 1 cubic yard	= 0.7646	cubic meter

(in units for cordwood, etc.)

16 cubic feet = 1 cord foot		
8 cord feet = 1 cord	= 3.625	cubic meters

Chain Measure

(for Gunter's, or surveyor's, chain)

7.92 inches = 1 link	= 20.12	centimeters
100 links or 66 feet = 1 chain	= 20.12	meters
10 chains = 1 furlong	= 201.17	meters
80 chains = 1 mile	= 1609.3	meters

(for engineer's chain)

1 foot = 1 link	= 0.3048	meter
100 feet = 1 chain	= 30.48	meters
52.8 chains = 1 mile	= 1609.3	meters

Surveyor's Measure

625 square links = 1 square pole	= 25.29	square meters
16 square poles = 1 square chain	= 404.7	square meters
10 square chains = 1 acre	= 0.4047	hectare
640 acres = 1 square mile or 1 section	= 259	hectares or 2.59 square kilometers
36 square miles = 1 township	= 9324.0	hectares or 93.24 square kilometers

Angular and Circular Measure

60 seconds = 1 minute
60 minutes = 1 degree
90 degrees = 1 right angle
180 degrees = 1 straight angle
360 degrees = 1 circle

APPENDIX J

Trade Associations, Standards-Generating Organizations, and Governing Authorities

Because of the massive amount of information required for any project, design professionals often utilize technical information and reference standards contained in publications produced by various organizations. Trade associations, standards-generating organizations, and governing authorities are invaluable sources of technical information, literature, and audiovisual aids. This information is specific, complete, and in-depth. It includes design, fabrication, processing, production, and installation data, with pertinent details. Usually, there is far more information than required, in that the testing and manufacturing procedures may be noted. Many items are provided gratis, but ask for a catalog, applicable price list for available items, and complete ordering information.

These documents are generally categorized as "reference standards." The data are promotional in nature, not directed toward sales, but toward understanding and the correct use and implementation of the products involved.

In lieu of repeating all of the necessary information on the drawings or in the specifications, professionals usually employ a system of referring to the required materials, often using acronyms or abbreviations to represent the full names of the organizations involved. Following is a partial list of many such organizations; numerous other organizations exist that are not listed. Names and addresses are subject to change, but are believed to be accurate as of the date of production of this book. To verify or update information, readers are advised to consult one of the following:

Encyclopedia of Associations, published by Gale Research Company

National Trade and Professional Associations of the United States and Canada and Labor Unions, published by Columbia Books, Washington, DC

Volume 1 of the 1998 edition of the SWEET'S General Building & Renovation Catalog File, contains a section called "Sources of Information" (Sect. No. 01317). This is a 40-page listing, a large number of associations and professional organizations, which act as resources within rather restricted (narrow-scope) areas of design, construction, construction-related activities, and manufacturing.

ARCAT, published by The Architect's Catalog, Inc., Fairfield, CT

Architectural Graphics Standards, 8th Ed., manual published by John Wiley & Sons, Inc., New York, NY

In addition, most larger public libraries have a directory service (free) that will locate addresses and telephone numbers in various cities.

AA	Aluminum Association 900 Nineteenth Street NW, Suite 300 Washington, DC 20006 (202) 862–5100
AAA	American Arbitration Association 140 West 51st Street New York, NY 10020 (212) 484–4000
AABC	Associated Air Balance Council 1518 K Street NW, Suite 503 Washington, DC 20005 (202) 737–0202
AAMA	American Architectural Manufacturers Association 1827 Walden Office Square, Suite 104 Schaumburg, IL 60173 (847) 303–5664
AAMA	Architectural Aluminum Manufacturers Association 2700 River Road, Suite 118 Des Plaines, IL 60018 (312) 699–7310
AAN	(See ANLA)
AASHTO	American Association of State Highway and Transportation Officials 444 North Capitol Street, Suite 249 Washington, DC 20001 (202) 624–5800
AATCC	American Association of Textile Chemists and Colorists P.O. Box 12215, 1 Davis Drive Research Triangle Park, NC 27709 (919) 549–8141
ACI	American Concrete Institute 38800 Country Club Drive, P.O. Box 9094

	Farmington Hills, MI 48333 (810) 848–3700
ACIL	American Council of Independent Laboratories 1629 K Street NW Washington, DC 20006 (202) 887–5872
ACPA	American Concrete Pipe Association 222 West Las Colinas Boulevard, Suite 641 Irving, TX 75039 (214) 506–7216
ADC	Air Diffusion Council 11 South LaSalle Street, Suite 1400 Chicago, IL 60603 (312) 210–0101
AFPA	American Forest & Paper Council/American Wood Council (Formerly National Forest Products Association—NFoPA) 1111 19th Street NW, Suite 800 Washington, DC 20036 (202) 463–2700
AGA	American Gas Association 1515 Wilson Boulevard Arlington, VA 22209 (703) 841–8648
AGA	American Galvanizers Association 1200 E. Iliff Avenue, Suite 204 Aurora, CO 80014 (303) 750–2900
AHA	American Hardboard Association 1210 W. Northwest Highway Palatine, IL 60067 (847) 934–8800
AHAM	Association of Home Appliance Manufacturers 20 N. Wacker Drive, Suite 1500 Chicago, IL 60606 (312) 984–5800

AHMI	Appalachian Hardwood Manufacturers, Inc. P.O. Box 427 High Point, NC 27261 (910) 885–8315		ANLA	American Nursery and Landscape Association (Formerly American Association of Nurserymen) 1250 Eye Street NW, Suite 500 Washington, DC 20005 (202) 789–2900
AI	Asphalt Institute Research Park Drive, P.O. Box 14052 Lexington, KY 40512 (606) 288–4960			
AIA	American Institute of Architects 1735 New York Avenue NW Washington, DC 20006 (202) 626–7359		ANSI	American National Standards Institute 11 W. 42nd Street New York, NY 10036 (212) 642–4900
A.I.A.	American Insurance Association 1130 Connecticut Avenue, NW, Suite 1000 Washington, DC 20036 (202) 828–7100		APA	(See EWA)
			APFA	American Pipe Fittings Association 7297 Lee Highway, Suite N Falls Church, VA 22042 (703) 533–1321
AIHA	American Industrial Hygiene Association 2700 Prosperity Avenue, Suite 250 Fairfax, VA 22031 (703) 849–8888		API	American Petroleum Institute 1220 L Street NW Washington, DC 20005 (202) 682–8000
AISC	American Institute of Steel Construction One E. Wacker Drive, Suite 3100 Chicago, IL 60601 (312) 670–2400		ARI	Air-Conditioning and Refrigeration Institute 4301 N. Fairfax Drive, Suite 425 Arlington, VA 22203 (703) 524–8800
AISI	American Iron and Steel Institute 1101 17th Street NW, Suite 1300 Washington, DC 20036 (202) 452–7100		ARMA	Asphalt Roofing Manufacturers Association Center Park, Suite 505 4041 Powder Mill Road Calverton, MD 20705 (301) 348-2002
AITC	American Institute of Timber Construction 7012 S. Revere Parkway, Suite 140 Englewood, CO 80112 (303) 792–9559		ASA	Acoustical Society of America 500 Sunnyside Boulevard Woodbury, NY 11797 (516) 576–2360
ALI	American Lighting Institute 435 N. Michigan Avenue Chicago, IL 60611 (312) 644–0828		ASC	Adhesive and Sealant Council 1627 K Street NW< Suite 1000 Washington, DC 20006 (202) 452–1500
ALI	Associated Laboratories, Inc. 1323 Wall Street, P.O. Box 152837 Dallas, TX 75315 (214) 565–0593		ASCE	American Society of Civil Engineers World Headquarters 1801 Alexander Bell Drive Reston, VA 20191 (703) 295–6196
ALSC	American Lumber Standards Committee P.O. Box 210 Germantown, MD 20874 (301) 972–1700		ASHRAE	American Society of Heating, Refrigerating and Air-Conditioning Engineers 1791 Tullie Circle NE Atlanta, GA 30329 (404) 636–8400
AMCA	Air Movement and Control Association 30 W. University Drive Arlington Heights, IL 60004 (312) 394–0150		ASME	American Society of Mechanical Engineers United Engineering Center, 345 E. 47th Street

	New York, NY 10017 (212) 705–8500
ASSE	American Society of Sanitary Engineering
	28901 Clemens Road
	Westlake, OH 44145 (440) 835–3040
ASSEI	American Society of Safety Engineers, Inc.
	1800 East Oakton Street
	Des Plaines, IL 60016 (708) 692–4121
ASTM	American Society for Testing and Materials
	100 Barr Harbor Drive
	West Conshohocken, PA 19428
	(610) 832–9500
AWA	Fine Hardwoods—American Walnut Association
	5603 W. Raymond Street, Suite O
	Indianapolis, IN 46421
	(317) 244–3312
AWI	Architectural Woodwork Institute
	1952 Issac Newton Square
	Reston, VA 20190 (703) 733–0600
AWPA	American Wood Preservers Association
	3246 Fall Creek Highway, Suite 1900
	Granbury, TX 76049 (817) 326–6300
AWPB	American Wood Preservers Bureau (Organization Defunct)
AWS	American Welding Society
	550 NW LeJeune Road
	Miami, FL 33126 (305) 443–9353
AWWA	American Water Works Association
	6666 W. Quincy Avenue
	Denver, CO 80235 (303) 794–7711
BANC	Brick Association of North Carolina
	P.O. Box 13290
	Greensboro, NC 27415
	(919) 273–5566
BHMA	Builders Hardware Manufacturers Association
	355 Lexington Avenue, 17th Floor
	New York, NY 10017 (212) 661–4261
BIA	Brick Industry of America (Formerly Brick Institute of America)
	11490 Commerce Park Drive, Suite 300
	Reston, VA 22091 (703) 620–0010
BIFMA	Business and Institutional Furniture Manufacturers Association

	2680 Horizon Drive, SE, Suite A1
	Grand Rapids, MI 49546
	(616) 285–3963
BSI	Building Stone Institute
	420 Lexington Avenue
	New York, NY 10017
CAGI	Compressed Air and Gas Institute
	c/o Thomas Associates, Inc.
	1300 Sumner Road
	Cleveland, OH 44115 (216) 241–7333
CAUS	Color Association of the United States
	409 W. 44th Street
	New York, NY 10036 (212) 582–6884
CBM	Certified Ballast Manufacturers Association
	Hannah Building, Suite 402
	1422 Euclid Avenue
	Cleveland, OH 44115 (216) 241–0711
CDA	Copper Development Association
	600 Rocky Drive
	Boiling Springs, PA 17007
	(717) 258–3904
CGA	Compressed Gas Association
	1725 Jefferson Davis Highway
	Arlington, VA 22202 (412) 979–0900
CISCA	Ceilings and Interior Systems Construction Association
	1500 Lincoln Highway, Suite 202
	St. Charles, IL 60174 (630) 584-1919
CISPI	Cast Iron Soil Pipe Institute
	5959 Shallowford Road, Suite 419
	Chattanooga, TN 37421
	(423) 892–0137
CLFMI	Chain Link Fence Manufacturers Institute
	9891 Broken Land Parkway, Suite 300
	Columbia, MD 21046 (301) 596–2584
CLPA	California Lathing and Plastering Association
	25332 Narbonne, Suite 170
	Lomita, CA 90717 (213) 539–6080
CRA	California Redwood Association
	405 Enfrente Drive, Suite 200
	Novato, CA 94949 (415) 382–0662
CRI	Carpet and Rug Institute
	310 S. Holiday Avenue
	Dalton, GA 30722 (706) 278–3176
CRSI	Concrete Reinforcing Steel Institute
	933 N. Plum Grove Road

	Schaumburg, IL 60173 (847) 517–1200	FM	Factory Mutual Engineering and Research 1151 Boston-Providence Turnpike
CTI	Ceramic Tile Institute of America 12061 West Jefferson Boulevard Culver City, CA 90230 (310) 574–7800		Norwood, MA 02062 (617) 762–4300
C.T.I.	Cooling Tower Institute Box 73383 Houston, TX 77273 (713) 583–4087	FPRS	Forest Products Research Society 2801 Marshall Court Madison, WI 53705 (608) 231–1361
DASMA	Door & Access Systems Manufacturers Association International [Formerly DORCMA and NAGDM] 1300 Sumner Avenue Cleveland, OH 44115 (216) 241–7333	FTI	Facing Tile Institute Box 8880 Canton, OH 44711 (216) 488–1211
		GA	Gypsum Association 810 First Street NE, Suite 510 Washington, DC 20002 (202) 289–5440
DHI	Door and Hardware Institute (Formerly National Builders Hardware Association) 14170 Newbrook Drive Chantilly, VA 22102 (703) 222–2010	GAMA	Gas Appliance Manufacturers Association, Inc. 1901 North Moore Street, Suite 1100 Arlington, VA 22209 (703) 525–9565
DIPRA	Ductile Iron Pipe Research Association 245 Riverchase Parkway E, Suite O Birmingham, AL 35244 (205) 988–9870	GANA	Glass Association of North America (Formerly Flat Glass Marketing Association) 3310 S.W. Harrison Street Topeka, KS 66611 (785) 271–0166
DLPA	Decorative Laminate Products Association (Now part of KCMA)	HEI	Heat Exchange Institute c/o Thomas Associates, Inc. 1300 Sumner Avenue Cleveland, OH 44115 (216) 241–7333
EIA	Electronics Industries Association 2500 Wilson Boulevard, 4th Floor Arlington, VA 22201 (703) 907–7500	HI	Hydronics Institute P.O. Box 218 35 Russo Place Berkeley Heights, NJ 07922 (201) 464–8200
EIMA	EIFS Industry Members Association 402 N. Fourth Street, Suite 102 Yakima, WA 98901 (509) 457–3500		
ETL	ETL Testing Laboratories, Inc. c/o ITS/Warnock Hersey P.O. Box 2040 3933 U.S. Route 11, Industrial Park Cortland, NY 13045 (607) 753–6711	HMA	Hardwood Manufacturers Association 400 Penn Center Boulevard, Suite 530 Pittsburgh, PA 15235 (412) 829–0770
EWA	Engineered Wood Association (Formerly American Plywood Association) P.O. Box 11700 Tacoma, WA 98411 (206) 565–6600	HPVA	Hardwood Plywood & Veneer Association 1825 Michael Farraday Drive, P.O. Box 2789 Reston, VA 22090 (703) 435–2900
		HVI	Home Ventilating Institute 30 West University Drive Arlington Heights, IL 60004 (708) 394–0150
FCI	Fluid Controls Institute c/o Thomas Associates, Inc. 1300 Sumner Road Cleveland, OH 44115 (216) 241–7333	ICEA	Insulated Cable Engineers Association, Inc. P.O. Box 440 South Yarmouth, MA 02664 (617) 394–4424
FGMA	(See GANA)		

IEC	International Electrotechnical Commission (Available from ANSI)
IEEE	Institute of Electrical and Electronic Engineers 345 E. 47th Street New York, NY 10017 (212) 705–7900
IESNA	Illuminating Engineering Society of North America 120 Wall Street, 17th Floor New York, NY 10005 (212) 248–5000
IGCC	Insulating Glass Certification Council (See ETL Listing; co-located)
ILI	Indiana Limestone Institute of America Stone City Bank Building, Suite 400 Bedford, IN 47421 (812) 275–4426
IMSA	International Municipal Signal Association P.O. Box 539, 165 E. Union Street Newark, NJ 14513 (315) 331–2182
IRI	Industrial Risk Insurers 85 Woodland Street, P.O. Box 5010 Hartford, CT 06102 (203) 520–7300
ISA	International Society for Measurement and Control P.O. Box 12277 67 Alexander Drive Research Triangle Park, NC 27709 (919) 549–8411
KCMA	Kitchen Cabinet Manufacturers Association 1899 Preston White Drive Reston, VA 22091 (703) 264–1690
LIA	Lead Industries Association, Inc. 292 Madison Avenue New York, NY 10017 (212) 578–4750
LGSI	Light Gauge Structural Institute c/o Loseke Technologies, Inc. P.O. Box 560746 The Colony, TX 75056 (972) 625-4560
LPI	Lightning Protection Institute 3365 N. Arlington Heights Road, Suite E Arlington Heights, IL 60004 (847) 577–7200
LRI	Lighting Research Institute 120 Wall Street New York, NY 10005 (212) 248–5014

MBMA	Metal Building Manufacturers Association c/o Thomas Associates, Inc. 1300 Sumner Avenue Cleveland, OH 44115 (216) 241–7333
MCAA	Mechanical Contractors Association of America 1385 Piccard Drive Rockville, MD 20850 (301) 869–5800
MFMA	Maple Flooring Manufacturers Association 60 Revere Drive, Suite 500 Northbrook, IL 60062 (708) 480–9138
MHI	Material Handling Institute 8720 Red Oak Boulevard, Suite 201 Charlotte, NC 28217 (704) 522–8644
MIA	Marble Institute of America 30 Eden Alley, Suite 201 Columbus, OH 53215 (614) 228–6194
M.I.A.	Masonry Institute of America 2550 Beverly Boulevard Los Angeles, CA 90057 (213) 388–0472
ML/SFA	Metal Lath/Steel Framing Association (Division of NAAMM) 8 South Michigan Avenue, Suite 1000 Chicago, IL 60603 (312) 456–5590
MSS	Manufacturers Standardization Society of the Valve and Fittings Industry 127 Park Street NE Vienna, VA 22180 (703) 281–6613
NAA	National Aggregate Association 900 Spring Street Silver Spring, MD 20910 (301) 587–1400
NAAMM	National Association of Architectural Metal Manufacturers 8 South Michigan Avenue, Suite 100 Chicago, IL 60603 (312) 332–0405
NAMM	National Association of Mirror Manufacturers 9005 Congressional Drive Potomac, MD 20854 (301) 365–4080
NAPA	National Asphalt Pavement Association NAPA Building 5100 Forbes Boulevard Lanham, MD 20706 (301) 731–4748

NAPF National Association of Plastic
Fabricators (Now DLPA)

NAWIC National Association of Women in
Construction
327 S. Adams Street
Fort Worth, TX 76104 (800) 552–3506

NBGQA National Building Granite Quarries
Association
369 N. State Street
Concord, NH 03301 (603) 225–8397

NBHA National Building Hardware
Association (See DHI)

NCMA National Concrete Masonry
Association
2302 Horse Pen Road
Herndon, VA 22071 (703) 713–1900

NCRPM National Council on Radiation
Protection and Measurement
7910 Woodmont Avenue
Suite 800
Bethesda, MD 20814 (301) 657–2652

NDMA National Dimension Manufacturers
Association
1000 Johnson Ferry Road
Marietta, GA 30068 (404) 565–6660

NDPA National Decorating Products
Association
1050 North Lindbergh Boulevard
St. Louis, MO 63132 (314) 991–3470

NEC National Electric Code
(Available through NFPA)

NECA National Electrical Contractors
Association
3 Bethesda Metro Center, Suite 1100
Bethesda, MD 20814
(301) 657–3110

NEII National Elevator Industry, Inc.
185 Bridge Plaza North, Suite 310
Fort Lee, NJ 07024 (201) 944–3211

NEMA National Electrical Manufacturers
Association
2101 L Street NW, Suite 300
Washington, DC 20037
(202) 457–8400

NFPA National Fire Protection Association
Batterymarch Park, P.O. Box 9101
Quincy, MA 02269 (617) 770–3000

NFoPA National Forest Products Association
(Name change; see AFPA listing)

NHLA National Hardwood Lumber
Association
P.O. Box 34518
Memphis, TN 38184 (901) 377–1818

NAIMA North American Insulation
(Formerly Thermal Insulation
Manufacturers Association)
44 Canal Center Plaza, Suite 310
Alexandria, VA 22314 (703) 684–0084

NKCA National Kitchen Cabinet Association
(now KCMA)

NOFMA National Oak Flooring Manufacturers
Association
P.O. Box 3009
Memphis, TN 38173 (901) 526–5016

NPA national Particleboard Association
18928 Premiere Court
Gaithersburg, MD 20879
(301) 670–0604

NPCA National Paint and Coatings
Association
1500 Rhode Island Avenue NW
Washington, DC 20005
(202) 462–6272

NRCA National Roofing Contractors
Association
10255 W. Higgins Road, Suite 600
Rosemont, IL 60018
(847) 299–9070

NRDCA National Roof Deck Contractors
Association
600 S. Federal Street
Chicago, IL 60605 (312) 922–6222

NRMCA National Ready Mixed Concrete
Association
900 Spring Street
Silver Spring, MD 20910
(301) 587–1400

NSF NSF International
(Formerly National Sanitation
Foundation)
P.O. Box 130140
3475 Plymouth Road
Ann Arbor, MI 48113 (313) 769–8010

NSPE National Society of Professional
Engineers
1420 King Street
Alexandria, VA 22314
(703) 684–2800

NSSEA National School Supply and Equipment Association
8300 Colesville Road, No. 250
Silver Spring, MD 20910
(301) 495–0240

NSPI National Spa and Pool Institute
2111 Eisenhower Avenue
Alexandria, VA 22314 (703) 838–0083

NSWMA National Solid Wastes Management Association
1730 Rhode Island Avenue NW
Washington, DC 20036
(202) 659–4613

NTMA National Terrazzo and Mosaic Association
3166 Des Plaines Avenue, Suite 121
Des Plaines, IL 60018 (312) 635–7744

NWMA National Woodwork Manufacturers Association (Now NWWDA)

NWWDA National Wood Window and Door Association (Formerly NWMA)
1400 E. Touhy Avenue, Suite G54
Des Plaines, IL 60018 (847) 299–5200

PCA Portland Cement Association
5420 Old Orchard Road
Skokie, IL 60077 (847) 966–6200

PCI Precast/Prestressed Concrete Institute
175 W. Jackson Boulevard
Chicago, IL 60604 (312) 786–0300

PDCA Painting and Decoration Contractors of America
3913 Old Lee Highway
Fairfax, VA 22030 (703) 359–0826

PDI Plumbing and Drainage Institute
45 Bristol Drive, Suite 101
South Easton, MA 02375
(508) 230–3516

PEI Porcelain Enamel Institute
4004 Hillsboro Pike, Suite 224-B
Nashville, TN 37215 (615) 385–5357

PI Perlite Institute
88 New Dorp Plaza
Staten Island, NY 10306
(718) 351–5723

PPFA Plastic Pipe and Fittings Association
800 Roosevelt Road, Building C, Suite 20
Glen Ellyn, IL 60137 (630) 858–6540

PPI Plastic Pipe Institute
(Formerly The Society of the Plastics Industry, Inc.)
1801 K Street, NW, Suite 600L
Washington, DC 20006
(202) 974–5306

PWC Professional Women in Construction
342 Madison Avenue
New York, NY 10173 (212) 687–0610

RCSHSB Red Cedar Shingle and Handsplit Shake Bureau
515 116th Avenue NE, Suite 275
Bellevue, WA 98004 (206) 453–1323

RFCI Resilient Floor Covering Institute
966 Hungerford Drive, Suite 12-B
Rockville, MD 20805
(301) 340–8580

RIS Redwood Inspection Service
c/o California Redwood Association
405 Enfrente Drive, Suite 200
Novato, CA 94949 (415) 382–0662

RMA Rubber Manufacturers Association
1400 K Street NW Suite 900
Washington, DC 20005
(202) 682–4800

SAMA Scientific Apparatus Makers Association
1101 Sixteenth Street NW
Washington, DC 20036
(202) 223–1360

SDI Steel Deck Institute
P.O. Box 25
Fox River Grove, IL 60021
(847) 462–1930

S.D.I. Steel Door Institute
30200 Detroit Road
Cleveland, OH 44145 (216) 899–0010

SFPA Southern Forest Products Association
P.O. Box 64170
Kenner, LA 70064 (504) 443–4464

SGAA Stained Glass Association of America
Box 22642
Kansas City, MO 64113
(816) 333–6690

SGCC Safety Glazing Certification Council
(See ETL Listing; co-located)

SHLMA Southern Hardwood Lumber Manufacturers Association
(Now HMA)

SIGMA   Sealed Insulating Glass Manufacturers
Association
401 N. Michigan Avenue
Chicago, IL 60611 (312) 644–6610

SJI   Steel Joist Institute
3127 10th Avenue North
Myrtle Beach, SC 29577
(843) 626–1995

SMACNA   Sheet Metal and Air Conditioning
Contractors National Association
4201 LaFayette Center Drive
Chantilly, VA 20151
(703) 803–2989

SPIB   Southern Pine Inspection Bureau
4709 Scenic Highway
Pensacola, FL 32504 (904) 434–2611

SPRI   SPRI (Formerly Single-Ply Roofing
Institute)
200 Reservoir Street, Suite 309A
Needham, MA 02194
(718) 444–0242

SSPC   Society for Protective Coatings
(Formerly Steel Structures Painting
Council)
40 24th Street, 6th Floor
Pittsburgh, PA 15222 (412) 281–2331

SWI   Steel Window Institute
c/o Thomas Associates, Inc.
1230 Keith Building
Cleveland, OH 44115 (216) 241–7333

TCA   Tile Council of America
100 Clemson Research Boulevard
Anderson, SC 29625 (864) 646–8453

TIMA   Thermal Insulation Manufacturers
Association (Now NAIMA)

TPI   Truss Plate Institute
583 D'Onofrio Drive, Suite 200
Madison, WI 53719 (608) 833–5900

UL   Underwriters Laboratories
333 Pfingsten Road
Northbrook, IL 60062
(847) 272–8800

VA   Vermiculite Association, Inc.
600 S. Federal Street, Suite 400
Chicago, IL 60605
(312) 922–6222

WA   Wallcoverings Association
401 N. Michigan Avenue
Chicago, IL 60611 (312) 644–6610

WCLIB   West Coast Lumber Inspection
Bureau
P.O. Box 23145
Portland, OR 97281 (503) 639–0651

WCMA   Wall Covering Manufacturers
Association
66 Morris Avenue
Springfield, NJ 07081 (201) 379–1100

WIC   Woodwork Institute of California
P.O. Box 980247
Sacramento, CA 95798
(916) 372–9943

WRCA   Western Red Cedar Association
Box 120786
New Brighton, MN 55112
(612) 633–4334

WRCLA   Western Red Cedar Lumber
Association
1200–555 Burrand Street
Vancouver, BC, Canada
(604) 684–0266

WRI   Wire Reinforcement Institute
203 Loudoun Street SW
Leesburg, VA 20175 (703) 779–2339

WSC   Water Systems Council
Building C, Suite 20
800 Roosevelt Road
Glen Ellyn, IL 60137 (603) 545–1762

WSFI   Wood and Synthetic Flooring Institute
(Now MFMA)

WWPA   Western Wood Products Association
1500 Yeon Building
522 SW 5th Avenue
Portland, OR 97204 (503) 224–3930

W.W.P.A.   Woven Wire Products Association
2515 N. Nordica Avenue
Chicago, IL 60635 (312) 637–1359

Federal Government Agencies

Names and titles of federal government standards and specification-producing agencies are frequently abbreviated. The following acronyms and abbreviations as referenced in the contract documents indicate names of standards or specification-producing agencies of the federal government. Names and addresses are subject to change but are believed to be accurate.

CE	Corps of Engineers (U.S. Department of the Army) 20 Massachusetts Avenue, NW Washington, DC 20314 (202) 761–0660			Washington, DC 20401 (202) 401–0388
		FS	Federal Specifications Unit (Available from General Services Administration) 470 East L'Enfant Plaza SW, Suite 8100 Washington, DC 204076 (202) 619–8925	
CFR	Code of Federal Regulations (Available from Government Printing Office) Washington, DC 20401 (Material is usually first published in the *Federal Register*) (202) 512–0000			
		GSA	General Services Administration F Street and 18th Street NW Washington, DC 20405 (202) 708–5082	
CPSC	Consumer Product Safety Commission East West Towers 4330 East-West Highway Bethesda, MD 29814 1-(800) 638–2772			
		MIL	Military Standardization Documents (U.S. Department of Defense) Defense Printing Service 700 Robbins Avenue, Building 4D Philadelphia, PA 19111 (215) 697–2179	
CS	Commercial Standard (U.S. Department of Commerce) Government Printing Office Washington, DC 20402 (202) 512–1800			
		NIST	National Institute of Standards and Technology (U.S. Depart. of Commerce) Building 101, #A1134 Route I-270 and Quince Orchard Road Gaithersburg, MD 20899 (301) 975–2000	
DOC	Department of Commerce 14th Street and Constitution Avenue Washington, DC 20230 (202) 482–2000			
DOT	Department of Transportation 400 Seventh Street SW Washington, DC 20590 (202) 366–4000			
		OSHA	Occupational Safety and Health Administration U.S. Department of Labor/OSHA 200 Constitution Avenue NW Washington, DC 20210 (202) 219–8148	
EPA	Environmental Protection Agency 401 M Street SW Washington, DC 20460 (202) 260–2090			
		PS	Product Standards (National Bureau of Standards) (U.S. Department of Labor) Government Printing Office Washington, DC 20402 (202) 512–1800	
FAA	Federal Aviation Administration (U.S. Department of Transportation) 800 Independence Avenue SW Washington, DC 20591 (202) 366–4000			
		RUS	Rural Utilities Service (U.S. Department of Agriculture) 14th Street and Independence Avenue SW Washington, DC 20250 (202) 720–9560	
FCC	Federal Communications Commission 1919 M Street NW Washington, DC 20554 (202) 418–0126			
		TRB	Transportation Research Board 2101 Constitution Avenue NW Washington, DC 20418 (202) 334–2934	
FHA	Federal Housing Administration (U.S. Department of Housing and Urban Development) 451 Seventh Street SW			

USDA   U.S. Department of Agriculture
        14th Street and Independence
        Avenue SW
        Washington, DC 20205 (202)
        720–8732

USPS   U.S. Postal Service
        475 L'Enfant Plaza SW
        Washington, DC 20260 (202)
        268–2000

Other Sources

Names and titles of other standards, code, or specification-producing agencies are also frequently abbreviated. The following are subject to change but are believed to be accurate.

CSI   Construction Specifications
            Institute
            601 Madison Street
            Alexandria, VA 22314

EJCDC/NSPE Engineers Joint Contract
            Documents Committee
            of National Society of
            Professional Engineers
            1420 King Street
            Alexandria, VA 22314

ACEC   American Consulting
            Engineers Council
            1015 E. 47th Street
            New York, NY 10017

BOCA   Building Officials and Code
            Administrators International,
            Inc. (*National Building Code
            and Others*)
            4051 West Flossmoor Road
            Country Club Hills, IL 60477

NFiPA   National Fire Protection
            Association
            (*Life Safety Code, National
            Electric Code*, and other
            standards)
            Batterymarch Park
            Quincy, MA 02269

CABO*   Council of American Building
            Officials
            (*One and Two family Dwelling
            Code*)
            5203 Leesburg Pike
            Falls Church, VA 22041

SBBC   Southern Building Code
            Congress International
            (*Standard Building Code* and
            others)
            900 Montclair Road
            Birmingham, AL 35213

ICBO   International Conference of
            Building Officials
            (*Uniform Building Code* and
            others)
            5360 S. Workman Mill Road
            Whittier, CA 90601

* CABO now is also office for International Building Codes.

Magazine, Digest, and Research Sources

AIA   American Institute of Architects
(*Architectural Record* magazine)
Box 2063
Marion, OH 43305
Private *Architecture* magazine
1515 Broadway
New York, NY 10036

NIBS   National Institute of Building
Sciences (*Building Science Newsletter*)
1015 15th Street NW
Washington, DC 20005

NRC   National Research Council
(*Canadian Building Digest*)
Ottawa, Canada KIA OR6

CSI   Construction Specifications Institute,
Inc. (*Construction Specifier*)
601 Madison Street
Alexandria, VA 22314

NIST   National Institute of Standards and
Technology

(*Building Science Series*)
U.S. Superintendent
of Documents
Washington, DC 20402

HHFA   Housing and Home Finance Agency
(*Housing Research Papers*)
Washington, DC 20402

SHC   Small Homes Council—Building
Research Council
(*Reports*—Miscellaneous Topics;
send for listing)
University of Illinois
1 E. St. Mary's Road
Champaign, IL 61820

FPL   Forest Products Laboratory
(*Wood Handbook*, USDA
Handbook 72)
U.S. Government Printing Office
Washington, DC 20402
(202) 783–3328

Glossary

This glossary has been compiled to be as comprehensive as possible for students in Architecture, Engineering, and Construction Technology programs. It is *not* complete, inasmuch as each construction phase, system, trade, and material has its own jargon, and nomenclature, and many cases, definitions too. These number in the tens of thousands. Therefore, it is impossible to know them all, but, it is well to become familiar with them as the need arises.

In addition, it should be noted that things are often called by familiar names that are not accurate. for example, it is plastic laminate, not Formica; concrete, not cement; steel, not iron.

The following is a short list of resources and references that may provide the definitions of terms being sought by the student. Be advised that the latest editions should be verified with the publishers.

Construction Dictionary, **9th ed.**
Greater Phoenix Chapter
National Association of Women in Construction
P.O. Box 6142
Phoenix, AZ 85005
(602)263–7680

Dictionary of Architecture and Construction, **2d ed.**
By Cyrill M Harris
ISBN0–07-026756–1
Published by McGraw-Hill Book Company

Building News Construction
Dictionary Illustrated
Published by ENR/BNI Books
1221 Avenue of the Americas
New York, NY 10020

Construction Glossary **2d ed.**
By J.S. Stein
ISBN 0–471-56933-X
Published by John Wiley & Sons, Inc.

Means Illustrated Construction Dictionary
ISBN0–87629-218-X
Published by R.S. Means Co., Inc.
100 Construction Plaza
P.O. Box 800
Kingston, MA 02364

A Glossary of Construction Specifications Terminology
District of Columbia Metropolitan Chapter
Construction Specifications Institute
1777 Church Street NW
Washington, DC 20036

GLOSSARY

Many publications of the Trade and Professional organizations listed in Appendix J also provide definitions and descriptions specific to their products or services.

A

Abrasive
A hard substance, such as carborundum; small pieces (grits) are often used in terrazzo and concrete stairs to provide a nonslip surface; used to make rubbing stones for concrete wall finishing; also used for grinding and polishing.

Abut
To be adjacent to, and touching, on a side or an end.

Access flooring
A raised floor surface consisting entirely of relatively small (24 sq. ft.) individually removable panels, beneath which wiring, duct work, cabling, and other services may be installed; also called *computer floor* or *pedestal floor.*

Accessories
Trim pieces, reinforcement, anchors, and similar devices that aid and enhance various materials installation; vary in type; available for drywall, plaster, masonry, concrete, etc.

Acoustic(al)
Pertains to sound. In some buildings, it is necessary to include sound control, i.e., acoustical treatment; smooth, flat surfaces generally reflect sound; a soft, porous surface will absorb it. The finished surfaces of ceilings and walls are designed according to the need for acoustical treatment; floors may also be treated, as well as doors, windows, and mechanical systems.

Acoustic Materials
Composition board installed on ceilings or walls for the purpose of reducing sound reflection (or echo); board is generally the same as that used for ordinary insulating purposes or can be specially manufactured material for added acoustic capabilities. Acoustical tile for ceilings is often perforated or fissured to increase the area of sound-absorbing surface; may be boards, batts, blocks, foam, spray-on, panel, sheets, pads, or tile materials.

Acoustical ceiling
A ceiling of fibrous tiles or boards that are highly absorbent of sound energy.

Acre
A land area comprising 43,560 sq.

Acrylic
A transparent plastic material widely used in sheet form for glazing windows and skylights; highly resistant to breakage.

ADA (Americans with Disabilities Act)
Federal law requiring that an accessible route be established so all persons, including those impaired in any way, can access any public area or service in a building; accessible entrances, ramps, door locations/sizes, rest room layouts, etc. are addressed.

Adhesive
A natural or synthetic material, generally in paste or liquid form, used to fasten or glue material together, install floor tile, fabricate plastic laminate-covered work, or otherwise attach work items together.

Admixture
A substance other than portland cement, water, and aggregates, included in a concrete mixture for the purpose of altering one or more properties of the concrete; aids setting, finishing, or wearing of the concrete.

Adobe
Construction using sun-dried units, in manageable block form, of adobe soil for walls; usually found in southwestern United States.

A-frame
Structural system utilizing members that when fastened together resemble the letter A.

Aggregate
Hard, inert material, such as sand, gravel, and crushed stone, which is combined with portland cement and water to produce concrete; must be properly cleaned and well graded as required.

AIA
The American Institute of Architects; a professional organization of registered architects; provides various membership services, documents, lobbying efforts, government interface, information, education, and other professional services.

Air-dried lumber
Any lumber seasoned by drying in the open air instead of in a kiln or oven.

Air-entrained concrete
Concrete in which a small amount of air is trapped

634

by the addition of a special material (admixture) to produce greater durability in the finished concrete.

Air space
A space or void in a wall or other enclosed part of a building between structural members.

Air-to-air heat exchanger
A device that exhausts air form a building while recovering much of the heat from the exhausted air and transferring it to the incoming air.

Air lock
Enclosure inside a set of entrance doors to create a transition space; a vestibule, overheated to prevent flow of cold air into a building; can be ceilingless, but will duplicate entrance doors layout.

AISC
The American Institute of Steel Construction.

Alcove
A recessed area opening off a larger area (room); often used as a sitting area, coat room, or storage/equipment area.

Alloy
A substance composed of two or more metals, or of a metal and a nonmetallic constituent, to form a substance of increased attributes (strength, for example).

Altitude (of the sun)
The angle formed by the rays of the sun and the earth's surface; a consideration in the shading of surfaces, light control, etc.

Ampere
The unit of measure for the rate of electrical flow.

Anchor
Any of a number of devices/fasteners (usually metal) used to mechanically attach one item or material to another of the same or different qualities or composition.

Anchor bolt
A threaded rod inserted into masonry construction or concrete to anchor base, bearing, and sill plates to foundations, footings, sills, piers, walls, etc.

Angle brace
A support to stiffen or reinforce a frame; placed across a corner at an angle to the supported members.

Angle (iron)
A piece of rolled structural steel bent to form a 90-degree angle; may have equal or unequal legs; identified by the symbol "L".

Annealed
Cooled under controlled conditions to minimize internal stresses.

Anodizing
An electrolytic process that forms a permanent, protective oxide coating on aluminum, with or without added color.

Anticlastic
Saddle-shaped, or having a curvature in two opposing directions.

Apron
Wood trim piece under the stool of an interior window trim/casing; concrete slab approach to a garage.

Arcade
A series of arches supported by columns or piers to provide an open passageway.

Arch
A curved structure that will support itself and the weight of wall above the opening, by mutual pressure.

Architect
A person trained and skilled in designing and supervising the construction of buildings and properly registered for the practice of architecture.

Arc welding
A process of joining two pieces of metal by melting them together at their interface with a controlled additional amount of molten metal from a metallic electrode.

Area divider
A partition or screen to temporarily or permanently separate one space or area from others; also a curb to partition or divide a large roof area to allow expansion and contraction in the deck and membrane.

Areaway
An area recessed below grade (at least partially) around a foundation to allow light and ventilation into basement windows; requires walls, a formed shield to hold earth, and a drain or gravel bottom.

Arrester
Wire screen secured to the top of a chimney or stack to direct, defuse, and disperse sparks and other products of burning.

Arris
A sharp edge formed when two planes or surfaces meet; found on edges of moldings, doors, shelves, and in cabinet construction.

Ash dump
A door in the fireplace floor or wall that allows ashes from the fire box to be swept into a chamber below or to the outside, where they can be removed.

Ashlar
Squared and dressed stones used for facing a masonry wall; also short upright wood pieces extending from the attic floor to the rafters, forming a dwarf wall.

Asphalt
A mineral pitch insoluble in water and used extensively in building materials for waterproofing, roof coverings, shingles, floor tile, paints, and paving.

Asphalt expansion joint material
A composition strip of felt and asphalt material made to specified thickness and used to take up the expansion in concrete floors and sidewalks.

Asphalt floor tile
A manufactured floor covering made of asphalt composition; comes in 9" x 9" tiles and a variety of dark colors; an older material not widely used today.

Asphalt roofing
On a flat surface, roofing composed of alternate layers of roofing felt and hot-applied asphalt (called a built-up roof). Asphalt is the most widely used material for covering roofs because it possesses the characteristics needed for protection against weather and is easily applied at a relatively inexpensive cost.

Asphalt-saturated felt
Moisture-resistant sheet material, available in several thicknesses and weights, usually consisting of a heavy paper that has been impregnated with asphalt.

Asphalt shingles
Composition roof shingles made from asphalt-impregnated felt covered with mineral granules, reinforced with strands of fiberglass; available in several weights.

Assembly
Portion of a building in combination; for example, a roof/ceiling assembly or a ceiling/floor assembly, wherein different materials are combined, installed, and interfaced to form protectives and other aspects of construction for an entire building.

ASTM
Abbreviation for the American Society for Testing and Materials, a organization dedicated to the testing and standardization of building materials.

Astragal
Molding or trim piece used to cover a joint between a pair of doors hung in a single frame; serves as a door stop for the initial swing door when nailed to the second door; also used between casement windows.

Atrium
A central hall or open court within a structure; may be multistory in height and is usually glazed to large degree.

Attic
The space/area between the roof and top ceiling of a building.

Attic ventilators
In houses, screened openings provided to ventilate an attic space; located in the soffit area as inlet ventilators and in the gable end or along the ridge as outlet ventilation;can also consist of power-driven fans or turbines used as an exhaust system (see *louver*).

Attribute
The line or color characteristics assigned to an entity or group of entities.

Audiovisual equipment
When built into a building (not movable equipment), encompasses security, fire, signal, alarm, video control, and sound detection devices.

Auger
A helical tool for creating cylindrical holes by drilling, such as caisson shafts in the ground, holes in other materials.

Awning window
An outswinging window with all sash panels hinged at the top and acting in unison.

Axial
In a direction parallel to the long axis of a structural member.

Axis
A line around which something rotates or is symmetrically arranged.

B

Backfill
Coarse earth or granular material used to fill in and build up the ground level around a foundation wall to provide a slope for drainage away from the foundation wall.

Backer rod
A flexible, compressible rope or strip of plastic foam wedged into a joint to limit the depth to which sealant can be applied.

Backsplash
A vertical surface at the back of a countertop or fixture.

Backup
A material, usually not in view, that acts as a support, filler, or rigidity reinforcement for another material (example: concrete masonry units act as "backup" to face brick).

Baffle
Acoustical pads or panels to absorb sound, hung or attached to walls; vanes in air ducts to divert slow of air; any other device/material to preclude transfer of heat, sound, etc.

Balcony
A deck projecting from the wall of a building above ground or at floor level.

Ballast
A heavy material (usually gravel or stone) installed over a roof membrane to prevent wind uplift and to shield the membrane from sunlight; also aids water evaporation.

Balloon framing
Name of a system of light-wood or house framing characterized by the studs extending in one piece from the foundation sill to the roof plate; not widely used because it requires applied fire blocking and a let-in ribbon or the second floor framing; utilizes long pieces of lumber, not readily available; also called *Eastern framing*.

Balustrade
A series of balusters connected by a hand- or guardrail; generally used for porches and balconies.

Baluster(s)
Small vertical posts supporting a handrail; ore commonly known as *bannister spindles*.

Band joist (board)
Wooden joist running perpendicularly across the ends of the primary joists in a floor and closing of the floor platform at the outside face of the building.

Bar
Small rolled or drawn steel shape, round, square, or rectangular in cross section; a deformed steel shape used for reinforcing concrete.

Bar joists
Structural framing units made from bar- and rod-shaped steel and other lightweight members, for supporting moderate roof and floor loads; also known as *open-web steel joists* or *steel lumber*.

Bargeboard
Finish board along the top line of a gable roof after the siding has been applied.

Barrel shell
A scalloped roof structure of reinforced concrete that spans in one direction as a barrel vault and in the other as a folded plate.

Barrel vault
A segment of a cylinder, lying horizontally, and that spans as an arch.

Barrier-free design
Layout and design that provide an accessible route for all persons; meets requirements of ADA regulations, local building and safety codes, etc.

Base
The bottom part of any unit on which the entire item rests; can be a separate concrete pad under equipment; also slang for *baseboard*.

Baseboard
Interior wall trim at the floor line to cover the joint between wall and floor materials; strip of wood placed along the base of a wall or column to protect the finish from damage by shoes.

Base cabinet(s)
The lower, floor-mounted cabinets that support a work surface or countertop in kitchens or other work areas.

Base plate
A steel plate forming the bottom or base of a steel column; usually larger than the column, so as to disperse the imposed load, to allow proper anchorage to the bearing surface.

Base shoe
Small molding used next to the floor and applied to the face of a baseboard.

Batten
Narrow strip of wood, or other material, used to cover joints in sheets of decorative materials, plywood, or wide boards.

Batten seam
Seam in a sheet metal roof that encloses a wooden batten.

Batter boards
Horizontal boards set to exact elevations and nailed to posts outside the excavation for a new building; string- lines stretched across these boards locate the outline of the foundation and building walls for workers.

Batt insulation
Flexible blanketlike or roll of, insulating material (usually faced or unfaced fiberglass) used for thermal or sound insulation by installation between framing members in walls, floors, and/or ceilings.

Bay
Area of a building contained within four adjacent columns, which defines the structural layout of the area; also a projecting portion of a facade.

Bay window
Any fixed window space projecting outward from the walls of a building, either square or polygonal in plan.

Beam
A structural member that is normally subject to bending loads; usually a horizontal member carrying vertical loads (an exception to this is a purlin). Three types are

1. Continuous beam—has more than two points of support.
2. Cantilevered beam—supported at only one end and restrained against rotation and deflection by design and connection.
3. Simple beam—freely supported at both ends.

Beam ceiling
A type of construction in which the beams of the ceiling are exposed to view; beams may be true or false (nonbearing), but the appearance is the same.

Beam pocket
A slot or recess left in a wall in which the end of a beam or joist is placed for bearing.

Bearing plate
Steel plates set on grout bed (nonshrinking) under the end of a beam or other structural membrane; distributes the load carried on the member over a greater area of the wall; may also be a "pad" made of a block of plastic or synthetic rubber, which cushions the point at which members meet.

Bearing wall or partition
Wall that supports all or part of the floors, roofs, or ceilings in a building; partition that carries the floor joists and other partitions above it.

Bed joint
A horizontal mortar joint in brick or other masonry walls.

Bedrock
Unweathered, solid stratum of rock; excellent bearing surface for foundation systems.

Belt course
A layer of stone or molded work carried at the same level across or around a building; also a decorative feature such as a horizontal band around a building or a column.

Bench mark (BM)
A fixed point used as the basis for computing elevation grades; identified by marks or symbols on stone, metal, other durable surveying items/matter, permanently affixed in the ground, from which differences of elevation are measured; also referred to as a *datum* or *datum point*.

Bent
A rigid frame made of two vertical supporting members and a sloped or horizontal structural member fixed between them.

Bevel siding
Shaped wood boards, thicker on one edge than on the other; applied in such a way that the thick edge of one board overlaps the tin edge of the next one below.

Bibb
See *hose bibb*.

Bi-fold doors
Folding doors arranged so that a door panel is pivoted on each side of the opening and the doors fold toward the jambs.

Blind nailing
A method of fastening flooring in which the nail is driven into the edge of the board just above the tongue, at an angle, so that the head is concealed by the edge of the next board; also called *secret nailing*.

Bit
A device inserted into a drill chuck that will drill the required hole(s).

Bituminous concrete
An asphaltic compound with small aggregate placed in a thick liquid, which hardens into a paving surface; also called *blacktop*.

Blocking
Method of bonding two adjoining or intersecting walls not built at the same time; also, various wood members sized and shaped and used as fillers.

Board measure
A system for specifying a quantity of lumber; one unit is 1 board foot, which is the amount of wood in a piece 1"x12"x12".

Bollard
Sort stanchion(s) used to inhibit vehicle access, to direct pedestrian traffic, and/or as decorative (and illuminated) markers (not part of a sign system); also used as bumpers to protect buildings, fire hydrants, and similar obstacles.

Bolster
A device made of heavy bent wire used to hold several reinforcing bars in position; also an auxiliary brace or support under structural members (sometimes called a *haunch*).

Bond
Interlocking masonry units in the face of a wall by overlapping the units to break the continuity of vertical joints; also the adhesion of one material to another (for example, concrete to reinforcing steel).

Bond beam
Continuous reinforced concrete block courses in or around the top of masonry walls, to stabilize the walls.

Bond breaker
Chemical coating, or inert sheet divider, to prevent adhesion of one material to another; primarily used in sealant joints to prevent the sealant from adhering to the backer rod.

Bottom chord
Bottom horizontal member in a truss.

Box beam
A hollow structural member built up of plywood sheets and solid wood members.

Box sill
Wood frame sill construction wherein a header (band joist) is nailed, vertically, across the ends of the floor joists, closing off the voids between joists and ensuring proper spacing and stability.

Braced framing
Supporter framework of a house, especially at the corners; diagonal or let-in braces (wood or metal) form a triangular shape to make the frame rigid and solid; plywood sheets at corners provide the same function.

Bracing
Support members in framing that are used to make the major structural members more rigid.

Bracket
A projection from the face of a wall or column as a support for a structural or ornamental feature; a support for a shelf.

Brad
A small, thin nail with a small head; used when the head is to be sunken into the wood (a finishing nail).

Brick
Masonry unit(s) composed of clay or shale; formed into a rectangular prism while soft, then burned or fired in a kiln; can have voids or recessed panels to reduce weight and increase bond to mortar.

Brick veneer
Single wythe (thickness) of brick facing applied over wood frame construction or masonry other than brick; this facing is nonstructural.

Bridging
Method of bracing floor joists to distribute the weight over more than one joist; joins joists to act as a diaphragm unit rather than individually; prevents displacement and wracking. Usually two wood (1 in. thick) or light metal pieces criss-

crossed between joists; can also be wood stock of the same size as joists, called "solid bridging", must be installed continuously from end wall to end wall.

BTU (British thermal unit)
The amount of heat required to raise the temperature of 1 pound of water, 1 degree Fahrenheit (F).

Buck
The framing around an opening in a wall; *door buck* is another name for a door frame which encloses the opening in which a door is placed.

Buffer
A natural or man-made screening device to separate areas in an effort to modify or reduce noise, light, unsightliness, etc.

Building code
A series of legal requirements specifying minimum design and construction components to ensure the health and safety of the people using a building or structure.

Building line
Lines established and marked off by a surveyor that denotes the exterior faces of a proposed building; used by tradespeople as guidelines; surveyors get their information from the plans, specifications, and official records. A building line is generally extended and marked on batter boards placed about 6 ft outside the corners/lines of the building excavation.

Building paper
Heavy sheet material used between sheathing and siding/facing for insulation and windbreaking purposes; four types: (1) red rosin paper, (2) sisal paper, (3) plain asphalt felt paper (tar paper), and (4) plastic sheeting.

Building permit
Certificate that must be obtained from the local government by the property owner or contractor before a building can be erected or repaired; indicates proper review for compliance with various regulations; must be kept posted in a conspicuous place on-site until the job is completed and passed by the building inspector.

Built-up roof
A roof covering made of alternate layers of building (roofing) felt and hot liquid asphalt, with a final surfacing of gravel; laid on a low slope or comparatively level roof.

Bull nose
A rounded outside corner; brick, tile, or concrete masonry unit (CMU) with a rounded corner(s).

Butt
Type of door hinge that allows the edge of a door to butt into the jamb of the frame.

Butt joint
The junction of two members in a square-cut joint, end to end, or side to side (edge to edge).

Butt-joint glazing
Installation of glass sheets with butted vertical joints and no mullion; joints are sealed with silicone sealant; used or interior or exterior for clean, sleek range of glass without struts.

Buttress
Vertical masonry or concrete support, usually larger at the base, which projects perpendicularly from a wall; used to brace and strengthen walls.

Butyl rubber
A synthetic rubber compound used in caulking and various sheet materials.

C

Cable tray
Open or closed tray, tube, box, or rack for running wiring and cabling throughout a building; usually concealed, but may be exposed for access; called *wireway*, or *wire mold* in smaller sizes.

Caisson
A deep shaft drilled into the ground down to adequate bearing soil, then filled with concrete; used to support a column or to provide other structural foundation.

Call out
A note on a drawing with a leader line to the feature, location, material, or work item involved.

Camber
A slight upward arch placed in a beam or girder to counteract deflection caused by loading.

Cant strip
An angular board installed at the intersection of the roof deck and a wall, curb, or other penetrating item; used to avoid sharp right angles when the roof covering is installed.

Cantilever
Projecting beam or slab supported at one end/slab only.

Casework
Manufactured or custom-built cabinetry, including shelves, cabinetry, including shelves, cabinets (base and/or wall), countertops, and ancillary equipment; can be metal, wood, laminate covered, etc.

Casement window
A side-hinged window that opens outward by a crank device or push bar.

Casing
Molding of various widths, thicknesses, and profiles used to trim door and window openings at the jambs, head, and sills.

Cast-in-place concrete
Current and proper term for the placing of concrete into its forms on a job site; replaces the word *pour*, which has negative connotations relating to a watery mix inappropriate for construction use; also *Sitecast.*

Caulk(ing)
A waterproof material used to seal cracks and joints; also see *sealants.*

Cavity wall
A masonry wall made of two or more wythes of masonry units joined with ties, but having an air space between them.

Cementitious
Attribute of inorganic substances that have cementing properties.

Cement, portland
A gray, powdery material that, when mixed with water, will harden; used with aggregate of various sizes in concrete and mortar.

Centerline
Actual or imaginary line through the exact center of an object.

Center- to- center
Measuring distance from centerline to centerline of adjacent units; a term meaning "on center," as in the spacing of joists, studding, and other structural parts.

Centering
The temporary support for a masonry arch in process of being built; more generally it may refer to the forms for all supported concrete work (either permanent or temporary).

Chain
A unit of land measurement of 66 ft in length.

Chairs
Metal, heavy wire, or plastic supports to hold reinforcing steel i place during placing of concrete in forms; allow concrete to surround bars, and provide proper cover between bars and face of concrete member.

Chamfer
A corner beveled at an angle (usually 45 degrees); in concrete work, a three-cornered wood strip called *chamfer strip* is used to form the profile, e.g., at a corner of a column.

Channel
Structural section, steel or aluminum, shaped like a rectangle, but with one long side missing; C-shaped.

Chase
In masonry, a channel cut or built in the face of a wall to allow space for receiving pipes, conduits, etc.; also a recess in any wall to provide space for pipes and ducts, etc.

Chimney
A vertical shaft for drawing smoke from a heating unit, fireplace or incinerator and venting it to the outside.

Chord
Usually refers to the uppermost (top chord) or lowest (bottom chord) member in a truss; also a line drawn through a circle other than a diameter or radius.

Cladding
Any of several materials or systems used as exterior wall enclosures for a building.

Class A, B, C roofing
Roofing coverings classified by their resistance to fire, determined by ASTM E108; Class A highest, C lowest.

Cleat dimension; clear opening
Designation used to indicate the distance between opposing inside faces of an opening, frame, room, etc.

Clerestory
Portion of a room that extends above the adjoining roof, usually with glazing for light and ventilation.

Coating topping
Relatively thin material, such as paint, epoxy, etc., applied to surfaces for protection and/or decoration; topping is also applied to floors to smooth irregularities.

Collar beam
Horizontal member tying opposing rafters together below the ridge in roof framing.

Column
A vertical structural member supporting horizontal or sloped members; can also be purely decorative.

Column spiral
A continuous coil of reinforcing steel used to tie vertical re-bars together in a concrete column.

Combined sewer
Sewer line that carries both storm and sanitary drainage; not recommended (old technology) but still prevalent in many areas.

Common bond
Brick laid in a pattern consisting of five (5) courses of stretchers, followed by one (1) "bonding" course of headers.

Common rafter
Rafter extending from the top of a wall to the roof ridge.

Component
A unitized part of a house assembled before delivery to a building site.

Composite metal decking
Corrugated steel decking manufactured in such a way that it bonds securely to a concrete floor fill to form a reinforced concrete slab/deck.

Composite pile
A pile consisting of two different types of construction material in successive sections.

Composite wall
A masonry wall that incorporates two or more different types of masonry units, such as clay brick and concrete masonry units (CMUs).

Compression
A stress in a structural member caused by loading, which tends to "push together" or compress the member, parallel or at right angles to its axis.

Compression gasket
A synthetic rubber strip that seals around a sheet of glass or wall panel by being squeezed and compressed tightly against it.

Concave joint
A mortar joint tooled into a curved, indented profile.

Concealed grid
A suspended ceiling framework that is completely hidden by the tiles or panels it supports.

Concrete
A thick, pasty (but plastic/formable) mixture of portland cement, sand, gravel, and water; can be formed into any shape, which it retains when hardened and cured; mixes may be varied in proportioning, strength, and other attributes.

Concrete block
See *concrete masonry units (CMU)*.

Concrete brick
A solid concrete masonry unit of the same size and proportions as a modular clay brick.

Concrete cylinder test
A compression test on concrete. Wet (fresh from the delivery truck) samples of concrete are carefully placed in specially made cylinders, 6 in. in diameter and 12 in. high; cylinders are filled one-third full, and concrete is compacted by rodding, 25 strokes, with a bar; this repeated at two-thirds full and full. Two or more such cylinders are prepared i this manner; some to be tested 7 days after preparation, and the rest at 28 days after preparation. They are stripped of the cylinder shells and lab tested by being placed in a hydraulic press that measures the pressure required to crush the cylinders; the result is the "compressive strength" of the concrete.

Concrete masonry unit (CMU)
Units of hardened concrete formed to varying profiles, sizes, and strengths; some solid, others with hollow cores (voids); designed to be laid in same manner as brick or stone to form walls, partitions, etc.

Concrete slump test
A test to determine the plasticity of concrete. A sample of fresh concrete is placed in a con-shaped container, 12 in. high. concrete is compacted with 25 rod strokes at one-third, two-thirds, and completely full. The container is then slowly lifted; the concrete will "slump" as the form is removed. The flattened concrete is then measured to ascertain how much lower than the

12 in. original height remains, i.e., how much the concrete has slumped down from the 12 in. cylinder height. This slump will be specified, and the actual test results note the acceptability of the concrete (for use in a project). This test is completely site-accomplished. Usually a slump of 3 to 5 is required or acceptable; it varies as required to meet the various job conditions.

Conditions and restrictions
The term used to designate any condition(s) applicable to the use of land, where structures may not be placed, etc., and the penalties for failure to comply.

Conduit, electrical
A pipe, usually metal or plastic, in which wire is installed for electrical service.

Continuous ridge vent
A screened, water-shielded ventilation opening and cap strip that runs continuously along the ridge of a gable roof to provide ventilation to the attic space.

Contour line(s)
Lines on a site plan or topographic map that connect points of like (same) grade elevation above/below sea level or other datum point(s).

Control joint
An intentional, linear discontinuity in a structure or component, designed to form a plane of weakness where cracking can occur in response to various forces, so as to minimize or eliminate cracking elsewhere in the structure.

Contract
In construction, an agreement between two or more parties for the pursuit of work on a building or construction project; one part to perform the work, the other to pay for the work; used separately for both design work and the actual construction work.

Contractor
A person or company, which is party to a contract, that agrees to construct a building for a specified amount of money; also see *subcontractor*.

Convector
A heat exchange device that uses the heat in steam, hot water, or an electric resistance element to warm the air in a room; often called, inaccurately, a *radiator*.

Cooling tower
Roof- or ground-mounted unit through which heated water from healing, ventilation, and air-conditioning (HVAC) systems are routed for cooling purposes; usually a louvered or coiled unit of wood or metal construction.

Cope
In steel construction, to cut and remove a flange section in order to avoid interference with other members; in carpentry, to cut a piece of molding to fit the profile of another piece joining it at 90 degrees.

Coping
A cap or top covering of a masonry or other wall to close off the wall from moisture, etc; can be stone, brick, concrete, precast concrete, or formed metal.

Corbel
A decorative, stepped projection of masonry from the face of a wall; or a projecting bracket used to support weight from above; transition from a wall of one size to another.

Corner bead
A metal strip (angle) used to form, reinforce, and protect plaster or drywall corners.

Cornice
The molded projection of the roof overhang at the top of a wall; not in common use.

Corner brace
Diagonal brace at the corners of frame structures to stiffen and strengthen the wall and combat wracking.

Corrugated
Formed into a fluted, rippled, or ribbed profile.

Counterflashing
A flashing turned down from above to overlap another flashing (base flashing) turned up from below, so as to shed water and prevent leakage.

Course
A single continuous row of brick or stone.

Court
An open area surrounded partially by a building and/or walls (see *atrium*).

Cove base
A flexible strip of plastic, vinyl, or synthetic rubber used to finish the junction between resilient flooring and a wall.

Cove molding
A concave molding usually used on horizontal inside corners; also a rounded inside corner.

Cramp
Iron rod with ends bent at right angles; used to hold blocks of stone together or to attach them to backup material.

Crawl space
A space beneath a house or structure that lacks a basement, which allows access to utilities; may also refer to the space in an attic that is too low to walk in, but high enough to crawl through or store in.

Cricket
Small roof structure, single- or double-sloped, used to divert drainage around an obstruction (pipe or other vertical penetration) and toward a drain or downspout; see *saddle*.

Cripple
Structural members cut less than full length, such as a stud piece above or below a window or door opening.

Crown molding
Decorative molding used a the top of cabinets, at ceiling corners, and under a roof overhang soffit.

Cubic foot
Measure of volume that has three 12 in. dimensions—width, height, and depth; contains 1,728 cu in. (12″ × 12″ × 12″).

Cubic yard
Measure of volume that is 3 ft on each side—width, depth, and height; contains 27 cu ft (3′ × 3′ × 3′).

Cul-de-sac
A street or court with no outlet, but providing a circular turnaround for vehicles.

Cull
Building material (especially boards or brick) that is rejected because of mars, imperfections, defects, or below usable grade standards; also portions of brick broken or cut off from full unit (unusable salvage>

Cup
A curl in the cross section of a board or timber, caused by unequal shrinkage or expansion between one side and the other.

Cupola
Small, decorative structure built on a roof of a house; often placed over an attached garage; may be utilized for outside air intake for ventilation purposes.

Curb
Linear edging, raised or partially concealed around paved areas, at walks, around other areas; also a raised box installed around roof openings for passage of equipment, piping, devices, and the watertight mounting of same.

Curing
The slow chemical process that takes place in concrete after it is placed and as it attains its load-bearing strength over a period of time.

Curing compound
Liquid that when sprayed on the surface of newly placed concrete, forms a water-resistant layer to prevent premature dehydration of the concrete (which is detrimental to proper curing and strengthening).

Curtain wall
Non-load-bearing wall placed over the structural skeletal frame construction of a building; an exterior "skin" (a relatively thin wall).

Cut stone
Decorative, natural stone of various types, cut to given sizes and shapes (veneers, sills, and copings, for example).

D

Dado joint
Groove cut across the face of a piece of wood stock to receive and conceal the end of another board fitted into it; often used in quality shelf and cabinet construction.

Damper
Movable plate that regulates the draft of air in a stove, fireplace, or furnace.

Damproofing
Layer of impervious material, usually spread or sprayed on walls, to prevent moisture from passing through.

Darby
Stiff straightedge of wood or metal used to level the surface of wet plaster or concrete

Datum (point)
See *bench mark*.

Dead load
Load on a structure imposed by its own weight, i.e., the weight of the materials of which it is built, and other fixed loads.

Dead man
Reinforced concrete anchor set into earth tied to a retaining wall for stability; usually set on an angle to the unit being supported; can be wood.

Decible
Unit used to measure the relative intensity or loudness of sound; higher numbers indicate greater sound.

Deck
Exterior floor, similar to a concrete slab, patio, or porch; usually wood and extending out from building wall; usually slightly elevated above ground surface.

Deed
Legal document indicating that ownership of a parcel of land has been transferred from one party to another; gives legal description of the land and may contain applicable restrictions as to the use of the land (easements, for example).

Defect
In lumber, an irregularity occurring in or on wood that will tend to impair its strength, durability, or utility value.

Deflection
Amount of sag at the center of a horizontal structural member (between supports) when subjected to a load.

Dentil
An ornamental trim of repetitive square, toothlike blocks.

Design
The concept of a project developed to meet stated needs, desires, and goals of a client; drawn showing the plan, elevations, sections, and other features necessary in the construction of a new building. As used by architects, the term *plan* is restricted to the horizontal projection, and *elevation* applies to the vertical (or exterior) views.

Design professional
A person trained, skilled, and engaged in the actual planning, layout, and design of construction projects or parts thereof; usually refers to the registered (licensed) architects and engineers (of various disciplines) engaged on a project.

Detail
A term in architecture/construction applied to drawings of small parts or areas of a project, or special information about same; usually a sectional view of a special feature or intricate construction, drawn at a larger scale.

Diffuser
Grille or other terminal unit on an air duct that dispenses and directs the flow of air into a space; usually ceiling mounted and adjustable; also known as an *anemostat*.

Dimension lumber
Framing lumber that is 2 in. thick and from 4 to 12 in. wide.

Distribution panel
Electrical box that distributes incoming electrical service current into smaller circuits.

Divider strip
Strip of metal or plastic embedded vertically in terrazzo to form control joints and decorative patterns.

Dog-legged stairway
Term applied to stairs consisting of two or more successive flights rising in opposite directions and having level platforms or landings at the turns; a stair that "returns on itself."

Dome
Roof used over an entryway or complete structure in the form of a modified hemisphere.

Door check
Device to retard the movement of a closing door to guard against slamming (or banging), but which also ensures its closing; also called a *closer*.

Door jamb
Two vertical pieces of a door frame (wood or metal) held together by the head (top, horizontal piece) forming the inside lining of a door opening, into which the door itself is set.

Dormer
A rooftop projection built out from and above a sloping roof to provide greater headroom inside.

Double glazing
A sealed glass unit of two or more panes of glass, with air space between panes to provide added insulating value; also called *insulated glass*.

Double header
Two or more structural members joined together

for added strength; also the shorter framing of two members to create an opening in structural framing.

Double-hung window
A window unit having a top and bottom sash, each capable of moving up and down independently, bypassing each other.

Double-strength glass
Glass that is approximately 1/8 in. (3 mm) in thickness.

Double tee
A precast concrete member/element that resembles the letters TT in cross section; flat slab structural member with two vertical fins or webs.

Dowel
A pin that fits into a hole in an abutting piece and prevents slipping; in concrete, a re-bar projecting from a member that allows installation of additional re-bars contained within another member yet to be installed; also a *wood peg* or *stick*.

Downspout
A tube or pipe of plastic or sheet metal for carrying rainwater from a roof gutter to the ground or to a sewer connection; also called a *leader*.

Drainage
Flow or removal of water.

Dressed size
The actual size of lumber after machining and surfacing for construction use.

Drip
A projecting construction member, or groove in the underside of a member, to throw off rainwater.

"Dry" system
System of construction that uses little or no water during construction, as differentiated from systems such as masonry, plastering, and ceramic tile work, which are called "wet"; also fire protection (sprinkler) system where no water is stored in the distribution piping.

Drywall construction
Interior wall construction other than plaster; usually referred to as *gypsum board, wall board,* or *plasterboard*; sheets of material are applied to a stud framework.

Dry well
A pit located in porous ground, walled up with rock, that allows water to seep through; used for disposal of rainwater or the effluent from a septic tank.

Duct
In a building, usually round or rectangular metal pipe for distributing warm or conditioned air from the air-handling unit to the various rooms; may also be made of composition materials.

Duplex outlet
Electrical wall or floor outlet having two receptacles.

Dwarf wall/partition
A low, part-high (less than full height) wall built to retain an excavation or embankment.

DWV
Drain-waste-vent pipes; part of plumbing system of a building that removes liquid wastes and conducts them to a sewer or sewage disposal system.

E

Earth-sheltered dwelling (building)
A structure that is totally or partially underground; uses soil coverings to reduce heat loss (or gain).

Easement
An area of property where rights are given to (or taken from) another for the purpose of placing power lines, drains, sewers, access drives, and other specific uses; can be private, but usually are taken by government or utility functions; building of structures usually is prohibited in these areas.

Eaves
The projecting lower edges of a roof overhanging the walls of a building.

Edge bead
A strip of metal or plastic used to make a neat, durable edge where plaster or gypsum board abuts another material.

Efflorescence
Undesirable chalky white stains on masonry walls created by moisture from within.

EIFS (exterior insulation finish system)
A material, usually a polymer, used as an exterior finishing material applied over insulation foam; stucco-like coating in several colors that conforms to any profile cut and constructed in the foam backing; adds thermal performance and decreases air infiltration.

Elastomeric/plastomeric membrane
A rubberlike sheet material used as a roof covering.

Elevation
In surveying measurements, the height of a point above sea level or some other datum point. Used in drafting a drawing or orthographic view of the vertical sides or walls of a building, interior or exterior.

Ell
An extension or wing of building at right angles to the main section.

Encase
To fully enclose, such as totally covering an underground electrical conduit with concrete—top, bottom, and sides.

End bearing pile
Pile acting like a column; the point has a solid bearing in rock or other dense material.

End-match
To tongue and groove the ends of hardwood flooring so that the joints fit tightly; end-matched flooring must be laid in one direction, so end joins match as the floor is laid.

End nail
Nailing through the face of one piece of material into the end of another, as in lumber framing, nailing plates to studs.

Engineer
Person trained, skilled, and registered to practice in any of the construction engineering fields,such as civil, electrical, plumbing, fire suppression, HVAC, etc.

Engineered fill
Earth compacted in such a way that it has predictable physical properties, based on laboratory tests and specified, supervised installation procedures.

English bond
Pattern in brickwork consisting of alternate courses of headers and stretchers.

Entasis
Slight convexity of a column, designed to make it appear straight sided and pleasing to the eye.

Entrance (assembly)
Complex of construction, usually involving tubular wall framing (see *storefront construction*), which includes the entrance doors themselves.

EPDM
Ethylene propylene diene monomer, a synthetic rubber material used in roofing membranes.

Erect
To raise, construct a building frame; generally applied to prefabricated materials, such as structural steel, as they are installed on a job site.

Erector
The subcontractor who raises, connects, and accurately sets (plumb and level) a building frame from fabricated steel or precast concrete members.

Erosion control
Temporary, temporarily used, or permanent facilities installed to prevent/minimize erosion during construction; silt fences, straw bale lines, sheet plastic barriers used temporarily; permanent area for temporary storage of water (retention and detention ponds); riprap, swales, drainageways, culvert pipes, etc.

Escutcheon
Door hardware piece that surrounds and accommodates the knob and keyhole.

Excavation
A cavity or pit produced by digging and removing earth in preparation for construction.

Expanded metal lath
A thin sheet of metal that has been slit and stretched to transform it into a metal mesh; used as base for plaster applications.

Expansion bolt
A combination of a bolt and a sleeve used when an ordinary bolt is unsuitable. The sleeve is inserted into predrilled hole, the bolt is then inserted and turned to expand a V-shaped piece into the sleeve and forces the sleeve to become wider at the bottom; it is tightened until the assembly firmly anchored in the material.

Expansion joint
Joint in walls, floors, or other surfaces to permit and take up expansion caused by temperature changes without damage to surrounding surfaces. All materials expand in warm/hot weather and contract in cold; an expansion joint is provided for the resultant cracking at the joint where it is not noticeable and will cause the least damage.

Expansion shield

Any of several types of inserts placed in a wall material to receive fasteners; i.e., a screw can be turned into this insert, which expands it and creates a tight load-carrying attachment; used in wood, glass, masonry, plaster, drywall, tile, brick, concrete, metal, and other materials; can be made of tough jute fiber compressed into tubular form, lead, or plastic, with varying sizes, lengths, and configurations.

Exposed aggregate finish

Concrete surface in which the top of the aggregate (usually "pea gravel") is exposed; can be used in walks or wall panels.

Exposed grid

A framework for an acoustical ceiling system that is visible from below after the ceiling panel installation is complete.

Extrusion

The process of squeezing a material through a shaped orifice (a die) to produce a linear element with the desired cross-sectional profile; an element produced by this process.

Eyebrow

A dormerlike structure attached to a roof, usually at or near the overhang, for venting or decorative purpose.

F

Fabricator

Company that prepares materials or members (such as structural steel) for erection and installation to specific project conditions by cutting, fitting, punching, coping, and otherwise making ready to specific installations.

Facade

The face or front elevation of a building

Face brick

Brick of higher quality, made specifically for exposure to weather; usually hard-burned and frost-proof.

Face nailing

Nailing whereby a nail is driven through the side of one member into the side of another.

Facing

Any material attached to the outer portion of a wall and used as a finished surface.

Factor of safety

Ratio of the ultimate strength of a material to the maximum permissible stress in use; unused capacity ranges from two to five times that required.

Falsework

Temporary work that does not form a part of the final structure; concrete formwork and scaffolding, for example.

Fascia

The horizontal member on the edge of a roof or overhang; closes off ends of rafters/trusses and is backing for gutter.

Fasteners

General term for metal devices, such as nails, bolts, screws, etc., used to secure materials and members within a building.

Felt

A clothlike building paper made from matting wool fibers, hair, and recycled paper together by rolling and pressing; usually asphalt-impregnated for roofing and other water-resistant construction.

Fenestration

Arrangement, pattern, and sizing of doors and windows in a building.

Fiberboard

A building board made from fibrous material and used as an insulation board.

Fiberglass

Glass spun into fine threads and made into batting, which us used as an insulation material; can also be pressed into rigid board insulation; can be used for forms for, and fashioned into, intricate shapes.

Fill

Clean sand, gravel, or loose earth used to bring a subgrade up to desired level around a building, in a trench, etc.

Fillet

A narrow concave strip connecting two surfaces meeting at an angle; adds strength and beauty of design by avoiding sharp angles.

Fillet weld

A weld at the inside intersection of two metal surfaces that meet at right angles.

Finger joint

A glued end connection between two pieces of wood, using an interlocking pattern of deeply cut prongs or "fingers"; creates a large surface for glue bond to allow full development of tensile strength in the wood connected.

Finial

A slender (usually pointed) ornament at the top of a roof or spire.

Finish carpentry

Carpentry work that be exposed to view in the final project; casing of openings, running trim (base, chair rail, crown molds, etc.) bookshelves, paneling, and so forth (see *rough hardware* for contrast).

Finish floor (covering)

The floor material exposed to view as differentiated from the subfloor, which is the load-bearing floor material beneath.

Finish hardware

Devices and features of door hardware; in particular, knobs, rosettes, escutcheons, push/pull plates, closers, hinges, etc., which are exposed and have decorative finishes (see *rough hardware* for contrast).

Finish lumber

Good-quality lumber used to form surfaces that will be finished (often in natural finish) and exposed to view.

Finish plaster

Final or white coat of plaster.

Firebrick

A refractory brick that is especially hard and heat-resistant; for use i fireplace fire boxes and as smokestack linings.

Fire clay

A refractory mortar used to lay firebrick in the base and walls of a firebox.

Fire cut

An angled cut made on the end of a joist or wood beam (inserted into a masonry wall) to permit the member to rotate and drop away if burned through.

Fire Protection System

An interconnected system of devices, and equipment installed throughout a structure (for in specific hazardous areas) to detect a fire, activate an alarm, suppress or control a fire, or any combination thereof; fire alarm systems, sprinkler systems, and smoke detectors are examples.

Fireproofing

Material to protect portions of buildings, primarily structural members, against fire; can be stiff material (brick, concrete, tile, gypsum) or flexible (spray-on, wraps, paints).

Fire-rated doors

Doors designed to resist the passage of fire from one side to the other; constructed to match those tested in standard fire tests and subsequently awarded an hourly rating and label.

Fire rating

The comparative resistance of a material to failure, as stated in hours, when subjected to fire testing; ratings are standardized by fire underwriters (the Underwriters' Laboratories/UL, for example), who publish full data on tests, results, and material performance.

Fire-resistant

Incombustible; slow to be damaged by fire; forming a barrier to the passage of fire.

Fire-retarding material

Any material that will smolder but will not burn rapidly unless subjected to intense heat; insulation board, for example.

Fire-separation wall/partition

Wall required by building codes to separate two areas of a building as a deterrent to the spread of fire.

Fire-stop

Any material, even wood, placed to prevent the rapid spread of fire; used to block the passage of flames or air currents upward, or across and in concealed building part; includes draft-stops.

Fire-stopping system

Installation of a combination of fire-resistant wraps, packing, and sealants in holes around piping, etc., in walls and floors, to preclude the passage of fire and smoke.

Fire wall

Wall designed and constructed to remain in place, despite collapse of structure on either or both sides of the wall, to resist the spread and passage of fire from one portion of a building to another for an extended period of time (up to 4 hours).

Fixed window
Unit of glass mounted in an inoperable frame, mounted in a wall opening.

Fixture
One of many types of electrical and plumbing equipment (a bathtub, for example).

Flagstone
Flat, natural stone used for floors, steps walks, and walls.

Flame-spread rating
A measure of the rapidity with which fire will spread across the surface of a material, as determined by ASTM Test E84.

Flange
Horizontal bottom and top portions of an I-beam, wide-flange beam, or channel member.

Flashing
Sheet metal, or rubberized plastic material, used for making joints, openings, and connections in roofs and walls watertight; used in roof valleys, at dormers, chimneys, and other vertical penetrations through roofs; also at window and door openings; usually covered, at least in part, by finished material such as siding or roofing so that water is directed away from the areas in which leaks could occur.

Flat-slab construction
Type of reinforced concrete floor/roof construction having no beams, girders, or joists below the underside; requires thick slabs, moderate spans, and special reinforcement at columns.

Flemish bond
Pattern of bonding in brickwork consisting of alternate headers and stretchers in the same course.

Flitch beam
Built-up beam formed by a vertical steel plate sandwiched between two wood members and bolted together for additional strength.

Float
To bring concrete to a proper level before it starts to cure; utilized a trowel (called a "float") that has slightly rough surface.

Floor plan
Horizontal section view, "cut through" a proposed building/structure, approximately 4 ft above floor lines, and showing all features, layout, and details of the design and construction; most important source of information for other contract documents.

Flue
Space or passage in a chimney through which smoke, gasses, and fumes ascent; each fuel-burning appliance requires its own flue.

Flue lining
Special refractory clay or terra-cotta pipe, round or square, usually made in all ordinary flue sizes and in 3 ft lengths; used for inner lining of chimneys with brick or masonry work surrounding; runs from above the smoke chamber to several inches above the top of the chimney.

Fluid-applied roof membrane
A roof membrane applied in one or more coats of a liquified mastic material that cures to form a continuous impervious sheet.

Flush door
A door with two flat faces (no panels), resembling a slab can have a hollow or solid core; can have glass or louvered openings; can be fire-rated.

Foil-backed gypsum board
Gypsum wallboard with thin aluminum foil laminated to its back (unexposed) side as a vapor retarder and thermal insulator.

Folded plate
Roof structure whose strength and stiffness are derived from pleated or folded geometry.

Footing
Lowest part of a structure, generally of reinforced concrete; spread out flat to distribute the imposed load of the wall, column, grade beam, chimney, foundation wall, or other feature it supports, over a sufficient area of earth to provide stability.

Footing drain
System of clay tile or plastic piping circling building footings to carry underground water away from structure; 4 in. diameter.

Form
Temporary framing, basically, a "mold" into which concrete is placed; built of wood, plywood, or metal for holding and shaping concrete.

Form tie
Mesh, strap, or heavy wire/rod used to hold wall-forms in place, but of proper length to provide

specified width; spaced at intervals over the entire area of forms, as necessary.

Formwork
Temporary framework of wood, steel, or plastic that serves to give shape to cast-in-place concrete and to support it and keep it moist as it cures.

Foundation
Lowest portion of a structure, fully or partially below grade; substructure of building, consisting of a foundation system (walls, grade beams, etc.) and supports (caissons, footings, etc.).

Foundation bed
The layer of soil on which a building foundation and footings rest; solid rock is the best and strongest bed, but other types of soil, with sufficient bearing capacity, can be used to support structures of various sizes.

Framing
Process of putting the skeletal part (beams, columns, studs, etc.) of a building together; rough lumber, steel, or concrete frame including floors, roofs, and partitions; in light wood framing there are "platform" and "balloon" system.

Framing anchors
Sheet metal devices, of varied configuration, to connect various framing members to each other by nailing; hangers, straps, caps, bases, slings, etc.

French door
A symmetrical pair of doors with full glass panels, usually with small panes; side-hinged and decorative for residential use mainly.

Frost line
Depth to which frost penetrates the earth's surface; varies across different localities in the country and is usually denoted in building codes; building footings should be placed below this line, per code, to prevent upheaval.

Fuel-contributed rating
Measure of the extent to which a building material will add energy to a fire.

Furnish
Means to "supply, and deliver to the job site, ready for unloading, unpacking, assembly, installation, and similar operations" (see *Install* and *Provide*).

Furring
Narrow strips of wood or other material (metal channels) attached to a surface to provide a level and plumb plane for attachment of finish wall or ceiling materials; provides some added insulation space.

Furring channel
Light-gauge steel member in channel shape used in furring or for runners at top and bottom of light partitions, particularly plaster; can also be used for ceiling support.

Fuse
Soft metal link inserted in an electrical circuit; metal strip melts when overloading occurs, cutting off flow of electricity.

G

Gable
End wall of a building where the roof slopes on only two sides; a gable is that triangular part of the wall between the eaves and the ridge.

Galvanized iron
Sheet iron (steel) that has been dipped into and coated with molten zinc to protect it against rust.

Gambrel roof
Roof with its slope broken by an obtuse angle.

Gasket
Dry, resilient material used to seal a joint between two rigid assemblies/materials by being compressed between them; also heavy formed strips into which glass can be inserted and then installed in a frame.

Gauge
A uniform standard of measure for wire diameters and thicknesses of sheet metal, plates, etc.; also a measure of other materials in regard to spacing or thickness (see p. 234).

General contractor
A contractor who has responsibility for the overall conduct of the construction project, and control over the actual work and the subcontractors doing such work.

Geo-textile
Various mesh pads or stripping, made of interwoven plastic fibers, used to hold an earth covering (finish grading or open soil) to prevent erosion and denuding of the surface; aids establishment of ground covers and stability of slopes.

Girder
The larger of the principal structural members

of wood, steel, or concrete used to support concentrated loads at isolated points along its length, e.g., at the bearing points of a series of supported beams.

Girt(s)
Horizontal struts that run between structural members to brace the structure; also provide for attachment of siding and other features to the building frame.

Glass block
Hollow masonry unit made of glass; usually square, made of diffused or molded glass; translucent.

Glass fiber batt
Thick, fluffy, nonwoven insulating blanket of filaments spun from glass.

Glass mullion system
Method of constructing large glazed areas by stiffening the sheets of glass with perpendicular glass ribs.

Glazing
Placing glass or other such materials into windows and doors, or in tubular grid systems.

Glazing compound(s)
Mastics of various formulations used to bed small lights of glass in their frames; a variation of sealants.

Glue-laminated (glu-lam) timber
Timbers and rigid frames (arches) built up from a large number of small strips (laminations) of wood, glued together; used where solid wood timbers are not available for the loads and spans involved.

Government anchor
A V-shaped anchor, usually a 1/2 in. round bar, used to secure steel beams and joists to the masonry wall that supports them.

Grade
(1) Construction/building trade term used in referring to the ground level around a building; (2) lumber term to denote the quality and classification of the pieces related to their adaptability for different uses; (3) the slope or gradient of a roof, piece of land, ramp, etc.

Grade beam
Concrete foundation (wall) formed into a beam configuration (by pattern of reinforcement), which spans across isolated footings, piles, or caissons spaced at intervals; used where soil bearing pressure is inadequate for continuous support.

Grade wood
Designation given to indicate quality of manufactured lumber.

Gradient
Inclination or slope of a road, piping, ramp, ground level, etc.

Grain
In wood, the direction of the longitudinal axes of wood fibers, or the figure formed by the fibers.

Granite
Igneous rock with visible crystals of quartz and feldspar.

Gravel stop
Metal (usually) strip or piece formed with a vertical lip used to retain the gravel on a roof surface around the edge of a built-up roof; can be enlarged to act as the fascia also.

Green gauge
(1) Portion of shingle that is exposed; (2) unit of measure (wire, sheet metal); (3) instrument used for measuring, as a carpenter's gauge used to strike a line the parallel to a board's edge.

Grillage
Steel grid in foundations designated to spread a concentrated load over a wider area; generally enclosed in concrete.

Grille
Open mesh of bars or rods of metal (rolling, coiling, or sliding), which acts as a security screen by closing openings, e.g., front opening of shopping mall rental spaces; also terminus trim on air ducts for decorative and operational purposes (see *register*).

Ground-faced concrete masonry units (GFCMU)
Special CMUs made with variegated natural aggregates and with the faces ground to expose this aggregate; subsequently coated with an acrylic to accentuate the aggregate and seal the facing; ASTM units, sizes same as other CMUs, plus special shapes as required.

Ground fault circuit interrupter (GFCI)
An electrical device that detects current leaks in a circuit (current to load does not equal back

from load) and shuts off power to that circuit; usually used in areas that can be wet or moist (countertops, etc.).

Grounds
Narrow strips of wood nailed to walls as guides for plastering, and as a nailing base for interior trim.

Grout
A thin cement mortar used for leveling bearing plates and filling masonry cavities; usually a non-shrinking type is preferred.

Gunnable sealant
A sealant material of any formulation that is extruded in thickened liquid or mastic form under pressure from a caulking gun.

Gusset plate
Plywood or metal plate used to overlay adjacent/intersecting members in a truss joint to connect and strengthen the joint; plate is nailed in place.

Gutter
A U-shaped trough, along the roofline of a building of metal or plastic to receive and carry off various types of drainage, usually nonsanitary; flat areas adjacent to street curb for drainage.

Gypsum backing board
Board specifically manufactured to be located behind finish gypsum board i a multilayer drywall installation; can be water-resistant for backing of ceramic tile installations; also called *W/R, backer,* or *"green" board.*

Gypsum board
Sheet material having a gypsum core laminated between layers of heavy paper (exposed face is manila in color; the back-face is gray); also called *drywall* and *plasterboard.*

H

Half-lap joint
Joint formed by cutting away half the thickness of wood pieces and then overlapping them.

Hanger
Wire, rod, or bar (or other shape required for loading) suspended from roof or other structural members used to support and carry piping, balconies, runaways, etc.; stirrup like drop support attached to wall to carry ends of beam.

Hardboard
Sheet material composed of bonded wood fibers pressed together.

Hardware
A wide variety of items, in both rough and finished form, that provide various functions such as attachment, operation, etc.; see *rough hardware* and *finish hardware* for further distinctions.

Hardwood
Wood cut from broad-leaved trees or trees that lose their leaves annually; examples include oak, maple walnut, and birch; utilized in a number of construction and architectural items, primarily as finish carpentry.

H beam
Another name or designation for steel beam shapes; most often refers to an I beam used as column—"H column"; see *I beam* and *wide-flange section.*

Head
The top of a frame at a door, window, or other opening; also a standing depth of water that exerts downward pressure.

Header
(1) Doubled members installed perpendicular to trimmer joists on each end of openings for stairs, chimneys, or other features, for attachment of joists cut short to allow the opening; also wood lintels; (2) in masonry, units laid on a large flat face with small end exposed.

Heading bond
Pattern of brick bonding formed with headers.

Headroom
Vertical clear space in a doorway, or in the height between a stair tread and the ceiling overhead.

Hearth
The incombustible floor or covering extension in front of and in a fireplace (actual floor of firebox); can be brick, stone, or tile.

Heat pump
All electric heating and cooling unit that takes heat from outside air, or groundwater for heating, and reverses for cooling.

High chair
A heavy wire device for the support of reinforcing bar(s) to ensure proper placement and cover.

High-range sealant
A sealant capable of a high degree of elongation without rupture, as compared with low and medium-range sealants.

High-tension bolts
Steel bolts designed to be tightened, with calibrated wrenches, to high tensile strength; used as a substitute for conventional rivets in steel frame construction.

Hip rafter
Diagonal member, in roof framing, that extends from the corner of the wall top plate to the ridge, forming the hip.

Hip roof
Roof that rises by inclined planes from all four sides of a building.

Hod
Three-sided container, supported on a long handle, used to carry brick and mortar to the immediate work area (from storage or preparation areas on a site).

Hollow concrete masonry units
Concrete masonry units (CMUs) manufactured with open cores; ordinary concrete block units of various sizes.

Hollow core door
Door consisting of two wood veneer panels separated by a lightweight core (grid, egg crate, strips) installed to reinforce and stabilize the faces; solid wood framing members for stiles and rails.

Honeycomb
Rough surface in concrete that shows hollow spaces between gravel pieces; looks like popcorn; caused by dry, stiff concrete (insufficient water), not well mixed and/or consolidated (vibrated).

Hopper window
Window with sash pivoted along the sill; opens by tilting the top inward.

Hose bibb
A water faucet made for the threaded attachment of a hose; exterior bibbs should be frostproof.

House drain
Horizontal sewer piping within a building, which receives waste from the soil stacks and conveys it to the house sewer.

House sewer
Watertight soil/waste pipe extending from the exterior of the foundation wall (and connected to the house drain) to a public sewer or private disposal system.

I

I Beam
rolled structural steel section with a cross section resembling the letter "I"; (often called an "H-beam" when used as a column); usually higher than it is wide; can be made of wood in similar profile; used for larger spans across openings, etc.

Ice dams
Obstructions along the eave of a roof caused by the refreezing of water emanating from melting snow on the roof surface above.

Impact Insulation Class (IIC)
An index of the extent to which a floor assembly transmits impact noise from a room above to the room below.

Improvements
Changes and additions to a property that tend to increase its value; buildings, utilities, streets, etc.

Incombustible material
Material of various formulations that will not ignite or actively support combustion in a surrounding temperature of 1200°F during exposure of 5 minutes; will not melt when temperature is maintained at 900°F for at least 5 minutes.

Insert
Metal device around which concrete is poured; the exposed face creates an opening or anchor for bolts, fasteners, anchors, etc., which are then firmly held in place by the concrete.

Install
Usually means on-site operations of "unloading, unpacking, assembly, erection, placing, anchoring, applying, working to dimension, connecting, testing, finishing, curing, protecting, cleaning, and similar activities for proper and complete use/operation of area, equipment, appliance, or item.

Insulating board
Material, in board form of various sizes and thicknesses, for insulating purposes; usually manufactured from vegetable fibers or synthetic chemi-

cals, and pressed or caused to "foam" into a finished profile.

Insulating concrete
Concrete with vermiculite added to produce lightweight concrete with insulating properties; used for subfloor and roof fills.

Insulating glass
Multiple panes of glass, separated by air spaces (for insulation purposes) and sealed in a single frame/unit.

Insulation
A variety of materials designed and manufactured for protection from heat or cold, protection against fire, or reduction of sound transmission; usually paper, composition board, fiberglass, wools, foam products are good insulators (poor conductors).

Interior finish
Term applied to the total effect produced by the inside finishing of a building; includes not only the material used, but the means of their installation and decoration.

Interior trim
General term for all finish moldings, casings, baseboards, cornices, and other applied running and isolated trim pieces inside a building; installed by finish carpenters for fine fitting, finishing, and decorative expression.

Intumescent coating
Paint or mastic that expands to form a stable foamlike insulating char when exposed to fire, and acts as an insulating agent (against fire) for surfaces to which it is applied.

Inverted roof
Roof assembly in which a drain line must join a manhole or main for proper slope and drainage; refers to bottom inside edge of the pipe itself; also refers to elevation of bottom of manhole.

Invert elevation
Height at which a drain line must join a manhole or main or proper slope and drainage; refers to bottom inside edge of the pipe itself; also refers to elevation of bottom of manhole.

Isocyanurate foam
Thermosetting plastic foam with insulating qualities.

J

Jack rafter
Short (cut) rafter of which there are three types:

1. Hip jack—fills triangular space in roof between plate and hip rafter.
2. Valley jack—fills triangular space in roof between valley rafter and the ridge.
3. Cripple jack—fills space in roof between hip and valley rafters.

Jalousie
Type of window consisting of a number of along, thin hinged glass panels, which operate in unison—outswinging; can be used in doors or in isolated window units.

Jamb
Lining or frame mounted in a rough opening for installation of a door or window; side of an opening.

Joint
Line, point, or position where two items meet or adjoin each other; in masonry, the layer of mortar between the horizontal courses of units (tooled to raked, flush, weeping, concave, tooled, V, etc. shape).

Jointery
General woodworking term used for better-quality wood joint construction; carefully done carpentry work for tight, sure/proper fit of work to adjacent surfaces.

Joist
Horizontal member used with others as a support for floor, ceiling, or roof; identified by location/placement; usually smaller than a beam, and rests on same; can be wood, steel, or concrete.

Journeyman
Currently, worker or tradesperson who has learned a skilled trade sufficiently well to perform the ordinary work of that trade; in some trades, the highest level of qualification after a period of apprenticeship training.

Junior beam
Smaller, lightweight rolled structural steel section similar to an I beam; used for short spans and light loads, bracing, etc.

K

Keene's cement
White finish plaster that produces a very durable and moisture-resistant surface; used in bathrooms around bathtubs and showers and in areas of high pedestrian traffic wear or abuse; see *veneer plaster* and *gypsum backing board*.

Kerf
Saw cut made in a board; width of the cut is controlled by the set of the saw.

Keyway
Groove formed in the top of a concrete footing to anchor the foundation wall and prevent horizontal displacement; also any such groove in concrete for subsequent concrete placement.

Kicker
Block of wood in concrete formwork used to prevent the side of the form from springing out at the bottom.

Kick plate
A brass, stainless steel, or plastic fastened to the lower portion of a door to protect it from damage.

Kiln dried (KD)
Wood artificially seasoned in an ovenlike chamber, which hastens the drying process; a marking is stamped on such wood to identify it.

King post
Type of truss, with a center vertical member; also that center upright.

Kip
A unit of 1,000 lb used to simplify structural calculations; e.g., a 9,000 lb load is said to be "9 kips" in magnitude.

Knee wall
A low wall, in attic spaces, resulting from 1 1/2 story construction.

Knocked down
Unassembled construction units requiring assembly after being delivered to the job site.

Knot
Defect that can weaken lumber (depending on location and size); in framing members, knot should be turned to the top; large/bad knots are prohibited in scaffolding planks.

Kraft paper
A strong brown paper made of sulfate pulp; used for protection of surfaces, such as floors, and composition material.

L

Lag screw
Large wood screw with hexagonal or square head for turning/tightening with a wrench.

Lally column
A steel pipe column, with or without concrete/sand fill; used for loads up to moderate sizes, including residential floor loads.

Laminate
To form or build up materials from successive overlaying of thin sheets or plates; plywood is a laminated product made by gluing alternate sheets of wood veneer together; also see *plastic laminate*.

Laminated beam
A beam, arch or other member formed by pressure-gluing multiple layers or strips (laminations) together to form the shape and size desired/required; substitute for solid wood members swing to their limited availability (see *glue-laminated*).

Landing
Platform between two flights of stairs where they end or change direction as they run between floors of a building.

Lateral bracing
Diagonal or other bracing in structural systems to counteract wind pressures and other loads and to reduce spans; can be wood, metal, or plywood sheets.

Latex caulk
a low-range sealant formulated of synthetic latex material.

Lath
Material secured to framing on which plaster is applied; can be gypsum lath (solid or perforated) or metal lath, each providing a mechanical or chemical bond for the plaster.

Lattice
Open framework of crossed wood or metal slats; lightweight, usually, but can be heavy where used as bracing in structures.

Leader
Vertical pipe—downspout—that carries rainwater

drainage from a roof gutter to the ground or a storm sewer.

Ledger strip
Small piece of lumber attached to lower side(s) of beams, or girders, where joists can rest and be supported.

Legal description
Written indication of the location and boundaries of a parcel of land; refers generally to the recorded plat or survey in official files; usually includes restrictions (easements) taken by government or utilities.

Let-in braces
Braces, usually diagonal,in wood framing where a bracing member is set into notches cut in the framing members so that the faces of both are flush.

Level
(1) On a perfectly flat, horizontal line or plane; (2) tool used by workers to determine such level plane or line; (3) surveyor's instrument, similar to or a function of a transit, for establishing grade elevations.

Lift
In concrete, the dimension from the top of one "pour" in a form to the top of the next; e.g., "concrete to be placed in 8 in. lifts."

Lift slab
System of construction wherein the various floor slabs are poured at ground level and then subsequently lifted into proper position by hydraulic jacks working simultaneously at each column; cast-in steel collars are welded to steel columns to hold the slabs in place.

Light (Lite)
A pane of glass.

Light steel framing (LSF)
Construction method utilizing light-gauge steel members for the structure.

Lintel
Structural member (wood, steel, concrete, stone, etc.) placed horizontally across the top of an opening to support the wall above.

Live load
All furniture, persons, and other movable loads not included as a permanent part of a structure.

Load-bearing wall
Wall designed to support the weight (load) imposed on it from walls and structural members.

Lobby
An interior entrance area in a commercial building.

Loggia
Roofed, open gallery along the front of side of a building; a porch.

Lookout
Short wood framing members used to support the soffit of an overhanging eave; extends from wall to fascia or bottom edge of roof framing members.

Lot line
Establishable line (with transit) forming the legal boundary of a parcel, tract, or lot of property; also called *property line.*

Louver
Opening or slatted grille that allows ventilation while providing protection from rain, sight, sound, or light.

Low-range sealant
Sealant that is capable of only a slight degree of deformation or elongation prior to rupture.

Luminaire
An electric light fixture.

M

Mansard roof
Roof having two slopes on each of the four sides; top slopes are less steep than the lower.

Mantel
Shelf on the face of a fireplace, above the firebox opening; also, decorative trim around the opening.

Margin (factor) of safety
Comparative value between actual capacity required and that which the member possess; e.g., a beam that is capable of carrying 6,000 lb and is required to carry only 1,000 lb has a 5,000 lb margin of safety (see *factor of safety*).

Masonry
General term applied to construction made of brick, stone, concrete masonry unites, and similar materials; sometimes called "unit masonry."

Masonry cement
Factory-made mixture of portland cement and admixtures specially designed to increase the workability of mortar; usually better than site-mixed cement because of the control available at a plant.

Masonry unit
A brick, stone, or concrete masonry unit, glass block, or hollow clay tile intended to be laid in courses and embedded in mortar.

Masonry veneer
A single-wythe, non-load-bearing facing installed over a structural frame; e.g., brick veneer applied to a wood frame house.

Mastic
A thick, paste like adhesive or other coating material used for attachment, dampproofing, etc.

Mat foundation
Continuous monolithic reinforced concrete foundation constructed under an entire building as a unit; also called "raft" or "floating" foundation.

Matte finish
A muted finish with no gloss or highlights.

Medium-range sealant
A sealant material capable of a moderate degree of elongation before rupture.

Meeting rail
Wood or metal window frame member along which one operable sash seals against another.

Member
Individual element of a structure, such as a beam, girder, column, joist, piece of decking, stud, truss chord, brace, etc.

Membrane
Sheet or mastic material that is impervious to water and water vapor.

Membrane waterproofing
Tough fabric, sheet, or mastic material (seamless) that is made waterproof by saturating with liquid asphalt, or when applied and spread in a monolithic manner.

Metal lath
Steel mesh created by slitting sheet steel and pulling it out until it forms a grid or mesh; used primarily for, and provides an excellent plaster base owing to the mechanical "keying" of plaster around mesh wires.

Metal wall ties
Strips of corrugated sheet metal (galvanized) used to anchor (tie) brick veneer construction to the structural frame behind.

Mil
Unit of measure (thickness) for very thin sheets; one thousandth part of an inch (.001 in.).

Millwork
General term for interior woodwork and trim that is machined to profile, size, and finish; usually does not include flooring, ceiling, or siding materials; finished carpentry work, as opposed to rough carpentry (framing).

Mineral wool
Type of batt insulation consisting of many fine threads of a wood by-product; also used for fireproofing and acoustical treatment.

Miscellaneous iron work
All iron and steel members that cannot be classified as ornamental or structural; includes loose lintels, bucks, etc.

Miter joint
Joint made by closely fitting two pieces of material that have ends or edges cut to a 45-degree angle.

Modular housing
Buildings (ranging from small structures up to houses) fully constructed, built, and assembled in a factory and then transported to a site for final attachment and connections.

Modular measure
System of measurement designed to fit parts together on a grid of a standard 4 in. module.

Module
(1) A unit of measure established as 4 in.; (2) complete part of assembly for a building, such as a bathroom or kitchen, fitted and completed in a factory.

Moisture barrier
Material, plastic or specially treated paper, that retards the passage of moisture and vapor into walls and prevents condensation; see *vapor barrier*.

Molding
Single strip/piece, or series of pieces of material, cut, shaped, and finished to serve as an ornament; can be made of various materials—wood, stone, fiberglass, plaster, etc.

Monolithic
Term used for concrete and other materials placed or installed without joints; as one piece or a unit.

Mortar
A mixture of masonry cement, sand, and water used by masons as the bonding agent between masonry units; the "joint material" in masonry.

Mosaic
Small colored tile, glass, stone, or similar material, regular or irregular in shape, arranged to produce a decorative surface; used on walls or floors.

Mudsill
Lowest sill of a structure, as a foundation member placed directly on the ground or foundation.

Mullion
Structural member between window units placed in a continuous pattern.

Muntin
Small framing member separating and retaining the glass lights in a window or door; may be a removable grid installed over a single pane of glass.

N

Nail-base sheathing
Sheathing material, such as wood boards, panels, or plywood, to which siding can be attached by nailing; such nailing is not permitted by fiberboard or plastic foam materials used as sheathing (primarily for better insulation).

Nailer
Wood member, shaped to fit, in any of several places used to provide a nailing base for other members or materials; called *blocking* in some locations.

Nail popping
Loosening of nails in drywall work; shrinkage of wood studs tends to expel the nails, which then appear on the surface of the board.

Nail set
Hardened steel punch used to drive a nail head below the surface of the wood, for filling and finishing.

Needle beam
Steel or wood beam used for needling operation.

Needling
Series of steel or wood beams threaded through a bearing wall to support it while its foundation is underpinned.

Newel
Vertical terminal post at ends, angles, or turns in handrails and guardrails.

Nominal size
Size of material before final working and dressing; not the actual size; e.g., a 2×4 (nominal) is $1\frac{1}{2}$ in. $\times 3\frac{1}{2}$ in. (actual).

Nonbearing partition/wall
Term used for space-dividing partitions or other walls that carry no imposed floor or roof load.

Nonferrous metal
Metal containing no iron; copper, brass or aluminum, for example.

Nosing
Portion/edge of stair tread that projects beyond the riser below it; any other similar projection.

Notch
A three-sided slot, groove, or opening cut into a piece of material, usually along an edge.

O

Oculus
A circular, or round, window.

Offset line
Surveying term; where an actual line cannot be established because of obstructions, a parallel line set away (offset) from the actual is used.

Ogee
An S-shaped curve; usually in trim, gutters, etc.

On-center (O.C.)
Method of indicating spacing of framing members or other items; measurement is from the center of one object to the center of each of those adjacent.

One-way action
Operates in one direction only; in structural terms, action of a concrete slab that spans between two parallel beams or walls.

Open web (steel) joist
Prefabricated, light steel truss like member with a welded lattice like web; closely spaced for moderate spans; also called *bar joist* or *steel lumber*.

Operator
Device for operation of windows, doors, or other such equipment; manual crank or motor driven.

Ordinary construction
Building type with exterior masonry bearing walls and an interior structure of wood framing.

Orientation
(1) Direction in which a building or structure faces; (2) relationship to a direction or bench mark/line; (3) relating contact drawings to the actual structural.

Oriented-strand board (OSB)
Building panel composed of long shreds of wood fiber oriented in specific directions and bonded together with an adhesive matrix under pressure.

Outlet
Electrical system device, of various configurations, which allows current to be drawn from the electrical service system and carried to lights, appliances, equipment, etc.

Overhang
Area or portion of upper story, building part, or roof at the eave, that projects beyond the wall below.

Owner furnished/contractor installed (OFCI)
Equipment, material, or other components of a system or building that purchased by the owner, directly, and furnished to the contractor, who receives, stores, protects, installs, connects, and tests each such item; this procedure can be modified as necessary.

Oxidation
Corrosion; rust; rusting; creation of a mar or coating on a surface as the result of exposure to air pollution, etc.

P

Pad
Extra concrete slab installed on top of a floor slab as the mounting surface for mechanical or other equipment; adds some strength, but merely provides a better, slightly elevated surface for mounting the unit(s).

Pan construction
Method of forming a ribbed or waffle concrete floor/roof slab; see *pans*.

Panel
(1) A fabricated section of a wall, ceiling framing; (2) a sheet of material; (3) an electrical box device for current distribution, etc.

Panel door
Door constructed with thin panels installed between solid rails and stiles (perimeter frame).

Paneling
Thin sheet material of composite, synthetic, or wood composition that is used as a lining or interior wall finish; can be nailed or glued into place over various subsurfaces.

Panic hardware
Door latching/locking device that releases automatically when pressure is exerted against the bar or paddle mounted on the interior side; required in emergency exits.

Pans
Steel or fiberglass forms for concrete, shaped like inverted two- or four-sided pans; various depths used for forming ribbed or waffle (two-way) concrete floor and/or roof slabs; variation of slab and joist construction.

Parallel strand lumber (PSL)
Wood product made from veneers clipped into 1/2 in. stands, then combined with adhesives and curved under pressure using microwave-generated heat.

Parapet
The portion of a wall that extends above the top of the roof; usually in exterior walls or interior fire walls.

Parging (parge coat)
Thin coat of mortar applied to masonry walls for refinement/finishing of the surface for appearance or dampproofing.

Parquet floor
Usually "wood tiles" composed of strips of wood flooring, laid with grain of strips alternating to form various designs.

Partition
Interior wall, full or part-high for dividing, separating, or screening spaces from one another or for directing traffic.

Party wall
Single wall between and common to two adjoining buildings owned by different owners; also common walls between row houses.

Particle board
Composition board made from wood chips or particles bonded together in an adhesive matrix under pressure.

Passive solar heating
Capturing, storing, and using solar energy/radiation to heat a structure without the use of internal heating devices; can circulate air with fans or pumps for even distribution.

Patio
Paved, open area outside a house; also called a terrace, and can be a structure such as a deck.

Paver
Clay masonry (brick) made specially for finish floor surfaces, walks, drives, terraces, etc.; must be frostproof and serviceable for heavy traffic.

Paving
Concrete or asphaltic material (or composites) used as installed ground cover or as a hard-stand for vehicle access or parking; usually asphaltic concrete (blacktop) or cast-in-place concrete over a compacted gravel fill; can be light-duty or heavy-duty, depending on traffic requirements and construction.

Penetrometer
Device for testing the resistance of a material to penetration; usually used to make a quick, approximate determination of a material's compressive strength (e.g., soil bearing pressure).

Penny
Term used to indicate nail length; still used, but this is an archaic term that once meant the price for 100 nails; e.g., 10 penny nails cost 10 pennies (English) per 100; still indicated by letter "d".

Penthouse
A relatively small structure/enclosure, usually roof mounted, to enclose mechanical and/or elevator equipment without taking up valuable interior floor space.

Perimeter drain
See *footing drain.*

Perlite
Expanded volcanic rock particles used as a lightweight aggregate in concrete and plaster; also used as an insulating fill.

Pier
Vertical structural member, usually of concrete or masonry; also, short foundation columns, between window/door openings, and mass masonry supports such as for bridges, gates, and girders.

Pilaster
Rectangular pier engaged in a wall for the purpose of strengthening it; can also be decorative or act as a beam support (expanded bearing area at the wall).

Pile (piling)
Concrete, wood, or steel member driven into the ground to act as an undergrade column to support a building; used to carry the building load to sufficient bearing soil.

Pitch
Slope of roof or other inclined/sloped surface(s).

Plank
Long, flat wood members 2 in. to 4 in. thick and 6+in. wide.

Plaster
a cementitious material usually applied to gypsum or metal lath or masonry surfaces; formed of a gypsum or portland cement mixture; applied in paste form, which hardens into a hard, smooth surface (or other finish desired).

Plasterboard
See *gypsum board.*

Plaster ground
wood or metal strips placed around the base of and around openings in walls to be plastered; used to obtain a uniformly smooth surface with straight edges; also provided as backing for baseboards and other trim or wall-hung items.

Plastic laminate
Composite material made from compressing Kraft paper into phenolic resin layers to form a decorative material usually has a melamine exposed (decorated) surface; used for covering doors, countertops, wall paneling, cabinets, etc.

Plat
Drawing of a parcel or parcels of land based on and giving its legal description and perhaps other survey data; bay be filed as an official record of the land.

Plate
Horizontal members at top (doubled) and bottom of stud walls (sole plate); also refers to bearing, top, and base plates for structural steel members.

Plate glass
Glass of high optical quality produced by grinding and polishing both faces of the glass sheet; glass with parallel faces and minimal distortion.

Platform framing
System of light-wood framing for housing whereby each story is built on top of the one below, but framed independently (upper story rests on floor decking applied to top of first floor ceiling joists); also called *Western framing*; see and contrast with *balloon framing*.

Plinth block
Small block slightly thicker and wider than the casing of an interior door that is placed at the bottom of the door trim and against which the baseboard is butted.

Plot
Lot, parcel, or other piece of land (real estate) with specific dimensions; potential building/construction site.

Plumb
Absolutely vertical; straight up and down; a plum line is created when a weight (plumb bob) is tied on a cord and held vertically.

Plywood
Wood panel, of many varieties and types, composed of a number of thin veneers bonded together, glued under pressure; normally 4 ft wide by 8 ft, although longer lengths are available; has various face finishes and can be used as a finish or rough material.

Polybutene
A sticky, masticlike tape used to seal nonworking joints, especially between glass and frames or mullions; sealant in tape form.

Polycarbonate
Extremely tough, strong, usually transparent plastic used for window and skylight glazing, light fixture globes, and other applications; also see *acrylic*.

Polyethylene
Thermoplastic widely used in sheet form for vapor retarders, moisture barriers, and temporary construction enclosures.

Polystyrene
Thermoplastic foam with thermal insulating properties; mainly available in board form, with varying thicknesses.

Polyurethane
Large group of resins and synthetic rubber compounds used in sealants, varnishes, insulating foams, and roof membranes.

Polyvinyl chloride (PVC)
Thermoplastic material widely used in construction products, including plumbing pipes, floor tiles, wall coverings, and roofing membranes.

Portland cement
Very fine powderlike gray-colored limestone material (crushed and pulverized) made from burning compounds of lime, silica, and alumina together; is the bonding agent in concrete, grouts, etc.

Post-and-beam construction
Wall and roof construction system using widely spaced posts and beams as the frame; plank decking is applied transversely across the beams for stability and roof structure; a wood version of a rigid frame, in concept.

Potable water
Water of drinkable quality, for use in concrete, mortar, or other construction mixtures; not contaminated in any manner.

Pour
Outdated term, meaning to place concrete, casting concrete in place without interruption; not used today because of negative impression of a thin, watery, inadequate substance.

Powder-driven
Device or equipment driven, attached or inserted by a gunlike tool using energy provided by an exploding charge (blank) of gunpowder; e.g., powder-driven pins to secure sole plates to concrete floors.

Precast
Structural members shaped in a factory, then transported and installed in a building; include concrete joists, beams, tee-slabs, as well as nonstructural terrazzo, stair treads and risers, and miscellaneous trim such as copings, sills, etc.

Precut
Wood stock cut to exact dimensions at a mill, yard, or job site before using/installation; for standardizing building components and minimizing errors.

Prefabricated
Sections or component parts of a building built

in a factory and installed/assembled as a whole on the job site; see *modular housing*.

Pressure-treated lumber
Lumber that has been impregnated with chemicals under pressure for the purpose of retarding rot, decay, vermin infestation, and/or fire.

Prestressed concrete
Concrete produced by a system for utilizing fully the compressive strength of concrete by bonding it with highly stressed (tensile strength) stretched cables, wires, reinforcement.

Prime coat
First coat of paint applied to a material; provides better surface for application of final coats; can also be the "shop coat" applied in the plant, e.g., on structural steel to both protect the material and make other finishing easier.

Professional association society
An organization usually representing a given profession that combines single efforts (by members) into a larger and more extensive voice; presents educational and informational efforts, information and document sales, and other combined services to individual members; somewhat of a lobbying group that acts on behalf of members (see *trade associations*).

Provide
Means to furnish, pay for, and install in completely operational condition; see *furnish* and *install* for clarification.

Purlins
Smaller members of wood or steel that reduce the span between joists or rafters and support the roof decking to prevent sagging; the timbers spanning from truss to truss.

Push/pull hardware
Used in lieu of knob/latch sets; usually involves a pull bar/grip and a flat push plate attached to the door, along with a closer to ensure shutting of the door; used in high-traffic areas, such as rest rooms.

Q

Quarry tile
Unglazed machine-made tile used for floors with sanitary requirements and open to wet conditions; usually red or tan color, 6 in. x 6 in.

Quarter round
Small molding whose profile is a quarter circle.

Quarter sawn
Lumber, usually flooring or veneer, that has been sawn so that the medullary rays showing on the end grain are nearly perpendicular to the face.

Quoins
Large squared stone pieces, or slightly projected panels of brick, set in the corners of masonry walls for decorative purposes.

Queen post
One of two vertical posts in a roof truss.

R

R-value
Indicator of the ability of a material to resist the flow of heat.

Rabbet
Groove cut the surface or on the edge of a board to receive another member.

Raceway
Trays and/or closed channel/boxes, set in floors or routed overhead, to receive, contain, and distribute wiring, cabling.

Radiant heating
Method of heating, usually consisting of a forced hot water system with pipes placed in floor, wall, or ceiling; can also be a system of electrical cables placed in similar positions.

Rafter
A slopped/inclined structural roof member running from a wall to the ridge or top of the roof; designed to support the roof deck, roofing, and other loading; such rafters for a flat roof are called *joists*.

Rake
An incline or slope, as in a pitched roof.

Ramp
A sloped surface for walking or rolling equipment for easier access than stairs; required as access under the ADA regulations for disabled persons; can be utilized with stairs.

Random rubble
Stonework utilizing irregularly shaped units, with no indication of systematic course work.

Raze
To demolish or wreck work, usually to provide place for new construction.

Rc-bars
Contracted term indicating "reinforcing bars" (rods/steel); see *reinforcing steel*.

Receptor
A shallow base or basin used in a shower or as a mob sink; low curb height makes access and use easier (mop sink).

Register
Grille, with or without screening, installed at the open end of a duct that carries warm or cool air; many have adjustable vanes for directing air.

Reglet
A linear groove/recess either formed into a material or an applied trim piece to receive flashing, counterflashing, etc., or for decorative effect.

Reinforced concrete
A composite material in which steel bars are placed in the concrete to reinforce its tensile strength; material bonded together to act in unison with a combined capacity that of either material alone; various design principles utilize varying amounts of reinforcing.

Reinforcing steel (bars)
Steel bars (rods) deformed with projecting ridges to ensure bonding, placed in concrete to add tensile strength; bars are bent or straight, as required, and tied in shapes, grids, or other configurations as required for concrete member; come in various diameters; most are round, but some are square in cross section (also called "re-bars").

Re-shoring
Placing temporary supports under concrete members after the formwork has been removed, to prevent overloading of the members prior to full curing and strength in the members.

Resilient flooring
Manufactured sheet or tile flooring material of asphalt, vinyl, vinyl composition, polyvinyl chloride, rubber, cork, or other similar resilient materials; installed with adhesive.

Retaining wall
A wall that holds back an earth embankment; usually concrete, but can be wood, stone, or masonry.

Return
Change in a direction of a molding, cornice, or other design feature, without breaking the continuity of the profile.

Reveal
Side of an opening for a window or door in a masonry or wood structure; margin to which the casing is set on a jamb for appearance and to accommodate the door hinges.

Ribbon
In balloon framing, a board let-in (placed in a cut-out) the face of the studding (long dimension vertical) to support the joists.

Ridge/ridge board
The top edge of a roof where two slopes meet; also, the horizontal board between, to which opposing rafters are attached, running the length of the roof structure.

Rigid frame
A structural system that utilizes aligned beams and columns, rigidly connected, usually spanning across the entire building.

Riprap
Surfacing of moderate to large random stone/rock that is used to prevent erosion on an embankment; breaks up the flow of a strong, directed stream of water.

Rise
In stairs, the vertical height of a step or a flight of stairs; distance form one floor to the next for stair design is called "total rise"; also vertical height of a roof above the surrounding walls.

Riser
In general, the vertical part of a stair step; in plumbing, a vertical water supply line.

Rod
(1) A reinforcing bar (re-bar); (2) a brightly colored leveling stick that telescopes to greater length by sections and is used for sighting a line or grade elevation with a transit.

Rolled section
A structural steel member, such as an I beam or wide-flange section, that is formed to its final shape by hot rolling at the mill.

Roofing
Short name for roof covering; the material that constitutes the exposed roof surface, such as asphalt shingles, wood shakes, several plies (layers) of roofing felt or tar paper, synthetic membrane, metal, slate, etc.; also see *inverted roof*.

Roof saddle
High point between roof drains; on flat roofs,

added fill is required to create the saddles that direct water to the drains.

Roof sheathing
Boards or sheet material fastened to the roof framing (rafters/trusses, etc.), to which the shingles or other roof covering is attached; also called *roof deck* or *decking*.

Rough carpentry
The work of the carpenter trade that is, for the most part, concealed, such as framing, blocking, etc.; usually involves dimensioned lumber and rough hardware.

Rough hardware
All devices such as nails, screws, bolts, hangers, etc., that aid in the construction of the framing and rough construction of a project; also called *builders' hardware*; see *finish hardware*.

Roughing-in
The erection of the framing of a structure; in plumbing, the installation of the underground lines and all associated plumbing piping, but not the fixtures themselves.

Rough opening
Framing around a window or door opening that has been sized to accept the finished units, with allowances for fitting, shimmying, and leveling.

Rowlock
Method of laying brick on its long side so that the vertical ends appear in the face of the wall; a vertical header.

Run
Horizontal distance of a flight of stairs; also the horizontal distance from the top of a sidewall to the ridge of a roof.

Running bond
Brick bonding pattern consisting entirely of stretchers overlapping by 1/2 brick; i.e., vertical joints centered over the bricks below.

R-value
Measure of resistance to heat flow.

S

Saddle
Two sloping surfaces meeting in a horizontal ridge used behind vertical roof penetrations (chimneys, etc.) through a sloped roof to divert water for proper drainage; also called a *cricket*.

Safing insulation
Fire-resistant material inserted into space between piping, ducts, curtain walls, conduits, beams, columns, walls, floors, etc., where fire might pass through; packing behind fire penetration sealant used to close top of such openings and retard passage of fire and smoke.

Sandwich panel
Panel consisting of two outer faces of wood, metal, or concrete bonded to a core of insulating material.

Sanitary sewer (drain system)
Sewer, piping, and fixtures used to collect and dispose of sanitary waste(s), which includes all drainage other than natural storm (rainwater) drainage; this system should be self-contained and not made to carry other drainage.

Sash
Individual frames around glass in windows; movable part of a window.

Scab
Wood pieces, usually, joining members together; nailed across the joint on the face of the members.

Scale
Use of proportional measurements; i.e., using a small increment of measure to represent 1 ft (usually); also a drafting tool with markings at various intervals to permit measuring using different increments.

Scarfed joint
Wood joint made by mitering adjoining pieces so the ends overlap, which are firmly joined into one continuous piece; used in moldings and railings so that expansion does not produce an open joint.

Screed
Long, straight board or rod used to level concrete within forms; also pegs, stakes or rods installed to level at the top of flat concrete to control its depth and grade level.

Scribbing
Fitting of woodwork or other material to irregular faces of surfaces; fitting of a molding to another molding at an inside corner without a mitered joint.

Scupper
Opening through a wall for drainage of water from a floor or roof into a downspout; requires

careful and extensive flashing for watertight installation.

Scuttle
Opening in a ceiling or roof that provides access to an attic or roof.

Sealant
Thickened liquid or paste substance used to seal cracks, joints, and porous surfaces; must adhere to surrounding material and permit expansion and contraction without rupture; many varieties, chemical compounds, types, colors, and uses involved; may also be in tape or gasket form.

Section
Drawing showing interior features when an imaginary "cut" is made through a building or a portion of a building; both floor plans and details are section drawings, among others.

Segregation
Separation of the materials used for making concrete, caused by excessive handling or vibration (usually gravel will fall to the bottom).

Seismic load
Load on a structure caused by movement of the earth relative to that structure during an earthquake; varies by locale and history of earthquake incidents.

Select lumber
Lumber without knots or other deformities. This is the best lumber. In hardwood the term refers to a specific grade.

Set
The change in concrete and mortar from a plastic (semiliquid) to a solid (hardened) state.

Setback
A required minimum distance from the property line to the line; buildings prohibited in these areas.

Shakes
Hand-cut wood shingles.

Sheathing
The rough covering over the framing of a house; not exposed in complete building.

Sheeting
A stiff material used to retain the soil around an excavation; a material such as polyethylene in the form of very thin, flexible sheets.

Sheet metal
Flat rolled metal less then 1/4 in. (6.35 mm) thickness.

Shim
A thin piece or wedge of material placed between two parts to level a surface or fill a void.

Shiplap
Wood sheathing that is rabbeted so that the edge of the boards overlap and make a flush joint.

Shoe mold
The molding covering the joint between the flooring and the baseboard.

Shop drawings
Detailed plans prepared by a manufacturer or fabricator to guide the shop production of such building components as cut stonework, steel, or precast concrete framing, curtain wall panels, and cabinetwork.

Shore
Temporary vertical support for form work and fresh concrete.

Shoring
The placing of a shore under formwork; also refers to the bracing or sheeting used to hold back an earth bank.

Sidelight
A tall, narrow glazed panel on either or both sides of a door.

Siding
Boards placed over the outside wall of a frame building and nailed to the sheathing. Although wood or plywood is generally used, composition board is also popular. Wood siding is made in several different patterns, as are vinyl and aluminum.

Signage
The entire coordinated system or pattern of signs used on, around, and throughout a building, interrelated and color coded or coordinated.

Silicone
A polymer used for high-range sealants, roof membranes, and masonry water repellant.

Sill
In general, the lowest part of an opening in a wall, such as a door or window sill. In frame construction, the bottom rough structural member that rests on the foundation.

Sisal kraft paper
A paper reinforced with strands of sisal fibers. The strands of sisal are placed between two layers of paper stuck together with a coat of pitch. This paper has many uses in construction because of its toughness and durability.

Site
The area of land that is the location of a building project.

Site-cast concrete
See *cast-in-place concrete.*

Skylight
A window built into a roof or ceiling may be operable or fixed.

Slab
A thick slice of stone or other masonry material; the term is use in referring to a concrete floor; concrete pavements and sidewalks are also concrete slabs.

Slab-on-grade
A concrete surface lying upon, and supported directly by, the ground beneath.

Sleeper
A piece of timber, stone, or steel on or near the ground used to support a superstructure. When a concrete floor is covered by a wood floor, the flooring is nailed to crosspieces called *sleepers.*

Sleeve
A metal or fiber pipe extending through floor slabs and walls to provide an opening for the passage of plumbing and heating pipes to be installed later.

Slope
Ration between the rise and the run of a roof; the amount of incline on any nonlevel surface.

Slurry
A watery mixture of insoluble materials; a very lean concrete mix used as leveling fill.

Smoke chamber
The portion of a chimney flue located directly over the fireplace.

Smoke developed rating
An index of the toxic fumes generated by a material as it burns.

Smoke shelf
The horizontal area behind the damper of fireplace.

Snap tie
A patented wire wall tie for concrete wall forms. It is so made that the end of the wire may be twisted or snapped off after the forms have been removed.

Soffit
A lower horizontal surface such as the underface of eaves, cornices, or beams.

Soffit vent
An opening under the eave of a roof used to allow air to flow into the attic or the space below the roof sheathing.

Softwood
Wood produced from coniferous trees or trees that bear cones. Most commonly used are the pines, but also included are such trees as fir, spruce, redwood, and cedar. The term has no reference to the actual hardness or softness of the wood.

Soil boring
Holes drilled into subsurface soil for the purpose of investigating the load-bearing and stability characteristics of the earth under a building.

Soldier course
Course of brick consisting of brick set on end with the narrow side exposed.

Soleplate
The horizontal member of a frame partition or wall resting on the rough floor to which the studs are nailed.

Solid bridging
A solid member placed between adjacent floor joists near the center of the span to prevent joists from twisting.

Solid core door
A flush door with no internal cavities.

Sound transmission class (STC)
A means of specifying the ability of a material to resist the transmission of sound.

Span
The horizontal distance between supports for joists, beams, trusses, and other structural members.

Spandral
The wall area above a window.

Specifications
The written matter complementing and supplementing building plans; written by the architects and contains information that cannot be shown on the drawings. They also prescribe the materials that are to be used and indicate how they are to be handled and installed.

Spike
A nail more than 6 in. long. It differs from the common nail by having a larger diameter in relation to its length.

Splash block
A small precast block of concrete or plastic used to divert water, at the bottom of a downspout, away from the foundation.

Splice
The joining of two members to form one piece.

Spline
A small piece of corrugated metal or wood used to strengthen wood joints; it is driven into the two pieces of wood at the joint.

Spread footing
A concrete footing larger than the structural member it supports, constructed for the purpose of spreading the load over the bearing soil; used under piers, columns, and foundation walls.

Sprinklers
See *Fire protection systems.*

Square
Designates 100 sq ft and is used as a unit of measurement by roofers. Generally, roof area estimates are expressed in the number of squares of material required for application. Also indicates members set (at 90°) perpendicular.

Staging
Various types, styles, and sizes of scaffolding, "jump-up-boards," and other temporary falsework, used to facilitate and provide access to work and short-term storage of material; used in some cases for bracing, and always for reasons of safety.

Stairwell
A compartment extending vertically through a building, into which stairs are placed.

Staking out
The laying out of a building plan by driving stakes into the ground to show the location of the foundation.

Standing seam
A sheet metal roofing seam that projects at right angles to the plane of the roof.

Steel joist
A light steel truss made from bars, rods, or angles welded into rigid units.

Stile
Vertical framing member of a panel door.

Stirrup
A vertical loop of steel bar used to reinforce a concrete beam against diagonal tension forces.

Stool
The horizontal ledge or strip as part of the frame below an interior window; commonly called *sill.*

Stop
A wood strip used to hold a window place or against which a door closes.

Storefront construction
System of light aluminum tubular sections interconnected to form a network of glass frames, utilizing large glass panels; usually includes the entrance complex and acts as both wall and fenestration.

Storm sewer (drain)
A sewer, pipe, or other feature (natural or manmade) used to carry away surface water but not sewage.

Story
Space between two floors of a building; top of floor to top floor.

Story pole
A rod or pole cut to the proposed clear height between finish floor and ceiling. A story pole is often marked with minor dimensions for door trims, cabinet heights, etc.

Straightedge
A straight piece of lumber or metal used to strike off the surface of a concrete slab to grade screeds or other guides.

Strap
Lightweight, flat rolled iron or steel used as a connecting member.

Stratum (plural strata)
A sheetlike mass of rock or earth of one kind found in layers between beds of other kinds. (plural is strata).

Stressed skin
In frame construction, the outer surface of panels used for floors and roof decks. The skins have structural value. In steel construction, the cladding of steel structures designed to help support the structure.

Stretcher
Brick laid with its length parallel to the wall and its side exposed.

Striated
Textured with parallel scratches or grooves.

Strip flooring
Wood finish flooring in the form of long, narrow tongue-and-groove boards.

Strike plate
In a building, the part of a door lock that is fastened to the jamb. Sometimes called a *striking plate* or *keeper*.

Stringer
In general construction, the member of each side of a stair that supports the treads and risers. In reinforced concrete construction, horizontal structural member supports.

Structural glazed (clay) tile
Hollow clay tile with glazed faces; used for constructing interior partitions where sanitation or cleanliness is a concern.

Structural shapes
The H, I, and T beam, angle, channel, and plate.

Structural tubes
Usually welded-seam, hollow tubular sections of various sizes used as light columns, struts, and bracing; also, other structural and sometimes decorative installations; can be square or rectangular.

Strut
A member used to hold other members apart. It contrasts with a *tie*, which is used to hold members together. Also called a *spacer*.

Stucco
Most commonly refers to an outside plaster made with portland cement as its base.

Stud
In building an upright member, usually piece of dimension lumber, 2 x 4 x 6, used in the framework of a partition or wall.

Subcontractor
A company (or individual) who enters into an agreement with a general contractor. A subcontractor usually agrees to do certain specific skilled work on a building. Plumbing, heating, electrical work, and other portions of construction work are sublet to contractors who specialize in these particular kinds of work.

Subfloor
In carpentry, the flooring laid directly on the joists and serving as a work platform during construction. When all rough construction work is completed, a finish floor is laid over the subfloor.

Subgrade
A fill or earth surface on which concrete is placed.

Substantial completion
The point at which a building project is complete and ready for occupancy, except for a limited number of minor repairs or incomplete work items; point at which final payment can be made to contractor(s) and owner can move in.

Substructure
Foundation system and portion of structure/building below grade line; lowest support for superstructure.

Sump
A pit in a basement floor that collects subsurface water and into which a sump pump is placed to remove the water.

Superstructure
The aboveground portion of a building.

Survey
A description of the measure and configuration of land, including maps and field notes that describe the property.

Suspended ceiling
A ceiling hung below the underside of a building structure. Wire and channel sections are commonly used to support the ceiling material.

Swale
A low area between two higher sloping sections of earth, usually V-shaped, used for drainage.

Synthetic flooring
Any of a large number of floor covering materials, either applied or adhered to the substrate (usually a concrete slab); e.g., seamless (epoxy) coatings, mat-type sheeting (with welded seams), gymnasium materials, etc.

T

Tail joists
Relatively short (cut) joists that are framed between a header or trimmer in floor framing.

Tapered edge
The longitudinal edge of a sheet of gypsum board, which is sloped/tapered to allow room for reinforcing tape and joint compound.

Tee
A metal or precast concrete member with a cross section resembling the letter T.

Tempered glass
Glass that has been heat treated to increase its toughness and its resistance to breakage.

Template
A gauge or pattern, commonly a thin board or light frame, used as a guide for forming work to be done; plaster molding, hinge spacing, hardware layout, etc.

Tensile strength
The ability of a member to withstand forces tending to lengthen it.

Tension
A stretching force; to stretch.

Terne plate
Sheet iron coated with an alloy of four parts of lead to one part of tin, used for roofing.

Terrazzo
Wear-resistant flooring made of marble chips or small stones embedded in a cement matrix (paste), then polished smooth.

Threshold
A strip of wood or metal with beveled edges used over the joint between a finish floor and the sill of an exterior doors.

Tile
A fired clay product that is thin in cross section as compared with brick; either a thin, flat element (ceramic tile or quarry tile), a thin, curved element (roofing tile), or a hollow element with thin walls (flue tile, tile pipe, structural clay tile); also a thin, flat element of another material, such as an acoustical ceiling unit or a resilient floor unit.

Tilt up construction
A method of constructing walls, and sometimes floors, by pouring concrete or putting wooden walls together in flat panels. When complete, they are moved to the building site where they are tilted into permanent place.

Timber
Construction lumber larger than 4 in. x 6 in. (102 mm x 152 mm) in cross section.

Tinted glass
Glass that is colored with pigments, dyes, or other admixtures.

Toenail
To drive a nail diagonally across the corner of one board and into another.

Toggle bolt
A bolt used to fastening something to a hollow wall. The thin webs of a hollow will unit do not permit the use of a cinch anchor or other expansion bolt, for it would probably break the unit. A toggle bolt consists of a threaded bolt and a nut with attached spring arms. The unit is applied to the bolt, which is then placed in a hole drilled in the wall. On the inside surface of the wall the flexible arms spring out to form a T. The bolt is then tightened. This can also be used in plaster, drywall, and concrete block walls.

Toilet room accessories
Various items of equipment, such as towel dispensers, soap dispensers, waste receptacles, napkin and seat dispensers, robe hooks, tissue holders, etc., for installation in rest rooms.

Tongue and groove
A continuous projection on the edge of a board that fits into a groove formed on another board.

Topography
Usually refers to site characteristics such as contour of the land, trees, and other natural features.

Topping
A thin (2 in.) layer of concrete cast over a roof or floor deck.

Tract
A specified area of land.

Trade Association(s)
Organizations with a common interest in construction materials, methods, operations, etc.; usually single interest motivation in education, marketing, information, combined research and development, and representing numerous groups/manufacturing, etc., with single combined effort.

Transit-mixed concrete
Concrete mixed in a rotating drum on the back of a truck as it is transported to a building site.

Transom
A window placed above a door or permanent window, which is hinged for ventilation purposes.

Trap
A U-shaped pipe below plumbing fixtures designed to create a water seal and prevent sewer odors and gasses fro being released into habitable areas.

Tread
The horizontal board in a stairway on which the foot is placed.

Tremie
A large funnel with a tube attached, used to deposit concrete in deep forms or beneath water or slurry.

Trim
The finished woodwork of a structure. The term is also used in reference to painting and decorating.

Trimmer
A beam or stud into which a header is framed for a chimney, stairway, door, or window opening.

Truss
Structural steel or wood members fastened together to make a framework that will span long distances; utilizes principle of rigid triangular panels.

Two-way action
Bending of a slab or deck in which bending stresses are approximately equal in the two principal directions of the structure.

Two-way flat slab
A reinforced concrete framing system in which columns with mushroom capitals and/or drop panels directly support a two-way slab that is planar on both its surfaces.

Two-way ribbed slab
Structural concrete slab with ribs (joists) running in two directions between supports; also called *waffle slab*; can be left exposed and unfinished as a decorative texture/pattern for the ceiling of space below; light fixtures can be mounted in the voids, if desires.

Two-way slab
A concrete slab in which the reinforcing steel is placed into perpendicular directions; usually a structural floor or roof slab.

Type-X gypsum board
A fiber-reinforced gypsum board used where greater fire resistance is required; fire-rated board.

U

Ultimate strength
The strength of a material varies during the application of stresses; its ultimate strength occurs at the instant where the greatest strength is obtained.

Underlayment
Floor covering of plywood or fiberboard used to provide a smooth, level surface for carpet or other resilient flooring; any material that underlies and supports/strengthens another, primarily a finish material.

Underpinning
The process of placing new foundations beneath an existing structure.

Upside-down roof
A membrane roof assembly in which the thermal insulation lies atop the membrane; see *Inverted roof*.

Urea-formaldehyde
A water-based foam used as thermal insulation.

V

Valley
A depression in a roof where two parts of the roof at different slopes come together.

Valley rafter
The diagonal rafter at the intersection of two sloping roofs.

Vapor barrier
A watertight material used to prevent the passage of moisture or water vapor into and through walls and slabs.

Veneer
(1) A thin sheet of wood or other material. The outside sheet is generally of superior quality, chosen for its beauty. Plywood is made by gluing sheets of wood veneer together. (2) Brick veneer consists of one row of brick placed around a framework. Most brick houses have wood frames covered by veneer.

Veneer plaster
A wall finish system in which a thin layer of high-strength plaster is applied over a special gypsum board base.

Vent stack
A vertical soil pipe connected to the drainage system for ventilation and pressure equalization.

Vermiculite
Expanded mica used for loose fill insulation and as aggregate in lightweight concrete.

Vestibule
An open area at an entrance to a building

Vibrator
A mechanical device used in placing concrete to ensure that all voids are filled (a screed vibrator is a rotary surface vibrator); also compacts concrete as it is placed.

Vierendeel truss
A truss with rectangular panels and rigid joints. The members of a Vierendeel truss are subjected to strong nonaxial forces.

V-joint
A joint between two pieces of a material. The corners are beveled to form a joint profile resembling the letter "V."

Void
Air space between materials or between substances in material.

W

Waferboard
A building panel made by bonding together large, flat flakes of wood.

Waffle slab
A two-way concrete joist system (ribbed slab), formed with square pan forms; see *two-way ribbed slab*.

Wainscot
The lower section of a wall made of different material from the upper part; usually composed of wood, tile, or wall covering.

Wallboard
A general term referring to large, rigid sheets used to cover interior walls. It can be made of wood fibers, gypsum, or other material.

Wall tie
A small metal strip or steel wire used to bind wythes of masonry in cavity-wall construction or to bind brick veneer to the wood-frame wall in veneer construction.

Warp
To bend or twist out of shape.

Water-cement ratio
A numerical index of the relative proportions of water and cement in a concrete mixture.

Waterproof
To render a material or surface impervious to water. This is generally done by coating it with another material that will not let water pass through it. Tar, asphalt, mortar parging, and heavy-body cementitious paints are common waterproofing agents.

Water-resistant gypsum board
A gypsum board designed for use in locations where it may be exposed to occasional dampness; called *green board*.

Waterstop
A synthetic rubber strip used to seal joints in concrete foundation walls.

Water table
A horizontal member projecting from the surface of an exterior wall to throw off rainwater; also level of subsurface water.

Weatherstripping
A strip of fabric or metal fastened around the edges of windows and doors to prevent air infiltration; can be interlocking or spring fit.

Web
The single vertical portion of an I beam, wide-flange, or channel member between the flanges.

Wedge
A piece of wood, metal, or other material that tapers to a thin edge at one end.

Weep holes
Holes near the bottoms of masonry walls to allow the release of accumulated moisture; important in brick veneer work.

Weld
A joint between two pieces of metal formed by fusing the pieces together, usually with the aid of additional metal melted from a rod or electrode.

Weld-wire-fabric (WWF)
Steel wires welded together to form a grid for concrete slab reinforcing; commonly called *mesh*.

"Wet" systems
Construction systems that utilize considerable quantities of water on a construction site, such as masonry, plaster, and terrazzo.

Whaler (or waler)
A horizontal bracing member used in form construction to support the stud uprights on concrete forms; can also support sheeting.

Wide-flange section
Any of a wide range of steel sections rolled in the shape of a letter I or H, with different dimensions than I beams.

Wind brace
A diagonal structural member whose function is to stabilize a frame against lateral (wind) forces.

Winder
A triangular tread on a stair.

Wind load
Lateral forces acting against a building that, in particular, must be considered in the design of high-rise buildings.

Wired glass
Glass in which a large-gauge wire mesh has been embedded during manufacture.

Wood shakes (Shingles)
Individual wood roofing pieces, made of cedar (usually), which are hand split or machined to useable size; can be fire-rated for added protection.

Work
The tasks, construction, installation, etc., that must occur to build, finish, and produce a project anticipated and under contract.

Working drawings
Drawings containing design details; plans to which the actual construction is done; drawing portion of contract documents.

Working load
Those definite forces, used in design calculations, that act on structural members.

Wracking
Forcing out of plumb and/or square.

Wrought iron
A form of iron that is soft, tough, and fibrous in structure, containing about 0.1 percent carbon and 1 to 2 percent slag.

Wythe
A section of a masonry wall (in plan) which is 4 in. wide; pertains to the number of 4 in. sections in the full width of a masonry wall.

Y

Yard
Usually that area of a lot from the building to the property lines; in zoning, that minimum prescribed distance back from the property lines where building cannot occur (also called setbacks).

Z

Zoning
Building regulations that control size, use, location, and type of structures to be built in specific areas.

SUGGESTED READING

DRAFTING AND DRAWING

Allen, Edward: *Architectural Detailing*, John Wiley & Sons, New York 1993

Dagostino, Frank R.: *Contemporary Architectural Drawing*, Reston Publishing Co., Reston, VA, 1977.

Earle, James H.: *Engineering Design Graphics*, Addison Wesley Publishing, Reading, MA, 1969.

French, Thomas E., and Charles J. Vierch: *Engineering Drawing and Graphic Technology*, 12th ed., McGraw-Hill Book Co., New York, 1978.

Gieseke, Frederick E., et al.: *Technical Drawing*, 6th ed., The MacMillan Co., New York, 1974.

Goodban, William T., and Jack J. Hayslett: *Architectural Drawing and Planning*, 3d ed., McGraw-Hill Book Co., New York, 1979.

Hammond, Robert H., et al.: *Engineering Graphics for Design, Analysis, and Communication*, 2d Ed., The Ronald press, New York, 1971.

Hepler, Donald E., and Paul I. Wallach: *Architecture: Drafting and Design*, 4th ed., McGraw-Hill Book Co., New York, 1982.

Hooper, Lee: *Introduction to Construction Drafting*, Prentice-Hall, Englewood Cliffs, NJ, 1971.

Kicklighter, Clois E.: *Architecture, Residential Drawing and Design*, The Goodheart-Wilcox Co., South Holland, MI, 1973.

Lytle, R. J.: *American Metric Construction Handbook*, Structure Publishing, Farmington, MI, 1976.

McHugh, Robert C.: *Working Drawing Handbook*, Van Nostrand Reinhold, New York, 1977.

Muller, Edward J.: *Architectural Drawing and Light Construction*, 4th ed., Prentice-Hall, Englewood Cliffs, NJ, 1993.

Obermeyer, Thomas: *Architectural Technology*, McGraw-Hill Book Co., New York, 1976.

O'Connell, William J.: *Graphic Communication in Architecture*, Stipes Publishing, Champaign, IL, 1972.

Stitt, Fred A.: *Working Drawing Manual*, McGraw-Hill Co., New York, 1998.

Thomas, Marvin L.: *Architectural Working Drawing: A Professional Technique*, McGraw-Hill Book Co., New York, 1978.

Wakita, Osamu A., and Richard M. Linde: *The Professional Practice of Architectural Detailing*, 3rd ed., John Wiley & Sons, New York, 1999.

Weidhaas, Ernest R.,: *Architectural Drafting and Design,* 4th ed., Allyn & Bacon, Boston, 1981.

NEW TECHNIQUES

Books

Fotodraft, Automation Industries, Vitro Laboratories Division, Silver Spring, MD.

Daltry, C. D., and D. T. Crawshaw: *Working Drawings in Use,* Building Research Establishment, Garston, Watford, England.

Reprodrafting Overlay Register System for Architects and Engineers and *A Planning Guide for Overlay Drafting,* and *Reprodrafting Overlay Register System Seminar Brochure,* DuPont DeNemours, E. I. and Co., Inc., Wilmington, DE.

Foxhall, William B. (ed.): *Techniques of Successful Practice,* McGraw-Hill Book Co., New York, 1975.

Systems Drafting Manual for Reprographic Firms, Gresham and Smith, Nashville, TN.

Intergraphics, An Experiment in Architectural Communications, Jarvis-Putty-Jarvis, Inc., Dallas, TX.

Powers, R., and J. Quebe: *The Overlay Drafting System,* Archimedia, Inc., Philadelphia, PA, 1978.

Stitt, Fred A.: *Systems Drafting,* McGraw-Hill Book Co., New York, 1980.

Booklets

The Fotodraft User's Manual, Automation Industries, Inc., Silver Spring, MD.

Graphic Techniques for Design and Production and *HLM Production Systems,* Hansen, Lind and Meyer, Iowa City, IA.

Composite Drafting, Applique Drafting, Photodrafting, Overlay Drafting, Typewritten Notation, and *Freehand Sketch Drafting,* Guidelines Publications, Orcinda, CA.

Recommended Standards on Production Procedure, Volumes 1 and 2, Northern California Chapter, AIA, San Francisco, CA.

Photogrammetric Recording of Cultural Resources (024–005-00684–2), U.S. Government Printing Office, Washington, DC.

Blu-Ray Presentation Tips, Blu-Ray Inc., Essex, CT.

Never Draw It Twice, Nuarc Co., Chicago, IL.

Redraw Short-Cuts Through Reprodrafting, Keuffel & Essel Co., Morristown, NJ.

From Eastman-Kodak Company, Rochester, NY: *Overlay Drafting Techniques, Overlay Drafting for Architects, Kodak Products for Drawing Reproduction, Drawing Problems? Creative Solutions with Kodagraph Materials, Drawings Made Easy, What's a Photodrawing, Photoreproduction for Architects, Photodraphics—Specialists in Drawing Reproduction, Engineering Document Control, Guide to Overlays, Guide to Use and Preparation of Photodrawings.*

Journals

The Paper Plane, monthly, Archimedia, Inc., Philadelphia, PA.

The Reprodrafting Overlay Register System for Architects, E. I. DuPont Co., Wilmington, DE.

GAF Designer's Almanac, GAF Corporation, New York, NY.

Overlay Drafting for Architects, Eastman Kodak, Rochester, NY.

The Guidelines Letter, monthly, Guidelines, Orinda, CA.

Reprographics, monthly, Reprographics, New York, NY.

Repro Drafting Digest, monthly, St. Regis Publications, Inc., New York, N.Y.

Plan and Print, monthly, Plan and Print, Inc., Franklin Park, IL. Articles of interest in back issues: "Two Sides of the Coin," May 1979; "Selling Pin Graphics," May 1979; "Systems Drafting," June 1978; "Developing a New Production System," October 1978; "Expanding Services," October 1977; "Overlay Drafting Work," October 1977; "End to Repetitive Drafting," October 1977; "Delivering the Marketing Message," October 1977; "Overlay Drafting," June 1976; and "Keen Competitive Edge," February 1976.

Articles

"Using Photographs in Contract Documents on Restoration Work," by Cynthia J. Phifer, *AIA Journal,* February 1976.

"Saving Time and Money with Overlay Drafting," by C. William Semisch, *Repro Drafting Digest,* June 1977.

"Architectural Firms Use Half-Size Drawing System," *Architectural Record,* May 1971.

"Saving Drafting Hours and Money Through Re-prodrafting," by Brian Smith, *Reprodrafting Digest,* January 1977.

"Photodrawings in Industrial Modeling," by L. A. Nusslein, *Repro Drafting Digest,* October 1977.

"Graphic Techniques Workshop Strives for Production Savings," *Architectural Record,* Mid-October 1976.

"Photodrawings in Industrial Modeling," by L. A. Nusslein, *Repro Drafting Digest,* October 1977.

"Another Application for Pin-Registered Working Drawings," by Rolland D. Thompson, *Repro Drafting Digest,* May 1977.

"Overlay Drafting Technique Helps Reduce Errors and Omissions," by Philip M. Jones, *Architectural Record,* July 1976.

"Draw the Line Once," *Progressive Architecture,* August 1976.

"Team Drafting with Overlays," by Pat Giannico, *Plan and Print,* May 1977.

"A Design System That Produces Contract Drawings," by New H. Abrams, *AIA Journal,* March 1970.

"The Future Is Here—and It Works in Architectural Design and Drafting," by Fred A. Stitt, *Repro Drafting Digest,* January 1978.

"A Comprehensive Approach to Improving the Quality of Contract Documents," by Jerry Quebe, *AIA Journal,* February 1975.

"How to Get Informed on the New Reprodrafting Systems," by Fred A. Stitt, *Repro Drafting Digest,* April 1978.

"Pin Registration Drafting Saves Time, Assures Alignment," by Clay Eissler, *Consulting Engineer,* December 1977.

COMPUTER-AIDED DRAFTING AND DESIGN (CADD AND CAD)

Crosley, M. L.: *The Architect's Guide to Computer Aided Design,* John Wiley & Sons, New York, 1988.

Gerlach, Gary M.: *Transition to CADD,* McGraw-Hill Book Co., New York, 1987.

Kennedy, E. Lee: *CAD: Drawings-Design-Data Management,* Watson-Guptill, New York, 1986.

Potts, Jackie: *Computer-Aided Drafting and Design Using AutoCad,* Harcourt, Brace, Jovanovich, New York, 1989.

BUILDING CONSTRUCTION

Allen, Edward: *Fundamentals of Building Construction,* 3rd ed., John Wiley & Sons, New York 1998

ASTM Standards, American Society for Testing and Materials, 100 Barr Harbor Dr., West Conshohocken, PA 19428 USA

Ching, Francis D. K.: *Building Construction Illustrated,* 2d ed., Van Nostrand Reinhold, New York, 1991.

Egan, M. David: *Concepts in Building Firesafety,* John Wiley & Sons, New York, 1978.

Hornbostel, Caleb: *Construction Materials,* John Wiley & Sons, New York, 1978.

Hornbostel, Caleb, and William J. Hornung: *Materials and Methods for Contemporary Construction,* Prentice-Hall, Englewood Cliffs, NJ, 1974.

Huntington, Whitney C., and Robert E. Mickadeit: *Building Construction,* 6th ed., John Wiley & Sons, New York, 1987.

Merritt, Frederick S. (ed.): *Building Construction Handbook,* 3d ed., McGraw-Hill Book Co., New York, 1975.

Muller, Edward J.: *Reading Architectural Working Drawings,* Prentice-Hall, Englewood Cliffs, NJ, 1971.

Manual for House Framing (Wood Construction Data No. 1), National Forest Products Association, Washington, DC, 1970.

Olin, Harold B., et al.: *Construction: Principles, Materials and Methods,* 6th ed., John Wiley & Sons, New York, 1995

Parker, Harry, et al.: *Materials and Methods of Architectural Construction,* 4th ed., John Wiley & Sons, New York, 1966.

Principles of Clay Masonry Construction, Brick Institute of America, Washington, DC.

Przetak, Louis: *Standard Details for Fire-Resistive Building Construction,* McGraw-Hill Book Co., New York, 1977.

Ramsey, Charles G., and Harold R. Sleeper: *Architectural Graphic Standards,* 9th ed., John Wiley & Sons/AIA, New York, 1998 (Arch. Graphic Stds).

Ramsey, Charles G., and Harold R. Sleeper: *Architectural Graphic Standards,* Student Edition of 8th ed., John Wiley & Sons/AIA, New York, 1994.

Reiner, Laurence E.: *Methods and Materials of Construction,* Prentice-Hall, Englewood Cliffs, NJ, 1970.

Rubenstein, Harvey M.: *A Guide to Site Planning and Landscape Construction*, 4th ed., John Wiley & Sons, New York 1996

Small Homes Council-Building Research Council: *Circular Series*, University of Illinois, Urbana, IL. Various circulars published several times a year.

Smith, Ronald C.: *Principles and Practices of Light Construction*, 3d ed., Prentice-Hall, Englewood Cliffs, NJ, 1980.

Smith, Ronald C.: *Principles and Practices of Heavy Construction*, 4th ed., Prentice-Hall, Englewood Cliffs, NJ, 1993.

Steel Construction Handbook, 9th ed., American Institute of Steel Construction, New York, 1989.

Weaver, Gerald L.: *Structural Detailing for Technicians*, McGraw-Hill Book Co., New York, 1974.

GENERAL PRACTICE

Abbett, Robert W.: *Engineering Contracts and Specifications*, 4th ed., John Wiley & Sons, New York, 1963.

American Institute of Architects: *Current Trends in Architectural Practice*, AIA/Architectural Record Books, Washington, DC, 1976.

Architect's Handbook of Professional Practice, 12th ed., American Institute of Architects, Washington, DC, 1994.

Bennett, Philip M., and Harold J. Rosen: *Construction Materials Evaluation and Selection*, John Wiley & Sons, New York, 1979.

Clough, Richard H.: *Construction Contracting*, 3d ed., John Wiley & Sons, New York, 1975.

Clyde, James E.: *Construction Inspection*, 2d ed., John Wiley & Sons, New York, 1986.

Computerized Financial Management, AIA Journal, American Institute of Architects, Washington, DC, 1971–1972.

CSI Documents and Manual of Professional Practice, Construction Specifications Institute, Washington, DC, various dates/1992

Correale, William H.: *A Building Code Primer*, McGraw-Hill Book Co., New York, 1979.

Edwards, H. Griffith: *Specifications*, 2d ed., Van Nostrand Reinhold, Princeton, NJ, 1961.

Harper, G. Neil: *Computer Applications in Architecture and Engineering*, McGraw-Hill Book Co., New York, 1969.

Liebing, Ralph W.: *Construction Regulations Handbook*, John Wiley & Sons, New York, 1987.

Liebing, Ralph W.: *Construction Contract Administration*, Prentice Hall, Englewood Cliffs, NJ, 1997.

Lewis, Jack R.: *Construction Specifications*, Prentice-Hall, Englewood Cliffs, NJ, 1975.

Meier, Hans W.: *Construction Specifications Handbook*, Prentice-Hall, Englewood Cliffs, NJ, 1975.

Rosen, Harold J., and Paul Heineman: *Construction Specification Writing*, 4th ed., John Wiley & Sons, New York, 1998.

Smith, Ronald C.: *Materials of Construction*, 3d ed., McGraw-Hill Book Co., New York, 1979.

Watson, Don A.: *Construction Materials and Processes*, 3rd ed., Glencoe, 1994.

Williams, Harry: *Construction Practices*, Prentice-Hall, Englewood Cliffs, NJ, 1975.

Yatt, Barry D., *Cracking the Codes: An Architect's Guide*, John Wiley & Sons, New York, 1998.

Index

INDEX